palgrave macmillan law masters

business law

palgrave macmillan law masters

Series editor: **Marise Cremona**

Business Law   Stephen Judge
Company Law   Janet Dine and Marios Koutsias
Constitutional and Administrative Law   John Alder
Contract Law   Ewan McKendrick
Criminal Law   Jonathan Herring
Employment Law   Deborah J. Lockton
Family Law   Kate Standley
Intellectual Property Law   Tina Hart, Simon Clark and Linda Fazzani
Land Law   Joe Cursley, Mark Davys and Kate Green
Landlord and Tenant Law   Margaret Wilkie, Peter Luxton, Jill Morgan and Godfrey Cole
Law of the European Union   Jo Shaw
Legal Method   Ian McLeod
Legal Theory   Ian McLeod
Torts   Alastair Mullis and Ken Oliphant
Trusts Law   Charlie Webb and Tim Akkouh

palgrave macmillan law masters *focus*

Economic and Social Law of the European Union   Jo Shaw, Jo Hunt & Chloe Wallace
Evidence   Raymond Emson

palgrave macmillan law masters

business law

stephen judge
Formerly Lecturer in Law at the
University of Surrey

Fourth edition

Series editor: Marise Cremona
Professor of European Law
European University Institute
Florence, Italy

This edition first published 2009 by
PALGRAVE MACMILLAN

Palgrave Macmillan in the UK is an imprint of Macmillan Publishers Limited, registered in England, company number 785998, of Houndmills, Basingstoke, Hampshire RG21 6XS.

Palgrave Macmillan in the US is a division of St Martin's Press LLC, 175 Fifth Avenue, New York, NY 10010.

Palgrave Macmillan is the global academic imprint of the above companies and has companies and representatives throughout the world.

Palgrave® and Macmillan® are registered trademarks in the United States, the United Kingdom, Europe and other countries.

ISBN-13: 978–0–230–57572–1
ISBN-10: 0–230–57572–2

This book is printed on paper suitable for recycling and made from fully managed and sustained forest sources. Logging, pulping and manufacturing processes are expected to conform to the environmental regulations of the country of origin.

A catalogue record for this book is available from the British Library.

10   9   8   7   6   5   4   3   2   1
18   17   16   15   14   13   12   11   10   09

Printed and bound in Great Britain by
CPI Antony Rowe, Chippenham and Eastbourne

Contents

Business Law

The very term 'law' often gives rise to misapprehension and doubt in the minds of non-lawyers. The law is seen as belonging to a specialist world of jargon and professional flummery from which they are excluded. This is often accompanied by a feeling that the law is something in which they become involved at their peril, with its association with highly paid professionals and large bills.

In effect, this is largely because the involvement of the law is seen as something which occurs only when something has gone wrong, but otherwise is something which does not affect us.

In reality, as with any other human activity, the carrying on of a commercial, professional or business activity needs to be legally regulated for a number of purposes, including the following:

- Regulating the rights and duties of people carrying on a business in common to ensure that profits and losses are shared equally.
- Protecting persons dealing with the business as clients from harm caused by defective products or services produced or offered by the business organisation.
- Ensuring that the treatment of employees and workers is fair and non-discriminatory.
- Protecting investors in business to ensure that their rights as creditors or shareholders are respected.
- Regulating the dealings between the business and persons supplying it with goods and services to afford mutual protection of supplier and customer.
- Ensuring the protection of the public from those who have engaged in doubtful business practices.

The regulation of these and other aspects of the conduct of a commercial or business activity is ensured by a body of substantive rules of law relating to business, and, in addition, the establishment of forums to review any alleged breach of the rules ensures the enforcement of these rules – the aim being to prevent future abuses and to compensate any injured party.

The most obvious relevant forum is the official court system and the system of specialist tribunals to which parties can turn for adjudication. There is also the recognition and regulation of arbitration tribunals and private organisations providing for dispute resolution, including alternative dispute resolution (ADR) through mediation.

In certain trades and professions, regulation is also ensured by the existence of legally recognised business associations to which traders can belong and which require their members to abide by established codes of practice. These trade organisations also operate tribunals to adjudicate on disputes involving their members.

The law and the legal system should be seen in the same way as the rules regulating various sporting activities: professional football, ice dancing, synchronised swimming. They are the ever-present background to the activity but are often ignored until some questionable behaviour is alleged. The 'offside rule' may be understood by only a few, but it is important for everybody.

About this book

This is intended as a comprehensive text for a business law module as part of an undergraduate law degree. It is also suitable for students on Business Studies degree programmes and those undertaking courses to obtain professional qualifications such as those offered by the Institute of Chartered Secretaries and Administrators and the various professional accountancy bodies.

In this new and revised edition, many chapters have been completely rewritten to reflect major changes in the law. This is most obvious in the chapters on registered companies (chapters 6 to 12) which incorporate the major changes in company law as a result of the passing of the Companies Act 2006. The Act comes into force in its entirety in October 2009, but the chapters are written as if the legislation were already fully implemented. Another chapter which has been largely rewritten is chapter 21 on Consumer Protection. The legislation relating to unfair trading practices was completely reformed in 2008 with the transposition into UK law of the EU Directives aimed at harmonising the law in this area.

Business law syllabuses vary enormously. Some programmes concentrate on the organisational and relational aspects of business and deal with partnership and company law. Others may choose to concentrate on commercial relationships including agency, employment and consumer contracts. This text covers both of these approaches to the subject, and also includes a chapter on the rapidly developing field of e-commerce.

Students also vary greatly, and while law students will have knowledge of the general principles of English law through an earlier course of study, others may be embarking on legal studies for the first time. This divergence of knowledge is recognised by the inclusion of an introductory section on the workings of the legal system and English law, including arbitration and ADR.

In respect of the relevant 'law for business' material, the text is designed as a 'one-stop' source. The layout is non-linear, in the sense that it is designed so that students can select from it the topics of specific relevance to their particular course. There is extensive cross-referencing linking related topics. This allows for reference forward and back for further and deeper understanding or for revision.

The aim is to cover the widest possible range of business and commercial law topics to suit the widest possible range of courses and the widest possible range of students.

This is reflected in the contents and presentation of the material:

▶ The language used is as straightforward and as non-technical as possible without compromising accuracy
▶ Technical legal terms are defined at the outset and there is an extensive glossary of technical terms
▶ Cases are presented to serve as illustrations for the evolution and application of legal principles to business and commercial situations

- End of chapter summaries stress the main points to be retained by the student
- End of chapter questions offer the opportunity of applying the principles covered to practical business scenarios
- Extensive cross-referencing allows for reference back or forward to related topics for revision purposes or further development.

A dedicated website supports the book and provides further information on specific topics as well as suggested answers for the problem questions. This also allows the book to be regularly updated.

STEVE JUDGE
November 2008

Table of Cases

Table of Statutes

Table of European Legislation

Table of Statutory Instruments

Part I

Introduction to the English Legal System

This introductory section is mainly for students coming to legal studies for the first time. It will, however, be helpful revision for those who are already familiar with English law, but for whom the details have become blurred. Knowledge of legal rules and regulations governing the formation of a business organisation and the carrying on of a business is of vital importance for everybody involved in business. Ignorance of the law is never a defence.

In Chapter 1 we cover the sources of English law. The earliest source of the law was the common law, the body of case law built up over the centuries by decisions of judges. For the development of new rules relevant to the contemporary world the principal source is now legislation passed by Parliament. Common law is still of great importance, however, since these new legislative rules are interpreted and refined by judgments in the law courts.

The rules can establish criminal offences that result in the wrongdoer being prosecuted in the criminal courts and punished. The rules also, however, regulate relationships between persons where the non-compliance with the law by one party will allow the injured party to sue the wrongdoer in a civil court. In most cases the injured party will seek to claim compensation for any loss suffered as a result.

Since the UK became a member of the European Community in 1973, many of the initiatives for legislation affecting commercial affairs have come from Brussels. It is vitally important to understand the superior position of EU law and the way in which it brings about changes in UK law. A further influence is the European Convention on Human Rights 1951. The Human Rights Act 1998 makes the Convention rights enforceable in the UK courts. All UK legislation must be compatible with the Human Rights Convention.

Chapter 2 is concerned with dispute resolution. In a non-commercial context, disputes are usually regulated by the injured party bringing a legal action against the wrongdoer in a court of law. In the world of business, however, the parties may prefer to solve their differences outside the formal confines of a court of law. Many business contracts will provide that, in the event of a disagreement between the parties, the dispute will be resolved by referring the matter to be decided by arbitration, where the parties agree to be bound by the decision of the arbitrator. An increasingly popular method of resolving differences between business organisations is alternative dispute resolution (ADR), usually in the form of mediation.

In the USA, ADR includes binding arbitration, but in the UK, all forms of ADR are non-binding and, if resolution proves impossible, the parties are still free to litigate.

The Centre for Effective Dispute Resolution (CEDR) is a non-profit-making organisation created with the mission to encourage and develop cost-effective dispute prevention and dispute resolution in commercial and public sector disputes and in civil litigation. Model documents relating to ADR can be downloaded from the CEDR website at www.cedr.co.uk.

For example, in a dispute involving £120m between Texaco and Borden over breach of contract claims, after years of legal battles, the parties chose to use a mini-trial system where both vice-presidents sat together with a mediator and listened to an abbreviated version of the evidence. A deal was struck after three weeks with no money involved. The parties renegotiated supply agreements and continued trading together.

Another example is a CEDR-arranged mediation of a dispute involving a disputed claim for £27m and for which there was a planned 12-week hearing. The dispute was actually resolved in one day. In England, as in the USA, about 85–90 per cent of cases listed to appear in court are resolved before trial, and the incentive to use ADR is encouraged by the courts. The advantages of both arbitration and ADR are speed, an absence of publicity and lower costs.

Chapter 1

Introduction to the English legal system

Learning objectives

After reading this chapter you will know about:

- criminal and civil law
- natural and legal persons
- sources of English law
- supremacy of EU law
- the European Convention on Human Rights

Hot Topic . . .

A NEW SUPREME COURT FOR THE UK?

The Constitutional Reform Act (CRA) 2005 made major changes to the UK legal system, the most important being the creation of the Supreme Court of the United Kingdom to replace the Appellate Committee of the House of Lords as the final court of appeal from October 2009. The 12 judges will be called Supreme Court Justices and will be appointed by a high-powered appointments committee after having submitted an application. In a new departure, the 2005 Act has opened up the position to lawyers who have not prevously held judicial office.

In another change, the Lord Chancellor no longer sits as a judge or is the head of the judiciary, a position now held by the Lord Chief Justice. The Lord Chancellor's power to make judicial appointments was also transferred to a Judicial Appointments Commission. The Lord Chancellor is no longer required to be a lawyer or a Lord. The position is normally held by the Justice Secretary of the newly created Ministry of Justice. The qualities for appointment are listed in s.2 CRA 2005.

The highest level of jurisdiction in the UK is currently shared between the Appellate Committee of the House of Lords (House of Lords) which hears appeals from courts in England, Wales and Northern Ireland and in civil cases from Scotland, and the Judicial Committee of the Privy Council (JCPC), which hears appeals from ecclesiastical courts and ex-colonies which have not established their own final court of appeal. It also has jurisdiction to ensure that the devolved assemblies and the Scottish Parliament are within their legal powers. This jurisdiction will pass to the new Supreme Court.

The Law Lords and other holders of high judicial office are restricted from sitting and voting in the House of Lords for as long as they hold full-time judicial office.

The reforms are partly due to concerns over the role of the Law Lords as both judges and legislators, following the Human Rights Act 1998.

1.1 Criminal and civil law

English law is sub-classified into criminal and civil law, each with its own court system: the criminal and civil courts. Some courts, however, have criminal and civil jurisdiction and final appeals in criminal and civil cases are heard by the House of Lords.

Criminals are prosecuted in the name of the Queen by the Crown Prosecution Service (CPS). The purpose of criminal law is the punishment of the offender. If the victims of a crime want compensation for their injury or loss, they must bring an action in the civil courts. The civil courts exist to resolve legal disputes between persons. Claims are initiated by the injured party – the claimant – against the defendant.

1.2 Natural and legal persons

The term 'person' covers natural persons – individuals – and legal persons – bodies recognised as having a separate legal existence. In respect of commerce and business, the most important legal persons are limited liability companies and limited liability partnerships (LLPs). Legal persons are created by incorporation and are generally referred to as 'corporations'. A company is not an 'individual' under trust law: *Jasmine Trustees Ltd and Ors v. Wells & Hind and Anor* [2007] EWHC 38 (Ch). The word 'individual' refers only to natural persons.

(a) Natural persons – nationality and domicile

A person normally has one nationality, but may have dual nationality and can be stateless. Generally the law applies to both nationals and aliens. Nationality determines a person's public rights: the right to live in a state and voting rights.

Domicile relates to the permanent place of residence. Persons domiciled in England and Wales are subject to English law, and those domiciled in Scotland or Northern Ireland to Scots or Northern Irish law. Everybody has a place of domicile and can have only one domicile at any given time.

There are three types of domicile: (i) domicile of origin; (ii) domicile of choice; and (iii) dependent domicile. Domicile of origin is the person's domicile at birth. Domicile of choice arises where persons of full age and capacity establish a permanent home elsewhere than their place of birth. Abandoning the domicile of choice means an automatic reversion to domicile of origin unless and until a new domicile of choice is established. Dependent domicile applied to children and married women whose domicile was dependent upon their parents or husband. The Domicile and Matrimonial Proceedings Act (DMPA) 1973 allows married women to acquire a domicile separate from their husband: s.1 DMPA 1973, for children to acquire an independent domicile at 16, and to adopt the mother's domicile when parents separate or divorce: ss.3 and 4 DMPA 1973.

(b) Corporations

Corporations are generally formed by one or more natural or legal persons. There are various ways in which the incorporation can take place, and the law distinguishes between (i) chartered; (ii) statutory; and (iii) registered corporations, of which registered corporations are the most important in the business context:

- ▷ **Chartered corporations** are created by royal charter. The earliest trading corporations, the Hudson's Bay Company and the East India Company, were created in this way. Today, this is the format for professional bodies such as the Law Society, the Institute of Chartered Secretaries and Administrators (ICSA) and so on. The older universities are also chartered corporations.
- ▷ **Statutory corporations** are created by a special Act of Parliament. Local authorities are statutory corporations, as were the nationalised industries prior to their privatisation as registered corporations.
- ▷ **Registered corporations** are formed by complying with the registration requirements of the Companies Act 2006. The most important form of registered corporation is the

limited liability company limited by shares, either private or public. These are the normal vehicle for carrying on trade or business. Registered companies can also exist as unlimited liability companies or companies limited by guarantee. The former are rare since most members of a trading company will seek the protection of limited liability for the company's debts and liabilities. Companies limited by guarantee are more common but are used for non-commercial – often charitable – objects (see Chapters 6 and 8). The nationality and domicile of registered companies depend on the situation of the company's registered office: UK registered companies with registered offices in England or Wales are domiciled under English law, as opposed to those with registered offices in Scotland or Northern Ireland.

Other bodies with separate legal personality under the law include limited liability partnerships (LLPs) created by registration under the Limited Liability Partnerships Act 2000 (see Chapter 7).

Hot Topic . . .

NATIONALITY AND DOMICILE OF COMPANIES AND THEIR CONTROLLERS

The issue of domicile can be important, in respect of both the company and its controllers. The company will be liable for taxation in its place of domicile, as will the controllers. For this reason, many companies are established in tax havens to escape UK taxation: places like the Isle of Man, Jersey and Sark are geographically close examples. Other popular places include the Cayman Islands.

Philip Green is the controller of Arcadia plc, which owns the Top Shop and Dorothy Perkins chains. The vehicle used to acquire Arcadia in 2002 was Taveta Investments Ltd, a family-owned company incorporated in Jersey. In 2004, he formally passed control of the company to his wife who is resident in Monaco. This saved the family a liability of £150m in tax which would otherwise have been payable on the £460m dividend the retail group paid them that year. Mr Green's Bhs Group is ultimately controlled through Global Textile Investments Ltd, a family-held company, also registered in Jersey.

1.3 Unincorporated associations

These have no legal personality and their property is jointly owned by their members, who are also contractually and tortiously liable for them. Special rules relate to particular categories of unincorporated association: trades unions, employers' associations, and general partnerships (see Chapter 7).

1.4 The sources of English law

The major sources of English law are (i) case law; (ii) legislation; and (iii) EU law.

1.5 Case law

When a criminal or civil case is heard, the judge or judges reach a decision by applying the relevant law to the material facts of the case. Depending on the court's status, the statement of law establishes a precedent: a decision relevant for any future, identical dispute. This system is called the doctrine of binding precedent and relies on: (i) accurate and efficient law reporting and (ii) an established court hierarchy. It was fully implemented only at the end of the 19th century when a system of accurate reporting and a hierarchical court system were finally established.

(a)   Law reports

Civil cases are reported using the names of the claimant and the defendant. Criminal cases are generally indicated by the letter 'R' standing for Rex or Regina (king or queen) in place of the claimant as the action is brought by the state. The letters DPP (Director of Public Prosecutions) and AG (Attorney General) will also be found. The rest of the reference is an information retrieval code which gives:

▶ the year of the report. The presence of square brackets means that the date is the year in which the case was reported and not necessarily the year in which the case was heard, for example [1999]. The earliest reports give the date in round brackets which indicates the year in which the case was decided. Where the case citation gives a date in round brackets, the date is not significant for retrieving the case. The crucial information is the volume number and the series of the report. When citing cases, it is important to use the correct form of bracket.

▶ the name of the series of the report, including the volume number, for example 3 QB or 2 All ER.

▶ the page on which the report can be found, for example 542.

The official and most important body concerned with law reporting is the Incorporated Council of Law Reporting which is responsible for producing the *Law Reports*. Where there is an official report of a case, it is this report that should be cited in court rather than an alternative private report. In respect of the civil law, the *Law Reports* comprise a separate series of reports for each division of the High Court – Ch for Chancery Division, Fam for Family Division and QB (or KB) for Queen's Bench (or King's Bench) Division. Court of Appeal cases are reported under the name of the division where they were initially heard and House of Lords cases are reported as Appeal Cases (AC). The Council also publishes *Weekly Law Reports*, indicated by the letters WLR.

A number of private reports exist, of which the most famous are the *All England Law Reports*, indicated by the letters 'All ER'. This series of reports is frequently cited in this book since most public libraries will have a set of the *All England Law Reports*.

Unreported cases can be cited, provided they are vouched for by a barrister present when the judgment was delivered.

Decisions of the House of Lords from 1996 are available on the web two hours after the judgment is handed down at www.parliament.the-stationery-office.co.uk.

From 11 January 2001, a form of neutral citation was introduced in both divisions of the Court of Appeal and the Administrative Court of the High Court. From 14 January 2002, the practice of neutral citation was extended to all judgments by the High Court.

Judgments have an identification code and number: Court of Appeal (Civil Division) [2000] EWCA Civ 1, 2, 3 etc.; Court of Appeal (Criminal Division) [2000] EWCA Crim 1, 2, 3 etc.; High Court [2000] EWHC Admin 1, 2, 3 etc, [2002] EWHC 123 (QB), (Ch), (Fam), (Pat), (Comm) etc. The letters 'EW' stand for 'England and Wales' and the numbers refer to the first, second, third etc. judgment of that year. The unfamiliar letters in brackets refer to a number of finite specialist courts which exist within the three divisions of the High Court. The Commercial Court (Comm) is a specialist court of the Queen's Bench Division; whereas the Patents Court (Pat) and the Companies Court (Co) are specialist courts of the Chancery Division, presided over by specialist judges.

The main reason was to facilitate the publication of judgments on the web, and decisions of the High Court can be accessed via www.courtservice.gov.uk or www.hmcourtservice.gov.uk. Some recent cases are cited in this way in the following chapters.

The principal free source of UK case law is that of the British and Irish Legal Information Institute at www.baille.org.

Cases are also accessible through subscription databases, including Lexis (www.lexis-nexis.com.), Lawtel (www.lawtel.co.uk) and Westlaw UK (www.westlaw.co.uk).

(b)   The court hierarchy

The hierarchy of the courts can be seen in Figure 1.1. Binding precedent operates from the top down, with the more junior judges presiding over the inferior courts obliged to follow the decisions of their seniors presiding over the higher courts. Decisions of the lower courts (magistrates', county courts) are not reported and have no value as precedents. This is explained in more detail below.

1.6   The binding element in legal decisions

Reports detail facts, names of parties, a statement of the law forming the basis of the decision and the judgment. Only the statement of law forming the basis of the decision is binding. This is called the *ratio decidendi* (the reason for the decision).

Ratio decidendi – a statement of law applied to the legal problems raised by the material facts of the case as identified by the court upon which the decision is based.

Decisions may contain other statements of law which do not fall within this definition. These are merely persuasive and are called *obiter dicta* (singular *obiter dictum*) (a statement of law made by the way). There are two types of *obiter dictum:*

1. A statement of law based upon facts which were either not found to exist or, if found, were not found to be material.

In their judgment, the judges may give their opinion on what the law would be if the material facts of the case were different. This is a hypothetical statement of the law.

2. A statement of law which, although based on material facts of the case as identified by the court, does not form the basis of the decision.

This is a dissenting or minority judgment and can arise in the Court of Appeal or the House of Lords where there are an odd number of judges on the bench and where the outcome of the case will be the majority decision. The value of *obiter dicta* statements depends upon the reputation of the judges making them and their position in the judicial hierarchy.

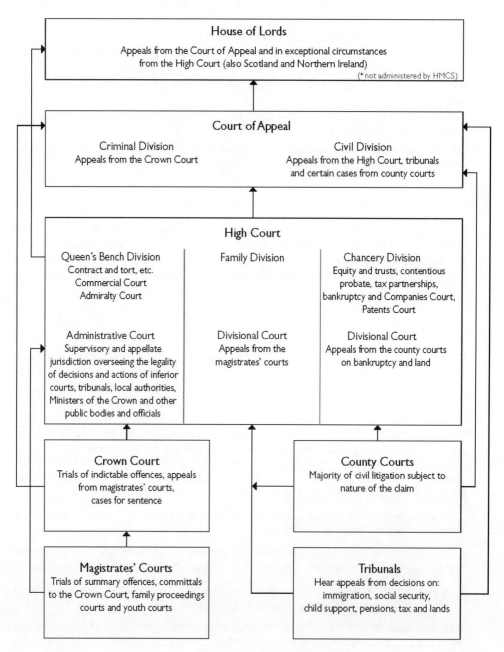

Figure 1.1   The Courts in England and Wales

Non-binding precedents include: (i) persuasive precedents; (ii) precedents which have been overruled; (iii) precedents which have been distinguished; and (iv) *per incuriam* precedents.

(a)   Persuasive authorities

The doctrine of binding precedent operates vertically downwards. Courts lower in the hierarchy are bound by decisions of courts of higher status but decisions of courts lower in the hierarchical system can be ignored or followed by the higher courts depending upon whether they agree or disagree with the statement of the law expressed.

   Decisions of Scottish, Irish, Commonwealth and foreign courts are of only persuasive value in respect of the English courts. In addition, decisions of the Judicial Committee of the Privy Council (JCPC) are also only persuasive. The JCPC hears final appeals from certain Commonwealth countries and ex-colonies which have not created their own final courts of appeal.

(b)   Precedents which have been overruled

Precedents can be overruled by a later decision of a higher court or by Act of Parliament. Judicial overruling is retrospective, whereas overruling by Act operates from the date when the Act comes into force unless the legislation is retrospective. The issue of whether the courts had the power to overrule a decision prospectively was exhaustively discussed in *National Westminster Bank plc v. Spectrum Plus Ltd* [2005] UKHL 41. The possibility was not ruled out in exceptional circumstances. Overruling guarantees the development of the law and must be contrasted with reversing. Overruling effects a retrospective change in the law, but the position of the original litigants is not affected. Reversing involves overturning a lower court's decision on appeal and directly affects the parties.

(c)   Precedents which can be distinguished

If the court finds a material difference in the facts of the case before it and those of the precedent it is urged to follow, it can refuse to be bound by the precedent. It is possible to distinguish virtually any precedent, since factual situations are almost never precisely the same. It ensures the flexibility and adaptability of the law.

(d)   Precedents made through lack of care

The Court of Appeal established that it was not bound to follow its own earlier decisions if they had been made through lack of care: *Young v. Bristol Aeroplane Co. Ltd* [1944] KB 718. These are called decisions made *per incuriam* and are where some relevant statutory provision or precedent had not been brought to the court's attention, making the decision flawed. This has been extended to other courts.

1.7   The operation of binding precedent

All lower courts are bound by decisions of superior courts, and some courts are bound by horizontal precedents at the same level (see Figure 1.1).

(a)   House of Lords/Supreme Court of the UK

Bound by decisions of the European Court of Justice (ECJ) and the Court of First Instance (CFI) in matters of EU law. Bound by its own decisions (*London Street Tramways Ltd v. LCC* [1898] AC 375), subject to the right to 'depart from' its own previous decisions 'when it appears right to do so' (*Practice Statement (Judicial Precedent)* [1966] 3 All ER 77).

(b)   The Court of Appeal (Civil Division)

Bound by decisions of the ECJ and CFI and the House of Lords/Supreme Court, and by its own decisions, subject to the following exceptions:

(i)   faced with two conflicting decisions of its own, the court may choose which it will follow;
(ii)   where a decision is inconsistent with a later decision of the House of Lords, the court must follow the House of Lords;
(iii) where the decision is flawed (*per incuriam*), the court is not bound to follow it.

It is also bound by decisions of the criminal division. Decisions by a full court of five or seven judges have no more weight, and decisions by a two-judge court have no less weight than the normal three-judge court: *Langley v. North West Water Authority* [1991] 3 All ER 610.

(c)   The Court of Appeal (Criminal Division)

Also bound by decisions of the ECJ/CFI, the House of Lords/Supreme Court and the Civil Division, subject to the usual exceptions. The Criminal Division is not bound by its own previous decisions where this would cause injustice: *R v. Gould* [1968] 2 QB 65. The size of the court seems to be more important regarding the decision's status. Established legal principles will generally only be overruled by a court of five or seven judges.

(d)   The divisional courts (appellate and judicial review)

These are bound by all the higher courts and their own earlier decisions. The Divisional Court of Queen's Bench (QBD) is now the Administrative Court.

(e)   First instance High Courts

These are bound by all the higher courts, including their own divisional court, but are not bound by their own previous decisions. Whether the failure to wear seat belts in a car constituted contributory negligence gave rise to 14 conflicting decisions between 1970 and 1975 until the Court of Appeal decision in *Froom v. Butcher* [1976] QB 286. Judges, however, have tended to follow their own decisions, and in *Colchester Estates (Cardiff) Ltd v. Carlton Industries plc* [1984] 2 All ER 601, it was stated that, faced with two conflicting decisions, judges should normally treat the second as being correct if made in full knowledge of the earlier one.

(f)   Inferior courts

Magistrates' courts, county courts and other inferior tribunals are bound by the decisions of all the superior courts. The position of the Crown Court depends on the presiding judge. When presided over by a High Court judge, it is presumably equivalent to a first instance High Court. Decisions of the inferior courts have no authority over higher courts or courts at the same level. There are three distinct tiers of Crown Court handling different levels of work:

- 1st tier – presided over by High Court judge (QB division): handles all serious criminal trials and civil hearings;
- 2nd tier – presided over by circuit judge or recorder: handles less serious criminal trials and serious trials released by 1st tier judge;
- 3rd tier – presided over by circuit judge and/or recorder with panel of lay justices (JPs): hears offences which could otherwise be tried in a magistrates' court (either way offences) and appeals on fact against decisions in magistrates' courts.

(g)   European Court of Justice (ECJ) and the Court of First Instance (CFI)

The ECJ/CFI are not bound by their own previous decisions, but they are binding on all courts in all the Member States.

1.8   Common law and equity

Anybody dealing with anything to do with the law will soon come across the terms 'common law' and 'equity' and it is important to understand their significance.

Common law refers to the vast body of law based on judicial precedent and derives from judgments of the common law courts from their earliest days in the 13th century. Initially, dissatisfied litigants could also petition the king where the common law was inadequate. These petitions were ultimately directed to the Lord Chancellor and led to the creation of the Court of Chancery, which developed a body of law which supplemented and corrected the defects of the common law and created new and improved legal remedies: specific performance, injunctions, rescission and rectification. It also developed areas of exclusive jurisdiction in competition with the common law: trusts and mortgages.

Following clashes between the systems, the supremacy of equity over the common law was established in the 17th century. At the end of the 19th century the old court system was abolished by the Judicature Acts 1873–5. The exclusive, equitable jurisdiction of the Court of Chancery was transferred to the Chancery Division of the High Court and all judges of the newly created, unified court system were authorised to apply equitable rules and remedies at their discretion. The supremacy of equity over the common law is set out in the Supreme Court Act 1981. Equitable rights and remedies differ from common law rights and remedies in the following ways:

- Equitable rights and remedies are discretionary and can be denied to undeserving claimants.
- Equity enforces the intentions of the parties and recognises leases and mortgages even though the legal formalities required by common law are not complied with.
- Equity enforces agreements to create leases or mortgages by a decree of specific performance.

▷ Equity prohibits persons from doing something which is unfair even though it is legal.

1.9   Legislation

Legislation is the major source of any new law. There are two forms of legislation: direct and indirect, or delegated. Direct legislation is in the form of Acts of Parliament passed by the two Houses of Parliament. Delegated legislation is passed by other bodies authorised by Parliament.

Direct legislation – Parliament has absolute legislative power to change the law, consolidate existing enactments, codify the law, implement treaties and introduce social legislation. Parliamentary sovereignty states that the freedom of future parliaments to legislate as they wish cannot be restricted by an Act of Parliament. Britain's membership of the European Community has seen this sovereignty diminish since 1973 (see p. 20) and the Human Rights Act 1998 also imposes restrictions (see p. 20).

Delegated legislation – by bodies authorised by Parliament to legislate. The legislation is binding if it is within the powers which Parliament has conferred (*intra vires*). Legislation in excess of those powers (*ultra vires*) is illegal and void.

Examples are:

Bylaws – by local authorities and other authorised bodies.
Statutory instruments – by government departments under authority given by direct legislation.
Orders in council – promulgated by the government through the Privy Council.

1.10   Statutory interpretation

Legislative texts, however carefully drafted, may not accurately reflect the intentions of the legislators. The Employers' Liability (Defective Equipment) Act 1969 made employers liable for supplying employees with faulty 'equipment'. The term has been interpreted to include a ship which sank due to construction defects (*Coltman v. Bibby Tankers Ltd* [1968] AC 276), and a defective flagstone which injured an employee when it fractured when handled (*Knowles v. Liverpool City Council* [1993] 4 All ER 32). Modifying adjectives can cause confusion: in the phrase 'public hospital or school', 'public' could refer to both 'hospital' and 'school' or merely the former. The courts have also been called upon to decide whether the term 'manufactured beverage' included a drink produced by hand squeezing a fresh orange: *Customs and Excise Commissioners v. Savoy Hotel Ltd* [1966] 2 All ER 299.

Ambiguity arises where the words are capable of two or more literal meanings, one technical and the other non-technical.

The Restriction of Offensive Weapons Act 1959 made it an offence to 'offer for sale' offensive weapons. In *Fisher v. Bell* [1961] 1QB 394, the accused was charged under the Act for displaying, for the purposes of sale, a flick knife in a shop window. This was not an offer for sale for the purposes of the Act but merely an invitation to treat, inviting a member of the public to make an offer for sale.

A court may also be called upon to extend legislation to situations which were unforeseeable when it was passed. The Telegraph Act 1869, which pre-dated the invention of the telephone, was held to confer powers over telephone messages on the Postmaster General: *A-G v. Edison Telephone Co.* (1880) 6 QBD 244.

The courts have a body of presumptions, rules and aids to which they can refer in deciding on the meaning of a statute.

(a) Presumptions

Presumptions are presumed to apply when a court is faced with a piece of legislation to interpret:

- *Territorial application:* legislation is applicable only within the UK but, unless otherwise specified, it applies to the whole of the UK.
- *Statute does not bind the Crown:* Acts which bind the Crown must state this fact expressly.
- *Against any alteration in the common law:* A statute can effect a change in the common law only by means of an express provision, not merely by implication.
- *Against imposition of strict liability:* in interpreting legislation imposing criminal liability, the court presumes that there must be evidence of criminal intention *(mens rea)* before a person can be guilty of an offence. Strict liability offences can be created only by express provision: *Sweet v. Parsley* [1969] 1 All ER 347.
- *Against removal of a vested right:* Acts authorising something which interferes with a person's enjoyment of their property do not remove their right of action against the nuisance unless expressly stated. This also presupposes that statutes do not have retrospective effect.

There are three fundamental rules relating to interpretation: (i) the literal rule; (ii) the golden rule; and (iii) the mischief rule.

(i) The literal rule
Legislative interpretation is in the ordinary and natural meaning of the words used. The Act must be read as a whole, with the words read in their context.

(ii) The golden rule
This a 'gloss on the literal rule' so that, where the statute permits two or more literal interpretations, the golden rule allows the court to adopt the interpretation which produces the 'least absurd or repugnant effect'.

(iii) The mischief rule
The mischief rule operates in the event of the failure of the literal rule. It is derived from *Heydon's Case* (1584) 3 Co Rep 7a, 7b. In *Jones v. Wrotham Park Settled Estates* [1980] AC 74, Lord Diplock identified three necessary conditions for the operation of the rule:

(i) it must be possible to determine precisely the mischief that the Act was drafted to remedy;

(ii) it must be apparent that Parliament had failed to deal with the mischief;

(iii) it must be possible to state the additional words that would have been inserted had the omission been drawn to Parliament's attention.

(b) Purposive and literalist interpretation

The purposive view looks to the intention behind the Act and seeks to interpret the text to effect the intention, even against the strict, literal meaning of the words. The literalist approach is bound by the literal meaning of the words used and believes that, if the wording is inadequate, the matter should be left to Parliament to give effect to the intention by amending the legislation. The purposive approach is the more modern approach, with its basis in the mischief rule.

(c) Other rules of interpretation

▷ Where a general term follows two or more specific words which form a genus, the general words are interpreted in the light of the specific words.

The effect is to limit the scope of the general words.

In *Powell v. Kempton Park Racecourse Co.* [1899] AC 143, the court held that in respect of a prohibition against betting in a 'house, office, room or other place' (s.1 Betting Act 1853), the words 'other place' did not include Tattersalls' enclosure at a racecourse as not being of the same genus as 'house, office, room'.

There must be at least two specific words to create a genus. In *Allen v. Emerson* [1944] KB 362, an Act referring to 'theatres and other places of amusement' extended licensing to funfairs, since no genus was established. This is called the *eiusdem generis* (of the same kind) rule.

▷ Words are to be interpreted in their proper context.

In *Pengelley v. Bell Punch Co. Ltd* [1964] 1 WLR 691, the court was required to interpret the meaning of the word 'floors' in a phrase in a statute which required 'floors, steps, stairs, passages and gangways' to be kept clear. The court, by analogy with the other words, limited its meaning to floor areas used for access. It did not cover a part of a factory floor used for storage.

▷ Where specific words are not followed by general words, the Act applies only to the specific instances mentioned.

An example is the express repeal of existing legislation by Acts of Parliament. Only the legislation listed is repealed.

▷ Penal provisions are construed narrowly.

An ambiguous penal provision is construed in favour of the defendant (see the presumption against the imposition of strict liability).

(d) Aids to interpretation

The Interpretation Act 1978 gives definitions of words and phrases and there are internal and external aids to help in interpreting legislation. Internal aids are found within the Act itself in the form of interpretation sections which define words for that Act. External aids include dictionaries, reports of the Law Commission and the various law reform committees and other Acts of Parliament. Where the legislation implements an international convention or EC Directive, the convention and the Directive can be looked at. Courts are also entitled to consult reports of parliamentary proceedings in Hansard where (a) legislation is ambiguous or obscure or leads to an absurdity; (b) the material relied upon consists of statements by a minister or other promoter; and (c) the statements relied upon are clear: *Pepper v. Hart* [1993] 1 All ER 42.

(e) The European dimension

There are special rules where the legislation implements a Directive or a decision of the European Court of Justice (ECJ). The ECJ stated: 'In applying the national law and in particular the provision of a national law specifically introduced in order to implement [a directive], national courts are required to interpret their national law in the light of the wording and the purpose of the directive in order to achieve the result referred to in [the Treaty]': Case 14/83 *Von Colson v. Land Nordrhein-Westfalen* [1984] ECR 1891. In keeping with this, in *Pickstone v. Freemans plc* [1989] 3 WLR 265, the House of Lords interpreted an Act as if it contained words which were not in fact there.

The ECJ has also held that national courts should interpret national law in furtherance of Community law principles whenever possible: Case C–106/89 *Marleasing SA v. La Commercial International de Alimentacion SA* [1990] ECR I–4135.

1.11 European Union law

The sources of EU law are legislation and case law. Certain Treaty provisions constitute primary legislation, whereas Regulations, Directives and Decisions of the Council and Commission under Article 249 of the EC Treaty (the Treaty of Rome, hereafter called the EC Treaty) are secondary or delegated legislation. In addition, the decisions of the European Court of Justice (ECJ) and the Court of First Instance (CFI) are binding on the national courts of Member States. Britain is bound not only by the Treaty provisions themselves and the secondary legislation made thereunder, but also interpretations given by the European Court: s.3(1) European Communities Act (ECA) 1972.

(a) Directly applicable and directly effective legislation

A directly applicable provision becomes part of the law of each Member State automatically without the need for direct or indirect national legislation.

A directly effective provision creates rights in favour of natural and legal persons enforceable by action in the national courts. All directly applicable provisions are also directly effective.

Provisions which are not directly applicable can be directly effective but they are enforceable only against the Member State or an organ of the state. They cannot be enforced against other persons, legal or natural. As a result, they are considered to have vertical direct effect, since the person is enforcing the provision upwards against the state or state agency.

Directly applicable provisions can be enforced against persons, legal or natural, at the same level (horizontal direct effect).

(h) Legislation

(i) Treaty provisions

Treaty provisions are directly applicable and directly effective, both horizontally and vertically, if they: (i) are not simply concerned with interstate relations; (ii) are clear and precise; (iii) are unconditional and unqualified and not subject to any further measures on the part of the Member State or the Community; and (iv) do not leave any substantial latitude or discretion to Member States. In respect of the equal pay provision in Article 141 EC Treaty, the Equal Pay Act 1970 was held to be contrary to Community law (see Chapter 17, p.396).

Under Article 249 EC Treaty, the Commission and the Council can make secondary legislation. Draft proposals for such legislation are initiated by the Commission and can be passed or rejected by the Council of Ministers where individual Member States are represented. In most of its business the Council proceeds by a qualified majority voting system, but some decisions are required to be unanimous.

(ii) Regulations

Regulations are defined as having 'general application' and 'being binding in [their] entirety and directly applicable in all Member States'. They 'not only … render automatically inapplicable any conflicting provision of current national law but … also preclude the valid adoption of new national legislative measures to the extent to which they would be incompatible with Community provisions'.

Regulations introduce major changes in Community law throughout the Community. They bind all Member States and take precedence over existing or future national legislation. Regulation rights are enforceable in the national courts of Member States.

(iii) Directives

Directives are 'binding as to the result to be achieved upon each Member State to which it is directed, but shall leave to the national authorities the choice of form or methods' (Art. 249).

Directives are used to harmonise systems throughout the EU and require a Member State to introduce legislation within a specific time limit to implement the Directive. See in particular examples in respect of employment law (Chapter 17).

Directives cannot be directly applicable, but where Member States fail to implement them within the period required actions can be brought against them in the national courts to claim the benefit of any right guaranteed by the Directive (vertical direct effect). Liability extends to local authorities and government agencies, including regional health authorities.

In Case C–152/84 *Marshall v. Southampton and South West Hampshire Area Health Authority (Teaching)* [1986] ECR 723, M was compulsorily retired from her job with the authority at the age of 62 when she wished to continue until 65. The retiring age was determined by the employee's entitlement to the state pension: 60 for women and 65 for men. M brought an action against the authority as an agent of the state on the ground that UK law conflicted with the EU Directive on equal treatment for men and women. UK legislation was held to conflict with EU law and was subsequently changed.

(iv) Decisions

A decision is 'binding in its entirety upon those to whom it is addressed' (Art 249).

Decisions are generally addressed to one or more Member States or individuals where, on investigation, it has been found that they are in breach of EU law. The ECJ has held that decisions addressed to Member States could give rise to directly effective rights in an individual, which must be protected by national courts.

(c) Case law

Case law arises from decisions of the Court of First Instance (CFI) and the European Court of Justice (ECJ). The CFI has three areas of jurisdiction, of which only actions for damages regarding implementation of competition rules to undertakings are relevant here. The most important, relevant jurisdiction of the ECJ for our purposes relates to requests by courts or tribunals of Member States for preliminary rulings concerning the interpretation of the EC Treaty under Article 234.

The ECJ has the sole responsibility for interpreting EU legislation and, when a judge in a Member State is called upon to interpret EU law, that judge may – and in some cases must – seek a preliminary ruling on the matter from the ECJ. This means suspending the hearing and addressing a question to the ECJ and awaiting the ECJ's decision. The law as interpreted is then applied by the judge in the reconvened case. Judges can generally use their discretion in the matter, but they must make a preliminary reference where the question is raised in a case 'pending before a court or tribunal ... against whose decisions there is no judicial remedy under national law' – in other words a court from which there is no right of appeal.

The following points are important in respect of the preliminary reference procedure:

- It is for the court to decide whether or not to refer a matter.
- Article 234 applies to all courts, statutory and arbitral tribunals and include the disciplinary committees of bodies such as the Jockey Club or the Football Association.
- There is an obligation to refer in respect of any court or tribunal at whatever level against whose decision there is no right of appeal: Case 6/64 *Costa v. ENEL* [1964] ECR 585. This does not apply to the Court of Appeal even though there is no 'right' of appeal from its decisions: *Chiron Corporation v. Murex Diagnostics Ltd* [1995] All ER (EC) 88.
- There is no obligation to refer where the point of law is sufficiently clear, even though it has not been interpreted by the ECJ.
- UK courts are bound to treat rulings as precedents by s.3(1) ECA 1972. Rulings on interpretation are generally retrospective.

Decisions of the European Court are officially reported in the European Court Reports (ECR), and most can also be found in the unofficial but authoritative Common Market Law Reports (CMLR). Cases can be accessed via www.baille.org.

1.12 The supremacy of Community law

Acts of Parliament are to be construed and have effect subject to Community provisions: s.2(4) ECA 1972. English courts must also interpret Community legislation using European methods (s.3(1)), and judicial notice must be taken of the treaties, the Official

Journal of the Communities (OJ) and decisions and opinions of the ECJ on matters of interpretation: s.3(2).

Lord Bridge stated that the supremacy of Community law over national law was: 'well established long before the UK joined the Community ... Under the European Communities Act 1972 it has always been clear that it was the duty of a UK court, ..., to override any rule of national law found to be in conflict with any directly enforceable rule of Community Law. Similarly, when decisions of the Court of Justice have exposed areas of UK law which failed to implement Council Directives, Parliament has always loyally accepted the obligation to make appropriate and prompt amendments. Thus there is nothing in any way novel in according supremacy to rules of Community law.': Case C–213/89, R v. Secretary of State for Transport, ex parte Factortame (No. 2) [1991] ECR I–2433. The Factortame case concerned the requirement under the Merchant Shipping Act 1988 that British-registered boats fishing for British quotas were to be British owned and managed. The Act was held to contravene Article 43 EC Treaty by discriminating against the nationals of other Member States.

In Stoke-on-Trent CC v. B & Q plc [1991] 2 WLR 42, Hoffmann J also stated: 'The EEC Treaty is the supreme law of this country, taking precedence over Acts of Parliament. Our entry into the European Economic Community meant that (subject to our undoubted but probably theoretical right to withdraw from the Community altogether) Parliament surrendered its sovereign right to legislate contrary to the provisions of the Treaty on matters of social and economic policy which it regulated'. In Fleming (t/a Bodycraft) v. Revenue and Customs Commissioners; Conde Nast Publications Ltd v. Same [2008] UKHL 2, the House of Lords held that regulation 29(1A) of the VAT Regulations 1995 was incompatible with EU law because it was retrospective and made no provision for transitional arrangements, and had to be disapplied. Their Lordships refused to rule on what was a reasonable transitional period. This was for Parliament or the Commissioners to decide.

Hot Topic . . .

MEMBER STATES' LIABILITY FOR DAMAGES FOR BREACH OF COMMUNITY LAW

In Joined Cases C–6 and 9/90 Francovich and Bonifaci v. Italian State [1991] ECR I–5357, Italian workers successfully claimed damages against the Italian state for its failure to implement a Directive to protect the wages of employees of an insolvent employer. The liability was clarified in two decisions heard together, Joined Cases C–46 and 48/93 Brasserie du Pêcheur SA v. Germany and R v. Secretary of State for Transport, ex parte Factortame Ltd (No. 3) [1990] ECR I–03905. The Brasserie du Pêcheur case concerned German laws on the purity of beer

which prevented the French brewery from selling its products in Germany in breach of Article 28 EC Treaty prohibiting 'quantitative restrictions on imports [between Member States] and all measures having equivalent effect'.

Liability for damages is subject to the following conditions:

▶ Where the legislature, judiciary or executive was responsible for losses arising from breaches of EU law – whether directly effective or not.
▶ Failure to transpose a Directive into domestic law.

Persons can claim compensation:

(i) where the rule breached is intended to confer rights upon them;
(ii) where the breach is sufficiently serious;
(iii) where there is a direct causal link between the breach and the damage.

Seriousness depends on whether the Member State clearly and gravely disregarded the limits on its discretion, taking into consideration:

(i) the clarity and precision of the rule;
(ii) the amount of discretion allowed the Member State;
(iii) whether the infringement and the damage were intentional or involuntary;

(iv) whether any error was excusable or inexcusable;

(v) any contribution of a Community institution towards the omission, adoption or retention of national measures contrary to Community law.

A breach is serious if it has persisted despite a judgment, preliminary ruling or precedent of the ECJ from which it is clear that it constituted an infringement.

Compensation is in accordance with national law, but the conditions must not be less favourable than for similar domestic claims or make it impossible or excessively difficult to obtain compensation.

▶ Compensation must not be conditional upon fault of the state organ.

▶ Compensation must be commensurate with the loss. The criteria must not be less favourable than for similar claims in domestic law, or make it impossible or excessively difficult to obtain.

▶ National legislation excluding loss of profit is incompatible with Community law (see 'Pure economic loss', Chapter 5, p.127).

▶ It must be possible to award exemplary damages if they may be awarded for similar domestic claims (see Chapter 5, p. 128).

▶ State liability cannot be limited to damage sustained after a judgment finding the infringement.

In Case C–392/93 *The Queen v. HM Treasury, ex parte British Telecommunications plc* [1996] ECR I–1631, BT sought annulment of part of some 1992 Regulations, which incorrectly implemented an EC Directive, and damages for losses in complying with those Regulations. The ECJ agreed that liability could arise from an incorrectly transposed Directive but held that, in this case, the breach was not sufficiently serious, since the relevant Article of the Directive was imprecise and capable of interpretation by the UK government. There had been no available guidance on interpretation from decided case law and the Commission had not raised the matter when the Regulations were adopted by the UK government. However, in *Byrne v. Motor Insurers' Bureau and Anor* [2007] EWHC 1268 (QB) the court held that failure of the UK to comply with the Second European Directive on motor insurance rendered it liable in damages.

1.13   The European Convention on Human Rights (ECHR)

The Human Rights Act 1998 incorporates the rights guaranteed by the ECHR into UK law and gives nationals the ECHR protection before the national courts rather than the Court of Human Rights in Strasbourg.

All courts and tribunals must interpret all primary and subordinate legislation 'so far as it is possible to do so' to be compatible with Convention rights: s.3(1). This does not, however, affect the validity, operation or enforcement of any incompatible primary legislation: s.3(2). The definition of primary legislation includes delegated legislation in the form of orders in council and statutory instruments, which are generally regarded as secondary.

If a compatible interpretation is not possible, a superior court (High Court and upwards) may make a 'declaration of incompatibility' which is 'not binding on the parties' and which does not affect the validity, operation or enforcement of the primary legislation: s.4. Parliamentary sovereignty is maintained by failure to allow the courts to set aside incompatible Acts of Parliament. In addition, all courts and tribunals in considering questions relating to Convention rights must 'take into account' decisions of the Commission and Court of Human Rights: s.2.

It is unlawful for public authorities (including courts and tribunals) to act in a way which is incompatible with Convention rights, unless primary legislation permits no other course of action: s.6. Actual or likely victims of such an 'unlawful act' may take proceedings in an appropriate court/tribunal, for example by application for judicial review: s.7. The courts/tribunals may provide 'such relief or remedy or make such an order within its jurisdiction as it considers just and appropriate', but damages are available only in civil courts with power to award damages: s.8.

The Act provides for a 'fast-track' procedure for amending primary legislation by statutory instrument ('remedial orders') to remove inconsistencies with Convention rights, when either a superior court or the Court of Human Rights has found a breach of the Convention: s.10. Before the second reading in respect of proposed legislation, the government minister responsible for introducing the Bill must either make a statement of his/her view that the Bill is compatible with Convention rights, or state that despite being unable to make that statement the government nevertheless wishes to proceed with the Bill: s.19.

The Convention freedoms are: the right to life (Art. 2); freedom from torture or inhuman or degrading treatment or punishment (Art. 3); freedom from slavery, servitude or forced or compulsory labour (Art. 4); the right to liberty and security of the person (Art. 5); the right to a fair trial (Art. 6); freedom from retroactive criminal offences and punishment (Art. 7); the right to respect for private and family life, home and correspondence (Art. 8); freedom of religion (Art. 9); freedom of expression (Art. 10); freedom of assembly and association (Art. 11); the right to marry and to found a family (Art. 12); the right to an effective national remedy (Art. 13); and freedom from discrimination in respect of protected rights (Art. 14). Article 15 allows for derogation from the rights in time of war or other public emergency.

In App. No. 62617/00 *Copland v. UK* [2007] ECHR 253, the European Court of Human Rights held that an employer's collection and storage of information of an employee's telephone, e-mail and internet usage at the workplace was, in the absence of any legal provisions, unjustified and a breach of Article 8 ECHR protecting the right for private life and correspondence. The Telecommunications (Lawful Business Practice) Regulations (SI 2000 No 2699) were not in force at the relevant time.

The First Protocol recognises the right to property (Art. 1); the right to education (Art. 2) and the right to free elections (Art. 3). The Fourth Protocol recognises the freedom from imprisonment for non-fulfilment of a contractual obligation (Art. 1); freedom of movement within a state and freedom to leave its territory (Art. 2); the right of a national not to be expelled from and to enter a state's territory (Art. 3); and the freedom of aliens from collective expulsion (Art. 4). The Sixth Protocol provides for freedom from the death penalty. The Seventh Protocol recognises the freedom from expulsion of individual aliens (Art. 1); the right to review in criminal cases (Art. 2); the right to compensation for miscarriages of justice (Art. 3); freedom from further trial or punishment for an offence for which a person has already been finally acquitted or convicted in accordance with the law of that state (Art. 4); and equality of rights of spouses (Art. 5).

1.14 Human rights and UK law

The fact that claimants can now raise the issue of compatibility of legislation and common law with the Human Rights Act has had an enormous effect on many areas of the law, including business law. An important example relates to the Crown's immunity from tortious liability under s.10 Crown Proceedings Act 1947 whereby members of the armed forces who were negligently exposed to asbestos and contracted a related disease were unable to claim damages from the Crown but were obliged to claim under a less favourable government-administered compensation system.

Even though s.10 was repealed by the Crown Proceedings (Armed Forces) Act 1987, the legislation was not retrospective and many victims of pre-1987 exposure were denied a right of action. In *Matthews v. Ministry of Defence* [2002] All ER 137, the High Court held that s.10 was incompatible with Article 6(1) ECHR, which provides that everyone is entitled to a fair hearing in respect of his civil rights.

In *Wilson v. First County Trust Ltd* [2003] 4 All ER 97, the House of Lords reversed the Court of Appeal's finding that s.127(3) Consumer Credit Act 1974 was incompatible with two of the rights guaranteed to a pawnbroker by the ECHR (see Chapter 20, p.480). In *R (Countryside Alliance and Ors) v. Attorney-General and Anor* [2007] UKHL 52 the House held that the Hunting Act 2004 was not incompatible with the ECHR.

The ECHR has been instrumental in developing the legal recognition of a right to privacy under Article 10. This was based on the notion of the reasonable expectation of privacy established in *Campbell v. Mirror Group Newspapers Ltd* [2004] 2 AC 457 when the claimant successfully claimed in respect of a photograph of her leaving a drug clinic. In *Murray v. Big Pictures UK Ltd* [2008] EWCA Civ 446 the court recognised that a child had a reasonable expectation that he would not be targeted in order to obtain photographs in a public place for publication. The child was the son of the author, J.K. Rowling.

A seminar in London in December 2004 considered the human rights responsibilities of international companies in the countries in which they operate. It took as its starting point the UN's 'norms' of the responsibilities of transnational enterprises including 'the obligation to promote, secure the fulfilment of, respect ... the rights and interests of indigenous peoples and other vulnerable groups'. Other norms specify rights to equal opportunity for all, regardless of sex, language, religion, social status or origin. The norm covering workers' rights stipulates that transnational corporations should 'provide a safe and healthy environment ... remuneration that ensures an adequate standard of living'.

End of chapter summary

In this chapter you have been introduced to the sources of English law including case law and domestic legislation, direct and indirect. You have also been shown how English law is influenced by EU law, and how the Human Rights Act 1998 has introduced into English law the rights guaranteed under the European Convention on Human Rights.

You should now be able to appreciate the following points which are of great significance and which you will need to know to understand the later chapters of the book:

- The court hierarchy and the doctrine of binding judicial decisions.
- The differences between direct and indirect legislation, with particular regard to statutory instruments.
- The sources and supremacy of EU Law.
- The reference mechanism of Article 234 EC Treaty for the preliminary interpretation of EU law.
- The significance of the Human Rights Act 1998.

To see examples of these factors in a business context, look particularly at the anti-discrimination legislation relating to employment in Chapter 17 to see how EC Directives have driven development in this area and how changes are incorporated into English law by statutory instruments.

Questions

1. Ted, the owner of 'Ted's Take-Away', is summoned for breach of a local authority by-law making it an offence 'to keep open any restaurant or other premises for the sale of tea, coffee or other drinks after 11.00 p.m.'. One evening at 11.30 p.m. Ted was seen selling bottles of Coca-Cola to passers-by through a hatch from his store, the door of which was locked. What risk does he run of being convicted of an offence?

2. What do you understand by the vertical and horizontal operation of the doctrine of binding precedent?

3. In respect of the elements in the precedent system which are claimed to maintain its flexibility, explain when a court can distinguish an earlier binding precedent. What is the difference between overruling and reversing?

4. Assuming that the Factories Act 1990 makes it a criminal offence 'to keep explosives in any factory, workshop or other place without a licence', would an offence be committed by a quarry owner keeping explosives in a caravan adjacent to the quarry?

5. Two Community law procedures are designed to standardise and harmonise the law throughout the EU. Identify and explain their operation.

6. What is the difference between direct applicability and direct effectivity? To what extent can EU legislation be directly effective if it is not at the same time directly applicable?

Chapter 2

Resolving disputes

Learning objectives

After reading this chapter you will know about:

- civil dispute resolution through the courts
- enforcement of judgment orders
- civil dispute resolution through arbitration
- alternative dispute resolution (ADR): advantages and disadvantages

Several different systems exist for resolving disputes between parties: tribunals; the courts; arbitration; and alternative dispute resolution (ADR).

2.1 Tribunals

Certain disputes must be referred to specialist statutory tribunals: claims by employees for unfair dismissal to an employment tribunal; fixing fair rents to a rent tribunal, claims in respect of social security payments to a national insurance tribunal and title disputes to registered land to a lands tribunal.

2.2 The civil courts

The principal civil courts are the High Court and the county courts. Certain cases must be brought in the county court, others in the High Court, and in other cases there is a choice. The Court structure and appeals system is shown in Figure 1.1 (p.10).

(a) The jurisdiction of the county court

County court jurisdiction is of three kinds: (i) exclusive; (ii) concurrent without financial limitation; and (iii) concurrent subject to financial limits.

(i) Exclusive to the county court

Exclusivity arises under various statutes and includes: (i) recovery of possession by landlords; (ii) actions on regulated consumer credit agreements under the Consumer Credit Act 1974 (hire purchase, conditional sale and credit sale agreements and consumer hire agreements); (iii) claims for unlawful racial, sexual and disability discrimination except in relation to employment which go to an employment tribunal; and (iv) mortgage possession proceedings outside London (except foreclosure when a £30,000 limit applies).

(ii) Concurrent jurisdiction without financial limits

Concurrent jurisdiction without financial limits includes: (i) contract and tort actions (excluding libel and slander); (ii) actions to recover a sum recoverable by statute; (iii) actions to recover land or involving a dispute as to title; (iv) financial provision applications from a deceased person's estate; and (v) tenants' applications against forfeiture for non-payment of rent.

Under Article 7 High Court and County Courts Jurisdiction Order 1991, actions for less than £25,000 are heard in the county court unless the court considers they should be transferred to the High Court and the High Court agrees, or they are commenced in the High Court which considers it ought to try the action. An action for £50,000 or more is heard in the High Court unless the High Court considers that it ought to transfer to the county court, or if the action was commenced in the county court and that court does not consider that it ought to be transferred. Where the claimant claims more than £15,000 for non-personal injuries, the claim may be started in the High Court. However, claims for personal injuries can be started in the High Court only where the claim is for more than £50,000.

Under an amendment order (SI.2008/2934) the county courts have jurisdiction over the EOP Regulation (1896/2006/EC, [2006] OJ L399/1) creating a European Order for Payment procedure up to £15,000, and above that amount jurisdiction is at either the county court or High Court. This came into force on 12 December 2008.

(iii)   Jurisdiction subject to financial limits

Jurisdiction subject to financial limits includes: (i) administration of estates up to £30,000, including contentious probate; (ii) execution, declaration and variation of trusts up to £30,000; (iii) foreclosure or redemption of mortgages up to £30,000; (iv) specific performance, rectification or cancellation of agreements for the sale, purchase or lease of property up to £30,000; and (v) certain courts outside London may be designated as bankruptcy courts with unlimited jurisdiction for personal insolvency and jurisdiction over company winding-up where the paid-up share capital does not exceed £120,000, and for partnerships where the assets do not exceed £30,000.

(iv)   Small claims

All disputes for up to £5,000 are automatically referred to arbitration by the district judge. This is an informal procedure and parties are discouraged from being legally represented since the successful party cannot recover costs. Under an amendment order (SI.2008/2934) the county courts also have jurisdiction under the ESCP Regulation (861/2007/EC, [2006] OJ L199/1) establishing a European small claims procedure. This applies in respect of civil and commercial matters where the value of the claim does not exceed € 2,000. The procedure applies to monetary and non-pecuniary claims. The rules in respect of the ESCP Regulation came into force on 1 January 2009.

(b)   The jurisdiction of the High Court

The jurisdiction of the High Court is split between three divisions.

(i)   Queen's Bench Division

This has concurrent jurisdiction with the county court in contract and tort, with exclusive jurisdiction for libel and slander. There are specialist courts relating to admiralty and commercial disputes relating to insurance, bills of lading, and negotiable instruments and so on.

A review in 2000 recommended a specialist court as part of the High Court to deal with public and administrative law cases. This led to the creation of the Administrative Court in place of the Queen's Bench Division Divisional Court (QBD Div Ct). It deals with appeals by way of case stated on points of law from criminal cases from the magistrates' and Crown Courts. It also has an important supervisory function through Judicial Review which includes the review of –

- Decisions of local authorities in respect of welfare benefits and special needs provision in education;
- Decisions of immigration authorities and the Immigration Appellate Authority;
- Decisions of regulatory bodies;
- Decisions relating to prisoners' rights.

(ii)   Chancery Division
This hears cases on the administration of estates, trusts, mortgages, partnerships, patents, trade marks and copyright and revenue matters, and the sale, exchange or partition of land. There are separate, specialist courts: Companies Court, Patents Court. A Divisional Court hears appeals from county courts on bankruptcy and land.

(iii)   Family Division
This hears defended matrimonial causes, decrees of death (where a spouse has disappeared for a number of years), legitimacy and nullity, the rights of children, such as adoption, wardship and actions between spouses for the ownership of property and occupation of the matrimonial home. A Divisional Court hears appeals on family matters from the magistrates' court.

(c)   Appeals from civil trial courts

(i)   Appeals from county courts

Appeals from a district judge normally go first to a circuit judge and then to the High Court (although exceptionally they will go to the Court of Appeal).

Otherwise, appeals are heard by the Court of Appeal which may affirm, vary or reverse the judgment. Appeals involve consideration of the trial judge's notes and other documentary evidence, rather than a re-hearing; the court is reluctant to overturn the trial judge's findings of fact. Further appeal is to the House of Lords with permission of the Court of Appeal or the House of Lords on a point of law of public importance. Bankruptcy appeals from county courts outside London are to the Divisional Court of the Chancery Division.

(ii)   Appeals from the High Court
Appeals on matters of fact and/or law are to the Court of Appeal. Further appeals are to the House of Lords with the permission of the Court of Appeal or the House of Lords in respect of a point of law of public importance. A 'leapfrog' procedure allows appeals direct to the House of Lords where the parties agree and the trial judge certifies that the case involves a point of law of public importance concerning either the construction of a statute or statutory instrument or, more usually, a matter upon which the Court of Appeal is bound by a previous ruling of the House of Lords and cases where the House of Lords itself gives leave.

(d) Bringing a civil action in the High Court or the county court

Proceedings are in accordance with the Civil Procedure Rules supplemented by Practice Directions. The rules encourage pre-trial settlements with litigation as a last resort. The courts promote settlement by way of alternative dispute resolution (ADR) and parties can request a stay of proceedings for one month to enable them to try to settle the case through ADR or other means.

(i) Claim form

Proceedings commence with a claim form served on the defendant by the court by first-class post, unless the claimant notifies the court that they will undertake service. The defendant must file an acknowledgement of service or a defence within 14 days or the claimant can enter judgment against the defendant in default. If the defendant files a defence, the court serves a questionnaire on each party to enable it to allocate the claim to one of the following three tracks:

- Small claims track for actions involving claims for less than £5,000;
- Fast track for actions concerning claims between £5,000 and £15,000;
- Multi-track for cases dealing with claims in excess of £15,000.

Allocation determines the time allocated for the following procedural stages, of which the next is disclosure.

(ii) Disclosure

Disclosure enables each party to seek more details of the claim or the defence from the other using a 'request for information'. Each side can inspect all relevant documents in the other party's possession unless they are protected by privilege and cannot be disclosed. To prevent the defendant from destroying evidence or disposing of assets or transferring them out of the court's jurisdiction, the claimant can have recourse to a freezing injunction and a search order. A county court may impose a freezing injunction only: (i) in its family proceedings jurisdiction; (ii) for the preservation, custody or detention of property which forms or may form the subject matter of proceedings; or (iii) to preserve assets until execution can be levied upon them. An application to the High Court for a search order or freezing order automatically transfers proceedings to the High Court for this purpose, but the action will be retransferred afterwards unless the High Court orders otherwise.

(iii) Freezing injunctions

Freezing injunctions prevent the defendant from 'removing from the jurisdiction of the High Court, or otherwise dealing with, assets located within that jurisdiction'. The words 'dealing with' include disposing of, selling or charging assets.

The application is generally made without notice to the defendant, sometimes even before issuing a claim form. Claimants must swear an affidavit in support of the application. The High Court may grant a freezing injunction 'in all cases in which it appears to the court to be just and convenient to do so': s.37(1) Supreme Court Act (SCA) 1981. However, claimants must establish: (i) that they have a good arguable case; and (ii) that the refusal of an application would involve a real risk that a judgment or award in their favour would remain unsatisfied because of the removal of the assets from the jurisdiction or dissipation of assets within the jurisdiction.

The service of an injunction on a bank or other body will freeze an account or other assets held for that party. The injunction may continue after judgment if the court fears that assets may be dissipated, and it may even be granted for the first time after the judgment.

The standard freezing injunction contains an express provision that it should be of no effect on a third party outside the jurisdiction of the court until it is declared enforceable or is enforced by a court in the relevant country. Claimants obtaining a worldwide freezing injunction must enforce the order in any local jurisdiction in which assets may be located.

(iv) Search orders

Search orders oblige defendants to allow claimants to enter their premises to inspect, remove or make copies of documents belonging to them or relating to their property. They may be obtained without notice where there is a danger of property being smuggled away or vital evidence destroyed and are most used in respect of copyright infringement or misuse of confidential information. Failure to allow access is contempt of court.

The claimant's only risk is paying the defendant's costs and for any damage caused. There are procedural safeguards: the claimant's solicitor must attend when the order is executed and, where entry is refused, no force should be used. Defendants must have the opportunity to contact their solicitor and be advised of their right to obtain legal advice. Applicants must make full disclosure of all relevant matters to the court, and failure to disclose material facts will cause the order to be discharged.

Defendants against whom a 'without notice order' has been made may apply to have it set aside and, pending the appeal, refuse to comply with the order. The danger is that, if their application fails, they will be in contempt of court and liable to severe penalties if they have acted in breach of the order by destroying records. In *Rank Film Distributors Ltd v. Video Information Centre* [1981] 2 All ER 76, the House of Lords held that a defendant could successfully resist the making of an order on the ground of privilege against self-incrimination, but s.72 SCA 1981 removes the privilege in relation to High Court proceedings for infringement of rights relating to intellectual property or passing off.

(v) Part 36 payment

Defendants will often try to settle a claim for debt or damages by making a payment of money into court. This puts claimants in a difficult position since, if they continue with the action and are awarded a smaller sum than that paid into court, they will be liable for their own and the defendant's legal costs from the date of the payment into court. The judge does not know how much money has been paid in. The defendant serves a notice of payment in on the claimant. This is a major reason for most actions to be settled out of court – more than 50 per cent just before the case is due to go to court.

If the case is not settled out of court, it will then proceed to trial.

(vi) The trial

Once a defence has been filed, trial dates are fixed and are difficult to postpone. The pace at which the various stages of the action proceed depends upon the designation of the action to one of the three tracks. Apart from cases allocated to the small claims track, cases will be designated as either fast-track or multi-track cases. Fast-track cases will normally be allocated to the county court and will involve claims for between £5,000 and £15,000. A typical timetable for such an action is given by a Practice Direction as follows:

▶ disclosure: four weeks from issue of claim form;
▶ exchange of witness statements: 10 weeks from issue of claim form;
▶ exchange of experts' reports: 14 weeks from issue of claim form;
▶ hearing: 30 weeks from issue of claim form.

Any change to the date of the trial requires an application to the court. The normal length of a trial is one day and the trial judge may dispense with an opening address by counsel. Witness statements will usually stand as evidence in chief, and expert evidence is restricted to one expert per party in any field of expertise and limited to two fields of expertise. The ultimate aim is for the introduction of pre-trial fixed costs in an attempt to reduce legal bills. Lord Woolf had recommended a limit on costs of £2,500.

For multi-track cases, the court can give management directions for the case, with a timetable established for the various stages. For more complex cases, the timetable may follow a case management conference or a pre-trial review or both. The trial date for the multi-track cases is fixed only as soon as it is practicable to do so. The High Court hears only multi-track cases.

The trial begins with an opening speech from the claimant's counsel outlining the facts and the relief sought. Counsel will then call the witnesses to give evidence by examination in chief; they will then be cross-examined by the defendant's counsel and re-examined by the claimant's counsel. The defendant's counsel will then present his case and call his witnesses who will also be cross-examined by the claimant's counsel and re-examined. The action terminates with the closing speech of the claimant's counsel, followed by that of the defence counsel.

The judgment is given either immediately or at a later time (a 'reserved judgment'). Normally the successful party's costs are paid by the other party, but the court has discretionary powers in the matter.

(vii) Small claims

Where the claimant commences a default action for £5,000 or less and the defendant files a defence, the action is automatically referred to the district judge for informal arbitration. Cases for larger sums can be treated in the same way if the parties agree. Automatic reference can be rescinded where the case involves a difficult question of law or exceptionally difficult questions of fact, where there is a charge of fraud, where it would be unreasonable, or where the parties agree to rescind the reference.

The case is heard in private by the district judge and the normal rules of procedure and evidence do not apply. The district judge will simply ask the parties about the nature of the dispute. The aim of the procedure was to enable claimants to bring actions in respect of minor matters without the need to be legally represented. In practice, anybody bringing an action on their own against a business will generally be faced by a solicitor or a barrister for the defence.

The major advantage is that, win or lose, parties will not have to pay the other party's costs or be able to recover their own costs, except for the costs of commencing the action and enforcing the district judge's award. The only exception is where parties have acted unreasonably, when they may be ordered to pay the costs of the other.

Under the Lay Representatives (Rights of Audience) Order 1992, a party can be represented by a non-lawyer – a lay person. The party to the action must also attend.

Appeals are rare, but it is planned to introduce a requirement for permission to appeal and give the parties the right to an oral hearing on the substantive appeal, which is treated more as a review than a rehearing.

(e) Enforcement of civil judgments

When defendants are unwilling to pay the damages awarded against them, claimants may need to enforce their judgment. Article 8 High Court and County Courts Jurisdiction Order 1991 provides that a judgment or order of a county court for the payment of money which it is sought to enforce by execution against goods shall be enforced: (i) only in the High Court if the sum is £5,000 or more; (ii) only in the county court if the sum is less than £2,000; and (iii) in either the High Court or a county court if the sum is between £2,000 and £4,999. Where the judgment is in respect of a regulated consumer credit agreement, the county court may enforce the judgment irrespective of the amount.

Since the methods of enforcing a judgment differ according to the position of the debtor, it is desirable for the creditor to find out something about the debtor's financial position. The rules provide for debtors to be means tested by a court officer.

(i) Claim of fieri facias (fi fa) or warrant of execution

Fieri facias (fi fa) – a claim addressed to the sheriff seeking him to 'cause to be made' a levy on the judgment debtor's goods for the sum due under a judgment.

This operates for a judgment by the High Court ordering the payment of money. As a result, the defendant's property will be seized and (unless the defendant pays up in the meantime) sold to satisfy the judgment, any costs awarded and the sheriff's costs. The county court equivalent is the 'warrant of execution' addressed to the county court bailiffs.

(ii) Attachment, 'third party debt proceedings'

This order prevents a third party paying a debt owed to the judgment debtor and makes it payable to the holder of the third party debt proceedings order.

These orders are frequently directed against the judgment debtor's bank in respect of credit balances held in bank accounts. Application is made without notice and the order *nisi* forbids the person named from paying the judgment debtor. The order is served on the third party and the judgment debtor and no less than 15 days later they all attend the court, when the order will be made absolute unless good reason is shown.

The problem is that these orders are ineffective if the account is empty at the time of the making of the order.

(iii) Charging orders

The judgment creditor may obtain a 'charging order' over land, stocks and shares or an interest in partnership property. The property can be disposed of to settle the judgment debt.

(iv) Appointment of a receiver

A receiver may be appointed where the debtor is in receipt of income, such as rent from tenants, which must be collected by an independent person.

(v) Bankruptcy and liquidation

The judgment creditor could consider making an individual judgment debtor bankrupt or, in the case of a general partnership, limited liability partnership (LLP) or registered company, petition for it to put into liquidation (see Chapter 13, p.290).

(vi) Attachment of earnings

The debtor's employer is ordered to pay into court such part of the earnings of the debtor as it thinks fit. The order can be discharged if the debtor loses or changes his employment. Application must be to the debtor's local county court: Attachment of Earnings Act 1971.

(vii) Claim or warrant of specific delivery

A judgment for the delivery of goods or chattels can be enforced by the issue of a claim or warrant of specific delivery depending on whether the claim is in the High Court or the county court. The sheriff or county court bailiff is ordered to seize the goods and deliver them to the successful litigant.

(viii) Claim of sequestration

Commissioners seize and retain the judgment debtor's property until the debtor complies with the court order. It is a punishment for contempt of court and has been used against the refusal of trade unions to comply with prohibitory injunctions.

(ix) Claim or warrant of possession

This enforces an order for possession of land and commands the sheriff or county court bailiffs to enter upon the land, evict those in unlawful possession and give possession to the claimant.

(x) Committal for contempt of court

The court may commit a person to prison for refusing to obey an injunction.

(f) The European dimension

Provisions unify the rules of conflict of jurisdiction in civil and commercial matters and ensure the rapid recognition and enforcement of judgments between Member States. The first was the Brussels Convention on Jurisdiction and the Enforcement of Judgments in Civil and Commercial Matters of 27 September 1968, followed by the parallel Lugano Convention of 16 September 1988. The matter is now regulated by Council Regulation (EC) No. 44/2001 but the Brussels Convention remains in force and regulates the issue for Denmark, which did not adopt the Regulation.

Generally, a person domiciled in a Member State has a right to be sued in the courts of that Member State and can be sued in the courts of another Member State only under the rules in sections 2–7 of Chapter II: Art. 2. A person domiciled in a Member State may be sued in another Member State in relation to a contract in the courts for the place of performance of the contract. This is, in the case of the sale of goods, the place in a Member State where the goods were or should have been delivered and, in the case of the provision of services, the place in a Member State where the services were or should have been provided: Art. 5(1). In respect of a tort the person may be sued in the courts for the place where the harmful event occurred or may occur: Art. 5(3). In respect of a dispute arising out of the operations of a branch, agency or other establishment, he may be sued in the courts for the place in which the branch, agency or other establishment is situated: Art. 5(5).

A person domiciled in a Member State may also be sued, where he is one of a number of defendants, in the courts for the place where any one of them is domiciled: Article 6(1); as a third party in an action on a warranty or guarantee or any other third party proceedings, in the court seised of the original proceedings: Art. 6(2); on a counterclaim arising from the same contract or facts on which the original claim was based, in the court in which the original claim is pending: Art. 6(3); in matters relating to a contract, if the action may be combined with an action against the same defendant in matters relating to rights *in rem* in immovable property, in the court of the Member State where the property is situated: Art. 6(4).

Jurisdiction in relation to insurance is dealt with by section 3: Arts 8–14. Jurisdiction over consumer contracts in section 4: Arts 15–17; and jurisdiction over individual contracts of employments in section 5: Arts 18–21.

Chapter III deals with recognition and enforcement of judgments, defined as any judgment given by a court or tribunal of a Member State whatever the judgment may be called. Essentially the Regulation provides that a judgment given in a Member State shall be recognised in the other Member States without any special procedure being required: Art. 33(1). The Regulation provides that a judgment given in a Member State and enforceable in that State shall be enforced in another Member State when, on the application of an interested party, it has been declared enforceable there: Art. 38(1). In the UK, a judgment shall be enforced in England and Wales, in Scotland, or in Northern Ireland when, on the application of any interested party, it has been registered for enforcement in that part of the UK: Art. 38(2). The procedure for making the application is governed by the law of the Member State in which enforcement is sought.

2.3 Arbitration

Arbitration is a quasi-judicial inquiry before a specialist arbitrator appointed by the parties to the dispute where the parties agree to abide by the decision of the arbitral tribunal.

Parties to a commercial contract will usually want to avoid any contract dispute being resolved by a civil court action, preferring settlement by arbitrators appointed by the parties by way of an arbitration clause in the contract. This specifies the time frame for any arbitration proceedings, the applicable law, the number of arbitrators and the manner of their appointment.

Arbitration agreements can be written or verbal; written arbitration agreements are covered by the Arbitration Act 1996 and include: (a) agreements made in writing (signed or unsigned); (b) those made by exchange of communications in writing (for example, by fax or telex); or (c) agreements evidenced in writing: s.5(1) and (2). Assignees of a contract are bound by the agreement: s.82(2).

Oral arbitration agreements are governed by the common law rules, which are preserved by s.81(1)(b), which also preserves any rule of the common law which is consistent with the provisions of Part I of the Act. Statutory references throughout this section are to the Arbitration Act 1996 unless otherwise stated.

An arbitration agreement is an agreement to submit to arbitration present or future disputes (whether contractual or not): s.6(1). The term 'dispute' includes a 'difference' (s.82(1)) and covers claims in tort, breaches of a statutory duty or fraud. The Act does not define what disputes are arbitrable and retains the common law rules: s.81(1)(a). The scope of the arbitral tribunal's powers will depend on the exact wording of the arbitration agreement. This will usually refer to 'disputes' 'in connection with' or 'arising out of' or 'under' the substantive contract. The significance of the wording is that a reference to disputes 'under this contract' will exclude tortious claims unless they are coextensive with a claim for breach of contract. References to all disputes arising 'under or in connection with this contract' encompass tortious claims. The words 'arising out of this contract' also cover claims for rectification of the contract.

A person sued in respect of a dispute covered by an arbitration agreement may apply for a stay of proceedings even where the reference is after the exhaustion of other dispute resolution procedures: s.9(1) and (2). The stay is mandatory unless the court is satisfied that the arbitration agreement is null and void, inoperative or incapable of being performed: s.9(4).

Unless otherwise agreed, an arbitration agreement which forms or was intended to form part of another agreement (whether or not in writing) shall not be regarded as invalid, non-existent or ineffective because that other agreement is invalid, or did not come into existence or has become ineffective, and it shall be regarded as a distinct agreement: s.7. This is the principle of separability of the arbitration agreement: its validity, existence or effectiveness is not dependent upon the validity, existence or effectiveness of the underlying substantive contract. Thus a breach or termination of the main contract will not affect the arbitration agreement.

In *Heyman v. Darwins Ltd* [1942] AC 356, the defendants appointed the claimant as their selling agent under a contract with a clause referring disputes 'in respect of this agreement' to arbitration. A court action was commenced by the claimant on the ground that the arbitration agreement had been terminated by the defendant's repudiation of the contract. The court ordered a stay of legal proceedings on the ground that the arbitration agreement was unaffected by the breach of contract.

Questions concerning the validity of an arbitration agreement cannot be referred to arbitration.

Subject to agreement, an arbitration agreement is not discharged by the death of a party and may be enforced by or against the personal representatives of that party: s.8(1). The death of the party appointing the arbitrator does not terminate the authority of an arbitrator appointed by him: s.26.

The Arbitration Act 1996 is not just a consolidating statute, but introduces changes designed to improve arbitration and enhance the position of the City of London as a world-preferred arbitration centre. It reflects the provisions of the United Nations Commission on International Trade Law (UNCITRAL) as well as 300 years of British expertise.

Section 1 sets out three principles as the basis of the interpretation of the Act:

▶ fair resolution of disputes by an impartial tribunal without unnecessary delay or expense;
▶ party autonomy subject only to safeguards necessary in the public interest;
▶ restricting the power of the court to intervene to regulate arbitrations within the Act.

(a) The arbitral tribunal: umpires and chairmen

A chairman attends all meetings and votes in respect of all decisions. An umpire makes a decision in place of the arbitrators where they cannot agree and replaces the arbitrators for the rest of the arbitration.

The number of arbitrators and whether there is to be a chairman or umpire are by agreement of the parties. Unless otherwise agreed, an agreement that there shall be two or any other even number of arbitrators requires the appointment of an additional arbitrator as chairman. Where there is no agreement on the number of arbitrators, the tribunal shall consist of a sole arbitrator: s.15. The parties are free to agree on the procedure for appointing the arbitrator and any chairman or umpire but, failing agreement, the Act provides a procedure: s.16. It is generally preferable to appoint a chairman or an umpire.

Where the parties agree that there shall be two or more arbitrators with no chairman or umpire, they can agree how the tribunal makes decisions, orders and awards but, in the absence of any agreement, they shall be made by all or a majority of the arbitrators: s.22. The chairman's view shall prevail in the absence of unanimity or majority: s.20. The parties can agree on the functions of an umpire and, failing agreement, the position is regulated by s.21.

The parties can also revoke the arbitrator's authority by agreement and the court also has power to revoke an appointment under s.18 or remove an arbitrator under s.24: s.23. If one party refuses or fails to appoint an arbitrator within the specified time, the other party, having already appointed an arbitrator, may serve written notice that its arbitrator shall be sole arbitrator. Unless the defaulting party appoints and serves notice of the appointment of an arbitrator within seven days of that first notice, the appointment of the sole arbiter will proceed and any award by the sole arbiter shall be binding on both parties subject to the defaulting party's right to apply for the appointment to be set aside: s.17.

Failing agreement, where there is a procedural failure to appoint the tribunal, any party may, on giving notice to the other parties, apply to the court to: (a) give directions as to the making of any necessary appointments; (b) direct that the tribunal shall be constituted by such appointments as have been made; (c) revoke any appointment already made; and (d) make any necessary appointments itself. An appointment made by the court has effect as if made with the agreement of the parties: s.18. The court shall take into consideration agreements regarding the arbitrators' qualifications: s.19.

In the event of the arbitrator's resignation, the parties can agree on their entitlement to fees or expenses, and any liability incurred by them. Failing agreement, arbitrators resigning may, on serving notice to the parties, apply to the court for relief from any liability and for an order respecting their right to fees or expenses or the repayment of fees or expenses already paid and, if their resignation was reasonable, the court may grant relief on such terms as it thinks fit: s.25. Arbitrators are generally in breach of contract if they resign, but may agree the terms of their resignation with the parties.

The arbitrator's authority is personal and ceases on death: s.26(1), but, unless otherwise agreed, the death of the appointee does not revoke his authority: s.26(2). In the event of a vacancy, the parties can agree (a) whether and how the vacancy is to be filled; (b) whether and to what extent the previous proceedings should stand; and (c) the effect, if any, on persons appointed by the arbitrator. Failing such agreement, there are statutory provisions relating to filling the vacancy: ss.16 and 18. The reconstituted tribunal shall then decide whether and to what extent the previous proceedings should stand. An arbitrator's loss of office does not affect their appointment (alone or jointly) of another arbitrator, umpire or chairman: s.27.

The parties are jointly and severally liable to pay the arbitrators such reasonable fees and expenses as are appropriate. Parties may, on serving notice on the other parties and the arbitrators, apply to the court for the fees and expenses to be considered and adjusted. The court may order repayment by the arbitrator of any excessive payment. This does not affect the liability of a party to any other party to pay all or any of the costs of the arbitration or any contractual right of the arbitrator regarding fees and expenses: s.28.

Arbitrators are not liable for acts or omissions in the discharge of their functions unless they are done in bad faith. This extends to their employees but does not affect liability incurred by resignation under s.25: s.29. There is also immunity for arbitral institutions and other persons who have been given responsibility for the appointment or nomination of an arbitrator for anything done or omitted in the discharge of that duty unless done in bad faith: s.74(1). In addition, the institution or person is not liable for the acts or omissions of the arbitrators or their employees or agents in the discharge of their arbitral functions: s.74(2).

The tribunal's duty is to act fairly and impartially and adopt procedures suitable to the circumstances, avoiding unnecessary delay and expense: s.33. The tribunal decides all procedural and evidential matters subject to any agreement between the parties. Unless otherwise agreed, the parties may be represented by a lawyer or other person: s.36, but they cannot delay proceedings by insisting on being represented by a particular person. A non-lawyer cannot claim professional privilege under this section. A foreign lawyer may represent a party in arbitration proceedings but not in an application to court.

Subject to agreement, the tribunal may appoint experts or legal advisers, or appoint assessors to assist it on technical matters and allow such persons to attend the proceedings: s.37(1). The arbitrators are liable for the fees and expenses of these persons, which constitute expenses of the arbitrators: s.37(2).

The parties can agree on the tribunal's powers and, failing agreement, the tribunal may order a claimant to provide security for the costs of the arbitration. It may give directions in relation to any property which is the subject of proceedings, owned or in the possession of a party. It may direct that a party or witness shall be examined on oath and it may give directions to a party for the preservation of any evidence in its possession: s.38. The tribunal can, by agreement of the parties, make provisional awards relating to the payment of money or the disposition of property, or an interim payment on account of the costs of the arbitration. Any such award must be taken into account in the final award: s.39.

The general duty of the parties is to do all things necessary for the proper conduct of the proceedings, including complying without delay with any decision of the tribunal: s.40. If, without sufficient cause, a party fails to attend or be represented at a hearing, or, where matters are to be determined in writing, fails to submit written evidence or make written submissions, the tribunal may continue the proceedings in that party's absence or without its written submissions and make an award on the basis of the evidence before it.

(b)   The award

The tribunal shall decide the dispute in accordance with the law chosen by the parties: s.46(1)(a); or, if the parties agree, in accordance with such other considerations as are agreed by them or determined by the tribunal: s.46(1)(b). This allows the parties to agree for their dispute to be decided in accordance with 'equity clauses'. This will exclude any right of appeal to the courts, since there is no point of law to appeal against. The choice of the country's laws refers to its substantive laws. If there is no choice or agreement, the tribunal shall apply the law determined by the conflict of law rules which it considers applicable in accordance with the Contracts (Applicable Law) Act 1990 which enacts the EC Convention on the Law Applicable to Contractual Obligations: s.46(3).

Unless otherwise agreed, the tribunal may make more than one award at different times on different aspects of the matters to be determined: s.47. Failing agreement to the contrary, the tribunal may make declarations or order the payment of a sum of money in any currency. It has the same powers as the court (i) to order a party to do or refrain from doing something; (ii) to order specific performance of a contract (other than one relating to land); and (iii) to order the rectification, setting aside or cancellation of a deed or other document: s.48. The parties may give the tribunal powers which are not available to the courts, but the remedies must not be contrary to public policy if they are to be enforced. Failing agreement, the tribunal may award simple or compound interest from such dates, at such rates and with such rests as it considers just: s.49.

Where there is a time limit for making an award, subject to parties' agreement the court may extend the time, but only after the parties have exhausted any arbitral process for agreeing an extension: s.50. If the parties reach a settlement during the proceedings, the tribunal shall, unless otherwise agreed, terminate the proceedings and record the settlement, which has the same status and effect as an award: s.51. Failing agreement to the contrary, the award shall be in writing signed by all the arbitrators or all those assenting and give the reasons for the award. This means that a hard copy of the award must be produced. Unless otherwise agreed, the parties shall be served with copies of the order without delay: s.55. The tribunal may, however, refuse to deliver an award pending full payment of the arbitrators' fees and expenses. In this event, a party may apply to the court, which may order the delivery of the award on the payment into court by the applicant of the fees and expenses demanded or such lesser amount as the court orders: s.56.

The parties can agree on the tribunal's powers to correct an award or make an additional award and, on its own initiative or on a party's application, it may correct an award to remove a clerical mistake or error, or remove any ambiguity, or make an additional award in respect of any claim which was presented to the tribunal but not dealt with in the award.

Application must be within 28 days or such longer period as the parties agree. A correction shall be made within 28 days of the application or, if made at the tribunal's initiative, within 28 days of the award or, in either case, any longer period agreed to by the parties. Any additional award shall be within 56 days of the original award or any longer period agreed by the parties: s.57. Unless otherwise agreed, an award is final and binding on the parties and any person claiming through or under them. This does not affect the right of a person to challenge the award by any available arbitral process of appeal or review.

(c) Costs of the arbitration

Agreements that a single party is to pay the whole or part of the costs in any event are valid only if made after the dispute has arisen: s.60. The tribunal may make an award of costs between the parties, subject to any agreement between them. Unless otherwise agreed, costs are awarded on the principle that they follow the event unless inappropriate: s.61.

(d)   Powers of the court in relation to the award

Arbitration awards are enforceable in the same manner as a judgment or order of the court and, where permission is given, a judgment may be entered in the terms of the award: s.66(1) and (2). A party may, on giving notice to the other parties and the tribunal, apply to the court to challenge any award of the tribunal as to its substantive jurisdiction; or for an order declaring an award to be of no effect in whole or in part because of lack of substantive jurisdiction. The tribunal may continue proceedings and make further awards while the application is pending. The court may confirm, vary or set aside the award: s.67. A party may also challenge an award on the ground of serious irregularity affecting the tribunal, the proceedings or the award, subject to s.73 and the restrictions of s.70(2) and (3): s.68.

Parties may appeal to the court in respect of an award on a question of law unless there is agreement to the contrary. An agreement to dispense with the giving of reasons for the award operates to exclude the court's jurisdiction. Appeals can only be brought subject to all-party agreement or the court's permission. The court will give permission only if satisfied: (a) that the determination of the question will substantially affect the rights of one or more of the parties; (b) that it is one which the tribunal was asked to determine; (c) that on the basis of the findings of fact in the award the decision is obviously wrong or the question is of general public importance and the decision of the tribunal is open to serious doubt; and (d) that it is just and proper for the court to determine the question. On an appeal, the court may confirm, vary, remit or set aside the award in whole or in part. Permission of the court is required for any further appeal, and it will be given only if the court considers that the question is one of general importance, or one which for some other special reason should be considered by the Court of Appeal: s.69.

In *C v. D (London arbitration clause)* [2007] EWCA Civ 1282, although the governing law of a liability insurance contract was that of New York, where the contract contained a London arbitration clause the parties were to be taken to have agreed that the award could be challenged only in English law proceedings under ss. 67 and 68 on the grounds of lack of jurisdiction and serious irregularity, the parties having agreed to exclude the right of appeal under s.69 on points of law. It was therefore not permissible for the defendant to bring proceedings in New York or elsewhere.

Applications challenging or appealing against awards may be brought only once the applicant or appellant has exhausted any arbitral process of appeal or review and any recourse under s.57 for the correction of the award or the making of an additional award: s.70(2). An application or appeal must be within 28 days of the date of the award or the date when the applicant or appellant was notified of the result of any arbitral process of appeal or review: s.70(3). The court may ask the applicant or appellant to provide security for the costs of the application or appeal: s.70(6).

2.4 Alternative dispute resolution (ADR)

Court hearings are not always the ideal way of resolving a dispute. Among the problems associated with court hearings are:

- The result of the hearing creates winners and losers;
- The adversarial nature of the hearing may result in the parties becoming enemies;
- The absence of relevant technical knowledge on the part of the judge;
- Inflexible rules of procedure;
- A court solution is imposed on the parties;
- The public nature of the hearing;
- The cost of legal proceedings.

Companies find litigation protracted, cumbersome and increasingly expensive: the cost of a two-year commercial dispute ending in a one- or two-month trial can run into millions of pounds. ADR can avoid all these disadvantages. ADR is not appropriate where legal precedents are involved, injunctive relief is sought or the facts are in dispute. It is also not suitable in cases where it is necessary to start or continue a legal action in order to get the other party to the negotiating table.

ADR takes various forms: mediation, conciliation or mini-trial.

Mediation is a flexible process conducted confidentially in which a neutral person actively assists parties in working towards the negotiated agreement of a dispute or difference, with the parties in ultimate control of the decision to settle and the terms of the resolution: Centre for Effective Dispute Resolution (CEDR) definition, 1 November 2004.

The mediation process can take whatever shape the parties want but, in the majority of cases, company representatives meet round a table with one or more independent advisers who listen to a short presentation of each side's case. The parties are then taken to separate rooms where the positions are discussed and reviewed. Negotiations continue until an agreement is reached to the satisfaction of both sides. Legally binding agreements are then drawn up and signed before either party has time to sleep on the decision.

In commercial cases, ADR offers many advantages over litigation, including a wider range of solutions, better control of risk and confidentiality. ADR can help to preserve the commercial relationship between the parties because it need not involve allegations of fault. Thus the final outcome can be a creative solution where there is no loser – otherwise known as win–win.

The benefits of ADR are most attractive in respect of costs. Costs at CEDR are based on the amount in dispute and range from several hundred pounds to over £1,000 a day. Most mediations, however, settle in one to three days.

Since its launch in 1990, CEDR has had a 85–90 per cent success rate with mediation. However, despite this and support from industry and consumer groups such as the National Consumer Council, ADR has not had the impact expected. This is partly attributed to the 'traditional adversarial mindset and culture of lawyers and clients in litigation'. In an effort to make mediation more available to small and medium-sized enterprises, CEDR has extended its membership to include trade associations. For ADR to produce savings for the civil justice system it needs to be extended beyond commercial disputes to cover all civil litigation, in particular personal injury actions. Moves have been made for greater use of ADR in medical negligence disputes, and a report in December 2002 by the law firm Nabarro Nathanson and the ADR Group suggested that local authorities could each save over £500,000 a year in legal costs if they referred their disputes to ADR.

Hot Topic . . .

UK AND PAN-EUROPEAN DEVELOPMENTS IN ADR

The growing significance of the need to attempt to use ADR to resolve disputes can be seen in the statement by Dyson LJ in *Halsey v. Milton Keynes General NHS Trust* [2004] EWCA Civ 576: '[a]ll members of the legal profession who conduct litigation should now routinely consider with their clients whether their disputes are suitable for ADR'. In addition, the Civil Procedure Rules (CPR) 1998 require the civil courts actively to encourage parties to use ADR, and in particular mediation, to resolve their disputes. This encouragement took on more significance after the Court of Appeal decision in *Dunnett v. Railtrack plc* [2002] EWCA Civ 302 which placed pressure on a party to mediate or face the prospect of a costs sanction on being found to have unreasonably refused to do so.

In the *Halsey* case, the Court of Appeal stressed that depriving successful parties of some or all of their costs on the ground that they refused to agree to ADR is an exception to the general rule that costs should follow the event. The court then held that rather than the burden being on the successful party to justify a refusal to mediate, the burden is on the unsuccessful party to justify why the general rule should be departed from. In order to succeed, the unsuccessful party must show that the other party acted unreasonably in refusing ADR. The court then set out some of the factors which should be considered in reaching a conclusion. These include the following:

- The suitability of the dispute for ADR – where a binding precedent would be useful, where parties need injunctive or other relief which is available only from the court.
- The merits of the case – where the party justifiably believes that it has a strong case.
- Other settlement methods have been tried – unreasonable refusal by the other party of settlement terms.

- Costs of mediation disproportionately high – where the sums in dispute are relatively small.
- Delay in proposing ADR – the other party's refusal may be justified if it will delay the trial.
- Whether mediation had a realistic prospect of success.

On 22 October 2004, the European Commission adopted a proposal for a Directive on certain aspects of mediation in civil and commercial matters which recognised that 'mediation holds an untapped potential as a dispute resolution method and as a means of providing access to justice for individuals and businesses'. The proposal contains two types of provision: one which ensures a sound relationship between mediation and judicial proceedings by establishing minimum common rules throughout the Community on a number of key aspects of civil procedure; and one which provides the necessary tools for the courts of the Member States actively to promote the use of mediation without making it compulsory or subject to sanctions.

End of Chapter Summary

In this chapter you have been introduced to the mechanisms for the resolution of legal disputes. Apart from the use of tribunals and the civil court, you have also seen that, in a commercial context, there are various alternatives to the court system for resolving disputes.

In this respect you should be aware of the following significant points:

- The existence of specialised tribunals with exclusive jurisdiction for the resolution of certain disputes. The most important of these in the business context are the employment tribunals to which extensive reference is made in Chapter 17.
- The jurisdiction of the civil courts and the appeals procedure.
- The importance of the freezing injunction in preventing defendants from removing their assets from the jurisdiction to frustrate possible judgments handed down by the court.

End of Chapter Summary cont'd

▶ The importance of the search order in enabling a claimant to find evidence of wrongdoing particularly in respect of actions involving breach of copyright and trade mark cases.
▶ The reasons which motivate recourse to arbitration and alternative dispute resolution (ADR) to resolve commercial disputes.

Questions

1. In what court could the following legal actions be heard:
   (i) a claim of £25,000 damages for breach of contract;
   (ii) a claim for £60,000 damages for injuries arising from negligence;
   (iii) a claim by a finance company for arrears under an HP agreement;
   (iv) a dispute concerning an insurance claim;
   (v) a claim by an employee alleging discrimination under the Race Relations Act?

2. What methods of enforcement for a judgment of £5,000 would be most suitable in the following situations?
   (i) A obtains judgment against B who runs a large car and has a cabin cruiser and two video recorders.
   (ii) C obtains judgment against D who has just sold his house and paid the money into a building society account.
   (iii) E obtains a judgment against F who has a large shareholding in British Telecom plc.
   (iv) G obtains a judgment against H who lives in rented accommodation but is in employment.

3. AB plc, an engineering company, specialises in rail maintenance work. One of its major sources of maintenance contracts is South Rail. Following the completion of a major contract for South Rail, the directors of AB plc are engaged in a dispute concerning the payment for the contracted work. AB plc claims that it was obliged to undertake extensive work at weekends and on bank holidays in order to complete the work by the time fixed by the contract due to the failure of its supplier to deliver replacement rails on schedule. AB plc claims that under the terms of the contract with South Rail it is allowed to charge for this extra work. South Rail denies that this is a correct interpretation of the contract and refuses to pay.

   Advise the directors of AB plc how they could resolve this dispute and the relative advantages and disadvantages of the possible methods.

4. Trak Records Ltd is considering legal action against Jake whom it accuses of pirating its records in his studios. There is evidence of a large number of pirate CDs on the market, but no clear evidence linking this to Jake except by reputation from industry sources.

   If the action is successful, Trak Records Ltd will be seeking extensive damages against Jake. It is known that Jake has several bank accounts in the UK into which he has paid the earnings from his pirating.

   Advise Trak Records Ltd as to the court in which any action will be brought and how it will be initiated. Are there any court processes which Trak Records Ltd should consider in respect of ensuring a successful outcome to any legal action?

Part II

Introduction to the Law of Obligations

Introduction to Part II

The fundamental legal basis of business relationships lies in contractual and tortious obligations. Students who have not so far undertaken any legal studies must understand the material in this section of the book in order to appreciate the rest of the material.

Contractual obligations are those which are voluntarily undertaken between two parties, as where one party agrees to supply goods or services to another against payment. Where one or other of the parties fails to perform their contractual obligations, the injured party will be able to sue for damages for breach of contract.

It is important, however, for businesspeople to realise the formalities surrounding contractual obligations, and Chapter 3 is concerned with the formalities of entering a contract, elements which may make the contract void, valid but avoidable by one of the parties, or merely legally unenforceable. It is also concerned with identifying what constitutes failure to perform contractual obligations and occasions when persons can be excused for refusing to perform their legal obligations.

Contractual relationships are fundamental to all areas of business: the formation of partnerships or limited companies, the relationship of agents and principals and employers and employees, contracts for the sale and supply of goods and services and consumer credit.

Tortious liability does not arise from agreement between the parties. A tort is a civil wrong – not a criminal offence – which can be committed against any number of persons. The most important tort is negligence: where a person is owed a duty of care to another and has acted in breach of that duty causing loss or injury, the injured party can sue for damages to compensate for the loss suffered.

In the world of commerce and industry, employers are liable to their employees for exposing them to dangers in the workplace and manufacturers and suppliers to their customers in respect of faulty goods or negligent services. Chapter 4 deals with a range of torts of specific importance to the business world.

Chapter 5 is concerned with the legal remedies for persons claiming in respect of breaches of contractual and tortious obligations. These are of crucial importance, and references to available remedies appear throughout the rest of the text.

Chapter 3

Contract law

Learning objectives

After reading this chapter you will know about:

▶ the essentials of a valid contract
▶ elements which can make contracts void, voidable or unenforceable
▶ express and implied contract terms and exclusion clauses
▶ discharge of contracts

Legal obligations arise in various ways, but two major ways are under the law of torts and the law of contract: **tortious** and **contractual** obligations.

Tortious obligations arise where a person commits a tort, a civil wrong, against another, giving rise to liability in an action by the injured party.

Contractual obligations arise from a legally enforceable contract between persons imposing mutual obligations on the parties. Failure by the parties to perform their contractual obligation gives rise to liability for breach of contract.

Obligations imply the existence of a person who is legally under the obligation and a person who benefits from the obligation. The fact that the beneficiary can enforce the obligation by legal action distinguishes the law of obligations from criminal law.

Obligations also arise under a trust where the trustee agrees to administer someone else's property. This book does not deal with the law of trust, but aspects of trust law are important since partners, company directors, principals and agents, employers and employees are subject to fiduciary duties. Thus partners are in a quasi-trustee position as regards the partnership property and their fellow partners (Chapter 7); directors are in a quasi-trustee position in respect of the company's property (Chapter 11). Agents owe fiduciary duties to their principal (Chapter 16), and employees and employers have duties of good faith to each other (see Chapter 17).

Trustees and quasi-trustees are liable for breach of their fiduciary duties, and third parties who knowingly assist in or profit from the breach of duty can be held liable as constructive trustees. This is of particular significance in respect of the misappropriation of company property by directors and third parties (see Chapter 9, p.214).

3.1 Essentials of a contract

There are three essential elements of a valid contract:

▶ a matching offer and acceptance;
▶ the promise must be by deed or supported by valuable consideration;
▶ the parties must have intended to create legal relations.

3.2   Matching offer and acceptance

(a)   Offers, invitations to treat and preliminary statements of price

An **offer** is the offeror's undertaking to be contractually bound by the terms of his/her offer; acceptance of the offer creates a binding contract if the other essentials are present. Offers can be made to a person, a group of persons, or the world at large as in *Carlill v. Carbolic Smokeball Co.* [1893] 1 QB 256 (see below).

An **invitation to treat** invites the making of an offer which can be accepted or rejected. In *Fisher v. Bell* [1961] 1 QB 394, the court held that the display of an article for sale in a shop window is not an offer for sale. Similarly, in *Pharmaceutical Society of Gt Britain v. Boots Cash Chemists* [1953] 1 QB 401, it was held that displaying goods for sale on a supermarket shelf was not an offer.

In *Partridge v. Crittenden* [1968] 2 All ER 421, Partridge was convicted of offering wild birds for sale by way of a classified advertisements column: the conviction was quashed since the advertisement was only an invitation to treat.

In *Harris v. Nickerson* (1873) LR 8 QB 286, a broker failed to recover damages for breach of contract after attending an auction when the advertised lots in which he was interested were withdrawn. In this case the lots were withdrawn before any bids were received. In an auction without reserve, however, where goods are withdrawn because the auctioneer considers that the bids are too low, the auctioneer is liable to pay damages to the highest bidder amounting to the difference between the bid and the market price of the goods: *Barry v. Davies (t/a Heathcote Ball & Co)* [2001] 1 All ER 944.

Brochures, price lists and so on are invitations to treat, as are quotations: *Scancarriers A/S v. Aetearoa International Ltd* (1985) 135 NLJ 79.

Advertisements by companies may constitute an offer. In *Carlill v. Carbolic Smokeball Co.* (1893), the defendants in a series of advertisements offered to pay £100 to any person who contracted influenza after using their patent 'smokeball' three times a day for two weeks and stated that they had deposited £1,000 in a bank to meet any claims. C sued for £100 and the court held that the deposit of the £1,000 indicated that the advertisement was an offer.

For **contracts for the sale of land**, there must be a clear intention to sell. In *Harvey v. Facey* [1893] AC 552, in reply to a telegram asking the defendant, 'Will you sell Bumper Hall Pen? Telegraph lowest cash price', the defendant replied, 'Lowest price … £900.' The appellants then telegraphed, 'We agree to buy Bumper Hall Pen for £900 asked by you. Please send your title-deeds in order that we may get early possession', to which they got no reply. The court held that the defendant's telegram was not an offer but a statement of the minimum price required for the property if it was eventually decided to sell it.

In *Clifton v. Palumbo* [1944] 2 All ER 497, the statement in a letter by the claimant, 'I am prepared to offer you … my … estate for £600,000 …' was held not to be an offer but a preliminary statement of price to enable negotiations to proceed.

Offers may be express or implied from conduct. A bus stopping at a bus stop is an offer and the passenger getting on is the acceptance: *Wilkie v. London Passenger Transport Board* [1947] 1 All ER 258 at 259. Taking a ticket at a car park barrier can also be analysed in terms of offer and acceptance.

Offers must be communicated. Persons can only accept offers of which they are aware, but their motive for accepting does not affect the validity of the contract. In *Williams v. Carwardine* (1833) 5 Car & P 566, W successfully sued for payment of a reward for information even though her motive was to clear her conscience when she thought she was dying.

Lapse of offer. Offers lapse: (i) on the offeror's death: *Dickinson v. Dodds* (1876) 2 Ch D 463; (ii) on the offeree's death: *Reynolds v. Atherton* (1921) 125 LT 690; (iii) on the expiration of the time for acceptance or a reasonable time: *Ramsgate Victoria Hotel v. Montefiore* (1866) LP 1Ex 109; and (iv) where there has been a radical change in the state of affairs, for example lapse of offer to buy a car on hire purchase when the car was vandalised before acceptance: *Financings Ltd v. Stimson* [1962] 3 All ER 386.

Revocation of offer. Offers can be revoked at any time before acceptance: *Financings Ltd v. Stimson* (1962). Revocation can be communicated by a third party, and is possible even where the offeror has promised to keep the offer open for a specified period unless there is a separate option contract with the offeree.

In *Dickinson v. Dodds* (1876) 2 Ch D 463, the defendant signed an agreement to sell a property to the claimant, '[t]his offer to be left over until Friday ...'. The claimant decided to buy the property on the Thursday but that afternoon heard from somebody else that the defendant had sold to a third party. That evening he delivered a formal acceptance but his claim for specific performance was refused since there had been an implied revocation of the offer by the sale to the third party.

Revocation is effective only when communicated; the postal rules of communication do not apply: *Byrne v. Van Tienhoven* (1880) 5 CPD 344 (see below).

Termination of offer. Offers automatically terminate: (i) where the offeree communicates rejection of the offer; and (ii) where the offeree makes a counter offer. A purported acceptance which seeks to introduce new terms is a counter offer. In *Hyde v. Wrench* (1840) 3 Beav 334, the defendant offered his property for £1,000 to the claimant who countered with an offer of £950 before purporting to accept the original offer. The court held that the counter offer had terminated the offer, which could no longer be accepted. In *Neale v. Merrett* [1930] WN 189, there was no valid acceptance of an offer to sell a property when the claimant introduced terms relating to payment by instalments.

In *Butler Machine Tool Co. Ltd v. Ex-Cell-O Corp (England) Ltd* [1979] 1 WLR 401, the parties were contracting, each using its own 'standard form' (that is, a pre-drafted contract). Butler's offer form included a price variation clause, but the buyer's order was placed on that firm's standard form, which did not include such a clause. The seller acknowledged the order by returning a tear-off slip from the buyer's form and the Court of Appeal held that the buyer had made a counter offer which had been accepted by the sellers and that the contract contained no price variation clause.

In *Stevenson, Jacques & Co. v. MacLean* (1880) 5 QBD 346, the claimant responded to an offer of goods by telegram to ask whether the sellers would spread delivery over two months. Receiving no reply, he accepted the original offer. The court held that a valid contract had been made and awarded damages against the defendants who had sold the goods to a third party.

(b) Acceptance

Subject to the exceptions discussed below, acceptance (i) must be communicated; and (ii) must comply with the terms of the offer.

Silence cannot constitute a valid acceptance. A contract does not arise due to the offeree's failure to reject the offer within a specified period. In *Felthouse v. Bindley* (1863) 1

New Rep 401, the claimant wrote to his nephew: 'If I hear no more about him I shall consider the horse mine at £30.15s'. There was no contract when the nephew failed to reply. This has been further developed in the Unsolicited Goods and Services Acts 1971 and 1975 as amended by the Consumer Protection (Distance Selling) Regulations 2000 (see Chapter 21). The need for communication is subject to two exceptions: (i) the postal rules of acceptance, and (ii) acceptance by action.

The postal rules of acceptance. Acceptance by post is effective from the time of posting even though the letter is delayed or lost, on condition that: (a) the post is a suitable means of communication; (b) the letter was properly stamped and addressed; and (c) it was properly posted: *Adams v. Lindsell* (1818) 1 B & Ald 681.

In *Household Fire and Carriage Accident Ins. Co. Ltd v. Grant* (1879) 4 Ex D 216, the defendant applied for shares and a letter of allotment was posted but never arrived. The court held that he was a shareholder from the time of the posting.

The rules apply to telegrams but not instantaneous forms of communication such as telephones, telex and fax machines. The cases of *Entores v. Miles Far Eastern Corp.* [1955] 2 QB 327 and *Brinkibon Ltd v. Stahag Stahl* [1983] AC 34 show the rule's importance in determining where the contract was made and the proper law of the contract. In *Brinkibon* a contract between a buyer in England and a seller in Austria accepted by a telex from England was subject to Austrian law, since acceptance was on receipt of the telex.

The postal rule can be excluded expressly or by implication. Thus an option to purchase exercisable by notice in writing required actual delivery: *Holwell Securities Ltd v. Hughes* [1974] 1 All ER 161. The rule does not apply to the revocation of offers.

In *Byrne v. Van Tienhoven* (1880) 5 CPD 344, VT in Wales sent a postal offer to B in New York on 1 October but revoked it by post on 8 October. The offer was received by B on 11 October, who telegraphed acceptance confirmed by post on 15 October. The notice of revocation was delivered on 20 October and before the letter of acceptance was delivered on 25 October. The revocation was ineffective, since the offer had already been accepted.

As regards acceptance by email, the Electronic Commerce (EC Directive) Regulations 2002 provide that an acceptance takes effect as soon as the offeree is able to access it, even if s/he has not yet gone online.

Acceptance by action. For unilateral contracts, the contract comes into existence on the completion of the act or non-act of another in response to it. Acting in response to the promise is both the acceptance and consideration: see *Carlill v. Carbolic Smokeball Co.* (1893).

Acceptance must comply with the terms of the offer. Where the acceptance method is specified, this can be a condition making other methods invalid: in *Compagnie de Commerce et Commission SARL v. Parkinson Stove Co. Ltd* [1953] 2 Lloyd's Rep 487, acceptance was required by a specific form with no other method being valid. Acceptance was by letter followed by a cancellation. The court held that there had been no valid acceptance. Alternatively, the stated method of acceptance can be merely an indication of the speed with which the acceptance should be communicated and an alternative, equally speedy method is valid: *Tinn v. Hoffman & Co.* (1873) 29 LT 271. Requiring acceptance by registered post is not generally a condition, and acceptance by ordinary post is valid: *Yates Building Co. v. Pulleyn* (1975) 119 SJ 370.

Acceptance 'subject to contract'. A contract will arise only when a formal contract is drawn up and agreed: *Winn v. Bull* (1877). Once the term is introduced it applies even though omitted in subsequent correspondence: *Cohen v. Nessdale Ltd* [1982] 2 All ER 97.

Tenders. Invitations to tender are invitations to treat, and the tenderer bears the cost of tendering, but persons tendering before the deadline are entitled to have their tender considered: *Blackpool and Fylde Aero Club Ltd v. Blackpool Borough Council* [1993] 3 All ER 25. Companies often invite tenders for the supply of goods over a fixed period to guarantee price stability. On acceptance, the company is not obliged to place orders, but orders placed must be with the tenderer. The tender is a standing offer and all orders are acceptances. The tender can be revoked at any time but the tenderer is in breach of contract for failing to supply pre-revocation orders: *Great Northern Railway Co. v. Witham* (1873) LR 9 CP 16.

Exceptional cases. Sometimes there is no discernible offer and acceptance.

In *Shanklin Pier Ltd v. Detel Products Ltd* [1951] 2 KB 854, the claimants entered into a contract for the repair and painting of the pier, specifying that the defendant's paint should be used for the job since the defendants had previously told the claimants that their paint had a life of between seven and 10 years. The claimants were able to sue the defendants for damages for breach of warranty of a collateral contract.

In *Clarke v. Dunraven, The Satanita* [1897] AC 59, two yacht owners entered a race undertaking to be bound by the club rules, one of which provided that an owner was liable for damage arising from breach of the rules. The court held that the owner of a damaged yacht could sue the other owner under an inferred contractual obligation.

In *G. Percy Trentham Ltd v. Archital Luxfer Ltd* [1993] Lloyd's Rep 25, the claimants (building contractors) negotiated the supply and installation of doors and windows with the defendants and the work was completed and paid for. In an action under the contract, the defendants denied the existence of a contract because of the lack of a matching offer and acceptance. The Court of Appeal held: (i) the test for the formation of a contract is objective, in this case 'the reasonable expectations of sensible businessmen'; (ii) a matching offer and acceptance are not necessarily required where a contract arises out of performance; (iii) performance of the contract precludes claims of lack of intention to create legal relations or the contract is void because of uncertainty; and (iv) if a contract arises during and as a result of performance, it impliedly covers pre-contractual performance. It was held that a contract had come into existence 'even if it cannot be precisely analysed in terms of offer and acceptance'.

3.3 Consideration

Consideration. '(a) An act or forbearance of one party, or (b) the promise thereof, is the price for which the promise of the other is bought, and the promise thus given for value is enforceable'. This definition distinguishes between executed and executory consideration.

In English law, promises are enforceable in law only where they are given in return for some action, forbearance or counter promise by the other party and are a bargain between the parties. The promises of one party have been bought by valuable consideration from the other party. Gratuitous promises are enforceable only if by deed.

Executed consideration. The promise is in return for an act or forbearance of the promisee and enforceable on complete performance of the consideration, which is also the acceptance of the offer.

An offer of a reward for finding a lost dog becomes a binding contract when a person who is aware of the offer finds and returns the dog. They can then sue in contract for the reward.

The fact that acceptance is achieved only on completion of the consideration means the offer can be revoked before complete performance, even after performance of the act of consideration has begun. However, in the Court of Appeal, Goff LJ stated that, once the offeree had embarked on performance, the offeror could not revoke his offer: *Daulia Ltd v. Four Millbank Nominees Ltd* [1978] Ch 231. There is still a problem where the payment is for the promisee to refrain from doing something.

Executory consideration, The promise is in return for a counter promise and a contract comes into being immediately, although the performance remains to be carried out in the future.

A, a singer, agrees with B to perform at a concert at a future date against the promise of payment and there is a binding contract between A and B from that moment on.

(a)   Consideration must exist but need not be of equal value

There must be something capable of being identified as valuable consideration, but the value of the consideration in relation to the promise is unimportant. A promise to let a house on payment of £1 *per annum* is enforceable: *Thomas v. Thomas* (1842) 2 QB 851; and wrappers from chocolate bars can be consideration: *Chappell & Co. Ltd v. Nestlé Co. Ltd* [1960] AC 87. The classic example is a lease of land for a peppercorn rent. There are restrictions on what constitutes valuable consideration.

(b)   Promise to perform a legal obligation

The orthodox position is that a promise to perform a pre-existing legal or contractual duty cannot be consideration. In *Collins v. Godefroy* (1831) 1 B & Ad 950, the claimant was promised payment for attending a court hearing as a witness. In effect, he was legally obliged to attend in this capacity and so could not enforce the promised payment. The rule can be defended on the ground that it prevented officials from extorting payments for the performance of their legal duties. Promises of payment in such cases could be enforced only where the person or official exceeded their legal duty. Thus, in *Glasbrook Ltd v. Glamorgan CC* [1925] AC 270, the defendants were able to recover promised payments for protecting the claimant's premises from strikers because they provided more police protection than legally required.

In addition, where a person was already under a pre-existing contractual duty to another, performance of that duty could not be consideration for a fresh promise by the other. In *Stilk v. Myrick* (1809) 2 Camp 317, the master of a vessel promised to divide the wages of deserting crew members among the remaining crew in consideration for their taking over the deserters' duties. The promise was not enforceable because the claimant had a contractual obligation to stand in for the deserters. An exception was where the promisees had exceeded their existing contractual obligations. Thus, in *Hartley v. Ponsonby* (1857) 7 E & B 872, the number of deserters left the ship dangerously undermanned and payment was enforceable since the crew members had exceeded their pre-existing contractual obligation.

The decision in *Stilk* survived several judicial attacks over the years and now appears to be effectively avoided.

In *Williams v. Roffey Bros & Nicholls (Contractors) Ltd* [1991] 1 QB 1, the defendant contractors were contracted to refurbish a block of flats. The carpentry work was subcontracted to the claimant for £20,000. Having completed part of the work, the claimant got into financial difficulties. It was in the defendants' interest to ensure that the work was completed on time because they would otherwise incur liability under a 'penalty' clause in the main contract. At a meeting between the claimant and the defendants, it was agreed that the defendants would pay the claimant an extra £10,300 at a rate of £575 per flat on completion. Having been paid only £1,500 for completing a further eight flats, the claimant sued for the £10,300 promised. The defendants relied on the *Stilk* decision, claiming that performance of pre-existing contractual duties was no consideration. The Court of Appeal rejected the defendants' argument and held that the defendants had obtained a practical benefit as a result of the claimant's promise.

The decision suggests that the rule is relaxed where parties agree to the modification of existing contracts as a way out of unanticipated problems. The position can be summarised as follows: where a party to a contract promises an additional payment to the other in return for a promise to perform his contractual obligations on time and thereby obtains some benefit or avoids a disbenefit, and the promise was not obtained by economic duress or fraud, then the promise will be legally binding.

A promise to perform a pre-existing contractual obligation to a third party is, however, valid consideration. Thus if A has a legal obligation to build a fence for B and he is later promised an extra sum by C for completing the work, A can sue C for payment.

In *Pao On v. Lau Yiu Long* [1980] AC 614, the claimants contracted with a public company (Fu Chip) to transfer shares in their private company against 4.2 million shares in Fu Chip and promised not to sell 2.5 million of the shares for a year so as not to depress the market. As a guarantee against the fall in the price of the shares, the defendants, the majority shareholders in Fu Chip, in a subsidiary agreement agreed to buy back 2.5 million shares within that year at $2.50 per share. The claimants realised that they had made a bad bargain if there was an increase in the share price and refused to carry out their promise under the main agreement unless the defendants replaced the subsidiary agreement with a true guarantee by way of indemnity if the shares fell below $2.50. The defendants refused to honour the indemnity when the share price collapsed and claimed an absence of consideration. The Privy Council held that the consideration was the promise to perform or the performance of Pao's pre-existing obligations to Fu Chip, and stated: 'a promise to perform, or the performance of, a pre-existing contractual obligation to a third party can be valid consideration'.

(c) Past consideration is no consideration

In the case of executed consideration, the action or forbearance which is the consideration must follow the promise. If it is before the promise, it is past consideration and not valid. Thus a promise by the heirs of an estate to pay £500 to the wife of one of them in consideration of improvements which she had already carried out to a property could not be enforced: *Re McArdle* [1951] Ch 669. There are exceptions where the act or forbearance was at the other party's request and payment for the service was implied.

In *Re Casey's Patents, Stewart v. Casey* [1892] 1 Ch 104, Casey had worked for two years at the request of the inventors to exploit their invention commercially. Having achieved this, they promised him a third share in the patent rights. The court upheld his claim: he had acted at the promisors' request and there was an implication that his services would be paid for. In the *Pao On* case, the Privy Council stated, 'An act done before ... a promise to make a payment or to confer some other benefit can sometimes be consideration for the promise. The act must have been done at the promisor's request, the parties must have understood that the act was to be remunerated ..., and payment ... must have been legally enforceable' (*per* Lord Scarman).

There are statutory exceptions to past consideration. Under the Limitation Act 1980 an action for breach of a simple contract is statute barred six years from the date of the breach and for contracts by deed and other specialty contracts the period is 12 years. However, a written acknowledgement of the statute barred claim by the party originally liable revives the right of action for a further period even with no consideration. A further exception is in relation to bills of exchange and cheques.

(d)　Consideration and third party rights

The common law doctrine of privity of contract meant that English law did not recognise third party contractual rights. Thus if A and B contracted to pay money to C, C could not sue to enforce payment. The Contracts (Rights of Third Parties) Act 1999 now provides that a third party to a contract may enforce a contract term if the contract expressly provides that he may or the term purports to confer a benefit on him: s.1(1).

In the latter case, the right to enforce the term does not apply if it appears that the parties did not intend the term to be enforceable by the third party: s.1(2). The third party must be expressly identified by name, as a member of a class or as answering a particular description, but need not be in existence when the contract was entered into: s.1(3): *Themis Avraamides and Anor v. Colwill and Anor* [2006] EWCA Civ 1533.

Where a third party has rights under s.1, the contracting parties 'may not, by agreement, rescind the contract, or vary it in such a way as to extinguish or alter his entitlement under that right without his consent if –

(a) the third party has communicated his assent to the term to the promisor,
(b) the promisor is aware that the third party has relied on the term, or
(c) the promisor can reasonably be expected to have foreseen that the third party would rely on the term and the third party has in fact relied on it': s.2(1).

The assent may be by words or conduct and, if sent to the promisor by post or other means, shall not be regarded as communicated until received by the promisor: s.2(2). The restrictions on rescission or variation under s.2(1) are subject to any express term under which the parties may rescind or vary the contract without the third party's consent or where the third party's consent is required in circumstances specified in the contract instead of those in s.2(1). The right of the third party under s.1 does not affect the promisee's right to enforce any term of the contract (s.4) and, where the promisee has recovered from the promisor a sum in respect of the third party's loss in respect of the term or the expense to the promisee of making good to the third party the default of the promisor in any proceedings brought by the third party, the court or arbitral tribunal shall reduce any award to the third party to an appropriate extent: s.5.

Agency is a recognised exception to the doctrine, and there are other judicial exceptions. Thus in *Jackson v. Horizon Holidays Ltd* [1975] 3 All ER 92, a party to a certain category of domestic contract can sue for damages in respect of a non-party, for example contracting for family holidays, meals in a restaurant or hiring a taxi. Other judicial exceptions include constructive trusts, quasi-contract and restrictive covenants.

(i)　Constructive trusts

In *Gregory & Parker v. Williams* (1817) 2 Mer 582, P assigned his property to W against a promise that W would pay P's debts to G. G and P could enforce this promise in equity as P was a constructive trustee for G.

Quasi-contract (unjust enrichment)
In *Shamia v. Joory* [1958] 1 QB 448, the defendant owed his agent £1,300 and promised to pay £500 of this to the claimant, the agent's brother, but later denied any liability. The claimant succeeded in his claim. The case established that, where A owes money to B or holds money on their behalf and promises B to pay the money to C, and confirms this obligation to C, then the law will enforce the payment in quasi-contract on the ground of the unjust enrichment of A.

(ii)   Restrictive covenants
In *Tulk v. Moxhay* (1848) 2 Ph 774, the claimant sold Leicester Square to Elms, who agreed to keep it 'as a pleasure garden and uncovered with buildings'. The land was eventually sold to the defendant, who claimed the right to build. The court granted an injunction since the defendant had acquired the land with notice of the restriction.

(e)   Equitable estoppel and consideration

Estoppel is a rule of evidence which applies in certain circumstances and stops a person denying the truth of a statement previously made by him.

In *Central London Property Trust Ltd v. High Trees House Ltd* [1947] KB 130, the defendants rented a block of flats from the claimants for a term of 99 years at a ground rent of £2,500 p.a. In 1940, when few of the flats were occupied because of the war, the claimants promised to reduce the rent to £1,250. The defendants continued to pay the reduced rent until 1945 when all the flats were let and the claimants claimed that the full rent was again payable. The court held that they were entitled to full rent from the time the flats were fully occupied. In a celebrated *obiter dictum*, Denning J held that had they claimed for the full rent between 1940 and 1945 they would have been estopped from asserting their strict legal right to demand payment in full.

The reasoning behind this statement was that when parties enter into an arrangement which is intended to create legal relations and in pursuance of such arrangement one party makes a promise to the other which he knows will be acted upon and which is in fact acted upon by the promisee, the promise is binding on the promisor to the extent that the law will not allow him to act inconsistently with it, although the promise is not supported by consideration in the strict sense.

In *Combe v. Combe* [1951] 1 All ER 767, a wife had obtained a decree *nisi* and her solicitors wrote to the husband's solicitors and obtained confirmation of the fact that he would allow her £100 *per annum*. The wife, in reliance on this promise, did not apply for maintenance but the husband did not observe his promise. Her claim for arrears of payment was rejected by the court since the husband had not asked her not to make an application for maintenance so there was no consideration for his promise. The wife could not use the doctrine to enforce the promise; the principle established in the *High Trees House* case must be 'used as a shield and not as a sword'. This has been confirmed by the Court of Appeal although Judge LJ considered that this might be reviewed in the future by the House of Lords: *Baird Textile Holdings Ltd v. Marks & Spencer plc* [2001] EWCA Civ 274.

The remedy is equitable and discretionary and the court will refuse to offer its protection where the party seeking relief has not acted fairly (see discussion under 'Accord and satisfaction and equitable estoppel', p.79).

The defensive nature of promissory estoppel should be contrasted with proprietary estoppel, which arises in respect of promises as to future rights over land where the promisee relies on the promise to his detriment. Thus in *Gillett v. Holt* [2000] 2 All ER 289 the Court of Appeal held that a promise to leave a farming business to the appellant on the respondent's death was enforceable by the appellant who had relied on the promise to his detriment.

3.4　Intention to create legal relations

The parties must intend that their agreement was to give rise to a legal relationship. For this purpose the courts distinguish between agreements between family and friends and commercial agreements.

(a)　Agreements between family and friends

There is a presumption that agreements between family and friends do not give rise to legal relations and persons seeking to enforce them must rebut this presumption.

In *Balfour v. Balfour* [1919] 2 KB 571, a husband and wife on leave from Ceylon agreed that the husband would pay the wife £30 a month maintenance while she stayed on in England. The court found there was no intention to create legal relations. In *Merritt v. Merritt* [1970] 2 All ER 760, the fact that an agreement between husband and wife for property and maintenance was concluded after they had separated and was in writing was evidence of legal intention.

Other cases relate to agreements to share winnings from bingo or agreements to divide prize money: *Simpkins v. Pays* [1955] 1 WLR 975, where the court found there was an intention; agreements in respect of lifts to work by a workmate: *Coward v. Motor Insurers' Bureau* [1963] 1 QB 259 and *Albert v. Motor Insurers' Bureau* [1972] AC 301; and an agreement by a mother to support her daughter during her legal studies: *Jones v. Padavatton* [1969] 2 All ER 616, where the court found no intention proved.

(b)　Commercial agreements

There is a presumption that commercial agreements give rise to contractual obligations, and persons claiming there is no contract must rebut this presumption. The presumption can be removed by the inclusion of a clause to the effect that the agreement is 'binding in honour only' – an 'honourable pledge clause'. It is difficult to rebut the legal presumption: thus the words 'ex gratia' in respect of a promise of redundancy payments for an airline pilot were not sufficient to rebut the presumption that the promise was binding: *Edwards v. Skyways Ltd* [1964] 1 WLR 349.

In *Rose and Frank and Co. v. Crompton (JR) & Brothers Ltd* [1925] AC 445, a supply contract stated: 'This arrangement is not entered into … as a formal or legal agreement, and shall not be subject to legal jurisdiction in the Law Courts' The court held that the agreement could not be enforced.

(c)   Collateral contract/lock-out agreements

In *Walford v. Miles* [1992] 1 All ER 453, the claimant was negotiating the purchase of the defendant's business. Negotiations reached a point where the claimant agreed to obtain a 'comfort letter' from the bank and not to withdraw from the negotiations. The defendant counter promised to break off negotiations with a third party, but ultimately sold the business to it. The House of Lords held that an agreement by the defendant not to consider further offers was a binding 'lock-out' agreement.

In *Pitt v. PHH Asset Management Ltd* [1993] 4 All ER 961, the claimant offered £185,000 for a property, which was accepted subject to contract by the defendant. The defendant then received an offer of £195,000 from Miss B and withdrew his acceptance. The claimant then offered £200,000, which was again accepted until Miss B offered £210,000, which was accepted. Following threats by the claimant to withdraw and inform Miss B (who would then have been able to lower her offer), the claimant and the defendant agreed orally that the defendant would stay with the claimant's offer of £200,000. This was confirmed by a letter stating: 'The Vendor will not consider any further offers for the property on the basis that I will exchange contracts within a period of two weeks of the receipt of that contract'. The defendant replied that, if the two-week deadline was not met, he would be free to consider other offers. The defendant later sold the property to Miss B for £210,000 in breach of this agreement, and the claimant sued for damages. The Court of Appeal found that the consideration for the defendant's promise was the claimant's undertaking to exchange in two weeks of the receipt of a draft contract. This will prevent 'gazumping' where there is a clearly stated period within which the purchaser will exchange contracts.

Hot Topic . . .

COLLECTIVE AGREEMENTS BETWEEN EMPLOYERS AND EMPLOYEES

Employers and trades unions regularly enter into collective agreements about rates of pay and conditions of employment. The legal status of these agreements is unclear. In November 2004, three appeal court judges tore up an agreement protecting MG Rover workers against compulsory job losses. The so-called jobs-for-life case was brought by a Longbridge worker under a deal negotiated between the unions at MG Rover and the company's previous owner, BMW, in 1997. This provided guarantees against compulsory redundancy in exchange for more flexible working practices. A regional official of the manufacturing union Amicus said that he was obviously extremely disappointed by the decision and was considering an appeal to the House of Lords. An MG Rover management spokesperson welcomed the decision as recognising the company's right to manage the business in the face of changing business conditions.

3.5   Elements causing the contract to be void, voidable or unenforceable

Agreements may not be valid if one or more of the following elements render it void, voidable or unenforceable:

▶ absence of true agreement owing to mistake, misrepresentation, duress or undue influence;

▶ contract illegal or impossible;
▶ contract in the incorrect form;
▶ terms of agreement insufficiently clear;
▶ parties lack capacity to contract.

Void contracts are void *ab initio* (from the beginning) and no rights arise under them. Voidable contracts are valid but can be avoided – or rescinded – by the injured party. Unenforceable contracts are valid but unenforceable due to lack of formality.

3.6   Mistake at common law

A contract is void at common law where the offer and acceptance are affected by mistake, and the defence is limited to the defined categories of operative mistakes of fact: (i) *non est factum*; (ii) unilateral mistake; and (iii) bilateral mistake.

(a)   Non est factum (not my deed)

This is where the party to a written contract signed the contract believing it to be a completely different document. The leading case of *Saunders v. Anglian Building Society* [1971] AC 1004 restricts its operation to situations where: (i) the document is fundamentally different from the contract intended; and (ii) the party signing has not been negligent. The doctrine also applies where a person signs a blank document of legal significance leaving it to be completed by somebody else: *UDT Ltd v. Western* [1976] QB 513.

In *Lloyds Bank v. Waterhouse* [1991] Fam Law 23, an illiterate person escaped liability on a guarantee which he had signed without reading it or telling the bank that he could not read. He had relied on the bank's representations as to its nature and also succeeded in fraudulent misrepresentation (see below).

(b)   Unilateral mistake

Mistake by one party to the knowledge – real or constructive – of the other party. There are two aspects: mistake as to identity, or mistake as to terms.

(i)   Mistake as to identity
If a party has obtained the agreement by pretending to be somebody else, the outcome depends on whether it was (i) a face-to-face contract; or (ii) one negotiated at a distance: by post.

Face-to-face contracts
In *Lewis v. Averay* [1972] 1 QB 198, a rogue pretended he was a well-known film star and persuaded the claimant to let him take away a car against payment by cheque. The cheque bounced and the claimant sought to recover the car from the defendant, who had purchased the car in good faith before the cheque had bounced. The court, following *Phillips v. Brooks* [1919] 2 KB 243 and distinguishing *Ingram v. Little* [1961] 1 QB 31, rejected a claim that the original contract was void for mistake but simply voidable because of fraudulent misrepresentation and recognised the defendant's title to the vehicle. This is covered by s.23 Sale of Goods Act 1979 (see Chapter 18, p.438).

Contracts at a distance

Contracts are void where claimants show that the other party's identity was vital and that they intended dealing with a different and real person. In *Cundy v. Lindsay* (1878) 3 App Cas 459, the claimant recovered goods from the defendant which he had purchased from a person supplied by the claimant believing him to be a well-known, reputable trader. It does not cover contracts where one person uses a fictitious alias: *King's Norton Metal Co. Ltd v. Edridge, Merrett & Co. Ltd* (1897) 14 TLR 98.

In *Shogun Finance Ltd v. Hudson* [2004] 1 All ER 215, the House of Lords considered the *Cundy* decision and two Law Lords favoured removing the artificial distinction between face-to-face contracts and those at a distance. The current position was, however, upheld by the majority.

(ii) Mistake as to terms

If the two elements of unilateral mistake exist, the contract will be void.

In *Webster v. Cecil* (1861) 30 Beav 62, the defendant had already rejected an offer for his property of £2,000. He then sent a letter to the claimant offering to sell it to him for £1,250. This was clearly a mistake for £2,250, which the claimant was aware of when he accepted. The court held that the contract was void for mistake.

In *Higgins (W) Ltd v. Northampton Corporation* [1927] 1 Ch 128, a contract was valid where the claimant had made an error of calculation in submitting a tender since the defendants had no knowledge of the error.

(c)   Bilateral mistake

It is possible to distinguish between a bilateral mutual mistake and a bilateral common mistake.

(i) Bilateral mutual mistake

In this category of mistakes, both parties are mistaken about the identity of the subject matter; in a contract for the sale of a car, the purchaser believes s/he is buying car A and the seller believes s/he is selling car B.

In *Raffles v. Wichelhaus* (1864) 2 H & C 906, the contract to purchase goods 'ex "Peerless" Bombay', was void when two ships of the same name were leaving at different times and there was confusion between the parties as to the exact ship. In *Scriven Bros & Co. v. Hindley & Co.* [1913] 3 KB 564, the parties' confusion as to whether the subject matter of the contract was tow or hemp rendered the contract void.

In borderline cases, the contract is enforced if the court can objectively establish the nature of the agreement. In *Tamplin v. James* (1880) 15 Ch D 215, the claimants auctioned a public house and some land and there were detailed plans of the lot on view. The defendant successfully bid for the property, mistakenly believing that the lot included the rear garden of the inn and claimed the contract was void for mutual mistake. The court allowed specific performance of the contract as there was no excuse for the mistake.

(ii) Bilateral common mistake

Both parties share the same mistaken belief: the seller and buyer of a ring contract in the mistaken belief that it is solid gold. Common law protection is limited to: (i) mistakes as to the existence of the subject matter of the contract; and (ii) contracts to acquire something the buyer already owns.

Contracts to buy something which no longer exists at the time of contracting are void: s.6 Sale of Goods Act 1979. If they cease to exist after the contract has been concluded, the contract is valid.

Where the mistake relates only to the quality of the subject matter, however fundamental, the contract is valid: a contract for a painting which both parties believed to be by Constable was not void for mistake: *Leaf v. International Galleries Ltd* [1950] 2 KB 86. The leading decision is *Bell v. Lever Bros* [1932] AC 161, where the court enforced an agreement whereby the defendants paid compensation to terminate the claimant's contract of service. Both parties thought the contract was valid but later discovered that it could have been terminated without compensation. Where parties contracted for a property in the shared belief that there was no preservation order, the contract was valid: *Amalgamated Investment & Property Co. Ltd v. John Walker & Sons Ltd* [1976] 3 All ER 509.

Equity allows for contracts which are void at common law to be rectified and for the specific enforcement of the rectified contract. This is possible if the written contract does not substantially represent the common intention of the parties, which continue unchanged until the contract is drawn up: *Joscelyne v. Nissen* [1970] 2 QB 86. Rectification is possible in respect of unilateral mistake.

Hot Topic . . .

CONTRACTS VALID AT COMMON LAW CANNOT BE VOIDABLE IN EQUITY

In *Great Peace Shipping Ltd v. Tsavliris Salvage (International) Ltd* [2002] 3 WLR 1617, the *Cape Providence* was in danger of sinking in the Indian Ocean. The defendants tried to locate ships in the vicinity to give assistance in a salvage operation. They believed the claimant's ship was very near and chartered it for five days at US$16,500 per day, with cancellation subject to payment of a minimum of five days' hire in any event. Unknown to both parties, the ship was several hundred miles away and would take around 39 hours to reach the sinking ship. The defendants cancelled the charterparty and refused to pay the minimum engagement fee, as the contract was void at common law or voidable in equity because of a common fundamental mistake. The court rejected the common law claim on the ground that the mistake was not sufficiently fundamental and stated that there was no equitable doctrine of mistake.

In dismissing the defendant's appeal, the Court of Appeal stressed the common origins of the doctrines of mistake and frustration. Mistake was contracting to do the impossible and frustration contracting to do something which becomes impossible. The requirements for mistake were stated as:

▶ A common assumption as to the existence of a state of affairs;
▶ The absence of any warranty by either party that that state of affairs exists;
▶ The non-existence of the state of affairs must not be attributable to the fault of either party;
▶ The non-existence of the state of affairs must render performance of the contract impossible;
▶ The state of affairs must be the existence, or a vital attribute, of the consideration to be provided or circumstances which may subsist if performance of the contractual adventure is to be possible.

In *Solle v. Butcher* [1950] 1 KB 671, Lord Denning had held that contracts which could not be void for common mistake at common law could be voidable in equity. The Court of Appeal upheld the trial judge's view that contracts could not be set aside in equity if they were valid and enforceable at common law and held that *Solle v. Butcher* was irreconcilable with the House of Lords' decision in *Bell v. Lever Bros*, due to a misunderstanding by Lord Denning.

The High Court held, however, that a mistake about an existing or pre-existing fact was capable of bringing the equitable jurisdiction into play provided that the mistake was of a sufficiently serious nature. Thus, where a person made a potentially exempt transfer (PET) of property to reduce or avoid liability for inheritance tax in February 2004 but was diagnosed as having lung cancer in autumn 2004 from which he died in April 2005, the court held that the disposition was voidable since it was made when he was suffering from lung cancer of which he was unaware: *Re Griffiths (deceased)* [2008] EWHC 118 (Ch).

In *A. Roberts & Co. Ltd v. Leicestershire County Council* [1961] Ch 555, the claimants tendered for work to be completed within 78 weeks, but the contract as drawn up by the defendants specified 30 months. This alteration benefited the defendants. The claimants signed and the discrepancy was not drawn to their attention. Rectification of the contract was ordered.

(d) Mistake of law

Until the decision of the House of Lords in *Kleinwort Benson Ltd v. Lincoln City Council* [1998] 3 WLR 1095 there was no possibility of recovery in the case of a mistake of law. The House of Lords, however, found that there was no reason why there should be no recovery where the recipient would otherwise be unjustly enriched. In *Deutsche Morgan Grenfell Group plc v. IRC* [2006] UKHL 49 the claimant, the UK subsidiary of a German parent company, paid advance corporation tax under the Corporation Taxes Act 1988 which allowed the payment of dividends without the subsidiary paying advance corporation tax only where the subsidiary and the parent were resident in the UK. On 8 March 2001 the ECJ held that this restriction was contrary to Community law and that Community law conferred a right of compensation or restitution in respect of payments of advance corporation tax already paid. The House of Lords stated that it recognised a restitutionary claim for tax paid under a mistake of law. It also held that the mistake could not have been discovered until the date of the ECJ's judgment and that the limitation period under s.32(1)(c) Limitation Act 1980 did not commence until that date. In a similar case, the House of Lords held that the claim for restitution should be measured by the award of compound interest at conventional rates during the relevant period: *Sempra Metals Ltd v. IRC* [2007] UKHL 34.

3.7 Misrepresentation

A representation is a statement of fact made by one party in the course of negotiations inducing the other party to enter into a contract. If the other party is induced into making the contract by the statement and the representation is false, the injured party can seek rescission of the contract and/or damages depending upon whether the misrepresentation was fraudulent, negligent or innocent.

(a) Statement of fact

The term 'statement' is not to be taken literally: a gesture, a nod or a wink can be a 'statement' of fact. Misrepresentation cannot arise from statements (i) of law; (ii) of intention; (iii) of opinion; and (iv) which are mere eulogistic commendations or sales puffs.

(i) Statements of law
In *Solle v. Butcher* [1949] 2 All ER 1107, the statement that a flat was outside the rent restriction legislation was regarded as a statement of fact (coupled with a proposition of law). In *André et Cie. S.A. v. Ets. Michel Blanc et fils* [1979] 2 Lloyds Rep 427, the court held that a misrepresentation as to foreign law was a misrepresentation of fact.

(ii) Statements of intention
Statements of intention are statements of fact if the intention never existed in the mind of the person making the representation. In *Edgington v. Fitzmaurice* (1885) 29 Ch D 459, the

claimant successfully sought to rescind an agreement to subscribe for debentures influenced by a statement in the prospectus that the directors intended to use the loan to expand the business since this had never been their intention.

(iii) Statements of opinion

Statements of opinion may be statements of fact if the speaker did not hold such an opinion or a reasonable person could not honestly have held it on the basis of the available information. An agent's statement that a property was leased to a person 'who is in our opinion a most desirable tenant' was a misrepresentation, since there was no evidence to justify it: *Smith v. Land and House Property Corp* (1884) 28 Ch D 7. However, in *Bisset v. Wilkinson* [1927] AC 177, the claimant's statement during negotiations for the sale of land that it would support 2,000 sheep was merely a statement of opinion and the contract could not be rescinded.

(iv) A 'mere eulogistic commendation' is not a representation of fact

Mere eulogistic commendations are statements made in the course of a sale regarded as being of no legal significance. This will not be the case if there are statements of fact. The Estate Agents Act 1979 has restricted the frequency of such statements in estate agents' property details.

(v) Silence is not generally a misrepresentation

There is no duty on the seller of goods to point out their defects. The rule is 'caveat emptor' – 'let the buyer beware'. There is a duty of disclosure, and silence or incomplete disclosure will be actionable where:

▷ Silence distorts a positive representation – factual pre-contractual statements must be full and frank and material omissions are a misrepresentation. In *Curtis v. Chemical Cleaning & Dyeing Co.* [1951] 1 KB 805, the client was informed that a form signed when leaving clothes for dry cleaning excluded liability for damage to beads and sequins, whereas it was much broader and the clause could not be relied on. Statements must be corrected once it is found that they are not true or no longer true. In *With v. O'Flanagan* [1936] Ch 575, the failure to correct a statement of business income to a prospective purchaser allowed the purchaser to rescind the contract.

▷ Contracts of utmost good faith – these are contracts where one party has a duty to make a full and frank disclosure of all material facts relating to the contract, for example completing a proposal form for life assurance (see Chapter 19).

▷ *Where parties are in a fiduciary relationship* – examples include agents–principals; director–company; partners; and solicitor–client. Executives owe a fiduciary duty to their employer: in *Sybron Corp v. Rochem Ltd* [1983] 2 All ER 707, failure by an executive to disclose subordinates' breaches of employment contracts (which would have revealed his own breach) was misrepresentation, enabling the employer to recover redundancy payments (see Chapter 17, p. 393).

(b)   The party must be induced to enter the contract

Misrepresentation is harmless if the claimant (i) did not know of its existence; (ii) did not allow it to affect their judgment; or (iii) knew that it was untrue. Contracts may be rescinded even if the misrepresentation was not the only inducement: in *Edgington v.*

Fitzmaurice (1885) 29 Ch D 459, the claimant could rescind the contract even though partly induced by his mistaken belief that the debenture was secured.

Claimants must always be prepared to prove that they were influenced by the misrepresentation, but once a misrepresentation is proved to have been made the burden of proof is on the person making it to prove that it did not influence the other party: *Brikom Investments Ltd v. Carr* [1979] QB 467. In *Smith v. Chadwick* (1884) 9 App Cas 187, the claimant failed in respect of a misrepresentation in a prospectus that a certain MP was to be a director when he admitted that he had no idea who the MP was. And in *Attwood v. Small* (1838) 6 Cl & Fin 232, an action to rescind the contract for the sale of a mine failed since the purchasers had relied on their own agents' reports. Parties can still succeed if they relied on the misrepresentation even though they were given material which would have proved it false if they had read it. In *Redgrave v. Hurd* (1881) 20 Ch D 1, the contract was rescinded because of a misrepresentation as to the income of a solicitor's practice, even though the claimant had been furnished with a set of accounts which revealed the true position.

3.8 Types of misrepresentation and remedies

Since the Misrepresentation Act (MA) 1967, misrepresentations can be (i) fraudulent; (ii) innocent but negligent; or (iii) wholly innocent. The distinction determines the remedies of the injured party.

(a) Fraudulent misrepresentation

Fraudulent misrepresentation is a false statement 'made (1) knowingly, or (2) without belief in its truth, or (3) recklessly, careless whether it be true or false': *Derry v. Peek* (1889) 14 App Cas 337. The burden of proof is on the claimant to prove fraud.

The remedies are (i) rescission of the contract and (ii) damages for the tort of deceit.

(b) Negligent misrepresentation

'Where a person has entered into a contract after a misrepresentation has been made to him by another person … and as a result … he has suffered loss, then, if the person making the representation would be liable in damages … had the misrepresentation been made fraudulently, that person shall be so liable … unless he proves that he had reasonable ground to believe and did believe up to the time the contract was made that the facts represented were true': s.2(1) MA 1967. There is a presumption that all misrepresentations are made negligently, and the person making them must prove that s/he was not negligent. The remedies are (i) rescission of the contract by the misled party; and (ii) damages under s.2(1) MA 1967.

In *Royscott Trust Ltd v. Rogerson* [1991] 3 WLR 57, the Court of Appeal held that damages recoverable under s.2(1) MA 1967 were tortious rather than contractual, and that a person can recover all losses occurring as a natural consequence of the misrepresentation, including unforeseeable losses, subject to the normal rules on remoteness (see Chapter 5).

(c) Wholly innocent misrepresentation

The burden of proof is on the person making the misrepresentation to establish that s/he had reasonable grounds for making the statement. The only remedy is rescission but the court can award damages in lieu of rescission under s.2(2) MA 1967 'if ... it would be equitable to do so'.

3.9   Misrepresentation and exclusion clauses

A contract term excluding or limiting (a) liability for misrepresentation or (b) any remedy for misrepresentation is null and void unless it satisfies the requirements of reasonableness under the Unfair Contract Terms Act 1977: s.3 MA 1967. This does not affect the principal's right to limit the otherwise ostensible authority of an agent.

In *Overbrooke Estates Ltd v. Glencombe Properties Ltd* [1974] 1 WLR 1335, the claimants instructed auctioneers to sell a property and the sale catalogue excluded the auctioneers' authority to make representations relating to the property. The auctioneers made representations concerning the property to the defendants, who then bought it. The information was inaccurate and they refused to proceed with the purchase. Specific performance was granted; the auctioneers' representations were not binding on the claimants.

3.10   Duress, undue influence and unconscionable bargains

Where a party's consent is the result of improper pressure, the contract can be avoided under the common law defence of duress or the equitable defence of undue influence. A related equitable remedy relates to unconscionable bargains.

(a)   Duress

Duress is any illegitimate threat which constitutes 'a coercion of the will, which vitiates consent': *Pao On v. Lau Yiu Long* [1980] AC 614.

Economic duress was recognised in *Universe Tankships Inc of Monrovia v. International Transport Workers Federation* [1983] 1 AC 366, where a shipowner was forced into a wage agreement when the crew occupied his ship, with potentially devastating economic results. Duress has two elements: (i) pressure amounting to compulsion of the will; and (ii) the illegitimacy of the pressure exerted. In this case the pressure was illegitimate because it was deemed to be secondary picketing.

In *Dimskal Shipping Co. SA v. International Transport Workers Federation (The Evia Luck)* [1992] 2 AC 152, the ship was boarded by ITWF agents, who informed the master and the owners that the ship would be blacked and loading would be continued only when the company entered into certain agreements with the ITWF. The company signed under pressure and sought a declaration that the agreements were void. The House of Lords held that, since English law was the proper law of the contract, the agreements could be avoided.

In *CTN Cash and Carry Ltd v. Gallaher Ltd* [1994] 4 All ER 714, G supplied CTN with cigarettes and arranged credit facilities which they had absolute discretion to withdraw. They delivered a consignment to the wrong warehouse and it was stolen. CTN paid for the consignment when the defendant threatened to withdraw credit facilities. CTN sought to recover the payment, alleging economic duress. The Court of Appeal held that, although a threat to perform a lawful act coupled with a demand for payment could amount to economic duress, it would be difficult to maintain such a claim in respect of arm's length commercial dealings where the party making the threat *bona fide* believed that its demand was valid. An extension of 'lawful act duress' would introduce an undesirable element of uncertainty into the commercial bargaining process.

(b) Undue influence

Claimants must show that they were subjected to influences which excluded free consent: under threat to prosecute the contracting party, or spouse or close relative: *Kaufman v. Gerson* [1904] 1 KB 591, *Williams v. Bayley* (1866) LR 1 HL 200.

Where the relationship between the parties means that one is in a dominant position over the other, undue influence is presumed unless the dominant party proves the other party was independently and competently advised before entering the contract. Relationships include: (i) parent and child: *Lancashire Loans Ltd v. Black* [1934] 1 KB 380; (ii) solicitor and client: *Wright v. Carter* [1903] 1 Ch 27; and (iii) religious leader and disciple: *Allcard v. Skinner* (1887) 36 Ch D 145. Others include doctor and patient, trustee and beneficiary, and any relationship of trust and confidence. This legal principle developed from *Allcard v. Skinner*, where Allcard made a generous gift of property to a religious order of which she was a member on the sole advice of the mother superior. In spite of the absence of pressure on Allcard, the court held that the gifts were made under a pressure which she could not resist.

In *National Westminster Bank plc v. Morgan* [1985] 1 All ER 821, M was a businessman in financial difficulties and planned to raise money by mortgaging the jointly owned family home. He persuaded the bank manager to assure his wife (wrongly) that the mortgage did not include his business liabilities. The wife executed the mortgage without independent legal advice. The Morgans fell into arrears and the bank obtained a possession order. The husband died with no business debts owing, so that the wife did not in fact suffer from the misleading advice. Rejecting the wife's claim to set aside the mortgage due to undue influence, Lord Scarman held that *Allcard v. Skinner* related only to gifts, and that for transactions the presumption of undue influence would arise only where the transaction is disadvantageous to the party seeking to set it aside. He held that the transaction provided 'reasonably equal benefits for both parties'. For further discussion and cases on undue influence and mortgages see Chapter 15, pp.341.

(c) Unconscionable bargains

Transactions can be set aside where one of the parties is in need of special protection through poverty or ignorance, or where unfair advantage is taken of them. In *Watkin v. Watson-Smith, The Times*, 3 July 1986, the defendant, a frail old man of 80, obtained relief after having agreed to sell his bungalow for £2,950 when the price should obviously have been £29,500.

3.11 Public policy and illegal contracts

Contracts may be void or void and illegal if their terms, purpose or performance are contrary to public policy at common law or under statute. This section concentrates on the common law. Contracts may be (i) illegal (and void) because they involve a degree of moral wrong; or (ii) void because their enforcement would be socially or economically harmful.

Hot Topic . . .

PRENUPTIAL AGREEMENTS

Contracts between couples about to marry have become increasingly popular in Britain but have no formal legal status as they have been traditionally seen as against public policy. In 1998, the government floated the idea of making them enforceable to reduce the cost of divorce but the idea was dropped in face of lack of enthusiasm from judges. Only a few cases involving prenuptial agreements have come to court but judges have been willing to enforce at least some terms of the agreements if they were considered to be fair. In 2000, the High Court upheld an agreement by a London property tycoon worth up to £150m, who had been reluctant to marry, and his pregnant wife-to-be, who had no job but a £1m trust from her father. In the divorce, she was awarded only the sum – £120,000 after a two-year marriage – which she had signed up to in the agreement and a home worth £1.2m which would revert to her husband when their son grew up. All she got on top of the agreement – which did not cover maintenance – was £15,000 *per annum* to run the house.

The Solicitors' Family Law Association (SFLA) report in November 2004 called for prenuptial agreements to be made legally binding.

On 11 June 2008, the Head of the Law Commission, Sir Terence Etherton, unveiled the latest programme of law reform. As part of the programme, the Law Commission will look into whether and in what circumstances prenuptial agreements should be upheld by the courts, with the aim of producing a draft bill on the issue by 2012. The project will look at the enforceability of agreements entered into before a marriage or a civil partnership, and after a marriage, taking into account the experiences of other countries such as the US, where prenuptial agreements are binding. It will also consider if and when post-marital agreements providing for the division of assets should be enforced. In a case in 2007, where a wife had had an affair, her husband asked her to sign such an agreement as a condition of reconciliation. The judge said post-marital agreements could be enforced, but refused to uphold the agreement in this case because the wife had been put under duress.

(a) Illegal contracts

A contract is illegal at common law if the terms of the contract or the intentions of either party involve the commission of one of the following.

(i) Contracts for the commission of a criminal offence or civil wrong

In *Dann v. Curzon* (1911) 104 LT 66 the claimants agreed to cause a disturbance to promote a play. Contracts to commit a civil wrong include (i) agreements to procure a breach of contract; (ii) agreements between principal debtor and creditor prejudicial to a guarantor/indemnor; and (iii) contracts where an agent takes a bribe.

(ii) Immoral contracts

The only immoral contracts void for public policy relate to sexual immorality and immoral publications. Prostitutes cannot enforce contracts for payment for their services, and in *Pearce v. Brooks* (1866) 1 Exch 213, a contract for the hire of a carriage to the defendant knowing that it was to be used to solicit was void. In respect of indecent publications, in *Armhouse Lee Ltd v. Chappell, The Times*, 7 August 1996, the Court of Appeal allowed the claimants to sue for the cost of advertisements in a magazine offering telephone sex lines and sex dating, stating that 'it was undesirable … for individual judges exercising a civil jurisdiction to impose their own moral attitudes'.

(iii) Contracts with enemy aliens or nationals living in enemy territory

Enemy aliens cannot contract with British subjects during wartime and cannot enforce rights under existing contracts, although they may defend the action if sued. British citizens may become enemy aliens by choosing to live in enemy territory. An English registered company may be an enemy alien if its controlling shareholders are enemy aliens: *Daimler Co. Ltd v. Continental Tyre and Rubber Co. (Great Britain) Ltd* [1916] 2 AC 307 (see Chapter 6, p.150).

(iv) Contracts illegal by the law of a friendly foreign country

A partnership agreement to import spirits into the USA contrary to prohibition laws was void: *Foster v. Driscoll* [1929] 1 KB 470. An agreement contrary to Indian laws against trading with South Africa was also void: *Regazzioni v. K. C. Sethia (1944) Ltd* [1958] AC 301.

(v) Contracts prejudicial to the administration of justice

A contract to prevent a prosecution to enable someone to escape the law of bankruptcy is illegal: *John v. Mendoza* [1939] 1 KB 141. Contracts to encourage a person to bring a civil action against a share in the proceeds are unenforceable.

(vi) Contracts tending to corruption in public life

These include contracts for the sale of public offices and contracts to procure titles.

(vii) Contracts to defraud the revenue

This applies to both national and local revenue. The effect of the illegality depends upon whether the contract is: (i) illegal on the face of it; or (ii) tainted by the improper intention of one or both of the parties.

(b) Effect of illegality

(i) Illegality on the face of the contract

Contracts are totally void, neither party obtains rights under them, and neither party can recover money or property transferred under them. This is subject to three exceptions:

1. Where the transferor can establish a right or title without relying on the illegal contract. In *Tinsley v. Milligan* [1993] 3 All ER 65, T and M had both contributed to the purchase of a house which was put into T's name to enable M to make false claims against the DHSS. The parties fell out and M claimed a share of the property. The House of Lords held that M should succeed. Her right to recovery arose from her contribution to the purchase price and did not depend upon reliance on the illegal contract. And in *Skilton v. Sullivan* [1994] LS 993 R 41, the claimant contracted to sell carp to the defendant, who paid a deposit. The claimant's invoice described the fish as trout, which were zero-rated for VAT. The claimant was entitled to sue for the balance: the contract itself was not illegal and he was not relying on his unlawful act.

2. Where the parties are not equally guilty
In *Hughes v. Liverpool Victoria Legal Friendly Society* [1916] 2 KB 482, an agent of the defendants falsely persuaded the claimant that she was entitled to take out life assurance against the lives of certain people and the policies were illegal and void. Hughes was able to recover the premium payments because she was not a guilty party.

3. Voluntary repentance before performance
In *Bigos v. Boustead* [1951] 1 All ER 92, the parties entered into an agreement illegally to avoid exchange control regulations and the defendant deposited a share certificate with the claimant as security. The court rejected his claim to recover his security because he had not truly repented his action.

Collateral contracts between the parties will also be void, as will those with third parties: *Spector v. Ageda* [1973] Ch 30. Thus a loan of money is illegal if the lender knows that it is to be used to perform an illegal contract, such as the payment of another illegal loan.

(ii) Contracts tainted by intention

Parties with improper intentions or knowledge at the time of contracting acquire no rights under the contract and cannot recover property or money transferred subject to exceptions (1) and (3) above.

In *Ashmore, Benson, Pease & Co. Ltd v. A. W. Dawson Ltd* [1973] 2 All ER 856, the defendant haulage company agreed to transport the claimant's equipment by road and overloaded its lorries, watched by the claimant's transport manager. One of the lorries overturned and the claimant's action for damages was refused: the contract was illegal as performed to the knowledge of the claimant's employee.

The innocent party can sue for:

(i) work done or goods supplied in quasi-contract;
(ii) recovery of money or property;
(iii) damages for breach of contract.

In *Mohamed v. Alaga & Co (a firm)* [1999] 3 All ER 699, the claimant sued to enforce an alleged oral contract with the defendant solicitors. He claimed that, in return for him introducing Somali asylum seekers to the defendants and helping them prepare and present their cases, the solicitors would pay him one-half of any fees received from the Legal Aid Board. The Court of Appeal held that an agreement by a solicitor to share his fees was contrary to rule 7 Solicitors' Practice Rules 1990 and illegal and unenforceable. However, since the plaintiff was less blameworthy, he was entitled to recover in quasi-contract reasonable remuneration for his professional services.

Collateral contracts will not necessarily be affected.

(c) Contracts void for public policy

The most important are: to oust the court's jurisdiction by removing a person's right of action and contracts in restraint of trade.

(i) Contracts to oust the jurisdiction of the courts

Contracts may legally contain a clause referring dispute to arbitration: *Scott v. Avery* (1856) 5 HLC 811 (see Chapter 2).

(ii) Contracts in restraint of trade

Contracts restraining persons from exercising their trade, business or profession are valid only if the restriction is reasonable. These are classified as (i) restraints on employees; and (ii) restraints on sellers of businesses.

Restraints on employees. Employment contracts may restrict employees' rights to work after leaving their employment. Restraints are only acceptable if in order to protect the employer's interests, such as trade secrets or goodwill. For trade secrets, employers must prove that employees have a substantial knowledge of some secret process. There is no right if the employee has only partial knowledge of the process, and is unable personally to exploit it. Any restraint clause must only be sufficient to ensure the employer's protection.

In *Commercial Plastics Ltd v. Vincent* [1965] 1 QB 623, V was employed to coordinate research and development of adhesive tape production. His contract provided that he would not 'seek employment with any of our competitors in the PVC calendering field, for at least one year after leaving our employ'. The restriction was wider than necessary for the claimant's protection since it was potentially worldwide and extended beyond the production of sheeting for adhesive tape.

Employers can protect their goodwill in respect of employees' knowledge of and influence over customers. Restraints have been upheld against: a solicitor's clerk: *Fitch v. Dewes* [1921] 2 AC 158; a tailor's cutter–fitter: *Nicoll v. Beere* [1855] 53 LT 659; a milkman: *Home Counties Dairies Ltd v. Skilton* [1970] 1 All ER 1227; and an estate agent's clerk: *Scorer v. Seymour Jones* [1966] 1 WLR 1419.

Clauses are invalid if they extend beyond the valid protection of the employer's goodwill unless the court agrees to sever the illegal part of the clause. In the *Home Counties Dairies* case, the clause prevented the defendant from selling milk and dairy produce and the court severed the reference to dairy produce, and enforced the rest of the clause.

In *Atwood v. Lamont* [1920] 3 KB 571, L had been employed as cutter and head of the claimant's tailoring department in Kidderminster. He was restrained from trading within a radius of 10 miles as a 'tailor, dressmaker, general draper, milliner, hatter, haberdasher, gentlemen's ladies' or children's outfitter'. The court refused to sever the illegal aspects and enforce the valid restraint.

In all cases, clauses are reasonable only where the restrictions relating to area and the duration are reasonable. The protection extends to indirect restraints. In *Bull v. Pitney-Bowes Ltd* [1966] 3 All ER 384, a contributory pension scheme provision for loss of pension rights for employees engaged in any activity or occupation in competition with or detrimental to the interests of the employer was held void.

In *Rock Refrigeration Ltd v Jones* [1997] All ER 1, the restraint of trade clause against J was stated to be effective after termination of the employment contract 'howsoever arising' or 'howsoever occasioned'. J resigned and started work with a competitor of the claimant. The Court of Appeal held that the clause was unreasonable and void because it could apply even after repudiation of the contract by the employer, in which case the employee would have been released from his obligation.

In *Countrywide Assured Financial Services Ltd v. (1) Smart (2) Pollard* (Ch D), 7 May 2004, P had worked for the appellant estate agent as a mortgage consultant. His contract of employment contained a number of restrictive covenants restricting P from working for any other estate agent within a three-mile radius of the appellant's office for three months, and a covenant that he would not solicit any of the appellant's clients for six months from termination. The court held that, since P had agreed not to solicit recent or existing clients, there was no separate interest for the area restriction.

Restraints on the seller of a business. The court is more prepared to accept a restraint on the future activities of the seller of a business. This is because the parties to the agreement have equal bargaining power and the restriction enables the seller to obtain the value of his goodwill. This is subject to the fact that:

- there must be a genuine sale of a business;
- protection is limited to the actual business sold;
- the restraint must only be sufficient to protect the purchaser's interest;
- the duration and area of operation are reasonable.

Restrictions may operate for the seller's lifetime: *Elves v. Crofts* (1850), and the area may range from the UK to the whole world: *Nordenfeldt v. Maxim Nordenfeldt Guns & Ammunition Co.* [1894] AC 535. Restraints may be subject to EU competition law.

(iii) Wagering contracts

In wagering contracts the parties have no interest in the outcome of a future or past event except the possibility of winning the wager. There must be the possibility of either party winning or losing, which excludes betting on the 'tote'. Wagering contracts, either verbal or in writing, were null and void: s.18 Gaming Act (GA) 1845. Parties could not sue on the contract nor recover money or property transferred. A subsequent contract to pay money lost was also unenforceable. In *Hill v. William Hill (Park Lane) Ltd* [1949] AC 530, Tattersalls decided that Hill should pay off his debts to WH by instalments. WH could not enforce the agreement as the debts were of 'money … alleged to have been won upon any wager' within s.18 GA 1845. The position is now changed by the Gambling Act 2005, which repealed s.18 GA 1845. The position for gaming contracts made after the coming into force of the Act is that 'the fact that a contract relates to gambling shall not prevent its enforcement': s.335 GA 2005.

Gambling is now regulated by the GA 2005, which established a Gambling Commission to license and regulate the gambling industry.

(d) Effect of a void contract

A contract is void only in so far as it conflicts with rules of public policy; money paid or property transferred is recoverable. Under the doctrine of severance the court may enforce the good part of the agreement. In *Goodinson v. Goodinson* [1954] 2 QB 118, a husband and wife agreed the husband would pay the wife an allowance in consideration that she would not 'commence or prosecute any matrimonial proceedings against the husband'. The court severed this part of the agreement and enforced the rest.

3.12 Absence of formalities

Some contracts must comply with certain formalities or they are unenforceable. Contracts for the sale or creation of interests in land must be in writing and signed by the parties. Deeds must be in writing and the signature of the party or parties must be witnessed. The Electronic Communications Act 2000 gives ministers the power to authorise or facilitate the use of electronic communication and electronic storage and electronic signatures (see Chapter 22). The Land Registration Act 2002 envisages the introduction of electronic conveyancing (see Chapter 14).

(a) Contracts which must be by deed

A lease for more than three years is required to be made by deed. Informal leases are valid between the parties in equity and can be protected by registration. All conveyances and charges of land must be by deed.

(b) Contracts which must be in writing

Contracts which must be in writing include: (i) cheques, bills of exchange and promissory notes; (ii) contracts of marine insurance; (iii) acknowledgements of statute-barred debts; (iv) consumer credit transactions under the Consumer Credit Act 1974; and (v) contracts for the sale of land: s.2 Law of Property (Miscellaneous Provisions)

Act 1989. This also includes options to buy land: *Spiro v. Glencrown Properties Ltd* [1991] 2 WLR 931.

(c) Contracts which must be evidenced by a memorandum in writing

This is the legal position of contracts of guarantee where writing is essential for the legal enforcement of contracts. The memorandum can be in any form, including an exchange of letters, and need exist only before the action is brought: s.4 Statute of Frauds 1677. Subject to that:

(i)   the memorandum must contain the names or a sufficient description of the parties;
(ii) the subject matter of the contract must be described so that it can be identified and the material terms of the contract must be stated;
(iii) there must be some consideration but the need to set it out was removed by s.3 Mercantile Law (Amendment) Act 1856;
(iv) it must contain the signature of the party to be charged or his agent (this may be printed, typed, a stamp, initial or an identifying mark).

In *Actionstrength Limited v. International Glass Engineering In.Gl.En.Spa and ors* [2003] UKHL 17 the House of Lords stressed the absolute requirement for a guarantee to be evidenced by a memorandum in writing and rejected a claim by the appellant that they could rely on promissory estoppel on the ground that this would be contrary to s.4. In *Re A Debtor (No. 517 of 1991), The Times*, 25 November 1991, the court held that an oral agreement varying the performance of a guarantee could be relied on by way of defence. The debtor had guaranteed performance of a debt by an associated company but claimed to have made an oral agreement with the creditor's representative that money advanced to the associated company through another company would count towards reducing or extinguishing his liability under the guarantee.

3.13　Capacity to contract

Special rules relate to corporations; children; the mentally unsound and drunks; and enemy aliens.

(a) Corporations

Contractual capacity depends on the way the corporation was incorporated. Chartered corporations created by royal charter have no limits to their contractual capacity, but may lose their charter if they act beyond their powers under the charter. Statutory corporations' powers are restricted by the statute by which they are created, and contracts beyond their powers are *ultra vires* and void. (For companies registered under the Companies Act 2006 see Chapter 8, p.193.)

(b) Children

Children are persons under 18 years of age: s.1. Family Law Reform Act 1969. This area of the law has been reformed by the Minors' Contracts Act 1987. Children's contracts are valid, voidable or unenforceable against the child.

Valid contracts are executed contracts for necessaries for the child and his/her family, and beneficial contracts of service.

Necessaries exclude goods or services which are pure luxuries, but may include luxurious utility items suited to the child's status. Goods are necessaries only if they are suitable (i) to the condition in life of the child; and (ii) to his/her actual requirements at the time of sale and delivery: s.3 Sale of Goods Act (SOGA) 1979. In *Nash v. Inman* [1908] 2 KB 1, the court found that fancy items of clothing could be necessaries but were not, since the child was already adequately supplied.

The obligation to pay arises only once the goods and services have been delivered or supplied, prior to which contracts can be repudiated. The child's liability is restricted to paying a reasonable price for goods and is subject to the contract being fair: s.3 SOGA 1979.

Beneficial contracts of service include contracts of employment, apprenticeship and training and analogous contracts. The contract must be generally beneficial for the child and, if so, will be enforced in spite of some non-beneficial clauses. In *Clements v. L. & N. W. Ry Co.* [1894] 2 QB 482, a service contract was enforced even though it obliged the child to renounce statutory rights to compensation for industrial injury in favour of cover by the employer's less advantageous insurance scheme.

Contracts permitting the child to earn money are equated with contracts of service, and the court has enforced a contract to enable a child to box professionally: *Doyle v. White City Stadium Ltd* [1935] 1 KB 110; a contract for writing memoirs: *Chaplin v. Leslie Frewin (Publishers) Ltd* [1966] Ch 71; and a contract where a child appointed a manager to look after his affairs: *Denmark Productions Ltd v. Boscobel Productions Ltd* [1969] 1 QB 699. Liability extends to executory contracts, and the court awarded damages against a child for repudiation of an agreement to undertake a world tour with a professional billiards player: *Roberts v. Gray* [1913] 1 KB 520.

Voidable contracts. Contracts to acquire an interest of a permanent nature, such as to buy shares, join a partnership or take a lease are valid unless avoided by the child during his minority or within a reasonable period after achieving adulthood. If the contract is repudiated, the child: (i) is not liable for future obligations; but (ii) cannot recover money paid unless there is a total failure of consideration. In *Steinberg v. Scala (Leeds) Ltd* [1923] 2 Ch 452, the claimant purchased partly paid shares in the defendant company and later repudiated the contract. Although not liable for future calls, she could not recover the money paid, since the share allotment constituted the consideration. A child who paid money under a partnership agreement recovered it when the partnership did not come into existence: *Corpe v. Overton* (1833) 10 Bing 252. There are conflicting decisions on leases concerning liability for unpaid rent for the period before repudiation, but logically there should be no liability.

Unenforceable contracts. Under the Minors' Contracts Act (MCA) 1987, contracts for loans, the supply of non-necessaries and accounts stated (such as IOUs) are enforceable by, but not against, the child. On achieving adulthood, the child can ratify the agreement or make a fresh agreement on the same terms. The Act abolishes the previous rule under *Coutts & Co. v. Browne-Lecky* [1947] KB 104, whereby a guarantee by an adult of a loan to a child was void: s.2 MCA 1987 (see Chapter 15, p.353).

The other party can recover property acquired under the contract or 'any property representing it': s.3 MCA 1987. This allows for the recovery of goods or money where the child has substituted or sold the original goods.

Contracts cannot be indirectly enforced through an action in tort. In *R. Leslie Ltd v. Sheill* [1914] 3 KB 607, a child who had obtained credit by fraudulently representing that he was an adult could not be sued for damages for fraud. Similarly, a child cannot be sued in tort for a wrong committed within the terms of the contract. In *Jennings v. Rundall* (1799) 8 TR 335, a contract to hire a horse specified that the horse should be ridden carefully. The child was not liable in tort for injuring the horse by riding it too fast, but, in a later case, was liable for causing the horse's death by jumping, since this was excluded in the contract: *Burnard v. Haggis* (1863) 14 CBNS 45.

(c) Contracts by the mentally unsound and drunks

The mentally unsound or drunks can avoid contracts if they can prove they were mentally unsound or drunk when the contract was made and the other party knew this. For executed contracts for necessaries they must pay a reasonable price: s.3 SOGA 1979.

3.14 Terms of the contract

Terms can be express or implied, and then be further classified as conditions and warranties. Express terms are those specifically incorporated into the contract, whereas implied terms are incorporated by custom, the court or statute. Conditions are fundamental terms, the breach of which entitles the injured party to repudiate the contract and sue for damages. A warranty is a less important term the breach of which merely allows the injured party to sue for damages.

(a) Terms implied by the court

Certain types of contract, including contracts of service, always contain judicially implied terms (see Chapter 17). The court can, however, imply terms into any contract to reflect the parties' presumed intention and give 'business efficacy' to it. *The Moorcock* (1889) 14 PD 64 concerned a contract for mooring a ship against a jetty for unloading. Both parties were aware that at low tide the ship would rest on the river bed, but there was no term in the contract warranting the suitability of the river bed. The ship was damaged and the wharf owners were held liable for breach of an implied term that the river bed was safe. In *McRae v. Commonwealth Disposals Commission* (1950) 84 CLR 377, the claimants contracted to salvage a ship sunk at a particular site but it was discovered that there was no wreck. They succeeded in an action for breach of an implied term in the contract that there was a wreck at the specific site.

The term must have been intended by both parties to be included. In *K C Sethia (1944) Ltd v. Partabmull Rameshwar* [1950] 1 All ER 51, a contract for the supply of jute was delivered one-third under the contract amount because of a government-imposed export quota. The court refused the supplier's claim that the words 'subject to quota' should be implied into the contract since the buyer was unaware of the quota restrictions. In *Ali v Christian Salvesen Food Services Ltd* [1997] 1 All ER 721, the Court of Appeal held that if any topic had been left uncovered in a carefully negotiated collective agreement, the natural inference was that the topic had been omitted on purpose.

(b) Terms implied by statute

Terms are frequently statutorily implied into contracts to ensure a minimum degree of protection for one of the contracting parties: including employees (see Chapter 17) and consumers (see Chapters 18 and 21).

(c) Classification of terms as conditions and warranties

Classification is done by the court following two alternative approaches:

(i) the probable intention of the parties at the time of contracting;
(ii) the seriousness of the breach (an approach used for terms not suitable for strict classification).

(i) In accordance with the probable intention of the parties at the time of contracting

The court defines the term once and for all as a condition or warranty and is not bound by the term's designation in the contract. In *L Schuler AG v. Wickman Machine Tool Sales Ltd* [1974] AC 235, a term in an agency agreement to the effect that the defendants would ensure that sales representatives would visit the six major motor manufacturers each week was held to be a breach of warranty, although described as a condition in the contract.

In *Bettini v. Gye* (1876) 1 QBD 183, the claimant contracted to sing and agreed to be in London six days before the commencement of the engagement for rehearsals. Due to illness, he missed the first four days and the defendant repudiated the contract. The court held this was a breach of warranty and awarded damages for wrongful repudiation. But in *Poussard v. Spiers & Pond* (1876) 1 QBD 410, the claimant, an opera singer, missed the final rehearsals and the first four nights of a three-month engagement. When she offered to turn up on the fifth night her services were refused. The court found she had broken a condition which justified repudiation by the defendants.

(ii) In accordance with the seriousness of the breach

The Court of Appeal has recognised the existence of certain terms, called *innominate* or *intermediate terms*, which were too complicated for straightforward classification and which must be classified according to the seriousness of the breach. In *Hong Kong Fir Shipping Co. Ltd v. Kawasaki Kisen Kaisha Ltd* [1962] 2 QB 26, the court held that a contract to charter a ship could not be repudiated for breach of condition because it was unseaworthy for 20 weeks out of a total charter period of two years. This approach has been criticised and not been extended to terms relating to the time when ships are to be ready to load, or the period of notice of loading required. In *The Mihalis Angelos* [1971] 1 QB 164, a clause that a ship was 'expected to be ready to load under this charter about 1 July 1965' was held to be a condition. And in *Bunge Corp., N. York v. Tradax Export S.A. Panama* [1981] 1 WLR 711, where the contract required 'at least 15 consecutive days notice of the probable readiness of the vessel', notice given on 17 June for sailing by the end of June was a breach of a condition allowing the injured party to repudiate the contract.

Terms relating to time for performance or delivery are usually conditions, but those relating to time for payment are merely warranties.

In *Union Eagle Ltd v. Golden Achievement Ltd* [1997] 2 All ER 215, a contract for the sale of land specified completion by a specific time, failing which the purchaser's deposit was forfeited as liquidated damages. The documents for the completion were delivered 10 minutes after the deadline. The JCPC held that the time for performance had passed, and performance by the purchaser was no longer possible.

(iii) Waiver of breach of condition

A breach of condition can always be treated as a breach of warranty, but waiver on one occasion does not prevent the term from being subsequently and unilaterally reintroduced as a condition on reasonable notice. In *Charles Rickards Ltd v. Oppenheim* [1950] 1 KB 611, the defendant ordered a car to be built on a Rolls-Royce chassis within the specified time. He waived a failure to deliver on a number of occasions but then served notice that, if the car was not delivered within four weeks, he would refuse to accept delivery. The court supported his claim. (For waiver in sale of goods contracts see Chapter 18, p.429.)

(iv) Conditions precedent and subsequent

A contract subject to a condition precedent will come into effect only when that condition is satisfied: *Aberfoyle Plantations Ltd v. Cheng* [1960] AC 115; and, where the contract contains a condition subsequent, it may be terminated: *Head v. Tattersall* (1871) LR 7 Ex 4.

3.15 Exclusion or exemption clauses

Contract terms frequently exclude one party either wholly or partially from liability for breaches of contract or tort. These terms are regulated by common law and the Unfair Contract Terms Act (UCTA) 1977, which prohibits their use against consumers in circumstances which are unfair.

(a) Common law protection against exclusion clauses

The common law attacks exclusion clauses in three stages:

(i)   denying that they were incorporated into contracts;
(ii)   limiting their scope by interpretation;
(iii) restricting their scope through the doctrine of privity of contract.

(i) The exclusion clause is not incorporated into the contract

The exclusion clause must be contained in the contract and not a mere receipt. In *Chapelton v. Barry UDC* [1940] 1 KB 532, it was held that an exclusion clause was not incorporated by a term on the reverse of a ticket issued on the hire of deck chairs. If the clause is in a contractual document, it is significant whether or not the contract was signed. If it is signed, it is generally impossible for the signer to escape the consequences of the clause in the absence of fraud or misrepresentation: *Curtis v. Chemical Cleaning & Dyeing Co.* [1951] 1 KB 805.

   If contained in a contract which is unsigned or in the form of a notice, the party must have had actual or constructive notice of the clause before or at the time of making the contract. Constructive notice can be achieved by prominent notices at the place where the contract is made. In *McCutcheon v. David MacBrayne Ltd* [1964] 1 WLR 125, the defendants were not protected from liability for loss of the claimant's car when the ferry carrying it sank, in spite of an exclusion clause being displayed in their office. Neither were they protected by a reference to the notice on a receipt given when the car was booked in, since this was issued after the contract was entered into.

In *Olley v. Marlborough Court Ltd* [1949] 1 KB 532, O booked into a hotel and property was later stolen from the room. The management claimed protection from liability by a notice displayed in the room. The court rejected their claim since the contract had been made before the claimant went to her room.

Similarly, a notice excluding the owners of a car park from liability for injury to users was not part of the contract since it was visible only once drivers had entered into a contract by passing through the automatic barrier: *Thornton v. Shoe Lane Parking Ltd* [1971] WLR 585.

In *Dillon v. Baltic Shipping Co. (The 'Mikhail Lermontov')* [1991] 2 Lloyd's Rep 155, the court held that the claimant was not bound by an exclusion clause contained in the tickets for a cruise which limited the liability of the shipping line for personal injury and death, since the issue of the tickets came after a firm contract was already in existence.

Clauses can be incorporated through a sufficient course of dealings in the past where there has been consistent use of the exclusion clause. In *J. Spurling Ltd v. Bradshaw* [1956] 2 All ER 121, the claimant was able to rely on the protection of an exclusion clause against loss of stored goods in spite of the non-validity of a notice on an invoice for the dealing in question, since the companies had had dealings over a number of years on the basis of an exclusion of liability. The use of the exclusion clause must, however, be consistent. The defendants were unable to succeed on this ground in *McCutcheon* since they had not regularly asked the claimant to sign a risk note excluding them from liability. The course of dealing must be more than three or four occasions during the previous five years, as in *Hollier v. Rambler Motors (AMC) Ltd* [1972] 2 QB 71.

(ii)   Limiting scope through interpretation

Where the clause is ambiguous, it is interpreted against the person seeking to rely on it. In *Thornton v. Shoe Lane Parking Ltd* [1971] 2 QB 163, the exclusion clause for a car park stated 'Cars parked at owners' risk', which could conceivably protect against damage to drivers as well as cars, but the court limited it to damage to vehicles.

In *Hollier v. Rambler Motors (AMC) Ltd* [1972] 2 QB 71, H's car was damaged by a fire caused by the negligence of the defendant, who claimed protection by a clause stating: '[t]he company is not responsible for damage caused by fire to customers' cars on the premises'. The court held that it did not extend to fires caused by the defendant's negligence.

(iii)   Restricting the scope of the protection

In *Adler v. Dickson* [1954] 3 All ER 396, a clause in a ticket issued by a shipping line to a passenger protected the company but, because of privity of contract, not the company's employee whose negligent action caused the passenger's injury. In *Scruttons Ltd v. Midland Silicones Ltd* [1962] 1 All ER 1, S Ltd, who were stevedores employed by a shipowner, claimed protection of an exclusion clause contained in the contract between the shipper and MS Ltd, the owners of the cargo, limiting the shipowner's liability to $500. They were not entitled to the protection of the clause since they were not parties to the contract.

(b)   Statutory protection: the Unfair Contract Terms Act (UCTA) 1977

The Act applies to different situations where exemption clauses attempt to modify future liability. It does not cover settlements and compromises on events which have already occurred: *Tudor Grange Holdings Ltd v. Citibank NA* [1991] 4 All ER 1. See also the discussion on the Unfair Terms in Consumer Contract Regulations 1999 (Chapter 21).

(i)   Avoidance of liability for negligence

As regards business liability, exclusion clauses cannot protect against negligence resulting in death or personal injury. For any other loss or damage, a clause is valid only where it 'satisfies the requirement of reasonableness' (see below): s.2(1) UCTA 1977.

This does not prevent agreements between the owner and hirer of industrial plant regarding their liability for negligence and excluding one from liability at the other's expense: *Thompson v. T. Lohan (Plant Hire) Ltd and Another* [1987] 2 All ER 631 (see p.99 below for the facts of the case).

(ii)   Liability in contract

In contracts where one party 'deals as a consumer' or where there is a standard form contract, exclusion clauses are subject to the 'requirement of reasonableness': s.3. A person deals as a consumer if (i) s/he does not contract in the course of a business or hold him/herself out as doing so; (ii) the other party does contract in the course of a business; and (iii) (in contracts for goods) the goods are of a type ordinarily supplied for private use or consumption. A person does not deal as a consumer in sales by auction or competitive tender.

There is no protection for contracts between dealers (unless they contract on one party's standard form) and the clause will be binding on the parties subject to common law rules, since there is equality of bargaining position. In *Photo Production Ltd v. Securicor Transport Ltd* [1980] AC 827, the House of Lords restated the principle in the *Suisse Atlantique* case (*Suisse Atlantique Société d'Armement Maritime SA v. NV Rotterdamsche Kolen Centrale* [1967] 1 AC 361), where clauses could operate to exclude parties even from a fundamental breach of contract. In the *Photo Production* case, Securicor were excluded from all liability for the destruction of the claimant's premises by a fire started by one of its security guards protecting the site.

(iii)   The 'requirement of reasonableness'

Exclusion clauses are judged 'having regard to the circumstances which were, or ought reasonably to have been, known to or in the contemplation of the parties when the contract was made'. The court interprets exclusion clauses strictly. In *Computer and Systems Engineering plc v. John Lelliott Ltd, The Times*, 21 February 1991, the contract excluded liability for flooding or burst pipes, while the damage was caused by a fractured sprinkler pipe. The court held that the damage was not within the meaning of the clause.

This area of the law is also covered by the Unfair Terms in Consumer Contracts Regulations 1999 (see Chapter 21, p.517).

3.16   Incomplete or inchoate agreements

Contracts may be unenforceable because they are unclear. In *G. Scammell & Nephew Ltd v. Ouston* [1941] AC 151, the defendant agreed to buy a van on terms that 'the balance of the purchase price can be had on hire purchase terms over a period of two years'. No precise meaning could be given to the term, since hire purchase contracts varied widely and there was no enforceable contract. The court may sever any meaningless clause if the sense of the contract is not damaged. In *Nicolene Ltd v. Simmonds* [1953] 1 QB 543, the court severed from a sale of goods contract the clause: 'I assume that we are in agreement that the usual conditions of acceptance apply'. There were, in fact, no such 'usual conditions'.

The court may otherwise resolve the problem by reference to a trade practice or course of dealing between the parties. In *Hillas & Co. Ltd v. Arcos Ltd* [1932] All ER 494, a contract for the supply of wood contained an option for the following year without specifying the kind of timber, the destination or manner of shipment. The court held that these points could be determined by reference to the previous dealings and normal trade practice.

The court may also imply a term into the agreement to give it efficacy, or the agreement may itself provide for the clarification of the contract by providing for reference to arbitration. In *Foley v. Classique Coaches Ltd* [1934] 2 KB 1, F contracted to supply petrol to the defendants 'at a price to be agreed by the parties in writing and from time to time'. It also provided that any dispute should be submitted 'to arbitration in the usual way'. The defendants could not repudiate the contract after three years on the ground of uncertainty, since the court implied terms whereby the petrol should be of reasonable quality and at a reasonable price and the contract provided an arbitration procedure to fix a price failing agreement.

In *Neilson v. Stewart* [1991] SC(HL) 22, an agreement for the sale of shares included a loan repayment which was to be deferred for one year, 'after which time repayment shall be negotiated to our mutual satisfaction'. The purchaser claimed that this clause rendered the whole agreement unenforceable, but the House of Lords held that the parties did not apparently intend the loan to be fixed as to time and manner of payment, that all loans were repayable on demand and it was not essential that interest should be payable.

Where contracts for sale and supply of goods and services make no provision as to price, the obligation to pay a reasonable price is implied by statute (see Chapter 18, p.447).

3.17   Discharge of contracts

Contracts are discharged by performance, by agreement, by acceptance of breach, and by frustration.

(a)   Discharge by performance

Whether a party can claim in respect of part performance of its contractual obligations depends on whether the contract is entire or divisible. In entire contracts, the performance must be complete and no claim can be made for part performance. In divisible contracts, the performance is broken down into smaller units and payment is claimable for the units performed. Employment contracts providing weekly or monthly payment are a typical example. Building contracts generally provide for staged payments on satisfactory completion of each stage, avoiding the problem in *Sumpter v. Hedges* [1898] 1 QB 673 (see below).

(i)   Exceptions to doctrine of proper performance for entire contracts
Payment for partial performance can be claimed where: (i) failure to complete is the fault of the other party; (ii) it has been accepted; and (iii) there has been substantial performance.

Failure to complete is other party's fault. In *Planché v. Colburn* (1831) 8 Bing 14, an author was entitled to part payment in respect of preparation of a manuscript when the editor cancelled the series.

Where partial performance has been accepted. Partial performance can always be rejected but, if accepted, there is liability to pay in quasi-contract for the work done or the goods supplied (see Chapter 5). Acceptance of part performance presupposes the possibility of rejection, so that part performance of a contract to build houses is impossible, even though another builder completes the work: *Sumpter v. Hedges* [1898] 1 QB 673. In *IBMAC v. Marshall (Homes) Ltd* (1968), IBMAC failed to recover in respect of part completion of a road building scheme.

Where there has been substantial performance. Where the contract is substantially but not exactly performed, the party which has substantially performed its contractual obligation is entitled to payment less an amount in respect of the work outstanding.

In *Hoenig v. Isaacs* [1952] 2 All ER 176, the value of the outstanding work on a contract for interior decoration was fixed at around £55 and the court ordered payment of the outstanding balance under the contract less the £55.

Where the value of the outstanding work is too great in relation to the total contract price, there is not substantial performance. In *Bolton v. Mahadeva* [1975] QB 326, the outstanding work to make a central heating system function was assessed at £174.50 against a total contract price of £560. There was no substantial performance.

(b) Discharge by agreement: accord and satisfaction

Accord and satisfaction: an agreement (accord) between parties to release each other from their contractual obligations is legally enforceable because the mutual release from their obligations constitutes consideration (satisfaction).

Where, however, one party has performed its obligations under the contract and promises unilaterally to release the other party from its, the promise is only binding if the other party has supplied valuable consideration or the promise is by deed.

Thus, if A owes B £100 under a contract, but B agrees to release A from the obligation to pay or to accept a lesser sum in complete satisfaction, B will be entitled at common law to sue for the unpaid balance in the future. This was established by *Pinnel's Case* (1602) 5 Co Rep 117a, and followed in *Foakes v. Beer* (1884) 9 App Cas 605. In this case, Mrs Beer obtained a judgment against Foakes ordering him to pay her £2,090. Foakes was unable to pay and, by a written agreement, agreed to pay £500 immediately and the balance by instalments. When the balance was paid, Mrs Beer sued to recover interest on the judgment debt. The House of Lords held that her claim should succeed because payment of the smaller sum was not consideration for the promise to accept this sum in satisfaction of the judgment debt.

In *Stour Valley Builders v. Stuart*, *The Independent*, 9 February 1992, a debtor sent a cheque for less than the total amount owed on condition that the creditor accepted it in full and final satisfaction. The creditor cashed the cheque and was later able to sue for the balance outstanding. In *Re Selectmove Ltd* [1995] 2 All ER 531, the company had offered to pay debts to the Inland Revenue (IR) by instalments and the inspector had agreed to inform the company if this was not acceptable. The company had begun to pay by instalments when the IR threatened to wind up the company if the arrears were not paid immediately. The company relied on *Williams & Roffey Bros v. Nicholls (Contractors) Ltd* [1991] 1 QB 1 that a promise to perform an existing obligation would be good consideration if there were practical benefits to the promissor (see p. 52 above). The argument was rejected as inconsistent with *Foakes v. Beer.*

A partial solution lies in equitable estoppel (see pp. 55) since, under this doctrine, where a person promises to release the other from a contractual obligation and the other acts in reliance on that promise, the promisee can use the promise as a defence against an attempt by the promissor to insist upon his/her original legal rights. The doctrine apparently covers only promises relating to the suspension rather than the termination of contractual rights. This seems to be confirmed by the *High Trees House* case (see p. 55) and later decisions.

In *Tool Metal Manufacturing Co. Ltd v. Tungsten Electric Co. Ltd* [1955] 2 All ER 657, the appellants granted the respondents a licence to import certain hard metal alloys for 10 years from 1937 and thereafter until determined on six months' notice. The respondents agreed to pay a royalty in respect of alloy used and an additional sum by way of 'compensation' if they used more than a specified amount. Shortly after the outbreak of the war, the payment of compensation was suspended. The appellants claimed for compensation payments under the original agreement from 1 January 1947. The court held they were entitled to resume their legal rights on giving reasonable notice.

The remedy is discretionary and the court will refuse to offer its protection where the party seeking relief has not acted fairly.

In *D & C Builders Ltd v. Rees* [1966] 2 QB 617, where the court refused to extend protection to the defendant who had forced the claimant, whom she knew to be in desperate need of funds, to accept £300 in complete satisfaction of a debt of £500, the issue of whether promissory estoppel would have covered the termination of contractual rights was not solved, since the decision was based on withholding the discretionary remedy on the ground of Mrs Rees's dishonourable conduct; but see economic duress (p. 64).

In *Ferguson v. Davies* [1997] 1 All ER 315, F sold records to D in consideration of the transfer to him by the purchaser of records worth £600, or a cash payment of £1,700. Records worth £143.50 and a payment of £5 were made by the purchaser. F sued for £486.50 and was sent a cheque for £150 expressed to be in full payment of the debt. F cashed the cheque but notified D that he was continuing his claim, now increased to £1,745.79. The county court judge dismissed F's claim on the ground that the acceptance of the £150 was a binding accord and satisfaction. The Court of Appeal held that acceptance of a lesser sum was not accord and satisfaction unless the claimant received some additional benefit by way of consideration.

(c)   Novation and notice

A contract can be replaced by another by way of novation, usually with different parties. Contracts of employment can be terminated by notice only in accordance with an express provision or the statutory minimum notice provisions under the Employment Protection (Consolidation) Act 1978, subject to the common law notion of reasonable notice (see Chapter 17, p.420).

(d)   Discharge by acceptance of breach

Where one party breaches a condition, the injured party can opt to regard him/herself as still bound by the contract, or can repudiate it. In either case it could sue for damages.

An anticipatory breach of a contract occurs before the time fixed for performance of the contract. This can be by way of a notice by one of the parties that he will not comply with the terms of the contract at the time fixed for performance or by his putting himself in a position which makes compliance with the contract impossible. Injured parties can treat the contract either as ongoing or as repudiated. In the latter case, they can sue for damages for breach of contract without waiting for the time fixed for performance. In *Hochster v. De La Tour* [1843–60] All ER Rep 12, H was informed on 11 May 1852 that he was no longer required as a courier contracted to start work on 1 June 1852. H was able to commence his action for breach of contract on 22 May 1852.

Failure to accept repudiation can cause problems. In *Avery v. Bowden* (1855) 5 E & B 714, B chartered A's ship and agreed to load her at Odessa within 45 days. The captain was informed on arriving that B would not load the ship, but stayed on, hoping that B would change his mind. The outbreak of the Crimean War made performance of the contract illegal and it was discharged by frustration, preventing a claim for damages for breach of contract.

Parties refusing to treat the contract as repudiated can treat the contract as valid and perform their contractual obligations. In *White & Carter (Councils) Ltd v. McGregor* [1961] 3 All ER 1178, the claimants refused to accept repudiation of a contract when no expenses had been incurred, performed their obligations and recovered damages for their subsequently incurred losses. This contradicts the obligation to mitigate one's loss, and later cases have taken a different approach. In *Clea Shipping Corpn v. Bulk Oil International Ltd, The Alaskan Trader (No. 2)* [1984] 1 All ER 129, a ship was chartered in October 1979 for two years. In April 1981, the charterers indicated for the second time that the ship was not needed and refused to give sailing instructions. The shipowners kept the ship at anchor with a full crew ready to sail until the charter expired. The arbitrator held that they should have accepted the repudiation in April 1981.

(d)   Discharge by subsequent impossibility: frustration

A contract is frustrated when performance is impossible because of some unforeseen happening beyond the control of the contracting parties, and neither party will be liable for breach of contract.

This exception to the common law principle of absolute contractual duties was first recognised in *Taylor v. Caldwell* (1862) 32 LJQB 164, where a contract to lease a theatre was frustrated by a fire which destroyed the theatre. The doctrine does not apply where the event should have been provided for, or where the contract is merely more difficult or less profitable to perform.

In *Davis Contractors Ltd v. Fareham UDC* [1956] AC 696, DC Ltd contracted to build 78 houses in eight months for a fixed price, but took 22 months because of labour shortages, and their claim that the original contract had been frustrated failed. In *Tsakiroglou & Co. Ltd v. Noblee Thorl GmbH* [1962] AC 93, a contract by the claimants to sell a consignment of groundnuts and deliver them to Hamburg was not frustrated by the closure of the Suez Canal, which forced them to be shipped via the Cape of Good Hope: '[a]n increase of expense is not a ground of frustration'.

Frustration has been recognised in the following cases:

(i)   Impossibility because of changes in the law: *Avery v. Bowden* (1855) 5 E & B 714 (outbreak of Crimean War);

(ii) Contracts for personal services discharged by death or permanent incapacity: *Condor v. The Barron Knights Ltd* [1966] 1 WLR 87 (contract discharged by insanity);

(iii) Where the contract depends upon a state of affairs which ceases to exist: *Taylor v. Caldwell* (1862) 32 LJQB 164 (destruction of theatre by fire); *Krell v. Henry* [1903] 2 KB

740; *Chandler v. Webster* [1904] 1 KB 904 (contracts to rent accommodation from which to watch the Coronation procession, which was later cancelled). But see *Herne Bay Steamboat Co. v. Hutton* [1903] 2 KB 603, where the defendant chartered the claimant's ship '[to view] the naval review and for a day's cruise round the fleet': the contract was not frustrated by the cancellation of the royal review, since the fleet was still available for inspection;

(iv) Where the commercial purpose of the contract is frustrated. In *Jackson v. Union Marine Insurance Co. Ltd* (1874) LR 10 CP 125, a ship was chartered to sail from Liverpool to Newport and load with a cargo for San Francisco. It ran aground and returned to Liverpool for repairs, which took eight months. The contract was frustrated and the parties were discharged.

Frustration does not apply where the frustrating event is self-induced. In *Maritime National Fish Ltd v. Ocean Trawlers Ltd* [1935] AC 524, a charter contract for fishing boats was not frustrated when the charterer was granted fewer fishing licences than he had applied for and he allocated those licences to his own vessels.

(v) The doctrine extends to leases and contracts for land. In *National Carriers Ltd v. Panalpina (Northern) Ltd* [1981] AC 675, the appellants leased a warehouse for 10 years. After five, the local authority closed the access road for two years. The court, while agreeing in principle that frustration could apply, refused to apply it in this case.

The effect of frustration is that the contract is void *ab initio* and the parties can (i) recover money paid; and (ii) claim payment for work performed prior to the frustration: Law Reform (Frustrated Contracts) Act 1943.

(i) Right to recover money paid

'All sums paid or payable to any party in pursuance of the contract before the time when the parties were so discharged shall, in the case of sums so paid, be recoverable from him as money received by him for the use of the party by whom the sums were paid, and, in the case of sums so payable, cease to be so payable.': s.1(2). This is qualified by allowing the person to offset expenses incurred in the fulfilment of the contract prior to the frustrating event.

(ii) Right to compensation for partial performance

A party who has 'obtained a valuable benefit before the time of discharge' is required to pay 'such sum ... as the court considers just having regard to all the circumstances of the case'. It is not clear whether this covers the facts in *Appleby v. Myers* (1867) LR 2 CP 651, where Appleby failed to recover damages under a contract to erect machinery on the defendant's premises where the premises and the machines were both destroyed by fire when the work was virtually complete. In *BP Exploration Co. (Libya) Ltd v. Hunt (No. 2)* [1983] 2 AC 352, the court suggested that *Appleby v. Myers* would still not be covered.

End of Chapter Summary

In this chapter you have considered the law of contract including: the formation; the vitiating elements; the terms and discharge of contracts.

The law of contract is fundamental to business law, and all these elements are important and will recur in other contexts in later chapters. This is particularly true in respect of the law of agency, the sale and supply of goods and services and contracts of employment. In chapters concerning the creating of securities for loans, the law relating to misrepresentation is particularly relevant where mortgages are created over a jointly owned matrimonial home in respect of the business debts of one of the spouses.

Of particular relevance to this chapter is the final chapter in the book on e-commerce where the rules relating to formation and terms are reconsidered in the context of virtual contracts.

Examples of practical situations relating to the application of the principles raised in this chapter can be seen in the following questions.

Questions

1. Max Ltd runs a factory requiring around 10,000 tons of steel annually. The company invited tenders 'for the supply during the coming 12 months of Grade 1 steel, not exceeding 10,000 tons in total, delivery to be made as and when demanded by Max Ltd'. Steely Ltd tendered at the price of £400 per ton and Max Ltd replied: 'I accept your tender'.

   Max Ltd ordered 1,000 tons of steel which was supplied by Steely Ltd without delay and later placed a further order with Steely Ltd for 1,000 tons. This second order coincided with a national steelworkers' strike and, as a result, the market price rose to £600 per ton.

   Steely Ltd seeks your advice concerning the obligation to deliver the second order and how the company can safeguard its position in the future if the price of steel remains higher than the price tendered.

   Advise Steely Ltd.

2. A offered a reward for the return of a lost watch by a notice in a shop window. After six months he revoked the offer by a replacement notice in the same window. Six months later, B, who saw the original notice but not the second, returned the watch and claimed the reward. Is B likely to succeed?

3. A writes offering to sell you a bike for £250; you accept the offer by post, enclosing a cheque for £50 payable immediately and a further four cheques for £50 postdated over the next four months. You have now discovered that A sold the bike to B before receiving your letter. Can you sue for damages for breach of contract?

4. Trekkers Ltd contracted with Tarzan to pay him £5,000 to act as expedition guide for a trip into a dangerous area of Africa. Before the departure of the expedition, a war broke out in the area between warring tribes and Tarzan refused to act as a guide unless Trekkers Ltd promised to pay him a further £2,500. Trekkers Ltd promised to pay the extra sum and the expedition left, guided by Tarzan. On the return of the expedition, Trekkers Ltd refused to pay the extra £2,500 to Tarzan.

   Advise Tarzan of his rights in respect of the extra money.

5. BH Ltd agreed to build a house for Clive for £250,000. However, it was later discovered that BH Ltd had made a mistake in its calculations and the cost of building the house was higher than anticipated and its profit margin would be virtually nothing.

Questions cont'd

6.   Bodger Ltd hired an excavator by telephone from Equipment Ltd. The excavator was to be used on marshy ground. The period of hire and the hire charges were agreed over the phone, but no other reference to the terms of the hire contract were made.

On the first day of hire, the excavator became bogged down in the ground and could no longer be used without its recovery by Equipment Ltd and extensive repairs.

On the day the excavator became bogged down, Equipment Ltd sent Bodger Ltd a copy of the conditions of the hire contract. These included the usual trade terms requiring the hirer to indemnify Equipment Ltd for all damage and expenses incurred by Equipment Ltd in connection with the recovery and repair of the excavator.

Advise Equipment Ltd whether it can enforce the terms against Bodger Ltd.

7.   Angus owed Brenda £500 in monthly instalments of £50. After paying eight instalments, Angus told Brenda that he had lost his job and could no longer keep up the payments. As a result, Brenda agreed to forgo the two final instalments.

Brenda later regretted her decision and claimed the unpaid balance from Angus.

Advise Angus whether Brenda is likely to succeed in her action.

Would it make a difference to your advice if you now discover that Angus had in fact lied about losing his job?

8.   P Ltd won a contract with BH Ltd for the installation of water systems in a housing estate being built by BH Ltd. Under the terms of the contract, BH Ltd promised P Ltd that the company would have site access to start work in January with work to be completed the following December.

P Ltd was able to gain access only in March and protested about the delay but attempted to complete the work in accordance with the contract.

In December, P Ltd abandoned the contract when it was three-quarters complete in order to start work on another project which it had earlier contracted to start in December in anticipation of the work for BH Ltd being completed.

BH Ltd has not paid for the work completed. Advise P Ltd of its rights.

Chapter 4

Tort law

After reading this chapter you will know about:

- the classification of torts and tortious liability
- general defences to tortious liability
- persons who can sue and be sued in tort
- establishing liability for negligence
- occupiers' liability to visitors and trespassers
- liability for private nuisance
- the rule in *Rylands v. Fletcher*
- torts affecting economic rights

4.1 Definition

A tort is an actionable, civil wrong entitling a person who suffers injury or loss to sue for unliquidated damages. Some torts are actionable *per se*, that is, without proof of damage. The word 'tort' comes from the French word for 'wrong'.

Tortious liability is important for businesses, particularly regarding employees' or agents' negligence, failure to ensure the safety of their premises and disturbances affecting neighbours.

(a) Torts affecting people

(i) *Negligence*
Breach of a duty of care owed to a person causing foreseeable injury to the person (see p. 92).

(b) Torts affecting property

(i) *Private nuisance*
Indirect interference with an occupier's use or enjoyment of land – structural damage caused by roots, vibrations and so on, as well as damage to enjoyment through smells, smoke and so on (see p. 103).

(ii) *Trespass to land*
Direct interference with a person's rights of possession to land. It includes entry onto property and placing things on property. The duty is owed to the possessor even if he is not the owner. The tort is actionable *per se*, that is, actionable without proof of damage.

Trespass can be at ground level, below ground and in the sky. In *Kelsen v. Imperial Tobacco Co. (of Gt Britain and Ireland) Ltd* [1957] 2 All ER 343, the trespass was by a sign which projected in the airspace over the claimant's shop; and in *Woolerton and Wilson v. Richard Costain (Midlands) Ltd* [1970] 1 All ER 483, a crane travelling in the airspace above the claimant's premises was trespass. There is an upper limit, however, and in *Bernstein v. Skyviews & General Ltd* [1977] 3 All ER 902, the court refused to recognise trespass caused by a plane flying at over 600 feet over the claimant's property, but suggested that constant air surveillance could be an actionable nuisance.

(iii)   *Trespass to goods*
Wrongful interference with another person's goods: including touching, marking or taking away.

(iv)   *Conversion*
Acts in relation to goods amounting to a denial of the owner's title – removing goods and denying the ownership of the person from whom they have been taken; sale of goods by a non-owner.

(v)   *Negligence*
Breach of a duty of care in respect of the property of another, causing foreseeable harm (see Chapter 5, p.124).

(vi)   *Rylands v. Fletcher*
The escape of things stored or collected on land which were not natural to the land causing damage to another's property – water escaping from reservoirs causing damage to neighbouring properties.
It is frequently used in cases relating to protection of the environment (see p.107).

(c)   Torts affecting economic rights

(i)   *Inducement of breach of contract*
Persuading others to breach their contract with another, or acting to prevent its performance (see p.111).
This is of commercial importance where one business tries to poach the employees of another business.

(ii)   *Conspiracy to cause wilful damage*
Two or more persons acting without lawful justification to cause wilful damage to the claimant resulting in actual damage (see p.112).

(iii)   *Passing off*
Passing off one's products or services as those of another, causing financial loss or damage to business reputation. Trading in a name similar to that of another business causing public confusion (see p.112).

(iv)   *Negligent misstatement causing loss*
Breach of duty of care in giving advice to people to whom one owes a duty of care, causing them foreseeable loss including purely economic loss (see p.94).

Accountants, solicitors or banks are particularly vulnerable to this tort, arising from negligent audits or negligent advice or, in the case of banks, negligent character references.

(d)   Torts affecting reputation

(i)   Defamation

'The publication of a statement which tends to lower a person in the estimation of right thinking members of society generally; or which tends to make them shun or avoid that person.' If the defamation is in permanent form it is a libel, which is actionable *per se* (without proof of damage); if it is in impermanent form, it is a slander, which is generally actionable only on proof of loss. Libel includes defamatory statements in writing or via the media (television, film, records, stage and so on), whereas slander is restricted to verbal statements.

(e)   Torts affecting rights generally

(i)   Public nuisance

Behaviour which materially affects the reasonable comfort and convenience of a class of people – carrying on an offensive trade; obstructing the highway (see p.103) and environmental damage.

4.2   Establishing tortious liability

Claimants must prove an actionable interference with their rights causing them harm or loss. Some torts – including trespass to land and libel – do not require proof of loss.

Legal actions do not become illegal simply because they are malicious, with the exception of the tort of nuisance (see below p.104). In *The Mayor of Bradford Corporation v. Pickles* [1895] AC 587, the defendant maliciously dug trenches on his land to stop the flow of water and force the council to buy his land for a high price. His intent did not make his action illegal. In *Wilkinson v. Downton* [1897] 2 QB 57, the defendant was liable for causing nervous shock to the claimant by telling her that her husband had broken his legs in spite of his defence that it was merely a practical joke. Some torts – malicious falsehood and malicious arrest – require malice to be established, and malice defeats the defences of fair comment and qualified privilege in defamation.

4.3   General defences to tort

Some defences are specific to certain torts: for defamation there are the special defences of justification, fair comment and privilege. Some defences relate to torts in general.

(a)   Consent

A wrong can never be done to a person who consents to it.

A person can consent to an intentional act or run the risk of accidental injury, including active participation in dangerous sports, or even as a spectator. It is important in respect of employees and rescuers (see below p.99).

(b)   Exclusion of liability

People can exclude or limit their tortious liability in negligence or under the Occupiers' Liability Act 1957, subject to the Unfair Contract Terms Act 1977 and the Unfair Terms in Consumer Contracts Regulations 1999 (see Chapter 21, p.517).

(c)   Inevitable accident

This relates to accidents which could not be avoided by taking reasonable precautions. In *Stanley v. Powell* [1891] 1 QB 86, the claimant was hit by a shot during a pheasant shoot when the shot glanced off a tree.

(d)   Act of God

This relates to a natural and unpredictable eventuality: in *Nichols v. Marsland* [1876] 2 Ex D 1, exceptional rainfall burst the banks of the defendant's artificial lakes, destroying a number of bridges.

(e)   Necessity

Intentional damage to prevent even greater destruction or in defence of the realm: destroying properties in the path of a fire to prevent its spread.

(f)   Mistake

Mistake of fact where the mistake is reasonable: wrongful arrest by the police.

(g)   Act of state

The state protects persons from liability for damage caused when carrying out their duty except in respect of injury to a British subject or a friendly alien. In *Nissan v. Att. Gen* [1967] 2 All ER 1238, the claimant, the British owner of a hotel in Cyprus occupied by British troops, recovered damages since 'act of state' was no defence against a British subject.

(h)   Statutory protection to a public authority

The extent of the protection depends on whether the authority is absolute or conditional. If absolute, there is no liability as long as the authority acted reasonably and there was no available, alternative course of action. Conditional authority is where there is the power to act but no duty to do so, and the act must not interfere with the rights of others. In *Vaughan v. Taff Vale Railway* (1860) 5 H & N 679, the defendants were not liable for fires caused by sparks from engines since they were obliged to operate a railway and had done so with proper care.

(i)   Self-defence

If the tort is committed by people to protect themselves, their families or their property or the public, there is no liability if the action is a reasonable response to the threatened harm.

4.4   Persons who can sue and be sued in tort

Special categories include children, corporations, married couples, trades unions and executors and administrators.

(a)   Children

Children can sue and be sued in tort, but must sue through an adult as next friend.

Parents may also be liable if they are the child's employer, where they encouraged the child to commit the tort and where the tort arises from their negligent supervision. The Congenital Disabilities (Civil Liability) Act 1976 extends protection to children born disabled due to the fault of a third person, other than the mother: through drugs and so on.

(b)   Corporations

Public sector corporations include local authorities, other public bodies and universities. Private sector corporations include companies registered under the Companies Act 2006 and limited liability partnerships (LLPs) registered under the Limited Liability Partnerships Act 2000. Corporations are vicariously liable for their employees' torts within the ordinary course of their employment (see p.90), and where the corporation instigated the tort.

Where liability requires intention on the corporation's part, the 'identification theory' can allow an officer of the company to be identified as the corporation (see Chapter 6, p.151).

(c)   Husband and wife

Married women are liable for their torts (Law Reform (Married Women and Tortfeasors) Act 1935). Husbands are only exceptionally additionally liable, as when the husband is the wife's employer. Husbands and wives can sue each other but the court may stay the action where no substantial benefit would accrue to either party (Law Reform (Husband and Wife) Act 1962).

(d)   Unincorporated associations

Unincorporated associations cannot be liable in tort either actually or vicariously. Where their employees commit a tort within the ordinary course of their employment or where liability arises under the Occupiers' Liability Act 1957 or 1984, liability usually falls on the management committee or the association's principal officer.

In *Artistic Upholstery Ltd v. Art Forma (Furniture) Ltd* [1999] 4 All ER 277, the court held that an unincorporated association could bring a legal action for damages for passing off where the defendant company by itself took on the running of a trade exhibition in the same venue and under the same name as previous exhibitions organised by the association. The court held that the association owned the goodwill in the name of the exhibition.

General partnerships are unincorporated associations but statutory provisions relate to tortious liability for the actions of partners and employees (see Chapter 7, p.166). Trades unions are unincorporated associations, but they can contract and sue and be sued in their own names: s.2 Trade Union and Labour Relations Act 1974. They are vicariously liable for the torts of their officers and employees. They enjoy certain immunity in the law of tort for torts committed during the furtherance of a trade dispute where the union has balloted its members before taking industrial action. They can otherwise be liable for inducing people to break their employment contracts.

(e) Executors and administrators

Claims survive the death of the victim, except for defamation, and actions can be started by the deceased's executors or administrators: Law Reform (Miscellaneous Provisions) Act 1934. Damages include loss of expectation of life and earnings.

There may also be additional liability to the deceased's relatives, including husband, wife (not divorced or common law), children (including those unborn), grandchildren, parents, grandparents, brothers, sisters, aunts and uncles and their issue: Fatal Accidents Act 1976. The Act provides that '[n]ot more than one action shall lie for and in respect of the same subject matter of complaint': s.2(3).

In *Cachia v. Faluyi* [2001] All ER 299, Mrs Cachia died in a car accident in 1988 leaving a husband and four children. A writ was issued on their behalf against the driver, but it was never served. In 1997, outside the limitation period for the husband and the eldest child, but within the limitation period for the other three children, another writ was issued. The defendants succeeded in striking out the claim under s.2(3). The Court of Appeal reconsidered the section in the light of the Human Rights Act (HRA) 1998 and Article 6(1) of the European Convention on Human Rights which provides: '[i[n the determination of his civil rights and obligations, everyone is entitled to a fair and public hearing'. The court held that the word 'action' must be a 'served process' so that s.2(3) was no bar to the children's claim.

Hot Topic . . .

EMPLOYERS' VICARIOUS LIABILITY

Employers are vicariously liable for their employees' tortious acts within the scope of their employment, but are only exceptionally liable for the torts of an independent contractor. Employers must have insurance cover against such vicarious liability: Employers' Liability (Compulsory Insurance) Act 1969.

In *Limpus v. London General Omnibus Co.* (1862) 1 H&C 526, the employers were liable when their employee, a bus driver, raced his bus contrary to their instructions, but in *Beard v. London General Omnibus Co.* [1900] 2 QB 530, they were not liable when the conductor

drove the bus, since this was outside his employment.

In *Twine v. Bean's Express Ltd* (1946) 175 LT 131, the defendant's employee, a driver, gave a lift to a third person who was killed because of his negligent driving. The defendants were held to be not liable, since the driver had exceeded the scope of his employment. However, in *Rose v. Plenty and Another* [1976] 1 All ER 97, the employer was liable for injuries to a young boy helping on a milk round in spite of a notice in the depot saying: 'Children must not in any circumstances be employed by you in the performance of your duties'.

Where employees commit criminal acts, the basic test for vicarious liability depends on whether the act is a wrongful and unauthorised mode of doing some authorised act. In *Warren v. Henleys* [1948] 2 All ER 935, the employer was not liable where a pump attendant at a petrol station punched a client, but in *Lloyd v. Grace, Smith & Co.* [1912] AC 716, a firm of solicitors was liable for its managing clerk's fraud in carrying out conveyancing in the course of his employment.

In *Trotman v. North Yorkshire CC* [1999] LGR 584, the Court of Appeal held that the employers of a teacher who had sexually assaulted a pupil were not vicariously liable since it was not an unauthorised way of doing an authorised act. The House of Lords in *Lister v. Hesley Hall Ltd* [2001] 2 All ER 769 stated that this case was wrongly decided and held the defendant school vicariously liable for the sexual abuse of pupils by a warden. It stressed that a broad approach should be taken to what was in the scope of a person's employment. In the case of intentional wrongdoing by an employee, an employer is liable even for unauthorised acts if they are so connected with authorised acts that they could be regarded as improper modes of doing them. The question is: 'is there a sufficient connection between the acts of the employee and the employment so that there should be vicarious liability?'.

In *Harrison v. Michelin Tyre Co. Ltd* [1985] 1 All ER 918, the test was 'whether a reasonable man would say either that the employee's act was part and parcel of his employment even though it was unauthorised and prohibited by the employer, ... , or ... so divergent from his employment as to be plainly alien to his employment'. In this case, the employers were liable when the claimant was injured when a duckboard on which he was standing was tilted by a handtruck pushed by another employee who was larking about. In *Hudson v. Ridge Manufacturing Co. Ltd* [1957] 2 All ER 229, the employers were liable when an employee tripped up another employee as a practical joke. The employee had a reputation as a practical joker and the company had not dismissed him. See also *Jones v. Tower Boot Co. Ltd* [1997] 2 All ER 406 (see p. 404).

In *Mattis v. Pollock (t/a Flamingo's Nightclub)* [2003] 1 All ER 10, the employer was vicariously liable for a violent assault by his employee, a bouncer. The bouncer had been chased from the club following an incident and had returned home to arm himself with a knife. On his way back, about 100 metres from the club, he bumped into people involved in the dispute and stabbed the claimant. The court stressed that 'where an employee is expected to use violence while carrying out his duties, the likelihood of establishing that an act of violence fell within the broad scope of his employment is greater than it would be if he were not'.

4.5   More than one person liable for the tort

(a)   Separate concurrent tortfeasors

Where separate tortious acts produce the same damage: a passenger is injured in a crash involving two cars due to the negligence of both drivers: *Drinkwater v. Kimber* [1952] 2 QB 281.

(b)   Separate tortfeasors causing different damage

Two or more persons causing different injury/damage to the claimant: a negligent motorist injures a pedestrian who is then the victim of negligent medical care.

(c)   Joint tortfeasors

Two or more persons committing the same tortious act: one person instigates another to commit a tort; the breach of a duty imposed on two or more persons; torts committed by one or some persons, involved in a 'concerted action to a common end'; vicarious liability of employers for their employees' torts while acting within the scope of their employment.

(d)   Liability of parties

For joint and separate concurrent tortfeasors, each person is liable for the whole damage subject to the right to claim contribution from the other(s) under s.1 Civil Liability (Contribution) Act 1978. Where two or more persons cause different damage, the court fixes the liability of each defendant and there is no right of contribution.

(e)　Termination of liability

The most important terminating event is lapse of time under the Limitation Act 1980 (see Chapter 5, p. 116). For defamation, liability is terminated by the claimant's death.

4.6　Negligence

Negligence relates to the protection of persons and property from involuntary but negligent interference.

Negligence is the breach of a legal duty to take care, resulting in unintended harm to the claimant. There are three essential ingredients: (i) a legal duty of care owed by the defendant to the claimant; (ii) a breach of that legal duty by the defendant; and (iii) injury or damage to property suffered by the claimant arising out of the breach of the duty.

(a)　The duty of care

This was famously expressed by Lord Atkin in *Donoghue v. Stevenson* [1932] AC 562: '[y]ou must take reasonable care to avoid acts or omissions which you can reasonably foresee would be likely to injure your neighbour'. Neighbours are 'persons who are so closely and directly affected by my act that I ought reasonably to have them in contemplation as being so affected when I am directing my mind to the acts or omissions which are called into question'.

In the *Donoghue* case, the manufacturer of a bottle of ginger beer was liable to the consumer who became seriously ill due to a partly decomposed snail in the bottle. The consumer was not the purchaser, and the decision was the basis of manufacturers' liability until the Consumer Protection Act 1987 (see Chapter 21).

The principle is infinitely adaptable. In *Lewis v. Carmarthenshire County Council* [1953] 1 WLR 1439, an education authority was held to owe a duty to road users to exercise reasonable supervision of children in a nursery adjoining the road. In *Bermingham v. Sher Brothers* 1980 SLT 122, a firefighter was a 'neighbour' of an occupier who owed a duty to warn of any unexpected danger of which he knew or ought to have known. And in *Ogwo v. Taylor* [1988] 1 AC 431, the occupier was liable to a firefighter for injuries suffered during a blaze at a house resulting from the occupier's negligence.

The scope of the duty of care was extended by a number of later decisions.

In *Ross v. Caunters* [1979] 2 All ER 97, the defendant solicitor was held to owe a duty of care to non-clients. The defendant had given his client negligent advice on making a will, failing to warn him that any bequest to a witness was void under s.15 Wills Act 1837.

In *Yianni v. Edwin Evans & Sons* [1981] 3 All ER 592, the defendant surveyors were liable to the claimant for a negligent survey carried out for the building society making a loan to the claimant who had been advised to obtain a separate survey but went ahead without one. In *JEB Fasteners Ltd. v. Marks, Bloom & Co.* [1983] 1 All ER 583, the defendant auditors were liable for a negligent audit for their client. The claimant had relied on the accounts in making a bid for the company. The court held that, in the circumstances, the defendants should have foreseen a possible takeover bid and that the bidder might rely on the accounts. In *White and Another v. Jones and Others* [1995] 1 All ER 691, a solicitor was liable to two beneficiaries through failure to incorporate a testator's new instructions received on 17 July. These were passed on by the managing clerk on 16 August, who went on holiday on 17 August. On his return, he made an arrangement to see the testator on 17 September, but the testator died on 14 September.

In *E.H. Humphries (Norton) Ltd and Thistle Hotels Ltd v. Fire Alarm Fabrication Services and Ors* [2006] EWCA Civ 1496 the court stated that in certain circumstances an independent contractor could owe a duty of care to employees of its subcontractor.

(i) Restricting the duty of care

The restriction is based on public policy and applies in particular to public officials. In *Hill v. Chief Constable of West Yorkshire* [1989] AC 53, the police owed no duty of care to the general public in the prevention or detection of crime in an action by the mother of the last victim of the 'Yorkshire Ripper' alleging negligence for failure to make an earlier arrest. This point of principle was restated in *Brooks v. Commissioner of Police of the Metropolis* [2005] 1 WLR 1495 and *Van Colle and Anor v. Chief Constable of the Hertfordshire Police; Smith v. Chief Constable of Sussex Police* [2008] UKHL 50.

It has also been held that the police owed no duty of care to victims when taking a decision whether or not to prosecute a suspected offender on the ground that it would not be reasonable to require prosecutors to weigh the private interests of the victim against their general duties: *Vicario v. Commissioner of Police for the Metropolis* [2007] EWCA Civ 1361.

In *Elguzouli-Daf v. Commissioner of Police of the Metropolis; McBrearty v. Ministry of Defence* [1994] 2 WLR 173, the defendants, accused respectively of rape and handling explosives, were detained for 22 and 85 days before the prosecution abandoned the case for lack of evidence. The Court of Appeal rejected their right to sue the Crown Prosecution Service (CPS) for negligence on the ground of public policy.

In *Barrett v. Enfield LBC* [1997] All ER 171, the claim that the local authority was in breach of its duty of care to act as a parent and show the standard of care of a responsible parent was rejected on ground of public policy. In *Capital and Counties plc v. Hants CC* [1997] 2 All ER 865, the Court of Appeal, deciding three separate appeals on similar grounds, held that the fire brigade does not owe a duty of care to owners or occupiers merely by attending and fighting a fire. It could, however, be liable where it had caused increased damage. Thus, the fire brigade was liable where the fire officer's decision to turn off the sprinkler system resulted in the total destruction of a building.

In *OLL Ltd v Secretary of State for Transport* [1997] All ER 897, coastguards were found to be under no enforceable private law duty to respond to an emergency call, nor, if they did respond, would they be liable if their response was negligent, unless it amounted to a positive act which directly caused greater injury than would have occurred had they not intervened at all. However, in *Neil Martin Ltd v. Revenue and Customs Commissioners* [2007] EWCA Civ 1041 where an employee of the Revenue had assumed responsibility to complete a tax-exemption registration form for the claimant and had completed it wrongly, as a result of which the claimant suffered economic loss, the court held it would be fair, just and reasonable that a common law duty of care existed.

In *Harris v. Perry and Anor* [2008] EWCA Civ 907 the Court of Appeal allowed an appeal by the defendants that they were liable to the claimant for severe injuries suffered when, aged 11, he was playing on a bouncy castle hired by the defendants. The court held that the trial judge had imposed an unreasonably high standard of care in holding that the children playing on the castle required uninterrupted supervision.

(ii)   Negligent misstatement

In *Hedley Byrne & Co. Ltd v. Heller & Partners Ltd* [1964] AC 465, the defendant bankers gave a negligent credit reference to the claimant, who lost over £17,000 when the client company went into liquidation. The House of Lords recognised that damages could be recovered for economic loss arising from a negligent misstatement where the advice was given by an expert in a relationship of sufficient proximity to the person being advised that he knew who was going to act in reliance on it and how.

In *Caparo Industries plc v. Dickman* [1990] 1 All ER 568, the court held that the company's auditors did not owe a duty to shareholders or members of the public purchasing shares in reliance on the audited accounts. Although it might be foreseeable that persons used the audited accounts for making investment decisions, and that these people might suffer financial loss if the accounts were inaccurate, this was insufficient to establish a duty of care. There had to be sufficient proximity between the claimant and the defendant, and the court had to consider it just and equitable to impose a duty of care. The person giving the advice or information had to be fully aware of the nature of the contemplated transaction, and that the claimant would rely upon the advice or information. The purpose of the auditor was to enable the shareholders as a body to make corporate decisions, not for individual shareholders making personal decisions whether or not to deal in the company's securities.

In *James McNaughton Paper Group Ltd v. Hicks Anderson & Co.* [1991] 1 All ER 134, auditors were not liable to the claimants, who had relied on accounts prepared by them for a group of companies in making a takeover bid for the group; there was not a sufficient proximity between the parties.

Damages for economic loss are recoverable only where there is: (i) a negligent misstatement; (ii) expertise; (iii) a duty of care; (iv) a special relationship; (v) knowledge of reasonable reliance; and (vi) foreseeable loss. In *Galoo Ltd v. Bright Grahame Murray and Another* [1995] 1 All ER 16, auditors were liable for the negligent preparation of accounts used as the basis of a decision to purchase shares in a company as they were aware that an identified bidder would rely on the accounts.

(b)   Breach of the duty of care

This is generally based on the objective test of a reasonable man taking into account the following factors: (i) the likelihood of harm; (ii) the seriousness of the risk and the risk of serious injury; (iii) the usefulness or importance of the defendant's activity, and (iv) the relationship between the risk and the measures taken. In the case of professional negligence, however, the test is the standard of the ordinary skilled man exercising and professing to have that professional skill.

(i)   The likelihood of harm

The care required increases with the likelihood that the action could cause harm. If this is only a remote possibility, persons will be acting reasonably even though they do not protect against the harm. In *Bolton v. Stone* [1951] AC 850, the claimant was standing in the road when she was hit by a ball from the defendant's cricket club. Her action failed since the probability of such an injury was not reasonably foreseeable because there had been only six occasions in 28 years when balls had been hit outside the ground.

(ii)   *The seriousness of the risk and the risk of serious injury*

Standards may be higher where the defendant is aware of the need for greater care. In *Paris v. Stepney Borough Council* [1951] AC 367, a one-eyed mechanic was totally blinded by a splinter of metal piercing his good eye while working under the defendant's vehicle. It was held that, although it was not normal practice to provide goggles to normally sighted workers, a higher duty of care was owed to this one-eyed employee.

In *Haley v. LEB* [1965] AC 778, the court held that a greater duty of care was owed to a blind pedestrian. The LEB had dug a hole in the pavement which was indicated by warning signs and a flashing light. Haley recovered damages after he fell into the hole and was injured.

(iii)   *The social importance of the defendant's activity*

The court considers the value to the community of the defendant's activity at the relevant time.

In *Watt v. Hertfordshire County Council* [1954] 1 WLR 835, a fireman was injured by a jack falling from a lorry not equipped to carry such heavy equipment. The lorry was the only available transport to take the jack to the scene of an accident, where a woman was trapped in the wreckage. The local authority was held not liable. Lord Denning MR stated: 'one must balance the risk against the end to be achieved' and 'the commercial end to make a profit is very different from the human to save life or limb'.

(iv)   *The relationship between the risk and the measures taken*

The measures to avoid the risk of harm must be balanced against the likelihood of the risk.

In *Latimer v. A.E.C. Ltd* [1953] AC 643, an exceptional storm flooded a factory, leaving the floor covered with a slimy mixture of oil and water. In spite of precautions to make the floor safe, the claimant was injured and alleged negligence for failure to close the plant. The court held that the risk did not justify such extreme measures.

(v)   *The burden of proof and* res ipsa loquitur

Res ipsa loquitur, 'the thing speaks for itself', that is, is evidence of negligence in the absence of an explanation by the defendant.

The claimant must establish breach of the duty of care except when the doctrine of *res ipsa loquitur* applies when a *prima facie* case of negligence is established which the defendant must rebut. The doctrine applies only when the following apply:

(i)   it is impossible to establish what negligent action or omission caused the injury;
(ii)   the cause must be something which would not have occurred if proper care had been exercised;
(iii) the defendant had control over the events alleged to be the cause of the injury.

Examples of the doctrine are: *Scott v. London and St. Katherine Docks Co.* (1865) 3 H & C 596, where the claimant was hit by falling bags of sugar as he was passing the defendant's premises; and *Chaproniere v. Mason* (1905) 21 TLR 633, where the claimant broke a tooth on a stone in a bath bun supplied by the defendant.

Cases illustrating point (iii) include *Gee v. Metropolitan Railway Co.* (1873) LR 8 QB 161, where the defendants were liable when the claimant fell from an improperly closed door minutes after the train left the station. But in *Easson v. L. & N. E. Ry. Co.* [1944] KB 421, the doctrine did not apply when the claimant fell from an express train a long time after a station stop. It was held that 'it is impossible to say that the doors of an express train travelling from Edinburgh to London are continuously under the sole control of the railway company'.

In *Pearson v. North Western Gas Board* [1968] 2 All ER 669, the claimant's husband was killed and her house destroyed by a gas explosion after the rupture of a gas main caused by a severe frost. The defendants were found to have rebutted the presumption of negligence since they had a team standing by to deal with any reported gas leaks, but there was no way of predicting or preventing explosions.

In *Ward v. Tesco Stores* [1976] 1 WLR 810, Ward slipped on some spilt yoghurt while shopping. The yoghurt was probably spilled by another customer but the defendants were liable because they failed to establish that they operated a non-negligent spillages system.

(c) Injury or damage due to negligence

(i) *The nature of the injury*
The injury can be physical and/or psychiatric. In *Page v. Smith* [1996] 1 AC 155, as a result of a car accident the claimant's myalgic encephalomyelitis (ME) became chronic and permanent and he was unable to work. The House of Lords held that once the defendant should have foreseen the claimant suffering personal injury, it was irrelevant whether it was psychiatric without external physical injury.

Hot Topic . . .

PSYCHIATRIC INJURY TO SECONDARY VICTIMS

These include family, friends, rescuers and persons involved in an accident caused by their employer's negligence. Liability was initially on the basis of foreseeability: in *King v. Phillips* [1953] 1 QB 429, a taxi driver carelessly reversed and ran over a little boy's tricycle and the little boy screamed. His mother, in an upstairs room, heard the scream, rushed to the window and saw the tricycle under the taxi and suffered from shock thinking her son was injured. The court held that no duty was owed to the mother. In *Boardman v. Sanderson* [1964] 1 WLR 1317, however, the defendant negligently reversed his car over the claimant's son's foot knowing that the claimant/parent was in earshot and likely to run to the scene. The claimant recovered damages for nervous shock.

This test was qualified in respect of psychiatric injury arising from the Hillsborough stadium disaster. In *Alcock and Others v. Chief Constable of South Yorkshire Police* [1991] 3 WLR 1057, the House of Lords stated that reasonable foresight of psychiatric injury was not sufficient; proximity was also required between the person claiming the injury and those involved in the disaster. This included all relationships based on love and affection at a comparable level to parents and spouse. For more distant relationships, the burden was on the claimant to establish the closeness of the relationship. The House of Lords found

that parents who had lost a son and a woman who had lost her fiancé were within the category, but brothers and brothers-in-law (and by extension sisters and sisters-in-law) were excluded in the absence of evidence of particularly close ties of love and affection.

In addition, the injury must be caused through sight or hearing of the event or its immediate aftermath, and viewing the scenes on TV did not qualify. This was subject to the fact that Lords Ackner and Oliver agreed with Nolan LJ in the Court of Appeal that simultaneous broadcasts of a disaster could be the equivalent of actual sight or hearing of the event or its immediate aftermath.

The immediacy of the aftermath was also stressed. The fact that the earliest identification was eight or nine hours after the disaster excluded it from the definition of 'immediate aftermath', as did subsequent visits to the mortuary for identification purposes. Lord Ackner stressed that the psychiatric injury must be the shock caused by the sudden appreciation by sight or sound of a horrifying event.

In *McFarlane v. EE Caledonia Ltd* [1994] 2 All ER 1, the claimant failed in his claim for psychiatric injury as a bystander on a support vessel during the Piper Alpha oil platform disaster. It was stated that: '[p]sychiatric injury to [the bystander] would not ordinarily … be within the range of reasonable foreseeability, but could not … be entirely excluded … if the … catastrophe occurring very close to him [was] particularly horrific'. The need for a close tie of love and affection

between the claimant and the primary victim was restated. In *Vernon v. Bosley (No. 1)* [1997] 1 All ER 577, the Court of Appeal approved damages for nervous shock to the father of two children drowned when the car in which they were travelling went off the road and the father watched the rescue attempts.

The same criteria do not apply where the secondary victims are employees. In *Frost and Others v. Chief Constable of South Yorks* [1997] 1 All ER 540, police officers claimed damages from their employer for psychiatric injury arising from the Hillsborough disaster, and the court found that their exposure to the horrific events resulted from the employer's negligence in breach of his duty of care.

The Law Commission report 'Liability for Psychiatric Illness' (Report Law Com No. 249 10 March 1998) and the draft Negligence (Psychiatric Illness) Bill propose to remove the restrictions on physical and temporal proximity to the accident and the means by which the secondary victim became aware of the injury to the primary victim. The need for a close tie of love and affection remains.

In *Chadwick v. British Transport Commission* [1967] 2 All ER 945, damages were recovered after the claimant was voluntarily involved in a rescue operation following a train crash. The court held that rescuers were owed a duty of care.

(ii)   *Causal link between negligence and injury*

There must be a factual link between the negligence and the injury. This is normally decided on the basis of the 'but for' test. If the injury would have occurred irrespective of the defendant's negligence, there can be no liability on the part of the defendant. In *Barnett v. Chelsea & Kensington Management Committee* [1969] 1 QB 428, the hospital negligently refused to examine a night watchman taken to hospital complaining of vomiting. He died a few hours later from arsenic poisoning. In spite of the hospital's negligence, there was no liability since he would have died from the poison in any event. In *Hotson v. East Berkshire Area Health Authority* [1987] AC 750, the defendant's negligence in diagnosing the claimant's injury was not the cause of his later disability which, on a balance of probability, would have resulted from the injury itself.

The test was widened to include situations where a defendant had made a material contribution to the claimant's injury which made the injury worse than it would have been. The defendant is liable for the proportionate damages reflecting the contribution to the disease. In *McGhee v. National Coal Board* [1973] 1 WLR 1, the defendant negligently failed to supply washing facilities so that the claimant could wash off abrasive brick dust, forcing him to cycle home before he could wash. This caused him to contract dermatitis. The fact that he had to cycle home materially added to the risk that he might develop the disease.

For dose-related illnesses like asbestosis, where the claimant's exposure to asbestos has been the fault of different persons on different occasions, liability is apportioned according to the period of exposure for which they have been responsible: *Holtby v. Brigham & Cowan (Hull) Ltd* [2003] 3 All ER 421.

The House of Lords' decision in *Fairchild v. Glenhaven Funeral Services Ltd* [2002] 3WLR 89 represents a major step away from the 'but for' test in situations where it is impossible to determine which of a number of possible employers were responsible for causing the claimant's disease. In the *Fairchild* case, the claimants had been exposed to asbestos dust by several employers and could not establish when and during which period of employment they had contracted mesothelioma, which is as likely to be triggered by a single fibre as multiple fibres. The court held that each employer had materially increased the risk of contracting the disease and all were liable.

If the employer has gone out of business by the time the claim is brought, the Third Parties (Rights against Insurers) Act 1930 provides a claim against the defunct company's insurers. There is statutory no-fault compensation for industrial diseases, including mesothelioma, by the Pneumoconiosis etc. (Workers' Compensation) Act 1979, but it offers less money than would be recovered in court and is available only if the employer has gone out of business.

Hot Topic . . .

STRESS-RELATED PSYCHIATRIC INJURY TO EMPLOYEES

A major new developing area of psychiatric illness is that caused by stress at work.

The guidelines for stress claims by employees were set out in *Hatton v Sutherland* [2002] All ER 1:

▶ The ordinary principles of employer's liability apply.
▶ An employer can assume that employees are up to the normal pressures of the job unless 'he knows of some particular problem or vulnerability'.
▶ No occupations are intrinsically dangerous to mental health.
▶ Relevant factors include:
  ▶ Whether the workload is excessive, or the work particularly intellectually or emotionally demanding.
  ▶ Whether unreasonable demands are made on the employee.
  ▶ Whether others similarly employed are suffering harmful levels of stress.
  ▶ Whether there is an abnormal level of sickness or absenteeism in the same job or same department.
  ▶ Whether there are signs of impending harm to the employee's health.
  ▶ Whether the employee has a particular problem or vulnerability

and a history of stress-related illness.
▶ Whether any recent uncharacteristic absence is attributable to stress.
▶ Employers can take what they are told by the employee at face value, unless there is good reason to think to the contrary.
▶ To trigger a duty to take steps, the indications of impending stress-related harm to health must be plain enough to alert a reasonable employer.
▶ Employers are in breach of duty only if they have failed to take reasonable steps, bearing in mind the size and scope of the operation, its resources and other employees' demands.
▶ Employers offering a confidential advice service, with reference to specialist counselling or treatment services, are unlikely to be in breach of duty.
▶ If dismissal or demotion is the only reasonable and effective step, the employer will not be in breach of duty in allowing a willing employee to continue in the job.
▶ Claimants must show that the breach of duty has caused or materially contributed to the harm suffered. It is not sufficient to show that occupational stress was the cause.
▶ Where the harm has more than one

cause, the employer should pay only for the part of the harm attributable to his breach of duty.
▶ Assessment of damages will take into account any pre-existing disorder or vulnerability.

Establishing causation is a problem if, as in *Garrett v London Borough of Camden* [2001] All ER 202, the main cause was the vulnerable personality of the employee of which the employer was unaware.

In *Daw v. Intel Corporation UK Ltd* [2007] EWCA Civ 70, D had worked for Intel for many years. Between late 2000 and early 2001, she had a heavy workload, was given insufficient assistance and worked excessive hours. She frequently complained of this and, in March 2001, one of her managers found her in tears, and she was asked to write down her concerns, which she did. She remained in post on an assurance that another employee would be recruited to assist her, but no appointment was made. In June she was signed off work by her doctor and attempted suicide the day after leaving the office. She was awarded damages for personal injury. Intel appealed against the award on the ground that it had discharged its duty by providing counselling services in reliance on Court of Appeal guidelines. The court held that a failure of management had created D's stress and breakdown and the failure to take action was not avoided by the provision of counsellors.

4.7 Defences to an action for negligence

(a) Exemption clauses

The general law of contract is relevant for determining the validity and scope of the exclusion clause. In addition, under the Unfair Contract Terms Act 1977 s.2(1) persons cannot exempt themselves from liability resulting in personal injury or death in respect of negligence in a business context.

In *Thompson v. T. Lohan (Plant Hire) Ltd and Another* [1987] 2 All ER 631, A hired an excavator plus driver to B. The terms of the contract of hire provided that 'drivers ... shall for all purposes ... in the working of the plant be regarded as the servants or agents of the hirer ... who alone shall be responsible for all claims arising'. One of B's workers was killed because of the negligence of the driver. The court held that A could claim protection of the exemption clause in an action against him by the widow of the person killed. The case establishes that, although s.2(1) prevents parties from excluding themselves from liability, it is possible for them to allocate responsibility between them.

(b) Consent to the risk

A person's consent to the risk of accidental injury is a bar to a negligence claim. The doctrine is important in a wide number of instances.

(i) Consent and spectators

Consent is a defence where the organiser of a sporting event has taken reasonable precautions against foreseeable risks. In *Hall v. Brooklands Auto Racing Club* [1933] 1 KB 205, two racing cars collided and one crashed through the iron railings set back from the edge of the track, causing injury to the claimant. It was the first accident of its kind in 23 years, it was a danger the defendants were not required to have anticipated, and the claimant had accepted the risk of such an accident. In *Murray v. Harringay Arena Ltd* [1951] 2 All ER 320, the defence of consent protected the defendant when a young spectator was struck in the eye by a hockey puck. The spectator's age was irrelevant.

(ii) Consent and rescue cases

A person voluntarily becoming involved in a rescue operation is exposed to this defence in the event of any injury depending on the reasonableness of the rescuer's actions. If they act reasonably, there is no consent to risk and greater risk-taking is justified where lives rather than property are threatened.

In *Haynes v. Harwoods* [1935] 1 KB 146, the defence did not apply to a policemen injured trying to control bolting horses to prevent injury to passers-by; whereas in *Cutler v. United Dairies (London) Ltd* [1933] 2 KB 297 it applied when the claimant was injured helping to capture a horse which had bolted but which was, at the material time, quietly grazing in a field.

(iii) Consent and employees

Mere knowledge of the danger is not sufficient, particularly in cases of danger at work.

In *Baker v. James Bros.* [1921] 2 KB 674, the defendants supplied their employee with a car with defective starting gear. He had complained repeatedly, but continued to use the car. The defence of consent failed; knowledge of the defect did not imply consent.

In *Smith v. Charles Baker & Sons* [1891] AC 325, although the claimant and his employer were aware of the risk of rocks falling onto him from a crane operating over his head, there was no consent.

Things would be different where the employee was receiving extra danger money to run the risk.

(iv) Consent and contributory negligence

In *Morris v. Murray and Another* [1990] 3 All ER 801, consent operated where the claimant spent all afternoon drinking with another man and then agreed to be a passenger in a plane piloted by that man in bad weather conditions. The court distinguished *Dann v. Hamilton* [1939] 1 All ER 59, where the claimant was injured while a voluntary passenger in a car driven by the defendant who was, to her knowledge, the worse for drink: 'the claimant was engaged in a quite ordinary social outing with a driver who was not … drunk until quite a late stage when it was not easy for the claimant to extricate herself without giving offence'. In *Dann v. Hamilton* damages would now be reduced on the ground of contributory negligence (see Chapter 5, p. 127).

4.8 Occupiers' liability

This is an aspect of the law of negligence relating to the occupier's duty to protect people from dangers inherent in premises and is covered by the Occupiers' Liability Acts (OLA) 1957 and 1984. Premises are defined as 'any fixed or moveable structure, including any vessel, vehicle or aircraft': s.1(3). This includes buildings, land and anything erected on that land including pylons, diving boards and grandstands, and includes cranes and scaffolding.

(a) Occupiers

Whether persons are occupiers depends on the degree of control arising from their presence or activity on the premises. Exclusive occupation is not required.

In *Wheat v. E. Lacon & Co. Ltd* [1966] AC 552, the defendants, the owners of a public house, were the occupiers in addition to the manager and his wife, who were in actual occupation. In *Stone v. Taffe* [1974] 1 WLR 1575, A owned a hotel of which B was the manager. Because of the low level of lighting on the stairs of the hotel, C, a guest, fell downstairs and was killed. Both the manager and the owner were occupiers.

An independent contractor engaged to do work on premises may be an occupier. In *Hartwell v. Grayson, Rollo and Clover Docks Ltd* [1947] KB 901, a contractor converting a ship was the occupier of the ship.

Persons may still be liable after they cease to be occupiers under the Defective Premises Act 1972. This imposes a duty of repair on landlords with the same duty owed to visitors and trespassers.

(b) Persons protected

People coming on to property are either authorised visitors or trespassers. Liability for visitors is governed by the OLA 1957 with the OLA 1984 covering trespassers.

(i) Duty to visitors

All visitors are owed the common duty of care, 'such care as … is reasonable to see that the visitor will be reasonably safe in using the premises for the purpose for which he is invited or permitted to be there': s.2(2). People entering premises in the exercise of a legal right are treated as being there with the occupier's consent for that purpose: s.2(6). There are special rules for children and people coming onto premises to carry out work.

Children
'An occupier must be prepared for children to be less careful than adults': s.2(3). Occupiers have a duty 'not merely not to dig pitfalls for them, but not to lead them into temptation'. This means not having on their property things which may act as an allurement or invitation to a child.

In *Glasgow Corporation v. Taylor* [1922] 1 AC 44, a boy aged 7 died from eating berries growing on a poisonous shrub in a public park. The court held that the berries were tempting in appearance to children and that the corporation knew they were dangerous but had taken no steps to warn children of the dangers of picking them. The concept of an allurement involves the idea of 'concealment and surprise, of an appearance of safety under circumstances cloaking a reality of damage'.

A heap of stones was not an allurement: *Latham v. Johnson & Nephew Ltd* [1913] 1 KB 398; and neither was a hole in the ground: *Perry v. Thomas Wrigley Ltd* [1955] 1 WLR 1164.

In *Phipps v. Rochester Corporation* [1955] 1 QB 450, where the claimant aged 5 (accompanied by his 7-year-old sister) fell into a 9 ft deep trench and broke his leg, the defendant escaped liability on the ground that it was reasonable to expect the child to be accompanied by a responsible person. In *Coates v. Rawtenstall BC* [1937] 3 All ER 602, the court held that a 14-year-old was a responsible person.

Professionals
Occupiers 'may expect that a person [coming on to the premises] in the exercise of his calling, will appreciate and guard against any special risks ordinarily incident to it, so far as the occupier leaves him free to do so': s.2(3)(b).

In *Roles v. Nathan* [1963] 1 WLR 1117, two chimney sweeps employed by the defendants to block up holes in a central heating flue attempted to do so while the boiler was lit and were killed by carbon monoxide gas. It was held that this was an incidental risk that they should have guarded against.

All circumstances are considered in determining whether occupiers have discharged their statutory duty, so that:

(i) where there has been a sufficient warning of the danger, the warning absolves the occupier from liability (in *Roles v. Nathan* the sweeps were warned of the danger by the occupier's agent);

(ii) where the danger is due to the faulty construction, maintenance or repair work by an independent contractor, the occupier is not liable if he acted reasonably in engaging the independent contractor, and was satisfied with the contractor's competence and that the work had been properly done.

In *Cook v. Broderip* (1968) 112 SJ 193, B's cleaner was injured when she plugged the vacuum cleaner into a socket negligently installed by D, a qualified electrician. B was not liable as long as he had no reason to believe that D was not skilled in his work. D would be liable in negligence.

The common duty of care does not make occupiers liable for risks to which the visitor has willingly consented and they are protected by the Law Reform (Contributory Negligence) Act 1945.

In *Bunker v. Charles Brand & Son Ltd* [1969] 2 All ER 59, B's employers were subcontractors of the defendants for tunnelling in connection with the construction of London's Victoria Line. B was injured as he carried out modifications to a digging machine while it was in operation. The defendants were occupiers and their defence of consent failed since knowledge of danger was not assent. B's damages were, however, reduced by 50 per cent in respect of his contributory negligence.

Occupiers may restrict, modify or exclude liability by prominently displaying a suitably worded notice at the entrance to the premises: s.2(1). For business premises, the Unfair Contract Terms Act 1977 prohibits exclusion from liability for personal injury or death: s.2(1). For other loss or damage, any restriction or exclusion is subject to the test of 'reasonableness': s.2(2). Non-business occupiers can continue to exclude for liability for personal injury and death. However, the liability of an occupier towards a person obtaining access for recreational or educational purposes is not a business liability unless that purpose falls within the occupier's business purposes.

(ii)   Liability for trespassers

Occupiers must take reasonable steps to protect reasonably foreseeable trespassers from any risk of injury through reasonably foreseeable dangers 'due to the state of the premises or things done or omitted to be done on them': s.1(1) Occupiers' Liability Act 1984. Injury covers 'death or personal injury, including any disease and any impairment of physical or mental condition': s.1(9). An occupier incurs liability if:

(a) he is 'aware of the danger or has reasonable grounds to believe that it exists';
(b) he 'knows or has reasonable grounds to believe that the other is in the vicinity of the danger concerned or ... may come into the vicinity of the danger'; and
(c) 'the risk is one against which, in all the circumstances of the case, he may reasonably be expected to offer the other some protection': s.1(3).

The duty is to 'take such care as is reasonable in all the circumstances ... to see that ... [he] does not suffer injury on the premises by reason of the danger concerned': s.1(4). The duty may be discharged by a warning of the danger concerned, or discouraging persons from incurring the risk: s.1(5). It does not extend to risks willingly accepted: s.1(6). There is no liability for loss or damage to property: s.1(8).

In *Tomlinson v Congleton BC* [2003] 3 All ER 1122, T, an 18-year-old, went thigh-deep into the water of a lake in a public park and dived from a standing position. He struck his head on the lake bottom and was paralysed from the neck down. T ignored signs erected by the council marked 'Dangerous Water: No Swimming'. The Court of Appeal upheld his claim for damages under s.1(3)(c) and (4) 1984 Act since the council had recognised the potential risk and had started a programme to cover the beach areas. The House of Lords held that it was unjust to prohibit the enjoyment of responsible people to safeguard irresponsible visitors. The fact that they ignored the warnings did not create a duty to take other steps to protect them.

In *Evans v. Kosmar Villa Holidays plc* [2007] EWCA Civ 1003 the claimant, then aged 18, went on a holiday booked through the defendant. In the early hours of the morning, he dived into the shallow end of the pool in the apartment complex and suffered incomplete tetraplegia. He claimed damages under an implied term in the contract with the defendants on the ground that the size and positioning of the 'no diving' signs were inadequate and that signage relating to the closure of the pool at night should have been explicit and enforced. The Court of Appeal held that decisions under the Occupiers' Liability Acts should be applied to people to whom a duty of care was owed under a contract and that the defendant had no duty of care to guard the claimant against the risk of diving into the pool and injuring himself.

4.9   Nuisance

Nuisance is a strict liability tort, and is not dependent on establishing that a person's conduct is intentional or negligent. The difference between private and public nuisance is important.

(a)   Public and private nuisance

Private nuisance is the interference with the claimant's occupation of his or her property, or their enjoyment of rights over the property. This includes the right to light, the right to support, or a private right of way, causing physical damage to land or substantially interfering with the use or enjoyment of land or an interest in land, where this interference can be said to be unreasonable. It includes indirect interference caused by smoke, vibrations, heat, noise, fumes and overhanging branches and roots of trees. Claims based on public nuisance are not linked with use of land.

Public nuisance is something which materially affects the reasonable comfort and convenience of life of a class of Her Majesty's subjects. Something which affects only one or two people cannot be a public nuisance. Examples include brothel-keeping; obstructing public highways or waterways, allowing a dangerous state of affairs to exist which threatens the public generally; and selling impure foods. It has been suggested that, in order to constitute a public nuisance, the interference with the public right must have continued for a considerable length of time.

In *Midwood & Co. Ltd v. Mayor of Manchester* [1905] 2 KB 597, a sudden explosion was held to constitute a public nuisance. This was justified in that the nuisance was not the explosion itself but the 'state of affairs' over a period of time, that is, the build-up of gas which resulted in the explosion.

Public nuisance is a crime, which private nuisance is not, and is tortious only in respect of claimants who have suffered greater damage than the community in general.

In *Campbell v. Paddington Corporation* [1911] 1 KB 869, the defendants were liable for public nuisance for erecting a stand blocking the highway for Edward VII's funeral. The claimant recovered damages, since the stand blocked the view from her windows and prevented her from letting out her rooms to spectators. In *Castle v. St. Augustine's Links* (1922) 38 TLR 615, C's windscreen was shattered by a golf ball and a piece of glass went into his eye. The ball had been struck by a player teeing off from a tee parallel with the main road which was a public nuisance. C was awarded damages.

(b) Nuisance and negligence

There is an overlap between nuisance and negligence, particularly where the alleged interference concerns things escaping from premises. Nuisance liability is based on the existence of a state of affairs foreseeably capable of resulting in damage to the neighbour. In *Bolton v. Stone* [1951] AC 850, a pedestrian was struck by a cricket ball hit over the club wall into the road. The court stated, 'The gist of such a nuisance ... is the causing or permitting of a state of affairs from which damage is likely to result'. The final decision was based on negligence and the club was held not liable (see p. 94). In *Miller v. Jackson* [1977] QB 966, the claimant sued a cricket club for damage caused by balls hit into his garden. The defendants were liable for negligence, since the risk of injury was both foreseeable and foreseen, and playing cricket constituted a nuisance.

(c) Examples of private nuisance

Private nuisance may cause material damage or a substantial interference with the enjoyment of the property.

(i) Material damage to property
There must be a physical deterioration, visible without recourse to scientific evidence, and a fall in the property's value. 'Property' includes chattels stored or kept on the land, and includes the value of a business carried out on the land.

In *St. Helen's Smelting Co. v. Tipping* (1865) 11 HL Cas 642, the claimant's shrubs were damaged by fumes from the defendant's copper-smelting plant, resulting in a fall in the property's value. In *Spicer v. Smee* (1946) 175 LT 163, the defective electrical wiring of the defendant's bungalow caused it to burn down, destroying the claimant's adjacent bungalow.

(ii) Interference with enjoyment of property
The interference must materially prejudice the ordinary physical comfort of human existence, not merely 'according to elegant or dainty modes and habits of living'. The loss of one night's sleep can be 'substantial interference' and there need not be injury to health.

(d) Factors taken into account in establishing nuisance

The court weighs the defendant's activity against the nature and extent of the interference to the claimant. It is an objective test and considers the defendant's purpose or motive.

(i) The defendant's malice
In *Christie v. Davey* [1893] 1 Ch 316, D hammered on the party wall, blew whistles, banged trays and shouted during music lessons and performances given by the claimant, his neighbour. His malice distinguished the noise he was causing from that of his neighbour

and made it a nuisance. In *Hollywood Silver Fox Farm v. Emmett* [1936] 2 KB 468, E maliciously fired shotguns on his own land to cause the foxes in the neighbouring farm to abort; the malicious intent made his action an actionable nuisance.

(ii)   Social value of defendant's activity

The more worthwhile the defendant's activity, the less likely it is to be held to be unreasonable. The court is more generous to power stations and factories than to speedway tracks or racecourses. But the fact of it being worthwhile will not automatically prevent it from being actionable.

(iii)   The locality

The court generally considers the character of the neighbourhood in deciding whether the disturbance constitutes a nuisance, but this cannot always be relied upon.

In *Pwllbach Colliery Co. Ltd v. Woodman* [1915] AC 634, the alleged nuisance was the settling of coal dust on the claimant's slaughterhouse and the meat and sausages inside. The Court of Appeal took the nature of the locality into consideration in rejecting liability. And in *Sturges v. Bridgman* (1879) 11 Ch D 852, in deciding that the activity of a confectioner whose noise disturbed a neighbouring physician was actionable nuisance, the court took notice of the fact that the area was extensively used by the medical profession and stated that what was a nuisance in Belgrave Square would not necessarily be so in Bermondsey. Other cases show less concern for suitability of the locality.

In *Adams v. Ursell* [1913] 1 Ch 269, the court granted an injunction against a fish and chip shop which had opened up next door to the claimant's house purchased five years before, even though it was in a working-class area and supplied a public need. In *Dunton v. Dover District Council* (1977) 76 LGR 87, the court awarded damages and granted an injunction restricting the opening hours of the playground and the age of the children playing there. In *Bone v. Seale* [1975] 1 All ER 787, the Court of Appeal awarded damages to the claimant in respect of smells coming from a neighbouring pig farm. In *Watson and Ors v. Croft Promosport Ltd* [2008] EWHC 759 (QB) the claimants brought proceedings for nuisance in respect of noise from adjacent land used as a motor circuit. The claimants sought injunctive relief to restrict the use of the circuit for racing which created high levels of noise on 140 days in a year to 20 days with 40 days being acceptable on payment of compensation for the difference between the two. The court held that the willingness to accept compensation as against an injunction indicated that it was not an appropriate case for granting an injunction and an award of damages was made.

(iv)   Cost of avoiding the nuisance

The court considers whether defendants could prevent the interference, and if it could be cured at a reasonable cost they will be acting unreasonably. Where claimants carry out work on the defendant's property for their joint benefit, the costs are shared in proportion to their share of the benefit and not their relative poverty or wealth: *Abbahall Ltd v. Smee* [2003] 1 All ER 465.

(v)   Sensitivity of the claimant

In *Robinson v. Kilvert* (1889) 41 Ch D 88, R's action for nuisance failed in relation to damage to particularly sensitive paper stored on his premises caused by heat from the defendant's cellar which would not have harmed less sensitive goods. And in *Bridlington Relay Ltd v. Yorkshire Electricity Board* [1965] 1 All ER 264, BR's action failed because they required exceptional freedom from disturbance to operate a television relay service.

(e) Who can sue in respect of private nuisance

Only persons with an interest in the affected land can bring an action which restricts claims to owners or lessees and excludes mere licensees: people who are there with the owner's permission but without a legal right to be there.

In *Malone v. Laskey* [1907] 2 KB 141, the defendants owned a house which they leased to a firm, which sublet it to another firm which employed the claimant's husband, who was allowed to live there. A flush cistern in the lavatory was loosened by vibrations from the defendant's electricity generator next door and negligently repaired by the defendants. The claimant was injured when it fell on her but her nuisance claim failed because she was only a licensee.

In two actions, *Hunter v. Canary Wharf Ltd* and *Hunter v. London Docklands Development Corporation* [1997] 2 WLR 684, the House of Lords rejected a right of occupiers to sue and restated the principle that only those with an interest in the land could sue. The first action alleged nuisance in respect of interference with TV reception, and the second dust deposits caused by road construction. In the first action, it was held that landowners were entitled to build on their land as they wished, subject to planning control, and were not, in the absence of an easement or agreement, liable if their building interfered with the neighbour's enjoyment of their land.

In *Delaware Mansions Ltd v. Westminster City Council* [2001] 3 WLR 1007, the claimant, Flecksun Ltd, sought damages for a private nuisance caused by the penetration under a block of flats of the roots of a plane tree. The claimant purchased the freehold reversion in June 1990, but the damage had largely been caused during the 1989 drought, but the claimant had paid for the underpinning work. The defendant claimed that the tort had been against the previous owner, claiming that purchasers cannot sue in tort for pre-purchase damage. The House of Lords held in favour of the claimant since 'where there is a continuing nuisance of which the defendant knew or ought to have known, reasonable remedial expenditure may be recovered by the owner who has had to incur it'.

People with a right to possession can sue where their interest has been interfered with. Landlords can sue in respect of permanent damage to leased property, as opposed to temporary interference.

There is no authority as to whether damages can be claimed for personal injuries, and decisions on damage to goods are inconclusive. In *Halsey v. Esso Petroleum Co. Ltd* [1961] 1 WLR 683, damages were recoverable for washing on a clothes line, but in *Cunard v. Antifyre Ltd* [1953] 1 KB 551, damages to furniture was refused.

(f) Persons liable

Generally the occupier will be the person creating the nuisance, but landlords can be jointly liable if they created the situation before leasing the property, where they expressly or impliedly authorise tenants to create or continue the nuisance, or where they knew or ought to have known about the nuisance before they let the premises. In *Harris v. James*

(1876) 45 LJQB 545, a landlord was liable for letting his field for quarrying lime, but in *Smith v. Scott* [1973] 3 All ER 645, the local authority was not liable for letting a house to offensive and undesirable tenants knowing they were likely to cause a nuisance, since it had not authorised the nuisance.

Employers are vicariously liable for nuisances created by their employees in the course of their employment.

Occupiers may be liable for a state of affairs caused by a trespasser if they knew, or ought to have known, of the nuisance; and one caused by nature or a previous occupier where they are aware of or could foresee the hazard: nuisance by self-sown trees or those planted by a previous owner.

(g) Prescription as a defence

A special defence for nuisance is that the activity has been continuously carried on for 20 years. In *Sturges v. Bridgman* (1879), the defence failed because the time ran only from the date the claimant had moved his consulting room to the end of his garden adjoining the confectioner and first became aware of the noise.

4.10 The rule in *Rylands v. Fletcher*

In *Rylands v. Fletcher* (1868) LR 3 HL 330, F, a mill owner, employed an independent contractor to build a reservoir on his land. The contractors encountered disused mine shafts which connected with mines worked by R in adjoining land. The contractors negligently failed to seal them up, and when the reservoir was filled, the mines were flooded. The basis of the defendant's liability was stated in the following terms: '[w]e think that the true rule of law is, that the person who for his own purposes brings on his lands and collects and keeps there anything likely to do mischief if it escapes, must keep it at his peril, and if he does not do so is prima facie answerable for all damage which is the natural consequence of its escape'. The House of Lords limited liability to things brought onto land in the course of non-natural use of the land.

Liability depends on establishing four things: (i) defendants must bring the thing onto their land for their own purposes; (ii) the thing must be likely to do harm if it escapes; (iii) the use of the land must be non-natural; and (iv) the thing must escape. Lessees and licensees can be liable as well as owners.

(a) Bringing on to the land

There is no liability for the escape of a thing naturally present on the land unless it constitutes nuisance or negligence: escape of weeds: *Giles v. Walker* (1890) 24 QBD 656; vermin: *Stearn v. Prentice Brothers Ltd* [1919] 1 KB 394; rocks: *Pontardawe RDC v. Moore-Gwyn* [1929] 1 Ch 656; and flood water: *Whalley v. Lancashire and Yorkshire Ry. Co.* (1884) 13 QBD 131. In *Leakey v. National Trust* [1980] 1 All ER 17, the defendants were liable in nuisance for failing to remove naturally occurring earth and debris. And in *Goldman v. Hargrave* [1966] 2 All ER 989, a landowner was liable in negligence for damage to a neighbouring property by the spread of fire he failed to put out when a tree was struck by lightning.

(b)   Escape must be likely to cause harm

In *Crowhurst v. Amersham Burial Board* (1878) 4 Ex D 5, damages were awarded against the defendants who planted a yew tree the leaves of which poked through the fence and were eaten by the claimant's horse, which died. In *Shiffman v. Venerable Order of the Hospital of St John of Jerusalem* [1936] 1 All ER 557, the defendants erected a casualty tent in Hyde Park and a flagpole supported by guy ropes. As a result of being interfered with by children, the flagpole fell and injured the claimant, who was entitled to damages for negligence and under the *Rylands v. Fletcher* ruling. In *Hale v. Jennings Bros* [1938] 1 All ER 579, a chair and its occupant broke away from a 'chair-o-plane' run by the defendant and injured the claimant, who owned a shooting gallery on adjoining ground.

The escape can be of something connected with the thing brought on to the land. In *Musgrove v. Pandelis* [1919] 2 KB 43, the defendant was liable for a fire in an adjoining property caused by a fire in the petrol tank of a car on his property. And in *Att. Gen. v. Corke* [1933] Ch 89, the owner of a disused brickworks who allowed people to live on the site in caravans was liable for their using the neighbouring property as a toilet.

(c)   Land use must be non-natural

Non-natural land use includes bulk storage of gas, water or electricity and sewage: *Smeaton v. Ilford Corporation* [1954] 1 All ER 923. The scope of the rule is restricted by the notion of benefit to the community. In *Read v. J. Lyons* [1946] 2 All ER 471, some of the Law Lords thought that running a munitions factory during wartime was a natural use. In *British Celanese v. A. H. Hunt (Capacitors) Ltd* [1969] 2 All ER 1252, the community benefit of the defendant manufacturing electrical components made the use of the land and the storing of strips of metal foil a natural use of the land.

In *Cambridge Water Co. v. Eastern Counties Leather plc* [1994] 1 All ER 53, Lord Goff stated that he did accept that the creation of employment as such, even in a small industrial complex, 'is sufficient of itself to establish a particular use as constituting a natural or ordinary use of land'. Cambridge Water Co. sued the operators of a tannery concerning spillage of organochlorines which had seeped into the soil below the tannery and polluted a borehole from which they extracted water. The appeal against liability was allowed on the ground that they could not have foreseen that the seepage could cause pollution of the borehole.

The *Cambridge Water Co.* case restricts the strict liability of the rule to situations where the defendant knew or ought reasonably to have foreseen that those things might, if they escaped, cause damage.

(d)   Thing must escape

In *Read v. J Lyons & Co Ltd* (1946), the House of Lords rejected the appellant's claim for damages for personal injury when she was injured by an exploding shell while working in the shell-filling shop of a factory, because the essential element of escape was missing. An escape from property occupied by the defendant on to that occupied by the claimant within the same area is sufficient: *Hale v. Jennings Brothers* (1938). The escape can be from one room of a house to another. In *Sochacki v. Sas* [1947] 1 All ER 344, where a fire in the defendant's room spread to the claimant's room destroying his furniture, the action failed only because the fire was a natural use.

(e) Persons who can sue and what they can claim

In *Read v. J Lyons & Co Ltd* (1946), it was stated that the rule in *Rylands v. Fletcher* 'derives from a conception of mutual duties of adjoining or neighbouring landowners' and that claims were restricted to damage to land and chattels. Since this decision, damages have not been given for personal injury.

(f) Defences to *Rylands v. Fletcher*

(i)   Act of God

The act of God defence succeeded in *Nichols v. Marsland* (1876) 2 Ex D 1, where exceptional rainfall caused flooding from artificial lakes on the defendant's land, but that decision is weakened by the decision in *Greenock Corporation v. Caledonian Ry. Co.* [1917] AC 556, where the corporation built a paddling pool in the bed of a stream, obstructing its natural flow. The defendants were liable when the stream overflowed, damaging the claimant's property even though the rainfall was 'extraordinary and … unprecedented'.

(ii)   Act of a stranger

The act of a stranger defence is where the escape is caused by the unforeseeable act of a stranger – as opposed to servants, family, independent contractors, and possibly guests. In *Rickards v. Lothian* [1913] AC 263, the claimant failed in his action when his premises were flooded when a water tap was turned on in the defendant's premises and 'this was the malicious act of some person'.

(iii)   Contributory negligence

There is no decision on contributory negligence, but it would undoubtedly be a valid defence.

(iv)   Statutory authority

Statutory authority to bring the thing on to and store it on the land excludes the doctrine. In *Pearson v. North Western Gas Board* [1968] 2 All ER 669, the claimant failed in her claim for damages under *Rylands v. Fletcher* arising from the death of her husband and the destruction of her home following a gas explosion when a gas main was fractured due to a movement of the earth caused by a very severe frost, as the defendants had a statutory duty to supply gas. She also failed in her claim in negligence since the defendants' actions to meet any disaster rebutted the presumption of negligence under the doctrine of *res ipsa loquitur*.

(v)   Consent

Consent is implied in two situations. In a landlord and tenant relationship, tenants are presumed to have consented to the presence of things brought on to the premises at the commencement of the lease. In *Peters v. Prince of Wales Theatre Ltd* [1943] KB 73, the tenant of a shop in the defendant's theatre could not claim when her shop was flooded by the freezing up of a sprinkler system.

The second case is where the claimant and the defendant share a building and something escapes from the defendant's part into the claimant's. In *Collingwood v. Home and Colonial Stores Ltd* [1936] 3 All ER 200, the claimant's action failed when a fire caused by faulty electric wiring in the defendant's premises damaged the claimant's shop. This has often been justified on grounds that the claimant took the premises as they were and must put up with the consequences.

(vi)   Remoteness of damage

The remoteness of damage defence was established in *Cambridge Water Co. Ltd v. Eastern Counties plc* [1994] 1 All ER 53.

(g)   Relationship with other torts

In the *Cambridge Water Co. Ltd* case, Lord Goff commented: 'there is no reason to suppose that Blackburn J intended to create a liability any more strict than that created by the law of nuisance; but … he must have intended that, in the circumstances specified by him, there should be liability for damages resulting from an isolated escape'. It is unlikely that the *Rylands v. Fletcher* defence extends to the escape of noise and vibrations in spite of *Hoare & Co. v. McAlpine* [1923] Ch 167, where the defendant was liable under the rule for damage to a hotel's foundations by vibrations from a pile driver. In nuisance there is no automatic liability for the acts of an independent contractor, which is clearly not the case in *Rylands v. Fletcher*.

Liability does not require proof of negligence, but the court's lack of enthusiasm for strict liability has allowed defences which bring the rule closer to claims for negligence, particularly through the concept of foreseeability.

Hot Topic . . .

NUISANCE, *RYLANDS V. FLETCHER* AND THE HUMAN RIGHTS ACT 1998

In *McKenna v. British Aluminium Limited* [2002] Env LR 721, there was a multi-party action by residents living round the defendant's factory who claimed that emissions and noise disturbed their occupation/enjoyment of their homes. The claims were originally under nuisance and the rule in *Rylands v. Fletcher* but were later amended to include negligence. The defendants applied for claims by children living with their parents to be struck out as they had no proprietary interest in the land to found an action in nuisance following *Hunter*, and under the rule in *Rylands v. Fletcher* following *Cambridge Water Co. Ltd*.

The claimants argued that Article 8 of the European Convention on Human Rights, incorporated into English law by the Human Rights Act 1998, required the court to take a fresh approach to the law of nuisance and *Rylands v. Fletcher*. Article 8 provides that: (1) everyone has the right to respect for his private and family life, his home and his correspondence. On this basis, Neuberger J decided that the claims should not be struck out but left the issue to be decided at the trial.

4.11   Torts affecting economic rights

(a)   Inducement to breach of contract and causing loss by unlawful means

The main principles of the tort of inducement to breach of contract were established in *Lumley v. Gye* [1843–60] All ER 208. In this case, the claimant, the manager of an opera house, contracted with Johanna Wagner, a soprano, for her exclusive services for a period of time. Gye induced Wagner to break her contract and sing for him. It was held that the right to sue in such cases was not confined to actions by masters for the enticement of their servants but extended to wrongful interference with any contract of personal service.

This case involved direct interference aimed at the other party to the contract. In other decisions, the courts extended the scope of the tort to include unlawful interference with intent to cause economic loss unrelated to inducement to breach of contract. In such cases, the court refused to grant a remedy where the effect was uncertain. In *Middlebrook Mushrooms Ltd v. TGWU* [1993] IRLR 232 women sacked from a mushroom farm after refusing new contracts which they claimed cut their pay proposed to leaflet customers at supermarkets to persuade them not to buy the farm's mushrooms. The Court of Appeal refused to grant an injunction to prevent this because it was possible for customers to ignore the campaign.

In *Proform Sports Management Ltd v. Proactive Sports Management Ltd and anor* [2006] EWHC 2812 (Ch) in December 2000 the claimant entered a two-year representation agreement with a well-known footballer when he was 15 years old. In June 2002, the player and his parents wrote to say that they would not renew the agreement. On 14 December, three days after its expiry, the first defendant entered into a representation agreement with the player. The claimant claimed damages against the defendant for unlawful interference with and/or the procuring of a breach of the 2000 agreement. The court held there could be no liability for inducing or facilitating the breach of a voidable contract with a minor.

In *OBG Ltd and anor v. Allan and ors / Douglas and anor v. Hello! Ltd and ors (No3)./ Mainstream Properties Ltd v. Young and ors* [2007] UKHL 21 the House of Lords considered three appeals principally concerned with claims in tort for economic loss caused by intentional acts. The House of Lords rejected the argument that there was a unified theory of economic torts which treated procuring breach of contract causing loss by unlawful means as part of a more general tort of actionable interference with contractual rights. It held that the tort of causing loss by unlawful means differed from that of inducing breach of contract in at least four respects: (i) unlawful means was a tort of primary liability not requiring a wrongful act by anyone else; (ii) unlawful means required the use of means which were unlawful under some other rule; (iii) liability for unlawful means did not depend upon the existence of contractual relations, it was sufficient that the intended consequence was damage in any form to the claimant's economic expectations; (iv) in unlawful means, the defendant had to intend to cause damage to the claimant, whereas in *Lumley v. Gye* the intention to cause a breach of contract was both necessary and sufficient.

The House of Lords held that, whilst there was no reason why the same facts should not give rise to claims under both headings, this did not make them the same tort. The distinction between direct and indirect interference was unsatisfactory and the unnatural union between the two should be dissolved and the two causes of action restored to independence.

In the first appeal, the defendants were receivers purportedly appointed under an invalid floating charge and took control of the claimant company's assets and undertaking. The claimant contended that this constituted unlawful interference with its contractual relations. The House of Lords held that the requirements for liability under each of the two possible causes of action had not been satisfied. It also held that the strict liability tort of conversion applied only to chattels and could not be extended to choses in action.

In the second appeal, the magazine *OK!* contracted for the exclusive right to publish photographs of a celebrity wedding. *Hello!* published photographs surreptitiously taken by an unauthorised photographer. *OK!* appealed against a decision that *Hello!* did had not have the necessary subjective intention to cause harm. The House of Lords held that it was entitled to bring proceedings for breach of an obligation of confidentiality and allowed the appeal.

In the third appeal, two employees of a property company, in breach of their contracts, diverted a development opportunity to a joint venture. The defendant, wrongly believing that they were not in breach of their duties, facilitated the acquisition by providing finance. The House of Lords held that the defendant in providing the finance had not intended to cause a breach of contract, nor was there any question of having caused loss by unlawful means.

(b)   Conspiracy to cause wilful damage

The principles of the tort were laid down in *Crofter Hand Woven Harris Tweed Co Ltd v. Veitch* [1942] AC 435. The dockers at Stornoway and the employees of spinning mills on the island of Lewis were members of the TGWU. The mills on the island produced Harris Tweed. The claimant company also produced tweed produced on the mainland which was also sold as Harris Tweed but did not bear a special stamp trade mark. The TGWU pressed the mill owners on the island to increase the wages of the employees and the owners claimed they could not because of the competition of the claimant. Veitch and other officials of the TGWU instructed dockers at Stornoway to embargo the claimant's goods. The claimant sought an injunction. The court rejected its claim as its purpose was to benefit the members of the union and the means employed were not unlawful. The case established the following principles:

▷ The tort covers acts which would be lawful if done by one person;
▷ The combination will be justified if the predominant motive is self-interest or protection of one's trade rather than injury to the claimant;
▷ Damage to the claimant must be proved.

(c)   Passing off

The civil wrong of passing off is committed by any person, company or organisation which carries on or proposes to carry on business under a name calculated to deceive the public by confusion with the name of an existing business. It also extends to the use of similar wrappings, identification marks and descriptions. Thus in *Reckitt & Coleman Products Ltd v. Borden* [1990] 1 All ER 873 the court found the defendants guilty of selling lemon juice in lemon-coloured and lemon-shaped containers misleading the public into thinking they were buying the 'Jif' brand of juice produced by the claimant.

The House of Lords in *Erven Warninck BV v. J Townend & Sons (Hull) Ltd* [1979] AC 731 established the four characteristics which must be present in order to succeed in a passing off action:

▶ There must be a misrepresentation
▶ This must be made in the course of a trade, profession or business
▶ It must be calculated to injure the business or goodwill of another trader as a foreseeable consequence
▶ It has caused actual damage to the business or goodwill or will probably do so.

In *Inter Lotto (UK) Ltd v. Camelot Group plc* [2003] EWCA Civ 1132 the claimant operated lotteries in public houses under the registered trade mark 'HOTSPOT', and chose the name 'HOTPICK' for a feature of the game in July 2001. Camelot chose the name 'HOTPICKS' in August 2001 and on 17 October 2001 it applied for registration of the name as a trade mark for lottery services. The application was opposed by Inter Lotto on 7 November 2002. Camelot's new 'Lotto Hotpicks' game began operation in July 2002 and in January 2003 Inter Lotto began proceedings for trade mark infringement and passing off, claiming damages for Camelot's use of the name between 4 August 2001 and July 2002. It was held that it could not claim in respect of the period after 17 October 2001 when Camelot applied for registration due to the retrospective effect given by English law to a registered mark back to the date of application under the Trade Marks Act 1994 (see Chapter 14, p.313).

End of Chapter Summary

This chapter has considered the law of torts, with particular reference to torts which are important in a business context.

Having read the chapter you should be familiar with the following topics which are of specific relevance to business:

▶ Vicarious liability in so far as it relates to the employer's liability for the torts committed by employees and agents in the course of their employment.
▶ The scope of the duty of care and the 'neighbour test'.
▶ Liability to secondary victims and the circumstances in which they have a right of action.
▶ The liability of persons in respect of their occupancy of property and the duties owed to vulnerable children and trespassers.
▶ The importance of the tort of nuisance in respect of indirect nuisance caused by noise, smells and vibrations.
▶ The significance of the tort in *Rylands v Fletcher* on the risks associated with bringing onto premises non-naturally occurring materials and the scope of liability in the event of their escape to neighbouring properties.
▶ The nature of and significance of the torts affecting economic rights: inducement to breach of contract, conspiracy to inflict wilful damage and passing off.

Questions

1. Alex is a doctor in the casualty department of a large hospital run by the Sana Health Trust. One night when she had been on duty continuously for 28 hours, Ernie, an electrician, came into casualty with an injured leg suffered when the platform on which he had been working collapsed. Ernie was employed by Sparks Ltd, an electrical contractor, but when the accident happened, he had been rewiring the premises of Utopia Ltd. The platform and other equipment used in rewiring Utopia Ltd's premises had been supplied by Utopia Ltd.

    Because Alex was so tired, she gave Ernie an anti-tetanus injection without administering a test dose. Ernie had a violent reaction to the injection, became uncontrollable and ultimately leapt from the window of the ward and was killed by the fall.

    The fall was videoed by Tariq and appeared as a news item at 6.00 a.m. the next morning. Ernie's wife Fay, who had been staying the night with a friend and was therefore uncontactable by the police, saw the news item and collapsed with nervous shock.

    Advise Fay of any claims that she may be able to bring in respect of her husband's death against any of the parties.

2. PH Ltd owns a number of buildings on a disused industrial estate. The estate borders on to a residential area. PH Ltd employed BC Ltd to demolish some of the properties and convert others into apartments. BC Ltd erected a low fence around the site and put up notices warning 'Danger, Keep Out'.

    Work on the site has been in progress for four weeks and is expected to last a further five months. Work begins early in the morning and continues until late in the evening. There is a good deal of noise from the site and disturbance from heavy lorries entering and leaving the site. The mud and dust from the work has blighted the enjoyment of the residents in the nearby houses.

    After work stopped one evening, Tracy, an 8-year-old girl, was able, as on several occasions in the past, to gain access to the site with some friends. Whilst playing in a partly demolished building, she fell through the floor of an upstairs room and injured her back.

    (i) Explain the rules of law applicable in determining liability for Tracy's injuries.

    (ii) What rights do the neighbouring tenants have in connection with the disturbance caused by the site operations?

3. Tipper Ltd runs an industrial waste disposal business. Its employees engaged in the disposal work have strict instructions to dump waste only at properly approved sites. Some drivers, however, occasionally dump waste on private land without permission.

    One of the drivers, Glen, dumped a load of toxic waste on a field which was part of Hal's farm. One of Hal's employees mentioned this to Hal but Hal took no action.

    Unusually heavy rainfall caused the waste to seep into the soil and pollute a stream which ran into neighbouring land farmed organically by Ian, causing a field to be unusable. Lois, a villager, took a short cut across Hal's field, examined the pile of waste and contracted a rash which is painful and requires treatment with strong creams.

    (i) Consider the claims which Ian may have against Hal and any defence Hal may have.

    (ii) Consider whether Hal will have any liability to Lois.

    (iii) Consider any liability of Tipper Ltd in respect of Glen.

Chapter 5

Remedies for contract and tort

Learning objectives

After reading this chapter you will know about:

- ▶ remedies for breach of contract and tort at common law and in equity
- ▶ the doctrine of remoteness of damages for tort and contract
- ▶ mitigation of loss in torts and contract

Hot Topic . . .

ACTIONS IN CONTRACT AND/OR TORT

All legal systems which recognise a law of contract and a law of tort face the possibility of concurrent claims arising under the two areas of law. There are two solutions: (i) force claimants to sue for breach of contract; or (ii) allow them to choose the remedy they prefer. In the UK, the problem of concurrent claims was generally ignored until the second half of the 20th century. Initially, the courts adopted the first solution, holding that a claim against a solicitor for negligence must be pursued in contract and, in *Groom v. Crocker* [1939] 1 KB 194, this was adopted firmly. In *Bagot v. Stevens Scanlon & Co. Ltd* [1966] 1 QB 197, Diplock ʟ adopted a similar approach in a claim against a firm of architects.

The question is not just of academic importance. If there is no concurrent liability, a claim based in contract may be statute-barred before a person is even aware of it. The consequences of the professional negligence may not be revealed until after the lapse of six years from the date of the breach of contract. The Latent Damages Act 1986, which postpones the accrual of the cause of action until after the claimant has the relevant knowledge, is limited to tortious negligence.

The first and most important move towards concurrent remedies in contract and tort came in *Hedley Byrne & Co. Ltd v.*

Heller & Partners Ltd [1964] AC 465. This provided the opportunity to reconsider the question of concurrent liability. The change of heart came in *Esso Petroleum Co. Ltd v. Mardon* [1976] QB 801, which concerned statements made by employees of Esso in precontractual negotiations with Mr Mardon, a potential tenant of a petrol station, concerning the throughput of the station. He suffered a serious loss when the throughput was less than predicted. The Court of Appeal held that he was entitled to recover damages on the basis of breach of warranty or negligent misrepresentation. Lord Denning held that, in addition to its liability in contract, Esso was liable in negligence.

In *Midland Bank Trust Co. Ltd v. Hett, Stubbs & Kemp* [1979] Ch 384, the court held that a solicitor could be liable for negligence to his client in tort or in contract, giving the claimant the advantage of a more favourable date of accrual of the cause of action. In that case, Oliver ɟ stated, 'There is not and never has been any rule of law that a person having alternative claims must frame his action in one or the other'.

In *Henderson and Others v. Merret Syndicates Ltd etc* [1994] 3 WLR 761, Lloyd's 'Names' (people in syndicates issuing insurance policies in respect of which they are personally liable without limit) sued their agents and sub-agents

for damages. Lord Goff held that the underwriting agents' duty of care to the Names in tort was not excluded by the terms of the contract with them. The Names could pursue their action in contract or in tort.

The court will not, however, impose concurrent liability in tort if the contracting parties intend their relationship to be governed solely by the contract. Thus in *Greater Nottingham Co-operative Soc. Ltd v. Cementation Piling and Foundations Ltd* [1989] QB 71 the claimants, who were owners of a building, entered into a building contract with a main contractor who then entered a contract with the defendant sub-contractors. Subsequently the claimants entered into a collateral contract with the defendants which did not impose liability for negligent performance of the contract. The claimants sued in the tort of negligence for physical damage and loss arising from the negligent operation of drilling equipment. The Court of Appeal held that entering into a collateral contract was inconsistent with liability in the tort of negligence.

Apart from different rules regarding limitation of actions, there are significant differences in the remedies between the two areas of law:

- ▶ specific performance and liquidated damages are limited to breach of contract;
- ▶ different tests apply to remoteness of damage and damages for mental distress;

▶ contributory negligence and exemplary damages are available only in tort;
▶ restitutionary damages are more readily available in tort than in contract.

Remedies compensate the injured party rather than punish the defendant, with the exception of exemplary damages in tort. Legal remedies are available as of right, whereas equitable remedies – specific performance, injunction, rectification and rescission – are discretionary. The remedies available are damages, equitable remedies and restitutionary remedies.

5.1 Limitation of actions in contract and tort

The Limitation Act 1980 provides that actions based on breach of contract or tort must be brought within a specific time after the cause of action arose. If an action is not brought within the time period allowed, the claimant is statute-barred and the action cannot be brought. There are different time limits applicable for actions in contract and in tort.

(a) Lapse of time for actions founded on tort

The general period of limitation for tort is six years from the date of the accrual of the cause of action: s.2 Limitation Act 1980. There are sometimes situations where there may be a dispute as to when the right of action accrued.

In *Byrne and Another v. Hall Pain & Foster (a firm) and others* [1999] 2 All ER 400, the second defendant, a chartered surveyor employed by the first defendants, produced a negligent survey report about a flat which the plaintiffs proposed to purchase. The plaintiffs exchanged contracts on the basis of their report on 8 July 1988 and the purchase was completed on 22 July. Subsequently defects in the property came to light and the plaintiffs issued proceedings against the defendants alleging negligence on 18 July 1994. The defendants pleaded that the plaintiffs' claim was barred by s.2 Limitation Act 1980. The Court of Appeal held that the cause of action accrued on exchange of contracts and the plaintiffs were statute-barred.

Where the action is in respect of damages for personal injuries arising from 'negligence, nuisance or breach of duty' the period is three years from the date the cause of action accrues, or the date of knowledge (if later) of the person injured: s.11(4)(a) and (b). The 'date of knowledge' is defined as the date on which the person first had knowledge of the various facts including 'that the injury in question was significant': s.14(2). Where s.11 applies, the court has discretion to extend the limitation period when equitable to do so: s.33. In *Stubbings v. Webb* [1993] AC 498 the House of Lords decided that s.11 did not apply to a case of deliberate assault.

This created an anomaly illustrated in *S v. W (Child Abuse: Damages)* [1995] 1 FLR 862 where the plaintiff's claim for damages for sexual abuse brought against the father for intentional assault nearly 10 years after the last act of abuse was struck out, whereas the claim against the mother for negligent failure to protect the plaintiff against the father fell under s.11 and was granted discretionary extension by the judge. In *A v. Hoare and other appeals* [2008] UKHL 6 the House of Lords overruled *Stubbings* and decided that actions for damages for intentional trespass to the person fell within s.11. The House of Lords also held that the test under s.14(2) for what counted as a significant injury was an entirely impersonal standard, external to the claimant and involved no enquiry into what he ought reasonably to have done. The question whether an actual claimant, considering his psychological state, could reasonably have been expected to institute proceedings was relevant to s.33.

Thus the date of exposure to asbestos dust through an employer's negligence is when the right of action accrues under s.11(4)(a), but the date when the employee is aware that he has developed lung cancer, which may be years later, is covered by (b). If the injured person dies before the period in s.11(4)(a) and (b) expires, the cause of action survives for the benefit of his/her estate for three years from the date of death or the date of the personal representative's knowledge, whichever is the later: s.11(5). Under the Latent Damages Act 1986, where a person's tortious negligence results in latent damage other than personal injury, the cause of action runs for six years from the date when the damage is discovered.

For torts of a continuing nature such as nuisance, an independent cause of action arises on each day that the tort is committed, so that, even though the wrong was first committed outside the limitation period, the claimant can sue in respect of the part committed within the limitation period. For children or persons suffering from mental disorder, the period does not start to run until their disability ends. The periods of limitation against the estate of a deceased tortfeasor are subject to the normal three-year or six-year rule from the accrual of the cause of action: Proceedings against Estates Act 1970.

In respect of any period of limitation under the Act, where any fact relevant to the plaintiff's right of action has been deliberately concealed from him by the defendant the period of limitation shall not begin to run until the plaintiff has discovered the fraud, concealment or mistake or could with reasonable diligence have discovered it: s.32.

For defamation or malicious falsehood, the right to bring an action expires one year from the date on which the cause of action accrued.

(b)   Lapse of time for actions founded on breach of contract

The general periods within which an action may be brought as laid down by the Limitation Act 1980 are as follows:

- Actions based on a simple contract may be brought within six years from the date when the cause of action accrued.
- Actions based on a contract made by deed may be brought within 12 years from the date when the cause of action accrued.

The cause of action arises at the time of the breach, not when the contract was made. If, however, the potential claimant was suffering from a disability by reason of being a child or unsound of mind, the limitation period runs once the disability is ended or on the person's death. Where persons are the victims of fraud or have acted under a mistake, the limitation period begins to run only once a person is aware of the situation or from the time when they should, with reasonable diligence, have become aware of it. In the case of a claim in equity for specific performance, the Court of Appeal has held that it was inappropriate to apply, by analogy, the limitation period which applied in law to the underlying contract: *P & O Nedlloyd BV v. Arab Metals Co and Ors (No 2)* [2006] EWCA Civ 1717.

(c)   Lapse of time for actions in respect of trust property

No period of limitation applies to an action 'in respect of any fraud or fraudulent breach of trust to which the trustee was party': s.21(1)(a) LA 1980. It has been held, however, that this exception applied only to a breach of trust by an express trustee and did not apply to a claim brought against a defendant alleging that she had dishonestly and knowingly assisted in the fraudulent breach of trust. In *Cattley and Anor v. Pollard and Anor* [2006] EWHC 3130 (Ch) judgment was entered against Mr Pollard for fraudulent misappropriation of trust assets between 1987 and 1996. In November 2005, the trustee brought new proceedings against Mrs Pollard for damages and equitable compensation arising from her knowingly and dishonestly assisting her husband in the breaches of trust. Her assertion that the claims were statute barred was upheld by the court.

5.2   Compensatory damages in contract

The aim is to put the claimant in the same position as if the contract had been performed. This is called *expectation loss*, and the claimant can claim for pecuniary loss assessed at the date of the breach of the contract. In *Golden Strait Corp v. Nippon Yusen Kubishika Kaisha* [2007] UKHL 12 the House of Lords held that the rule requiring damages to be assessed at the date of the breach did not, however, require subsequent events occurring before the actual assessment to be ignored. The parties had entered a charterparty in 1998 for a period of seven years with both parties able to cancel if war or hostilities broke out between a number of countries including the US, the UK and Iraq. In December 2001, the charterers repudiated the contract and this was accepted by the owners. The owners' claim for damages was referred to arbitration and the arbitrator found in their favour. The matter of damages went back to the arbitrator in March 2003 by which time the second Gulf war had broken out. The arbitrator held that no damages were recoverable from March 2003. The House of Lords held that the damages should be assessed at the date of the breach by valuing the chance that the contingency would occur and the charter cancelled. In the instant case, however, the war was an accomplished fact and the arbitrator had been correct in taking it into account.

(a)   Failure to deliver or accept goods or render a service

Where the goods are readily obtainable elsewhere, damages are the difference between the contract price and the market price when the goods should have been delivered. If the buyer pays above the market price for the substitute goods, the extra amount cannot be claimed. The same applies to a refusal to accept delivery and when the seller sells the goods below market price.

Where there is no available market for goods which have been repudiated, loss of anticipated profit can be claimed.

In *Thompson (W. L.) Ltd v. Robinson (Gunmakers) Ltd* [1955] Ch 177, the defendants repudiated a contract to buy a new car after one day and the claimants obtained damages for loss of profit on the deal, since there was no demand for the vehicle. In *Charter v. Sullivan* [1957] 2 QB 117, in similar circumstances damages for loss of profit were not awarded, since there were more buyers than cars available. In *Lazenby Garages v. Wright* [1976] 2 All ER 770, the court rejected a claim for loss of profits where a buyer repudiated a contract to purchase a second-hand car, which the seller subsequently sold for a higher price. The dealer claimed that, but for the repudiation, he would have sold two cars.

For services, damages are the difference between the contract price and the cost of substituted performance at a date determined by the court.

(b)   Supply of defective goods or services

Damages are the difference between what was contracted for and what was delivered, and are based on the cost of cure (putting the defect right) or diminution in value. Generally the cost of cure is granted unless it is shown that the claimant has no intention of carrying out the work. In *Tito v. Waddell (No. 2)* [1977] Ch 106, the defendant had promised to replant trees on an island after mining operations. Damages based on the difference in value of the island with and without trees were awarded since there was no clear intention of the islanders to replant. In *Radford v. De Froberville* [1977] 1 WLR 1262, where the claimant sold the defendant land on the basis that the defendant would erect a dividing wall, damages were the cost of building the wall rather than the difference in value (which would have been almost nothing), since the court was satisfied that the claimant intended to build the wall.

In *Ruxley Electronic v. Forsyth* [1995] 3 All ER 268, the claimants built a swimming pool for the defendant which was to be 7'6" at the deep end for diving. The finished pool was only 6'9" at the deep end and 6' at the natural diving point. The trial judge held that this made no difference to the pool's value, that it would cost £21,000 to cure, and it was unlikely and unreasonable that Mr Forsyth would carry out the alterations. He awarded damages of £2,500 for loss of amenity. The Court of Appeal reversed the decision and awarded the full cost of the cure. The House of Lords upheld the trial judge. The decision reflects the feeling that damages of £21,000 would overcompensate Mr Forsyth and that it was necessary to find a figure which, together with a usable pool, would leave him in the same position as he would have been.

(c)   Loss of profits

The claimant may claim loss of profits if within the reasonable contemplation of the defendant.

(d)   Loss of an opportunity

Damages are awarded even though loss of opportunity is difficult to assess. In *Chaplin v. Hicks* [1910] 2 KB 486, the court awarded damages for the loss of the opportunity to be auditioned for a part in a show offered as part of the prize of a competition. Similarly, in *Simpson v. London and North Western Rly Co.* (1876) 1 QBD 274, the claimant recovered damages for loss of custom when the defendant failed to deliver samples in time for a show, even though no precise assessment of loss was possible.

The award will take into consideration the fact that the claimant would have been liable for tax on those benefits: *Beach v. Reed Corrugated Cases Ltd* [1956] 2 All ER 652; and *British Transport Commission v. Gourley* [1956] AC 185.

As an alternative to expectation losses, the claimant may claim for losses incurred through acting in reliance on the defendant's promise – *reliance losses.*

In *Anglia Television v. Reed* [1972] 1 QB 60, the claim was in respect of expenditure on the preproduction costs of a film when the defendant broke his contract to appear.

In all cases it must be shown that the losses were within the reasonable contemplation of the defendant.

Reliance loss is useful when it is difficult to establish a foreseeable expectation of profit.

In *CCC Films v. Impact Quadrant Films* [1984] 3 All ER 298, the claimant's claim was not based on profits lost, but on recovering his initial investment in respect of distribution rights of certain videos. Recovery is not possible where it can be shown that the reliance expenditure would have been lost in any event. Thus a tenant could not recover the cost of improvements to a rented property on a six-month renewable licence: *C & P Haulage v. Middleton* [1983] 3 All ER 94.

(e) Consequential and incidental loss

The claimant may suffer equally foreseeable but less immediately obvious loss as a result of the breach of contract. Thus defective goods supplied under a contract may damage people or property, and losses following unfair dismissal may extend to pension rights, free health insurance, a company car and so on (see Chapter 17, p.411).

As a general rule in respect of ordinary commercial contracts, damages are not recoverable for injury to feelings, mental distress or damage to reputation arising from a breach of contract. Thus in *Addis v. Gramophone Co Ltd* [1909] AC 488 the claimant was unable to recover damages for the harsh and humiliating way in which he had been dismissed as manager of the defendant company. Where, however, a major or important object of the contract is either to give pleasure or enjoyment to the other party, or to provide compensation for physical inconvenience arising from the breach, non-pecuniary losses are recoverable if the breach causes discomfort or distress . The position was reconsidered and restated by the House of Lords in *Farley v. Skinner* [2001] 3 WLR 899.

Thus, in *Jackson v. Horizon Holidays Ltd* [1975] 3 All ER 92, the claimant recovered damages for his disappointment and that of his wife and children as a result of a disastrous holiday. In *Jackson v. Chrysler* [1978] RTR 474, damages were awarded for 'inconvenience and disappointment' after a holiday was ruined by repeated car breakdowns.

In *Heywood v. Wellers* [1976] QB 446 the claimant employed the defendant solicitor to obtain and enforce an injunction to prevent her being molested by a man. Due to the solicitor's negligence, she was molested on three or four occasions. The court awarded damages for mental distress. In *McLeish v. Amoo-Gottfried & Co., The Times*, 13 October 1993, the High Court awarded damages for distress and mental anxiety where the claimant's solicitors acted negligently in his defence. The court stated that the very essence of the contract had been to ensure his peace of mind by taking all appropriate steps, and that it was foreseeable that the claimant would suffer mental distress. The court was, however, unwilling to give an award for injury to reputation as a separate head of damages.

In *Farley v. Skinner* the court awarded damages against a surveyor who was asked to inspect a house on behalf of the claimant, paying particular attention to whether the property was affected by aircraft noise from nearby Gatwick airport. The surveyor reported positively about this aspect of the property as a result of which the claimant purchased it. In effect, the property was greatly affected by aircraft noise and the claimant sued for damages for mental distress and disappointment. The House of Lords confirmed an award of damages of £10,000 although it was considered to be on the high side.

5.3 Remoteness of damage in contract

Even where the loss arises from the breach, the claimant's claim may fail if the loss/damage is too remote.

The test was established by *Hadley v. Baxendale* (1854) 9 Exch 341. The claimant ran a mill and, when the crankshaft of the mill broke, contracted with the defendant carriers to deliver the shaft the following day to a manufacturer as a pattern for making a replacement. Delivery was not made until a week later and the mill was closed for longer than anticipated. The case established liability for (i) losses arising naturally from the breach of contract; or (ii) 'losses such as may reasonably be supposed to have been in the contemplation of the parties at the time the contract was made as a probable result of the breach of it'. The claim for damages because of the extended closure of the mill was neither a natural consequence of the breach nor one within the fair and reasonable contemplation of the parties, since it was conceivable that there was a replacement part.

The test was refined in *Victoria Laundry (Windsor) Ltd v. Newman Industries Ltd* [1949] 2 KB 528 to loss being recoverable where it was 'reasonably foreseeable at the time the contract was made as liable to result from the breach'. The defendants were liable for loss of normal profits because the laundry was closed for a longer period than contemplated caused by their delay in replacing boilers, but not for the loss of exceptional dyeing contracts which the claimants were forced to turn down.

A purchaser of goods for resale cannot claim loss of anticipated profit unless the other party was expressly or impliedly notified or could be presumed to have known that the goods were to be resold.

In *Koufos v. Czarnikow Ltd, The Heron II* [1969] 1 AC 350, shippers contracted to deliver a consignment of sugar to Basra. In breach of their contract the sugar reached Basra nine days late, when its market value had fallen between the due date for delivery and the actual date of delivery, The shippers were held liable for damages for loss of profit even though they did not know what the charterers intended to do with the sugar. They knew there was a market for sugar in Basra and must have realised that it was not unlikely that the sugar would be sold on arrival, and that in any ordinary market prices fluctuated daily with an even chance that the fluctuation would be downwards.

The remoteness rule was considered by the House of Lords in *Jackson v. Royal Bank of Scotland* [2005] UKHL 3 where the defendant bank, in breach of its duty of confidentiality, wrongly sent documents to the claimant's principal client which revealed the substantial mark-up on goods imported by the claimant and sold on to its client. As a result, the client terminated its contract with the claimant who sued for damages for loss of future business. The House of Lords held that the case fell under the first part of the rule in *Hadley v. Baxendale* – losses arising naturally from the breach – and disagreed with the Court of Appeal's decision that the claimant's losses should be restricted to one year's worth of future business. It restored the order made by the trial judge that four years' of lost business was recoverable on a reducing basis.

5.4 Mitigation of loss

A person cannot claim for losses which s/he could reasonably have avoided, and claimants have a duty to take all reasonable steps to minimise their loss. An employee who is unfairly dismissed must seek alternative employment: *Brace v. Calder* [1895] 2 QB 253, although this does not mean accepting re-employment in a position of lower status: *Yetton v. Eastwoods Froy Ltd* [1967] 1 WLR 104. A seller of goods faced with a repudiation of the contract must attempt to find a second buyer: *Lazenby Garages v. Wright* (1976) (see above). For damages for anticipatory breach see *White & Carter (Councils) Ltd v. McGregor* [1961] 3 All ER 1178 (see Chapter 3, p. 81).

5.5 Contributory negligence

In *Barclays Bank plc v. Fairclough Building Ltd and Others* [1995] 1 All ER 289, the claimants appealed against the extension of the defence of contributory negligence to contractual liability. The claimants had engaged the defendants to carry out work including cleaning roofs made of corrugated asbestos sheeting. Because of negligence by a subcontractor, the premises were contaminated with asbestos dust, requiring remedial work of £4m. The defendants claimed contributory negligence, since the work had been supervised by the claimants' own property services division. The Law Reform (Contributory Negligence) Act 1945 s.1(1) provides for reduced damages where the damage is partly the claimant's fault and partly the fault of another. 'Fault' is defined in s.4. to include 'negligence, breach of statutory duty, or other act or omission which [give] rise to a liability in tort or would, apart from this act, give rise to a defence of contributory negligence'. The Court of Appeal held that contributory negligence was not a defence to a claim for damages founded on a strict contractual obligation, even though the defendant might have a parallel liability in tort for such a failure.

5.6 Non-compensatory damages in contract

Hot Topic . . .

LIQUIDATED AND UNLIQUIDATED DAMAGES: PENALTY CLAUSES IN BUSINESS CONTRACTS

Business contracts may contain a 'penalty clause' setting out the sum payable by way of damages in the event of breach. This fixes the level of damages for any breach of contract and enables the injured party to claim the predetermined amount without proof of loss.

The clause will be contractually enforceable as liquidated damages without a need to establish actual loss only where it is seen as a genuine pre-estimate of the likely loss from the breach

of contract. Where the court decides that it is merely a threat held over the other party *in terrorem*, it cannot be relied on and the parties will have to prove their loss. The burden of proof of showing that a clause is a penalty and not unliquidated damages lies with the defendant. In reaching a decision, the court follows rules established in *Dunlop Pneumatic Tyre Co. Ltd v. New Garage Ltd* [1915] AC 847.

The rules for establishing liquidated damages are as follows:

▶ Where the amount is extravagant and arbitrary in comparison with the greatest loss which could possibly follow the breach, it will not be valid.

▶ If the breach for which the damages are payable is a failure to pay a sum of money and the damages are greater, it will not be valid.

▶ Subject to the above, if the damages arise only in the event of a specific and identified breach, it is valid: *Law v. Redditch Local Board* [1892] 1 QB 127.

▶ If the damages are payable on the happening of one or more or all of several events, of which some may cause serious damage while others may cause insignificant damage, there is a presumption that the damages are invalid as a penalty: *Ford Motor Co. v. Armstrong* (1915) 31 TLR 267; *Bridge v. Campbell Discount Co. Ltd* [1962] AC 600 (see Chapter 20).

If the clause is valid it will be enforced even though the claimant has suffered greater loss.

In *Cellulose Acetate Silk Co. Ltd v. Widnes Foundry Ltd* [1933] AC 20, the claimants' claim of £5,850 for actual loss caused by the 30-week delay in the defendant installing plant was rejected. They were entitled to only £20 per week as per a clause in the contract.

(a)   Nominal damages

Where there is an infringement of a contractual right but no quantifiable loss the court will award nominal damages: see *Lazenby Garages v. Wright* [1976] 2 All ER 770 (see above) where the claimant received £2 damages.

In *Surrey County Council v. Bredero Homes Ltd* [1993] 1 WLR 1361, the defendants had been granted two separate planning permissions for a site and covenanted with the claimant to develop in accordance with the first, but completed within the terms of the second and built 77 instead of 72 houses. The claimants claimed the profits made by the defendants in breaking the contract, but were awarded nominal damages since they had suffered no loss. In *Veitch and Anor v. Avery* [2007] EWCA Civ 711 the court held that any loss caused by a solicitor's negligence in wrongly advising his client that he was in default under a loan agreement with his bank was to be assessed on the date of the breach of duty. A claimant client who, on the facts, had no chance of trading himself out of his difficulties even had the solicitor not behaved negligently was entitled to only nominal damages.

5.7   Compensatory damages in tort

Damages are classifiable as (i) general damages; and (ii) special damages. General damages are presumed to have resulted from the tortious act, whereas special damages will have to be specifically proved by the claimant. A person suffering permanent physical or mental injury can be awarded damages under a variety of heads. General damages for personal injuries can be grouped under (i) pain and suffering; (ii) loss of enjoyment of life or amenity; (iii) loss of expectation of life; and (iv) loss of earnings (both actual and prospective).

In *Bee v. Jenson (No 2)* [2007] EWCA Civ 923 it was held that a claimant whose car had been damaged by the defendant's negligence could recover the reasonable cost of a replacement while his own car was being repaired, even though the cost of the hire had been paid directly to the hire company by the claimant's own insurers rather than by the claimant himself.

Credit has to be given for benefits received by the claimant as a result of the defendant's wrongdoing, but some collateral benefits are exempt, including money received through benevolence and the proceeds of insurance.

In *Parry v. Cleaver* [1970] AC 1, the claimant's claim for damages for personal injury was not reduced by the amount of the proceeds of disability insurance. The rule has now been extended to the law of contract in *Hopkins v. Norcros plc* [1994] IRLR 18.

In personal injury claims since 1987 the courts have used structured settlements, where the damages are paid in a series of tax-free payments. Such awards are facilitated by the Damages Act 1996.

5.8 Remoteness of damage in tort

The previous test for remoteness of damage, in *Re Polemis and Furniss Withy & Co.* [1921] 3 KB 560, made the defendant liable for all the direct consequences of his negligence, whether foreseeable or not. This was overruled by the JCPC in 1961.

The overruling was in *Overseas Tankship (UK) Ltd v. Morts Dock Engineering Co. Ltd, The Wagon Mound (No. 1)* [1961] 1 All ER 404, where the defendants carelessly discharged oil from their ship in Sydney Harbour. The oil was carried to the claimant's wharf about 200 yards away where some welding was being carried out and was continued after assurances that it was safe to continue. A spark set light to some cotton rags floating on the water; this caused the oil to catch fire and the result was that the wharf was seriously damaged. The defendants were not liable because they could not reasonably have foreseen that the claimant's wharf would be damaged by fire when they negligently discharged the oil into the harbour; '[i]t is thus a principle of civil liability … that a man must be considered to be responsible for the probable consequences of his act. To demand more of him is too harsh a rule, to demand less is to ignore that civilised order requires the observance of a minimum standard of behaviour' (Viscount Simonds).

From subsequent decisions the following points emerge:

▶ If the nature of the physical damage was reasonably foreseeable, its extent and the manner in which it occurs do not need to have been foreseeable.

  In *Vacwell Engineering Co. Ltd v. BDH Chemicals Ltd* [1971] 1 QB 88, the defendants were liable in respect of failing to label a chemical which they supplied with a warning that it was liable to explode in water. The fact that damage arising from a minor explosion was foreseeable meant they were liable even when the damage was more extensive than could have been reasonably foreseen.

  In *Muirhead v. Industrial Tank Specialities Ltd* [1985] 3 WLR 993, the supplier of a defective pump was liable for the loss of the entire stock of the claimant's lobsters kept in a fish tank. Goff LJ stated, 'If he had found that damage of that type was reasonably foreseeable, then the fact that, by reason of the full stocking of the relevant tank, the fish died more quickly or in a greater quantity was of no relevance, unless it … constituted the sole or contributory cause of the disaster which took place.'

  In *Tremain v. Pike* [1969] 3 All ER 1303, the claimant failed in his action for damages when he contracted the rare Weil's disease from contact with rats' urine, since it was completely different from the foreseeable outcome of a rat bite or food poisoning.

▶ The doctrine conflicts with the principle that a tortfeasor takes his victim as he finds him. This states that if, owing to some peculiar weakness, the victim suffers injury beyond that which is foreseeable, the defendant will be liable for the injury suffered.

  In *Smith v. Leech Brain & Co. Ltd* [1961] 3 All ER 1159, a man particularly susceptible to cancer was struck on the lip by some molten metal at work, contracted cancer and died as a result. The widow recovered damages for his death. In *Robinson v. Post Office* [1974] 2 All ER 737, the defendants were liable when the claimant suffered a minor injury as a result of his employer's negligence and was given an anti-tetanus injection and, owing to an allergic reaction, developed encephalitis resulting in permanent brain damage and disability.

▶ The doctrine does not protect against liability where the injured party is rich or the object damaged is of exceptional value. Thus the fact that the victim earns a large salary or that the damage was to an object of exceptional value such as an old master engraving rather than a reproduction does not excuse the tortfeasor from liability to pay damages. In addition, there is only a low degree of foreseeability required to establish tortious liability as compared with the remoteness test in the law of contract: *Koufos v. Czarnikow Ltd, The Heron II* [1969] 1 AC 350.

▷ Remoteness of damages does not apply to the tort of deceit. In *Doyle v. Olby (Ironmongers) Ltd* [1969] 2 QB 158, Lord Denning said, 'The defendant is bound to make reparation for all the actual damages directly flowing from the fraudulent inducement'. This decision has since been upheld by the House of Lords.

In *Smith New Court Securities Ltd v. Citibank N.A.* [1996] 3 WLR 1051, concerning fraudulent misrepresentation relating to a contract to purchase shares, Lord Browne-Wilkinson laid down a seven-point rule for assessment of damages where the claimant had been induced by fraudulent misrepresentation to buy property:

(1) the defendant is bound to make reparation for all the damage directly flowing from the transaction;

(2) although such damage need not have been foreseeable, it must have been directly caused by the transaction;

(3) in assessing such damage, the claimant is entitled to recover the full price paid by him, but he must give credits for any benefits which he has received as a result;

(4) as a general rule, the benefits received by him include the market value of the property acquired as at the date of acquisition; but such general rule is not to be inflexibly applied where to do so would prevent him obtaining full compensation;

(5) the general rule will normally not apply where either (a) the misrepresentation has continued to operate after the date of the acquisition of the asset so as to induce the claimant to retain the asset or (b) the circumstances are such that the claimant is, by reason of the fraud, locked into the property;

(6) in addition, the claimant is entitled to recover consequential losses caused by the transaction;

(7) the claimant must take all reasonable steps to mitigate the loss once he has discovered the fraud.

No view was expressed on the adoption of the *Doyle* measure of damages under the Misrepresentation Act 1967 in *Royscot Trust Ltd v. Rogerson* [1991] 3 WLR 57.

The same principle may apply for other intentional torts.

5.9 Intervening cause

Liability is limited where intervening natural events break the chain of causation. In *Carlogie SS Co. Ltd v. The Royal Norwegian Government* [1952] AC 292, the claimant's ship was damaged in a collision, repaired and then sailed to the USA and was extensively damaged because of the heavy weather. The House of Lords found the defendants not liable for storm damage, since it was not a consequence of the collision. In *Pearson Education Ltd v. Charter Partnership Ltd* [2007] UKEAT 0635 06 2307, architects who designed an inadequate drainage system for a warehouse were liable in negligence to the occupiers for flood damage where a third party had discovered the inadequacy following an earlier flood but had not informed the occupiers. The court held that the first flood and the following inspection neither placed the claimants outside the range of any duty of care owed by the architects nor broke the chain of causation between the architects and the damage suffered by the claimants.

A specialised instance of this involving a human intervening act is *novus actus interveniens*. This is a fresh act by someone other than the defendant which intervenes between the alleged wrong and the damage in question. It allows the defendant to escape liability if able to prove that the claimant's injury was the result of the claimant's or another person's subsequent and intervening event breaking the chain of causation linking the injury to their tortious act.

In *Davies v. Liverpool Corporation* [1949] 2 All ER 175, the defendants were vicariously liable for the negligence of a tram conductor who remained upstairs, allowing another passenger the possibility of ringing the bell while the claimant was still boarding the tram. The action of the passenger did not break the chain of causation between the wrongful act of the conductor and the injury suffered by the claimant.

Where the action of the claimant is alleged to break the chain of causation, there will be no break in the chain if the claimant acts reasonably. The decisions are sometimes difficult to reconcile.

In *McKew v. Holland and Hannen and Cubitts (Scotland) Ltd* [1969] 3 All ER 1621, the claimant had suffered an industrial injury through his employer's negligence, resulting in his leg giving way unexpectedly; he fell when his leg gave way while going downstairs without a handrail, but the court held that his action was unreasonable and broke the chain of causation. In *Wieland v. Cyril Lord Carpets Ltd* [1969] 3 All ER 1006, the claimant recovered damages for injuries after falling downstairs at her home. She had previously been injured at work because of the negligence of the defendant and was obliged to wear a neck support, which interfered with her use of her bifocal spectacles, resulting in the later fall.

In *Corr v. IBC Vehicles Ltd* [2008] UKHL 13 the claimant's husband was badly injured in 1996 in an accident caused by his employer's negligence. As a result, he suffered post-traumatic stress disorder and severe depression. In 2002, he was assessed as a significant suicide risk and committed suicide later that month. It was held that the defendant owed the deceased a duty of care embracing psychological as well as physical injury, and that he had acted in a way in which he would not have done but for the injury. The defence's claim of *novus actus interveniens* causing a break in the chain of causation was rejected.

5.10   Mitigation of damages

Damages are subject to mitigation. Thus damages for defamation may be reduced where the defendant was provoked. Mitigation also applies where claimants increase the loss suffered by their own actions.

In *Luker v. Chapman* (1970) 114 Sol Jo 788, the claimant lost his right leg as a result of an accident partly caused by the defendant's negligence. He was unable to carry on working as a telephone engineer, refused a desk job for less money and took up teacher training instead. The defendant was not liable for damages for the total loss of earnings during teacher training, since the claimant should have accepted the office job.

However, in *Moore v. DER Ltd* [1971] 1 WLR 1476, the claimant was able to claim for a new car when his 3-year-old car had been written off in an accident caused by the negligence of the defendant's employee, and for the cost of hiring a vehicle while awaiting delivery of the new car. The court was influenced by the claimant's need to have a reliable vehicle for his work. This appears contrary to the law relating to mitigation.

Hot Topic . . .

CONTRIBUTORY NEGLIGENCE

The Law Reform (Contributory Negligence) Act 1945 provides: '[w]here any person suffers damage as a result partly of his own fault and partly of the fault of any other person or persons … the damages recoverable in respect thereof shall be reduced to such extent as the court thinks just and equitable having regard to the claimant's share in the responsibility for the damage': s.1(1). The court assesses the situation and, provided the defendant caused the situation from which the claimant suffered, then s/he is liable, but the amount of compensation is reduced according to the degree to which the claimant contributed to his/her own injuries.

Contributory negligence can arise: (i) by the claimant contributing to the accident, for example both the claimant and the defendant were driving negligently when the accident occurred; and (ii) by the claimant making the injury or damage suffered more serious, for example by failing to wear a seat belt in a car or a crash helmet on a motorcycle: *O'Connell v. Jackson* [1972] 1 QB 270.

In *Sayers v. Harlow UDC* [1958] 1 WLR 623, the claimant became trapped in a public lavatory and attempted to climb out of the cubicle by placing her foot on the toilet roll holder. The roller turned and she fell and was injured, but her damages were reduced by 25 per cent since she was contributorily negligent in standing on the toilet roll holder.

In *Froom v. Butcher* [1976] QB 286, the claimant's damages were reduced by 20 per cent through failing to wear a seat belt, and in *Owens v. Brimmells* [1976] 3 All ER 765 by 20 per cent because the claimant knew that the defendant was driving under the influence of drink.

A person liable for deceit is not entitled to plead as a defence that his victim was guilty of contributory negligence: *Alliance & Leicester Building Society v. Edgestop Ltd; Same v. Dhanoa; Same v. Samra; Mercantile Credit Co. Ltd v. Lancaster* [1993] 1 WLR 1462. This was affirmed by the House of Lords in *Standard Chartered Bank v. Pakistan National Shipping Corp.* [2002] UKHL 43 (see p. 154).

In *Barclays Bank plc v. Fairclough Building Ltd and Others* [1995] 1 All ER 289, the Court of Appeal held that contributory negligence was not a defence to a claim for damages founded on a strict contractual obligation, even though the defendant might have a parallel liability in tort for such a failure.

5.11   Pure economic loss

The claimant can recover damages in respect of:

- physical injury, mental suffering and nervous shock where the damage is not too remote;
- monetary loss caused by physical harm to their property which is the foreseeable result of the defendant's negligence, but not for pure economic loss, except in the case of negligent misstatement.

The distinction between monetary loss arising from damage to property and pure economic loss is shown in the following case.

In *Spartan Steel and Alloys Ltd v. Martin & Co. Ltd* [1973] QB 27, the defendant's employees negligently damaged an underground electricity cable, cutting off power to the claimant's factory, which caused him to pour away molten metal from a furnace and to lose production time. The claimant recovered damages for loss of the metal and loss of profit on it, but failed to recover damages for loss of profit arising from the interruption to production, which was pure economic loss.

The refusal to allow claims for pure economic loss is on the grounds of public policy relating to the 'floodgates argument'. The rationale for this policy is best expressed in the much-cited words of the American judge, Cardozo CJ. In *Ultramares Corp v. Touche* (1931) 174 NE 441, in respect of the liability of accountants and auditors to third parties, he stated that allowing claims for pure economic loss would lead to liability 'in an indeterminate amount for an indefinite time to an indeterminate class'.

Claims for pure economic loss are restricted to liability for negligent misstatement which was severely restricted by the House of Lords decision in *Caparo Industries plc v. Dickman* [1990] 1 All ER 568 (see Chapter 4, p.94).

5.12 Non-compensatory damages in tort

Non-compensatory damages can be nominal, contemptuous, aggravated and exemplary:

▷ Nominal damages are awarded in cases where the tort is actionable *per se* without proof of loss, for example trespass to land and libel.

▷ Contemptuous damages are rarely awarded other than by a jury in a defamation case. They indicate that the claimant does not deserve more than a technical acknowledgement of having established an infringement of their rights.

▷ Aggravated damages are awarded where the court thinks them justified. Thus, in *Bisney v. Swanston* [1972] 225 EG 2299, aggravated damages were awarded where the defendant spitefully parked a trailer in the car park of the claimant's transport café to cause the greatest possible business interference.

▷ Exemplary damages are intended to make an example of the defendant or punish him. In *Rookes v. Barnard* [1964] AC 1129, the House of Lords limited the award to cases where: (i) the claimant is the victim of arbitrary and oppressive conduct by a government official: *Arora v. Bradford City Council 1990* [1991] 3 All ER 545; (ii) the defendant calculatedly makes a profit which exceeds the claimant's loss; or (iii) damages are awarded by statute. In *Cassell & Co. Ltd v. Broome* [1972] 1 All ER 808, where the publisher and author of a book knew that the money to be made would probably exceed the damages arising from a libel action, £25,000 exemplary damages were awarded in addition to the £14,000 compensatory damages.

Hot Topic . . .

THE FUTURE OF EXEMPLARY DAMAGES

In its report *Aggravated, Exemplary and Restitutionary Damages* (Law Com No. 247) (1997), the Law Commission recommended that the availability of exemplary damages should be extended.

In *Kuddus v. Chief Constable of Leicestershire* [2001] 3 All ER 193, the House of Lords reconsidered some aspects of the topic. In this case, K had been burgled and reported the fact to a police constable. Two months later, the constable forged K's signature on a statement purporting to withdraw the complaint of theft and the investigation was dropped. K sued for damages, including exemplary damages, for the tort of misfeasance in public office. The trial judge and the Court of Appeal struck out the claim for exemplary damages and K appealed to the House of Lords.

The main issue was whether exemplary damages were generally available whenever the case fell into either of Lord Devlin's categories in *Rookes v. Barnard* or available only when there was previous authority for an award of exemplary damages for that particular tort. The latter approach had been set out and applied by the Court of Appeal in *AB v. South West Water Services Ltd* [1993] QB 507. The House of Lords, in allowing the appeal, adopted the 'category' rather than the 'cause of action test'.

In the *Kuddus* case, the chief constable himself had done nothing wrong and was merely being sued for vicarious liability. The issue whether exemplary damages could be awarded against a defendant who was only vicariously liable was not argued before the court, and Lord Scott was the only member of the House to deal with this aspect. He regarded the objection to exemplary damages in vicarious liability cases as 'fundamental'. Lord Scott also stated that exemplary damages should no longer be part of English law and that the Practice Statement of 1966 (Practice Statement (Judicial Precedent) [1966] 3 All ER 77) allowed the court to depart from its decision in *Rookes v. Barnard*.

5.13 Equitable remedies in contract

Equitable remedies of rescission, rectification, specific performance and injunction may be ordered in respect of contract. For rectification see Chapter 3, p.60.

(a) Rescission

Rescission allows an injured party to the contract, as a result of misrepresentation, duress, undue influence or any situation where the contract is voidable as a result of some vitiating element, to avoid the contract and be restored to the position s/he was in prior to the contract. The remedy can be lost in the following instances.

(b) The injured party affirms the contract

The injured party affirms the contract when, with full knowledge of the vitiating element, s/he declares him/herself bound by the contract or acts in some way so as to imply affirmation. Lapse of time may be treated as evidence of affirmation

(c) There is lapse of time

A claim for rescission can be defeated under the maxim 'Delay defeats equities' (the doctrine of *laches*). In *Leaf v. International Galleries Ltd* [1950] 2 KB 86, a five-year delay was considered too much; and in *Allcard v. Skinner* (1887) 36 Ch D 145, an eight-year delay was considered too much. The acceptable period may be only weeks.

(i) *Restitutio in integrum is impossible*
The parties must generally be able to be restored to their pre-contract positions but, where complete restitution is not possible, the court may order rescission, subject to the payment of balancing compensation.

(ii) *Third party rights have arisen*
In *Phillips v. Brooks* [1919] 2 KB 243, jewellers were unable to recover a ring obtained by a buyer on a fraudulent misrepresentation once it had been acquired in good faith by a pawnbroker (see Chapter 18, p.438). Where the claim is in respect of a contract to purchase shares induced by misrepresentation, the remedy is lost when the company goes into liquidation: *Oakes v. Turquand and Harding* (1867) LR 2 HL 325.

(d) Specific performance

In specific performance, the court orders the party in breach to perform the contract. Specific performance will not be ordered in the following instances.

(i) *Where damages are an adequate remedy*
Generally, specific performance will be available only where the subject matter of the contract is unique, as with land, artworks or ships. The category of unique goods has been extended to include goods needed for the buyer in his/her business and not available elsewhere. Thus, in *Sky Petroleum Ltd v. VIP Petroleum Ltd* [1974] 1 All ER 954, an oil company was ordered to supply petrol to a garage during a petrol shortage.

(ii) *For contracts for personal services*

No court can compel an employee to work by ordering specific performance of the contract or restraining the breach of such a contract by injunction.

(iii) *For contracts where there is no valuable consideration*

This also applies to legally binding contracts by deed: *Cannon v. Hartley* [1949] Ch 213. The rule is that equity will not aid a volunteer.

(iv) *Where the performance requires supervision by the court*

The court refused to enforce an obligation by a landlord to have a porter constantly in attendance: *Ryan v. Mutual Tontine Association* [1893] 1 Ch 116. However, in *Posner v. Scott Lewis* [1986] 3 All ER 513, the court specifically enforced a covenant to provide a resident porter.

In *Co-operative Insurance Society Ltd v. Argyll Stores (Holdings) Ltd* [1997] 3 All ER 297, the House of Lords reversed an order for specific performance of a covenant in a lease to keep a shop open during normal business hours since this would require constant supervision. It could also unjustly allow the claimant to enrich him/herself at the defendant's expense if the latter were forced to run a business at a loss.

Contracts to build or deliver goods by instalments will not be specifically enforced.

(v) *Where there is no mutuality*

The court will not order specific performance against the defendant if it cannot at the same time ensure that the unperformed obligations of the claimant will also be specifically performed. Thus, if A promises to convey a house to B if B promises to work for him for 10 years, B cannot get specific performance against A because his own promise to work cannot be specifically enforced.

In addition, the remedy will be granted only where it is 'just and equitable to do so' and may be refused where (a) the contract is unfair; (b) the claimant has behaved unreasonably; (c) the defendant would suffer undue hardship; (d) the defendant made a *bona fide* and reasonable mistake; or (e) there has been undue delay in seeking the remedy.

The court may order damages in lieu of or in addition to specific performance: Supreme Court Act 1981 s.50.

(e) Injunction

An injunction may be prohibitory and order the person to refrain from doing something, or mandatory and compel him/her to carry out some action, for example to pull down a house built in breach of a restrictive covenant: *Wakeham v. Wood* (1982) 43 P&CR 40. An injunction can be granted where a wrong has already been committed to prevent its continuance, but equally an injunction can be to prevent an anticipated legal wrong, although none has occurred at present.

An injunction can be interlocutory or perpetual.

An interlocutory injunction is granted at an early stage of the proceedings and generally expressed to stay in force until the trial of the action. Similar to this is the interim injunction, which is usually granted in cases of urgency pending the seeking of an interlocutory injunction. The perpetual injunction is granted at the trial or hearing at which the final judgment is given.

Injunctions are used to enforce a negative promise in a contract, such as a promise not to build or not to compete. However, even where a contract does not contain an express negative stipulation, there may be an implied negative stipulation.

In cases of exclusive contracts of service, the court will enforce an express negative stipulation only where it encourages but does not compel performance of the contract. Thus in *Lumley v. Wagner* (1852) 5 De GM & G 604, the defendant agreed to sing at the claimant's theatre twice weekly for three months, and also promised not to perform at any other theatre during that period. She was restrained by injunction from singing elsewhere.

In *Warner Bros. Pictures Inc. v. Nelson* [1937] 1 KB 209, Bette Davis was restrained from breaking her exclusive service contract with the claimant by an injunction preventing her from working for another studio. The court held that, since she was a multi-talented woman with many possibilities open to her, the injunction did not compel her to work for the claimant. In *Page One Records Ltd v. Britton* [1968] 1 WLR 157, the court refused an injunction against the pop group the Troggs, restraining them from working for anyone but the claimant. The court held that, since performing as a group was all that the defendants were able to do, they would in fact be compelled to work for the claimant. Injunctions are sought to prevent breaches of confidence or a restraint of trade covenant.

5.14   Equitable remedies in tort

Prohibitory injunctions are appropriate to prevent the continuation or repetition of a tort, and are available for any tort. But prohibitory permanent injunctions have generally been sought in relation to nuisance and trespass to land.

In respect of nuisance, the court is very careful in exercising its power to grant an injunction. Where temporary noise and disturbance are caused by building operations, such as demolitions, conversions or repairs, no tort will be committed as long as the work is carried out with reasonable care for the neighbours, but in *De Keyser's Royal Hotel Ltd v. Spicer Brothers Ltd* (1914) 30 TLR 257, the claimant obtained an injunction preventing the defendants operating a pile-driver between 10.00 p.m. and 6.30 a.m. And in *Kennaway v. Thompson* [1980] 3 All ER 329, the Court of Appeal replaced an award of damages for future interference caused by motor boat races and water-skiing on the lake near the claimant's house with an injunction restricting the racing activities and the noise level of boats.

In *Miller v. Jackson* [1977] QB 966, the Court of Appeal refused an injunction to stop the playing of cricket on a village green, since the houses to which it constituted a nuisance had been built later where they were clearly vulnerable to interference, and the claimant bought the house knowing that cricket was played on the green. The refusal was also out of respect for the interests of the village as a whole.

5.15   Restitutionary remedies

Restitutionary remedies reverse unjust enrichment and include an account of profits, an action for money had and received, and restitutionary damages. The essence of restitution is that the defendant has acquired a benefit or has negatively benefited by saving an expense which would otherwise have been incurred where the enrichment derives from the breach of contract or tort.

(a) Restitutionary remedies in contract

Restitutionary remedies in contract cover recovery of money or recompense in quasi-contract.

(i) Recovery of money

Money paid under a contract may be recovered: (i) where there has been a total failure of consideration; (ii) where a contract is rescinded; (iii) under the Law Reform (Frustrated Contracts) Act 1943; or (iv) where the contract was invalid, for example void for mistake.

In *Nurdin & Peacock plc v. D B Ramsden & Co Ltd* [1999] 1 All ER 941, the court held that the plaintiff was entitled to recover money which had been overpaid in respect of rent on the ground that the money had been paid under a mistake of law. In a dispute concerning the amount of rent payable to the defendant under a lease, the plaintiff's solicitor had advised it to pay the higher amount claimed by the defendant pending resolution of their dispute since, in the event of its being successful, it would be entitled to recover the amount overpaid. In fact, there was no such legal right since the plaintiff was aware that it might not have been due.

(ii) Recompense in quasi-contract

The right to payment of a reasonable sum for goods or services supplied may arise in the following situations:

(a) Where a contract to supply goods or services does not fix the price, the seller/supplier is entitled to a reasonable price/remuneration: see Sale of Goods Act 1979 s.8(2); Supply of Goods and Services Act 1982 s.15 (see Chapter 18, p.447). This also applies where the contract is void for uncertainty.

(b) Where the parties have agreed remuneration under a contract which is void: *Craven-Ellis v. Canons Ltd* [1936] 2 KB 403.

(c) Where the contract has been frustrated.

(d) Where the court ignores the contract price and orders payment of a reasonable sum, for example necessaries have been sold and delivered to a minor: Sale of Goods Act 1979 s.3.

(e) Under the exceptions to complete performance.

(b) Restitutionary remedies in tort

(i) An action for money had and received

The most obvious application is in the tort of conversion, where the defendant derives a benefit from the claimant's property or the proceeds from it. Other cases arise out of the tort of trespass to goods and to land. Thus, in *Oughton v. Seppings* (1830) 1 B & Ad 241, the claimant recovered the proceeds of the sale of a horse which had been wrongfully seized by a sheriff's officer and later sold.

(ii) Restitutionary damages

In *Strand Electric Engineering Co. Ltd v. Brisford Entertainments Ltd* [1952] 2 QB 246, the claimant was awarded damages representing the reasonable hire of property for the period in which it had been wrongly retained and used by the defendant. And in *Penarth*

Dock Engineering Co. Ltd v. Pounds [1963] 1 Lloyd's Rep 359, the claimants won damages assessed on the basis of the benefits derived by the defendant by failing to remove his pontoon from the claimant's dock, by which he became a trespasser. A similar approach was taken in *Swordheath Properties Ltd v. Tabet* [1979] 1 WLR 285, when damages for trespass were calculated on the ordinary letting value of the property.

(iii) Account of profits

This equitable remedy is available for infringements of intellectual property rights, patents, copyrights, trade marks, passing off and breach of confidence (see Chapter 14).

End of Chapter Summary

This chapter has explained the legal and equitable remedies which are available in respect of breaches of contract and torts. After having read and understood the chapter, you should be fully acquainted with the following important points:

- The fact that, in respect of the negligent performance of a contractual obligation, the claimant has the choice of bringing an action for breach of contract or negligence in tort and the reasons for choosing one over the other.
- The distinction between expectation loss and reliance loss arising from a breach of contract and the reasons for claiming under one head or the other.
- The distinction between unliquidated and liquidated damages in the law of contract.
- The doctrine of remoteness of damage in contract as compared to tort.
- The importance of the obligation on the part of an injured party in contract and tort to mitigate its loss.
- The limitation in the law of tort in respect of claims for pure economic loss.
- The equitable remedies in contract and tort.

Most of the material that you learned in this chapter will have application in later chapters, in particular Chapters 18 and 19.

Questions

1. Hal owns a delicatessen and sells his own home-made duck paté. He sold paté to Ian, Jane and Leo and all three became ill with food poisoning. The illness lasted for a week, after which all three made a full recovery. Ian is a retired teacher. He spent the week in bed reading. Jane is a famous actress. She was unable to audition for a starring role in a new musical. The musical, starring another actress, has become a huge hit. Leo is a self-employed salesman who usually earns £1,000 per week from commission.

   Assuming that Hal is in breach of contract, advise him as to the likely measure of his liability.

2. B Ltd agreed to build a warehouse for S. Ltd for £400,000. Under the terms of the contract, the work was to be completed by 31 January. The contract included a term to the effect that, in the event of failure to complete in accordance with the contract, B Ltd would compensate S Ltd at the rate of £1,000 for every day for the first two weeks after 31 January, and thereafter at the rate of £5,000 for every subsequent day of delay.

   The building was completed four weeks late and S Ltd claims the following amount of damages:

Questions cont'd

14 x £1,000 = £14,000
14 x £5,000 = £70,000
TOTAL: = £84,000.

Advise B Ltd of its liability.

3. Angela contracted with Sports Ltd, a publisher, to write a book about the 2008 Olympics for a fixed fee of £20,000. She travelled to the Games, but halfway through the event the publishers contacted her to inform her that they had cancelled the contract. Advise Angela.

4. T Ltd contracted with H Ltd to transport a consignment of video recorders from London to Newcastle: 'to reach the destination on the day of departure from London'. Nothing was said about the ultimate purpose in sending the video recorders to Newcastle, but T Ltd knew that H Ltd ran a hire business. The video recorders were not delivered until four days after leaving London. As a result of the delay, H Ltd lost the profit on the hire of the machines for the four-day period. Advise H Ltd about a possible claim for damages for loss of income.

5. D Ltd is a car dealer selling new and second-hand cars. On 31 January, Fiona agreed with D Ltd to buy a second-hand MG TF for £15,000. On returning home, she found that she had just won a new sports car in a national competition and phoned to cancel the order. Later the same day, D Ltd sold the car to another purchaser for the same price. Advise the dealer of any claim against Fiona.

Part III

Business Organisations

Introduction to Part III

In this part of the book you are introduced to the various UK forms of business organisation as vehicles for carrying on a business. The choice of vehicle is fundamentally important to the would-be entrepreneur, irrespective of the scale of the planned business. The options available to entrepreneurs are discussed in Chapter 6.

At the simplest level, a person can begin to engage in a business activity without any formality whatsoever by trading as a sole trader. However, the downside to set against the absence of formality is that no distinction made between the individual's business and private assets, and in the event of the failure of the business, the private assets can be seized by business creditors and the individual can be made bankrupt.

This unlimited, personal liability for business debts is also a feature of the general partnership, which is a possible choice where two or more persons are going into business together. Once again, there are minimal formalities but disadvantages. The partnership does not have a separate legal existence and the partners have personal liability for the firm's debts and obligations. The position is somewhat different in Scotland where partnerships have a legal personality distinct from that of the members but the partners still have unlimited personal liability for the firms' debts and obligations.

Most people going into business opt for a form which provides the protection of limited liability for business debts, which will tend to result in the formation of a limited liability company. This can be formed by one person and, by the purchase of a ready-made, off-the-shelf company, can be achieved for less than £200 and without delay. There is a single company law code for England and Wales, Scotland and Northern Ireland in the Companies Act 2006. The only differences relate to terminology to take into account the fact that Scotland has a different legal system. There are separate Registrars of Companies for England and Wales and for Scotland and Northern Ireland.

Where there are two or more people involved in the start-up, an alternative form is the limited liability partnership (LLP). This has the advantage of limited liability but otherwise offers many of the advantages of the general partnership. It should always be remembered, however, that limited liability may well be illusory unless the capital base of the company or LLP is sufficiently strong. If the business is undercapitalised, suppliers of goods and services and lenders will generally require the entrepreneur to provide security, usually by way of a mortgage over personal assets. Securing loans against business or the personal assets of the entrepreneur is discussed in Part IV Chapter 15. In effect, in most small family-owned limited liability companies, capital is frequently secured by a mortgage on the entrepreneur's matrimonial home.

Chapter 7 looks in detail at the law relating to general partnerships and LLPs. The general partnership is the oldest form of UK business organisation and widely used. The more recent LLP, based on the model developed in the USA, has, however, become increasingly popular and threatens to replace the general partnership in the future.

In recognition of their position as the first-choice business vehicle, the following three chapters are devoted to the law relating to limited liability companies. Chapter 8 examines the legal significance of the articles of association as the company's constitution and the company's contractual capacity and the contractual authority of the directors.

Chapter 9 deals with raising capital through the issue of shares and Chapter 10 considers the different classes of shares, the rights of shareholders and their protection against unilateral variation of their class rights. It also deals with the important topic of the protection of minority shareholders against any abuse of their position by the company's controllers. Chapter 11 discusses the law relating to the appointment and disqualification of directors and their duties toward the company.

Chapter 12 concerns loan capital and considers the way in which companies can create fixed and floating charges over their assets. Finally, Chapter 13 deals with the topic of corporate insolvency.

Chapter 6

The business forms available under UK law

Learning objectives

After reading this chapter you will know about:

- sole traders, general partnerships, limited liability partnerships and limited companies
- public and private companies
- separate legal personality and the veil of incorporation
- essential differences between general partnerships, LLPs and limited companies

6.1 Introduction

The UK business organisations are **sole traders**, general **partnerships, limited liability partnerships (LLPs)** and **registered companies with limited liability.** For the entrepreneur, the choice of vehicle for carrying on the business is usually determined by the desire to limit their liability in the event of the failure of the business to the amount of the capital invested. This is impossible in the case of the sole trader and the general partnership, where the proprietor and the partners have unlimited liability for the debts of the business. Limited liability protection for entrepreneurs is possible only with LLPs or limited liability companies which are separate legal persons in law. The business is, in effect, carried on by the legal person which is fully liable for the business debts while the partners' or shareholders' liability is limited to their capital investment.

LLPs must not be confused with limited partnerships under the Limited Partnerships Act 1907 which have general partners with unlimited liability who run the business and limited partners with liability limited to their capital contribution but whose protection is lost if they become involved in running the business. This is an obsolete form of business organisation and will not be discussed.

6.2 Sole traders

Proprietors may employ other people, but they have sole responsibility for the success or failure of the enterprise. The business capital is usually raised by bank loans secured by a mortgage on the matrimonial home, life insurance policies or shares. Proprietors have unlimited liability for all business losses, and any legal action in respect of the business is brought against the proprietor.

An individual can carry on trade using his surname with or without his forename or initials. He can also indicate that the business is carried on in succession to a former owner: s.1192 Companies Act 2006. If, however he chooses to trade under a business name, Part 41 of the Companies Act 2006 applies and there are statutory restrictions on choosing a name suggesting a connection with the government or a local authority (s.1193) or which contains sensitive words or expressions for which approval is required: ss.1194 and 1195.

There are also restrictions on using names containing an inappropriate indication of company type or form (s.1197) and one giving a misleading indication of the nature of the business: s.1198. Persons trading under a business name must comply with the disclosure requirements of Chapter 2, Part 41, of the Act and there are criminal and civil consequences for failure to comply: ss.1205 and 1206. Where the person trades under a business name, legal actions will be brought against him in the form 'XY trading as (t/a) Just Desserts'.

Disadvantages of this business form include: (i) limited capital; (ii) limited borrowing; (iii) problems with holidays and sickness; and (iv) limited scope for expansion.

6.3 General partnerships

A partnership is 'the relation which subsists between persons carrying on a business in common with a view of profit': Partnership Act 1890 s.1(1).

Partnerships allow for an increased capital base, improved borrowing and reduce the problems relating to holidays and sickness. They are formed and regulated under the Partnership Act (PA) 1890. There must be at least two persons and the term 'business' includes any 'trade, profession or occupation': s.45 PA 1890. The stipulation relating to carrying on the partnership 'with a view of profit' means that partnerships cannot be used as a vehicle for charitable or non-commercial purposes.

A partnership is not a separate legal person, and partners are jointly liable for the firm's debts and obligations without limit: s.9 PA 1890. They are also jointly and independently liable for torts committed by partners and employees: s.12 PA 1890 – even those who play no part in the management ('sleeping partners'). A partnership is, therefore, unsuitable as a vehicle for a person who wishes to invest in a business without exposure to risk (for a full discussion see Chapter 7).

For taxation purposes, partners are self-employed and are taxed under Schedule D for partnership profits and capital gains from the disposal of partnership assets.

6.4 Limited liability partnerships (LLPs)

The Limited Liability Partnerships Act (LLPA) 2000 created a new, hybrid form between the general partnership and the registered company. An LLP is a body corporate (with legal personality separate from that of its members): s.1(2) LLPA 2000 the members of which enjoy limited liability. It is created by registration at Companies House, and a certificate of incorporation is the birth certificate of the firm. LLPs are regulated by the Companies Act (CA) 2006 in the same way as private limited companies except that there is no statutory management structure. This can be fixed by the partnership agreement.

LLPs were created following pressure from the large firms of accountants and solicitors, where major negligence claims exposed the partners to the risk of major financial loss.

The first LLP to be registered was the large accountancy firm Ernst & Young LLP. Since then, however, a large number of small, non-professional businesses have registered as LLPs. Their popularity is due to the fact that they offer commercial advantages over general partnerships, with enhanced credibility among customers and suppliers. LLPs also have enhanced borrowing powers since they can secure loans by means of a floating charge over their assets like a registered company. The management structure is more flexible than for a registered company and the fact that their accounts must be registered does not appear to have been a deterrent (for full details see Chapter 7).

The registration of an LLP is in accordance with s.2 LLPA 2000 and involves:

(a)   two or more persons associated for the purpose of carrying on a lawful business with a view to profit subscribing their names to an incorporation document;

(b)   delivery to the registrar of the incorporation document or a copy authenticated as required;

(c)   delivery to the registrar of a statement in the approved form, made either by a solicitor engaged in the formation of the LLP or anyone who has subscribed his name to the incorporation document, that the requirement of paragraph (a) has been complied with.

The certificate of incorporation is conclusive evidence that the requirements of s.2 are complied with and that the LLP is incorporated by the name specified in the incorporation document: s.3(4) LLPA 2000.

In a general partnership, the partnership property is jointly owned by all the partners. With regard to an LLP, new ss. 118ZA–118ZD of the Income and Corporation Taxes Act 1988 mean that a trade, profession or business carried on by an LLP shall be treated as if carried on by the members of the LLP in partnership, and the property of the LLP is to be treated as partnership property. The result is that the members of an LLP are taxed under Schedule D, and the LLP itself is not liable to any tax, such as corporation tax. By s.13, the members are also liable to Class 4 national insurance contributions on their share of the profit.

Where an LLP carries on a trade or business, its assets are treated for capital gains tax (CGT) purposes as belonging to the members: 59A Taxation of Chargeable Gains Act 1992. Where it is not carrying on a trade or business, however, the LLP is liable 'as if it were a company' (that is, to corporation tax): s.59A(2). In addition, the property, business, etc. is treated as if the LLP were a partnership and its incorporation, change of membership or dissolution is treated as the formation, alteration or dissolution of a partnership. Any transfer of value by or to an LLP is treated as if made by or to the members as partners: s.267A Inheritance Act 1984.

In an LLP, 'members have such liability to contribute to its assets on winding up as is provided for by virtue of this Act': s.1(4) LLPA 2000. There are no further provisions in the Act, but s.15 allows for regulations to apply any law relating to companies to LLPs. It further provides that the law relating to partnerships does not apply to an LLP: s.1(5) LLPA 2000.

6.5   Registered companies

A company is formed by one or more persons subscribing their names to a memorandum of association and complying with the registration requirements of the Companies Act 2006. They can form an incorporated company, with or without limited liability, and, in the case of a company limited by shares, one which is either public or private: ss.3 and 4 CA 2006.

(a) Unlimited liability companies

Members have unlimited liability for company debts, and companies are exempt from public disclosure through the Annual Return to the Registrar of Companies (ROC), and the annual audit of their accounts.

(b) Limited liability companies

These exist in two forms: the company limited by guarantee, and the company limited by shares.

(i) Companies limited by guarantee

Members agree to contribute to the company's assets on liquidation the amount guaranteed when they became members: s.3(3) CA 2006. Such companies are vehicles for charitable, educational or scientific purposes: the League Against Cruel Sports, the British Ski Club and universities created in the 1990s out of polytechnics.

(ii) Private and public companies limited by shares

These are the usual form of trading company and the only form which can be private or public. The members' liability is limited 'to the amount, if any, unpaid on the shares held by them': s.3(2) CA 2006.

Private companies cannot invite the public to subscribe for shares or debentures (loan stock) (ss.755–760 CA 2006) and are restricted to raising their capital from banks or the sale of shares by private treaty, or members of the families of shareholders or employees. Public companies are those whose Certificates of Incorporation state that they are public companies; all others are private: s.4(2) CA 2006. There is a minimum share capital requirement of £50,000 (or prescribed euro equivalent) for public companies (ss.761–767 CA 2006) and they are subject to greater regulation to protect the investing public.

Differences between public and private limited companies include:

- Private companies have the word Limited (Ltd) as the last word of their name, whereas public companies have the words Public Limited Company (plc).
- Private companies need have only one director, whereas public companies must have at least two: s.154 CA 2006.
- Directors of public companies are to be voted on individually: s.160 CA 2006.
- Private companies are not required to have a company secretary (s.270 CA 2006) but public companies must have a qualified company secretary (ss.271–273 CA 2006).
- Private companies are less strictly regulated, including: restrictions on loans to directors (ss.197–214 CA 2006), and the regulation of the raising and maintenance of capital.
- Disclosure requirements in the annual return are less onerous (s.380 CA 2006) where the private company (or group) is classified as either 'small' (ss. 382–384) or 'medium' (ss.465–467 CA 2006).
- Small private companies may be exempt from the statutory audit of their accounts: s.477 CA 2006.
- Private companies can enjoy deregulation, which enables them to dispense with formal meetings of their shareholders. This is by way of regulations allowing written and elective resolutions: ss.288–300 CA 2006.

Companies are generally incorporated as private companies and they 'go public' when they need access to the financial markets to raise capital. There are two main markets for company securities regulated by the stock exchange. Companies seeking to join the London Stock Exchange's official list must comply with strict requirements regarding capital size, length of trading record and the percentage of shares in public hands, which must be at least 25 per cent. The Alternative Investment Market (AIM) has no restrictions on capital, length of trading record or minimum percentage of shares in public hands. Companies listed on the AIM can apply to join the official list after two years. The vast majority of limited liability companies are private.

(iii) Community Interest Companies

Community Interest Companies (CICs) were created by the Companies (Audit, Investigations and Community Enterprise) Act 2004 and the Community Interest Company Regulations 2005. The CIC aims to meet the needs of organisations which:

- Trade with a social purpose (social enterprises) or carry on other activities which benefit the community; and
- Wish to enjoy the benefits of limited company status; and
- Want to make it clear that they are established for the benefit of the community rather than their members; but
- Are not able, or do not wish, to become charities.

Responsibility for CICs rests with the CIC Regulator who is an independent public office holder appointed by the Secretary of State for Business Enterprise and Regulatory Reform (BERR).

CICs were created following a 2002 report which pointed to a gap in the range of options available to social enterprises which wished to be incorporated as companies. The new framework is to support the social enterprise sector by way of a modern and appropriate legal vehicle to help raise its profile. CICs can be companies limited by guarantee or limited by shares. They are quick and easy to set up because the Regulator provides a model constitution which includes an assets lock. This is a fundamental feature of the CIC and is statutory and cannot be removed. Transparency of operation is ensured by the fact that CICs have to deliver an annual community interest company report about their activities for the public record. The CIC has greater flexibility than a charity in terms of its activities. There are no trustees and directors can receive reasonable remuneration. Regulation is light touch. Further information about the work of the Regulator and CICs can be found at www.cicregulator.gov.uk.

Hot Topic . . .

PRIVATE COMPANIES AS A MAJOR VEHICLE OF CONTROL

Private companies are important in that they are frequently used as the controlling vehicle for large public companies. This enables the controller to exercise enormous power over the group whilst escaping from the regulation and supervision associated with publicly quoted companies. Thus we referred in Chapter 1 to the fact that the ultimate control of Arcadia plc and the Bhs Group is through private companies registered in Jersey: Taveta Investments Ltd and Global Textile Investments Ltd respectively. Similarly, Richard Desmond, controller of the media empire which includes Express

Newspapers, operates the empire through the operating holding company Northern & Shell Network Ltd (N&SN). In 2004, N&SN paid £31m into Richard Desmond's pension as a way of reducing taxes ahead of a government clampdown in 2006. The company paid its founder and chairman a total of £46.2m in 2003. If it were a public company, shareholders would seek justification for the size of the package. But N&SN is a private company with Mr Desmond its only shareholder.

Other well-known examples include the Dyson company, which is wholly owned by Mr Dyson and his family. Mr Dyson and his wife received £17m in dividends in 2003, the year after the company moved production from the UK to Malaysia with the loss of 800 jobs. The public company MG Rover was controlled by Phoenix Venture Holdings Ltd the shareholders in which were four Birmingham businessmen. Originally heralded as saviours of MG Rover, they were later criticised for the way in which the group was reorganised and its ultimate collapse into administration.

The recent popularity of private venture capital has resulted in many large public companies passing into the private sector. One of the best known is Boots Pharmaceuticals.

(iv) Changes in company form

Companies can change from limited to unlimited liability companies and vice versa by means of the procedure in ss.102–104 CA 2006. Only one change is allowed.

Changes of form from a public to private company or vice versa are also possible: private to public under ss.90–96 CA 2006; public to private under ss.97–101 CA 2006. Some public companies do re-register as private companies: an example was Virgin Records Ltd.

(v) Groups of companies: holding and subsidiary companies

A 'group' is the term used to describe a number of related companies. A holding company is at the head of a group of companies, all of which are subsidiaries of the holding company. The relationship between holding companies and subsidiaries may be very complex. 'A company is a subsidiary of another company if that other company

(a) holds a majority of the voting rights in it; or
(b) is a member of it and has the right to appoint or remove a majority of its board of directors; or
(c) is a member of it and alone, pursuant to an agreement with other shareholders or members, controls a majority of the voting rights in it, or if it is a subsidiary of a company which is a subsidiary of that other company' (s.1159 CA 2006).

A 'wholly-owned subsidiary' is one which has no members except that other company and that other's wholly-owned subsidiaries or persons acting on their behalf: s.1159(2) CA 2006.

A holding company must prepare consolidated, group accounts: ss. 399–402 CA 2006. A subsidiary may not be a member of its holding company: s.136 CA 2006; and cannot give financial assistance to persons wishing to buy shares in its public holding company: ss.678–679 CA 2006.

6.6　Registration formalities for registered companies

The formalities for registering a company are laid down in the Companies Act 2006. Under this Act, a company is formed by one or more persons:

(a) subscribing their names to a memorandum of association (s.8), and
(b) complying with the requirements of this Act as to registration (ss.9–13). (s.7(1))

A company may not be formed for an unlawful purpose (s.7(2)).
   A memorandum of association is a memorandum stating that the subscribers:

(a) wish to form a company under this Act, and
(b) agree to become members of the company and, in the case of a company which is to have a share capital, to take at least one share each (s.8(1)).

The memorandum of association must be delivered to the appropriate registrar (s.9(6)) together with a application for registration and the supporting documents required, and a statement of compliance in accordance with s.13: s.9(1) CA 2006. The application for registration must state:

(a) the company's proposed name,
(b) whether its registered office is to be in England and Wales, in Scotland or Northern Ireland,
(c) whether the liability of the members is to be limited and, if so, whether by shares or by guarantee, and
(d) whether the company is private or public: s.9(2) CA 2006.

   For companies having a share capital, there must be a statement of capital and initial shareholdings in accordance with s.10 (see Chapter 9, p.200). For companies limited by guarantee, a statement of guarantee in accordance with s.11; there must also be a statement of the proposed officers in accordance with s.12: s.9(4).

6.7 Registration of company names

This is covered by Part 5 Companies Act 2006. A company must not be registered by a name if, in the opinion of the Secretary of State, its use would constitute an offence, or it is offensive: s.53. In respect of company names and the use of sensitive words and expressions, the approval of the Secretary of State is required for registration of a company by a name which would be likely to give the impression that it was associated with Her Majesty's Government (including Scotland and Northern Ireland), a local authority, or any public authority specified by regulations made by the Secretary of State: s.54(1). In addition, approval is required for a company to be registered by a name which includes a word or expression specified by the Secretary of State in regulations under the section: s.55. In respect of both provisions, the Secretary of State may require the applicant to seek the view of a specified Government department or other body: s.56.

   The name is required to indicate the company type or legal form. Thus the name of a public company must end with 'public limited company' or 'plc' (s.58(1)), while a private limited company must have a name ending in 'limited' or 'ltd': s.59(1). There are exceptions in each case for Welsh companies, which may end with the Welsh equivalent, and for community interest companies (CICs).

   A private company may be exempt from the requirement to have a name ending in 'limited' or 'ltd' if it (a) is a charity, (b) is exempt from the requirement by regulations made by the Secretary of State, or (c) qualifies for continuation of existing exemption for companies limited by shares (s.61) or companies limited by guarantee (s.62). Companies ceasing to be entitled to exemption can be ordered to change their name by the Secretary of State in writing: s.64. The Act also regulates inappropriate use of indications of company type or legal form: s.65.

The company name must not be the same as another in the registrar's index of company names: s.66. The Secretary of State can order the change of a name which is too similar to an existing name (s.67), the order must be within 12 months of the company's registration and specify the period within which the change must be effected, failing which an offence is committed by the company and every officer in default: s.68.

Third parties can object to a registered name if it is the same as, or sufficiently similar to, a name associated with them in which they have goodwill, so that its use in the UK would be likely to mislead the public by suggesting a connection between the company and the third party: s.69. For such cases, the Secretary of State can appoint company names adjudicators (s.70) who, within 90 days of an application under s.69, must make their decision and their reasons for it available to the public: s.72. If an application for a name change under section 69 is upheld, the adjudicator can make an order requiring the respondent company to change its name (s.73) subject to a right of appeal to the court against the adjudicator's decisions: s.74.

The Secretary of State can also order a company to change its name if misleading information has been given for the purpose of registration by a particular name, or an undertaking given for that purpose has not been fulfilled: s.75(1). Directions must be within five years of registration and specify the period within which the company is to change its name: s. 75(2). If the company's name also gives a misleading indication of the nature of its activities, the Secretary of State may order it to change its name within six weeks or any longer period: s.77.

A company may change its name by special resolution or by other means provided for by the company's articles: s. 77(1). In each case, the company must notify the registrar and the resolution must be forwarded to the registrar or the notice must be accompanied by a statement that the change of name has been made by means provided by the company's articles: ss.78 and 79. If the registrar is satisfied that the new name complies with the statutory requirements, he must enter the new name on the register in place of the former name and issue an altered certificate of incorporation: s.80. The change of name is effective from the date on which the new certificate is issued, and the change does not affect any rights or obligations of the company, and any legal proceedings which may have been continued or commenced against it in its former name may be continued against it in its new name: s.81.

The name may also be changed under s.64 (change to comply with the direction of the Secretary of State); s.73 (on the determination of a new name by a company names adjudicator); s.74 (appeal against decision of company names adjudicator); and s.1033 (company's name on restoration to the register). Any change must comply with the requirements of Part 5 of the Act.

The Secretary of State may make regulations requiring companies to display and publicise their names: s.82. The civil consequences for failure to comply with the Secretary of State's disclosure requirements are that any legal action brought by the company arising out of a contract at a time when the company was in breach of s.82 will be dismissed if the defendant shows that he has been unable to pursue a claim against the company, or that he has suffered some financial loss in connection with the contract because of the breach: s.83. There is also criminal liability for breach of s.82 in respect of the company and every officer in default: s.84. Minor variations in form are excluded for these purposes: s.85.

Provisions in the Insolvency Act (IA) 1986 were designed to stamp out the 'phoenix' company. This is where the company controllers place a failed company in liquidation and form a new company with the same or similar name and recommence trading, often on the same premises and with the assets of the failed company, to the detriment of the public. Under these provisions, persons who were directors or shadow directors during the 12 months prior to a company going into insolvent liquidation are prohibited for five years from that date from forming another company with the same or a similar name to that of the failed company unless they have the court's permission: s.216 IA 1986. In the event of breach, the directors are personally liable for the company's debts: s.217 IA 1986.

It was, however, felt that directors would not be in breach of the law if they – through ignorance – 're-used' a company name without any intention to deceive the public. This is not, however, the case which was seen in *Ricketts v. Ad Valorem Ltd* [2003] EWCA Civ 1706. Ricketts was a former director of Air Equipment Co Ltd (AEC) which went into creditors' voluntary liquidation in 1998. He was also director of another company which changed its name to Air Component Co Ltd (ACC) in 1998 and went into creditors' voluntary liquidation in 1999. The assignee of ACC's debts, Ad Valorem, succeeded in an action to make Ricketts personally liable for the debts under s.217. The court held that ss.216 and 217 applied to a wider set of circumstances than merely attempts to exploit the goodwill of a previously insolvent company. It is clear that it can also apply in a group structure where directors sit on the boards of several group companies with indistinguishable names where one goes into insolvent liquidation and they continue as directors of the surviving company or companies: *Thorne v. Silverleaf* [1994] 1 BCLC 637.

In *Churchill and Anor v. First Independent Factors and Finance Ltd* [2006] EWCA Civ 1623 the court held that to avoid personal liability prospective notice had to be given to creditors of the acquisition of an insolvent company by a similarly named 'phoenix' company which was to carry on trading under the same management. In this case the directors had given notice within 28 days of the acquisition in reliance on rule 4.228 Insolvency Rules (SI 1986 No 1925). The court held that notice could not be given retrospectively.

6.8 The registered office

The situation of the registered office establishes the domicile/nationality of the company. The actual address is also supplied on application for registration.

The registered office is the official address at which legal documents, notices and other communications are formally presented. The following statutory books must be kept there and be available for inspection by members free of charge during business hours for at least two hours a day (creditors may inspect the register of charges free of charge and members of the general public may examine the books, subject to some exceptions, on payment of a prescribed fee):

(i)   the register of members;
(ii)   the register of charges;

(iii)   copies of instruments creating registrable charges;
(iv)   the minute books;
(v)   the register of directors and secretary;
(vi)   the register of directors' interests in shares or debentures of the company;
(vii)   the register of debenture holders;
(viii) the register of substantial shareholdings;
(ix)   copies of directors' service contracts;
(x)   accounting records.

If satisfied that the registration requirements are complied with, the registrar (Part 35 CA 2006) registers the documents (s.14) and issues a Certificate of Incorporation in accordance with s.15. This is conclusive evidence of compliance with registration requirements (s.15(4)): *Jubilee Cotton Mills Ltd. v. Lewis* [1924] AC 958.

The registration has the effect that the subscribers to the memorandum and subsequent members are a body corporate 'by the name in the certificate of incorporation': s.16(2). The body corporate is capable of exercising all the functions of an incorporated company: s.16(3).

6.9 The company as a separate legal person: the rule in *Salomon v. Salomon*

In *Salomon v. Salomon & Co. Ltd* [1897] AC 22, S, a manufacturer of boots and shoes, incorporated the defendant company with a registered capital of £40,000 to take over the business. The law required seven subscribers to the memorandum, and S, his wife and five children subscribed, taking one share each. S then sold his business, valued at over £39,000, to the company in return for £20,000 in fully paid shares, £10,000 in cash and £10,000 in debentures secured on the company's assets. When the company collapsed into insolvent liquidation, the liquidator claimed that S should indemnify the company's creditors.

The High Court held that the company had a right of indemnity against S. Since the other signatories were S's nominees, the company was S in another form. He used the company as his agent. The Court of Appeal also held that the company was agent of and trustee for S. The House of Lords held that '[t]he company is at law a different person altogether from the subscribers to the memorandum: and … the company is not in law the agent of the subscribers or trustee for them'. S was not liable to indemnify the company's creditors.

This decision, in effect, recognised the validity of 'one-man companies' ahead of their legal introduction in 1992.

A person can be controller, managing director and also an employee of the company under a separate contract: *Lee v. Lee's Air Farming Ltd* [1961] AC 12. This principle of the 'veil of incorporation' separates the incorporators of a company from the company itself. The veil of incorporation also operates between the companies in a group, so that each company is regarded as a separate legal entity. Thus in *Lonrho Ltd v. Shell Petroleum Co. Ltd* [1980] 1 WLR 627, the claimant failed in an action against the defendant company to obtain disclosure of documents which were held by a subsidiary.

The registered company owns its own property, and no member of the company has any interest in it. The consequences can be unexpected and disturbing.

In *Macaura v. Northern Assurance Company* [1925] AC 619, the claimant, the owner of a large timber estate in County Tyrone, formed a company in which he was the principal shareholder, the other shares being held by his nominees, and transferred his estate to the company. Subsequently, when the timber was destroyed by fire, he claimed against the defendant company under an insurance policy held in his own name. The court held that, as a shareholder and creditor of the company, he had no insurable interest in the timber, which was exclusively the property of the company. In *Tunstall v. Steigman* [1962] 1 QB 593, Mrs S ran a business in one of a pair of shops of which she was the landlord. The other shop was leased to Mrs T. Mrs S sought to terminate Mrs T's lease to expand her own business into the second shop. She had to establish that she needed the premises to carry on a business run by her. She had earlier transferred her business to a limited company, of which she was the controller, and the court rejected her application on the ground that the business was owned and operated by the company and not by her.

There are judicial and statutory exceptions when the corporate veil between the registered company and its members is lifted or pierced. This allows for the separation between shareholders and company, or between parent and subsidiary companies, to be ignored.

(a) Judicial lifting of the veil

In 1985, the Court of Appeal declared that: 'the cases ... show that the court will use its power to pierce the corporate veil if it is necessary to achieve justice': *Re A Company* [1985] BCLC 333. This was rejected, however, in *Adams v. Cape Industries plc* [1990] Ch 433, which rationalised the judicial lifting of the veil. The case concerned an attempt to enforce against the UK registered parent company, Cape Industries plc, an American judgment against its wholly owned subsidiary in the USA. This involved piercing the corporate veil between the two. The court considered the occasions when it would lift the veil under three headings:

(i)   where the companies were a 'single economic unit'
(ii) where one company was a mere 'façade'
(iii) where one company was an agent for the other.

In addition to these three exceptions, there are three other cases where the court will pierce the corporate veil.

(i) Single economic unit

This was restricted to cases involving the interpretation or construction of a statute, contract or other document. In *The Roberta* (1937) 58 Ll L R 159, a parent company was held to be liable in respect of bills of lading signed by a subsidiary, since the subsidiary was a separate legal person 'in name only and probably for the purposes of taxation'. And in *Holdsworth & Co. v. Caddies* [1955] 1 WLR 352, the defendant's claim that, as managing director of the parent company, he could not be ordered to devote his energies solely to the affairs of the subsidiaries since they were separate legal persons was rejected as too technical.

In *Revlon Inc. v. Cripp & Lee Ltd* [1980] FSR 85, where the court was prepared to regard the parent company as proprietor of a trade mark actually registered in the name of a wholly owned subsidiary, the court found that the mark 'is an asset of the Revlon group of companies regarded as a whole'.

The decision in *DHN Food Distributors Ltd v. Tower Hamlets LBC* [1976] 1 WLR 852 involved the statutory interpretation of compulsory purchase compensation provisions. The parent company, DHN, operated a cash and carry business and had two wholly owned subsidiaries. One subsidiary owned the property in which the business was carried on and the other owned the transport. The subsidiary's property was compulsorily acquired and compensation paid to the subsidiary for loss of the freehold. The local authority, however, rejected a claim from DHN for loss of the business, since DHN used the land as a mere licensee and not under a lease. Lord Denning MR stated, 'The three companies should, for present purposes, be treated as one and the parent company, DHN, is that one'. The decision was greatly criticised but its scope has now been limited by the *Adams* case.

(ii) Façade companies

The veil can be pierced where the company is a mere façade to enable the corporators to perpetrate a fraud or avoid the consequences of a valid contractual obligation.

In *Gilford Motor Co. Ltd v. Horne* [1933] Ch 935, H had been employed by the claimant company and was bound by a restraint of trade clause which prevented him from soliciting his employer's clients once he had terminated his employment. On leaving, he attempted to avoid the effect of the clause by trading as a company controlled by nominees. The court held that the company was a sham and the covenant was enforced by way of an injunction against both H and the company.

Another example is *Jones v. Lipman* [1962] 1 WLR 832, where Lipman sought to escape specific performance of a contract for the sale of land by transferring the land to a company.

In *Re FG (Films) Ltd* [1953] 1 All ER 615, the court rejected the company's claim that the film it had made could qualify as a British film. The company had a share capital of 100 £1 shares, of which 90 were held by the US company which financed the film. FG (Films) Ltd was an agent of the American company and the film was an American film. This could be seen as a façade case.

(iii) One company as agent of another

A subsidiary may be the agent of a parent company, but only where there is an express agreement. Agency is not implied merely from the fact that one company controls another.

In the *Adams* case, the court rejected all three grounds. Slade LJ stated that: '[n]either in this class of case nor in any other class of case is it open to this court to disregard the principle of *Salomon v. Salomon & Co. Ltd* [1897] AC 22, merely because it considers it just to do so'. This was restated in *Yukong Line Ltd of Korea v. Rendsburg Investments Corpn of Liberia (No. 2)* [1998] 1 WLR 294, where the judge refused to pierce the corporate veil and find the company controller the undisclosed principal in a charterparty repudiated by the company, where he had frustrated a freezing injunction by transferring the company's assets to another company within his control.

(iv) To identify nationality of company in time of war

The veil is lifted to identify the company's nationality in terms of its dominant shareholders. In *Daimler Co. Ltd v. Continental Tyre and Rubber Co. (Great Britain) Ltd* [1916]

2 AC 307, the Continental Tyre and Rubber Co. was an enemy alien because its shareholders (with one exception) were German nationals resident in Germany.

(v)   To determine residence for the purposes of liability for tax

The company resides at the true place of its management. In *Unit Construction Co. Ltd v. Bullock (Inspector of Taxes)* [1960] AC 351, three companies registered in Kenya were wholly owned subsidiaries of a UK registered company and, since the parent exercised real management control of the subsidiaries, they were 'resident in the UK' for the purposes of the Finance Act 1953 s.20(9).

(vi)   To establish the company's tortious or criminal liability

Where it is necessary to establish criminal or tortious intention, the *identification theory* attributes the intention or knowledge of a person or persons controlling the company to the company.

In *Lennard's Carrying Co. Ltd v. Asiatic Petroleum Co. Ltd* [1915] AC 705, the appellant shipowners were sued for damages for the loss of a cargo in a fire caused when a ship ran aground because its defective boilers made it unseaworthy. A defence existed if the company could show that the loss happened without its 'actual fault or privity'. The House of Lords ruled that fault and privity could be established in respect of a company by establishing the existence of fault or privity in the mind of a person who was 'the directing mind and will' of the company. The company was liable because of the failure of the dominant director to rebut the presumption of liability by establishing that he was not aware of the unseaworthiness of the ship.

Where a corporate landlord was held capable of an intention to occupy premises, Denning LJ stated, 'A company may ... be likened to a human body. It has a brain and nerve centre which controls what it does. It also has hands which hold the tools and act in accordance with the directions from the centre. Some of the people in the company are ... nothing more than hands to do the work ... Others are directors and managers who represent the directing mind and will of the company, and control what it does. The state of mind of these managers is the state of mind of the company and is treated by the law as such': *HL Bolton (Engineering) Ltd v. T. J. Graham & Sons Ltd* [1957] 1 QB 159.

Criminal liability of companies was established for the first time in 1944 when companies were convicted of intent to deceive: *DPP v. Kent and Sussex Contractors Ltd* [1944] KB 146: and conspiracy to defraud, *R v. ICR Haulage Ltd* [1944] KB 551. The identification theory can operate only where the intention is identified at the level of the board, the managing director and other superior officers or people to whom they have delegated full discretion to act independently of instructions. A branch manager was not the company's representative for the purposes of liability for misleading pricing under the Trade Descriptions Act 1968: *Tesco Supermarkets Ltd v. Nattrass* [1971] 2 All ER 127 (see Chapter 21, p.501).

Since there is a statutory penalty of life imprisonment, companies cannot be guilty of murder. They can, however, be guilty of manslaughter: *R v. HM Coroners for East Kent, ex parte Spooner* (1987) 3 BCC 636 (DC). This was established as a point of legal principle in a case arising from the loss of the ferry, *Herald of Free Enterprise*, resulting in the deaths of nearly 200 passengers. Subsequently, P&O Ferries, the ferry operator, and five senior company managers were charged with manslaughter. The prosecution, however, failed to establish the necessary *mens rea* (guilty mind) to establish the guilt of any of the managers. The judge also rejected the prosecution's arguments that the knowledge and intentions of the individual managers should be aggregated to establish the criminal intention of the company. As a result, the case against the company collapsed: *R v. P&O Ferries (Dover) Ltd* (1990) 93 Cr App Rep 72. The first conviction for corporate manslaughter arose from the deaths of four teenagers on a canoeing trip at sea against a company operating an activity centre. The managing director's *mens rea* was established by his failure to heed previous warnings of potential danger by the company's instructors. This criminal intention was then attributed to the company by the identification theory: *R v. OLL Ltd, The Times*, 9 December 1994. This highlighted the fact that it is easier successfully to prosecute a small company than a large one.

Hot Topic . . .

REFORMING CORPORATE MANSLAUGHTER

Following large-scale disasters, such as Zeebrugge, the King's Cross fire and the Paddington and other rail disasters, there was considerable pressure to reform the law on corporate manslaughter. The government's ideas on reform were set out in *Reforming the Law on Involuntary Manslaughter: The Government's Proposals* (2000) which proposed a special crime of corporate manslaughter.

This resulted in the Corporate Manslaughter and Corporate Homicide Act 2007 which came into force on 6 April 2008 and creates a statutory offence of corporate manslaughter (corporate culpable homicide in Scotland).

The offence is concerned with the way in which an organisation's activities were managed or organised and whether an adequate standard of care was applied to the fatal activity. A substantial part of the failing must have occurred at senior management level i.e. those making significant decisions about the organisation or substantial parts of it including those carrying out HQ functions as well as those in senior operational management roles. The identification of senior management will depend on the nature and scale of the organisation's activities. Apart from directors and similar senior management positions, roles likely to be considered include regional managers in national organisations and managers of different operational divisions.

The Act applies to:

▶ Companies incorporated under the Companies Acts or overseas
▶ Other corporations including:
  ▶ Public bodies incorporated by statute: Local Authorities, NHS bodies and a wide range of non-departmental bodies;
  ▶ Organisations incorporated by Royal Charter;
  ▶ Limited liability partnerships
▶ All other partnerships and trade unions and employers' associations if the organisation is an employer
▶ Crown bodies such as Government departments
▶ Police forces.

It does not apply to individual directors, senior managers or other individuals, and it is not possible to convict an individual of assisting in or encouraging the offence: s.18. Prosecutions will be brought against organisations which will be represented in court by their lawyers; individual directors, managers and employees may be called as witnesses. In the case of partnerships, the prosecution will be brought against the firm in the firm's name and any fine will be payable from partnership funds, meaning that partnerships will be dealt with in a similar manner to companies and other incorporated defendants. A parent company cannot be convicted under the Act for failures within a subsidiary, but

the new offence applies to all companies and other corporate bodies operating in the UK, whether incorporated in the UK or abroad. The new offence will also apply to charities and voluntary organisations which are incorporated in or which operate as any other form to which the Act applies.

The Act applies across the UK and the new offence can be prosecuted if the harm occurs:

▶ In the UK
▶ In the UK's territorial waters in incidents involving commercial shipping or leisure craft
▶ On a British ship, aircraft or hovercraft
▶ On an oil rig or other offshore installation already covered by UK criminal law

The Act will not apply to British companies etc responsible for deaths abroad.

The organisation concerned must have owed a 'relevant duty of care' to the victim in respect of systems of work and equipment used by employees, the condition of worksites and other premises occupied by an organisation and products or services supplied to customers. These duties are already owed in the civil law of negligence. Relevant duties are set out in s.2 and include:

▶ Employers' and occupiers' duties
▶ Duties connected to:
  ▶ Supplying goods and services
  ▶ Commercial activities
  ▶ Construction and maintenance work

Using or keeping plant, vehicles or other things.

Duties relating to holding a person in custody.

Statutory duties owed under health and safety law are not relevant duties for the offence although there is a significant overlap between these types of duty. It is for the judge to decide whether a relevant duty of care is owed: s.2(5). In certain circumstances, however, where the person cannot be sued under the law of negligence, the offence will apply where a statute has replaced liability with a 'no fault' scheme for damages, and also where an organisation is engaged jointly in unlawful conduct with another person (e.g. illegal employment) and where a person has voluntarily accepted the risks involved: s. 2(4) and (6).

There are statutory exemptions which mean that the offence will not apply to deaths connected with the management of particular activities. The exemptions are of two types: comprehensive and partial. Comprehensive exemption applies to:

Public policy decisions (s.3(1)), e.g. strategic funding decisions and matters involving competing public interests but not decisions about how the resources were managed.

Military combat operations including potentially violent peacekeeping operations, and dealing with terrorism and violent disorder including support and preparatory activities and hazardous training: s.4.

Police operations dealing with terrorism and violent disorder including support, preparatory activities and hazardous training: s.5(1) and (2).

For partial exemptions, the new offence does not apply unless the death relates to the organisation's responsibility as employer or as an occupier of premises. These partial exemptions include:

Policing and law enforcement activities: s.5(2).

Emergency responses of:
  Fire authorities and other emergency response organisations;
  NHS trusts (including ambulance trusts) – not including duties of care relating to medical treatment other than triage decisions;
  The Coastguard, Royal National Lifeboat Institution and other rescue bodies; the armed forces.

Carrying out statutory inspection work (s.3(3)): child-protection functions or probation activities: s.7.

The exercise of 'exclusively public functions' (s.3(2)):
  Functions carried out by the government under prerogative powers i.e. acting in a civil emergency; and
  Functions which by their nature cannot be independently performed by a private body but require statutory or prerogative authority i.e. licensing drugs or conducting international diplomacy.

Private bodies carrying out public functions are broadly in the same situation in this respect as public bodies. Organisations convicted of the offence can receive:

A fine for which there is no upper limit.

A publicity order requiring them to publicise the conviction and details of the offence as specified by the court.

A remedial order requiring them to address the cause of the fatal injury. This can be made only on the application of the prosecution accompanied by the proposed terms of the order after consultation with the appropriate regulatory authority or authorities: Health and Safety Executive, Office of Rail Regulation, Food Standards Agency or local authority. Organisations failing to take the action set out in the order are liable to prosecution and an unlimited fine can be imposed on conviction.

In England and Wales and in Northern Ireland the consent of the relevant Director of Public Prosecutions is needed before a case can be taken to court. In Scotland all prosecutions are initiated by the Procurator Fiscal. Subject to this, in England and Wales and in Northern Ireland individuals will be able to bring a private prosecution for the new offence.

In England and Wales and in Northern Ireland it is no longer possible to bring proceedings for gross negligence manslaughter against a company or other organisation to which the offence applies. This part of the common law is abolished: s.20. In Scotland, the common law will continue in force and the Procurator Fiscal will determine the appropriate charge to be brought according to individual circumstances.

(b)   Statutory lifting of the veil

The principal statutory exceptions are ss.212, 213, 214 and 217 of the Insolvency Act 1986. Directors can be personally liable to contribute to company debts beyond the limit of any shares which may be held under s.212 (misfeasance), s.213 (fraudulent trading) and s.214 (wrongful trading) (see Chapter 13, p.297). Companies cannot exempt directors from such liability (s.232 CA 2006), but directors may take out insurance against such liability and the company can take out the policy and pay the premiums (s.233), subject to disclosure in the directors' report: s.236. In addition, a copy must be available for inspection (s.237) and members have a right to inspect it without charge and to request a copy on payment of a fee: s.238. Identical provisions apply to LLPs.

Hot Topic . . .

DIRECTORS' PERSONAL LIABILITY

A series of decisions caused fear among company directors of the development of a major tear in the veil of incorporation concerning personal liability of directors for company contracts and negligent misstatements made in the conduct of the company's business.

In *Fairline Shipping Co. v. Adamson* [1974] 2 All ER 967, Game & Meat Ltd, the owner of a cold meat store, failed to keep the store at the correct temperature and Fairline's meat perished. When Game & Meat Ltd went into liquidation, Fairline sued Adamson, the managing director, personally. All correspondence was on A's personal notepaper, and he had indicated that the business was his own. The court held that he was liable since the contract had become his personal contract rather than the company's.

In *Williams v. Natural Life Health Food Ltd* [1998] 1 WLR 830, W had been induced by negligent economic forecasts to buy the health food shop franchise from NLHF Ltd. Following NLHF's liquidation, W sued Mr Mistlin, the sole shareholder and director, personally. The High Court held that M had assumed a personal duty to W because the projections were based on his personal experience. This was in spite of the fact that M had no direct contact with W, all the documents were on the company's notepaper and W believed that he had contracted with the company. The

projections were the work of a company employee.

The Court of Appeal held that an assumption of responsibility could be implied if M had played an important, although behind the scenes, role in preparing the projections. The House of Lords reversed the decision and held that whether a director had assumed personal responsibility depended on an objective test whether 'the director, or anybody on his behalf, conveyed directly or indirectly ... that the director assumed personal responsibility towards the prospective franchisees'. A director has no reason to fear personal liability for the company's misstatements or negligent advice even if, in reality, he was personally negligent, unless he does something leading to a reasonably held belief that he was personally accepting responsibility to the claimants.

In *Standard Chartered Bank v. Pakistan National Shipping Corp.* [2002] UKHL 43, O Ltd agreed to sell bitumen to a Vietnamese buyer, payment being by letter of credit issued by a Vietnamese bank confirmed by SCB. The letter of credit required shipment before 25 October 1993 and presentation of documents before 10 November. Loading was delayed but Mr. Mehra, the managing director of O Ltd, agreed with the shipping agents and the shipowners (Pakistan National Shipping) that

documents with a false shipping date should be supplied. SCB accepted these documents and authorised payment, even though the documents had been presented late. SCB was unable to obtain the money from the Vietnamese bank because it had failed to notice that the documents were not in order and wrongly assumed that it would be able to conceal the late presentation of the documents.

SCB sued PNO and Mr Mehra for deceit, and the court found Mr Mehra personally liable. It distinguished *Williams* on the ground that there had been an assumption of responsibility by Mr Mehra. It was also held that Mr Mehra could not claim contributory negligence by SCB as a defence.

It has been stated that the *Williams* test should be applied in respect of the personal liability of members of an LLP where negligent misstatement leads to economic loss. However, the situation could not arise. Where a member of an LLP is liable for a wrongful act or omission in the course of the LLP's business, the LLP is liable to the same extent as the member: s.6(4) LLPA 2000. The only reason to claim against a member would be where the LLP had become insolvent. However, under s.1(4) LLPA 2000, '[t]he members of an LLP have such liability to contribute to its assets in the event of it being wound up as is provided by virtue of this Act'. It appears that the negligent member could be liable to contribute to the LLP's assets as well as being personally liable under s.6(4).

6.10 Some major distinctions between business organisations

(a) Change in business

General partnerships can carry on any legal business and can change their business activity by agreement. The same is true for LLPs. Companies registered under Companies

Acts prior to the Companies Act 2006 are restricted by the objects clause in their articles (unless they change their constitution and remove the limitation by special resolution: s.21 CA 2006). Companies formed under the Companies Act 2006 have unrestricted objects unless they are specifically restricted: s.31 (1) CA 2006 (see Chapter 8, p.193).

(b) Perpetual succession

Failing contrary agreement, general partnerships are dissolved by the death or bankruptcy of one of the partners or on his giving notice: s.32 PA 1890. They are also terminated by the retirement of a partner: s.26(1) PA 1890. They can also be dissolved by the court on other grounds: s.35 PA 1890. Changes in the company's membership, and even the death of all of the shareholders, has no effect on its existence unless and until it is wound up under the Insolvency Act 1986. This enables its control to change by mergers or take-overs.

(c) Participation in management

All partners in a general partnership have a right to take part in the management of the business: s.24(5) PA 1890.

For an LLP the rights and duties of the members are governed by agreement between the members, or the LLP and its members, which can be made before its incorporation and are binding on it: s.5(2) LLPA 2000. Failing agreement, the relationship is governed by regulations under s.15 by which 'every member may take part in the management'.

The management of a company is delegated to the board of directors. This allows investors to escape managerial obligations but can be a problem where a shareholder wants to be involved, since directors can be removed by ordinary resolution of the general meeting with special notice: s.168 CA 2006.

In *Bushell v. Faith* [1970] AC 1099, three shareholder/directors each held 100 shares. An attempt by two of them to remove the third from the board was frustrated by a provision in the articles that, in the event of a resolution to remove a director, the shares held by that director should, on a poll, have three votes per share as opposed to the normal one vote per share.

This decision is criticised as allowing the promoters of the company to bypass the law relating to the removal of directors by ordinary resolution.

Directors of a quasi-partnership company may claim that their exclusion from management entitles them to petition for the just and equitable winding-up of the company under s.122(1)(g) Insolvency Act 1986: *Ebrahimi v. Westbourne Galleries Ltd* [1973] AC 360; or to petition under s.994 CA 2006 on the ground that the exclusion is 'unfairly prejudicial to the interests of the members', and request the court to order that the member's shares be bought by the other members or by the company under s.996(2)(e) CA 2006 at a value to be fixed by the court (see Chapter 10, p.229).

(d) Public scrutiny

The affairs of a general partnership are private. This is not the case for an LLP or limited liability company. Both are required to notify the registrar of changes of membership, designated members, directors and registered office address. In addition, s.854 CA 2006 applies to companies and LLPs, and they are required to file an annual return to the Registrar of Companies. This is filed at the Companies Registry, to which the public has access.

Another aspect of scrutiny is the need for limited companies to deliver to the registrar for each financial year the accounts and reports required by ss.444–447 CA 2006. The Companies Act specifies reduced filing obligations for small companies and groups of companies (s.444) and for medium-sized companies and groups (s.445) as opposed to other unquoted companies (s.446) and quoted companies: s.447 CA 2006.

Companies are classified as small or medium-sized according to three criteria (shown below), and companies must comply with two out of three every other year to qualify for exemption. The same exemptions apply to groups of companies and LLPs. The criteria are set out in ss.382 and 383 for small companies and ss.465 and 466 for medium-sized companies.

Criteria	Small	Medium
Turnover	£5.6m (net)	£22.8m(net)
	£6.72m (gross)	£27.36 (gross)
Assets	£2.8m (net)	£11.4m(net)
	£3.36m (gross)	£13.68 (gross)
Employees	50	250

However, companies which qualify as small companies under s.382 can claim exemption from the statutory audit. The same provisions apply to LLPs.

This regime does not apply to a small company which is or was within the current financial year a public company, or an authorised insurance company, a banking company, an e-money issuer, an ISD investment firm or a UCITS management company, or a company which carries on an insurance market activity or is a member of an ineligible group as defined in s.384(2): s.384. Medium-sized companies are excluded under similar provisions: s.467.

(e) Entry of new partners or members

Partners in a general partnership need unanimous consent to transfer their partnership share, which makes a partner's share difficult to transfer. For LLPs, no person may be introduced as a member or voluntarily assign an interest in an LLP without the existing members' consent, and Companies House must be notified of membership changes: s.9 LLPA 2000.

For a limited liability company the capital is divided into freely transferable shares, so that potentially there is no control over changes in membership. In practice, however, most small private companies restrict transferability of their shares in the articles of association. This may provide that members must obtain the other members' consent to transfer their shares or that the shares should first be offered to existing members. There may even be an obligation on the other members or directors to buy up the shares: *Rayfield v. Hands* [1960] Ch 1.

A private company's articles will often give directors an absolute discretion to refuse to register share transfers, in which case the court will not intervene unless the power has been exercised in bad faith: *Re Smith & Fawcett Ltd* [1942] Ch 304, with the burden of proof on the person applying for registration: *Charles Forte Investments Ltd v. Amanda* [1963] 2 All ER 940.

(f)   Securing loans

A partnership is restricted to raising loans on the security of fixed charges, whereas companies and LLPs can create floating charges over the whole undertaking or a part of the undertaking, including circulating assets such as stock and book debts (see Chapter 12, pp.261).

(g)   Limits on size

For non-professional partnerships, there is a maximum of 20 partners, but no restriction on the number of shareholders in a registered company, whether private or public. For some 15 types of professional partnerships the limit is removed by statute or regulation. The Department of Trade and Industry (now the Department of Business, Enterprise and Regulatory Reform (BERR)) recommended the abolition of the restriction. There is no limit to the number of members of an LLP.

End of Chapter Summary

In this chapter we have discussed the four main forms of UK business organisation: sole trader, general partnership, limited liability partnership (LLP) and registered company limited by shares, both private and public.
  Having read and understood this chapter, you should be aware of the following important facts:

- The nature of the liability of partners in a general partnership.
- The advantage of trading in a business organisation with a separate legal personality.
- The possibility of the veil of incorporation being lifted where there has been abuse of the corporate form.

The knowledge in this chapter is important in so far as these business organisations recur through the following chapters. In particular, this knowledge will be built on in the succeeding chapters which examine the law relating to general partnerships, LLPs and registered companies.
  The knowledge is also crucial to an understanding of corporate insolvency in Chapter 13.

Questions

1.   'The single most important consequence of incorporation is the separate legal personality which the company acquires' (Mayson, French and Ryan, *Company Law*).
     (i) What are the advantages and disadvantages of a separate legal personality?
     (ii) What judicial and statutory exceptions are there to this rule?

2.   'Ever since the decision in *Salomon v Salomon* … attempts have been made to weaken or lift the veil of incorporation which is drawn over a limited company to protect its identity as an independent entity, distinct and in isolation from the personality of its directors, shareholders or other subsidiary companies. Whilst statutory deviations to the principle of corporate entity exist, these do little to undermine the general principle of corporate personality. As to common law exceptions, it is difficult to perceive in what form they are conceived other than by the generalised and indefinable equitable spirit of fairness and justice'. Discuss.

Questions cont'd

3.   'It is said that the two advantages for a small business of forming a company are the concepts of legal personality and limited liability. In practice, however, for small companies these concepts may prove to be as much of a handicap as a blessing, and in some respects may prove irrelevant.' Discuss.

4.   'The concept of limited liability as we have known it for the past century may soon be a thing of the past when a company goes into insolvent liquidation.' Discuss.

5.   Ben set up a business baking cakes for local restaurants from leased premises. He later formed Just Desserts Ltd to take over the business and was issued with 10,000 £1 shares in consideration of the transfer to the company of the catering business and assets. Ben is the sole shareholder and director. He signed a contract of employment with the company and drew a salary. When the company began to have financial problems and Ben was unable to pay his suppliers, he lent the company £5,000 secured by a floating charge over the company's assets. In a fire at the premises caused by faulty wiring, Ben was injured and the building damaged. Ben's insurance policy on the building and contents was taken out in his name. The company is now in insolvent liquidation.
     Advise Ben:
     (i)   whether he can claim under his policy for the damage to the building;
     (ii)   whether he can claim against the company for compensation for his injuries;
     (iii) of his rights and liabilities in the liquidation.

6.   Paradise Ltd imports furniture from India. Adam is the managing director and there are three other directors. The board decided to set up a retail business and created a wholly owned subsidiary, Indus Ltd, for the purpose. The registered office of Indus Ltd is the same as that of Paradise Ltd and Paradise Ltd is the sole director of Indus Ltd.
     The retail business was initially successful but later traded at a loss and suppliers continued to supply the company only on Adam's assurance that Paradise Ltd would give Indus Ltd financial support. Ultimately, Indus Ltd could not pay its debts as they fell due but continued trading for a further six months when it went into insolvent liquidation.
     Advise the liquidator of Indus Ltd of any common law or statutory liability of Paradise Ltd and its directors for Indus Ltd's debts.

7.   Edna, Fred and Gabor run a business buying and selling antiques as a partnership. They have been advised to form a private company to run the business. They seek your advice on the major differences between their present partnership and the proposed company.
     They are particularly concerned to know:
     (i)   to what extent their liability for the company's debts will be limited;
     (ii)   whether they will be able to exercise the same control over the membership as with a partnership;
     (iii) the extent to which they will have the same right to be involved in the management of the company.
     Advise them.

Chapter 7

Partnerships

Learning objectives

After reading this chapter you will know about:

- ▶ the nature and formation of general partnerships and LLPs
- ▶ the rights and duties of partners
- ▶ the contractual powers of partners
- ▶ the partners' liability for business debts and torts
- ▶ the dissolution of partnerships
- ▶ the liability of members of an LLP

7.1 General partnerships

The characteristics of a general partnership are 'the relation which subsists between persons carrying on a business in common with a view of profit': Partnership Act (PA) 1890 s.1(1). These are: (i) the existence of a business; (ii) which is carried on in common; (iii) with a view of profit.

Partnerships are not organisations with a separate legal personality, a fact which is, however, contradicted by the way in which they are treated in law. Firms can sue and be sued in their own name, but judgments against them are binding on the partners. The Insolvent Partnerships Order 1994 (SI 1994/2421) treats partnerships as legal entities which can enter into arrangements with their creditors in the same way as limited companies (see Chapter 13). In addition, partnerships in Scotland are separate legal entities, but partners do not enjoy limited liability. In *R v. W. Stevenson & Sons* [2008] EWCA Crim 273 the court held that, inasmuch as business activities were conducted in the name of a partnership and the partnership had identifiable assets which were distinct from the personal assets of the partners, there was no reason why a partnership should not be treated for the purposes of criminal law as a separate entity from the partners. It held that the Sea Fishing (Enforcement of Community Control Measures) Order 2000 drew a clear distinction between a partnership and an individual partner and made it clear that a partnership could be independently liable without any liability attaching to a partner unless the offence had been committed with his consent, connivance or due to his neglect. It thereby followed that, where a partnership alone was indicted, any fine could be levied only against the partnership assets and confiscation proceedings could not be brought against the partners' personal assets. As a result, the individual partners had not been convicted and had no standing to appeal against conviction.

Partnership law is contained in the Partnership Act (PA) 1890, and all statutory references in this part of the chapter are to this Act unless otherwise stated. With the exception of s.23, the Act was generally a statement of the law as it existed at the time. All the provisions concerning the rights and duties of the partners can be varied by the consent of the partners, and many other areas can be excluded where a contrary intention is established.

There are no formalities for the creation of the partnership and, while the partners can draw up a formal deed of partnership or written articles, a partnership can be created by oral agreement or implication. In *Walker West Developments v. F J Emmett* [1979] 252 EG 1171, a landowner and a builder entered into a development contract which provided for sharing the profits from the development. The court held that this constituted a partnership. The absence of agreement as to the division of losses was not important, since, in the absence of agreement to the contrary, they would be shared equally under the Partnership Act 1890 provisions.

(a)   Business in common

There must be a shared business activity which includes 'every trade, occupation or profession': s.45. The definition excludes relationships based on joint ownership of property without any common commercial venture: s.2(1). A partnership can be formed, however, for carrying through one transaction.

In *Keith Spicer Ltd v. Mansell* [1970] 1 All ER 462, the defendant and another person intended to set up a company to run a restaurant owned by the defendant. They opened a bank account in the proposed company's name leaving off the word 'Limited'. Goods were ordered on the company's behalf but the company was never formed. The supplier sued the defendant for the goods, claiming that the parties were partners. The Court of Appeal held that they were merely in the process of forming a company but not 'carrying on a business in common with a view of profit'.

There must be at least two persons actively engaged in the business activity. In *Britton v. The Commissioners of Customs & Excise* [1986] VATTR 204, the court refused to recognise a partnership between a husband and wife where the wife merely helped in the husband's business as an aspect of the domestic relationship.

In *Saywell v. Pope* [1979] STC 824, Saywell and Pope were partners and their wives did some work for the firm. In 1973, the firm expanded and the wives took a more active part in the business. The firm's accountant suggested that the four should draw up a partnership agreement; but the agreement was not signed until June 1975. Between 1973 and June 1975, the bank mandate still covered only Saywell and Pope, the creditors and customers were not notified of any change in the firm's constitution, and the wives contributed no capital. A share of the profits had been credited to them for 1973 and 1974 but they had never drawn on them. In April 1973, the significance of joining the firm had been explained to them and they had not objected to liability for the firm's debts. The court agreed with the Inland Revenue that the wives became partners only in 1975 since, prior to signing the agreement, the wives had never acted in the capacity of partners and had never been integrated into the firm.

(b)   With a view of profit

Sharing in the profits of a business is the major test for partnership. Indeed, prior to *Cox v. Hickman* (1860) 8 HL Cas 268, the mere receipt of a share of the profits was sufficient. The case involved a partnership in financial difficulties where the creditors allowed the partners to run the business under their supervision as trustees, taking a percentage of the annual profits until their debts were discharged. The court held that the creditors were not partners in the firm. This is reflected in s.2(3): '[t]he receipt by a person of a share of the profits of a business is *prima facie* evidence that he is a partner in the firm, but receipt of such a share, or of a payment contingent on or varying with profits of the business, does not of itself make him a partner in the business'.

In *Britton v. The Commissioners of Customs & Excise* (1986), the business profits were credited to a joint account which was both a business account and the domestic account from which the wife drew. The court held that '[t]he profit was Mr Britton's and Mrs Britton as his wife had access to it'. Sharing profits did not of itself create a partnership.

In the *Saywell v. Pope* case, the fact that the wives did not draw on the share of profits credited to them was regarded as evidence of absence of receipt of those profits, which required something more than a mere entry in the accounts.

While the sharing of the profits may not itself be sufficient to establish a partnership, the sharing of the losses is strong evidence of such a relationship, but once again not conclusive. It was not a significant factor in *Walker v. Hirsch* (1884) 27 Ch D 460, where the claimant and the defendant had entered into an agreement under which the claimant made a loan of £1,500 to the business and was to be paid £180 *per annum* and receive one-eighth of the net profits and bear one-eighth of any net losses. He served four months' notice to terminate the relationship in accordance with the agreement, and petitioned for the winding-up of the firm as a partner. The court held that he was an employee; this was merely a contract for a loan repayable when he left the firm's employment.

The Act attempts to clarify the position and identifies five particular situations when a partnership will not arise: s.2(3):

(a) The payment of a debt by instalments out of the profits of a business.
(b) Remuneration of a servant or agent by a share of the profits.
(c) Payment to a widow, widower, surviving civil partner or child of a deceased partner of a portion of the profits by way of an annuity.
(d) The advance of a loan to a person engaged or about to engage in any business on a contract that the lender shall receive:
   (i) a rate of interest varying with the profits; or
   (ii) a share of the profits, provided that the contract is in writing and signed by the parties thereto.
(e) Payment to the vendor of a business of a portion of the profits by way of an annuity or otherwise in respect of the sale of the goodwill of the business.

It is important to distinguish between partners and creditors, covered by s.2(3)(a) and (d) above. The first presents no problems but, in respect of s.2(3)(d), the court basically looks to the intention of the parties. In *Re Megavand, ex parte Delhasse* (1878) 7 Ch D 511, D lent £10,000 to a business repayable only on the firm's dissolution. The agreement expressly stated that he was not a partner, but he received a fixed percentage of the profits and had the right to inspect the accounts and dissolve the firm. The court held that he was a partner. The court was influenced by the fact that the 'loan' was the capital basis of the firm.

In *Pooley v. Driver* (1877) 5 Ch D 458, the loan agreement contained a promise by the partners and the lender to observe the covenants of the partnership agreement which gave the lender equal rights with the partners in enforcing the agreement, and this and the profit-sharing made him a partner. In *Re Young, ex parte Jones* [1896] 2 QB 484, Jones and Young entered into an agreement under which Jones would lend £500 to Young to be repaid at the rate of £3 per week out of the profits. Jones was to help in the office, have control over the money he had advanced and be entitled to draw bills of exchange. He also had a right to enter into a partnership within seven months. He was held not to be a partner.

The stipulation in (d) was construed literally in *Re Fort, ex parte Schofield* [1897] 2 QB 495, where Smith LJ said that, 'if the benefit of the section is desired by the lender, then, under the proviso, the contract must be in writing'.

In *Pratt v. Strick* (1932) 17 TC 459, a medical practitioner assigned his practice to someone else on terms that he would live for three months in the house where the practice was carried on and introduce patients, during which time he was entitled to half the profits and liable for half the expenses. The court held there was no partnership; the practice had passed to the purchaser from the date of the assignment.

Persons receiving money under (d) and (e) above are deferred creditors of the partnership: s.3; and will not be repaid their debts unless and until all other creditors of the firm have been paid: s.3, *Re Fort, ex parte Schofield* [1897] 2 QB 495.

The sharing of gross returns can never give rise to a partnership: s.2.(2). In *Cox v. Coulson* [1916] 2 KB 177, the defendant, the lessee of a theatre, made an agreement with the manager of a group of travelling players to present a play in the theatre. The defendant was to provide the theatre and pay for lighting and advertising and receive 60 per cent of the box office receipts. The claimant was injured by a shot during a performance. The defendant was not liable.

7.1 Forming a partnership

(a) Persons who can be partners

A limited liability company can be a partner if authorised by its memorandum of association: *Newstead (Inspector of Taxes) v. Frost* [1980] 1 All ER 363. An enemy alien cannot be a partner.

A minor can be a partner but can repudiate the agreement at any time during minority or during a reasonable period thereafter, but will be unable to recover any money paid under the partnership agreement unless there is a total failure of consideration. In *Steinberg v. Scala (Leeds) Ltd* [1923] 2 Ch 452, the claimant purchased shares in the defendant company, paying money on application and on one further call made by the company. She later repudiated the contract while still a minor and sought to recover the sums already paid. The claim failed as there had been no total failure of consideration.

In *Corpe v. Overton* (1833) 10 Bing 252, the claimant, while a minor, agreed to enter a partnership and deposited £100 as security for due performance of the contract. He rescinded the contract before the partnership came into being and was able to recover the deposit since there was total failure of consideration.

Minors will not be liable for any of the firm's debts during minority but can ratify them on majority: Minors' Contracts Act 1987. Capital invested by a minor can be used to meet the firm's debts. Minors can bind the firm and the other partners as a general agent even though lacking contractual capacity.

People who are of unsound mind can escape from partnership agreements if they can show that they were unsound of mind when they entered into them and that the other partner(s) knew that they could not understand the nature of the agreements. The fact that a partner is unsound of mind is a ground for the other partner(s) to petition for the firm's dissolution.

Hot Topic . . .

SALARIED PARTNERS

Many firms of solicitors have 'salaried partners'. Their names are listed on the stationery but they do not share in the profits. Their position is not covered by the Act. In *Stekel v. Ellice* [1973] 1 WLR 191, Megarry J contrasted people who were employees whose only qualification was being held out as a partner with a situation where there was a partnership deed with all the partners sharing the profits except one who was paid a fixed salary. The person could be a true partner if entitled to a share of the profits on winding-up. He concluded: 'it seems to me that one must in every case look at the terms of the relationship'.

In *Nationwide Building Society v. Lewis* [1997] 1 WLR 1181, Mr Lewis, a solicitor trading as a sole principal, was joined by W as a salaried partner and W's name was added to the letterhead. L handled a matter for the claimant but the final report to them was on stationery with both L's and W's names. W claimed that he was not a partner and not liable for L's negligent acts. The High Court held that the title of salaried partner did not create a partnership and that W was not liable as a partner for L's actions. The court's decision that W was, however, liable under s.14(1) as having been held out as a partner was overruled on appeal (see p.168).

(b) Firm and firm name

'Persons who have entered into a partnership … are … called collectively a firm': s.4. The firm can sue and be sued in its firm name but any judgment is against the partners. Unless the name is a combination of the partners' surnames plus permitted additions, Chapter 1 of Part 41 Companies Act 2006 applies, as does the common law tort of passing off.

The chapter does not prevent individuals carrying on a business in partnership under a name consisting of the surnames of all the partners plus the permitted additions of the forenames or initials of those forenames, or where two or more partners have the same surname, the addition of an 's' at the end of that surname, or an addition indicating that the business is carried on in succession to a former owner of the business: s.1192 CA 2006.

In other cases, there is a restriction on the use of words which might suggest a link with central or local government: s.1193 CA 2006. In addition, it is an offence to carry on business under a name which includes a word or expression specified in regulations made by the Secretary of State: s.1194 CA 2006. By regulations under ss.1193 and 1194, the Secretary of State may require that, in connection with an application for the approval of the Secretary of State, the applicant must seek the view of a specified Government department or other body: s.1195 CA 2006. In either event, the Secretary of State may withdraw any approval by notice in writing: s.1196 CA 2006. Further restrictions apply to names giving an inappropriate indication of company type or form (s.1197) or a misleading indication of activities (s.1198 CA 2006).

Where a partnership is carried out under a business name, meaning a name other than the surnames of all the partners who are individuals or the corporate names of all partners which are bodies corporate (apart from permitted additions), there is a legal requirement to disclose the name and address of each member of the partnership: s.1200 CA 2006. The disclosure is required on all business documents as identified in s.1202 CA 2006. There is an exception in the case of large partnerships of more than 20 persons, subject to certain conditions being met: s.1203 CA 2006. There is also a requirement for disclosure of the information at any business premises: s.1204 CA 2006. There are criminal and civil consequences for breach of these provisions: ss.1205 and 1206 CA 2006. The civil consequences are the power to dismiss legal proceedings on any contract made whilst in breach of the law unless the court is satisfied that it is just and equitable to permit the proceedings to continue: s.1206 CA 2006.

The firm name must not be so like that of an existing business as to cause confusion in the mind of the public.

In *Ewing v. Buttercup Margarine Co. Ltd* [1917] 2 Ch 1, the claimant, who traded in dairy products in the north of England and Scotland as the Buttercup Dairy, successfully obtained an injunction against the defendant company, which was registered in London. Normally the two concerns must also carry on the same business but this is not absolutely necessary. In *Annabel's (Berkeley Square) v. G Schoek (trading as Annabel's Escort Agency)* [1972] RPC 838, the claimant was able to obtain an injunction to prevent the defendants from using their name in a way which would damage the goodwill of its nightclub.

Firm names may consist of the proper names of the partners despite possible confusion with another business, provided goods are not advertised or marked so as to confuse the public. Persons can be prevented from trading under their own name if there is an intention to deceive the public: *Croft v. Day* (1847) 7 Beav 84. Persons may trade under an acquired or 'pet name': *Jay's Ltd v. Jacobi* [1933] All ER 690.

(c) Illegal partnerships

Partnerships can be illegal because of the nature of the business. In *Foster v. Driscoll* [1929] 1 KB 470, shipping alcohol into the USA during prohibition was illegal as it was contrary to the laws of a friendly foreign state. The illegality can also arise from carrying on business without the necessary qualifications or authorisation. In *Dungate v. Lee* [1967] 1 All ER 241, D and L set up in business as bookmakers. Only L had a permit, but D had no dealings with clients. The court held that the law did not require each partner to have a permit. A partnership with more than the legal number of partners is an illegal association. The maximum is 20 for trading partnerships. Solicitors, accountants and stockbrokers are not subject to any limitation, and most other professional firms are also exempt by statutory instrument, including patent agents, surveyors, auctioneers, valuers, estate agents, land agents, actuaries, consulting engineers, building designers and loss adjusters.

7.3 The relationships of partners to persons dealing with them

(a) Partners' power to bind the firm

Under s.5, every partner is an agent of the firm and the other partners for the purpose of the partnership business; and the acts of every partner in the usual way of the business carried on by the firm bind the firm and the partners. There is an exception where the partner has, in fact, no authority in the particular matter, and the person with whom they deal knows that they have no authority, or does not know or believe them to be a partner. For the firm to be liable the act must be:

1. in relation to the partnership business;
2. for carrying on business in the usual way;
3. done as a partner and not as an individual.

In respect of (1), the firm is not bound where a partner 'pledges the credit of the firm for a purpose apparently not connected with the firm's ordinary course of business' unless 'specially authorised by the other partners': s.7. The partner in question is personally liable in such cases.

In respect of (2), where a partner borrowed a sum of money at 60 per cent *per annum* interest instead of between 6 and 10 per cent, the firm was not liable: *Goldbergs v. Jenkins* (1889) 15 VLR 36.

In *United Bank of Kuwait v. Hammoud* [1988] 1 WLR 1051, on the evidence from an ex-president of the Law Society, the Court of Appeal held that it was usual for a firm of solicitors to give a bank undertakings on behalf of a client that the client's money in the firm's account would be transferred to the bank.

If, by agreement between the partners, a restriction is placed on the power of the partner to bind the firm, no act in contravention of the agreement is binding on the firm with respect to persons having notice of the agreement: s.8. This means that partners can bind their firm and the other partners within the scope of their usual authority unless the third party is aware of their restricted authority. In *Watteau v. Fenwick* [1893] 1 QB 346, W supplied cigars on credit to the manager of a hotel, who was expressly forbidden to buy cigars on credit. Since this was within the scope of the manager's usual authority, the defendant was liable.

(b) Actual and usual authority of partners

Actual or real authority is the partner's actual authority under the partnership agreement. Usual or implied authority is that normally attributed by law to persons in the partner's position. It is rare for partnership agreements to set out the partner's actual authority, but common for there to be a statement of restrictions: junior partners may be subject to financial limits when contracting for goods or services.

Usual authority varies according to whether the firm is a trading or non-trading firm. In *Wheatley v. Smithers* [1906] 2 KB 684, Ridley J said, 'trading implies buying or selling' and held that an auctioneer was not a trader. This was approved in *Higgin v. Beauchamp* [1914] 3 KB 1192, where cinema proprietors were held to be a non-trading partnership. The usual authority of partners has been established as follows.

(i) Trading partnerships

In the absence of express prohibitions, the partner is authorised to:

(i)   sell partnership goods;
(ii)   pledge the partnership goods;
(iii)   buy goods on the firm's account;
(iv)   borrow money on behalf of the firm;
(v)   contract debts on behalf of the firm;
(vi)   pay debts on its account;
(vii)   receive and give receipts for debts due to it;
(viii) draw, make, sign, endorse, accept, transfer, negotiate and procure the discounting of negotiable instruments;
(ix)   create an equitable mortgage of the firm's land or buildings;
(x)   engage and discharge employees;
(xi)   retain a solicitor to recover debts due or defend an action against the firm.

In *Mercantile Credit Co. Ltd v. Garrod* [1962] 3 All ER 1103, G was the dormant partner in a business concerned in the letting of garages and repairing cars. The agreement prohibited the buying and selling of cars but the active partner, P, sold a car to the credit company to be let on hire purchase to a customer. P did not own the car and the claimants claimed the £700 paid for it from G. The court held that P had implied authority to sell the car and G was liable.

(ii)　Non-trading partnerships

A partner cannot accept, make or issue negotiable instruments other than cheques and cannot borrow or pledge the partnership property.

(iii)　Acts for which there is no implied authority

Partners, whether in a trading or non-trading partnership, have no implied authority to:

(i)　execute a deed unless authorised by deed;
(ii)　give a guarantee in the firm's name;
(iii)　submit a dispute to arbitration;
(iv)　accept property in lieu of money in satisfaction of a firm debt;
(v)　make their partners partners of another firm;
(vi)　authorise a third person to use the firm's name in legal or other proceedings.

(c)　Partners' liability for debts and contractual obligations

All partners are jointly liable with the other partners for all debts and obligations of the firm incurred while they were partners; and after their deaths their estates are severally liable for such debts and obligations, in so far as they remain unsatisfied, but subject to the prior payment of their separate debts: s.9. This no longer applies in the event of the winding-up of an insolvent partnership (see Chapter 13, p. 300).

Joint liability means interdependent liability with the other partners, but not individual, separate (or several) liability. Joint liability initially gave rise to only one right of action in respect of the firm debt. If this right of action had been used against one or some of the partners only and not against all of them or against the firm, then no further right of action existed against a partner excluded from that action, even though the judgment remained unsatisfied. The position now is that '[j]udgment recovered against any person liable in respect of any debt or damage shall not be a bar to an action … against any other person who is … jointly liable with him in respect of the same debt or damage': s.3 Civil Liability (Contribution) Act 1978. Consolidated actions against all parties are, however, encouraged by way of a 'sanction of cost': s.4.

Persons dealing with a firm usually provide for joint and several liability of partners. Where a partnership bank mandate provides for joint and several liability, the bank can set off credit balances in the partners' personal accounts held at the same bank, even if not at the same branch.

(d)　Liability for torts and other offences

Firms are liable for the general torts of partners: s.10, and for the misapplication of money and property of third persons under s.11. They are also vicariously liable for their employees' torts under the normal common law rules (see Chapter 4, p. 90). Partners are jointly and severally liable for torts committed while they were partners: s.12.

The firm is liable for a wrongful act or omission of a partner acting only (i) 'in the ordinary course' of the firm's business; or (ii) with the co-partners' authority resulting in loss or injury to any person not being a partner. In *Dubai Aluminium Co. Ltd v. Salaam and Others* [2003] 1 All ER 97, the House of Lords held that the words 'wrongful act or omission' were not confined to common law torts and covered the equitable wrong of participating in a breach of trust or fiduciary duty.

In *Hamlyn v. John Houston & Co.* [1903] 1 KB 981, a partner of the defendant bribed a clerk of a rival firm to disclose confidential information, causing loss to that firm. The Court of Appeal held the defendant liable as it was in the ordinary course of business to obtain information about a trade rival even by illegal means. In *Arbuckle v. Taylor* (1815) 3 Dow 160, the partners were not liable where a partner had begun criminal proceedings against the claimant alleging theft of partnership property. This was not within the scope of the firm's activities, even though the case concerned partnership property.

Liability for the criminal acts of fellow partners is not so far-reaching. 'Innocent' partners may be liable for offences by fellow partners under the Consumer Protection from Unfair Trading Regulations 2008 which largely replace the Trade Descriptions Act 1968. Thus, in *Parsons v. Barnes* [1973] Crim LR 537, the other partners were liable where a partner recklessly made a false trade description (see Chapter 21). Partners will be liable for a partner's fraud only in exceptional circumstances. Liability does not extend to 'innocent' partners where the offence was committed by the partner 'on a frolic on his own', where the offence requires a particular *mens rea*, or where the criminal partner has committed one of the more serious offences.

Innocent partners are jointly and severally liable to make good any losses sustained by a third party where a dishonest partner has misapplied the third party's money or property. Liability arises in two cases:

(i) where one partner acting within the scope of his/her apparent authority receives the money or property of a third person and misapplies it, the firm is liable to make good the loss: s.11(a);
(ii) where the firm in the course of its business receives money or property of a third person, and it is misapplied by one or more of the partners while it is in his/her custody: s.11(b).

In practice there is little difference between the two. In *Rhodes v. Moules* [1895] 1 Ch 236, Rhodes mortgaged his property. He was told by a partner in the firm of solicitors that the mortgagees required additional security and handed over share warrants which the partner misappropriated. The firm was liable under s.11(b), since the warrants had been received by the firm in the ordinary course of business. In *British Homes Assurance Corpn Ltd v. Patterson* [1902] 2 Ch 404, the claimant appointed a solicitor in a partnership to act for it in mortgage transactions. The solicitor later notified them that he had taken the defendant into partnership and the firm name was changed. Subsequently the company sent a cheque to the solicitors in the old firm name and, when the cheque was misappropriated, sued Patterson under s.11(a). The court held that he was not liable, since the claimant had dealt with the solicitor in his personal capacity and not as a partner in the firm. In *Cleather v. Twisden* (1884) 28 Ch D 340, trustees deposited bearer bonds with a partner in a firm of solicitors and he misappropriated them. The other partners were held not liable, since it was not part of the business to accept such securities for safe custody. In addition, they did not know of the deposit.

If a partner improperly employs trust property, then the firm is liable to make good the deficiency only if the other partners knew of the breach: s.13.

(e)   Holding out: the liability of the quasi-partner

'Everyone who by words spoken or written or by conduct represents himself, or who knowingly suffers himself to be represented as a partner in a particular firm is liable as a partner to anyone who has on the faith of any such representation given credit to the firm': s.14(1). Mere carelessness or negligence will not, however, constitute holding out: *Tower Cabinet Co. Ltd v. Ingram* [1949] 2 KB 397 (see below, p. 169). Continued use of the old firm name after the death of one of the partners does not make the dead partner liable simply because his/her name is part of the firm name: s.14(2). Retiring partners risk liability if they consciously allow their old association to be treated as if continuing.

In *Bass Brewers Ltd v. Appleby and Another* [1997] 2 BCLC 700, A practised on his own account in Sunderland as a chartered accountant and licensed insolvency practitioner under the firm name Latham Crossley & Davis, which he had the right to use under a 'group management agreement' with others carrying on business in various parts of the UK. A sold a property as a receiver for the claimants, and a cheque payable to the firm was sent to A by the claimant's solicitors. Although initially paid into the client account, it was later transferred to A's overdrawn practice account and never recovered. The claimants obtained a judgment against A and were given the right to enforce the judgment against the members of the group management agreement. They appealed on the ground that A was not a member of the firm and that the money had been received by A in his personal capacity. Alternatively they claimed that, if the money had been received by the firm, the payment into the practice account was a breach of trust for which they could be liable under s.13 only if they had notice of the breach of trust. The court held that they had allowed themselves to be held out as members of the firm and that the cheque drawn payable to the firm and paid into an account in the name of the firm had been received by the firm. The court also held that the money had then been misapplied by A under s.11 and not s.13.

The basis of liability under s.14(1), originally established in *Lynch v. Stiff* (1943) 68 CLR 428, was restated by the Court of Appeal in *Nationwide Building Society v. Lewis and Another* [1997] 3 All ER 498. The court held that a salaried partner of a firm of solicitors was not liable in respect of a negligent report submitted by his employer on a letterhead on which his name appeared as a partner. Liability required evidence that the client relied on the holding out and, although this could be inferred, the burden of proof was on the claimant.

(f)   Liability of incoming and outgoing partners

By retiring, a partner does not cease to be liable for debts or obligations incurred before retirement: s.17(1), and an incoming partner is not liable in respect of debts or obligations incurred before becoming a partner: s.17(2). Novation agreements, however, may release the retiring partner and transfer liability for the debts or obligations to an incoming, replacement partner: s.17(3).

Retiring partners can continue to be liable for post-retirement debts and obligations unless serving actual notice of their departure to existing customers: s.36(1), and constructive notice to potential, future customers by an advertisement in the *London Gazette*: s.36(2). The constructive notice for potential future customers is restricted to people who, although not having previously dealt with the firm, are aware of its existence and the fact that the retiree was a partner: s.36(3). Subsections (1) and (2) do not apply to partners who have died or become bankrupt.

In *Tower Cabinet Co. Ltd v. Ingram* [1949] 2 KB 397, Ingram and Christmas set up a furniture business called 'Merry's' in January 1946. In April 1947, the partnership was dissolved by mutual agreement and Christmas continued to run the business. Ingram notified the firm's bankers of his departure and arranged that Christmas would notify existing clients. No advertisement of Ingram's departure was placed in the *London Gazette*. In 1948, without Ingram's knowledge, Christmas ordered furniture from the claimants, confirmed on a letterhead bearing Ingram's name. The claimants, who had obtained a judgment against Merry's, applied to levy execution against Ingram under ss.14(1) and 36(2). Ingram was not liable under s.36(2), since the claimants did not know him to be a partner before the dissolution; neither was he liable under s.14(1).

7.4 Relationships between partners

The partnership agreement overrides any conflicting provisions in the Act, which operate by default if the agreement is incomplete. The partnership agreement can, however, be changed expressly or by implication: s.19.

In *Pilling v. Pilling* (1865) 3 de G. J. & Sm 162, a father entered into partnership with his two sons. The articles provided that a mill and machinery belonging to the father should not be brought into the partnership and that he should receive 4 per cent interest *per annum* on his capital before profits were calculated. For a period of 10 years, each partner was credited with interest on capital. The court held that this was evidence of a new agreement and the mill and machinery were partnership property.

Variation by implication can apply even to a formal deed of partnership.

7.5 Partnership property

This is held and applied by the partners exclusively for the purposes of the partnership and in accordance with the partnership agreement (s.20) and includes property originally brought in and subsequently acquired property. Land is held on a trust for land under the Trusts of Land and Appointment of Trustees Act 1996.

There is generally no problem in identifying partnership property where the partnership agreement is clear. Failing agreement, the Act provides that there is no presumption that property has been brought into the partnership, but all property bought with the firm's money is deemed partnership property, even if conveyed to or taken in the name of one partner only.

In *Miles v. Clarke* [1953] 1 All ER 779, M, a freelance photographer, joined C as a partner in an existing photography business. The agreement provided for sharing the profits equally and for payment of a salary to M. On winding up the business, M claimed a share of the assets, including premises leased by the defendant and other equipment he had installed. The court held that the lease and other equipment belonged to C, and that M retained the value of his personal goodwill. The stock in trade and other consumable items purchased by the firm were partnership assets.

A writ of execution against partnership property is possible only on a judgment against the firm: s.23(1). A judgment creditor of a partner can, however, apply to the High Court or a county court for a charging order on the partner's interest. A receiver of that partner's share of the profits and any other money coming to him in respect of the partnership can also be appointed: s.23(2). The other partner(s) may redeem the property or, where it is ordered to be sold, purchase it: s.23(3) and apply for the partnership to be dissolved: s.33(2).

7.6 Partners' rights

Section 24 gives rights to partners. Subject to agreement to the contrary:

(1) Partners share equally in the capital and profits of the business and must contribute equally to the losses: s.24(1).

Thus, even where there is an unequal capital contribution, the partners will receive an equal share of the profits and be equally liable for any losses, including losses of capital. For example, A, B and C are partners, A contributes £10,000, B £5,000 and C know-how. If on dissolution the surplus assets after payment of debts are only £6,000, in other words a capital loss of £9,000, A, B and C will each be liable to contribute £3,000. Where one of the partners is insolvent and unable to contribute to lost capital, the position is covered by the rule in *Garner v. Murray* [1904] 1 Ch 57 (below, p.176).

In *Popat v. Shonchhatra* [1997] 3 All ER 800, P and S were partners in leasehold premises in joint names. P's capital contribution was £4,564 (£2,700 as a loan from S); S's was £23,064. The partnership was determined and S continued as sole trader. He acquired the freehold and later sold the business at a profit. P's claim for an equal share in the capital and profits was upheld by the Court of Appeal as, in the absence of any agreement to the contrary, P and S were entitled to equal shares.

(2) Partners must be indemnified by the firm for payments made and personal liabilities incurred for necessary actions taken to preserve the firm's business or property: s.24(2)(a) and (b).

(3) Partners making an advance beyond their capital contribution are entitled to interest of 5 per cent *per annum*: s.24(3).

(4) Partners are not entitled to interest on their capital contributions: s.24(4).

In practice, agreements usually provide for payment of interest on capital and an equal share of the profits.

(5) Every partner may take part in the management of the business: s.24(5).

(6) Partners are not entitled to remuneration for acting in the partnership business: s.24(6).

Remuneration is, in fact, normally paid to working partners before the profits are calculated so that they receive more than non-working partners.

(7) No person may be introduced as a partner without the consent of all existing partners: s.24(7).

(8) Differences as to ordinary matters of partnership business may be decided by majority decisions of the partners, but changes to the partnership business require the unanimous consent of all partners: s.24(8).

(9) Partnership books are to be kept at the place of business, and all partners are to have access to inspect and copy them: s.24(9).

This right can be delegated to a valuer or any other person to whom no reasonable objection could be taken.

Partners cannot be expelled by a majority decision of the partners unless there is an express power to do so: s.25. Where the agreement states that 'if a partner is guilty of misconduct, the others may expel him', the power cannot be exercised by one partner alone: *Re A Solicitor's Arbitration* [1962] 1 All ER 772. Powers of expulsion must be exercised in good faith, but notice of expulsion can be served without a warning or an opportunity to offer an explanation: *Green v. Howell* [1910] 1 KB 846.

7.7 Partners' duties

Partners are in a fiduciary relationship with other partners and contracts between them require full disclosure. The duty is owed to other partners or their legal representatives: s.28. In *Law v. Law* [1905] 1 Ch 140, the claimant succeeded in an action for misrepresentation against the defendant where he had sold his share in the partnership but later discovered that certain assets had not been disclosed. In *Conlon and anor v. Simms* [2006] EWCA Civ 1749 the court held that a prospective partner, in negotiating a partnership agreement, owed a duty to the other negotiating parties to disclose all material facts of which he had knowledge and of which the other negotiating parties might not be aware, and that where the breach of duty was fraudulent a party who had suffered loss as a result of the breach could recover damages in the tort of deceit.

(a) Duty regarding secret profits

Partners must account to the firm for any personal benefit they derive from transactions concerning the partnership property, or use of the partnership property, name or business connection without the other partners' consent: s.29(1). In *Bentley v. Craven* (1853) 18 Beav 75, B and C were partners in a sugar refinery. C bought sugar cheaply and sold it to the firm at the market price. The firm was entitled to C's secret profit.

This provision covers transactions after the dissolution of the partnership by the death of a partner and before the affairs have been wound up: s.29(2).

In *Pathirana v. Pathirana* [1966] 3 WLR 666, the parties were partners in a petrol station in Ceylon. The defendant gave notice determining the partnership, but before the termination date he obtained a new agreement with the petrol supplier, giving himself the sole agency. He continued to trade at the same premises under his own name. The claimant discovered the new agreement and claimed a share of the profits. The Privy Council held he was able to claim under s.29(1).

In *Thompson's Trustee in Bankruptcy v. Heaton* [1974] 1 All ER 1239, T and H were partners holding the lease of a farm. The firm was dissolved by mutual consent and the farm occupied by H, and later by a limited company controlled by H and his wife. On

H's death, T claimed a half-share of the lease, and in the same year H's executors acquired the freehold reversion and later sold the farm. T's trustee in bankruptcy successfully sought a declaration that the executors held the reversion as trustees for themselves and T.

In *Aas v. Benham* [1891] 2 Ch 244, B was a member of a firm of shipbrokers. He assisted in the formation of a shipbuilding company and in that connection used his experience and information as a shipbroker and, from time to time, wrote letters on the firm's letterhead. He was paid a fee and became a director of the company. The other partners' claim for an account of the fee and salary was rejected on the ground that B was permitted to use information gained from the partnership for purposes outside the scope of the business.

This is, however, contrary to *Boardman v. Phipps* [1967] 2 AC 46, where the appellants acted as agents for a trust which held shares in a private company. As a result of information gained as trustees, the agents purchased nearly all the other issued shares in the company without the prior consent of the trustees and, as a result of their management skills, the shares increased in value to the benefit of the trust and themselves. The House of Lords held that the agents were accountable to the trust for the profit made by them since their opportunity for making a profit arose from their position as the trustees' agents. This is consistent with decisions relating to secret profits made by directors (see Chapter 11, p.248).

(b) Duty not to compete with the firm

Partners competing with the firm without the other partners' consent must account to the firm for all their profits: s.30. Agreements usually prohibit competition and it is a ground for expelling the partner or terminating the partnership.

7.8 Rights of assignee of partnership share

If partners assign their partnership share, the assignee is not entitled to interfere in the management of the business, or request any accounts or inspect the books, but only to receive the partner's profit share. Assignees must accept the partners' account of profits: s.31(1). They cannot object to the payment of *bona fide* salaries to partners, even though this reduces their share of the profits: *Re Garwood's Trusts, Garwood v. Paynter* [1903] 1 Ch 236. On the firm's dissolution, assignees are entitled to the partner's share of the assets.

7.9 Dissolution of partnership

(a) Dissolution without a court order

(i) ***By expiration or notice***
Subject to agreement, a partnership is dissolved under s.32 PA 1890:

(1) if for a fixed term by the expiration of that term:
(2) if for a single undertaking by the termination of the undertaking;

(3) if for an undefined time by any partner giving notice to the other or others of his intention to dissolve the partnership.

For a partnership at will (3), the dissolution is effective from the date in the notice or, if not dated, the date of the communication of the notice: *McLeod v. Dowling* (1917) 43 TLR 655. Where the partnership can be terminated 'by mutual arrangement only', one partner serving notice will not effect a termination: *Moss v. Elphick* [1910] 1 KB 846. Once given, notice cannot be withdrawn except with the consent of all the partners: *Jones v. Lloyd* (1874) LR 18 Eq 265.

(ii) By death, bankruptcy or charge

Subject to agreement, every partnership is dissolved by the death or bankruptcy of any partner: s.33 (1) PA 1890. Where one partner has died, the articles frequently provide that the surviving partners may continue the business. Partners can dissolve the partnership where a partner allows his/her partnership share to be charged: s.33(2).

(iii) Dissolution by express provision

An express clause in the agreement may make any event grounds for the firm's dissolution, including unsoundness of mind, physical incapacity, incompatibility and dishonesty (both in connection with and outside the scope of the business).

In *Carmichael v. Evans* [1904] 1 Ch 486, the court held that a junior partner in a draper's firm convicted of travelling on a train without a ticket (on more than one occasion) could be expelled from the partnership where the agreement provided for expulsion for flagrant breach of partnership duties. It was inconsistent with his position as a partner and would adversely affect the firm's business.

(iv) Dissolution by reason of illegality

Partnerships are automatically dissolved if it becomes unlawful for the firm's business to be carried on, because of either the nature of the business or the status of the partners: s.34. In *Hudgell, Yeates & Co. v. Watson* [1978] QB 451, the partnership became illegal on the lapse of a partner's practising certificate as solicitor.

(b) Dissolution by order of the court

The court can dissolve a firm on the application of a partner in the following cases: s.35.

(i) Mental disorder

This power is contained in Part VII of the Mental Health Act 1983, s.94(2).

(ii) Permanent incapacity

This refers to physical incapacity as opposed to incapacity by reason of mental disorder: s.35(b).

(iii) Conduct prejudicial to the business

Where a partner is guilty of such conduct that is calculated prejudicially to affect the business: s.35 (c). In *Essell v. Hayward* (1860) 30 Beav 130, the partnership was dissolved where a partner was liable to criminal prosecution for fraudulent breach of trust, but in

Snow v. Milford (1868) 16 WR 654, an order was refused where a partner in a banking firm was guilty of adultery.

(iv) Persistent breach of partnership agreement

'Where a partner ... wilfully or persistently commits a breach of the partnership agreement, or otherwise so conducts himself in matters relating to the partnership business that it is not reasonably practicable for the other partner or partners to carry on the business with him' (s.35(d)).

(v) Carrying on business at a loss

When the business of the firm can only be carried on at a loss: s.35(e). It must be a practical impossibility for the firm to make a profit: *Handyside v. Campbell* (1901) 17 TLR 623.

(vi) Just and equitable grounds

This includes the breakdown of the relationship between the partners and other such situations. Examples from company law dissolution of quasi-partnerships include *Re Yenidje Tobacco Co. Ltd* [1916] 2 Ch 426, where the court ordered the winding-up of a company where there had been a complete breakdown in communication between the controlling shareholders arising from one party bringing an action for fraudulent misrepresentation against the other. Dissolution takes effect from the date of the court order.

(c) Dissolution by arbitrator

If the articles contain a clause referring disputes to arbitration and the dispute concerns a claim for dissolution, the arbitrator is empowered to dissolve the partnership just as the court might: *Vawdrey v. Simpson* [1896] 1 Ch 166. But the court has discretion to decide whether the matter will be tried or referred to arbitration where one partner brings an action for dissolution: *Olver v. Hillier* [1959] 2 All ER 220 and *Belfield v. Bourne* [1894] 1 Ch 521.

7.10 The consequences of dissolution

The partners have certain rights and may exercise authority in certain respects for the purposes of winding up the firm. On the dissolution of the firm or the retirement of one partner, any partner may publicly notify the same, and may require the other partners to concur in all necessary or proper acts to achieve that purpose: s.37. The authority of each partner continues so far as may be necessary to wind up the affairs of the partnership and complete transactions begun but unfinished at the date of dissolution.

In *Welsh v. Knarston* 1972 SLT 96, a solicitor's firm contracted to sue a third party on behalf of the claimant. The firm failed to perform the contract after it was dissolved, causing the action to become statute-barred. The court found the firm liable for damages for negligence.

Partners will not bind the firm in respect of new transactions (s.38). In *Re Bourne* [1906] 1 Ch 113, Bourne and Grove carried on a partnership business. When Grove died, the firm owed money to its bankers. Bourne continued the business for 18 months. He deposited the title deeds of partnership assets to secure an overdraft in order to wind up the business and later died insolvent. In a dispute between Grove's executors and the bank, the court held that the bank could assume that the dealings were for the purpose of the winding-up of the business. Firms are not bound by the acts of a bankrupt partner unless they have represented themselves or have knowingly allowed themselves to be represented as still being partners of the bankrupt.

Every partner is entitled to have the partnership property applied in payment of the debts and liabilities of the firm, and to have the surplus assets applied in payment of what may be due to the partners, after deducting sums which partners owe the firm. In order to achieve this purpose, partners may apply to the court to wind up the business and affairs of the firm: s.39. The section creates a lien as a personal right against co-partners and their representatives.

Where one partner has paid a premium on entering into a partnership for a fixed term and the partnership is dissolved before the expiration of that term, the court may order repayment of the whole or part of the premium as it thinks just. But the court cannot order the return of any part of the premium if:

(i)   dissolution is wholly or chiefly due to the misconduct of the partner who paid the premium;
(ii) the partnership has been dissolved by agreement containing no provision for return of any part of the premium;
(iii) the dissolution is due to the death of a partner: s.40.

7.11   Treatment of assets on dissolution

(i)   The firm may be sold as a going concern
The sale of a going concern may be to outsiders or the other partners. Where the firm is sold, the purchaser may use the firm name and restrain outgoing partners from using it or soliciting their former customers. Partners are not prevented from carrying on a business in competition with the purchaser, but can be prevented by injunction from soliciting old customers and representing that they are carrying on the actual business sold: *Trego v. Hunt* [1896] AC 7.

(ii) The assets may be divided among the partners
When assets are divided among partners, any partner may use the firm name so long as s/he does not involve his/her former partners in liability. In the event of disagreement about division, the court will order the sale of the business.

(iii) Application of assets on dissolution
Failing agreement to the contrary, assets are distributed as follows:

(i)   by paying debts and liabilities of the firm to non-partners;
(ii) by repaying partnership loans;
(iii) by repaying capital;
(iv) by dividing the residue among the partners in the proportion in which profits were divisible: s.44(b).

If the assets are not sufficient to satisfy creditors, partners' advances and the repayment of capital, the deficiency is to be made up:

(i)   out of profits brought forward from previous years;
(ii) out of partners' capital;
(iii) by the partners individually in the proportion in which they were entitled to share profits.

Where a partner is insolvent and the assets are not sufficient to repay the creditors and partners' loans, this deficiency must be made up by the solvent partners in the ratio in which they were entitled to share profits.

Where the assets are insufficient to repay partners' capital, then each partner must contribute in the proportion in which s/he shares profits, except that where a partner is insolvent, the other partners need pay in only their own share and the insolvent partner's portion of the deficiency falls on the solvent partners in the ratio of their last agreed capitals: *Garner v. Murray* [1904] 1 Ch 57.

Consider, for example, A, B and C who are partners. Last agreed capital was £6,000, £4,000 and £700. After repayment of debts there is a balance of £8,000: that is, a capital deficiency of £2,700. There is therefore a liability of each partner to contribute £900. C is insolvent and cannot pay and he loses his right to £700, but there is still a deficiency of £200. The loss of this £200 is divided between A and B in proportion to their last agreed capital. Therefore A loses £120 and B £80. A receives £4,980 and B £3,020.

7.12 Profits made after dissolution but before winding-up

Where, after the dissolution of the firm or retirement of one of the partners, the surviving or continuing partners carry on the business of the firm with its capital or assets before any final settlement of accounts, the outgoing partner or his estate is entitled to:

(i)   such a share of the profits made since dissolution as the court finds to be attributable to the use of his share of the partnership assets: see *Pathirana v. Pathirana* [1966] 3 WLR 666 and *Popat v. Shonchhatra* [1997] 3 All ER 800 (above); or
(ii) interest at 5 per cent *per annum* on the amount of his share: s.42(1): *Manley v. Sartori* [1927] 1 Ch 157.

7.13 Rescission of partnership agreement

Where the agreement is rescinded on the ground of fraud or misrepresentation of one of the parties, the injured party is entitled:

(i)   to a lien on the surplus assets of the firm for any sum of money paid by him/her for the purchase of a share in the partnership and any surplus capital contributed by him/her;
(ii) to be subrogated to the rights of the creditors of the firm for any payment made by him/her in respect of the firm's liabilities; and
(iii) to be indemnified by the guilty person against all the debts and liabilities of the firm: s.43.

7.14 Dissolution of insolvent partnership

The Insolvent Partnerships Order 1994 (SI 1994/2421) provides that the partnership is wound up as an unregistered company under Part V of the Insolvency Act 1986 (see Chapter 13, p. 300). Partners are now liable for disqualification under the Company Directors Disqualification Act 1986.

7.15 Limited liability partnerships (LLPs)

The Limited Liability Partnerships Act (LLPA) 2000 created a completely new type of organisation. The LLP is a hybrid between the existing general partnership and the limited liability company. There must be at least two members of the firm but there is no legal maximum.

LLPs are corporate bodies and their members have full limited liability; however, the business and property of the firm remain those of the members. The LLP is created by registration at Companies House, resulting in the issue of a certificate of incorporation. There is no requirement to register a written partnership agreement so that the details of the relationship of members and their rights and duties remain private. As for the general partnership, there is no need for a written partnership agreement.

The Limited Liability Partnerships Regulations 2001 (SI 2001/1090) provide that LLPs are subject to the same rules as a private limited company for the registration of accounts at Companies House and for the auditing of their accounts. The exemptions which apply to small and medium-sized private limited companies apply to LLPs: reg. 3. The remaining provisions of the Companies Act 2006 and the Company Directors Disqualification Act 1986 are also extended to LLPs: reg. 4. The Insolvency Act 1986 is also extended to LLPs: reg. 5 (see Chapter 13, p. 272).

Unlike with the private limited company, no fixed management structure is imposed on LLPs. There are no statutory provisions for general meetings, directors, company secretary, share allotments and so on. These matters are entirely regulated by the partnership agreement. In the absence of any agreement, implied terms regulate the rights and duties of the members.

(d) Choice of name

Rules concerning the names of LLPs are contained in Schedule 1 to the Act. The name must end with either the words 'limited liability partnership' or the letters 'llp' or 'LLP', or their Welsh equivalents. The other rules regulating the acceptability of the chosen name are equivalent to those applicable for registered companies.

An LLP can change its name at any time. There is no equivalent to the procedural requirements for obtaining approval for this change of name, but the change must be notified to Companies House by one of the designated members and is effective from the moment the registrar issues a change of name certificate. The same regulations apply on change of name as applied on initial registration, and the change of name of the LLP does not affect its rights or the rights of third parties.

The Secretary of State may also order an LLP to change its name as in the case of registered companies. It is a criminal offence for anybody other than an LLP to use the term 'limited liability partnership' on any contract.

All changes to the registered information about the LLP must be notified to Companies House, including changes in membership, the identity of the designated members and the address of the registered office.

(e)   Membership of an LLP

The initial members are the subscribers to the incorporation document: s.4 LLPA 2000. Subsequently, other persons can become members subject to the agreement of the existing members in accordance with the partnership agreement. In the absence of any contrary provision in the partnership agreement, no person may be introduced as a member without the consent of all existing members. A person may cease to be a member in accordance with any agreement with the other members or, in the absence of such agreement, by giving reasonable notice. The use of the term 'person' in respect of membership means that a company can be a member of an LLP.

At least two members of the LLP must be named as 'designated members', who accept responsibility for sending information to Companies House for registration: s.8 LLPA 2000. If Companies House is not notified of the identities of the designated members, all the members are designated members: s.8(2). The designated members may be changed from time to time by notification on the prescribed form.

In place of the concept of the 'shadow director' of company law, there is instead the concept of the 'shadow member' with similar consequences in respect of the LLP (see Chapter 11, p. 236).

(f)   Relationship of the members to each other

The Act provides that, except as far as otherwise provided by the Act or any other enactment, the mutual rights and duties of the members of an LLP, and those of the LLP itself and its members, are governed by agreement between the members, or between the LLP and its members: s.5 LLPA 2000. These agreements can be made prior to incorporation of the LLP and made binding on it: s.5(2) LLPA 2000. In the absence of such an agreement, the relationship between the members shall be governed by provisions in regulations made under s.15. This is broadly the equivalent of the implied terms provided by s.24 Partnership Act 1890 in respect of a general partnership.

The mutual rights and duties of the members and the mutual rights and duties of the LLP and the members shall be determined subject to the provisions of the general law and to any agreement, express or implied, between the members, or between them and the LLP, by the following rules:

1. All the members are entitled to share equally in the capital and profits of the LLP.
2. The LLP must indemnify every member in respect of payments made and personal liabilities incurred by him:
   (a) in the ordinary and proper conduct of the business of the LLP; or
   (b) in or about anything necessarily done for the preservation of the business or property of the LLP.
3. Every member may take part in the management of the LLP.
4. No member shall be entitled to remuneration for acting in the business or management of the LLP.

5. No person may be introduced as a member or voluntarily assign an interest in an LLP without the consent of all existing members.
6. Any difference arising as to ordinary matters connected with the business of the LLP may be decided by a majority of the members, but no change may be made in the nature of the business of the LLP without the consent of all members.
7. No majority of the members can expel any member unless a power to do so has been conferred by express agreement between the members.
8. The books and records of the LLP are to be made available for inspection at the place of business of the LLP (or the principal place if there is more than one) and every member of the LLP may, when he thinks fit, have access to and inspect and copy any of them.
9. Each member shall render true accounts and full information on all things affecting the LLP to any member or his legal representative.
10. If a member, without the consent of the LLP, carries on any business of the same nature as and competing with the LLP, he must account for and pay over to the LLP all profits made by him in that business.
11. Every member must account to the LLP for any benefit derived by him without the consent of the LLP from any transaction concerning the LLP, or from any use by him of the LLP property, name or business connection.

(g) Members' fiduciary duties

Even though it is not expressly stated in the legislation, since the LLP is a corporate body its members will owe fiduciary duties to it. In the absence of any statutory provision to that effect, it is unclear whether the members of the LLP will owe a duty of good faith to each other. After consultation, the DTI decided not to impose a general fiduciary duty by regulations on either the LLP or the members of it.

(h) Minority protection

No mandatory buyout procedures for a minority member have been included in the legislation, although it is possible for such provisions to be included in any partnership agreement.

The unfair prejudice remedy under s.994 Companies Act 2006 is extended to include LLPs, subject, however, to the possibility that the provision may be expressly excluded by the partnership agreement. This would extend not only to the initial members of the LLP but to members joining at a later date.

(i) Members as agents

The Act, in a similar provision to s.5 Partnership Act 1890, provides that every member of an LLP is an agent of it, but the LLP is not bound by anything done by a member if the member had no authority to act and the person he is dealing with either knows that fact or does not know or believe him to be a member: s.6 LPPA 2000.

Where persons cease to be members of an LLP, a person dealing with the LLP can regard the ex-member as still being a member unless he has had notice of the fact, or the cessation of membership has been notified to Companies House.

(i) Conversion of a general partnership into an LLP

This will involve a conversion process similar to that of converting a general partnership into a limited liability company. There will have to be a transfer of the partnership assets from the partners to the LLP, but there is a provision to the effect that no stamp duty is chargeable in respect of the transfer where the members of the LLP are the same as the original partners of the general partnership, and they hold the assets in the same proportions (or different proportions provided this is not to avoid liability to tax or stamp duty): s.12 LLPA 2000.

There is no statutory provision for the conversion of an LLP into a limited liability company.

End of Chapter Summary

Having read and understood this chapter you should have a detailed knowledge of the law relating to general partnership and be aware of the advantages of the LLP format which threatens to replace it. Of particular importance are the following:

▷ The lack of formalities involved in the creation of the general partnership and the tests used by the court for determining whether a partnership exists.
▷ The significance of the provisions of the Partnership Act 1890 as a default constitution regulating the rights and duties of the partners to each other in the absence of specific agreement in a separate partnership agreement.
▷ The contractual authority of individual partners to bind the firm and the other partners and the nature of the contractual and tortious liability of partners.
▷ The fact that all partners – whether sleeping or active partners – share the same contractual and tortious liability renders the partnership form unsuitable for someone who simply wants to invest without exposure to risk.

The knowledge gained from this chapter will be further developed in Chapter 13 concerning corporate insolvency since insolvent partnerships are now subject to the same insolvency procedures as registered companies.

Questions

1. The distinction between partners and creditors of a firm can be very fine, and some creditors, even though not partners, will, as a result of the nature of their relationship with the firm, be deferred creditors in the liquidation of the firm. Who are these deferred creditors?

2. The articles of an accountancy firm impose a limit on a partner's authority to bind the firm of £4,000. Partner P contracts in the name of the firm to buy (i) a relevant software package for £7,000; and (ii) £1,000-worth of golf clubs. Is the firm liable on these contracts?

3. Partners are jointly liable for the debts and obligations of the firm, and jointly and severally liable for the firm's torts. What is the significance of joint, or joint and several liability?

4. In what circumstances is a person liable as a quasi-partner or an apparent partner, and what is the difference between them?

5. Gwen and Vernon formed a general partnership. The partnership agreement contained a clause to the effect that Vernon would have the power to introduce into the partnership any of his children on their attaining the age of majority. Vernon's daughter, Halima, is 18 and Vernon wishes to bring her into the firm as a partner. Gwen refuses to consent. Advise Vernon.

Questions cont'd

6. Jane and Jamil carry on business in common designing and making exclusive millinery under the name Hats A'hoy! in premises owned by their brother, Austin. On starting up the business they were lent a large sum of money by Diana, a friend and client. The loan agreement provides for repayment of principal plus 7 per cent interest *per annum* out of the profits. In the event of the profits falling below a certain level in any year, the agreement provides that Diana will receive a nominal payment in place of the interest. Diana is very artistic and she regularly dresses the windows of the business against no payment.

The business is now unable to pay it debts. Advise Jane, Jamil, Austin and Diana on their liability for the business debts.

7. Blown Dry is a firm of hairdressers with three partners: Bloggs, Khan and Kant. Advise on the following matters.
   (a) The articles say that a partner cannot borrow money on the firm's behalf. Bloggs, without obtaining authority, borrowed £10,000 from Y Bank for the firm's business. The loan has not been repaid, and Y Bank seeks advice on whether the firm and the other partners are liable for the debt.
   (b) Khan retired from the firm to be replaced by Shah. The firm failed to serve notice to its existing clients of the change in the partnership and place an advertisement in the *London Gazette*. Jake Paxton, an old client, had a perm and tint at the premises and his hair was ruined. He is a well-known TV presenter and successfully sued the firm for £50,000 damages. The firm has no insurance. Against whom can Jake enforce the judgment?
   (c) When the partnership was created, Bloggs owned the leasehold business premises. On Khan's retirement, Khan claimed a share of the value of this property. Advise him.
   (d) The firm closed down following Jake's legal action. After payment of the debts, there was not enough money to return the capital in full. Bloggs had put in £9,000, Shah £7,000 and Kant £2,000. The capital remaining was £6,000. Kant is bankrupt. Advise how the capital will be distributed.

Chapter 8

Registered companies: constitution and contracts

Learning objectives

After reading this chapter you will know about:

▶ the articles of association and their constitutional role
▶ contractual capacity of companies: *ultra vires* and unauthorised contracts

Each part of the chapter is followed by questions on the relevant topics.

8.1 Company law in the UK

There is a single company law code for England and Wales, Scotland and Northern Ireland in the form of the Companies Act 2006. The only differences relate to terminology to take into account the fact that Scotland has a different legal system. The Scottish Parliament has no competence to legislate in respect of company law (Scotland Act 1998 ss.29 and 30 and Schedule 5). There are separate registrars of companies (ROCs) for England and Wales, Scotland and Northern Ireland.

The Companies Act 2006 is the result of an extensive review which began in November 1992 when the Department of Trade and Industry (DTI) (now the Department of Business Enterprise and Regulatory Reform (BERR)) established working groups for each aspect of company law. These working groups produced a number of consultation documents available at: www.open.gov.uk/cld/condocs.htm. Particular topics were referred to the Law Commission and the Scottish Law Commission, and their consultation papers and reports can be consulted at the Law Commission's website: www.open.gov.uk/lawcomm.

A more extensive review began in March 1998 and reported in June 2001. The Company Law Review Steering Group produced a first consultation document, *Modern Company Law for a Competitive Economy: the Strategic Framework* (URN 991654) (London: DTI, 1999). The document summarised the overall approach (para. 2) as follows:

> The objective is a modern law supporting a competitive economy, in a coherent and accessible form, providing maximum freedom for participants to perform their proper functions, but recognising the case for high standards and for ensuring appropriate protection for all interested parties. Account needs to be taken of current change, particularly globalisation, the impact of the EU's company law harmonisation programme, modern patterns of regulation and ownership, changing asset structures and the importance of small and closely held businesses. In principle there should be presumptions:
>
> ▶ against interventionist legislation and in favour of facilitating markets, including provision for transparency of information, wherever possible;
> ▶ in favour of minimising complexity and maximising accessibility of the rules – complexity should only arise where the substance demands it; and
> ▶ in favour of allocating jurisdiction to the most suitable regulatory bodies, avoiding duplication and effort.

The final report was published in July 2001 (*Modern Company Law for a Competitive Economy: Final Report* (URN 011942 and 011943) (London: DTI, 2001)). One recommendation was that there should be a permanent Company Law and Reporting Commission to keep company law and governance under review and to submit an annual report to the Secretary of State (*Final Report*, vol. 1, paras 5.21–5.37).

Hot Topic . . .

COMPETITION BETWEEN EUROPEAN COMPANY LAW REGIMES

There are no plans for a uniform company law in Europe and there are significant differences between the company law systems of the Member States. This means that entrepreneurs could effectively choose between the systems on offer throughout Europe.

In Case C–212/97 *Centros Ltd v. Erhvervs- og Selskabssfyrelsen* [1999] ECR I–1459, two Danish citizens registered Centros Ltd in the UK. The intention was that the company would not trade in the UK but through a branch in Denmark. They chose the UK because there is no minimum capital requirement for private companies, whereas under Danish law companies must have a minimum registered capital of DKr200,000 (about £20,000). The Danish authorities refused to register the company's Danish branch on the ground that this would enable the couple to evade Danish law. The European Court of Justice held that the refusal to register the branch contravened Article 43 EC Treaty, which prohibits restrictions on the freedom of establishment of nationals of one Member State in the territory of another Member State. Article 48 also requires companies or firms formed in accordance with the law of a Member State, and having their registered office, central administration or principal place of business within the EU, to be accorded the same rights of freedom of establishment as natural persons who are nationals of Member States.

It remains to be seen whether the result of this decision will be a movement of the incorporation of private companies away from countries imposing minimum capital requirements: France, Austria, Denmark and Germany. Whilst there has been no sign of a Member State setting out to become a European Delaware by designing its company law to make it attractive to incorporators, France has reformed its company law since 1999 to counter the threat of French companies reregistering in more liberal countries, inside and outside the EU.

8.2 The constitution of a UK registered company

The company's constitution was previously divided between the memorandum of association (external aspects) and the articles of association (internal aspects, including the balance of power between the board of directors and the general meeting).

Under the Companies Act 2006, references to a company's constitution include:

(a) the company's articles, and
(b) any resolutions and agreements to which Chapter 3 applies (see s.29): s.17 CA 2006.

The resolutions and agreements referred to include:

▶ any special resolution;
▶ any resolution or agreement agreed to by all the members that would not otherwise have been effective unless passed as a special resolution
▶ any resolution or agreement agreed to by all the members of a class of shareholders that would not otherwise have been effective unless passed by a particular majority or in some particular manner;

▷ any resolution or agreement that effectively binds all members of a class of shareholders though not agreed to by all those members; and

▷ any other resolution or agreement to which Chapter 3 of Part 3 of the Act applies.

(a) The articles of association

Companies must register articles of association (s.18(1)) contained in a single document divided into consecutively numbered paragraphs: s.18(3). The Secretary of State can set out model articles (s.19) which may be adopted in whole or in part: s.19(3). As previously, if no articles are registered, or in so far as they do not exclude or modify the model articles, the model articles apply by default: s.20. The current model articles are contained in Table A of the Companies (Tables A to F) Regulations 1985 as amended. There is a set of articles for public companies limited by shares and another set for a private company limited by shares. The latest versions came into operation on 1 October 2007. Where reference is made to the articles throughout this text, it will be to the default articles under Table A.

The articles regulate the rights and duties of the members and the administration of the company and deal with:

▷ share capital and variation of rights;
▷ liens and calls on shares;
▷ transfer and transmission of shares;
▷ forfeiture of shares;
▷ conversion of shares into stock;
▷ reduction of capital;
▷ general meetings;
▷ proceedings and voting rights at general meetings;
▷ power of general meeting over the board;
▷ appointment, retirement, rotation and disqualification of directors;
▷ powers of the board of directors, and delegation of powers;
▷ proceedings of directors' meetings;
▷ the company secretary.

(b) Alteration of the articles

Articles can be amended by special resolution (s.21(1)). They may also be changed by a unanimous informal decision of the members: *Cane v. Jones* [1980] 1 WLR 1451, and private companies may alter their articles by resolution in writing signed by or on behalf of all the members entitled to vote: ss.288–300.

Prior to the Companies Act 2006, when the company's constitution was split between the memorandum of association and the articles of association, in addition to the clauses required by statute, other clauses could be stated to be unalterable and thus embedded in the memorandum. This would not have been possible if they had been included in the articles since all individual articles could be varied or removed by special resolution under s.9(1) CA 1985. Under the Companies Act 2006, 'entrenched provisions' can now be included in the articles to allow companies the same possibility to embed provisions in their constitution.

The company's articles may contain provisions ('provision for entrenchment') to the effect that specified provisions of the articles may be amended or repealed only if conditions are met, or procedures are complied with, which are more restrictive than those applicable in the case of a special resolution: s.22(1). Provisions for entrenchment may be made in the articles only on formation, or by an amendment of the articles agreed to by all the members: s.22(2). Provision for entrenchment does not, however, prevent amendment of the articles by agreement of the members, or by order of the court or other authority having power to alter the company's articles: s.22(3). The registrar of companies must be notified of provisions for entrenchment and also of their removal: s.23.

Companies formed under earlier companies legislation are subject to s.28, which provides that provisions in the company's memorandum are to be treated as provisions of the company's articles, including provision for entrenchment for embedded clauses: s.28(3).

In respect of the alteration of non-entrenched provisions, amendments must not:

▷ Conflict with the Companies Act, e.g. directors removable only by special resolution.
▷ Be illegal.
▷ Deprive members of statutory protection (variation of class rights).
▷ Force members to take/subscribe for more shares or increase liability to contribute without written consent, and
▷ Be an abuse of majority power.

Where the proposed alteration constitutes a variation of class rights, it cannot be made under s.21(1), but only in accordance with s.630 which requires alteration in accordance with a variation provision in the company's articles (s.630(2)) or, where there is no such provision, if the holders of shares of that class consent to the variation either by (i) consent in writing of the holders of three-quarters of the issued shares, or (ii) a special resolution at a separate class meeting: s.630(4)

The most important restriction on companies' freedom to alter their articles is where the court decides that the alteration is not *bona fide* for the benefit of the company as a whole but is an abuse of majority power.

The court may reject an alteration as an abuse of majority power unless it is 'bona fide for the benefit of the company as a whole': *Allen v. Gold Reefs of West Africa Ltd* [1900] 1 Ch 656. The court will intervene only where the majority has acted in bad faith and applies a subjective test to decide whether the shareholders honestly believed they were acting in good faith in the company's interests. In *Shuttleworth v. Cox Bros. & Co. (Maidenhead) Ltd* [1927] 2 KB 9, the court approved an alteration to the effect that a director should resign on a written request of all his co-directors, stating: '[t]he only question is whether or not the shareholders ... honestly intend to exercise their powers for the benefit of the company'.

In *Greenhalgh v. Arderne Cinemas Ltd* [1951] Ch 286, the company's articles contained a pre-emption clause which prevented shares being transferred to a non-member so long as there was a member willing to buy them at a fair value. The majority shareholder wished to sell to a non-member and a resolution was passed allowing a transfer to any person if sanctioned by an ordinary resolution. The court held that the special resolution was valid. Evershed MR stated: 'it is now plain that "bona fide for the benefit of the company as a whole" means ... that the shareholder must proceed upon what, in his honest opinion, is for the benefit of the company as a whole [and] the phrase "the company as a whole" ... means the corporators as a general body' and 'a special resolution of this kind would be liable to be impeached if the effect of it were to discriminate between the majority shareholders and the minority shareholders, so as to give the former an advantage of which the latter were deprived'.

In *Clemens v. Clemens Bros Ltd* [1976] 2 All ER 268, the court held that a scheme by the majority shareholder holding 55 per cent of the shares to increase the capital with the effect of reducing the stake of the other shareholder from 45 per cent to below 25 per cent was not for the company's benefit. In such cases the most usual remedy is for the minority to petition for unfair prejudice under s.994 (see Chapter 10, p. 229).

(c) The company's right to limit its statutory powers

In *Punt v. Symons & Co. Ltd* [1903] 2 Ch 506, the articles gave the founder sole power to appoint directors and, after his death, gave the power to his executors. In a separate contract the company agreed that this provision could not be altered. The court held that companies could not restrict their members' right to alter the articles by contract. Where, however, the alteration is in breach of contract, the injured party may sue for damages.

In *Southern Foundries (1926) Ltd v. Shirlaw* [1940] AC 701, Shirlaw was appointed managing director for a term of 10 years, with the articles allowing premature removal of a managing director 'subject to the provisions of any contract between him and the company', and providing that if he ceased to be a director he would automatically cease to be the managing director. Later, new articles were adopted which allowed for the removal of a director by a written instrument signed by two directors and the secretary. Shirlaw was removed from the board under the new articles and succeeded in an action for damages for breach of an implied term in his contract that he would not be removed as director during the period of his appointment as managing director. The court stressed, however, that Shirlaw could not have obtained an injunction.

In *Cumbrian Newspapers Group Ltd v. Cumberland & Westmorland Herald Newspaper & Printing Co. Ltd* [1986] BCLC 286, an agreement by a company not to alter its articles could not be implied. In this case the defendant sought to remove under s.9(1) CA 1985 (now s.21(1) CA 2006) provisions in its articles that, for as long as the claimant held 10 per cent of its shares, it could appoint a director and had pre-emption rights on any share issue. The rights were held to be class rights of the claimant alterable only under s.125 CA 1985 (now s.630 CA 2006) by the claimant's written consent or approval at a class meeting.

(d) Binding effect of company's constitution

The provisions of a company's constitution bind the company and its members as if there were covenants on the part of the company and each member to observe those provisions: s.33(1). Money payable by a member to the company under its constitution is a debt due to the company which in England and Wales is of the nature of an ordinary contract debt: s.33(2). The constitution is enforceable by:

▶ Company against member
▶ Member against member
▶ Member against company *in respect of membership rights.*

The articles are not subject to normal contractual rules. They are not subject to rectification: *Scott v. Frank F. Scott (London) Ltd* [1940] Ch 794, and mistake and duress do not apply. In *Bratton Seymour Service Co. Ltd v. Oxborough* [1992] BCLC 693, the court held that terms could not be implied into articles to give effect to intentions of members.

In *Equitable Life Assurance Soc v. Hyman* [2000] 3 All ER 961, however, the House of Lords held that an implied term should be read into the appellant society's articles. The relevant article (art. 65) gave the directors a wide discretionary power to pay bonuses on its members' policies, and, in exercise of this power, the directors had paid some policy holders a larger bonus than others, contrary to 'guarantees' given when certain members took out their policies. Lord Steyn said that the articles should be read as containing an implied term that the directors would not exercise their discretion 'in a manner which deprived the guarantees of any substantial value'. This was described as being a 'purely constructional' implied term.

(i) Rights enforceable by the company against a member

In *Hickman v. Romney Marsh Sheepbreeders' Association* [1915] 1 Ch 881, the company's articles provided that disputes between the company and its members should be referred to arbitration and the court ordered a stay of proceedings where a member brought an action against the company.

In *Beattie v. E. & F. Beattie Ltd* [1938] Ch 708, however, an application for a stay of proceedings on an action brought by a director was rejected, since the arbitration clause applied only to company disputes with members, whereas this was a dispute in the claimant's capacity as director.

(ii) Rights enforceable by a member against another member

In *Rayfield v. Hands* [1960] Ch 1, a private company's articles provided that 'every member who intends to transfer shares shall inform the directors who will take the said shares equally between them at a fair value'. The court held that the articles bound the directors as members, and this was a personal obligation which could be enforced by other members directly.

(iii) Members' limited rights of enforcement against the company

Members can enforce their membership rights including their right to vote: *Pender v. Lushington* (1877) 6 Ch D 70, and their right to be paid a dividend in cash: *Wood v. Odessa Waterworks Co.* (1889) 42 Ch D 636. It has also been held that they can enforce their constitutional rights to have the company run through the proper organs. Thus, in *Re H R Harmer Ltd* [1958] 3 All ER 689, the claimants, who were shareholders and directors, could enforce their rights as members for the company to be run by the board and not by simple diktat by the founder, thus indirectly enforcing their rights as directors.

Members cannot, however, sue to enforce purely outsider rights contained in the articles. In *Eley v. Positive Govt. Sec. Life Assurance Co.* (1876) 1 Ex D 88, the claimant could not enforce an article that he should be solicitor to the company for life, even though he was a shareholder. This artificial limitation has been criticised, but is still generally accepted.

The definition of outsider rights extends to directors' salary rights contained in the articles. However, if directors take office in reliance on remuneration provisions in the articles, the term may be enforceable as an implied term in their contracts of service: *Re New British Iron Co.* [1898] 1 Ch 324. Where a person is appointed a managing director under a separate contract, there may be an implied term that they will not be removed as director during the period of the contract: *Nelson v. James Nelson & Sons Ltd* [1914] 2 KB 770; and *Southern Foundries (1926) Ltd v. Shirlaw* [1940] AC 701. Where provisions are an implied term in the contract of service, however, they can be altered under s.21(1) but not retrospectively: *Swabey v. Port Darwin Gold Mining Co.* (1889) 1 Meg 385.

(e) Shareholder agreements

The articles may be supplemented by a shareholders' agreement – usually a formal contract entered into at the time of the company's formation or subsequently – between all the current members, which restricts the use of shareholder agreements to small companies. The company may be a party, but the risk is that it may be held to have illegally fettered its statutory powers.

In *Russell v. Northern Bank Development Corporation* Ltd [1992] 3 All ER 161, soon after its incorporation in 1979 an agreement was made between the five shareholders and the company that no further share capital would be issued without each party's consent. In 1988, the board proposed an increase in capital by way of a rights issue. The House of Lords held that the agreement was binding on the claimant's fellow shareholders (although not on the company itself).

Even if the company is not a party, it may be able to rely on the agreement as a defence. In *Snelling v. John G Snelling Ltd* [1973] QB 87, the shareholders had lent the company money and had agreed that none of them would require repayment while certain other funding arrangements were in place. The court refused to allow a shareholder to sue for repayment in breach of the agreement.

The shareholder agreement may be to the effect that:

▸ each shareholder is entitled to appoint a director
▸ no shareholder shall vote for alteration of articles or capital unless all members agree;
▸ shareholders will not demand repayment of loans to the company except in certain circumstances.

The advantages of shareholder agreements are:

▸ they cannot be altered by majority vote or special resolution (cf. articles)
▸ they are, in principle, enforceable as of right – where appropriate by injunction (rights under the articles may not be enforceable by minority).

Courts may imply the existence of a shareholders' agreement. Thus, in *Pennell Securities Ltd v. Venida Investments Ltd* (25 July 1974, unreported), the directors proposed a rights issue, knowing that the claimant (with a 49 per cent shareholding) could not take up the issue, so reducing his holding to below 10 per cent. The court granted injunctions against the violation of a tacit agreement between the members that the claimant's minority stake should remain at 49 per cent.

In *Re A & BC Chewing Gum Ltd* [1975] 1 All ER 1017, an agreement that a corporate investor with one-third of the capital should have a 50-50 say in management was enforced in equity under the ruling in *Ebrahimi v. Westbourne Galleries Ltd* [1973] AC 360, but should have been enforced as a legally binding shareholder agreement.

If shareholders enter valid agreements restricting or determining the way in which they exercise their voting rights, these may be enforced by mandatory injunction. In *Greenwell v. Porter* [1902] 1 Ch 530, the defendants agreed to do all in their power to secure the election of two named persons as directors and vote for their re-election. They later tried to oppose the re-election of one of the two. The court restrained them from voting against the terms of their agreement.

A disadvantage of shareholder agreements is that they are binding on immediate parties only, and not on persons becoming shareholders later. In *Greenhalgh v. Mallard* [1943] 2 All ER 234, it was stated: '[i]f the contract ... only imposes an obligation to vote in respect of whatever shares the parties happen to have available, it follows that directly they sell their shares the contract is at an end ... in the hands of the purchaser there can be no question of a continuing obligation' (Lord Greene MR at p. 239).

Shareholder agreements are standard practice for joint ventures and management buyouts.

(f) Avoidance of rules on restriction of statutory powers

In reality there are ways in which companies can avoid the rules against restricting their statutory powers. In the *Russell* case, the court held that, although the agreement could not impose a restriction on the company, it could operate validly as a shareholder agreement under which shareholders agreed that they would never support a resolution to increase the company's capital. Similarly, as in the *Cumbrian Newspapers* case, provisions can be rendered invariable by being designated as class rights. Rights can also be entrenched by the use of 'weighted' voting, as in *Bushell v. Faith* (see Chapter 6, p.155). Banks wanting to prevent companies to which they have made loans from reducing their share capital while the loans are outstanding can provide that the loans are repayable if the company calls a meeting to consider such a reduction.

Hot Topic . . .

THE EUROPEAN PUBLIC LIMITED LIABILITY COMPANY – *SOCIETAS EUROPAEA* (SE) AND THE PROPOSED EUROPEAN PRIVATE COMPANY – *SOCIETAS PRIVATE EUROPAEA* (SPE)

(a) The *societas europaea* (SE)
From 8 October 2004, it has been possible to register a societas europaea (SE) in any Member State. The SE gives companies operating in more than one Member State the option of being established as a single company under EU law rather than establishing separate operating subsidiaries in each Member State in which they carry on business. This enables them to operate throughout the EU with one set of rules and a unified management and reporting system, rather than those of all the different national laws of each Member State in which they have subsidiaries. For companies active across the internal market, the SE offers the prospect of reduced administrative costs and a legal structure adapted to the internal market as a whole.

SEs will be primarily governed by a Council Regulation, supplemented by a Directive on worker participation. They will, however, be registered in the registries of the Member State in which they are incorporated and subject to national legislation. The legal position of SEs is regulated in the UK by the European Public Limited Liability Company Regulations 2004 (SI 2326). SEs can be set up in one of four ways:

▶ Merging two or more existing public limited companies from at least two different Member States;

▶ Forming an SE as a holding company for public or private limited companies from at least two different Member States;
▶ Forming an SE as a subsidiary of companies from at least two different Member States;
▶ Transforming a public limited company which has had a subsidiary in another Member State for at least two years.

An SE is a European public limited liability company with a share capital of at least €120,000. It must be registered in the Member State where it has its administrative head office. The EC Regulation provides detailed requirements in respect of the SE's board structure, the transfer of its registered office and employee involvement, but otherwise it is governed by the laws applicable to public companies in the Member State in which it is registered. UK registered SEs are subject to UK rules on tax, intellectual property, maintenance of capital, insolvency, accounting, directors' liabilities and pensions.

The potential advantages of SEs are:

▶ They facilitate cross-border mergers or functioning as joint venture vehicles for pan-European projects;
▶ They can transfer their registered offices to another Member State;
▶ One has the choice of a one- or two-tiered board structure – management board and supervisory board;
▶ Increased participation of employees.

(b) The proposed European Private Company – *societas private europaea* (SPE)

On 25 June 2008, the European Commission presented a proposal for a Statute on a European Private Company (SPE) to enable small and medium-sized enterprises (SMEs) to do business throughout the EU, with the aim of cutting costs and encouraging growth in this area. The SPE has been designed to address the current onerous obligations on SMEs operating across borders, which need to set up subsidiaries in different company forms in every Member State in which they want to do business. The SPE would mean that SMEs can set up their company in the same form whether they do business in their own or in another Member State. The proposal will be submitted to the European Parliament and Council.

End of Topic Summary

Having read and understood this part of Chapter 8, you should have a sound understanding of the significance of the articles of association and the way in which they regulate the operation of the company.

In particular, you should have knowledge of the following matters of particular interest:

▷ The restrictions, both statutory and judicial, on changing the company's constitution and the binding nature of the articles on the company and the members;
▷ The way in which the constitution can be drafted to prevent directors being removed and to protect the interests of specific investors;
▷ The significance of separate shareholder agreements.

These issues are of significance in the day-to-day running of a company.

Questions on the company constitution

1. The Companies Act 2006 provides that a company may alter its articles of association by special resolution: s.21(1). What restrictions are there on this power? Illustrate your answer with references to decided cases.

2. 'The articles of association form a contract between a company and its members. This contract is, however, an unusual one, limited both in its scope and permanence.' Discuss.

3. The articles of Module Limited contain the following clauses:
   (i) Norman should have the right to nominate a director;
   (ii) Olive should be the company secretary for life;
   (iii) The company's sales manager shall receive an annual bonus equal to 5 per cent of the company's profits.

Paul, the majority shareholder, has just sold his 75 per cent holding of shares to Quentin who proposes to alter the articles so that all the directors should be appointed by the general meeting and that the annual bonus payable to the sales manager shall be reduced to 2 per cent. He also intends to appoint Frieda as company secretary. The sales manager has a contract with the company which makes no provision for the payment of any bonus. Norman has a contract with the company stating that the company will not alter its articles so as to affect his rights without his consent.

Advise Quentin.

4. Under s.17 Companies Act 2006, references to a company's constitution include the company's articles and any resolutions and agreements to which Chapter 3 applies.

In this context, analyse the reference to resolution and agreements, and any other agreements which impact on the company's constitution.

8.3 Company contracts

This section is concerned with three types of company contract: pre-incorporation contracts, contracts beyond the company's capacity and contracts beyond the authority of the directors. All three topics were regulated by the Common Law until the law was radically reformed by the First Company Law Directive 68/151/EEC, [1968] JO L65/8. This resulted in legislation to transpose the Directive into company law beginning with the European Communities Act 1972 and continuing up to and including the Companies Act 1989. The legal position has been drastically changed in the Companies Act 2006 as regards contracts beyond the company's capacity, but is unchanged in respect of contracts beyond the directors' authority, in spite of the fact that the post-1989 position was, in some respects, unsatisfactory. The statutory material is in Part 4 Companies Act 2006: 'A Company's Capacity and Related Matters', ss.39–52.

8.4 Pre-incorporation contracts: s.51

Prior to the issue of the certificate of incorporation, the company has no contractual capacity and cannot be bound by pre-incorporation contracts negotiated on its behalf. In addition the company cannot 'by adoption or ratification obtain the benefit of a contract purporting to have been made on its behalf before the company came into existence': *Natal Land Co & Colonization Ltd v. Pauline Colliery and Development Syndicate Ltd* [1904] AC 120.

At common law, the person signing as agent on behalf of company was personally liable on the contract: *Kelner v. Baxter* (1866) LR 2 CP 174. The position was complicated where the contract purported to be executed by the non-existent company, in which event the contract was void: *Newborne v. Sensolid (GB) Ltd* [1954] 1 QB 45.

This was the position until the implementation of Article 7 Council Directive 68/151/EEC ([1968] JO L65/8) in s.9(2) European Communities Act (ECA) 1972. This was superseded by s.36C CA 1985 as amended by the Companies Act 1989. The law is now contained in s.51 CA 2006 which provides for the personal liability of 'the person purporting to act for the company or as agent for it' unless otherwise agreed: s.51(1). This applies (a) to deeds in England and Wales or Northern Ireland, and (b) to 'the undertaking of an obligation' in Scotland: s.51(2).

Section 9(2) ECA 1972 was applied in *Phonogram Ltd v. Lane* [1982] QB 938 where the defendant signed a contract in the name of a company which he intended to form but which was never incorporated. The Court of Appeal rejected defence arguments on the basis of the French text of the directive which appeared to limit its effect to companies in the process of being formed.

The provision was held not to apply to a situation where a company traded under a new name before the change of name became operative: *Oshkosh B'Gosh Inc v. Dan Marbel Inc. & Craze* [1989] BCLC 507. In *Badgerhill Properties Ltd v. Cottrell* [1991] BCLC 805 it was held not to apply where a company had been incorporated but had been described by an incorrect name. In another case, the defendant had contracted in the name of W Ltd unaware that the company had been previously struck off the register of companies in 1981 under s.652 CA 1985. A new company, W Ltd, was incorporated in 1989 to continue the business. The court held that the defendant could not be personally liable under s.36C because he had purported to make the contract on behalf of the old company. No one had thought of forming the new company at the time of the making of the contract: *Cotronic (UK) Ltd v. Dezonie* [1991] BCLC 721.

In *Rover International Ltd v. Cannon Films Ltd* [1989] 1 WLR 912, the Court of Appeal held that the common law position still applied to companies registering outside GB (in this case Guernsey).

The English text of Article 7 does not use the word 'contract' but refers to an 'action', which is wider in scope than the word 'contract'. The Article also presupposes the company's right to ratify pre-incorporation actions since the personal liability of the agent or the person purporting to act for the company arises only if 'the company does not assume the obligation arising from such action'. UK law does not allow for ratification by a company of pre-incorporation contracts.

It is doubtful whether the Article has been fully implemented except in Scotland. In England, Wales and Northern Ireland, s.36C CA 1985 (now s.51) was extended to apply to quasi-contract: *Hellmuth,Obata & Kassabaum Inc. v. Geoffrey King*, 29 September 2000, unreported.

While the provision clarified the position on the enforceability of pre-incorporation contracts, it did not cover the question of the identity of the person able to enforce it. This matter was addressed in *Braymist Ltd v. Wise Finance Co Ltd* [2001] EGCS 35. The claimant company contracted to sell land to the defendants on 28 January 1993 but it was incorporated only on 5 March 1993. At the time of the contract, the property was owned by Plumtree Ltd., a wholly owned subsidiary of Pique Holdings plc, in which Colin Pool held 75 per cent of the shares. Braymist Ltd was a wholly owned subsidiary of Plumtree Ltd. Mr. Pool instructed the solicitors to sign the contract 'as Solicitors and Agents' for Braymist Ltd. The purchasers claimed that they were not bound by the contract since Braymist had not been incorporated at the time, but the court held there was a binding contract under s.36C. The court further held that only the solicitors qualified as the 'deemed contracting vendor' with the power to enforce the contract.

The position is further complicated by the Contract (Rights of Third Parties) Act 1999, which allows a non-party to enforce a term of the contract in certain circumstances, provided that person is sufficiently identified.

By s.1(1) and (3) of the Contract (Rights of Third Parties) Act 1999, a contract may be enforced by a person who is not a party to it if 'the contract so provides or the contract purports to confer a benefit on him, and the contract expressly identifies that person by name ... or as answering to a particular description', whether or not the person is in existence when the contract is entered into. This would allow the company to claim the benefit of a contract signed on its behalf (see Chapter 3, p.54).

8.5 Contracts beyond the company's capacity

The topic of contracts beyond the company's capacity – *ultra vires* contracts – has had a long and glorious history in English company law since the decision in *Ashbury Railway Carriage & Iron Co v. Riche* (1875) LR 7 HL 653, which provided that contracts outside a company's objects were illegal, void and unratifiable. Over the following years, this led to lawyers drafting the objects of a registered company to extend their scope in an attempt to bypass the doctrine.

The effect of these drafting innovations led to an extended objects clause where, in a series of sub-clauses, companies' objects were extended to cover all manner of trading activities, including powers which had previously been left to be implied: the power to borrow etc. The court attempted to prevent this development by means of the identification of the company's main object and granting a winding-up petition against companies which had abandoned their main object. The main object was often identified as being the first object in a series of sub-clauses relating to separate objects, and often by reference to the corporate name. This was ruled out following the decision in *Cotman v. Brougham* [1918] AC 514, which recognised the validity of an additional sub-clause making each separate object in each sub-clause an equal and independent object and excluding identification of a 'main object' by reference to the corporate name.

Following the decision in *Bell Houses Ltd v. City Wall Properties Ltd* [1966] 1 QB 207 a subjective objects clause was added to the effect that – in addition to the objects listed – the company could carry on any other trade or business which 'in the opinion of the directors' could be carried on alongside the other business of the company. By the mid 20th century, the doctrine of *ultra vires* caused problems in only a limited number of cases.

A further decision in *Re Horsley & Weight Ltd* [1982] 3 All ER 1045 allowed for the company's objects to include non-commercial objects: charitable donations, *ex gratia* payments etc. In the absence of a clause covering non-commercial activities, *ex gratia* payments, political and charitable donations had to be incidental to the company's business: *Evans v. Brunner, Mond & Co.* [1921] 1 Ch 359; *Parke v. Daily News Ltd* [1962] 2 All ER 927; *Simmonds v. Heffer* [1983] BCLC 298. The position regarding political donations is now specifically regulated (Part 14, ss.362–379), as are *ex gratia* payments to employees and ex-employees: s.247 CA 2006.

Under the changes introduced by the Companies Act 1989, companies could, as an alternative to the complex, multi-objects clause, be registered with the object 'to carry on a business as a general commercial company', in which case the objects allowed the company 'to carry on any trade or business whatsoever', and 'to do all such things as are incidental or conducive to the carrying on of any trade or business': s.3A CA 1985. This allowed the company to change its business activities without the need to change its objects.

The Companies Act 2006 adopts an entirely new approach to the company's objects which the government says 'amounts to the removal of all that remains of the old *ultra vires* rule': *Modernising Company Law* (Cm 5553-1, 2002, part III, para. 5).

Companies formed under the Act have unrestricted objects unless the objects are specifically restricted by the articles. This means that unless a company takes a deliberate decision to restrict its objects, the objects will have no bearing on what it can do. Charitable companies will still need to restrict their objects (under charities legislation) and some community interest companies (CICs) may choose to impose a restriction.

The new position is covered by s.31(1) CA 2006. Companies incorporated under previous companies legislation will still operate under their old constitutional provisions (now regarded as part of the articles: s. 28) unless they change them into unrestricted objects under s.21(1).

8.6   Contracts beyond the powers of directors to bind the company

The company's constitution may also impose restrictions – particularly financial restrictions – on the power of its directors to bind the company. If such limitations were breached, the result at common law was that the contract could be avoided by the company. Since there was no provision for personal liability of the director – other than breach of an implied warranty of authority – the position was that third parties dealing with the company were in a vulnerable position.

The common law protection in that event lay in the rule in *Turquand's Case* and the doctrine of ostensible authority.

(i)   The rule in Turquand's Case – indoor management rule

The rule applied to protect outsiders where the articles allowed individual directors to enter contracts on the company's behalf subject to obtaining prior approval by a board resolution or ordinary resolution of the general meeting. The outsider was entitled to assume that the director had complied with the internal management rules of the company and obtained the necessary approval: *Royal British Bank v. Turquand* (1856) 6 E & B 327. The rule operated for other officers and executives as well as directors subject to the fact that persons claiming protection had to:

(a) Be outsiders and not insiders: *Hely-Hutchinson v. Brayhead Ltd* [1968] 1 QB 549.
(b) Have dealt with the company's agent within the limits of their usual authority: *Kreditbank Cassel GmbH v. Schenkers Ltd* [1927] 1 KB 826, and
(c) Have no notice, express or constructive, of failure to obtain permission: *Rolled Steel Products Ltd v. British Steel Corporation* [1986] 2 Ch 246.

The protection could be claimed even though the third party failed to read the articles prior to the transaction: *Freeman & Lockyer v. Buckhurst Park Properties Ltd* [1964] 2 QB 480.

It used to be held that the rule could not operate to bind a company in respect of a forged document: *Ruben v. Great Fingall Consolidated* [1906] AC 439. This no longer appears to be the case, and the company may be liable where the forgery is authenticated by an official acting within the scope of his actual or apparent authority.

(ii) Doctrine of ostensible, or apparent, authority

Ostensible, or apparent, authority is the authority of an agent as it is represented to persons dealing with the company. It arises where the principal, by words or conduct, has represented that the agent has the requisite actual authority, and the party dealing with the agent has entered into a contract with him in reliance on that representation: *per* Lord Keith of Kinkel in *Armagas Ltd v. Mundogas SA* [1986] AC 717 at p. 777. Having represented that the agent has this authority, the principal is then 'estopped' (or precluded) from claiming that the agent did not have the authority as represented.

Managing directors are company agents with actual authority to bind the company, whereas directors can bind the company only if authorised by the board. There is an exception where the director has been 'held out' by the board as having ostensible authority to bind the company in a particular transaction. In this case, the company is liable for the director's unauthorised acts where the third party establishes that:

- there was a representation or 'holding out' of authority in respect of the director/agent;
- the representation was made by the company;
- the third party relied on the representation;
- the transaction entered into was within the director/agent's usual authority: *Freeman & Lockyer v. Buckhurst Park Properties (Mangal) Ltd* [1964] 2 QB 480.

In *Freeman & Lockyer v. Buckhurst Park Properties (Mangal) Ltd*, the company's business was run by one of four directors, acting as if he was the managing director although not in fact appointed as such. He entered into a contract with the claimants, a firm of architects, for a property development, but the scheme collapsed when planning permission was refused, and the director left the country. The defendant company denied liability on the ground that it had not authorised the contracts. The court held it was liable as the director had been held out as its agent. It was not important that the claimants, the firm of architects, had not previously read the articles of association, but merely sufficient that the articles provided for the delegation of board authority to a managing director.

Allowing directors to act as if they were the managing director may give rise to liability by ostensible authority (*Freeman & Lockyer*). It may also be taken as the implied appointment of the director to the position of managing director, giving them actual authority. In *Hely-Hutchinson v. Brayhead Ltd* [1968] 1 QB 549, the second defendant, Richardson, acting as *de facto* managing director, agreed that the defendant company would indemnify the claimant in respect of any liability as guarantor of his company's bank account. The defendants denied liability and the Court of Appeal held that R had actual authority to bind the company.

8.7 Third party protection for contracts beyond the company's capacity or the directors' authority

The First EC Company Law Directive 68/151/EEC, [1968] JO L65/8 also required Member States to protect third parties dealing with companies, making the company liable even on contracts beyond its capacity or the authority of its directors: Art. 9. At the time of the passing of the Directive there was no official English language text since it was drafted before the UK was a member of the EEC. This provoked problems in transposing the text of the Directive into English law to give effect to it.

The official English text regarding *ultra vires* contracts refers to 'acts carried out by the organs of the company', and, in respect of contracts beyond the directors' authority to 'limits on the powers of the organs of the company'. The term 'organs' appears to be a translation of the French word *'organes'*. In UK company law the term 'organ' is used only in respect of the identification theory for fixing a company with criminal or tortious liability. In s.9(1) ECA 1972, the term was transformed into the phrase 'decided on by the directors', which had no counterpart in the Directive.

This terminological problem led to several attempts effectively to transpose the Directive into UK law. Section 9(1) ECA 1972 became s.35 of the Companies Act 1985, which was in turn revised and expanded by the Companies Act 1989, which added ss. 35A and 35B into the 1985 Act.

Regarding *ultra vires* contracts, the Directive was successfully transposed into UK law by s.35 as revised.

The provision is now contained in s.39 CA 2006, which is virtually identical to s.35(1) CA 1985: '[t]he validity of an act done by a company shall not be called into question on the ground of lack of capacity by reason of anything in the company's constitution': s.39(1). The success of the section in implementing the changes envisaged by the Directive is achieved by abandoning any attempt to translate the term 'organs'. In other ways the law has been greatly simplified by the Companies Act 2006.

Thus, whereas s.35 Companies Act 1985 provided a right of members to bring an action to restrain any future act which would be beyond the company's capacity (s.35(2) CA 1985), this is no longer required since companies can have unrestricted objects: s.31. There was also a provision to the effect that it was the directors' duty to observe limitations on their powers arising from the objects clause, and providing for their personal liability unless relieved from liability by a separate special resolution: s.35(3) CA 1985. This obligation and subsequent personal liability are now covered by the statutory duty of directors to act in accordance with the company's constitution (s.171(a)) and the enforcement of this duty under s.178.

In respect of unauthorised acts of directors, the position was and is more complicated. The term 'organs' was translated as 'the power of the board of directors' in s.35A CA 1985. This is now 'the power of the directors' in s.40: '[i]n favour of a person dealing with a company in good faith, the power of the directors to bind the company, or authorise others to do so, is deemed to be free of any limitation under the company's constitution': s.40(1).

The section gives a broad definition of 'dealing with the company in good faith', and provides that there is no duty to enquire as to limitations on the directors' powers to bind the company or authorise others to do so, and there is a presumption that the person acted in good faith unless the contrary is proved, and a person is not acting in bad faith simply by knowing that an act is beyond the directors' powers: s.40(2). Members still have the right to bring proceedings to restrain the doing of an action beyond the powers of the directors except in respect of an act in fulfilment of a legal obligation arising from a previous act of the company: s.40(4). Directors remain liable for acts beyond their powers: s.40(5).

It has always been claimed that the section failed to protect third parties dealing with a company through an individual director (except the managing director) where the director was not authorised by the board. The problem is in the wording 'the power of the directors to bind the company, or authorise others to do so'. It has been suggested that this should have been 'the power of the director or an individual director to bind the company, or authorise others to do so' in order to be effective in implementing the Directive.

It was suggested that the subsection should be interpreted to give effect to the Directive. This was the approach adopted by Browne-Wilkinson V-C in respect of s.9(1) European Communities Act 1972. In *TCB v. Gray* [1986] Ch 621, he stated that 'the manifest purpose of both the directive and the section is to enable people to deal with a company in good faith without being adversely affected by any limits on the company's capacity or its rules for internal management ... s.9(1) achieves this in two ways: first it "deems" all transactions to be authorised; second it deems that the directors can bind the company without limitations'.

In the House of Lords debate on s.35A, Lord Wedderburn argued that a constitutional requirement that the board should be quorate would be a limitation on the powers of the directors for the purposes of s.35A(1). The significance of the quorum requirement was confirmed in *Smith v. Henniker-Major & Co.* [2002] EWCA Civ 762, [2002] 2 BCLC 655. S, a company director, sued the defendant solicitors for negligence in the conduct of a land acquisition, claiming the company had suffered financial loss by losing the opportunity to purchase the land. He claimed the company had assigned the cause of action to him. The company had two directors and its articles required a quorum of two. The other director did not attend the meeting, but S minuted that the board authorised the assignment of the cause of action to himself. The issue was whether s.35A(1) validated the assignment. Rimer J held that s.35A only applied to powers exercisable by the directors when they gathered together and acted as a board.

Where an inquorate board attempts to transact business the transaction will be a nullity: *EIC Services Ltd and anor. v. Phipps and others* [2003] 3 All ER 804. The result is that third parties may still need to seek protection under the rule in *Turquand's Case* or the doctrine of apparent authority.

Where there is a transaction the validity of which depends on s.40, and where the parties to the transaction include a director of the company or its holding company, or a person connected with any such director, there is also a need to consider s.41. This provides that the transaction is voidable by the company: s.41(2). Whether it is avoided or not, parties to the transaction and directors of the company authorising the transaction are liable to account to the company for any direct or indirect gain, and to indemnify the company for any resulting loss or damage: s.41(3). A person other than a director is not liable if he shows that at the time of the transaction he did not know that the directors were exceeding their powers: s.41(5).

Persons connected with the directors include:

▷ Members of the director's family including a spouse or civil partner, any other person of the same or a different sex with whom the director lives as partner in an enduring family relationship, the director's children or step-children; any children or step-children under the age of 18 of the person with whom the director lives as partner in an enduring family relationship, and the director's parents: s.253.

▷ A body corporate with which the director is connected (s.252(2)(b)), defined as one in which he and the persons connected with him together are interested in at least 20 per cent of the equity share capital, or are entitled to exercise or control the exercise of more than 20 per cent of the voting power at a general meeting: s.254.

▶ A trustee of a trust the beneficiaries of which include the director or a person connected with him, or where the terms of the trust confer a power on the trustees which may be exercised for the benefit of the director or any such person: s.252(2)(c).

▶ A partner of the director or a person connected with that director (including a connected company or a trustee): s.252(2)(d).

▶ A firm which is a legal person and in which the director is a partner, a partner is a person connected with the director, or a partner is a firm in which the director is a partner or in which there is a partner with whom the director is connected: s.252(2)(e).

The equivalent measure for contracts with a sole member who is also a director is in s.231 under which, unless the contract is in writing, the company must ensure that the terms of the contract are either (a) set out in a written memorandum, or (b) recorded in the minutes of the first meeting of the directors following the contract: s.231(1). Shadow directors are treated as directors: s.231(5).

8.8 Form of company contracts

A contract may be made: (a) by a company, by writing under its common seal, or (b) on behalf of a company, by any person with express or implied authority; Contracts are subject to the same formalities as individuals unless a contrary intention appears: s.43 CA 2006. A document is executed by a company affixing its common seal, or by signature in accordance with s.44; There is, however, no requirement of common seal: s.45(1).

End of Topic Summary

Having read and understood this part of Chapter 8, you should have a clear understanding of the law relating to the contractual capacity of the company and the contractual authority of the board of directors and individual directors.

You should particularly understand the position regarding the following matters of special importance:

▶ The position with regard to contracts entered into before the incorporation of the company and the changes made to the common law by the First Company Law Directive.

▶ The significance of the memorandum and articles in respect of the contractual capacity of the company.

▶ The reforms in respect of *ultra vires* and unauthorised contracts as a result of the First Company Law Directive.

These are all issues of significance in the day-to-day running of the company, as can be seen from the following questions.

Questions on company contracts

1. How has the law relating to pre-incorporation contracts been changed by the transposition into UK Law of Article 7 of the First Company Law Directive and to what extent can it can be argued that the Directive has not been fully implemented in the UK?

2. Trekkers Ltd was incorporated under the Companies Act 2006 and carries on business as an adventure travel agency. The articles provide that the board may delegate authority to a managing director or individual directors, who may contract on behalf of the company up to a limit of £50,000, beyond which the board's prior authority must be obtained.
    The following agreements have been entered into on behalf of the company:
    (a) The board agreed to sponsor a local student to attend a three-year course unrelated to the company's business at a nearby university at a cost of £10,000.
    (b) Adam, the acting managing director who has not been formally appointed as such, contracted for a computer network installation for £55,000 without obtaining the prior authority of the board.
    (c) Eve, a director, contracted with Viper Ltd for the installation of a £60,000 air-conditioning system in the head office. She is the major shareholder in Viper Ltd and no prior board authority was obtained.
    Advise as to the validity of these transactions and the liability of the company and/or the board and the individual directors.

3. 'The companies legislation has abolished the doctrine of *ultra vires* and made it impossible for a company to limit the powers of directors to enter contracts on its behalf.' Discuss.

4. Amber Ltd carries on business importing amber from Russia. The directors have recently made three payments from company funds. The first was to a local pressure group campaigning for lower bank charges for small businesses. The second was to Nest-Egg Ltd, a company controlled by Amber Ltd's directors, for financial advice. The third payment was to the Green Party.
    Discuss the validity of these payments and the liability of the recipients and the directors.

Chapter 9

Registered companies: share capital

Learning objectives

After reading this chapter you will know about:

▶ the categories of share capital
▶ the principle of share capital as the creditors' guarantee fund
▶ the doctrine of raising and maintenance of share capital as applied to private and public companies

All references are to the Companies Act (CA) 2006, unless otherwise stated.

9.1 Categories of share capital

The most obvious change as a result of the CA 2006 has been to abolish the requirement of authorised share capital. Companies registered under the CA 2006 must include a statement of capital and initial shareholdings as part of the registration documentation submitted to the ROC. This constitutes a 'snapshot' of the company's share capital. The statement of capital and initial shareholding must contain the following information:

▶ The total number of shares of the company to be taken on formation by the subscribers to the memorandum;
▶ The aggregate nominal value of those shares;
▶ For each class of shares: prescribed particulars of the rights attached to those shares, the total number of shares of that class and the aggregate nominal value of shares of that class; and
▶ The amount to be paid up and the amount (if any) to be unpaid on each share (whether on account of the nominal value or by way of any premium).

The reference to the prescribed particulars of the rights attached to the shares is to such particulars as may be prescribed by the Secretary of State by statutory instrument (see s.1167).

A statement of capital is required whenever there has been a variation of class rights and whenever a company makes an alteration to its share capital.

The Act then gives definitions for different categories of share capital as follows:

(a) Issued capital: s.546(1)(a);
    Aggregate of nominal value of shares issued; aggregate of unissued shares is unissued capital.
(b) Called-up capital: s.547
    So much of share capital as equals the aggregate amount of calls made on its shares (whether or not those calls have been paid), together with:
    (a) any share capital paid up without being called, and

(b) any share capital to be paid on a specified future date under the articles, the terms of the allotment of the relevant shares or any other arrangements for payment of those shares.

(c) Uncalled capital: s.257
To be construed in relation to the definition of called-up capital. This relates to sums so far unpaid in respect of partly paid shares. The company can call in this capital as required unless the articles or terms of issue establish a schedule for payment at fixed future dates.

The aggregate nominal amount of share capital is credited to the Share Capital Account (SCA). On formation and before the company begins to trade, the amount credited to the SCA equals the net assets of company. Once the company begins to trade, the net assets will fluctuate according to the success or otherwise of the company. The SCA, however, does not fluctuate and will remain the same unless and until the company formally increases or reduces its capital. Thus, unlike the business capital of a sole trader or a general partnership which fluctuates over time and reflects the net worth of the business at any one time, the share capital of a registered company has ceased to be the name given to the fluctuating net worth of the business.

If shares are issued for cash or non-cash consideration at a premium (above their nominal value) the aggregate of premiums must be credited to the share premium account (SPA). The share premium is not credited to the shareholder who contributed it, it does not attract dividends and is not returnable to the shareholder on the dissolution of the company (for the status of the share premium account see below).

9.2 Capital as the creditors' guarantee fund

Because creditors of limited liability companies have no claims against the shareholders; all that they can claim against the company is the company's capital. There are complicated rules to ensure (i) the company has actually raised and received the capital it claims to have received and (ii) the capital is not subsequently returned, directly or indirectly, to the shareholders. The capital is the creditors' guarantee fund, and the body of rules is called the doctrine of raising and maintenance of capital.

The courts in the 19th and 20th centuries elaborated detailed rules to ensure that companies raised and maintained their capital.

The rule relating to raising capital was established in *Ooregum Gold Mining Co. of India v. Roper* [1892] AC 125 which established that a company could not issue its shares at a discount to their nominal value. It was also established that companies could not allot their shares for past consideration: *Re Eddystone Marine Insurance Co.* [1893] 3 Ch 9. The creditors' protection was, however, weakened by the fact that companies were allowed to allot their shares for non-cash consideration and that companies could buy property at any price they thought fit in consideration of an issue of fully paid shares. In this event, unless the transaction was fraudulent, the actual value received by the company for its shares could not be inquired into: *Re Wragg Ltd* [1897] 1 Ch 796.

In respect of maintenance of capital, the decision in *Trevor v. Whitworth* (1887) 12 App Cas 409 established that a company limited by shares could not buy its own shares since this would in effect be a reduction of the company's capital. This reduction could be achieved only through a formal, statutory procedure.

The doctrine also operated to prohibit companies from paying dividends out of capital. Dividends could only be paid out of profits: *Re Exchange Banking Co., Flitcroft's Case* (1882) 21 Ch D 519. There was, however, no restriction on paying them out of current trading profits without making provision for the depreciation of fixed assets: *Lee v. Neuchatel Asphalte Co* (1889) 41 Ch D 1. Neither were companies obliged to make good losses in fixed capital: *Verner v. General & Commercial Investment Trust* [1894] 2 Ch 239; or to make good past revenue losses: *Ammonia Soda Co. Ltd v. Chamberlain* [1918] 1 Ch 266. In addition, dividends could be paid out of unrealised profits: *Dimbula Valley (Ceylon) Tea Co. Ltd v. Laurie* [1961] Ch 353.

The Second EC Company Law Directive (No 77/9/EEC, [1977] OJ L26/1), required the UK to make specific provisions relating to capital maintenance and the payment of dividends. The rules were implemented in the Companies Act 1980. In respect of raising capital, the law was drastically changed in respect of public limited companies allotting their shares for non-cash consideration. The old common law rules still apply, however, for private companies.

In respect of capital maintenance, the common law rules relating to payment of dividends were replaced by new statutory provisions which distinguish between private and public companies, with the latter being more severely regulated. The Companies Act 1981 radically changed the law by allowing companies to purchase their own shares in controlled circumstances. This was in addition to the power which had existed since 1929 to redeem (buy back and cancel) shares issued as redeemable preference shares. The power to issue redeemable shares was also extended to all types of shares and not restricted to preference shares.

The result was that the rule in *Trevor v. Whitworth* still exists in statutory form but subject to a number of exceptions. The old prohibition on companies acquiring their own shares is replaced by permission subject to complex regulatory rules which bear more heavily on public companies. These ensure that creditor protection is maintained, whilst allowing companies greater flexibility.

It is only by understanding the underlying doctrine that sense can be made of the complex rules now contained in the Companies Act 2006.

9.3 Raising capital

The fundamental rule for all companies is that shares cannot be issued at a discount: s.580(1). In contravention of this, the allottee must pay the company an amount equal to the discount with interest at the appropriate rate (s.580(2)) which is 5 per cent *per annum* or any other rate specified by the Secretary of State: s.592. Shares and any premium may be paid up in money or money's worth (including goodwill and know-how: s. 582(1)).

(a) Shares issued for cash

Shares are paid up or allotted for cash if the consideration is:

- cash received by the company,
- cheques which the directors have no reason to suspect will not be paid,
- release of a corporate liability for a liquidated sum,
- undertakings to pay cash at a future date, or

▶ payments by any other means giving rise to a present or future entitlement to a payment, or credit equivalent, in cash: s.583(3).

Payment or an undertaking to pay cash to a third person is not cash consideration: s.583(5). 'Cash' includes foreign currency: s.583(6). Shares in a public company allotted to subscribers to the memorandum must be paid up in cash: s.584.

(b) Shares issued for non-cash consideration

(i) Private companies

There are no statutory requirements for valuation of the consideration, and it is only when it is clearly inadequate or where there is evidence of fraud that the court will intervene: *Re Wragg Ltd* [1897] 1 Ch 796. The consideration can be an undertaking to transfer assets or to perform future personal services and there is no maximum period for transfer or performance, and no minimum payment before shares can be allotted. The only control is the filing of a report of the issue with the ROC to alert potential investors and creditors.

(ii) Public companies

A public company must not accept in payment of its shares or any premium an undertaking by a person that he or another should do work or perform services for the company or any other person: s.585(1). In breach of this, the holder is liable to pay the aggregate nominal value and the whole of any premium and interest at the appropriate rate: s.585(2).

A public company must not allot shares unless paid up to at least one-quarter of their nominal value and the whole of any premium: s.586(1). In the event of any contravention, the shares are treated as if the statutory minimum had been received, and the allottee is liable to pay any shortfall with interest at the appropriate rate: s.586(3).

A public company must not allot shares if the consideration is or includes an undertaking which is to be, or may be, performed more than five years after the allotment: s.587(1). In breach of this, the allottee is liable to pay the aggregate of the nominal value and any premium with interest at the appropriate rate: s.587(2). Allottees have the same liability where the consideration is or includes an undertaking to be performed within five years which is not performed within that time: s.587(4).

Third parties who subsequently become holders of shares allotted in contravention of these provisions resulting in financial liability by another are jointly and severally liable to pay (s.588(1)) unless they are purchasers for value without actual notice of the contravention at the time of purchase, or derived their title (directly or indirectly) from a subsequent holder who was not financially liable under subs. (1): s. 588(2).

Allottees and subsequent holders can apply to be exempted in whole or in part from liability, but only if and to the extent that it is just and equitable, having regard to whether the applicant has paid or is liable to pay any amount in respect of any other statutory liability in respect of those shares, or any other undertaking to pay, whether another person has paid or is likely to pay, or whether the applicant or another person has performed or is likely to perform in whole or in part any undertaking, or had done or is likely to do anything in payment or part payment for the shares: s.589(1), (2) and (3). In *Re Bradford Investments plc (No. 2)* [1991] BCLC 688, four partners converted a dormant private company into a public company and transferred the partnership business to it in return for the allotment of fully paid shares. Their claim for relief against payment of the issue price of £1,059,000 was rejected because the court felt that the business had no value when it was transferred.

Contravention of those provisions is a criminal offence by the company and every officer in default and they are liable to a fine: s.590(1) and (2). Undertakings to do work or perform services are enforceable by the company notwithstanding the contravention of the Act: s.591. The appropriate rate of interest is 5 per cent *per annum* or such other rate as is specified by the Secretary of State: s.592(1).

Public companies must not allot shares for non-cash consideration unless the consideration has been independently valued and the valuer's report delivered to the company in the six months preceeding the allotment and a copy sent to the proposed allottee: s.593(1). Failure to comply makes the allottee liable to pay the aggregate of the nominal value and any premium and interest at the appropriate rate: s.593(3).

Subsequent holders of the shares are jointly and severally liable to pay (s.605(1)) unless they were purchasers for value without actual notice of the contravention at the time of the purchase, or derived their title from a subsequent holder who was not financially liable. The court can also relieve allottees and subsequent holders in similar circumstances to those in s.589 (above): s.606. In *Re Ossory Estates plc* [1988] BCLC 213 the vendor of property to the company received 8 million shares as part of the consideration. No valuation and report on the property had been made and a claim was made against him for £1.76 million in respect of the shares. The court granted relief on the ground that the company had sold some of the property at a substantial profit and had received money or money's worth at least equal to the aggregate nominal value of the shares and any premium.

Failure to comply with the valuation requirement gives rise to criminal liability of the company and every officer in default: s.607. Undertakings to do work or transfer assets are enforceable in spite of contravention of any statutory control or allotment for non-cash consideration: s.608. The appropriate rate of interest is 5 per cent: s.609.

The valuation report must give the nominal value of the shares and the amount of any premium, a description of the consideration, the valuation method and the date of the valuation and the extent to which the shares and any premium are to be treated as paid up by the consideration and in cash: s.596(2). Where the valuation was made by another person there must be a declaration that it was reasonable to accept the valuation, that the valuation method was reasonable, that there has been no subsequent material change in the value, and that the value, together with any cash, is not less than the aggregate nominal value and the premium: s.596(3).

The company must file a copy of the report with the ROC when it files the return of the allotment under s.555: s.597(1) and (2). Failure to do so is a criminal offence on the part of every officer in default subject to their right to apply for relief: s.597(3) to (6).

Additional restrictions apply to companies incorporated at the outset as public companies which, in the initial period after incorporation, agree to transfer shares for a non-cash consideration which amounts to at least one tenth of the company's issued capital: ss.598–604.

(c) Shares issued at a premium

If shares are issued at a premium, whether for cash or otherwise, a sum equal to the aggregate amount or value of the premiums on those shares must be transferred to the share premium account (SPA): s.610(1), *Henry Head & Co. Ltd v. Ropner Holdings Ltd* [1952] Ch 124. The SPA can be used to write off (a) the expenses of the issue of those shares; (b) any commission paid on the issue of those shares: s.610(2). It may also be used to pay up new shares to be allotted to members as fully paid bonus shares: s.610(3). Subject to these exceptions, the provisions of the Companies Acts relating to the reduction of the company's share capital apply as if the SPA were part of its paid up capital: s.610(4) (see below – maintenance of capital).

Section 610 has effect subject to the following exceptions: s.611 – group reconstruction relief; s.612 – merger relief; *Shearer v. Bercain Ltd* [1980] 3 All ER 295; s.614 – power to make further provisions by regulations.

The share premium account is an anomalous form of quasi-capital account because:

▶ no dividend is paid on it;
▶ it is not attributable to any shareholder;
▶ it is not part of the nominal capital;
▶ the ordinary investor does not regard it as capital.

Any percentage dividend is calculated on the basis of the nominal value, which is also the amount shareholders are entitled to on liquidation where assets remain after the payment of debts. The aggregate of the nominal capital is in the share capital account.

9.4 Maintenance of capital

The old rule in *Trevor v. Whitworth* is now contained in Part 18, ss.658 and 659 CA 2006. A limited company must not acquire its own shares, whether by purchase, subscription or otherwise, except in accordance with the provisions of this Part: s.658(1). In the event of breach, the company and every officer in default commit an offence and the purported acquisition is void. Persons convicted of an offence are liable, on indictment, to imprisonment for up to two years or a fine (or both) and on summary conviction to imprisonment for up to 12 months or a fine not exceeding the statutory maximum (or both): s.658(2) and (3). The exceptions to the general rule listed in s.659 are:

▶ Acquisition of fully paid shares otherwise than for valuable consideration: s.659(1);
▶ Acquisition of shares in a reduction of capital duly made under Part 17, Chapter 10, ss. 641– 657: s.659(2)(a);
▶ Purchase in pursuance of a court order under various sections including ss.994–996 (protection of members against unfair prejudice),
▶ The forfeiture of shares or the acceptance of shares surrendered in lieu in pursuance of the articles for failure to pay any sum in respect of the shares: s.659(2)(c).

A further exemption relates to the power of companies to redeem redeemable shares under rules in Part 18, Chapter 3, ss.684–689. Companies also have the power to purchase their own shares under Part 18, Chapter 4, ss.680–708. In respect of both of these exceptions, private companies have the power to redeem or purchase their own shares out of capital under Part 18, Chapter 5, ss.709–723.

Related to the rules relating to maintenance of capital is the statutory prohibition against the provision by a company or its subsidiary of financial assistance for the acquisition of shares in a public company under Part 18, Chapter 2, ss.678–680.

The rules relating to maintenance of capital also extend to regulate the payment of dividends under Part 22, Chapter 1, ss.829–847.

(a)   Power to redeem own shares

A limited company with a share capital may issue shares which are to be or are liable to be redeemed at the option of the company or the shareholder: s.684(1). This is subject to the proviso that a private company may exclude or restrict the issue of redeemable shares in its articles (s.684(2)) and that a public limited company may issue redeemable shares only if authorised by its articles: s.684(3). No redeemable shares may be issued when there are no issued shares of the company which are not redeemable: s.684(4).

The directors may fix the terms, conditions and manner of redemption if authorised by the articles or by a resolution: s.685(1). This may be an ordinary resolution even though it amends the articles: s.685(2). Where they are so authorised, the directors must fix the terms, conditions and manner of redemption before the shares are allotted and the obligation to set out in a statement of capital the rights attached to the shares covers the terms, conditions and manner of redemption: s.685(3). If the directors have no such authority, the terms, conditions and manner must be stated in the articles: s.685(4).

Shares may not be redeemed unless they are fully paid, and the shares must be paid for on redemption unless the terms of redemption provide for the possibility of payment at a later date: s.686.

In respect of financing the redemption, the statute makes a distinction between private and public companies. A private limited company may redeem its shares out of capital in accordance with Part 18, Chapter 5 (see the discussion on purchase of own shares below). Apart from this exception, the redemption must be out of distributable profits of the company, or the proceeds of a fresh issue of shares made for the purpose of redemption: s.687(2). Any premium payable on redemption must be out of distributable profits (s.687(3)) subject to the proviso that, where the shares were issued at a premium, any premium payable on redemption may be paid out of the proceeds of a fresh issue of shares up to an amount equal to the aggregate of the premiums received on the issue of the shares redeemed, or the current amount of the company's share premium account, whichever is the less: s.687(4).

Redeemed shares are treated as cancelled and the company's share capital is diminished by the nominal value of the shares redeemed: s.688. Within a month of the redemption the company must notify the ROC and send in a revised statement of capital. Failure to comply is an offence by the company and every officer in default: s.689.

Where the redemption is wholly or partly out of distributable profits, companies must transfer the aggregate par value of the shares redeemed out of distributable profits to a capital redemption reserve (CRR): s.733. This is subject to the capital maintenance rules but may be used for the allotment of fully paid bonus shares: s.733(5) and (6).

The CRR protects the company's creditors against a reduction in the company's capital. It is not necessary where shares are redeemed from the proceeds of a fresh share issue, since the new capital replaces the old. Companies normally issue redeemable preference shares and redemption from a fresh issue means that the company can replace issued redeemable preference shares with shares with a lower fixed dividend. The shares do not give the shareholders the right to vote, and the balance of power in the company is not upset.

(b)   Power to purchase own shares

A limited company with a share capital may purchase its own shares (including redeemable shares) subject to the provision of Part 18, Chapter 4, and any restrictions or prohibitions in the company's articles, unless the result would be that the only issued shares remaining were redeemable or treasury shares (see below): s.690. Shares may be purchased only when they are fully paid up and the shares must be paid for on purchase: s.691.

Private companies may purchase their own shares out of capital in accordance with Part 18, Chapter 5 (s.692(1)), subject to any restriction or prohibition in the company's articles: s.709(1). The 'permissible capital payment' is such an amount as, after applying for that purpose any available profits of the company and the proceeds of any fresh share issue made for the purpose of the redemption or purchase, is required to meet the price of redemption or purchase: s.710. The available profits are defined in s.711 and the amount of available profits is determined in accordance with s.712.

In order for a payment out of capital to be lawful, it must comply with the four conditions set out in s.713.

The directors must make a statement of the permissible capital payment and state that immediately following the payment the company will not be unable to pay its debts, and that in the year following, the company will be able to continue to carry on business as a going concern and pay its debts as they fall due during that year. Annexed to the statement is a substantiating report to the directors by the company's auditors: s.714. If the directors have no reasonable grounds for the opinion expressed, they are guilty of a criminal offence: s.715.

The payment must be approved by a special resolution on or within the week immediately following the date of the directors' statement: s.716. Where the resolution is proposed as a written resolution, a member who holds shares to which the resolution relates is not an eligible member (s.717(2)), and where it is proposed at a meeting it is not effective if a member holding shares to which the resolution relates exercises the voting rights carried by any of those shares in voting on the resolution, and the resolution would not otherwise have been passed (s.717(3)) whether voting on a poll or otherwise: s.717(4). The resolution is ineffective unless there has been prior disclosure to the members of the directors' statement and the auditor's report: s.718.

Within a week following the resolution, the company must give notice in 'the *Gazette*' and an appropriate national newspaper of the proposed payment, and deliver to the registrar a copy of the directors' statement and the auditor's report: s.719. In addition, the directors' statement and auditor's report must be available for inspection by members or creditors without charge at the company's registered office or a place specified under s.1136 from the date of the public notice until five weeks from the date of the resolution: s.720.

A member of the company (other than one who consented to or voted in favour of the resolution) and a creditor may apply to the court for the cancellation of the resolution within five weeks of the resolution. In this event, the court may adjourn the proceedings to achieve an arrangement for the purchase of the interests of the dissentient members or the protection of the dissentient creditors, and give directions and make orders for facilitating such an arrangement. Subject to that, the court must either cancel or confirm the resolution on such terms and conditions as it thinks fit: s.721. The registrar must be notified of the court application or order: s.722.

The payment out of capital must be no earlier than five weeks and no more than seven weeks after the resolution, subject to the court's powers to alter or extend time where the resolution is confirmed after objection: s.723.

Subject to the right of private companies to make payments out of capital, the purchase of shares can only be out of the distributable profits of the company or the proceeds of a fresh issue of shares made for the purpose of financing the purchase. In addition, any premium must be paid out of the distributable profits of the company: s.692(2). This is subject to the same exception as for the payment of premiums on redemption of redeemable shares: s. 692(3).

The purchase of shares may be off-market under a contract approved in advance under s.694 or by a market purchase under s.701: s.693(1). Section 693(2) and (3) defines both an off-market and a market purchase.

(i) Off-market purchases

An off-market purchase can only be under a prior contract approved under s.694. The terms must be authorised by a special resolution before the contract is entered into, or must provide that no shares may be purchased until the terms have been so authorised: s.694(2). The contract may be a contingent contract under which the company may become entitled or obliged to purchase the shares: s.694(3). The authority may be varied, revoked or from time to time renewed by special resolution (s.694(4)), and in the case of a public company, a resolution conferring, varying or renewing authority must specify a date on which the authority is to expire, which cannot be later than 18 months from the date on which the resolution is passed: s.694(5).

Where the resolution is proposed as a written resolution, a member who holds shares to which the resolution relates is not an eligible member: s.695(2). Where proposed at a meeting of the company, it is not effective if any member holding shares to which the resolution relates exercises the voting rights carried by any of those shares in voting on the resolution, and the resolution would not otherwise have been passed: s.695(3).

A copy of the contract or a memorandum setting out its terms must be available to members, in the case of a written resolution, by being sent or submitted to every eligible member at or before the time at which the proposed resolution is sent or submitted to him; and, in the case of a resolution at a meeting, by being made available for inspection by members both at the registered office for not less than 15 days prior to the meeting, and at the meeting itself: s.696(2). The resolution is not valid if this is not complied with.

A company 'may only agree' to a variation of a contract authorised under s.694 if the variation is approved in advance by special resolution. The authority may be varied, revoked or renewed by special resolution, but in the case of a public company the resolution must specify a date on which the authority is to expire, which must not be later than 18 months from the passing of the resolution: s.697. There are identical voting restrictions as under s.695 (s.698), and identical requirement for disclosure of details of the variations as in s.695: s.699.

Agreement by a company to release its rights under a contract under s.694 is void unless authorised by special resolution. The authority can be varied, revoked or renewed by special resolution with the usual requirement for a public company to specify a date within 18 months on which the authority expires. The resolution is subject to restrictions on the exercise of voting rights under s.698 and disclosure of details of variation under s.699: s.700.

(ii) On-market purchases

Since the purchase is regulated by the market, only an ordinary resolution is required: s.701(1). The authority may be general or limited to the purchase of shares of a particular class or description; and be unconditional or subject to conditions: s.701(2). It must state the maximum number of shares to be acquired, determine the maximum and minimum prices paid: s.701(3). This can be a particular sum, or a basis or formula for calculating the price but without reference to any person's discretion or opinion: s.701(7).

The authority may be varied, revoked or renewed, but where varied, conferred or renewed it must specify a date on which it is to expire, which must be not later than 18 months after the date on which the resolution is passed: s.701(4) and (5). A company may purchase its own shares after the expiry of the time limit if the contract of purchase was concluded before the authority expired, and the terms of the authority permitted the company to make a purchase contract which would or might be executed wholly or partly after its expiration: s.701(6).

Where companies have entered into a contract authorising off-market or market purchase, the company must keep a copy or a written memorandum of the contract available for inspection for 10 years from the date when the purchase of all the shares is completed, or the date when the contract determines. The copy or memorandum must be at the registered office or a place specified under regulations under s.1136 and the company must notify the registrar where it is kept or of any change in that place. The copies are open for inspection free of charge to members of private companies and for any person in the case of a public company: s.702. There are criminal penalties for the company and every officer in default for non-compliance: s.703.

Companies cannot assign their right to purchase their own shares (s.704), and payment for the shares is to be made out of distributable profits: s.705. The shares acquired by the company must be treated as cancelled and the issued share capital reduced by the nominal value of the shares cancelled except where s.724 relating to treasury shares applies, in which case the shares can be held and dealt with in accordance with Part 18, Chapter 6 (see below).

The company must make a return to the registrar within 28 days of the purchase of its own shares distinguishing between treasury shares and shares to be cancelled (s.707); it must also send notice of the cancellation within 28 days of the shares being delivered to it: s.708.

(c) Treasury shares

Where a company purchases its own shares out of distributable profits and the shares are qualifying shares in that they are:

- Included in the official list under Part 6 Financial Services and Markets Act 2000,
- Traded on the Alternative Investment Market (AIM),
- Officially listed in an EEA State, or
- Traded on a regulated market,

the company may hold the shares (or any of them), or deal with any of them, in accordance with s.727 or 729. The company must be entered in its register of members as the holder of the shares: s.724.

Where a company has only one class of share, the aggregate nominal value held as treasury shares must not exceed 10 per cent of the nominal value of the issued share capital (s.725(1)), and where there are shares of different classes the aggregate nominal value of the shares of any class must not exceed 10 per cent of the nominal value of that class (s.725(2)), otherwise the company must dispose of the excess shares within 12 months: s.725(3). The company must not exercise any right in respect of the shares and any purported exercise is void: s.726(2). This applies to any right to attend or vote at meetings. No dividend may be paid, and no other distribution in cash or otherwise of the company's assets including on a winding up may be made to the company: s.726(3). This does not prevent an allotment of bonus shares or the payment of money on the redemption of redeemable treasury shares. Shares allotted as bonus shares are treated as if purchased at the time of allotment: s.726(4) and (5).

The company can sell the shares at any time or transfer them in respect of an employees' share scheme: s.727(1). If the company receives a notice under s.979 (takeover offers; right of offeror to buy out minority shareholders) of a desire to acquire the shares, the company must not sell or transfer them except to that person: s.727(4). Where shares are sold or transferred, the company must notify the registrar within 28 days of their disposal: s.728(1).

The company may at any time cancel some or all of the shares, and must do so if they cease to be qualifying shares. On cancellation, the company's share capital is reduced accordingly (s.729); on cancellation the company must notify the registrar within 28 days and the notice must be accompanied by a statement of capital: s.730.

If the proceeds of sale of treasury shares are equal to or less than the purchase price, the profits are treated as a realised profit of the company. If the proceeds exceed the purchase price an amount equal to the price paid is treated as a realised profit, and the excess must be transferred to the company's share premium account: s.731.

Any contravention of this Chapter (except for s.730) is an offence by the company and every officer in default: s.732.

(d) Reduction of capital

A limited company with a share capital may reduce its share capital under Chapter 10 of Part 17. The Act distinguishes between private and public companies and provides that a private company may reduce its capital by special resolution supported by a solvency statement under ss.642–644: s.641(1)(a). In the alternative, private and public companies may reduce their capital by special resolution confirmed by the court under ss.645–651: s.641(1)(b). A reduction under either method cannot take place if the result would be that there would be no longer any member holding shares other than redeemable shares: s.641(2).

Companies can reduce their capital (i) when they have excess capital, and (ii) to write off losses. In the case of excess capital the company may extinguish or reduce the liability in respect of share capital not paid up, or, with or without extinguishing or reducing liability of its shares, repay any paid-up excessive share capital: s.641(4)(a) and (b)(ii). In writing off losses, the company may, either with or without extinguishing or reducing liability on any of its shares, cancel any paid-up capital which is lost or unrepresented by available assets:

s.641(4)(b)(i). The special resolution may not provide for a reduction to take effect later than the date on which the resolution has effect (s.641(5)). The statutory rules in the Chapter (with the exception of s.641(5)) are subject to any article provision restricting or prohibiting the reduction of the company's capital: s.641(6). A reduction to write off losses is merely a paper exercise to reduce the nominal value of the shares to reflect the company's assets value. There is no direct or indirect return of capital to the shareholders. This type of reduction may be necessary to enable a public company to pay dividends.

(i) Private companies: reduction of capital supported by a solvency statement

A private company may pass a written resolution or one proposed at a meeting. If it is a written resolution, a copy of the directors' solvency statement must be sent or submitted to every eligible member at or before the sending or submission of the proposed resolution. For resolutions at a general meeting, a copy of the statement must be available for inspection throughout the meeting. Failure to comply with this disclosure does not, however, affect the validity of the resolution: s.642.

A solvency statement is to the effect that each of the directors thinks that there is no ground on which the company could then be found to be unable to pay its debts; and also, if it is intended to wind up the company within the next 12 months, that the company will be able to pay its debts in full within 12 months of the commencement of the winding up; or that the company will be able to pay its debts as they fall due during the following year: s.643(1). If the statement is made without reasonable grounds and the statement is delivered to the registrar, an offence is committed by each director in default: s.643(4).

Within 15 days of the resolution, the company must deliver to the registrar a copy of the solvency statement, a statement of capital and the copy of the resolution: s.644(1). The registrar must register the documents, and the resolution does not take effect until they are registered. The company must also deliver to the registrar within the 15 days a statement by the directors confirming that the solvency statement was made not more than 15 days before the passing of the resolution and provided to the members in accordance with s.642(2) or (3): s.644(3)–(5). Failure to deliver the documents within the time limit or to comply with subsection (5) does not invalidate the resolution but is an offence by the company and every officer in default: s.644(6) and (8).

(ii) Reduction of capital confirmed by the court

Having passed a resolution for reducing share capital, a company may apply to the court for an order confirming the reduction. If the reduction involves diminution of liability in respect of unpaid share capital or the payment to a shareholder of paid-up share capital, the creditors are entitled to object to the reduction under s.646 unless the court orders otherwise: s.645. Under s.646, every creditor who, at the date fixed by the court, has a debt or claim against the company which would be admissible in proof against the company if that date were the commencement of the company's winding up is entitled to object: s.646(1). The court settles a list of creditors entitled to object and, if a creditor on the list whose debt or claim is not discharged or has not determined does not consent to the reduction, the court may dispense with their consent on the company securing payment of the debt or claim: s.646(4). The debt or claim is secured by payment of the following amounts: if the company admits the debt or is willing to provide for it, the full amount of the debt or claim; if the company does not admit and is not willing to provide for the full amount, or, if the amount is contingent or unascertained, an amount fixed by the court as if the company were being wound up by the court: s.646(5).

The court may confirm the reduction on such terms and conditions as it thinks fit but must not unless satisfied that every creditor entitled to object either has consented or his debt or claim has been discharged, determined or been secured: s. 648(1) and (2). The company may be ordered to publish the reasons for the reduction or other information to inform the public of the causes leading to the reduction: s.648(3). The court may also order that for a specified period the company should add to its name the words 'and reduced': s. 648(4).

The registrar must register the order and a statement of capital (s.649(1)) except where the order relates to a public company and brings the nominal value of its allotted share capital below the authorised minimum. In that case the registrar must not register it unless ordered to by the court or the company is first re-registered as a private company: s.650. There is an expedited procedure for re-registration under s.651.

The resolution for reducing capital, as confirmed by the court, takes effect on registration of the order and statement of capital unless it forms part of a compromise or arrangement under Part 26. The registrar certifies the registration and this is conclusive evidence that the requirements of the Act have been complied with and that the company's share capital is as stated in the statement of capital: s. 649(5) and (6).

If a creditor entitled to object is not entered on the list due to his ignorance of the proceedings or of their nature and effect and, after the reduction, the company is unable to pay his debt or claim, every person who was a member of the company at the date when the resolution took effect is liable to contribute an amount not exceeding that which he would have been liable to contribute if the company had commenced to be wound up on that date: s.653(1) and (2).

Where there has been no sanction or an improper sanction by the members, the burden of proof is on the company to establish that the proposed scheme is fair; otherwise it is on those seeking to establish that the scheme is unfair: *Re Holders Investment Trust Ltd* [1971] 2 All ER 289.

A company with ordinary and preference shares may decide to reduce its capital selectively by buying in and cancelling the preference shares. If this does not involve a variation of the preference shareholders' class rights, there is no need to obtain their approval (see Chapter 10, p.223 below).

(e)   The payment of dividends

The payment of dividends is covered by the law relating to distributions made by the company under Part 23. A distribution means every distribution of a company's assets to its members, whether in cash or otherwise, excluding the issue of bonus shares, the reduction of capital by extinguishing liability in respect of share capital or repaying paid-up capital, the redemption or purchase of the company's own shares and a distribution of assets to members on winding up: s.829.

Distributions can only be out of profits available for the purpose, defined as 'accumulated, realised profits, so far as not previously utilised by distribution or capitalisation, less its accumulated, realised losses, so far as not previously written off in a reduction or reorganisation of capital duly made': s.830(1) and (2). Public companies are further restricted, in that they cannot make distributions which would reduce the net assets below the aggregate of the called-up capital and undistributable reserves: s.831(1). The undistributable reserves are:

(i)   the share premium account;
(ii) the capital redemption reserve;
(iii) the revaluation reserve, that is, the amount by which the company's accumulated, unrealised profits exceed its accumulated, unrealised losses;
(iv) any other reserve which the company is prohibited from distributing: s.831(4).

This ensures capital maintenance. Treating the revaluation reserve as undistributable prevents the distribution of unrealised profits.

Shareholders must repay any distribution where they knew or had reasonable grounds for believing that it was in breach of the Act: s.847.

9.5 Financial assistance for the purchase of own shares

Financial assistance can be by a gift, guarantee, security or indemnity or by way of release or waiver: s.677. It can also be by way of a loan or the novation of or the assignment of rights arising under a loan, or any other financial assistance where the company's net assets are materially reduced or where the company has no assets.

Financial assistance is prohibited in connection with the acquisition of shares in a public company: s.678. The prohibition relates to direct and indirect financial assistance by the company or by a subsidiary of the company, and covers contemporaneous financial assistance given for the purposes of the acquisition before or at the same time as the acquisition takes place (s.678(1)) or subsequent financial assistance after the shares have been acquired for the purpose of reducing or discharging any existing liability: s.678(3).

The prohibition does not apply to a parent company in respect of a subsidiary, and foreign subsidiaries are not prohibited from giving financial assistance for the purchase of shares in an English parent: *Arab Bank plc v. Mercantile Holdings Ltd and Another* [1994] 1 BCLC 330.

Direct or indirect, contemporaneous and subsequent financial assistance by a public company is also prohibited in connection with the acquisition of shares in a private company where the public company is a subsidiary of that company: s.679.

Companies contravening the prohibitions are guilty of a criminal offence and liable to a fine, and every officer in default is liable to imprisonment or a fine, or both: s.680.

The share purchase itself is valid, but contracts in breach of the law and securities issued in contravention of the law are void: *Heald v. O'Connor* [1971] 1 WLR 497. The courts may sever the illegal aspect of the transaction, however, and anything not affected by the illegality is valid and enforceable: *Carney v. Herbert* [1985] AC 301.

(a) Exceptions to the general rule

Contemporaneous financial assistance is not prohibited if the principal purpose is not for the purpose of an acquisition of shares or, if it is, it is an incidental part of some larger purpose of the company, and given in good faith and in the interests of the company: ss.678(2) and 679(2). Subsequent financial assistance is not prohibited if the principal purpose is not to reduce or discharge any liability incurred by a person for the purpose of the acquisition or, if it is, it is an incidental part of some larger purpose of the company and in good faith and in the best interests of the company: ss.678(4) and 679(4).

The exception was originally introduced following *Belmont Finance Corpn Ltd v. Williams Furniture Ltd (No. 2)* [1980] 1 All ER 393 to validate *bona fide* company transactions with an incidental aim of providing financial assistance: the *bona fide* purchase of assets where the consideration paid enables the vendor to purchase shares in the company. The exception has been severely limited by the House of Lords' decision in *Brady v. Brady* [1988] BCLC 20, which stressed that there must be an identifiable principal and subsidiary purpose at the same time for the exception to operate. The court rejected the idea that the exception validated financial assistance as part of a company reconstruction or to avoid management deadlock. The case concerned the division of a group into two separate businesses between the two brothers who controlled it and who had fallen out.

The Act also sets out a number of unconditional exceptions including a dividend lawfully made or a distribution in the course of the company's winding up, the allotment of bonus shares, a reduction of capital under Chapter 10 of Part 17, a redemption and purchase of shares under Chapters 3 and 4 of Part 18: s.681(1) and (2).

Sections 678 and 679 do not prohibit a transaction under s.682(a) if the company giving the assistance is a private company, or (b) if the company giving the assistance is a public company and (i) the company has net assets that are not reduced by the giving of the assistance, or (ii) to the extent that those assets are so reduced, the assistance is provided out of distributable profits. The transactions are:

▷ The lending of money in the ordinary course of the company's business where the lending of money is part of the ordinary course of the company's business;

▷ The provision in good faith in the interests of the company or its holding company of financial assistance for the purposes of an employees' share scheme;

▷ The provision of financial assistance for the purposes of anything done by the company (or another company within the same group) to enable or facilitate transactions involving the beneficial ownership of shares by *bona fide* employees or former employees of that company or another company within the same group, or spouses, civil partners, widows, widowers, surviving civil partners, minor children or step-children of such employees or ex-employees;

▷ The making of loans to persons (other than directors) employed in good faith by the company to enable them to acquire fully paid up shares in the company or its holding company: s.682(2).

(b) Civil liability arising from financial assistance

Directors must account to the company in respect of their breach of trust, and persons who have knowingly been accessories to the directors' misapplication of corporate property are liable to account as constructive trustees. Liability as an accessory requires dishonesty on the part of the accessory, whether or not the directors are also acting dishonestly. If the directors misapply corporate assets in honest reliance on the advice of a dishonest third party, the third party is liable to account even though the directors are not liable: *Royal Brunei Airlines Sdn Bhd v. Tan Kok Ming* [1995] 2 AC 378. Third parties knowingly receiving misapplied corporate funds or property are also liable as constructive trustees. As regards the requisite knowledge of misapplication for liability as a constructive trustee, Peter Gibson J identified five kinds of mental state:

(i)   actual knowledge;

(ii) wilfully shutting one's eyes to the obvious;

(iii) wilfully and recklessly failing to make such enquiries as an honest and reasonable man would make;

(iv) knowledge of circumstances which would indicate the facts to an honest and reasonable man;

(v)   knowledge of circumstances which would have put an honest and reasonable man on enquiry: *Baden Delvaux & Lecuit v. Société Générale pour favoriser etc.* [1983] BCLC 325.

Liability as a constructive trustee in either respect requires knowledge within the first three categories – there must be a degree of intentional wrongdoing. A claim based on constructive knowledge or notice (categories (iv) and (v)) will fail.

The company can also sue the directors for damages for conspiracy: *Belmont Finance Corpn Ltd v. Williams Furniture Ltd* [1979] Ch 250. Minority shareholders can bring a derivative action under s.260(1) or petition under s.994 (see Chapter 10, pp.228 and 229).

9.6 Public companies taking charges over their shares

A lien or other charge of a public company on its own shares is void: s.670(1). This is, however, subject to the following exceptions: any company may take a charge on partly-paid shares for an amount payable in respect of the shares (s.670(2)); in the case of a company the ordinary business of which includes the lending of money or the provision of credit or the bailment of goods under a hire-purchase agreement or both, a charge is permitted whether the shares are fully paid or not if it arises in connection with a transaction in the ordinary course of that business (s.670(3)) and, in the case of a company which has been re-registered as a public company, a charge is permitted if it was in existence immediately before the re-registration application: s.670(4).

End of topic summary

This is an enormously complex and difficult topic, but the main thing to retain is the basic concept which underlies all these detailed rules. The basic concept is that, since the creditors of the company can only claim against the company and the company's creditworthiness lies essentially in its share capital, the company must actually raise and then maintain the share capital.
   Matters of particular importance are as follows:

▷ The issue of shares for non-cash consideration and the distinction in this respect between public and private companies.

▷ The reduction of capital and the distinction between reductions which return capital to the shareholders or reduce their liability to contribute in the future and reductions which merely write off losses.

▷ The rules in respect of dividend payments and the way in which they ensure that public companies maintain their capital.

▷ The reason behind the prohibition against public companies providing financial assistance to the purchasers of their shares.

These are issues of significance in the day-to-day operation of companies as the following questions show.

Questions

1. 'Companies must not issue shares at a discount but they can issue them at a premium.'
   Discuss with regard to the position of private and public limited companies.

2. Utopia plc has issued the following fully paid shares:
   (a) To Avril 5,000 shares in consideration for her valuable work in developing new markets for the company's products on the continent over the previous 10 years.
   (b) To Mohammed 5,000 shares in consideration of his services to the company as design consultant for the next three years. The shares have since been transferred to Tariq, the current shareholder.
   (c) To Sasha 10,000 shares in consideration of the transfer to the company in seven years' time of her leasehold industrial premises.
   Advise on the legal consequences of these transfers.

3. Prontaprint plc issued 2,500,000 £1 ordinary shares to Adam in consideration of the transfer to the company of four printing machines valued at £750,000 each and Adam's services as a design consultant for one year valued at £50,000. The first machine was delivered when the shares were allotted, but the others are to be delivered over the next two years, as Adam's own printing business is run down. Adam later transferred 500,000 of these shares to his wife, and 100,000 to each of his four children.
   Consider the legality of the share issue and the potential liability of Adam and his family.

4. The rules relating to raising and maintenance of capital of a limited liability company are designed to protect the company's creditors for whom the company's capital is a guarantee fund.
   In this context you are required to explain:
   (a) The adequacy of the legal controls on the issue of shares for a non-cash consideration for private and public companies.
   (b) The operation of the capital redemption reserve in the redemption or purchase by a company of its own shares.

5. Spiceworld plc has 1,500,000 issued paid-up shares. Owen, the sole director, holds 800,000. He wishes to sever his links with the company. Martin and Angela are interested in buying the shares.
   On behalf of Spiceworld plc, Owen purchases a consignment of spices from Paul. The ostensible intention of the company is to sell the spices at a profit. As a result of the settlement of this contract by Spiceworld plc, Paul is now in a position to lend Martin the money to enable him to buy 50 per cent of Owen's shares in Spiceworld plc.
   Angela borrowed money from her bank to enable her to buy Owen's remaining shares. Subsequent to the purchase, as directors of the company Angela and Martin created a debenture secured on Spiceworld plc's assets in favour of the bank as security for the loan to Angela.
   Consider (a) the legality of these transactions entered into by Spiceworld plc and the rights, and (b) the liabilities of Owen, Paul, Angela and Angela's bank arising from these transactions.

Chapter 10

Registered companies: shares and shareholders and minority protection

Learning objectives

After reading this chapter you will know about:

- Registered and bearer shares
- Classes of shares and class rights
- Protection of members against unilateral variation of their class rights
- Minority protection: derivative actions and petitions against unfair prejudice

All references are to the Companies Act 2006 unless otherwise stated.

10.1 A company's members

The shareholders of a company are generally described as its members and, in the case of registered shares, which are the UK norm, the list of shareholders required to be kept by the company is generally referred to as the list of members.

The subscribers to a company's memorandum are deemed to have agreed to become members of the company, and on its registration become members and must be entered as such in its register of members: s.112(1). Every other person who agrees to become a member of a company and whose name is entered on its register of members is a member of the company: s.112(2).

10.2 Shares and share capital of a company

In the Companies Acts 'share', in relation to a company, means a share in the company's share capital: s.540(1). The shares or other interest of a member in a company are personal property and are not in the nature of real estate: s.541. Shares in a limited company having a share capital must each have a fixed nominal value, and an allotment of shares which does not have a fixed nominal value is void: s.542(1) and (2). Shares may be denominated in any currency, and different classes of shares may be denominated in different currencies (but see s.765): s.542(3). Each share must be distinguished by its appropriate number, except in the following circumstances.

If at any time:

(a) all the issued shares in a company are fully paid up and rank *pari passu* for all purposes, or
(b) all the issued shares of a particular class in a company are fully paid up and rank *pari passu* for all purposes,

none of those shares need thereafter have a distinguishing number so long as they remain fully paid up and rank *pari passu* for all purposes with all shares of the same class for the time being issued and fully paid up: s.543.

Shares are transferable in accordance with the company's articles subject to the Stock Transfer Act 1963 and regulations under Chapter 2 of Part 21 (enabling title to be evidenced and transferred without a written instrument): s.544.

The shareholder is the proportionate owner of the company, but he does not own the company's assets which belong to the company as a separate and independent legal entity: *Macaura v. Northern Assurance Co.* [1925] AC 619. A share has been defined as 'the interest of the shareholder in the company measured by a sum of money, consisting of a series of mutual covenants entered into by all the shareholders *inter se* and made up of various right contained in the contract in the articles': *Borland's Trustee v. Steel Bros & Co. Ltd* [1901] 1 Ch 279.

10.3 Allotment of shares: general provisions

The directors of a company must not exercise any power of the company:

(a) to allot shares in the company, or
(b) to grant rights to subscribe for, or to convert any security into, shares in the company,

except in accordance with s.550 (private company with single class of shares) or s.551 (authorisation by the company): s.549(1). There is an exception in respect of the allotment of shares in respect of an employee's share scheme or to the grant of a right to subscribe for, or to convert any security into, shares so allotted: s.549(2).

Where a private company has only one class of shares, the directors may exercise any power of the company (a) to allot shares of that class, or (b) to grant rights to subscribe for or to convert any security into such shares, except to the extent that they are prohibited from doing so by the company's articles: s.550.

The directors of a company may exercise a power of the company (a) to allot shares, or (b) to grant rights to subscribe for or to convert any security into shares, if authorised to do so by the articles or by a resolution: s.551(1). Authorisation may be for a particular exercise of the power or for its exercise generally, and may be unconditional or subject to conditions: s.551(2). Authorisation must state the maximum number of shares that may be allotted under it, and specify the date on which it will expire, which must not be more than five years from (i), in the case of authorisation in the articles, the date of original incorporation; (ii) in any other case, the date on which the resolution is passed: s.551(3). Authorisation may be renewed or further renewed for a further period of up to five years, and be revoked at any time by resolution: s.551(4). A resolution to give, vary, revoke or renew authorisation may be an ordinary resolution, even though it amends the company's articles: s.551(8).

10.4 Allotment of equity securities: existing shareholders' right of pre-emption

'Equity securities' means (a) ordinary shares in the company, or (b) rights to subscribe for, or to convert securities into, ordinary shares in the company. 'Ordinary shares' means shares other than shares which as respects dividends and capital carry a right to participate only up to a specified amount in a distribution: s.560.

A company must not allot equity securities to a person on any terms unless:

(a) it has made an offer to each person who holds ordinary shares in the company to allot to him on the same or more favourable terms a proportion of those securities which is as nearly as practicable equal to the proportion in nominal value held by him or the ordinary share capital of the company, and

(b) the period during which any such offer may be accepted has expired or the company has received notice of the acceptance or refusal of every offer so made.

Shares held by the company as treasury shares are disregarded for the purposes of this section: s.561(4).

The section is subject to:

(a) ss.564–566 (exceptions to pre-emption right – bonus shares/issue for non-cash consideration/securities held under an employees' share scheme),

(b) ss.567 and 568 (exclusion of rights of pre-emption – exclusion by private companies/articles conferring corresponding right),

(c) ss.569–573 (disapplication of pre-emption rights – private company with one class of shares/directors acting under general authorisation/by special resolution/sale of treasury shares), and

(d) s.576 (saving for certain older pre-emption procedures): s.561(5).

No allotment shall be made of shares of a public company offered for subscription unless (a) the issue is subscribed in full, or (b) the offer is made on terms that the shares subscribed for may be allotted (i) in any event, or (ii) if specified conditions are met (and those conditions are met): s.578(1). The section further provides for repayment of all money received from applicants. An allotment in contravention of s.578 is voidable at the instance of the applicant within one month after the date of the allotment, and not later. It is voidable even if the company is in the course of being wound up: s.579(1) and (2).

10.5 Certification and transfer of securities

A certificate under the common seal of the company specifying any shares held by a member is *prima facie* evidence of his title to the shares: s.768(1). A company must within two months after allotment of any of its shares complete and have ready for delivery the certificates of the shares allotted: s.769(1). A company may not register a transfer of shares in the company unless (a) a proper instrument of transfer has been delivered to it, or (b) the transfer is an exempt transfer within the Stock Transfer Act 1982, or is in accordance with regulations under Chapter 2 of this Part of the Act: s.770(1). There is an exception in respect of registering persons to whom the right to shares has been transmitted by operation of law. When a transfer of shares has been lodged, the company must either (a) register the transfer, or (b) give the transferee notice of refusal to register the transfer, together with reasons for the refusal, as soon as practicable and in any event within two months after the date on which the transfer was lodged with it: s.771(1). The same applies on an application lodged by the transferor: s.772.

In the case of private companies, the directors will generally have an absolute discretion to refuse to register a transfer of shares. The only restriction on this power is that it must be exercised in what the directors consider to be the best interests of the company: *Re Smith & Fawcett Ltd* [1942] Ch 304. Private companies' articles will generally also contain pre-emption clauses requiring an existing shareholder to give first refusal to other members before the shares can be offered to outsiders. The pre-emption clause may even require the directors to purchase the shares: *Rayfield v. Hands* [1960] Ch 1; *Tett v. Phoenix Propery & Inv. Co. Ltd* [1986] BCLC 149, *Champagne Perrier–Jonet SA v. H.H. Finch Ltd* [1982] 3 All ER 713.

The certification by a company of an instrument of transfer of any shares in the company is to be taken as a representation by the company to any person acting on the faith of the certification that there have been produced to the company such documents as on their face show a *prima facie* title to the shares in the transferor's name in the instrument: s.775(1). The certification is not to be taken as a representation that the transferor has any title to the shares: s.775(2). Where a person acts on the faith of a false certification by a company made negligently, the company is under the same liability to him as if the certification had been made fraudulently: s.775(3). An instrument of transfer is certificated if it bears the words 'certificate lodged' (or words to the like effect): s.775 (4)(a). On transfer the company must issue certificates within two months after the transfer is lodged with the company: s.776(1).

In *Longman v. Bath Electric Tramways Ltd* [1905] 1 Ch 646, B became the registered holder of shares but two certificates made out in his name were not sent to him since, on the same day, B presented to the secretary for certification a transfer of the shares to H and M. Subsequently the secretary, by mistake, returned the original certificates to B, who lodged them with L as security for a loan. In an action by L to be registered as holder, the court held that the company owed a duty of care only to the transferee in respect of a share certificate lodged for certification, and that the proximate cause of the loss was the improper use by B of the certificates.

Chapter 2 of Part 21 allows the Treasury and the Secretary of State to make regulations for enabling title to securities to be evidenced and transferred without a written instrument: ss.783–790.

10.6 Estoppel by share certificate

Share certificates contain two statements of fact:

▶ of the name of the registered holder
▶ of the extent to which the shares are paid up.

If a company issues certificates which are incorrect and the statements are relied on by a third party, the company is estopped from denying the truth of the statement. In *Re Bahia and San Francisco Rly Co.* (1868) LR 3 QB 584, T, the registered holder of five shares, left the share certificate with her broker. Later a forged transfer purporting to be executed by T in favour of S and G was sent to the company for registration and a certificate issued to S and G. They later sold the shares to B. The company was ordered to restore T's name and B was awarded damages because the company was estopped from denying that S and G were the legal holders.

There must be an act in reliance on the false statement; thus the company is not generally liable to persons to whom the share certificate is issued. However, in *Balkis Consolidated Co. v. Tomkinson* [1893] AC 396, Tomkinson, acting in reliance on his supposed title to the shares, entered into a contract to sell them. When the company refused to register the transfer, he purchased more shares to honour his contract and successfully claimed damages against the company.

The company can claim an indemnity from the person sending in the forged transfer even though the person is totally innocent: *Sheffield Corporation v. Barclay* [1905] AC 392; and *Yeung Kei Yung v. Hong Kong & Shanghai Banking Corpn* [1981] AC 787. In *Bloomenthal v. Ford* [1897] AC 156, the appellant lent money to a company on the security of 10,000 £1 fully paid shares in the company. He was ordered to be removed from the list of contributories in respect of the shares on which nothing had been paid up on the ground of estoppel.

In *Ruben v. Great Fingall Consolidated* [1906] AC 439, it was held that a company could not be estopped by a forged share certificate issued by the company secretary, but the position now appears to be that a company is bound where a share certificate is authenticated by a company officer acting within the scope of his authority.

10.7   Information about interests in a company's shares

Public companies may give notice to persons that they know or have reasonable cause to believe (a) to be interested in their shares or (b) to have been interested during the three previous years, requiring them to confirm whether this is indeed the case and to give any further information in accordance with s.793. The shares in question are those carrying rights to vote in all circumstances at general meetings and include treasury shares held by the company: s.792.

10.8   Registered and bearer shares

Shares issued by a company limited by shares can be registered or bearer. The company must be authorised to issue bearer shares in its articles and may issue in respect of fully paid shares a share warrant stating that the bearer is entitled to the shares specified in it: s.779(1). This entitles the bearer to the shares specified, and the shares may be transferred by delivery of the warrant: s.779(2). The company may provide (by coupons or otherwise) for the payment of dividends on the shares: s.779(3). Bearer shares are extremely rare in the UK. On the issue of a share warrant the company is required to enter in the register of members the fact of the issue, a statement of the shares included in the warrant and the date of the issue of the warrant and, if necessary, amend the register so that no person is named as the holder of the shares specified in the warrant: s.122(1). If the articles provide, the bearer of the warrant may be deemed a member of the company: s.122(3).

For registered shares title is through the entry of the shareholder's name on the Register of Members, and transfer of title is under the Stock Transfer Act 1963, with the transferee replacing the transferor on the Register.

The CREST system for electronic registration of ownership and transfer of shares operates for listed securities. Investors can (i) choose to continue to use paper certificates, or (ii) be sponsored members of CREST and remain registered holders of securities; transfers will be through the sponsoring broker, or (iii) transfer shares to a nominee company operated by a CREST member (bank, stockbrokers, solicitors) to hold and deal in securities on their behalf. In this case, the shareholder is no longer the registered shareholder. Absence of paper certificates may make mortgaging the shares difficult. Handing the share certificate to the mortgagee is the normal way of creating an equitable mortgage. A legal mortgage involves transferring the legal title to the shares to the mortgagee subject to an obligation to retransfer the shares on repayment of the loan and interest.

In contrast to legal mortgagees of shares, equitable mortgagees are at a disadvantage (see Chapter 15, p.349)

10.9 Classes of shares and class rights

Prima facie, all shares enjoy equal rights, and where a company has different classes of shares, the presumption of equality applies unless rebutted. Where there are different classes of shares, companies can describe them in any way which seems appropriate. Shares with the same designation will, therefore, vary in respect of their rights between companies. The most frequently encountered classes of share are ordinary and preference shares. There is also a class of shares called deferred shares, but these are rare. All shares may be issued as redeemable shares, although redeemable preference shares are more usual. Shares are of one class if the rights attached to them are in all respects uniform: s.629(1).

(a) Ordinary shares

Unless otherwise indicated, all shares issued by a company are presumed to be ordinary shares. The implied rights of an ordinary shareholder by law are (i) to be paid an unlimited, non-cumulative dividend where the company makes a profit and a dividend is declared – after payment of any preference dividends; (ii) to receive notice of and attend and vote at company general meetings; and (iii) the return of capital and share in any surplus capital on winding-up.

(b) Preference shares

The defining characteristic of preference shares is that the holders always have a priority right to payment of a fixed dividend ahead of the payment of a dividend to the ordinary shareholders. There is a presumption that the right to a dividend is cumulative, but the right to a dividend only arises when the dividend is declared, and arrears of undeclared cumulative dividends are not provable in a winding-up but are paid out of surplus assets after payment of the company's debts.

Preference shareholders frequently have a right to prior repayment of capital on winding-up. They normally have no right to receive notice of company meetings and will not have a right to vote except where the articles provide for a right to vote where the dividend payment is in arrears.

(c) Deferred shares

Also known as management or founders' shares, they usually entitle their holders to multiple voting rights and an unlimited dividend deferred until a fixed minimum percentage is paid to the ordinary shareholders. Capital repayment is also deferred and the deferred shareholders have exclusive rights to surplus assets. The prospectus must give details of any deferred shares. They are rarely issued.

10.10 Variation of class rights

Rights attached to a class of a company's shares may be varied only:

(a) in accordance with provision in the company's articles for the variation of those rights, or
(b) where the company's articles contain no such provision, if the holders of shares of that class consent to the variation in accordance with s.630: s.630(2).

The consent required on the part of the holders of a class of a company's shares is:

(a) consent in writing from the holders of at least three-quarters in nominal value of the issued shares of that class (excluding treasury shares), or
(b) a special resolution passed at a separate general meeting of the holders of that class sanctioning the variation: s.630(4).

Any amendment of a provision contained in a company's articles for the variation of the rights attached to a class of shares or the insertion of any such provision into the articles is itself to be treated as a variation of those rights: s.630(5).

Where the rights attached to any class of shares are varied under s.630, the holders of not less in the aggregate than 15 per cent of the issued shares of the class (being persons who did not consent to or vote in favour of the resolution for variation) may apply to the court to have the variation cancelled. Treasury shares are disregarded for this purpose: s.633(1) and (2). If an application is made, the variation has no effect until confirmed by the court: s.633(3). Application must be made within 21 days after the date on which the consent was given or the resolution was passed, and may be made on behalf of the shareholders by one or more of their number as they may appoint in writing: s.633(4). The company must within 15 days of the court order forward a copy of the order to the registrar: s.635(1).

Where a company assigns a name or other designation or a new name or other designation to any class or description of shares, it must within one month deliver to the registrar a notice giving particulars of the name or designation: s.636(1). Where the rights attached to any shares are varied, the company must within one month deliver to the registrar a notice giving particulars of the variation: s.637(1).

(a) Variation of class rights and preference shares

A series of decisions has established that, where a class of shares is given express rights in respect of dividends, voting or return of capital, these rights are an exhaustive statement of those rights. In *Will v. United Lankat Plantations Ltd* [1914] AC 11, it was held that the right to a 10 per cent fixed dividend ruled out claims to participate in a higher dividend to the ordinary shareholders. This meant a presumption that preference shares were not participating preference shares, making them less desirable for investors.

In *Scottish Insurance Corporation Ltd v. Wilsons & Clyde Coal Co. Ltd* [1949] AC 462, following the nationalisation of the coal industry, WCC Ltd transferred its mines to the National Coal Board in return for compensation. Before going into liquidation, the company reduced its capital by paying off and cancelling the preference shares to deprive the preference shareholders from sharing in the distribution of surplus assets. The court held that the preferential right to return of capital was an exhaustive statement of the preference shareholders' rights on liquidation and that the ordinary shareholders had sole claim to surplus assets.

The court also held that the proposal to cancel the preference shares was perfectly legal. In the House of Lords Lord Simonds stated, 'Whether a man lends money to a company at 7 per cent or subscribes for its shares carrying a cumulative preferential dividend at that rate, I do not think that he can complain of unfairness if the company ... proposes to pay him off.'

The decision further diminished the status and value of preference shares. In a similar case involving another coal-mining company which, post-nationalisation, was to continue in business in Northern Ireland, the reduced business could no longer support the burden of the preference shareholders' dividend rights, and the company proposed cancelling them. The court held that, on a capital reduction, a company had a legal obligation to respect the preferential right to return of capital; and that, if a company was unable to meet the preference shareholders' dividend rights, it would be negligent if it failed to cancel them: *Re Chatterley-Whitfield Collieries Ltd* [1948] 2 All ER 593, affirmed in *Prudential Assurance Co. Ltd v. Chatterley-Whitfield Collieries Ltd* [1949] AC 512.

The effect was to make preference shareholders vulnerable to a selective capital reduction at any time. As long as the shareholders received the same rights on reduction as they were entitled to on a winding-up, there is no variation of their class rights and they have no right to be consulted on the decision.

In *Re Saltdean Estate Co. Ltd* [1968] 1 WLR 1844, the company proposed a selective reduction to remove the preference shareholders prior to a large dividend distribution to the ordinary shareholders. It was held that the risk of prior repayment is 'part of the bargain between the shareholders and forms an integral part of the definition or limitation of the bundle of rights which make up a preferred share'.

The House of Lords endorsed this decision in *House of Fraser plc v. ACGE Investments Ltd* [1987] AC 387, which also approved of the Court of Appeal's statement: '[i]n our opinion the proposed cancellation of the preference shares would involve fulfilment or satisfaction of the contractual rights of the shareholders, and would not involve any variation of their rights': *Re House of Fraser plc* [1987] BCLC 293.

In *Re Northern Engineering Industries plc* [1994] 2 BCLC 704, the articles provided that the rights attached to any shares shall be deemed to be varied by 'the reduction of the capital paid up on those shares'. The company proposed to pay off and cancel the preference shares. The Court of Appeal refused to confirm the reduction on the ground that it constituted a variation of class rights and that the shareholders had not consented. The company had argued that the clause covered only a reduction to a lower nominal value and not their cancellation.

(b)   The judicial definition of a variation of class rights

The courts distinguish between a direct variation of the rights and indirect variation by changing the environment in which those rights exist. The latter is not considered a variation of class rights.

In *White v. Bristol Aeroplane Co.* [1953] Ch 65, an increase in capitalisation which diluted the control of the existing class of preference shareholders was not a variation of their class rights; neither was a proposed bonus issue of ordinary shares to defeat the voting control of preference shareholders: *Re John Smith's Tadcaster Brewery* [1953] Ch 308.

In *Greenhalgh v. Arderne Cinemas Ltd* [1946] 1 All ER 512, a resolution by AC Ltd, with two classes of share, 10p and 50p, both carrying a right to vote, to split its 50p shares into five 10p shares and destroy the previous control over special resolutions held by G in respect of his 10p shares was not a variation of class rights.

Similarly, a rateable reduction of capital which affected the dividend rights of the preference shareholders was not a variation of class rights: *Re Mackenzie & Co. Ltd* [1916] 2 Ch 450. It is now worth considering whether these decisions would not be grounds for a petition under s.994 (see below p.229).

In *Cumbrian Newspapers Group Ltd v. Cumberland & Westmorland Herald Newspaper & Printing Co. Ltd* [1986] BCLC 286, the claimant company acquired over 10 per cent of the shares in the defendant company the articles of which gave special rights to prevent the defendant from being taken over without the claimant's consent. The court held that where specific rights were conferred on members in their capacity as members, the shares for the time being held by those members constituted a 'class of shares' and the rights were class rights for the purposes of s.125 (now s.630).

In *Harman and Another v. BML Group Ltd* [1994] 1 WLR 893, a company had 190,000 B shares held by B and 310,000 A shares, 260,000 of which were held by H and M. Under a shareholders' agreement the two classes of shares ranked equally except for certain specified pre-emption rights, and a shareholders' meeting was inquorate unless a B shareholder or proxy was present. The Court of Appeal held that B's right to be present in a quorum was a class right.

10.11 Ways of ceasing to be a member

- Transfer
- Forfeiture or surrender
- Sale by the company under its power of lien
- Transmission
- Redemption of redeemable shares.

10.12 The register of members

Every company is required to keep a register of its members giving their names and addresses, the dates on which they were registered as members and the dates on which they ceased to be members. For a company limited by shares, the register must identify the shares held by class: s.113. The register is to be available for inspection at its registered office or at a place specified in regulations under s.1136: s.114. Every company with more than 50 members must keep an index of the names of the members and make necessary alterations to the index within 14 days of an alteration in the register. The register must at all times be available for inspection in the same place as the register of members: s.115. The register and index must be open to inspection by any member without charge and any other person on payment of the prescribed fee. Any person may require a copy of the register or part of it on payment of the prescribed fee: s.116. Where the company receives a request under s.116, it must comply with the request or apply to the court within five working days. If the court is satisfied that the inspection or copy is not sought for a proper purpose, it shall direct the company not to comply with the request and with any other requests for a similar purpose; otherwise the company must immediately comply with the request: s.117. Refusal of inspection or default in providing a copy otherwise than in accordance with a court order is an offence committed by the company and every officer in default: s.118. It is also an offence for a person seeking a right to inspect or request a copy under s.116 knowingly or recklessly to make a statement which is misleading, false or deceptive in a material particular: s.119. When a person inspects the register or is provided with a copy of it, the company must inform him of the most recent date on which alterations were made and that no further alteration are intended to be made: s.120. Entries relating to former members may be removed 10 years from the date on which they ceased to be members: s.121.

In the case of limited companies with a single member, the company's register must contain a statement that the company has only one member: s.123. Where a company holds its own shares as treasury shares, the company must be entered in the register as the member in respect of those shares: s.124.

If a person's name is entered in or omitted from the register without sufficient cause, or there is default or unnecessary delay in entering on the register the fact that a person has ceased to be a member, the aggrieved person or a member of the company or the company may apply to the court for rectification of the register. The court may refuse the application or order rectification and payment by the company of any damages sustained by any aggrieved party. In so doing, the court may decide any question relating to the title of a person who is a party to the application to have his name entered in or omitted from the register: s.125. No notice of any trust, express, implied or constructive, shall be entered on the register or be receivable by the registrar: s.126. The register is *prima facie* evidence of any matters which are directed or authorised to be inserted in it by the Companies Act 2006: s.127. Liability of the company arising from making or deleting an entry or from failure to make or delete an entry is not enforceable more than 10 years after the date on which the entry was made or deleted or the failure first occurred: s.128.

10.13 Restrictions on transfers

The articles of private companies may allow the directors to refuse to register transfers of shares. Where the refusal is not on specified grounds, the directors do not have to justify their refusal, which can be queried only where there is evidence that they acted in bad faith or had not considered the question at all: *Re Coalport China Co.* [1895] 2 Ch 404. Where directors have an absolute discretion to refuse to register a transfer without justification, the power is subject only to the duty of the directors to act in good faith in what they consider to be the company's best interests: *Re Smith & Fawcett Ltd* [1942] Ch 304. The burden of proof is on the person seeking to establish bad faith: *Charles Forte Investments Ltd v. Amanda* [1963] 2 All ER 940.

Public companies can have restrictions on free transferability except where their shares are dealt with on the stock exchange or the alternative investment market (AIM). The most frequent restriction provides that shares cannot be transferred to a non-member as long as there is an existing member prepared to purchase them at a fair price. Where articles provide that shares must first be offered to existing members before they can be transferred to an outsider, a transfer to an outsider without the members' knowledge is invalid: *Tett v. Phoenix Property & Inv. Co. Ltd* [1986] BCLC 149.

Articles may provide that other members are bound to buy the shares of a member wishing to transfer them: *Rayfield v. Hands* [1960] Ch 1, and a company enforcing a power of sale under a lien must comply with the clause: *Champagne Perrier–Jonet SA v. H H Finch Ltd* [1982] 3 All ER 713.

10.14 The register of substantial shareholdings

There are provisions for disclosure of substantial shareholdings carrying unrestricted voting rights. If a person obtains an interest in at least 3 per cent of the nominal value of that share capital or disposes of the same, s/he has an obligation to notify the company in writing within two days. The company must make the necessary entry within three days in a special register: ss.198–219.

End of topic summary

Having read and understood this part of the chapter, you should have a detailed knowledge of the different classes of shares which a company can issue and the rights generally attached to those shares.

In particular you should have knowledge of these matters of special importance:

▷ The limited rights of the holders of preference shares as opposed to ordinary shares and their position as quasi-creditors of the company.
▷ The protection offered by the Companies Act in respect of unilateral variation of class rights and the way in which this protection is reduced by the judicial definition of class rights.
▷ The ways in which the free transfer of shares in a private limited company is generally restricted by the constitution.

The following questions are practical illustrations of the principles relating to this topic.

10.15 Minority protection

The basic rule in respect of the control of companies is that of majority rule. If there is a wrong against a company or an alleged irregularity in its internal management which can be confirmed by a simple majority of the members, the court will not interfere at the suit of a minority, which must accept the decision of the majority. This rule of the common law was established in *Foss v. Harbottle* (1843) 2 Hare 461. The attitude was that the minority could attempt to convert the majority to its view by the process of persuasion and otherwise to sell its shares.

This principle was restated in *Edwards v. Halliwell* [1950] 2 All ER 1064. The rule had two aspects: (i) the proper claimant in an action in respect of a wrong alleged to be done to a company is *prima facie* the company; and (ii) where the alleged wrong is a transaction which may be made binding on the company and all its members by a simple majority of the members, no individual member of the company is allowed to maintain an action in respect of that matter.

In *Stein v. Blake* [1998] 1 All ER 724, the Court of Appeal, applying *Prudential Assurance Co. Ltd v. Newman Industries Ltd (No. 2)* [1982] 1 All ER 354, ruled that a shareholder was not entitled to sue in respect of an alleged misappropriation of companies' assets by the other shareholder, and that it was only the companies, or their liquidators, which could bring the actions.

This is based on the reflective loss principle whereby the shareholder's loss is a reflection of the company's loss and the action should be brought by the company. Thus, where the shareholder's loss is the collapse in the share value following a wrong to the company, this will be redressed if the company recovers damages from the wrongdoer. The principle was endorsed by the House of Lords in *Johnson v. Gore Wood & Co* [2001] 1 All ER 481. Where the shareholder's loss is separate and distinct from the company's, however, each may sue in respect of his loss. In addition, a shareholder can sue where the wrong to the company prevents it from suing the wrongdoer.

In *Giles v. Rhind* [2002] 4 All ER 977, a company formed by G and R was driven into administrative receivership after R diverted a major contract to his new business and the company had to abandon its claim against R. The Court of Appeal allowed G to sue for the collapse in the value of his shareholding, even though this was reflective of the company's loss. He was also able to claim in respect of loss of future remuneration, pension contributions and other benefits in his capacity as a past employee.

10.16 Statutory derivative claims by members

Under the Companies Act 2006, members have a statutory right to bring derivative claims in respect of a cause of action vested in the company, and seek relief on behalf of the company: s.260(1). These actions can only be brought under Chapter 1 of Part 11 or by way of proceedings for unfair prejudice: s.994.

A derivative claim may be brought in respect of a cause of action arising from an actual or proposed act or omission involving negligence, default, breach of duty or breach of trust by a director: s.260(3). It is immaterial whether the cause of action arose before or after the person seeking to bring or continue the derivative claim became a member of the company: s.260(4).

Members bringing a derivative claim must apply to the court for permission to continue it (s.261(1)), and if the application and evidence filed do not disclose a *prima facie* case for permission, the court must dismiss the application: s.261(2). If the application is not dismissed, the court may give directions as to the evidence to be produced by the company and adjourn the proceedings to enable evidence to be obtained: s.261(3).

Permission must be refused if the court is satisfied that a person acting in accordance with s.172 (duty to promote the company's success) would not seek to continue the claim. In addition, the court refuses permission where the action arises from a prospective act or omission which has been authorised by the company or, where it arises from an existing act or omission, that it was previously authorised by the company or subsequently ratified: s.263(2).

In considering whether to give permission, the court must take into account in particular: whether the member is acting in good faith in seeking to continue the claim; the importance that a person acting to promote the success of the company would attach to continuing it; whether in the case of a proposed act or omission it would be likely to be authorised or ratified and, where it is an existing act or omission, whether it could be, and would be likely to be, ratified; whether the company has decided not to pursue the claim; and whether the act or omission gives rise to a personal cause of action for the member: s.263(3).

The Act also covers applications from a member to continue an action as a derivative action where the company has brought the claim but has failed to prosecute the claim diligently: s.262. The Act also provides for a member to take over a derivative action claim initiated by another member, or from a member who has continued as a derivative claim one initiated by the company, or from a member who has abandoned a derivative claim which was taken over from another member under s.264.

In conclusion, the statutory remedy is wider in that it encompasses negligence. The fact that claims can also be brought in respect of wrongs committed prior to a person becoming a shareholder merely reiterates the common law position. The need for permission to continue the claim also reflects the common law, as do the circumstances when permission must be refused as well as the criteria to be taken into account in giving permission.

The requirement that the claimant act in good faith reflects the equitable nature of the common law derivative claim, and the provisions relating to adopting claims commenced by the company or another member are also merely clearly spelled out, as opposed to radically new.

The one area of radical change is in respect of the court ordering the company to produce evidence and adjourning the proceedings while the evidence is acquired: s.261(3). This is a major improvement on the common law, where obtaining evidence of wrongdoing was always a problem for the claimant. This should facilitate derivative claims in the future.

Finally, the emphasis on whether the act or omission has, is likely to be or can be ratified reflects the principle of majority control which gave birth to the rule in *Foss v. Harbottle*.

10.17 Petition against unfair prejudice

'Any member of a company may apply to the court by petition for an order under this section on the ground that the affairs of the company are being or have been conducted in a manner which is unfairly prejudicial to the interests of its members generally or some part of its members (including at least himself) or that any actual or proposed act or omission of the company (including an act or omission on its behalf) is or would be so prejudicial': s. 994(1).

The court can make any order on the petition, but s.461(2) gives some examples. These include (i) regulating the conduct of the company's affairs in the future; (ii) requiring the company to refrain from doing or continuing an act complained of or conversely ensuring the action of a company where the petitioner complains of a failure to act; (iii) authorisation of civil proceedings in the name and on behalf of the company; and (iv) the purchase of a member's shares by other members or by the company itself.

Where purchase of shares is sought, their valuation can be either as a proportionate part of the company without discount for the fact of being a minority holding, or at the discounted market value. The Court of Appeal favoured the first solution where the petitioner is being forced out of a quasi-partnership company: *Re Bird Precision Bellows Ltd* [1986] 2 WLR 158.

In *Re Cumana Ltd* [1986] BCLC 430, Vinelott J chose to value the shares at the time of the presentation of the petition, and on appeal the Court of Appeal held that 'the date for valuation … is a matter for the … trial judge's discretion'. It also rejected the inclusion in the order of an 'escape clause' to cover a situation in which the party was unable to find the necessary money to purchase the shares.

It is important to identify what is meant by unfair prejudicial conduct and the nature of the interests of the members capable of unfair prejudice.

The court has suggested that the basic test is whether the value of the member's shareholding has been seriously impaired: *Re A Company* [1983] 2 All ER 36. In *Re Bovey Hotel Ventures Ltd* (1981), Slade J added that the test of unfairness is objective and not subjective. It is not necessary for the petitioner to show that the persons complained of acted in the conscious knowledge that what they were doing was unfair. The test is whether a reasonable bystander would regard the actions as unfairly prejudicial to the petitioner.

In *Re Elgindata Ltd* [1991] BCLC 959, the court rejected a petition alleging mismanagement. However, in *Re Macro (Ipswich) Ltd* [1994] 2 BCLC 354, the court stated that where the mismanagement was sufficiently significant to cause loss to the company, then it could constitute the basis for finding unfair prejudice.

The fact that the petitioner's own behaviour is not unimpeachable is not an automatic bar to relief under s.459 since it is not an equitable remedy. The behaviour may, however, be significant. Thus in *Re R. A. Noble & Sons (Clothing) Ltd* [1983] BCLC 273, the court held that the petitioner's exclusion from management was justified by his own neglect of his responsibilities and his s.459 petition was rejected. In *Re London School of Electronics Ltd* [1986] Ch 211, the court held that the petitioner's misconduct did not disqualify him from petitioning since it was in reaction to the unfairly prejudicial conduct on which the petition was based. The court indicated, however, that in such a case this could influence the nature of the relief accorded to the petitioner.

The first reported decision on s.459, *Re A Company* [1983] 2 All ER 36, followed s.210 Companies Act 1948 in limiting the right to cases where the unfair prejudice affected a person as a shareholder. This would have barred petitions based on exclusion from management, as in *Ebrahimi v. Westbourne Galleries Ltd* [1973] AC 360 (see p. 231). However, in *Re A Company* [1983] 2 All ER 854, Vinelot J stated obiter, 'It seems to me unlikely that the legislature could have intended to exclude from the scope of s.459 a shareholder in the position of Mr Ebrahimi in the Westbourne Galleries case'. And in *Re A Company* [1986] BCLC 376, Hoffmann J said, 'In the case of a small private company in which two or three members have ventured their capital ... on the footing that each will earn his living by working for the company as a director ... [the] member's interests ... may include a legitimate expectation that he will continue to be employed as a director and his dismissal from that office and exclusion from the management of the company may therefore be unfairly prejudicial to his interests as a member'. Relief has been obtained where the petitioner complained of removal from office among other things (*Re Bird Precision Bellows Ltd* (1986); *Re Cumana Ltd* (1986); and *Re London School of Electronics Ltd* [1986] Ch 211).

In *Re Ghyll Beck Driving Range Ltd* [1993] BCLC 1126, a father and son in December 1990 set up a company with two others to run a golf range. Each was an equal shareholder and director. By June 1991 the parties had fallen out, with the petitioner being increasingly isolated. Following a scuffle between him and his father, the business was run without reference to the petitioner. The court held that he had been unjustifiably excluded from a joint venture where it was contemplated that the business would be managed by all four for their mutual benefit.

In *Re A Company* [1986] BCLC 376, the court refused to strike out a petition on the ground that it related only to the petitioners' interests as vendors and employees. Hoffmann J stated, 'the interests of a member are not necessarily limited to his strict legal rights under the constitution of the company'. And in *Re Sam Weller & Sons Ltd* [1990] Ch 682, the court held that a company which had followed the same dividend policy for 37 years was unfairly prejudicial to members of the company who relied on the dividend for their income, as opposed to those shareholders remunerated as directors. The court held that holders of the same class of shares can have different interests. In respect of the petitioners, Gibson J stated, 'As their only income from the company is by way of dividend, their interests may be not only prejudiced by the policy of low dividend payments, but unfairly prejudiced'.

Successful actions have been brought in respect of breaches of fiduciary duties including conflict of interests: *Re Bovey Hotel Ventures Ltd*, 31 July 1981, unreported, excessive remuneration and a rights issue regarded as an attempt to dilute the interest of a shareholder: *Re A Company (No. 002612 of 1984)* [1985] BCLC 80; and *Re Cumana Ltd* [1986] BCLC 430.

10.18 Just and equitable winding-up

The court has a wide discretionary power to wind up a company on a petition presented by a member under s.122(1)(g) IA 1986.

In the leading case of *Ebrahimi v. Westbourne Galleries Ltd* [1973] AC 360, Lord Wilberforce stressed that in his view the general words should not be reduced to the sum of particular instances, and most of the old cases could be subsumed by the criteria established in *Ebrahimi*. In this case, E had been in a partnership with N and they later formed a company to take over the business, and became the only directors and shareholders, each holding 500 shares. When N's son joined the business, E and N transferred 100 shares to him and he became a director. E was removed from the board and petitioned for the just and equitable winding-up.

The House of Lords held that the exercise of legal rights was subject to equitable considerations which might make it unjust or inequitable for a person to insist on exercising his/her strict legal rights, that E and N had formed the company to perpetuate their previous partnership, and that E's exclusion was unjust.

Lord Wilberforce suggested that the remedy applied to a small private company where one or more of the following factors was present: (i) it was an association formed or continued on the basis of a personal relationship, involving mutual confidence; (ii) there was an agreement that all or some of the shareholders should participate in the management of the business; and (iii) there were restrictions on the transfer of the members' shares.

This decision has been applied in a number of cases. In *Re A & BC Chewing Gum Ltd* [1975] 1 All ER 1017, the minority shareholder was entitled under the articles and by virtue of a separate agreement to appoint one director. When the majority refused to give effect to the appointment, the court held that the company should be wound up.

In *Re North End Motels (Huntly) Ltd* [1976] 1 NZLR 446, the court ordered the company to be wound up where a minority shareholder/director was consistently outvoted at board meetings. It was influenced by the fact that the petitioner had had no independent advice before joining the company and had very little business experience, and the majority shareholder had the final word as to share valuation.

The equitable principles of *Ebrahimi* have been applied outside the framework of a winding-up petition. Thus in *Clemens v. Clemens Bros Ltd* [1976] 2 All ER 268, the court set aside an issue of additional shares aimed at diluting the claimant's holding. However, in *Bentley-Stevens v. Jones* [1974] 2 All ER 653, the court held that a director could not claim reinstatement under *Ebrahimi*.

The link between these petitions is clear from *Re R A Noble & Sons (Clothing) Ltd* [1983] BCLC 273, where the petitioner was refused relief under s.459 since his exclusion from management was prejudicial but not unfair, but obtained a winding-up order under s.122(1)(g), under the *Ebrahimi* criteria. Similarly, in *Jesner Ltd v. Jarrad Properties Ltd* [1993] BCLC 1032, the petitioner obtained a just and equitable winding-up, having failed to establish unfair prejudice. A petition for unfair prejudice is to be preferred, but the right to petition for just and equitable winding-up seems wider.

A petition under s.994 is not restricted to small companies, but its application to large companies has not been very successful. In *Re Tottenham Hotspur plc* [1994] 1 BCLC 655, the court rejected a claim to reinstate V pursuant to an agreement that S would be chairman and V a director and chief executive. The just and equitable petition is restricted to small companies.

10.19 DTI investigations

The DTI may appoint inspectors on the application of 200 members or members holding not less than one-tenth of the issued shares: CA 1985, s.431; or where there are circumstances suggesting fraud, illegality, unfair prejudice to members, misfeasance or other misconduct of the company's officers, or the wrongful withholding of information from members: CA 1985, s.432(2). This is more useful since there is no minimum of members required. The Secretary of State must also appoint inspectors where the court so orders: CA 1985, s.432(1).

Inspectors may question directors and other officers and requisition documents, whereas it is frequently difficult for a minority shareholder to establish his/her allegations against the controllers. Where the inspection produces sufficient evidence, the Secretary of State can proceed to petition for the winding up of the company or petition against unfair prejudice in the same way as a member under s.460. The report furnished by the inspectorate may also lead to the disqualification of directors. Investigations tend to be used for corporate insolvency investigations, and minority shareholders are unlikely to obtain relief.

End of Topic Summary

Having read this section of the chapter, you should have a clear idea of the nature of the legal protection offered to minority shareholders against the abuse of their position by the majority shareholders and controllers – including abuse by the directors.

The most important weapons at the disposal of the minority shareholder are to petition under s.994 CA 2006 and the new statutory derivative action under s.260 which has cleared up most of the uncertainties of the old common law remedy it replaces.

There is an obvious overlap between a petition for unfair prejudice and a petition for just and equitable winding-up under the IA 1986. The tendency to combine the two petitions as an alternative is discouraged since a winding-up petition triggers serious consequences including a complete suspension of trading unless the court otherwise orders. This is discussed in Chapter 13.

The procedure under s.459 CA 1985 (now s.994) was criticised as being costly since cases can run for many weeks. The position would appear to be unchanged.

Questions on shares and shareholders

1. Premier Hotels plc has a share capital of two million £1 ordinary shares and one million £1 7 per cent cumulative preference shares. The preference shares have the following rights under the articles:

   (a) a right to participate rateably with the ordinary shareholders in the profits of the company

   (b) a preferential right to dividends and repayment of capital on winding-up.

   Following the sale of Elyseum Hotels, the directors decide that the company has capital surplus to its requirements and that, operating a reduced business, it will be difficult to support the payment of the preferential dividend. The sale of the hotel chain leaves the company with sufficient reserves to enable it to reduce its capital selectively by buying in the preferential shares.

   The ordinary shareholders have passed a special resolution proposing to reduce the issued share capital by repaying the preference shares at par in spite of the fact that they stand at a premium in the market. The preference shareholders have not yet received a dividend in respect of the previous financial year.

   Advise Sid, a preference shareholder who does not wish to lose his shares, whether (i) he can prevent Premier Hotels plc from going through with the scheme and otherwise (ii) whether he is entitled to arrears of cumulative dividend prior to being bought out.

2. To what extent does the law protect shareholders against a variation of their class rights? Are there any weaknesses which can be identified in the current system as a result of the judicial definition of what constitutes variation? To what extent has it offered protection to preference shareholders?

Questions on minority protection

1. Brenda, Charles and Diana set up a catering business, Fancy Cakes. The business expanded and they registered a company in the same name to which the business was transferred. They each held a third of the shares and were the sole directors of the company.

   Charles became involved in a new venture and neglected his duties. Brenda and Diana decided to remove Charles from the company. The articles of association provide that 'in the event of a resolution to remove a person from the board, the shares held by that director shall on a poll have three votes per share instead of the usual one'.

At a meeting of the company, which Charles failed to attend, a resolution was passed to increase the capital by a 1 for 2 rights issue. Brenda and Diana took up their shares but Charles did not because he had no spare cash, a fact of which Brenda and Diana were aware when the plan was conceived.

A later meeting passed resolutions to remove the weighted voting provision from the articles and remove Charles from the board.

Advise Charles of the legality of these actions and any statutory remedies available to him.

2. Mark is a shareholder in a company owned and controlled by two families which have inherited the company from the founder. Mark and the other members of his family own 45 per cent of the shares. The other family owns the remaining 55 per cent of the shares and the directors of the company are appointed from the members of the family.

The board has recently resolved that the company will not pay a dividend at the end of the financial year but that the directors will receive increased fees. At the same board meeting, it was decided that the company would make a rights issue. The board was aware that Mark and the other members of his family would be unlikely to be able to afford to take up the offer and that this would result in their stake in the company being reduced from 45 per cent to 10 per cent.

Mark believes that the company has made sufficient profits to justify a dividend and that the fresh injection of capital is not required.

Advise Mark as to any rights and remedies which he may have under the law.

3. Section 994 Companies Act 2006 enables a member of a company to petition for an order on the ground that the company's affairs are being or have been conducted in a manner which is 'unfairly prejudicial to the interests of its members generally or of some part of its members'. Explain:
   (i)   the meaning of the term 'unfairly prejudicial';
   (ii) the way in which the behaviour of the petitioner affects the success of the petition;
   (iii) the relationship between s.994 and s.122(1)(g) IA 1986.

4. Explain the ways in which the statutory right of members to bring a derivative claim mirrors the old common law derivative claim whilst at the same time widening its scope.

Chapter 11

Registered companies: directors and directors' duties

Learning objectives

After reading this chapter you will know about:

▶ corporate governance
▶ directors: appointment, retirement and disqualification
▶ directors' duties to the company, shareholders and creditors
▶ enforcement of directors' duties.

All references are to the Companies Act (CA) 2006, unless stated otherwise.

Hot Topic . . .

CORPORATE GOVERNANCE IN THE UK

The financial scandals of the 1980s and 1990s led to the questioning of the corporate governance mechanisms and a series of reports to strengthen the self-regulatory codes applicable to large, publicly quoted companies:

▶ Cadbury Report 1992
▶ Greenbury Report 1995
▶ Hampel Report 1998
▶ Higgs Report 2003

The Cadbury Report examined the financial aspects of corporate governance and favoured self-regulation. The recommendations were summarised in a Code of Best Practice and included shortening the length of directors' contracts of employment to three years. The recommendations of the Report can be summarised under three headings.

Under the heading of recommendations for structural and functional alterations, the Report recommended the following:

▶ That the board of directors should contain a minimum of three non-executive directors (NEDs) to exercise a supervisory function and bring 'an independent judgement ... on issues of strategy, performance, resources, including key appointments, and standards of conduct'.
▶ That there should be a separation of the roles of chairman and chief executive.
▶ That audit committees should be created to provide a direct link between auditors and NEDs.
▶ That remuneration committees composed entirely or mainly of NEDs should be created to oversee board remuneration.
▶ That the company secretary should have enhanced status to ensure that board procedures were followed and regularly reviewed.

The Report was also concerned with the issue of the assumption of responsibility, making those governing the company aware of their responsibilities and ensuring that the responsibilities were effectively discharged. To this end the Report recommended:

▶ That there should be a statement of directors' responsibilities for the company's accounts and the auditors' responsibilities in carrying out the audit.
▶ That directors should make a statement in the accounts regarding ensuring a proper system of control over the company's financial management.
▶ That there should be a policy statement on the part of institutional investors about the exercise of their voting power and the monitoring of the board's performance.

The Report also recommended that there should be enhanced disclosure to ensure the effective working of financial reporting and the audit. It recommended an amendment to the listing rules to require a compliance statement by the board in respect of the Code of Best Practice and any reasons for non-compliance with the Code.

The Greenbury Report followed an outcry against board remuneration and contained a Code of Best Practice for Directors' Remuneration. It reinforced the Cadbury Report on remuneration committees and required audit committees to report annually to shareholders on the company's remuneration policy. It required more detail about remuneration packages.

Service contracts were restricted to one-year rolling contracts with two-year rolling contracts in exceptional cases.

The Hampel Report produced a draft set of principles and a code covering the work of the two previous committees and its own work. The London Stock Exchange issued the Combined Code, subtitled 'Principles of Good Governance and Code of Best Practice', on 25 June 1998 as an appendix to the listing rules. In March 2000, a survey showed that 93 per cent of FTSE All Share Index companies had boards with one-third or more NEDs.

The Higgs Report followed on from the Enron scandal in the USA and led to a revision of the Combined Code from July 2003.

11.1 The directors

(a) Definition

In the Companies Act 2006, a director is defined as including 'any person occupying the position of a director, by whatever name called': s. 250. There are three categories of director: *de jure* directors; *de facto* directors and shadow directors. Shadow directors are defined as persons 'in accordance with whose directions or instructions the directors of the company are accustomed to act', but excluding persons giving advice in a professional capacity: s.251. There is a proviso that 'a body corporate is not to be treated as a shadow director of any of its subsidiary companies by reason only that the directors of the subsidiary are accustomed to act in accordance with its directions or instructions'.

The Company Directors Disqualification Act (CDDA) 1986 contains a similar definition of a director (s. 22(4)) and shadow director (s.22(5)), as does the Insolvency Act (IA) 1986 (s. 251). The proviso excluding parent companies in respect of their subsidiaries is missing from the IA 1986, however, and parent companies can be shadow directors of subsidiaries for the purposes of s.214 and wrongful trading and are subject to statutory disqualification.

(b) *De facto* and shadow directors

The parties most vulnerable to claims of being *de facto* or shadow directors are major shareholders, creditors (including banks) and consultants, and they are the subjects of most of the legal decisions considered below.

Early UK decisions attempt to define and distinguish between *de facto* and shadow directors. Sir Nicolas Browne-Wilkinson V-C likened a shadow director to an *eminence grise*: *Re: Lo-Line Electric Motors Ltd* [1988] Ch 477. And Harman J referred to the shadow director as 'the puppet master controlling the actions of the board' and the boards as the 'cat's paw' of the shadow director: *Re: Unisoft Group Ltd* [1994] 1 BCLC 609.

In *Re a Company (No 005009 of 1987) ex parte Copp* [1989] BCLC 13 it was claimed that a bank which imposed terms on a corporate client as a condition of allowing a technically insolvent company to continue to trade was a shadow director, although the claim was not pursued at the subsequent hearing: *Re M. C. Bacon Ltd* [1990] BCLC 324. Another claim against a bank occurred in *Kuwait Asia Bank EC v. National Mutual Life Nominees Ltd* [1991] 1 AC 187. The Kuwait Bank and another company held 80 per cent of the shares in AIC Securities Ltd (AICS). By agreement between them, AICS was to have five directors, two nominated by the bank and three by the other company. The bank's nominees were bank employees. Rejecting a claim that the bank was a shadow director of AICS as its board was accustomed to act in accordance with its instructions, Lord Lowry stated, '[the bank's nominees] were two out of five directors … And there is no allegation … that the directors … were accustomed to act on the direction and instruction of the bank.' This is authority that a person could be a shadow director only if all the board as a whole was accustomed to act on its directions or instructions.'

In *Re Hydrodam (Corby) Ltd* [1994] 2 BCLC 180, the liquidator of Hydrodam, a wholly-owned subsidiary of Eagle Trust Plc, applied for orders against 14 defendants under s.214 IA 1986 including Eagle Trust plc, one of its subsidiaries and all of its directors, maintaining that they were shadow or *de facto* directors of Hydrodam, which had two corporate directors. Millett J agreed that s.214 liability extended to *de facto* as well as shadow directors, but held there was an essential difference between the two, seeing them as alternatives and 'in most and in perhaps all cases…mutually exclusive'.

According to Millet J, a *de facto* director was held out as a director, claimed to be a director although never actually appointed as such and undertook functions which only a director could properly discharge. In contrast, a shadow director was a person who did not claim to be a director and was not held out as such. In order to establish that a person was a shadow director, the following points needed to be established: (i) the identity of the directors of the company – *de facto* or *de jure*; (ii) that the person alleged to be a shadow director directed the directors how to act; (iii) that the directors acted in accordance with such directions; and (iv.) that they were accustomed to do so.

The Court of Appeal did not make the distinction in *Re Tasbian Ltd (No 3)* [1991] BCLC 792 referring to a 'company doctor' brought in to rescue a failing company as either a *de facto* or a shadow director for the purposes of disqualification proceedings.

In respect of *de facto* directors, Robert Walker J in *Re Kaytech* [1999] 2 BCLC 351 (CA) stated that the court should take account of all external and internal factors as a question of fact rather than a single test. Shadow and *de facto* directors had in common the fact that they exercised real influence (otherwise than as professional advisers) on the governance of a company, that this could be concealed or open and even a combination of both.

The Court of Appeal considered the definition of shadow director in *Secretary of State for Trade and Industry v. Deverell* [2000] 2 WLR 907 in respect of disqualification orders against two men who claimed to be 'consultants'. It was established that both men regularly gave advice which the board followed as a matter of course. Morritt LJ, finding that the two defendants were shadow directors, stated that the issue was who had real influence in the company regardless of labels and forms of communication, and that 'shadow director' was to be broadly construed to give effect to the parliamentary intention of public protection. The aim was to identify those, apart from professional advisers, with real influence in the company. He agreed with Robert Walker J in *Re: Kaytech* that this did not have to be over the whole field of its corporate activities, but must cover essential matters of corporate governance including financial affairs. Whether a communication was a direction or instruction was to be objectively ascertained from all the available evidence. The label attached to the communication by either or both parties was only one factor to consider and non-professional advice was sufficient, since the concept of 'advice' is not excluded by the terms 'direction' and 'instruction', all three having in common the feature of 'guidance'. While it was certainly sufficient to show that some or all of the directors placed themselves in a subservient role or surrendered their discretion to the shadow director, it was not a necessary requirement. Describing the board as the cat's paw, puppet or dancer to the shadow director's tune suggested a degree of control in excess of the statutory requirement. Neither was it necessary for a shadow director to lurk in the shadows.

The two Court of Appeal decisions substantially widen the category of persons who may be considered to be shadow and *de facto* directors.

In conclusion, whilst recognising the value of the extended definition of directors, it is arguably counter-productive to attempt to distinguish between shadow and *de facto* directors.

Hot Topic . . .

MANAGEMENT STRUCTURE OF PLCS AND SES

UK registered public companies always have a one-tier board structure to manage the company's business. In continental jurisdictions like France and Germany, where public companies can have a two-tier board structure, there is a clear division between the roles and functions of the two boards into a management and a supervisory function, and legislation regulates the relationship between the two boards and prescribes corporate actions which the management board may not undertake without the supervisory board's approval.

The possibility now exists in the UK for the promoters of SEs to choose between a one-tier board (an administrative organ) and a two-tier board (consisting of a management organ and a supervisory organ).

One-tier board

The administrative organ manages the day-to-day business of the SE. UK Regulations require a minimum of two members, appointed by the shareholders in general meeting. Where, however, there is employee participation in the administrative organ, there must be at least three members. The board meets at least once every three months at intervals laid down in the constitution. Subject to the constitution, members may be appointed for a term of up to six years and are eligible for re-appointment.

Two-tier board

The management organ reports to the supervisory organ at least once every three months. The supervisory organ has no power to manage the SE but supervises the work of the management organ. The members of the supervisory organ are appointed by the shareholders in general meeting and appoint the members of the management organ. The UK Regulations stipulate a minimum of two members for the management and supervisory organs, with no person being a member of both organs at the same time. Where there is employee participation on one or both of these boards, the representatives will be appointed by the employees' representative council.

Two-tier boards and UK registered SEs
The UK has not attempted to regulate the two-tier board system as in continental systems and the UK Regulations merely provide that any reference in the Companies Act 2006 and other UK legislation to 'directors' applying to a UK registered, two-tier SE refer to members of both the management and supervisory organs. As the supervisory organ has no power to manage, however, the DTI has stated that certain provisions of UK law do not apply to its members. An example is s.213 Companies Act 2006 penalising directors who knowingly permit a company to make a loan to any of its directors in breach of s.197 (see below p.254). Liability will attach only to the members of the management and administrative organs of an SE, as the members of the supervisory organ have no authority to enter into a loan on behalf of the SE. Deciding whether other provisions of UK legislation (for example, the Health and Safety at Work Act 1974) apply may not be as straightforward.

The UK approach is to place the onus of defining the different duties and responsibilities of the management and supervisory organs on the SE's constitution. The result may be that it is more likely that UK registered SEs will adopt a one-tier board.

11.2 Appointment and retirement of directors

All private companies are required to have at least one director, and public companies must have at least two (s.154) and must have at least one who is a natural person: s.155. In the event of breach, the Secretary of State can order appointments in accordance with ss.154 and 155: s.156. For public companies, the appointment of directors must be voted on individually: s.160.

A person may not be appointed as a director under the age of 16 (s.157(1)) subject to the Secretary of State's power to provide for exceptions: s.158. Existing under-age directors not falling within any exception cease to be directors on the coming into force of s.157.

Notwithstanding the subsequent discovery that a there was a defect in a director's appointment, that he was disqualified, that he had ceased to hold office or that he was not entitled to vote on the matter in question, the acts of a person acting as director are valid: s.161. This also applies where there is a breach of the requirement that

the appointment of directors to public companies must be voted on individually: s.161(2).

Those named in the statement of first directors and secretary are deemed appointed: s.10(2). Subsequent appointments are governed by the articles, which usually provide for appointment in general meeting by ordinary resolution; the board generally has a power to fill casual vacancies.

For a private company the rules relating to subsequent appointments of directors are currently in Table A Arts. 76–79. The position of public companies regarding subsequent appointments is more complex and contained in Table A Arts. 73–80. At the first AGM of a public company all directors retire, and at every subsequent AGM one third or the number nearest to one third must retire, being those who have been longest in office since appointment or reappointment. Where persons are appointed on the same day, those to retire are decided by lot: Table A Arts. 73 and 74. If the vacancy is not filled at the AGM, the director shall be deemed reappointed unless it is resolved not to fill the vacancy, or unless a resolution for reappointment has been proposed and lost: Table A Art.75. A director retiring at an AGM remains in office until the meeting appoints a replacement, or until the end of the meeting: Table A Art. 80. No person other than a director retiring by rotation shall be appointed or reappointed a director at any general meeting unless he is recommended by the directors or unless a member entitled to vote at the meeting has given at least 14 days' notice of the intention to propose that person: Table A Art. 76. Members must be given at least seven days' notice before the date of the meeting of any person who is recommended by the directors for appointment or reappointment at the meeting: Table A Art. 77. Subject to this, the company may by ordinary resolution appoint a person to be a director either to fill a vacancy or as an additional director, and may determine the rotation in which any additional directors are to retire: Table A Art. 78. The directors may also appoint a person to be a director either to fill a vacancy or as an additional director, provided the appointment does not cause the number of directors to exceed any number fixed as a maximum. In this case, the director shall hold office only until the next following AGM and, if not reappointed at the AGM, shall vacate office at the conclusion of the AGM: Table A Art.79.

Directors can appoint a person to act for them as an alternate director who is entitled to receive notice of all meetings of directors and of all meetings of committees of directors of which his appointor is a member, to attend and vote at any such meeting at which the appointing director is not personally present. The position of alternate directors is regulated by Table A Arts. 65–69.

11.3   Register of directors

The Act provides that every company must keep a register of its directors: s.162(1). and sets out the particulars which must be registered for individuals (s.163) and corporate directors and firms: s.164. There is also a requirement for the company to maintain a register of directors' residential addresses giving the usual residential address of each director: s.165. The Secretary of State has power to make regulations amending or adding to the particulars to be registered under ss. 163–165: s.166. Companies have a duty to inform the registrar within 14 days of any changes to the register of directors: s.167.

11.4   Removal of directors

Directors can be removed by ordinary resolution requiring special notice: s.168. The director has a right to protest against removal: s.169. The special notice requirement means that the resolution is effective only if notice of it has been given to the company at least 28 days before the meeting: s.312(1). The company must, where practicable, give members notice of such resolutions in the same manner and at the same time as giving notice of the meeting: s.312(2) Where that is not practicable, the company must give at least 14 days' notice before the meeting by advertisement in an appropriate newspaper, or in any other manner allowed by the articles: s.312(3). If, after notice to move such a resolution has been given, a meeting is called for a date 28 days or less after the notice, it is deemed to have been properly given: s.312(4).

It would appear that the company can still refuse to give notice of the resolution, arguing that the obligation to circulate members' resolutions is covered exhaustively in ss.314 and 315: *Pedley v. Inland Waterways Assoc. Ltd* [1977] 1 All ER 209. It is always possible for the provision relating to removal on an ordinary resolution to be frustrated by the inclusion of a provision in the articles, as in *Bushell v. Faith* [1970] AC 1099.

11.5   Disqualification of directors

Directors can be disqualified from acting by statute or under the terms of the articles. Statutory disqualification is more important, and the number of directors being disqualified has recently increased, although there is still criticism that people who should be disqualified are escaping because of the lack of vigilance of the BERR.

(a)   Statutory disqualification

Under the CDDA 1986 the court may (and under ss.6 and 9A *must*) disqualify persons. Disqualified persons cannot, without leave, be directors, liquidators or administrators of a company, or be receivers or managers of a company's property or in any way, directly or indirectly, be concerned or take part in promotion, formation or management for a specified period: s.1 CDDA 1986.

The Act does allow a certain discretion, which has led to the court making partial disqualification orders against directors, under which they may be disqualified in respect of one or more companies but be allowed to continue to operate as a director of another, subject to controls: *Re Mathews Ltd* (1988) 4 BCC 513; *Re Majestic Recording Studios Ltd* [1989] BCLC 1; *Re Lo-Line Electric Motors Ltd* [1988] BCLC 698; and *Re Chartmore Ltd* [1990] BCLC 673 (see Chapter 13, p.299).

(i)   Conviction of an indictable offence

A director may be disqualified when convicted on an indictment or summarily of an offence in connection with the promotion, formation, management or liquidation of a company, or receivership or management of the company's property for a maximum period of five years (summary) or 15 years (on indictment): s.2 CDDA 1986. In *R v. Goodman* [1994] 1 BCLC 349, the Court of Appeal held that insider dealing was an offence 'in connection with the ... management ... of a company' for the purposes of s.2(1) CDDA 1986. In *R v. Creggy* [2008] EWCA Crim 394 the defendant solicitor had allowed a company which was obtaining money dishonestly from an investor to use its client account at the solicitor's office to receive and pay out money. The defendant pleaded guilty to an offence of money laundering and his sentence included a seven-year disqualification under s. 2(1). The defendant's appeal on the ground that this was not an offence in connection with the management of a company was rejected.

(ii)   Persistent breaches of companies legislation

Directors can be disqualified for breaches relating to any return, account or other document to be filed with, delivered or sent, or notice of any matter to be given, to the Registrar of Companies: s.3 CDDA 1986. Three or more defaults in five years constitute persistent breach: s.3 (3). The maximum period of disqualification is five years.

(iii)   Fraud and so on in winding-up

The court may make a disqualification order if a person:

(a)   has been guilty of an offence (whether convicted or not) under s.993 CA 2006 (fraudulent trading);

(b)   has been guilty of fraud in relation to the company or breach of his/her duty (this includes shadow directors). The maximum period of disqualification is 15 years: s.4 CDDA 1986.

(iv)   Disqualification on summary conviction

In connection with filing a return, account or other document, the court may make a disqualification order for a maximum period of five years: s.5 CDDA 1986.

(v)   Duty to disqualify unfit directors of insolvent companies

The court must impose a minimum disqualification of two years if a person is or has been a director of a company which has become insolvent, where his conduct as a director (including conduct as director of another company) makes him unfit: s.6 CDDA 1986.

Unfitness is defined in Schedule I, Part II, as responsibility for the company becoming insolvent or for transactions which are voidable preferences: s.9.

Other factors that the court takes into consideration are:

- continuing to carry on business in spite of a large number of outstanding debts: *Re Dawson Print Group* [1987] BCLC 596; *Re Stanford Services* [1987] BCLC 607; *Re Churchill Hotel (Plymouth) Ltd and Others* [1988] BCLC 341; *Re Lo-line Electric Motors Ltd* [1988] BCLC 698; and *Re Sevenoaks Stationers (Retail) Ltd* [1990] 3 WLR 1165;
- general breaches of the standard of care as a director for which an objective test is applied: *Re Bath Glass* [1988] BCLC 329; *AB Trucking and BAW Commercials*, 3 June 1987, unreported; *Re DKG Contractors Ltd* [1990] BCC 903; *Re Civicia Investments Ltd* [1983] BCLC 456; and *Re Crestjoy Products Ltd*, 18 October 1989 (Lexis).

The court also takes mitigating factors into consideration: *Re Rolus Properties Ltd & Another* (1988) 4 BCC 446 (reliance on professional advice); and *Re Chartmore* [1990] BCLC 673 (youth).

Application is by the Secretary of State only, but s/he can direct the Official Receiver to apply where a company is being wound up by the court. Except with the court's consent, application must be made within two years from the company becoming insolvent. Where an extension is sought, the court must consider (i) the length of the delay; (ii) the reasons for the delay; (iii) the strength of the case against the director; and (iv) the degree of prejudice caused to the director by the delay, but before considering these points the application should be refused if the applicant's case is so weak that it could not lead to a disqualification: *Re Polly Peck International plc (No. 2)* [1994] 1 BCLC 574. Liquidators, administrators or administrative receivers have a statutory duty to report to the Secretary of State if aware of evidence of a director's unfitness: s7(3). 'Director' includes shadow directors. The maximum period of disqualification is 15 years.

In *Re Sevenoaks Stationers (Retail) Ltd* [1990] 3 WLR 1165, the Court of Appeal divided a 15-year period into three: 10 or more years reserved for particularly serious cases; two to five years where the case is relatively not very serious; and six to 10 years for serious cases not meriting the top bracket. In *Re Seagull Manufacturing Co. Ltd (No 2)* [1994] 1 BCLC 273, the court held that s.6 extended both to foreigners out of the jurisdiction and conduct which occurred out of the jurisdiction.

(vi) Disqualification after investigation of company

Persons may be disqualified from acting as directors following investigation by DTI inspectors under s.432, or where information from documents obtained under ss.447 and 448 satisfies the court of unfitness under Schedule I, Part I: s.8 CDDA 1986. This includes misfeasance, breach of fiduciary or other duty; misapplication or retention or any other conduct giving rise to an obligation to account for money or other property; and failure to comply with statutory regulations concerning registration. Application is restricted to the Secretary of State. In *Re Looe Fish Ltd* [1993] BCLC 1160, the allotment of shares by a director to maintain control of the company was evidence of unfitness for s.8.

In *Re Blackspur Group plc* [1998] 1 WLR 422, in disqualification proceedings under ss.6 and 8 CDDA 1986 the applicant accepted that he was likely to be disqualified for 10 years.

He applied for a stay of proceedings against his undertaking never to be a director or be involved in a company's management. The Court of Appeal held that an undertaking did not have the same effect, and refused to stop proceedings.

(vii) Competition disqualification order

The court must make a disqualification order against a person for a period of up to 15 years if satisfied (i) that the person is a director of a company which has committed a breach of competition law, and (ii) the court considers that his conduct makes him unfit to be concerned in the management of a company.

A breach of competition law is an infringement of the Competition Act 1998 or the competition provisions of the EC Treaty. Applications can be made by the OFT or a specified regulator: s.9A. The person can also consent to a disqualification order without the need for court involvement by way of a competition undertaking. The OFT and regulators have the same investigatory powers as those relating to the investigation of a suspected infringement of the Competition Act 1998. Before making an application, prior notice must be given to the person to give him/her the opportunity to make representations: s.9C.

(viii) Participation in wrongful trading

Directors ordered to contribute to a company's assets under s.213 or s.214 IA 1986 can be disqualified for a maximum of 15 years without the need for an application: s.10.

(ix) Undischarged bankrupts or persons subject to a bankruptcy restriction order

Undischarged bankrupts or persons subject to a bankruptcy restriction order (BRO) cannot act as directors of, or directly or indirectly take part in or be concerned in the promotion, formation or management of, a company except with the leave of the court: s.11. This is a strict liability offence. In *R v. Brockley* [1994] 1 BCLC 606, the defendant was liable for acting as a company director having been advised by a paralegal employed by his solicitors that he had been discharged. The same applies to failure to pay under a county court administration order under s.429 Appropriation Act 1986: s.12.

(x) Consequences of contravention

Breach of a disqualification order (or an offence under ss.11 and 12 CDDA 1986) incurs criminal penalties: s.13. Where the offence is committed by a body corporate with the connivance or consent of or the offence is attributable to the neglect of any officer, that person can be prosecuted: s.14. A person acting in breach is jointly and severally liable for the company's debts: s.15. The Secretary of State keeps a register of disqualification orders which can be inspected on the payment of a fee: s.18.

(b) Disqualification under the terms of the articles

The articles usually provide that the office of a director shall be vacated if:

- he ceases to be a director by virtue of any provision of the Act or he becomes prohibited by law from being a director; or
- he becomes bankrupt or makes any arrangement or composition with his creditors generally; or

▶ he is or may be suffering from mental disorder and either:
  ▶ he is admitted to hospital under the Mental Health Act 1983 or the Mental Health (Scotland) Act 1960
  ▶ a court order is made for his detention or for the appointment of a receiver etc to exercise powers in respect of his property or affairs; or
▶ he resigns office by notice to the company; or
▶ he is absent without permission of the directors from directors' meetings for more than six consecutive months, and the directors have resolved that his office be vacated: Table A Art. 81.

Where directors are automatically disqualified or their appointment is defective, any acts carried out by them are valid in spite of the defective appointment or lack of qualification: s.161.

11.6 Directors' duties

The Law Commission recommended in *Company Directors: Regulating Conflicts of Interests and Formulating a Statement of Duties* (Law Com No 261, 1999) a statutory codification of the principal duties of company directors.

The resultant partial codification is in Chapters 2 and 3 of Part 10 Companies Act 2006; ss.170–187. Section 170 refers to the scope and nature of the general duties, stating that they are owed by the director to the company: s.170(1). It further provides that a person who ceases to be a director continues to be subject to the duty to avoid conflicts of interest (s.175) as regards the exploitation of any property, information or opportunity of which he became aware at a time when he was a director, and to the duty not to accept benefits from third parties (s.176) as regards things done or omitted by him before he ceased to be a director: s.170(2).

The general duties are based on common law rules and equitable principles and have effect in place of those rules and principles as regards the duties owed by a director: s.170(3). And 'shall be interpreted and applied in the same way as common law rules or equitable principles, and regard shall be had to the corresponding common law rules and equitable principles in interpreting and applying the general duties': s.170(3). The general duties apply to shadow directors where, and to the extent that, the corresponding common law rules or equitable principles so apply: s.170(4).

The existing rule that the duties are owed to the company and not to individual shareholders is preserved.

This position was initially stated in the decision in *Percival* v. *Wright* [1902] 2 Ch 421, where the claimants offered to sell shares to the directors at a specific price. After the sale they discovered that the directors had been negotiating for the sale of the company at that time, and that they had placed a higher value on the shares. The court refused to rescind the contract for non-disclosure and held that there was no fiduciary relationship between directors and the shareholders individually.

There are exceptional situations where directors have been held to owe a duty to shareholders individually. In *Allen* v. *Hyatt* (1914) 30 TLR 444 the directors entered into merger negotiations with the directors of another company. They induced the other shareholders to give them options to buy their shares at par, representing that it was necessary to have the consent of the majority in order to effect the merger. The shareholders were not informed that the directors were buying the shares on their own account. The directors exercised the options and made a large personal profit. The JCPC affirmed the decision of the Ontario Court of Appeal that the directors must be taken to have held themselves out to the individual shareholders as acting for them as agents, and were bound to account to their principals for the profit.

In *Coleman v. Myers* [1977] 2 NZLR 225 the defendants were directors of a family company. The first defendant made a take-over offer to the other shareholders and succeeded in acquiring total control of the company. The plaintiff minority shareholders had reluctantly agreed to sell only when the first defendant invoked statutory compulsory purchase powers equivalent to ss.979–982 CA 2006. They alleged breach of a fiduciary duty owed to them as shareholders. The New Zealand Court of Appeal held that the defendants were liable to compensate the plaintiff, but only because the minority shareholders had habitually looked to the defendants for business advice, and information on the true value of the shares had been withheld from them by the defendants.

This was approved in *Re Chez Nico (Restaurants) Ltd* [1992] BCLC 192 where Browne-Wilkinson V-C said, 'Like the Court of Appeal in New Zealand, I consider the law to be that in general directors do not owe fiduciary duties to shareholders but owe them to the company: however, in certain special circumstances fiduciary duties, carrying with them a duty of disclosure, can arise which place directors in a fiduciary duty vis-à-vis the shareholders'. *Coleman* was also followed in *Platt v. Platt* [1999] 2 BCLC 745 where the shareholders of a BMW dealership were three brothers. All the ordinary shares were held by one brother who was the only one involved in running the business. When the company's financial position was weak, this brother persuaded the other two to sell their entire preference shareholdings to him for £1, representing that this was necessary to enable the business to be sold at the insistence of BMW. The finances subsequently improved and BMW did not require the business to be sold. The brothers successfully claimed on the basis of misrepresentation and breach of fiduciary duty.

In *Heron International Ltd v. Lord Grade* [1983] BCLC 244, the Court of Appeal found that the directors of a company which was the target of two rival takeover bids owed duties to their shareholders. The orthodox view was, however, restated in *Multinational Gas & Petrochemical Co. v. Multinational Gas & Petrochemical Services Ltd* [1983] 2 All ER 563; and in *Dawsons International plc v. Coats Patons plc* (1988) 4 BCC 305, and *Stein v. Blake* [1998] 1 All ER 724.

The basic principle of *Percival* was also upheld by the Court of Appeal in *Peskin v. Anderson* [2001] 1 BCLC 372.

The general duties are set out in seven sections:

(a) Duty to act within powers

The Act requires directors to '(a) act in accordance with the company's constitution [see s.257], and (b) only exercise their powers for the purposes for which they are conferred': s.171.

This preserves the common rule against directors abusing their powers whilst the requirement that they must act in accordance with the constitution reflects on the simplified s.39 (validity of acts beyond the company's capacity). In place of the extended s.35 CA 1985, this section ensures the directors' liability for acts beyond the company's capacity.

The existing decisions relating to directors abusing their powers will still be valid. Thus directors must exercise the powers they are given by the articles for the proper purpose. The power to allot shares must not be used to create or destroy majorities or for perpetuating the directors' power. In *Piercy v. S. Mills & Co. Ltd* [1920] 1 Ch 77, the directors allotted unissued shares to defeat the claimant's attempt to become a director; in *Hogg v. Cramphorn Ltd* [1967] Ch 254, and *Bamford v. Bamford* [1970] Ch 212, the same powers were used to frustrate takeover bids which the directors thought were not in the best interests of the company. In these cases the court allowed the company to ratify this exercise of their power.

In *Howard Smith Ltd v. Ampol Petroleum Ltd* [1974] 1 All ER 1126, directors issued shares to the claimant, preferring the company to be taken over by the claimant, rather than by the defendant company and an associate company which currently controlled the company and sought to make it a wholly owned subsidiary. The court held that this was an abuse of the directors' powers.

This area of abuse is severely curtailed by statutory restrictions on the directors' power to allot shares (ss.550 and 551) and the pre-emption rights of existing members in respect of the allotment of equity shares: Part 17 Chapter 3, ss.560 and 561(4).

(b)   Duty to promote the success of a company

The Act requires directors to act in good faith in a way most likely to promote the success of the company for the benefit of its members as a whole and to have regard (amongst other matters) to:

a. The likely consequences of any decision in the long term,
b. The interests of the company's employees,
c. The need to foster the company's business relationships with suppliers, customers and others,
d. The impact of the company's operations on the community and the environment,
e. The desirability of the company maintaining a reputation for high standards of business conduct, and
f. The need to act fairly as between members of the company: s.172.

The duty is subject to any enactment or rule of law requiring directors to consider or act in the interests of the company's creditors.

As regards the interests of creditors, the previous decisions concerning the paramount importance of the creditors' interests where the company is insolvent or on the verge of insolvency remain valid. Lord Templeman stated, 'A duty is owed by the directors to the company and to the creditors of the company to ensure that the affairs of the company are properly administered and that its property is not dissipated or exploited for the benefit of the directors themselves to the prejudice of the creditors': *Winkworth v. Edward Baron Development Co. Ltd* [1987] 1 All ER 114. The issue was also addressed in *Brady v. Brady* [1988] BCLC 20, where Nourse LJ stated, 'in a case where the assets are enormous and the debts minimal it is reasonable to suppose that the interests of the creditors ought not to count for very much. Conversely, where the company is insolvent, or even doubtfully solvent, the interests of the company are in reality the interests of existing creditors alone.'

Where there is an identifiable breach of duty to creditors, this may then be the subject of misfeasance proceedings under s.212 IA 1986. In *Re Purpoint Ltd* [1991] BCLC 491, the court made an order in respect of money used to purchase a car on hire purchase when the company was insolvent, and where the evidence suggested that the car was not for the company's business but for the director's new business venture. The issue of whether directors owed duties to creditors was disputed by the court in *Kuwait Asia Bank EC v. National Mutual Life Nominees Ltd* [1991] 1 AC 187, which makes developments difficult to predict.

The same is true for the decisions requiring directors to act *bona fide* in the interests of the company as a whole. In *Re W & M Roith Ltd* [1967] 1 All ER 427, the managing director altered the articles to enable pensions to be paid to directors, employees and their widows and, when no longer in good health, entered into a service agreement guaranteeing his widow a pension in the event of his dying in office. The court found in favour of the liquidator, who contested the right of the widow of the deceased managing director to prove as a creditor in respect of the value of the pension, since the service agreement was not made for the benefit of the company but for that of Mrs R. A similar decision was reached in *Re Lee Behrens & Co. Ltd* [1932] Ch 46 where, five years after the death of a former managing director, the company covenanted to pay his widow an annuity of £500 *per annum*.

The test is subjective, in that it is what the directors consider to be in the interests of the company, not the court: *Re Smith & Fawcett Ltd* [1942] Ch 304.

The reference to the interests of employees enshrines decisions such as *Re Welfab Engineers Ltd* [1990] BCLC 833.

(c) Duty to exercise independent judgement

The Act requires directors to exercise independent judgment, but specifically excepts acting in accordance with agreements entered into by the company which restrict the future exercise of discretion by its directors, or in ways authorised by the company's constitution.

Directors must not fetter their discretion or act as mere puppets on the instructions of another. In *Selangor United Rubber Estates Ltd v. Cradock (No. 3)* [1968] 1 WLR 1555, the directors of a company who, as nominees of the controlling shareholder, acted in accordance with his instructions were given constructive knowledge of his fraudulent intentions and were liable to account for money which they withdrew from the company's bank account in a transaction which constituted illegal financial assistance.

However, in *Fulham Football Club Ltd and Others v. Cabra Estates plc* [1994] BCLC 363, undertakings by directors of the football club to the defendant to use their powers as directors and shareholders to act in support of the defendant's planned development of the football ground were not in breach of their fiduciary duty not to fetter their discretion.

The previous flexibility of the common law is ensured in the above decisions.

(d) Duty to exercise reasonable care, skill and diligence

This means the care, skill and diligence which would be exercised by a reasonably diligent person with:

a. The general knowledge, skill and experience that may reasonably be expected of a person carrying out the functions carried out by the director in relation to the company, and
b. The general knowledge, skill and experience that the director has: s.174.

The common law position of non-executive directors being subject to the same standards as executive directors applies: *Dorchester Finance Co. Ltd v. Stebbing (1977)* [1989] BCLC 498.

Directors who have acted negligently may still escape liability through ratification of their negligent act by an ordinary resolution in general meeting even where the majority of the shares are held by the directors.

In *Re Horsley & Weight Ltd* [1982] Ch 442, where two out of five directors purchased a retirement pension policy for a retiring director and the company went into liquidation a year later, the court held that it was clearly outside the powers of the two directors to purchase the policy, and their decision could be effective only if ratified. The two directors were also the sole shareholders and the court held that, since they both assented to the transaction, the transaction was binding and unassailable by the liquidator.

In this case, Templeman LJ stated, 'I am not satisfied that the directors could excuse themselves because two of them held all the issued shares in the company and as shareholders ratified their own gross negligence as directors.' These doubts were rejected by dicta in *Multinational Gas & Petrochemical Co. Ltd v. Multinational Gas & Petrochemical Services Ltd* [1983] 2 All ER 563, which held that, where the directors are carrying out the shareholders' instructions, they cannot be negligent, since the shareholders owe the company no duty of care.

In *Re D'Jan of London Ltd* [1994] 1 BCLC 561, D'Jan was sued by the company's liquidator for negligence in signing an insurance proposal which enabled the insurers to avoid liability when the company's stock was destroyed by fire. The principle in *Multinational* required the shareholders to have mandated or ratified the act. It was not sufficient that they probably would have ratified it if they had known or thought about it before the liquidation. D'Jan's 99 per cent shareholding was not sufficient.

In some cases the incompetence might constitute breach of a tortious or contractual duty of care. In *Extrasure Travel Insurances Ltd v. Scattergood & Beauclair* [2003] 1 BCLC 598, the trial judge stated, 'A fiduciary may also owe tortious and contractual duties … but that does not mean that those duties are fiduciary duties … crass incompetence might give rise to a claim for breach of duty of care, or for breach of contract, but not for breach of fiduciary duty'.

The subjective and objective test is identical to that for wrongful trading: s.214 IA 1986. This influence on common law was first heralded in *Norman v. Theodore Goddard (a firm)* [1991] BCLC 1028 and *Re D'Jan of London Ltd* [1994] 1 BCLC 561.

(e) Duty to avoid conflicts of interest

This requires directors to avoid situations in which they have, or can have, a direct or indirect interest which conflicts, or possibly may conflict, with the interests of the company, in particular to the exploitation of property, information or opportunities (and it is immaterial whether the company could take advantage of the property, information or opportunity). The section specifically excludes conflicts of interest arising in relation to transactions or arrangements with the company: s.175(2). These are specifically covered by ss.175 and 182.

The duty is not infringed if the situation cannot reasonably be regarded as likely to give rise to a conflict of interest; or if the matter has been authorised by the directors. The section provides conditions under which the directors may authorise such conflicts.

The section covers the existing equitable principles relating to secret profits derived by directors from their position as director and specifically taking personal advantage of corporate opportunities. The section appears to take the absolute no-conflict no-profit position established in *Regal (Hastings) Ltd v. Gulliver* [1942] 1 All ER 378 and to have rejected a move towards adopting the more flexible corporate opportunity approach adopted in the USA, Australia, New Zealand and Canada.

In *Regal (Hastings) Ltd v. Gulliver*, the claimant company decided to form a wholly owned subsidiary company to acquire two further cinemas and sell the cinema business as a going concern. The owner of the cinemas refused to assign the leases unless the subsidiary had a minimum capital of £5,000. The company could not raise this amount so the directors personally invested in the subsidiary to raise the necessary minimum capital. When the cinemas were acquired, the whole group was transferred to new owners. In the transfer the directors made a personal, undisclosed profit on their investment. The new owners brought an action for an account of these profits. The High Court and the Court of Appeal rejected the claim on the grounds that the directors had acted in good faith and in the absence of fraud and that their profits had not been made at the company's expense. In the House of Lords, Lord Russell of Killowen stressed that these factors were irrelevant: '[t]he liability arises from the mere fact of a profit having … been made. The profiteer, however honest and well-intentioned, cannot escape the risk of being called upon to account.'

In *Industrial Development Consultants Ltd v. Cooley* [1972] 2 All ER 162, the defendant was obliged to account to the company, of which he had been the managing director, for the whole of the benefits derived by him under a contract entered into in breach of his duties despite the fact that the company itself could never have competed successfully for the contract.

Directors fraudulently taking personal advantage of corporate opportunities will have to account for any profit or be deemed to hold the contracts on trust for the company. In the alternative they may be liable to compensate the company.

In *Cook v. Deeks* [1916] 1 AC 554, three directors negotiated a contract on behalf of the company but signed it in their own names and, as controlling shareholders, passed a resolution that the company had no interest in the contract. They were held to hold the contract for the company's benefit, and the purported ratification was a fraud on the minority.

Influenced by the USA doctrine of corporate opportunity which is less rigid than that laid out in the *Regal* case, courts in the Commonwealth have developed new strategies for these situations. This has led to signs of a more flexible approach in the UK.

In *Canadian Aero Service Ltd v. O'Malley* (1973) 40 DLR (3d) 371, the president and executive vice-president were liable where, having obtained a contract on behalf of the company, they resigned and acquired the contract for the benefit of their new company.

In finding that they acted in breach of their duties, the following factors were held to be significant: (i) the contract diverted was a 'maturing business opportunity' of the company; (ii) they had negotiated the contract on the company's behalf; (iii) their resignation was motivated by the desire to take over the contract; and (iv) securing the contract for themselves was not a result of a fresh initiative but of their position within the company.

In *Island Export Finance Ltd v. Umunna and Another* [1986] BCLC 460, U, as managing director of the claimant company, had secured a contract in 1976 from the Cameroon postal authorities for the supply of post boxes. In 1977 U resigned because of general dissatisfaction, and subsequently set up in business on his own and obtained orders from the Cameroon postal authorities for his own company. IEF Ltd claimed that U was liable to account for breach of fiduciary duties and breach of confidentiality. On the breach of fiduciary duties, the court recognised that directors continue to owe a fiduciary duty to their company even after they have left. They were influenced, however, by the fact that, while U may have contemplated the Cameroon postal authorities as a potential future source of business, this was neither a primary nor an important motive for his resignation. In addition, both at the time of resigning and when U secured his orders with them, the possibility of IEF Ltd obtaining further orders could not realistically be seen to be a maturing business opportunity. The court also found that obtaining the contract was a result of U's fresh initiative. As a result, U was not held liable to account.

The strict approach of *Regal* still holds sway, however. In *Re Bhullar Bros Ltd* [2003] EWCA Civ 424, two directors of BB Ltd, a company with interests in property development, acquired a property adjacent to a property held by BB Ltd but in their own company's name. At the time, BB Ltd was in the process of trying to split its properties between the two groups of shareholders, and it had been agreed that it should acquire no further property. The Court of Appeal nevertheless held that the action of the two directors was in breach of their fiduciary duties and ordered that the property should be held by their company on trust for BB Ltd. The courts stated that the fact that the acquisition of the property had not been a maturing business opportunity of BB Ltd did not rule out that there had been a breach of fiduciary duties.

In another move away from the rigid approach of the UK courts, it has been held that, where the corporate opportunity has been *bona fide* rejected by the board, a director is free to take up the opportunity personally. This is a precedent of doubtful worth in the UK.

In *Peso Silver Mines Ltd v. Cropper* [1966] SCR 673, the defendant took up an offer of mining claims rejected by the claimant company. The court held that he was not liable to account to the company (now under different control). The court was influenced by the fact that the director was not abusing any confidential information in respect of a hypothetical case and by a dictum of Greene MR in *Regal (Hastings) Ltd v. Gulliver* in the Court of Appeal in which he imagined a scenario similar to that in *Peso* and drew the same conclusion.

Where the secret profit was not fraudulent or in bad faith, directors as shareholders can ratify the transaction. In *Regal* the court stated obiter that, had the profit been disclosed and ratified in general meeting, there would have been no liability to account, whereas in *Cook v. Deeks* the attempted ratification was regarded as ineffective.

The section would appear to cover breach of confidentiality by directors as reflected in the following decisions. It had previously been accepted that there was no legal objection to directors holding directorships in competing companies. The legal issue of overlapping directorships was raised initially in *London and Mashonaland Exploration Company Ltd v. New Mashonaland Exploration Company Ltd* [1891] WN 165 where the plaintiff company sought to restrain its chairman and director from acting as director of a rival company. The judgment of Chitty J initially approached the issue by looking for any contractual restraint, and concluded that there was nothing in the articles which required him to give any part of his time, much less the whole of his time, to the business of the company, or which prohibited him from acting as a director of another company. He then identified the problem as one of confidentiality, stating that no case was made out that the chairman was about to disclose to the defendant company any confidential information gained from his position. This decision was cited with approval by Lord Blanesborough in *Bell v. Lever Bros* [1932] AC 161 at p.195.

The issue was raised again in the light of the decision in *Hivac Ltd v. Park Royal Scientific Instruments Ltd* [1946] Ch 169, in which the court held that employees could be restrained from working for a business competing with that of their employer. Following this decision, doubts were expressed whether *Bell v. Lever Bros* still accurately reflected the law: *per* McDonald J in *Abbey Glen Property Corpn v. Stumborg* (1975) 65 DLR (3d) 235 at p. 278.

The issue was dealt with in *Plus Group Ltd v. Pyke* [2002] EWCA Civ 370; [2002] 2 BCLC 201, where the Court of Appeal approved the trial judge's statement that 'it is not a breach of fiduciary duty for a director to work for a competing company in circumstances where he has been excluded effectively from the company of which he is a director'.

The court, however, seemed to indicate that, in general, the holding of competing directorships would require the approval of the companies in question; but there was no rigid rule that a director could not be involved in the business of another company which was in competition with the company of which he was a director, and stressed that the situation was 'fact specific'. In this case the court referred to *Scottish Co-operative Wholesale Society Ltd v. Meyer* [1959] AC 324 which, while not entirely relevant to the situation, shows the problems which can arise regarding owing fiduciary duties to more than one company, although the situation in that case concerned the problem of the nominee director.

There clearly is a problem where confidential information learned in one company is conveyed to another. *Island Export Finance Ltd v. Umunna and Another* [1986] BCLC 460 established that information acquired in the course of a directorship is classifiable in the same way as for an employee, as in *Faccenda Chicken Ltd v. Fowler* [1987] Ch 117 (see Chapter 17, p.393). The duty could not be so wide as to categorise any use by former directors of non-confidential knowledge acquired in the course of their work as a breach of fiduciary duties unless prevented by a valid restraint of trade clause.

(f)   Duty not to accept benefits from third parties

This prohibits directors from accepting benefits from third parties conferred by reason of their being directors, or their doing (or not doing) anything as directors: s.176. The section excepts benefits which cannot reasonably be regarded as likely to give rise to a conflict of interest.

(g)   Duty to declare interest in proposed transaction or arrangement

This requires directors to declare the nature and extent of any interest – direct or indirect – in proposed transactions or arrangements with the company to the other directors: s.177.

The declaration can – but does not need to – be made at a meeting of the directors and can be by notice in writing under s.184 or by general notice under s.185. The declaration must be made before the company enters into the transaction or arrangement, and further declarations are required if the original declaration proves to be, or becomes, inaccurate or incomplete. Declarations of interest are not required where the director is unaware of the interest or of the transaction or arrangement. No declaration is required if it cannot reasonably be regarded as likely to give rise to a conflict of interest; if, or to the extent that, the other directors are already aware of it; or if, or to the extent that, it concerns terms of his service contract which have been or are to be considered by a meeting of the directors or a committee of the directors appointed for the purpose.

This relates to the duty imposed in *Aberdeen Rly Co. v. Blaikie Bros* (1854) 23 LT OS 315 (HL), which established the no-conflict rule whereby 'no one … shall be allowed to enter into engagements in which he has, or can have, a personal interest conflicting, or which possibly may conflict, with the interests of those whom he is bound to protect'. In that case, a contract was placed by the company with a firm for the supply of cast-iron benches. The company chairman was also a partner of the supplier. The company was able to avoid the contract even though there was no evidence of any actual conflict of interests.

The section removes some confusion from the law following several contradictory decisions concerning to whom the declaration had to be made. The provision must be seen in conjunction with the identical requirement of disclosure in s.182 for existing transactions or arrangements. Related sections cover declaration of interest in a company with a sole director (s.186), as in *Neptune (Vehicle Washing Equipment) Ltd v. Fitzgerald* [1995] 1 BCLC 352, and declaration of interest in existing transactions by shadow directors: s.187.

Under the articles, and subject to the statutory disclosure of their interest, directors can generally contract with the company, either directly or indirectly, and retain any profits and commission. Table A Art. 85 further provides that interested directors cannot vote in respect of the contract (Table A Art. 94), in which case they are not counted for quorum purposes (Table A Art. 95). Most private companies exclude these restrictions. The quorum may be fixed by the directors but, unless fixed at another number, shall be two: Table A Art. 89.

Where a company has entered a contract in which a director has an interest, the contract is ratifiable and the interested director can vote as a shareholder: *North-West Transportation Co. Ltd v. Beatty* (1887) 12 App Cas 589. Failure to make the statutory disclosure also makes a contract voidable: *Hely-Hutchinson v. Brayhead Ltd* [1968] 1 QB 549.

(h) Civil consequences of breach of general duties

The consequences of breach (or threatened breach) of ss.171–177 are the same as if the corresponding common law rule or equitable principle applied and the duties in those sections (with the exception of s.174) are enforceable in the same way as any other fiduciary duty owed by directors: s.178.

11.7 Directors' liabilities

Provisions which purport to exempt directors from any liability in respect of negligence, default, breach of duty or breach of trust are void: s.232(1), Part 10, Chapter 7, as are provisions by which companies directly or indirectly provide indemnity for directors of the company, or an associated company, against any liability in connection with any negligence, default, breach of duty or breach of trust. Exceptions relate to s.233 (provision of insurance); s.234 (qualifying third party indemnity provision) or s. 235 (qualifying pension scheme indemnity provision). Any qualifying indemnity provision must be disclosed in the directors' report (s.236), and a copy of the qualifying indemnity provision must be available for inspection (s.237). Members have the right to inspect and request a copy: s.238.

Ratification of acts giving rise to liability is possible by resolution of the members. Where the resolution is proposed as a written resolution neither the director (if a member of the company) nor any member connected with him is an eligible member: s.239(1)–(3). Where the resolution is proposed at a meeting, it is passed only if the necessary majority is obtained, disregarding votes in favour of the resolution by the director (if a member of the company) and any member connected with him. This does not, however, prevent the director or any such member from attending, being counted towards the quorum and taking part in the proceedings at any meeting at which the resolution is considered: s.239(4). The term 'director' includes former directors and shadow directors. Connected persons are defined in s.252.

11.8   Transactions with directors requiring approval of members

These are contained in Part 10, Chapter 4, of the Act and require members' approval for a number of transactions between the company and directors. For the purposes of these transactions, a shadow director is treated as a director: s.223. The relevant transactions include:

(a)   Directors' service contracts

Where a director's service contract contains a provision under which it is or may be longer than two years, a company may not agree to such provision unless it has been approved by resolution of the members of the company, and in the case of a director of a holding company, by resolution of the members of that company: s.188. In contravention of s.188 the provision is void to the extent of the contravention and the contract is deemed to contain a term entitling the company to terminate it at any time by the giving of reasonable notice: s.189.

(b)   Substantial property transactions

A company may not enter into an arrangement under which a director of the company, or a person connected with him/her, acquires or is to acquire from the company directly or indirectly a substantial non-cash asset, or the company acquires or is to acquire a substantial non-cash asset (directly or indirectly) from a director or a connected person unless the arrangement has been approved by a resolution of the members of the company or is conditional on such approval being obtained: s.190. A substantial non-cash asset is one the value of which exceeds 10 per cent of the company's assets and is more than £5,000 or exceeds £10,000: s.191. This is subject to certain exceptions: ss.192–194. Where the company enters into an arrangement in contravention of s.190, the arrangement and any transaction entered into in pursuance of it is voidable at the instance of the company, unless restitution is no longer possible, the company has been indemnified for the loss or damage suffered or rights acquired in good faith, for value and without actual notice have been acquired by third parties: s.195(2).

Whether or not the arrangement or any such transaction is avoided, the following persons are liable to account to the company for any gain made directly or indirectly, and are jointly and severally liable with any other person liable to indemnify the company for any loss or damage suffered thereby: s.195(3). The persons liable are (a) any director of the company or its holding company with whom the company entered into the contravening agreement, any person with whom the company entered into the contravening arrangement who is connected with a director of the company or its holding company, the director of the company or of its holding company with whom any such person is connected, and any director who authorised the arrangement or any pursuant transaction: s.195(4).

In *Re Duckwari plc* [1997] 2 WLR 48, the court considered a claim for damages suffered by D plc in an action under s.322(3)(b) CA 1985 (now s.195 CA 2006). The land had been purchased when the property market was buoyant but it subsequently collapsed. D plc claimed compensation for the loss in value. The court held that avoidance of the contract is the primary remedy for breach of s.320 CA 1985 (now s.190 CA 2006). Where the company cannot, or elects not to, avoid the contract, the recoverable loss is the difference between the market value at the date of the transaction and the price paid or received. There was no right to compensation for subsequent loss of value.

In *BRDC Ltd v. Hextall Erskine & Co.* [1997] 1 BCLC 182 the claimants obtained damages for their solicitors' negligent advice in relation to a joint venture between B Ltd and the second claimant, S Ltd, when they failed to advise that prior approval of the general meeting was required under s.320 CA 1985 (now s.190 CA 2006). It was impossible to rescind the transaction and the company sued for the subsequent loss. The court held that the defendants had deprived the company of the protection of the approval of the general meeting. The negligence of the directors in making a bad investment could not be attributed to the company as contributory negligence.

(c) Loans, quasi-loans and credit transactions to directors

Private companies cannot make loans to directors of the company or their holding company or stand as guarantor/surety for a third-party loan unless the transaction has been approved by a resolution of the company: s.197(1). If the director is a director of the company's holding company, the transaction must also have been approved by a resolution of the members of the holding company: s.197(2). No approval is required if the company is not a UK registered company, or is a wholly-owned subsidiary company of another body corporate: s.197(5).

For public companies or companies associated with a public company the need for approval extends to quasi-loans or credit transactions, or to giving a guarantee or providing security in connection with a quasi-loan or credit transaction: ss.198 and 201. It also extends to loans and quasi-loans and credit transactions to persons connected with the directors (for loans and quasi-loans) for credit transactions: s.201(2).

A 'quasi-loan' is a transaction under which the creditor agrees to pay, or pays otherwise than in pursuance of an agreement, a sum for another or agrees to reimburse, or reimburses otherwise than in pursuance of an agreement, expenditure incurred by another party for the borrower on terms that the borrower will reimburse the creditor, or in circumstances giving rise to a liability on the borrower to reimburse the creditor: s.199(1). This covers the operation by the company of credit cards for the director and connected persons.

A credit transaction is one under which the creditor (a) supplies goods or sells land under a hire-purchase agreement or a conditional sale agreement, or (b) leases or hires land or goods in return for periodical payments, or (c) otherwise disposes of land or supplies goods or services on the understanding that payment is to be deferred: s.202. This covers the company purchasing land, goods and services for the director and connected person for which it is to be reimbursed in the future.

There is special exemption for loans etc. to provide the director of the company or of its holding company, or a connected person with funds to meet expenditure incurred or to be incurred for the purposes of the company, or for the purpose of enabling him properly to perform his duties, or to enable any such person to avoid incurring such expenditure. For these purposes the aggregate of the value of the transaction and any other relevant transactions or arrangements must not exceed £50,000: s.204.

Another exception relates to providing the director with funds to meet expenditure incurred in defending any criminal or civil proceedings in connection with alleged negligence, default, breach of duty or breach of trust in relation to the company, or in connection with an application for relief or to enable a director to avoid incurring such expenditure: s.205. A similar exception applies in respect of expenditure in connection with regulatory action or investigation: s.206.

An exception also exists in relation to minor and business transactions where the loan or quasi-loan is restricted to £10,000 and credit transactions are limited to £15,000: s.207(1) and (2). The same section also provides an exception for credit transactions if they are entered into by the company in the ordinary course of the company's business and the value is not greater, and the terms on which they are entered into are not more favourable, than it is reasonable to expect the company to have offered to a person of financial standing but unconnected with the company: s.207(3).

There is an exception in relation to intra-group transactions (s.208) and in respect of loans and quasi-loans by a money-lending company if the transaction is entered into in the ordinary course of the company's business and the value is not greater, and the terms not more favourable, than would have been offered to a person of the same financial standing but unconnected with the company: s.209(1). In respect of 'home loans' to facilitate the purchase of a house and land for use as the only or main residence, or for the purpose of improving a house, or in substitution of an existing loan in relation to the purchase or improvement of a main dwelling, the loan is subject to an exception in favour of a director and an employee if such loans are ordinarily made by the company to its employees and the terms of the loan are no more favourable than those on which such loans are ordinarily made: s.209(3) and (4).

Transactions in breach of s.197, 198, 200, 201 or 203 are, subject to conditions, voidable by the company: s.213. Whether the transaction is avoided or not, the persons listed in subsection (4) are liable to account to the company for any gain made directly or indirectly, and to indemnify the company for any loss or damage: s.213(3). Subsection 4 includes (a) a director of the company or its holding company with whom the company entered into the transaction in contravention of the Act, (b) connected persons with whom the company entered into a transaction in contravention of the Act, (c) the director of the company or its holding company with whom any such person is connected, and (d) any other director of the company or its holding company who authorised the transaction. Persons listed under subsections 4(b) and (d) have a possible defence if they can show that they did not know at the time of the transaction the relevant circumstances constituting the contravention: s.213(7).

Where a transaction in contravention of the Act is affirmed within a reasonable time, the transaction can no longer be avoided under s.213: s.214.

(d)   Payments for loss of office

Payments for loss of office means payments made to a director or past director of a company (a) by way of compensation for loss of office as director, (b) by way of compensation for loss, while director of the company or in connection with ceasing to be a director, of any other office or employment in connection with the management of the company's affairs or any subsidiary company, (c) as consideration for, or in connection with, his retirement from office as a director, or as consideration for or in connection with his retirement, while director of the company or in connection with his ceasing to be a director, from any other office or employment in connection with the management of the company's affairs or the affairs of a subsidiary: s.215(1). Compensation or consideration includes benefits otherwise than in cash (s.215(2)) and payments to connected persons or to any person at the direction of, or for the benefit of, a director or a person connected with him are treated as payment to the director: s.215(3).

A company may not make a payment for loss of office to a director of the company or of its holding company unless the payment has been approved by a resolution of the members of the company or of each of these companies in the case of directors of the holding company: s.217(1) and (2). A resolution can be passed only if a memorandum setting out the details of the proposed payment is made available to the member whose approval is sought: s.217(3). Approval is not required for non-UK registered companies or wholly owned subsidiaries of another body corporate: s.217(4).

There are special provisions relating to payments in connection with loss of office arising in connection with the transfer of the whole or part of the undertaking or property of the company (s.218), and in connection with a transfer of shares in the company, or in a subsidiary of the company, resulting from a takeover bid: s.219. In these cases, if in connection with a transfer, (a) the price to be paid to the director for any shares in the company held by him is in excess of the price which could at the time have been obtained by other holders of like shares, or (b) any valuable consideration is given to the director by a person other than the company, the excess, or the money value of the consideration is taken to have been payment for loss of office: s.216.

If a payment is made in contravention of s.217 it is held by the recipient on trust for the company making the payment, and any director who authorised the payment is jointly and severally liable to indemnify the company for any resulting loss: s.222(1). Payments made in contravention of s.218 are held by the recipient on trust for the company whose undertaking or property is or is proposed to be transferred: s.222(2). Payments made in contravention of s.219 are held on trust by the recipient for persons who have sold their shares as a result of the offer, and the expenses in distributing that sum amongst those persons shall be borne by the recipient and not retained out of that sum: s.222(3).

There are exceptions in respect of payments in discharge of legal obligations which cover liability under contracts of service: *Taupo Totara Timber Co. Ltd v. Rowe* [1977] 3 All ER 123: s.220. A further exception relates to small amounts not exceeding £200: s.221.

11.9 Directors' service contracts

Directors' service contracts are covered in Part 10, Chapter 5, as defined in s.227. Copies of contracts or a memorandum of terms are to be available for inspection: s.228. There is a statutory right of members to inspect and request copies of the contracts or memoranda: s.229. The provision covers shadow directors: s.230.

Hot Topic . . .

EMPLOYEE INVOLVEMENT IN SES

Participating companies planning to establish an SE must enter negotiations with the representatives of the companies' employees and agree the employee involvement arrangements, which must cover consulting and providing information to employees and may extend to participation on the SE's board.

The employees' representatives are elected by ballot and form a special negotiating body (SNB). The SNB must try to reach a 'voluntary' agreement with the management of the participating companies. Negotiations must start as soon as the SNB has been formed and may continue for six months (and for a further six months if the parties agree). Although the Directive on worker participation imposes some minimum requirements as to the content of the voluntary agreement, these are 'without prejudice to the autonomy of the parties'. The agreement must provide for the establishment of a 'representative body' similar to a European works council or, failing that, specify the information and consultation procedures to be followed.

If no voluntary agreement is reached at the end of the negotiation period, or the SNB decides not to open negotiations or terminates them early, the SNB may decide by a two-thirds majority vote to rely on the national information and consultation rules in the Member State(s) where the SE has employees. All Member States, including the UK, have operated in accordance with these rules from March 2005, when the Information and Consultation (I&C) Directive (2002/14/EC, [2002] OJ L80/29) was transposed into UK law.

If no voluntary agreement is reached and the SNB decides not to rely on national I&C rules – and assuming the participating companies still wish to form the SE – the 'standard rules' of the Member State in which the SE wishes to register will apply. The UK's are contained in Schedule 4 to the UK Regulations and provide for information and consultation via a representative body, and employee participation on the administrative or supervisory organ of the SE in specified circumstances (for example where there is already employee participation in one of the participating companies).

In the case of a UK registered SE, where the employees have the right to participate in the administrative or supervisory organ, the employees will exercise far greater influence than they would over a UK plc. Employees may, however, be discouraged from assuming this degree of participation due to the potentially heavy liabilities attaching to directorships of large companies.

In the context of the European Private Company (SPE) the Commission proposal foresees that the general principle for board-level participation will be that the SPE is subject to the rules of the Member State in which it is registered. In this context, it should be remembered that worker participation in small companies exists in only a few Member States (e.g. Sweden and Denmark).

11.10 Insider dealing

Part V of the Criminal Justice Act (CJA) 1993 establishes the offence of insider dealing. It is an offence for an individual who has information as an insider to deal on a 'regulated market', or through or as a professional intermediary, in 'securities' the price of which would be significantly affected if the inside information were made public: s.52(1) and (3) CJA 1993. It is also an offence to encourage insider dealing and disclose inside information. No offence is committed unless there is some connection with the UK, which includes dealing on a regulated market which has been identified as being 'regulated in the United Kingdom'.

The Insider Dealing (Securities and Regulated Markets) Order 1994 (SI 1994/187) as amended by SI 2002/1874 specifies the securities to which the insider dealing provisions apply, and identifies what are a regulated market and a market regulated in the UK.

Directors are one category of 'insider' for the purposes of this legislation.

11.11 The company secretary

Private companies are not required to have a company secretary (s.270), but public companies must have a qualified company secretary: ss.271–273.

Company secretaries are the company's chief administrative officers and their duties include attending and minuting board and general meetings, authenticating certain documents, recording transfers of shares, keeping the company's books and registers, and making necessary returns.

In *Panorama Developments (Guildford) Ltd v. Fidelis Furnishing Fabrics Ltd* [1971] 2 QB 711, the company secretary hired cars in the company's name ostensibly for company business. In fact he used them himself. The court recognised that the company secretary had ostensible authority to enter into contracts connected with the administrative side of the company's affairs 'such as employing staff, ordering cars and so forth', and the company was liable to pay.

Authority does not extend to commercial or trading contracts, and the company would not be liable for money borrowed in its name.

Company secretaries owe duties to the company similar to those of a director and are liable to specific criminal penalties if they default in their statutory duties.

End of Topic Summary

The matters to retain particularly at the end of this topic are as follows:

▶ The distinction between *de jure*, *de facto* and shadow directors.
▶ The developments in respect of the persons to whom directors are held to owe a duty: the company, the shareholders, employees and creditors.
▶ The nature and scope of the fiduciary duties, with particular attention to conflicts of interest, secret profits and the duty of care and skill.
▶ An appreciation of the fact that the definition of the directors' duty of care and skill has been influenced by the duties in respect of wrongful trading.

The issues raised in this topic are of great practical importance and concern in all companies, large and small. The following questions are examples of practical situations in which these principles apply.

Questions

1. Infocon plc specialises in IT installations in the retail trade. The board was approached by Dr Boffin who offered a revolutionary new piece of software to the company for £1m plus a percentage of future profits over the next 10 years. The board of directors rejected the proposal due to the company's lack of research and development funds.

    Tariq, a director of Infocon plc, was at the board meeting and agreed with the decision to reject Dr Boffin's proposal. Tariq later discussed the matter with a fellow IT expert, Jasmin, and they decided to form a syndicate with Dr Boffin and a wealthy investor friend to develop and market the software. The syndicate formed a company, Input Ltd, for the purpose.

    When the software was launched, Tariq personally contacted a number of Infocon plc's clients. The launch led to many orders.

    (a) Advise the board of Infocon plc of any breaches of duty to the company committed by Tariq, and any remedies available against him. He is still a director of Infocon plc.
    (b) Would your answer be different if he had resigned his directorship when he formed Input Ltd?

2. Paradise plc, a listed company with articles in the form of Table A, produces fresh organic fruit. There are three executive directors, Adam, Eve and Barry, as well as three other non-executive directors. Three years ago, Pluto Ltd approached the board of Paradise plc and offered to sell the company a plot of land adjoining one of its principal market gardens.

    Because of current uncertainties and a large debt burden, the board rejected the proposal. Subsequently, Adam and Barry, acting through AB Properties Ltd, of which they are the only shareholders and directors, acquired the land in the name of their company for the original asking price of £250,000.

    Owing to the recent fall in interest rates and optimistic forecasts by the CBI, the board of Paradise plc regretted its initial failure to acquire the property, which was back on the market at £350,000, and the board contracted on behalf of Paradise plc to acquire the property from AB Properties Ltd. At the board meeting at which this decision was taken only Adam, Eve and Barry were present.

    Eve was negotiating a five-year contract to supply organic produce to Safebury, a national supermarket chain. Before the deal was publicised, Barry instructed his stockbroker to purchase 10,000 shares in Paradise plc on the market. He also advised his friend Norman to acquire shares, which he did.

    Before closing the deal with Safeburys, Eve was involved in a major dispute at a board meeting of Paradise plc and resigned her directorship. Within two months of this she became director of a rival producer, Eden plc. Using her influence with the managing director of Safeburys, she secured the signing of the five-year supply contract for Eden plc.

    Consider the criminal and civil liabilities of Adam, Eve, Barry and Norman.

Chapter 12

Registered companies:
loan capital

Learning objectives

After reading this chapter you will know about:

▶ Debentures and debenture stock
▶ Fixed and floating charges
▶ Registration of charges

All statutory references are to the Companies Act (CA) 2006 unless otherwise stated.

12.1 Debentures and debenture stock

Companies and LLPs borrowing on a long-term basis will generally do so against the issue of a debenture acknowledging the debt and specifying the terms under which the loan is made. Most debentures will also create charges over the assets of the company. The term 'debenture' is not precisely defined. It is not limited to loans secured on the assets of the company, except for quoted securities, where otherwise the term 'unsecured loan stock' is always used. A debenture is defined in s.738 as including 'debenture stock, bonds and any other securities of a company, whether or not constituting a charge on the assets of the company'. A debenture can also be defined as: a written acknowledgement of indebtedness, usually by deed and usually secured by a charge on the assets of the company. It can exist in the form of a single debenture or one of a series ranking *pari passu* (on equal footing). It includes debenture stock.

Debentures in a series and debenture stock are created by trust deed to trustees for the debenture holders who, in the case of debenture stock, will be issued with a debenture stock certificate. The trust deed enables the company to create legal charges over its property and allows for variation of the assets charged and greater protection to the debenture holders, whose interests will be protected and enforced by the trustee, usually a trust corporation or an insurance company.

Debentures can be registered or bearer and can be redeemable or irredeemable. A debenture can be perpetual, in that the Act provides that debentures or a deed for securing debentures are not invalid by reason only that the debentures are made (a) irredeemable, or (b) redeemable only (i) on the happening of a contingency (however remote) or (ii) on the expiration of a period (however long), any rule of equity notwithstanding: s.739. The reference to the rule of equity is to the rule against clogs on the equity of redemption of a mortgage, i.e. making it impossible for the mortgagor to redeem the mortgage beyond a reasonable time.

In *Knightsbridge Estates Trust Ltd v. Byrne* [1940] AC 613, the House of Lords held that a mortgage of a freehold property by the appellants to B with a covenant to repay the money by 80 half-yearly instalments was a debenture and not a mortgage, and the postponement of the right to redeem for 40 years was not void as a clog on the equity of redemption.

Debentures can also be convertible into shares, in which case they cannot be issued at a discount. Otherwise there is no restriction on the issue of debentures at a discount.

12.2 Charges over company assets

Charges can be either fixed or floating, and a debenture can be secured by a combination of the two. The essential distinction between the two is one of 'management autonomy' or 'control'. The hallmark of a fixed charge is that the assets over which it is secured are appropriated to the security immediately or at the time the chargor acquires an interest in the asset. A charge is floating if the chargor, either under the terms of the instrument creating the charge or in actual fact, has management autonomy over the assets which are subject to the charge.

(a) Fixed charges

Fixed charges are a charge over the specific assets of the company which the company cannot subsequently deal with or dispose of without the chargee's consent, since the chargee's rights against the property accrue at the moment of the creation of the charge.

Fixed charges can be either legal or equitable (formal or informal) and the holder of a fixed charge ranks above all other creditors of the company or LLP – including the receivership, administration or liquidation expenses, and the preferential creditors – in the event of liquidation, administration or receivership (see Chapter 13).

(b) Floating charges

A floating charge can only be equitable and is defined by its characteristics in *Re Yorkshire Woolcombers Assoc. Ltd* [1903] 2 Ch 284.

A floating charge:

- is a charge on a class of assets of the company present and future;
- these assets change from time to time in the ordinary course of the business of the company;
- until the chargeholder takes some step to enforce the security, the company may carry on its business in the ordinary way as far as concerns the particular class of assets.

The floating charge 'hovers' over the assets to which it relates but never becomes specifically attached to an asset or group of assets until the charge crystallises. A floating charge over stock leaves the company free to deal in and dispose of the property covered by the charge, including the right to create further charges ranking in priority above the floating charge, and this ceases only on crystallisation, when the rights of the chargee will vest in the stock then owned by the company and the company no longer has the right of free disposal of the property charged. Floating charges are created over the whole undertaking or a group of assets – stock in trade, book debts and so on.

(i) Crystallisation of floating charges

Crystallisation occurs:

- when a receiver (or administrative receiver) or administrator is appointed by the chargeholder under the terms of the debenture, or by the court;
- on the commencement of winding-up;
- where a company ceases to be a going concern: *Re Woodroffes (Musical Instruments) Ltd* [1985] 3 WLR 543;
- under the terms of an automatic crystallisation clause.

On crystallisation, a floating charge fixes on the assets charged, which are owned by the company at the moment of crystallisation, and it becomes a fixed equitable charge over those assets. This does not, however, affect its priority in the liquidation or administration of the company, since a floating charge is a charge 'which, as created, was a floating charge': s.251 IA 1986. This definition operates in conjunction with s.175 IA 1986, under which preferential creditors have priority over floating charges.

The same is true in the event of the company going into receivership, where s.40 IA 1986 also provides for the priority of the preferential creditors.

The crystallising event in the form of an automatic crystallisation clauses is a reference to the inclusion of clauses in the debenture providing for the automatic crystallisation of the charge on the happening of a specified event or events, for example the creation of a charge in priority to the floating charge or the insolvency of the company. The advantages of such clauses are also negatived by ss.251, 175 and 40 IA 1986 but they can be important in relation to unsecured creditors.

In *Re ELS Ltd* [1994] 3 WLR 616, the court held that where the unsecured creditors of the company seized the company's property in the execution of a judgment subsequent to the automatic crystallisation of a floating charge over the property, the effect of the crystallisation completed the assignment of the property to the chargee and the charged assets ceased to be 'the goods of the company'.

Hot Topic . . .

FIXED OR FLOATING?

Fixed charges were historically limited to charges over freehold and leasehold property, both present and future, fixed plant and machinery, and goodwill. In these cases, a restriction on the chargor's power to deal with or dispose of the property presented no problems. Because of the advantages of the fixed charge, there were, however, many attempts to create fixed charges over book debts and chattels. The ultimate power to determine the nature of the charge created, irrespective of how it is described in the instrument creating it, rests with the court: *Re Armagh Shoes Ltd* [1982] NI 59.

A major decision in this respect was the recognition of a fixed first charge in favour of a bank over 'all book debts and other debts now and from time to time due or owing'. The debenture provided that all monies received should be paid into the company's account and could not be assigned or charged without the bank's prior written consent: *Siebe Gorman & Co. Ltd v. Barclays Bank Ltd* [1979] 2 Lloyd's Rep 142. Similarly, the court recognised a fixed charge over book debts in favour of a bank where the monies were to be paid into a designated account to be withdrawn only on approval of an officer of the bank: *Re Keenan Bros Ltd* [1986] BCLC 242. Where the chargee was not a bank, a 'first specific charge' over book debts and other debts was held to be a floating charge in the absence of any restriction on the company dealing with and disposing of the monies once received: *Re Brightlife Ltd* [1987] Ch 200.

A sophisticated solution to the problem was the recognition by the Court of Appeal of a debenture creating a fixed charge over book debts while they remained uncollected, which became a floating charge over the money once paid into a specified bank account, if the chargee failed to give instructions as to how the money was to be dealt with: *Re New Bullas Trading Ltd* [1994] 1 BCLC 485.

On an appeal from the New Zealand Court of Appeal which condemned *New Bullas*, having already rejected the decision in *Siebe Gorman*, the JCPC held that the rationale in *New Bullas* was 'fundamentally mistaken': *Agnew v. Commissioners of Inland Revenue* [2001] 2 AC 710. The issue was resolved by the House of Lords which overruled *Siebe Gorman* and agreed that *New Bullas* was fundamentally flawed: *National Westminster Bank plc v. Spectrum Plus Ltd* [2005] UKHL 41. This presumably means an end to attempts to extend fixed charges to circulating assets generally.

(a) The disadvantages of floating charges

Floating charges are subject to a number of disadvantages and are only beneficial to the company creating them, since they allow it to use as security a fluctuating group of assets which are not capable of being secured by a fixed charge. The disadvantages are discussed under the following five headings.

(i) Priority disadvantage

On liquidation or receivership, a fixed chargeholder has a prior claim over all creditors in respect of the assets charged, whereas a floating chargeholder has a prior claim over all creditors in respect of the assets charged, except for preferential creditors and the expenses of the liquidation: ss.175 and 40 IA 1986 (see Chapter13).

Until crystallisation, the claims of the holder of a floating charge are postponed to subsequent specific charges, which rank in priority over earlier floating charges, subject to any negative pledge restriction. They are also postponed to the claims of (i) a landlord who has distrained for rent; (ii) a creditor who has obtained a third party debt proceedings order; (iii) an execution creditor who has seized and sold goods under a distress warrant; and (iv) the creditor under a hire purchase contract.

In addition, under s.176A IA 1986, the liquidator, administrator or receiver is required to make a prescribed part of the company's net property available for the satisfaction of unsecured debts, and cannot distribute that part of the company's assets to the holder of a floating charge except in so far as it exceeds the amount required for the satisfaction of unsecured debts. This does not apply where the company's net property is less than the prescribed minimum, and the liquidator, administrator or receiver thinks that the cost of making the distribution to the unsecured creditors would be disproportionate to the benefits.

(ii) Chargeholder's rights subject to set off, liens and retention of title

The chargeholder has the same rights over the property charged as the company. Thus, where a charge exists over book debts, creditors of the company can claim set-offs and liens against the chargeholder in the same way as they would be able to claim them against the company: *Rother Iron Works Ltd v. Canterbury Precision Engineers Ltd* [1974] QB 1; and *George Barker (Transport) Ltd v. Eynon* [1974] 1 WLR 462 (see Chapter13, p.275).

(iii) Company's power to dispose of assets charged

By the time chargeholders take action to enforce their charge, there may be insufficient assets remaining to provide adequate security. To guard against this, the chargeholder should require periodical certificates as to liquid assets and liabilities. The disposal of assets may be total where the company transfers its assets in exchange for shares in another company: *Re Borax Co.* [1901] 1 Ch 326.

(iv) *Increased vulnerability to avoidance*

In addition to the risk of being avoided as a voidable preference under s.239 IA 1986, a floating charge is further vulnerable to total or partial avoidance under s.245 IA 1986. This affects floating charges made to unconnected persons within one year before the commencement of winding-up or administration, or connected persons within two years (see Chapter13, p.295).

(v) *Increased vulnerability to administrator*

The administrator may dispose of or take action relating to property subject to a floating charge as if it were not subject to the charge. Where the property is disposed of, the holder of the floating charge shall have the same priority in respect of acquired property as he had in respect of the property disposed of. Acquired property means property which directly or indirectly represents the property disposed of: para. 70, Schedule Bi, IA 1986 (see Chapter13, p. 283).

(vi) *Duty of chargeholder with regard to authority of company and officers*

The chargee must ensure that the charge is not void as financial assistance for the acquisition of shares in a public company under ss.678–681 CA 2006, and that the directors' authority is not compromised by conflict of interest (see pp. 212 and 248).

12.3 The registration of charges

Charges created by a company falling within the scope of s.860 must be registered before the end of the period allowed for registration: s,860(1). Failure to register is an offence by the company and every officer in default: s.860(4). The section applies to the following charges:

(a) a charge on land or any interest in land, other than a charge for any rent or other periodical sum issuing out of land,

(b) a charge created or evidenced by an instrument which, if executed by an individual, would require registration as a bill of sale,

(c) a charge for the purpose of securing any issue of debentures,

(d) a charge on uncalled capital of the company,

(e) a charge on calls made but not paid,

(f) a charge on book debts of the company;

(g) a floating charge on the company's property or undertaking;

(h) a charge on a ship or aircraft or any share in a ship,

(i) a charge on goodwill or on any intellectual property:s.860(7).

Category (a) seems to refer to the issue of a series of debentures rather than operating to catch any form of charge not specifically mentioned. The reference to a charge on land in (d) covers legal and equitable mortgages of land even if the land is overseas. Thus an equitable charge created by memorandum and deposit of title deeds is registrable and, if not, the charge is void and the chargee cannot claim a lien over the deeds and documents:

Re Molton Finance Ltd [1968] Ch 325. In addition, an agreement to create a mortgage or charge over land is registrable as an equitable mortgage, and any mortgage or charge created subsequently is also registrable. Where an equitable charge is registered and is later converted to a legal charge under a term of the mortgage, the legal charge does not require registration: *Re William Hall (Contractors) Ltd* [1967] 2 All ER 1150. Book debts (e) are debts connected with and arising in the course of trade of any business, due to the proprietor of the business and entered in books. Charges over the company's bank account are not book debts: *Re Brightlife Ltd*.

The term 'book debts' has been largely replaced by the term 'receivables'. Receivables are defined as 'any amounts due or to become due to a company in respect of goods supplied or to be supplied or services rendered or to be rendered by a person ... in the course of that person's business'.

Rights of escrow in respect of a bank account are not a registrable charge: *Lovell Construction Ltd v. Independent Estates plc & Others* [1994] 1 BCLC 31.

Specific charges on registered land must be registered at the Companies Registry and also at the Land Registry. Floating charges over registered land must be protected by a notice. When the debenture creates both a fixed and a floating charge over registered land, it will be registered as a charge in respect of the fixed charge, whereas the floating charge will be protected by a notice.

Where a company acquires property which is subject to a charge of a kind which would, if it had been created by the company after the acquisition of the property, have required to be registered, the company must register the charge within the required period: s.862.

The period allowed for registration of a charge created by the company is 21 days from the day after the day on which the charge is created or, if the charge is created outside the UK, 21 days from the day after the day on which the instrument by which the charge is created or evidenced could, in due course of post (and if dispatched with due diligence), have been received in the UK: s.870(1).

The period allowed for registration of a charge to which property acquired by the company is subject is 21 days from the day after the day on which the acquisition is completed. If the property is situated and the charge was created outside the UK, the 21 days run from the day after the day on which the instrument by which the charge is created or evidenced (or a copy of it) could, in due course of post (and if dispatched with diligence), have been received in the UK: s.870(2).

The period allowed for registration of particulars of a series of debentures under s.863 is (a), if there is a deed containing the charge, 21 days beginning with the day after the day on which the deed is executed, or (b), if there is no such deed, 21 days beginning with the day after the day on which the first debenture of the series is executed: s.870(3).

(a) The register of charges

The Registrar shall keep a register of charges for each company: s.869(1). In respect of all charges (other than charges or debentures in a series) the registrar enters the following particulars:

(a) if created by the company, the date of its creation and, if it is one on property subsequently acquired by the company, the date of the acquisition,
(b) the amount secured by the charge,

(c) short particulars of the property charged, and
(d) the persons entitled to the charge: s.869(4).

In respect of a series of debentures under s.863, the particulars required by the registrar are:

(a) the total amount secured by the whole series, and
(b) the dates of the resolutions authorising the issue of the series and the date of
(c) the covering deed (if any) by which the series is created or defined, and
(d) a general description of the property charged, and
(e) the names of the trustees (if any) for the debenture holders.

In addition, where any commission, allowance or discount has been paid or made by a company to any person in connection with the issue of debentures, the particulars must include the amount or percentage rate of the commission etc.: s.864.

The registrar must give a certificate stating the amount secured by the charge (s.869(5)); the certificate is signed by the registrar or authenticated by his official seal. The certificate 'is conclusive evidence that the requirements of this Chapter as to registration have been satisfied': s.869(6)(b).

In respect of an issue of debentures, a copy of every certificate of registration given under s.869 is to be endorsed on every debenture or certificate of debenture stock issued by the company: s.865.

The effect is that inaccuracy in the registered particulars and in the Registrar's certificate does not affect the validity of the charge, even where the date of the charge and the particulars were inaccurate and the Registrar has accepted for registration documents which were out of time.

In *Re Eric Holmes Ltd* [1965] Ch 1053, a charge created on 5 June which was dated as having been created on 23 June and registered within 21 days of that date was not void for non-registration under s.395(1).

In *Re C L Nye Ltd* [1971] Ch 442, a charge created on 28 February 1964, dated 18 June 1964 and registered on 3 July 1964 was valid.

The charge is also valid even if the particulars are defective, but the terms are as stated in the instrument itself, not in the register.

In *Re Mechanisations (Eaglescliffe) Ltd* [1966] Ch 20, the company created two legal charges over freehold land to secure sums amounting to £18,000, plus any further sums owing in respect of goods supplied and interest. The certificate issued on the basis of incorrect particulars supplied showed a limit of £18,000 and did not refer to further sums for goods supplied. In the liquidation, the mortgagees claimed to be secured creditors for a total of £23,000. The court held that the charges were valid for the whole amount and that the registered particulars and the certificate did not avoid the security in respect of the excess over the amount of £18,000 mentioned.

(b) Rectification of the register

If the court is satisfied that the failure to register a charge before the end of the registration period, or the omission or misstatement of any particular with respect to the charge, was accidental or due to inadvertence or to some other sufficient cause, or is not of a nature to prejudice the position of creditors or shareholders of the company, or that on other grounds it is just and equitable to grant relief, it may order that the period for registration shall be extended or that the omission or misstatement shall be rectified: s.873. This can be on such terms and conditions as are just and expedient. In the case of extension of the registration period, the effect will be that the charge will be regarded as void until registered, which will affect the priority of the charge in respect of other secured creditors whose charges have been created and registered in the period during which the charge was void. *Re Telomatic* [1994] 1 BCLC 90.

The court will generally add to the order allowing late registration the following formula: '[t]hat the time for registering the charge be extended until the ... day of ... 19...; and this order is to be without prejudice to the rights of the parties acquired during the period between the date of the creation of the said charge and the date of its actual registration'. This indicates that the failure to register within 21 days causes the charge to become void *ab initio* until registered under an order made under s.404, when it becomes valid from the date of registration. The wording was introduced after the decision in *Watson v. Duff Morgan and Vermont (Holdings) Ltd* [1974] 1 All ER 794. Where a subsequent charge is created subject to a prior unregistered charge, the second charge will be postponed to the first when the register is rectified. The formula does not protect unsecured creditors.

An order to allow late registration of a charge after the company has gone into liquidation is made only in exceptional circumstances. Charges can be registered out of time after the application for an administration order and after the appointment of an administrator (see Chapter 13, p.277).

(c)   Effect of registration

Failure to register a charge under s.860 results in the charge being void against:

(a) a liquidator of the company,
(b) an administrator of the company, and
(c) a creditor of the company: s.874(1).

When a charge becomes void under this section, the money secured by it immediately becomes repayable: s.874(3).

(d)   Priority of charges

An unregistered charge which is void under s.874 loses its priority. Registration of a charge under s.860 gives rise to deemed notice of the existence of the charge. Thus, in respect of fixed charges, the priority of the charges will depend on the order of registration, irrespective of the nature of the charge, legal or equitable, since the registration of the equitable charge constitutes notice of its existence to the subsequent legal chargee.

In the case of floating charges, charges will rank in the order in which they are registered, except that a floating charge over the whole undertaking may be postponed to a floating charge over a part where the first floating charge enables subsequent floating charges over a part of the assets to be created, ranking in priority to it: *Re Automatic Bottlemakers Ltd* [1926] Ch 412.

Where there is a combination of fixed and floating charges, the floating charge will always be postponed to fixed charges even though the fixed charges were created subsequently. It is, however, common for floating charges to contain a clause restricting the company from creating subsequent charges ranking in priority above them. The mere fact of the restriction being contained in the floating charge will, however, have no validity against the holder of a subsequent fixed charge, since there is no constructive notice of the contents of the charge. If the restrictive clause is endorsed on the registered particulars, some degree of inferred knowledge could be argued but, generally, a subsequent chargee, aware of the existence of a floating charge, will request a copy of the charge and have knowledge of the restriction. Where the subsequent chargee of a registered fixed charge has knowledge of the existence of an earlier floating charge which contains such a restriction, it will not rank in priority over that earlier floating charge.

A registered charge has priority over an earlier unregistered charge, even though the holder of the registered charge has notice of the unregistered security: *Re Monolithic Building Co.* [1915] 1 Ch 643.

(e) Satisfaction and release

The Registrar, on receipt of a statutory declaration in the prescribed form verifying that the debt has been repaid or satisfied in whole or in part, or that part of the property or undertaking has been released or ceased to form part of the company's property or undertaking, may enter on the register a memorandum to that effect and, where there is a memorandum of satisfaction in whole, the Registrar shall, if required, send a copy to the company: s.872.

12.4 The remedies of the debenture holders

The remedies available to the company's secured creditors are:

(i)   to sue for the principal and interest;
(ii) to petition for the winding-up of the company;
(iii) to appoint a receiver or administrator;
(iv) to exercise any power of sale over charged property contained in the debenture.

The holders of debenture stock are not strictly creditors of the company and the trust deed will generally restrict the right of any action to the trustee (for discussion of (ii) and (iii) see Chapter13).

12.5 Application to LLPs

Limited liability partnerships also have the power to create fixed and floating charges over their assets in the same way as registered companies, and are therefore subject to the same regulation as set out in this chapter.

End of chapter summary

Having read and understood this chapter you should have a thorough knowledge of the following points:

▶ The significance of the role of the debenture and debenture stock in respect of the acknowledgement and securing of loans to companies and LLPs;
▶ The charges which can be created over their business assets by companies and LLPs and the distinction between fixed and floating charges;
▶ The disadvantages of floating charges as opposed to fixed charges in the event of the insolvency of the company creating the charge;
▶ The significance of the register of charges in ensuring the priority of charges.

Questions

1. Companies wishing to borrow money may do so on the security of a debenture secured by fixed and floating charges over the assets of the company. Explain:
    (i)   the difference between a floating charge and a fixed charge;
    (ii) the factors which cause a floating charge to crystallise;
    (iii) the way in which a subsequent liquidation of the company can affect the validity of both fixed and floating charges;
    (iv) what you understand by 'book debts' and the types of charge which can be created in respect of them.

2. With regard to the registration of charges, explain the effect of:
    (i)   the conclusive nature of the certificate issued by the Registrar of Companies;
    (ii) the possibility of out of time registration.

3. Bashir and Brenda formed Junk Bonds Ltd and ran a shop selling luxury goods in the city. The business expanded, the company went public and operated a chain of retail outlets throughout the UK.
    With the collapse in the market for luxury goods, the company was technically insolvent. On 1 May, Natbest plc demanded that Junk Bonds plc should create a charge in its favour over the fixed and floating assets of Junk Bonds plc to secure its unsecured overdraft of £500,000. The charge was created and registered in May.
    Yuppy Ltd, a major supplier to Junk Bonds plc, was owed £50,000 and refused to supply further goods unless the debt was settled. In July, Junk Bonds plc agreed to create a floating charge over its assets to Yuppy Ltd. for £100,000 to cover past and future liabilities. The charge was executed and registered in September but Yuppy Ltd delivered goods to the value of £20,000 to Junk Bonds plc in August in reliance on the charge. The goods were supplied under a standard contract containing a reservation of title clause.
    The following February the Inland Revenue presented a petition for the compulsory winding up of Junk Bonds plc.
    Advise the liquidator as to:
    (i)   the validity and priority of the charges to Natbest plc and Yuppy Ltd;
    (ii) the ownership of stocks of unsold goods supplied to Junk Bonds plc by Yuppy Ltd;
    (iii) any personal liability and other consequences which may result for Brenda and Bashir.

Questions cont'd

4. Paradise Ltd is a wholly owned subsidiary company of Eden Ltd which is itself controlled by Adam, the principal shareholder and managing director. Paradise Ltd suffered a financial crisis, and it was agreed in January that Eden Ltd would pay off its outstanding debts and advance a further £50,000 on the security of a floating charge on Paradise Ltd's assets. Eden Ltd settled the debts and made the first payment to Paradise Ltd in March, although the debenture containing the charge was not actually executed until July. The charge was registered within 21 days of its creation.

    The company had a major supplier, Viper plc, which in September refused to deliver further supplies to Paradise Ltd since it was already owed £40,000 for previous deliveries during the year. Viper plc agreed to continue to supply Paradise Ltd, but only on condition that Paradise Ltd created a combination fixed and floating charge to cover the debt of £40,000. It was created in October and registered within 21 days.

    Paradise Ltd went into voluntary creditors' liquidation in March 2003. Advise the liquidator of the validity of the charges to Eden Ltd and Viper plc.

5. Hernando's Hideaway Ltd (HH Ltd) ran a salsa nightclub. In June 2000, Lola Bank plc (LB plc) refused to allow HH Ltd to operate an overdraft unless it had some security. HH Ltd agreed to execute a debenture for the agreed overdraft maximum secured on a combination of fixed and floating charges over the company's assets.

    The debenture creating the charges was executed in June. The company secretary of HH Ltd meant to register it but forgot to do so. The failure to register the debenture was discovered in January when the secretary changed the date on it to one in January and sent it for registration the following day. The Registrar of Companies subsequently issued a certificate of registration.

    In June, following a petition by the Inland Revenue, HH Ltd was wound up.

    Advise the liquidator of HH Ltd whether he can successfully claim that the debenture in favour of LB plc is invalid.

Chapter 13

Registered companies: corporate insolvency

Learning objectives

After reading this chapter you will know about:

- ▶ receivership: administrative receivers and other receivers
- ▶ administration
- ▶ company voluntary arrangements (CVAs)
- ▶ voluntary and compulsory liquidation (winding-up)
- ▶ liquidators' powers
- ▶ directors: liability and disqualification
- ▶ insolvent partnerships.

13.1 Introduction

The changes in corporate insolvency law in 1985, later consolidated in the Insolvency Act (IA) 1986, were inspired by developments in the late 1970s in the USA and the insolvency administration known as 'Chapter 11 bankruptcy'. Under Chapter 11, businesses which had run into financial problems were able to place themselves under the protection of the bankruptcy laws in an attempt to hold their creditors at bay while they attempted to solve their financial problems. The procedure enabled the directors to remain in control of the company while the rescue plan was worked through. The success of the procedure was a source of inspiration for the Cork Committee, whose report was the basis of the reform of insolvency law, and UK corporate insolvency law was reoriented towards saving sick businesses – giving rise to a culture of corporate rescue. The same inspiration was behind the reform of corporate insolvency law elsewhere in the world including Australia and France.

There are informal and formal ways to resolve the problem of insolvent companies. Small companies with few creditors may informally negotiate a debt extension, and larger companies in multi-bank situations may use the London Approach, involving the banks remaining supportive and continuing banking facilities while seeking a solution involving rescheduling and a possible debt-for-equity swap.

The danger of informal procedures is that there is no protection from action by other creditors while the terms of a workout are being agreed.

The formal options available for an insolvent company are as follows:

Receivership – the remedy of secured creditors placing the charged assets in the hands of a receiver for the purpose of realising those assets to satisfy the creditors' claims.

Administration – an alternative to liquidation, placing the company in the hands of an administrator with the aim of rescuing the business.

Company Voluntary Arrangement (CVA) – the company is placed in the hands of a supervisor who seeks to reach agreement with the creditors to ensure the continuation of the company and the protection of creditors.

Liquidation – the company is placed in the hands of a liquidator who winds up the company's business, realises assets, pays off debts and dissolves the company.

The IA 1986 also created an enhanced form of receiver, the administrative receiver, in an attempt to ensure the survival of the company's business. 'Administrative receivers are defined as receivers or managers of the whole (or substantially the whole) of a company's property appointed by or on behalf of the holders of any debentures … secured by a … floating charge': s.29(1). Prior to the Enterprise Act 2002, administrative receivership competed with administration, since creditors entitled to appoint administrative receivers could veto the appointment of an administrator. But the holders of most floating charges are prohibited from appointing an administrative receiver (s.72A) and must appoint an administrator under paragraphs 14–21, Schedule B1, IA 1986 (see below p.278). There are only six specialist categories of creditor who can appoint an administrative receiver: capital market creditors: s.72B; public–private partnerships: s.72C; utilities: s.72D; project finance creditors: s.72E; financial market creditors: s.72F; and registered social landlords: s.72G. For this reason, this chapter will not consider the role of the administrative receiver and will concentrate on the Law of Property Act receiver.

The administration procedure was also streamlined and simplified, most notably by the removal of the need to apply to the court.

All references in this chapter are to the Insolvency Act 1986 and the Insolvency Rules 1986, as amended, unless otherwise indicated.

The provisions applying to companies are extended to limited liability partnerships (LLPs) by regulation 5 of and Schedule 3 to the Limited Liability Partnerships Regulations (SI 2001/1090). The provisions of the Company Directors Disqualification Act 1986 are also extended to LLPs by regulation 4.

13.2 Law of Property Act receivers

Secured creditors may appoint receivers under a power contained in the security instrument or by application to the court. The receiver's primary functions are to realise the secured assets and, after deduction of their expenses, to apply the proceeds in discharging the secured loan. The surplus proceeds or unrealised assets are then returned to the company, which may carry on or go into liquidation.

The term 'receiver' includes a receiver or manager, or a receiver of only part of the property and a receiver only of the income arising from the property or part of it: s.29(1).

Hot Topic . . .

INSOLVENCY AND PENSIONS CRISIS – EUROPEAN INITIATIVE

A major topic of the 21st century has been the plight of employees faced with the loss of some or all of their pensions when their employer became insolvent. A particular case was that of the employees of Allied Steel and Wire (ASW) which collapsed in 2002. Some of the workers lost up to 80 per cent of their pension. Similar problems arose in 2004 at Turner & Newal and Courts, the furniture retailer, and, in January 2005, the collapse into administration of Allders, the retail chain, left 3,200 members of the pension scheme, including 560 already drawing a pension. Only the latter are fully protected against loss.

In relation to protection of pension rights in the event of an employer's insolvency, Article 8 of the EC Insolvency Directive 1980 (80/987/EEC, [1980] OJ L283/23) provides:

Members States shall ensure that the necessary measures are taken to protect the interests of employees and of persons having already left the employer's undertaking or business at the date of the onset of the employer's insolvency in respect of rights conferring on them immediate or prospective entitlement to old-age benefits including survivor's benefits under supplementary company or inter-company pension schemes outside the national statutory social security schemes.

In response to the plight of the ASW workers, ministers set up the Pension Protection Fund (PPF) to safeguard millions of members of final salary schemes if their employers become insolvent. Established by the Pensions Act 2004, the PPF operated from 6 April 2005 and was intended to implement a 2002 EC Directive (2002/74/EC, [2002] OJ L270/10) amending a 1980 Directive (80/987/EEC, [1980] OJ L66/11). The scheme covers:

► Pensioners: those who have reached normal pension age under their schemes at the assessment date, or have retired early on ill health grounds, are covered for 100 per cent of their pension; all other pensioners will be covered for 90 per cent. Limited cover is provided for pension increases.
► Actives and deferreds: they are covered for 90 per cent of their pension entitlement at the assessment date plus revaluation at limited price indexation (up to 5 per cent) from then to normal pension age. There is also limited cover for pension increases.
► Dependants: spouses and civil partners are covered for, broadly, half the amount of cover which would have been available to the pensioner or active/deferred member under the PPF.

In addition, the amount of compensation is restricted to a maximum of £25,000 at age 65. The cap is expected to increase annually. The board of the PPF runs the scheme.

For the purposes of the provision, insolvency will include not only liquidation but also administration where the employer is insolvent.

When Allied Steel & Wire (ASW) became insolvent in 2002, the company's pension scheme was left in deficit, with the result that deferred members suffered substantial reductions in their pension benefits. The ASW scheme members brought a claim before the High Court seeking compensation from the government on the ground that the government had failed adequately to implement the 1980 Insolvency Directive in breach of European and UK law. The government denied that it had breached its duty on the ground that the measures it had taken, including introducing the Minimum Funding Requirement and requiring scheme funds to be kept separate from those of the employer under the Pensions Act 1995, provided sufficient protection. More recent measures under the Pensions Act 2004 which created the PPF were not relevant as they were introduced after the insolvency of ASW. The High Court referred various questions on the interpretation of the Directive to the ECJ. Specifically it asked whether the Directive required the government itself fully to fund pensions in the event of the employer's insolvency, whether the government had adequately implemented the Directive and, if not, what test the English Court should apply to decide whether the government should pay damages.

On 13 July 2007 the Advocate General delivered her opinion in Case C–278/05, *C M Robins and Others v. Secretary of State for Work and Pensions*. She concluded that the government's duty under the Directive was to ensure 'full' protection of pension rights and

rejected the government's claim that something less than full protection was required, but left open the possibility that in exceptional circumstances something less might be justified. She did not feel that the government itself should cover any shortfalls, but concluded that the level of protection offered to ASW members was inadequate to comply with the Directive. Although not required to express a view, she doubted whether the breach was sufficiently serious to make the government liable for damages.

In its final judgment on 25 January 2007, the ECJ ruled that, while EU law did not explicitly insist that 100 per cent of the benefits should be paid out, providing less than half of that entitlement 'cannot be considered to fall within the definition of the word "protect" used in the Directive'. The ECJ noted that in 2004 some 65,000 members of British pension schemes suffered the loss of more than 20 per cent of expected benefits, and some 35,000 of those suffered losses exceeding 50 per cent. The ECJ referred the case back to the High Court to decide whether the government should make up the shortfall in this case.

Thousands of members of other pension schemes in similar circumstances have issued claims for damages against the government in anticipation of the outcome of the ASW case.

On 28 November 2008, it was reported that the PPF may be forced to increase its levy on profitable companies to boost its finances. This followed the announcement that the Woolworths pension scheme was likely to end with a deficit of £250m. The PPF compensation will not cover the entire deficit, and Woolworths pensions could still be reduced by as much as an estimated 20 per cent according to an independent pensions consultant. Currently the PPF collects a levy of £675m a year.

(a) Powers of receivers

The powers of receivers are governed by common law and the Law of Property Act (LPA) 1925: s.109. Their task is to demand and recover the income of the property by any means provided by the law. For that purpose they can use the name of the mortgagor or the mortgagee and give effectual receipts. They can exercise any power delegated by the mortgagee under the Act and have limited powers of insurance. Power to sell the mortgaged property exists only if granted in the security instrument. A receiver who is wrongfully appointed is a trespasser against the company's assets and risks heavy damages: *Ford & Carter v. Midland Bank* (1979) 129 NLJ 543; but the court has discretionary powers under s.34 to order the appointor to indemnify an invalidly appointed receiver.

(b) Invalidity of receiver's appointment

The receiver's appointment may be invalid as the result of the invalidity of the security. Charges can be illegal as financial assistance: ss.678–680 CA 2006, or vulnerable as a voidable preference, or under provisions for the avoidance of floating charges: ss.239 and 245, IA 1986, and are void for non-registration: s.860 CA 2006.

The power to appoint a receiver must arise and be validly exercised. The power of appointment will usually be stated in the debenture and will generally arise on (i) the presentation of a petition for winding-up or administration; (ii) calling a meeting to pass, or the passing of, a resolution for winding-up; (iii) the levying of distress or execution against company assets; (iv) breach of a term of the debenture; (v) cessation of trading; (vi) the assets charged being in jeopardy; and (vii) the inability of the company to pay its debts under s.123, IA 1986, or otherwise.

A demand for payment of the outstanding debt and interest may be required before appointment is possible: *Crine v. Barclay's Bank, Byblos Bank v. Al-Khudhainy* [1987] BCLC 32, in which event a demand for 'all sums due' is sufficient: *Bank of Baroda v. Panessar* [1986] BCLC 497. The company must be given the opportunity to comply with the demand, and the demand and notice of appointment should not be handed over at the same time. The period allowed to comply is hours and not days: *Cripps (Pharmaceuticals) Ltd v. Wickenden* [1973] 1 WLR 944.

(c) Formalities of appointment of receivers

A body corporate cannot act as a receiver: s.30, nor can an undischarged bankrupt: s.31. Legal requirements for appointment will depend upon the security instrument, but appointment under s.109 LPA 1925 must be in writing, which does not include telex or fax. Receivers must accept appointment before the end of the next working day after they receive it or it will not be valid: s.33. Acceptance is normally in writing, but this is not required if there is written confirmation of the acceptance within seven days. Acceptance/confirmation must state the time and date of receipt of the instruments of appointment and of acceptance: s.33, Rule 3.1. Once accepted, the appointment is effective from the date of receipt of the instrument of appointment: Rule 3.1(5). After appointment the receiver must within seven days lodge the appropriate form at Companies House. All invoices, business letters and so on must indicate that a receiver has been appointed: s.39.

(d) Effect of the receivership

The company's undertakings and assets are controlled by a new agent, but ownership and contracts are unaffected. Assets covered by the floating charge under which the receiver is appointed are protected against unsecured creditors levying execution, including third party debt proceedings and charging orders. But landlords can distrain for rent arrears if the receiver remains in occupation.

(e) Contracts of employment

Receivers appointed by the court are not agents of the company and their appointment terminates all contracts of employment with the company, even though they carry on the business of the company. Appointment out of court does not terminate contracts of employment, which remain in force unless the appointment is incompatible with employees' functions.

In *Mack Trucks (Britain) Ltd* [1967] 1 WLR 780, an employee was given notice and instantly re-employed by the receiver on the same terms. The court held that the appointment of the receiver out of court did not automatically terminate current service contracts, and that the new contract accepted by the employee was offered by the receiver as agent for the company and there was no break in the employee's continuity of employment for the purposes of the length of notice.

In *Griffiths v. Secretary of State for Social Services* [1973] All ER 1184, the appointment of the receiver was not inconsistent with the continued employment of the managing director.

Receivers appointed under the security instrument are not personally liable in respect of contracts of employment existing at the date of appointment unless they 'adopt' them, but acts or omissions within 14 days of their appointment do not constitute adoption: ss.37(1) and (2) and 44(1)(b) and (2). In *Re Paramount Airways (No. 3)* [1994] BCC 172, the Court of Appeal rejected the legality of the practice whereby receivers used to avoid adopting contracts by issuing a letter to employees stating that, although their services were being retained, this was not to be taken as an adoption. This meant that retaining employees after the 14-day period constituted adoption. Receivers who are exposed to liability are protected by the right of indemnity.

Employment contracts are terminated if a winding-up order is made against the company and if the receiver, having sold off the assets, closes the business. If, however, the business is sold as a going concern, employment contracts are transferred under the Transfer of Undertakings (Protection of Employment) (TUPE) Regulations 1981 (see Chapter 17, p.417).

Directors remain in office and retain their powers subject to the duty to give effect to the receiver's directions in relation to the company's assets.

(f) Liability on contracts

Receivers are personally liable on contracts entered into by them unless liability is excluded in the contract, subject to a right of indemnity from the company's assets: ss.37(1)(a) and (b) and 44(1)(b) and (c); they are not generally liable on pre-existing contracts, but these contract claims can be specifically enforced against the receiver.

In *Rother Iron Works Ltd v. Canterbury Precision Engineers Ltd* [1974] QB 1, a bank appointed a receiver under a debenture containing a floating charge on the assets and undertaking created by the claimants, who had previously contracted to sell goods to the defendant for £159 while already owing them £124 under a previous contract. The court approved the validity of the defendant's action in setting off the two claims, even though the goods were delivered after the receiver's appointment. The court held that the debenture holder could not be in a better position than the claimant.

It is different where the set-off claimed does not arise out of the same contract (or is not closely associated with it) and does not arise until after the receivership.

In *Business Computers Ltd v. Anglo-African Leasing Ltd* [1977] 1 WLR 578, the claimant company went into receivership on 13 June 1974, being owed £10,587.50p by the defendants in respect of the purchase of two computers. The claimants had also contracted to buy a computer on hire purchase (HP) from the defendants under a third contract. The repudiation of the HP contract by the receiver was accepted on 8 August. The defendants' claim to set off £32,000 damages under the HP contract against their liability of £10,587.50p was refused, since the right did not arise until after the receiver's appointment.

It is the same in respect of liens. In *George Barker (Transport) Ltd v. Eynon* [1974] 1 WLR 462, the claimant transport contractors had a general lien under a contract for collecting goods and delivering them to consignees. On 2 September they collected a consignment, when they learned that the bank had appointed a receiver on 31 August. They were entitled to claim their right of lien against the receiver, since the contract survived the receivership and their right had arisen when the contract was concluded. It was immaterial that it had not been exercisable until after that date.

Pre-receivership VAT liability can be set off against a post-receivership VAT refund.

(g) Duties of the receiver

The primary duty of receivers is to realise the assets in the interests of the debenture holder. Their duty to the company and its guarantors to obtain the best possible price for assets is discussed at Chapter 15, p.346. Receivers have no duty to take instructions from the company, or to disclose information to the company which might harm the debenture holder's interests.

Receivers must respect the rights of any creditors ranking in priority over the debenture holder: s.40, but owe no duty to ordinary creditors.

(h) Conclusion of receivership

Receivership terminates when all the assets have been realised and payment has been made to the preferential creditors, prior chargees and the appointing creditor. Surplus funds are returned to the company. Receivers must make payments in the following order:

(i)   the costs of realising the assets, collecting debts, and claims against third persons;
(ii) all other proper expenses of the receivership, including the receiver's remuneration;
(iii) the costs and expenses of the trustees of the trust deed and their remuneration if the trust deed gives it priority;
(iv) the costs of the debenture holder's action;
(v)   where the loan is secured by a floating charge, the debts and liabilities which would be preferential in a liquidation of the company;
(vi) any prior encumbrances ranking in priority;
(vii) the loan secured by the security instrument, together with interest.

13.3 Administration

Administration is regulated by Schedule B1 IA 1986. All references in this section are to this schedule unless otherwise stated. Administrators can be appointed:

- by court order under paragraph 10;
- by the holder of a floating charge under. paragraph 14;
- by the company or its directors under paragraph 22.

The purpose of administration is to:

- rescue the company as a going concern;
- achieve a better result for the company's creditors as a whole than would be likely if the company were wound up;
- realise property in order to make a distribution to one or more secured or preferential creditors: paragraph 3(1).

Administrators exercise their functions in the interests of the company's creditors as a whole (para. 2, subject to sub-para. (4)) and are officers of the court however appointed (para. 5). They must be licensed insolvency practitioners (LIP) (para. 6).

(a) Appointment by the court

The court may make an administration order only if satisfied:

(a) that the company is or is likely to become unable to pay its debts, and
(b) that the administration order is reasonably likely to achieve the purpose of the administration (para. 11).

Application can be made only by:

(a) the company,
(b) the directors,
(c) one or more creditors,
(d) the chief executive of a magistrates' court in respect of a fine imposed on the company, or
(e) a combination of (a) to (d).

As soon as is reasonably practicable after the making of the application the applicant shall notify any person:

(a) who has appointed an administrative receiver,
(b) who is or may be entitled to appoint an administrative receiver,
(c) who is or may be entitled to appoint an administrator under paragraph 14, and
(d) other prescribed persons (para. 12).

On hearing the application the court may:

(a) make the administration order;
(b) dismiss the application;
(c) adjourn the hearing conditionally or unconditionally;
(d) make an interim order;
(e) treat the application as a winding up petition and make any order under s.125;
(f) make any other appropriate order (para. 13(1)).

The appointment of an administrator takes effect at a time appointed by the order or when the order is made (para. 13(2)).

(b) Appointment by the holder of a floating charge

The holder of a qualifying floating charge may appoint an administrator. A floating charge qualifies if it is created by an instrument which:

(a) states that this paragraph applies to the floating charge,
(b) purports to empower the holder of the charge to appoint an administrator,
(c) purports to empower the holder of the charge to appoint an administrative receiver.

A person is holder of a qualifying floating charge if he holds one or more debentures secured:

(a) by a qualifying floating charge relating to the whole or substantially the whole of the company's property,
(b) by a number of qualifying floating charges which together relate to the whole or substantially the whole of the company's property, or
(c) by charges and other forms of security which together relate to the whole or substantially the whole of the company's property and at least one of which is a qualifying floating charge (para. 14(3)).

The holder of the qualifying floating charge must have given at least two business days' written notice to the holder of any prior floating charge which satisfies paragraph 14(2) unless the holder has consented in writing to the appointment: paragraph 15(1). Administrators may not be appointed in respect of an unenforceable floating charge (para. 16) or where a provisional liquidator has been appointed or an administrative receiver is in office (para. 17). The person appointing the administrator is required to file notice of the appointment in the prescribed form with the court together with statutory declarations concerning his right to appoint an administrator and a statement by the administrator of willingness to serve: paragraph 18. The appointment takes effect when these requirements are satisfied: paragrah 19. Where the appointment is invalid, the court may order the appointor to indemnify the appointee against any consequential liability: paragraph 21.

(c) Appointment by company or directors

Appointment can be by the company or by the directors (para. 22). This is subject to certain restrictions including those following the moratorium period for a CVA under

Schedule A1 (para.24), if a petition for the winding up of the company has been presented or an administration application has been made and is not yet disposed of, or an administrative receiver has been appointed: paragraph 25. Persons seeking to appoint an administrator under paragraph 22 must give at least five business days' written notice in the prescribed form to persons who are or may be entitled to appoint an administrative receiver, and persons who are or may be entitled to appoint an administrator under paragrah 14: paragraph 26. Persons giving notice must file a copy of the notice and accompanying documents with the court as soon as is reasonably practicable together with a statutory declaration in the prescribed form and within the prescribed period:

(a) that the company is or is likely to become unable to pay its debts,
(b) that the company is not in liquidation, and
(c) that the appointment is not prevented by paragraphs 23–25, and
(d) to such additional effect, and giving such information, as may be prescribed (para. 27).

Persons appointing an administrator under paragraph 22 must file with the court notice of the appointment and other documents as prescribed together with statutory declarations in the prescribed form of their entitlement to make the appointment and a statement of consent to the appointment by the administrator: paragraph 29. The appointment takes effect when the paragraph 29 requirements are satisfied: paragraph 30. Where the appointment is invalid, the court may order the appointors to indemnify the appointee against consequential liability: paragraph 34.

(d) Administration application – special cases

Where the application is made in reliance on paragraph 35 by the holder of a qualifying floating charge in respect of the company's property, the court may make an order whether or not satisfied that the company is or is likely to become unable to pay its debts, but only if satisfied that the applicant could appoint an administrator under paragraph 14 (para. 35). Where the administration application is by a person who is not the holder of a qualifying floating charge in respect of the company's property, and the holder of a qualifying floating charge applies to the court to have a specified person appointed as administrator, the court shall grant the latter application unless it thinks it right to refuse because of the particular circumstances of the case (para. 36).

Where the holder of a qualifying floating charge in respect of the company's property could appoint an administrator except for the fact that the company is in liquidation following a winding-up order, that person may make an administration application and, if the court makes an administration order, the court shall discharge the winding-up order and make provision for such matters as may be prescribed and other consequential provisions: paragraph 37. The liquidator of a company may make an administration application and, on the making of an administration order, the court shall discharge the winding-up order and provide for such matters as may be prescribed and make other consequential provisions: paragraph 38.

Where there is an administrative receiver of a company, the court must dismiss an administration application unless:

(a) the person by or on behalf of whom the receiver was appointed consents to the making of the administration order,

(b) the court thinks that the security by virtue of which the receiver was appointed would be liable to be released or discharged under ss.238–240 if an administration order were made,

(c) the court thinks that the security by virtue of which the receiver was appointed would be avoided under s.245 if an administration order were made.

(e) Effect of Administration

(i) Dismissal of all pending winding up petitions

This suspension operates following the making of an administration order and during the administration following an appointment under paragraph 14. There are exceptions in respect of petitions presented under s.124A (public interest) and s.367 Financial Services and Markets Act 2000 where the petition is by the Financial Services Authority (FSA). In the case of these two, the administrator must apply to the court for directions under paragraph 63 (para. 40).

(ii) Dismissal of administrative or other receiver

Any administrative receiver shall vacate office and any receiver of part of the company's property shall vacate office if the administrator so requests (para. 41(1) and (2)).

(iii) Moratorium on insolvency proceedings

Where a company is in administration, no resolution can be passed and no order can be made for its winding up. This is subject once again to the exceptions in respect of ss.124A IA 1986 and 367 FSMA 2000 where the administrator is required to seek directions under paragraph 63 (para. 42).

(iv) Moratorium on other legal processes

The following steps can take place only with the consent of the administrator or the permission of the court:

▶ Steps to enforce security over the company's property.

▶ Steps to repossess goods in the company's possession under a hire purchase agreement.

▶ Peaceable re-entry by a landlord in the exercise of a right of forfeiture in relation to premises let to the company.

▶ Any legal process (including legal proceedings, execution, distress and diligence) instituted or continued against the company or its property.

Where the court gives permission under this paragraph, it can impose a condition or requirement in connection with the transaction. 'Landlord' includes a person to whom rent is payable (para. 43).

(v) Interim moratorium

The provisions of paragraphs 42 and 43 shall apply:

- Where an administration application has been made and:
  - (a) the application has not yet been granted or dismissed, or
  - (b) the application has been granted but the administration order has not yet taken effect
- From the time when a copy of a notice of intention (in the prescribed form) to appoint an administrator under paragraph 14 is filed with the court until:
  - (a) the appointment of the administrator takes effect, or
  - (b) the period of five business days beginning with the date of filing expires without an administrator having been appointed.
- From a time when the notice of intention to appoint an administrator is filed with the court under paragraph 27(1) until:
  - (a) the appointment of the administrator takes effect, or
  - (b) the period specified in paragraph 28(2) expires without an administrator having been appointed.

Where there is an administrative receiver of the company, the provisions of paragraphs 42 and 43 shall not begin to apply until the person by or on behalf of whom the receiver was appointed consents to the making of the administration order.

Paragraph 44 does not prevent or require the court's permission for:

- (a) the presentation of a petition for the winding up of the company under s.124A IA 1986 or s.367 FSMA 2000,
- (b) the appointment of an administrator under paragraph 14,
- (c) the appointment of an administrative receiver of the company, or
- (d) the carrying out by an administrative receiver (whenever appointed) of his functions (para. 44).

During the entire period when the company is in administration, every document issued by or on behalf of the company or the administrator must state the name of the administrator and that the affairs, business and property of the company are being managed by him (para. 45).

(f) Process of administration

On his appointment, the administrator must as soon as is reasonably practicable notify the company, the creditors and the registrar of companies of his appointment: paragraph 46. As soon as is reasonably practicable the administrator shall require one or more persons specified in paragraph 47(3) to provide him with a statement of the affairs of the company. That person must do so within a period of 11 days from receipt of the notice: paragraph 47.

The administrator then produces a statement setting out proposals for achieving the purpose of the administration, which may include a proposal for a voluntary arrangement or for a compromise or arrangement under s.895 CA 2006. The statement shall be sent to the registrar of companies, every creditor of whose claim and address he is aware, and every member of whose address he is aware. This distribution must be as soon as is reasonably practicable and within eight weeks from the start of the administration. This period can be varied under paragraph 107 (para. 49).

The administrator's statement of proposals sent to creditors must be accompanied by an invitation to attend a creditors' meeting except where the administrator thinks that:

(a) the company has sufficient property for each creditor to be paid in full,
(b) the company has insufficient property to pay unsecured creditors other than by virtue of s.176A(2)(a), or
(c) neither objective specified in paragraph 3(1)(a) or (b) can be achieved;

The meeting must be held as soon as is reasonably practicable and, in any event, within 10 weeks from the commencement of administration, subject to extension of this time limit under paragraph 107. The administrator must present a copy of his statement of proposals to an initial creditors' meeting. The administrator is required to summon an initial creditors' meeting if so requested by creditors whose debts amount to at least 10 per cent of the company's total debts (para. 52). The administrator's proposals are presented to the creditors at the initial creditors' meeting, and they may approve them without modification, or approve them with modification to which the administrator consents (para. 53).

Where the proposals have been approved but the administrator proposes a substantial revision of them, the administrator must summon a creditors' meeting sending each creditor a statement of the proposed revision with the notice of the meeting; send a copy of the proposed revision to each member of whose address he is aware and present a copy of the statement to the meeting. The creditors' meeting may approve the revision without modification or with modification to which the administrator consents. After the creditors' meeting the administrator shall as soon as is reasonably practicable report any decision to the court, the registrar of companies and other prescribed persons: paragraph 54.

The creditors' meeting may establish a creditors' committee to carry out the functions conferred on it by or under this Act. The committee may require the administrator to attend on the committee at any reasonable time on seven days' notice, and provide the committee with information about the exercise of his functions (para. 57).

Where the administrator reports to the court that the initial creditors' meeting has failed to approve his proposals or a creditors' meeting has failed to approve their revision, the court may terminate the administrator's appointment, adjourn the hearing conditionally or unconditionally, make an interim order, make an order on a petition for winding up suspended by virtue of paragraph 40(1)(b), or make any other appropriate order: paragraph 55.

(g)   Functions of the administrator

(i)   General powers

The administrator may do anything necessary or expedient for the management of the affairs, business and property of the company (para. 59(1)), and persons dealing with the administrator in good faith and for value need not enquire whether the administrator is acting within his powers: paragraph 59(2). The administrator's powers are laid down in Schedule 1 (para. 60) and include the power to remove a director and appoint a director: paragraph 61. The administrator may call a meeting of members or creditors (para. 62) and apply to the court for directions in connection with his functions: paragraph 63. A company in administration or an officer of a company in administration may not exercise a 'management power', meaning a power which could interfere with the exercise of the administrator's powers and whether conferred by enactment or an instrument, without the consent of the administrator, and the consent can be general or specific: paragraph 64.

(ii) Distribution
The administrator may make a distribution to a creditor of the company, but s.175 shall apply in relation to such a distribution as in relation to a winding up. A payment may not be made to a creditor who is neither secured nor preferential unless the court gives permission: paragraph 65. The administrator may make a payment otherwise than in accordance with paragraph 65 or paragraph 13 of Schedule 1 if he thinks it is likely to assist in achieving the administration's purpose: paragraph 66.

(iii) General duties
On his appointment the administrator takes custody or control (custody is physical possession but control indicates that he has control over assets held by others) of all the property to which the company is entitled (para. 67) and he shall manage the company's affairs, business and property in accordance with any proposals approved under paragraph 53, including a non-substantial revision made by him and substantial revisions approved under paragraph 54. This is subject to the fact that the administrator must comply with any instructions given by the court in connection with his management of the affairs, business or property: paragraph 68. In exercising his function the administrator acts as the company's agent (para. 69).

(iv) Charged property: floating charge
The administrator may dispose of or take action relating to property subject to a floating charge as if such property were not charged. Where the property is disposed of, the holder of the floating charge has the same priority in respect of acquired property, meaning property which directly or indirectly represents the property disposed of: para. 70.

(v) Charged property: non-floating charge and hire-purchase property
The court may allow the administrator to dispose of such property as if it were not charged where the court thinks the disposal would be likely to promote the administration's purpose. This is conditional on the administrator applying towards the discharge of the debt secured:

(a) the net proceeds of disposal of the property, and
(b) any additional money required to produce the amount determined by the court as the net amount which would be realised on a sale of the property at market value: paragraph 71.

An identical provision applies to disposals of the company's property under a hire-purchase agreement: paragraph 72.

(h)   Protection for secured or preferential creditor

An administrator's statement of proposals may not include any action which:

(a) affects the right of a secured creditor to enforce his security,
(b) would result in a preferential debt being paid otherwise than in priority to non-preferential debts, or
(c) results in one preferential creditor being paid a smaller proportion of his debt than another.

This does not apply where the relevant creditor consents to a proposal for a voluntary arrangement or for a compromise or arrangement under s.895 CA 2006: paragraph 73.

(i)   Challenge to administrator's conduct of company

A creditor or member may apply to the court claiming that the administrator:

(a) is acting or has acted so as unfairly to harm the interests of the applicant (whether alone or in common with some or all other members or creditors), or
(b) proposes to act in a way which would unfairly harm the interests of the applicant (whether alone or in common with some or all other members or creditors): paragraph 74(1).

They may also apply claiming that the administrator is not performing his functions as quickly or as efficiently as is reasonably practicable: paragraph 74(2).

In either case, the court has wide powers to make an order as long as it does not impede or prevent the implementation of an approved voluntary arrangement, a compromise or arrangement under s.895 CA 2006, or proposals or revisions approved under paragraph 53 or 54 more than 28 days before the date of the application: paragraph 74(6).

The court may examine the conduct of a person who is or purports to be or who has been or has purported to be the administrator of a company on the application of the official receiver, the administrator, the liquidator, a creditor, or a contributory. The application must allege that the administrator has misapplied or retained money or other property of the company, has become accountable for money or other property of the company, has breached a fiduciary or other duty in relation to the company, or has been guilty of misfeasance. The court may order that person to repay, restore or account for money or property; to pay interest; or to contribute a sum to the company's property by way of compensation for breach of duty or misfeasance: paragraph 75.

(j)   Ending administration

The administrator's appointment terminates at the end of one year from commencement, but on the administrator's application the court may extend the term of office for a specified period, and the term of office may be extended for a specified period not exceeding six months by consent: paragraph 76. An order can be made in respect of an administrator whose term of office has already been extended by order or by consent, but not after the expiry of the administrator's term of office: paragraph 77.

The court can also terminate the administration on the administrator's application where he thinks the administration's purpose cannot be achieved, that the company should not have entered administration, or that a creditors' meeting requires him to make such an application: paragraph 79. The administrator appointed pursuant to an administration order shall also make such an application if he thinks the purpose of administration has been sufficiently achieved.

Where he has been appointed under paragraph 14 or 22, the administrator may file a notice with the court and the registrar of companies if he thinks that the administration's purpose has been sufficiently achieved: paragraph 80. His appointment will then automatically cease. The court may terminate an administration on the application of a creditor alleging an improper motive on the part of the applicant for an administration order or on the part of the person appointing the administrator: paragraph 81.

Further paragraphs relate to the potential clash between a public interest winding-up petition against a company in administration (para. 82); moving from administration to a creditors' voluntary winding up (para. 83); moving from administration to dissolution (para. 84); and discharge of the administration order by the court where the administration ends (para. 85).

(k)   Replacing the administrator

Paragraph 97 provides for the administrator's resignation (para. 87); removal of the administrator from office where the administrator ceases to be qualified to act (para. 89); filling a vacancy in the office of administrator (para. 90); substitution of an administrator appointed by a qualifying floating charge-holder with one appointed by the holder of a prior qualifying floating charge (para. 96); and substitution of one appointed by the company or the directors by one appointed by the creditors at a creditors' meeting (para. 97).

There is also provision for discharge from liability in respect of any action as administrator where the person ceases to be an administrator for any reason: paragraph 98(1). In this event, the former administrator's remuneration and expenses shall be:

(a) charged on and payable out of property of which he had custody or control immediately before cessation, and

(b) payable in priority to any security to which paragraph 70 applies (para. 99(3)).

A sum payable in respect of a debt or liability arising out of a contract entered into by the former administrator or a predecessor before cessation shall be:

(a) charged on and payable out of property of which the former administrator had custody or control immediately before cessation, and

(b) payable in priority to any charge arising under sub-paragraph (3) (para. 99(4)).

Sub-paragraph (4) shall apply to a liability arising under a contract of employment adopted by the former administrator or a predecessor before cessation; and for the purpose:

(a) action taken within the period of 14 days after an administrator's appointment shall not be taken to amount or contribute to the adoption of a contract,

(b) no account shall be taken of any liability which arises, or in so far as it arises, by reference to anything which is done or which occurs before the adoption of the contract of employment, and

(c) no account shall be taken of a liability to make a payment other then wages or salary (para. 99(5)).

Paragraph 99(6) defines 'wages or salary' for this purpose. In *Re The Leeds United Association Football Club Ltd* [2007] EWHC 1761 (Ch) the court held that where administrators adopted contracts of employment and the company subsequently became liable to pay damages for the wrongful termination of those contracts, the damages were not payable in priority to other expenses since that liability was not within the words 'wages or salary'.

(l) General

The final section covers a number of points of which the most important relate to the appointment of more than one person as administrator and defining whether they are required to act jointly or individually: paragraphs 100–103. There is also a presumption of validity for any act carried out by an administrator in spite of a defect in his appointment or qualification: paragraph 104. Paragraphs 107–109 concern the extension of time limits in respect of the administration.

13.4 Company voluntary arrangements (CVAs)

CVAs were introduced to provide a simple procedure to allow companies to enter into arrangements with their creditors and exist alongside the complex and expensive procedure that already existed under s.425 CA 1985 (now s.895 CA 2006).

The procedure is regulated by ss.1–7A and can be used before or after the commencement of administration or the making of a winding-up order. The administrator, liquidator or the board puts forward a proposal to the company and its creditors for a composition or a scheme of arrangement of its affairs. Where the proposal is by the directors, there is no need for the company to be insolvent. CVAs cannot be proposed by creditors or members and they do not vary members' rights.

The proposal provides for a supervisor of the scheme, known as 'the nominee', who must be a qualified insolvency practitioner. There must be a short explanation of why a CVA is desirable. Where the nominee is not the liquidator or administrator, within 28 days they must submit to the court a report as to whether the proposal should be submitted to meetings of the company and creditors: s.2. Where the nominee is the liquidator or administrator, they summon meetings of the company and creditors at such time, date and place as they think fit: s.3(2).

If both meetings accept the proposals – in whole or as modified – then they are binding on all notified creditors and the company: s.4. There is no need for class meetings of members or creditors and no formal approval of the court is required; the chairpersons of the meetings simply report the result to the court: s.4(6). Proposals affecting the rights of secured or preferential creditors cannot be approved without their consent: s.4(3) and (4).

Acceptance by the creditors' meeting is by a majority representing 75 per cent in value of the creditors present in person or by proxy and voting on the resolution; acceptance at the members' meeting is by simple majority unless otherwise fixed by the articles.

On approval by both meetings, the CVA takes effect as if made at the creditors' meeting: s.5(2)(a), and binds dissenting creditors and all creditors with notice of and entitled to vote at the meeting: s.5(2)(b). Those entitled to vote at either meeting or their nominees, the liquidator or administrator can apply to the court for the revocation or suspension of the approvals or for summoning further meetings for reconsideration of the original proposal or a revised proposal on one or both of the following grounds namely:

(a) that a voluntary arrangement approved by the meetings unfairly prejudices the interests of a creditor, member or contributory of the company;
(b) that there has been some material irregularity at or in relation to either of the meetings: s.6.

Once the arrangement is approved, the court can stay all winding-up proceedings, discharge any administration and give directions to facilitate the composition or scheme: s.7. The supervisor must submit accounts or, if there is no trading, a progress report to the court, Registrar of Companies and all affected parties at least every 12 months. On completion of the CVA, the supervisor notifies all creditors and members of its full implementation, together with a financial report, with copies to the Registrar of Companies and the court.

A criticism of the original CVA was the absence of any moratorium after the making of the proposal to prevent creditors from proceeding against the company pending approval. There is now the right to apply for a 28-day moratorium (the period can be extended) for companies which qualify as small private companies under ss.382 and 383 CA 2006: s.1A. The only way of obtaining moratorium protection for larger companies is by way of administration.

The supervisor has also been given powers to report any past or present officer of the company who has been guilty of an offence in connection with the moratorium or the CVA to the Secretary of State: s.7A. Supervisors do not, however, have the investigative powers or power to reopen transactions enjoyed by administrative receivers, administrators and liquidators.

The provisions under s.895 CA 2006, which are expensive and appropriate only for major reconstructions, exist alongside this new mechanism but are rarely used.

13.5 Company winding-up

There are two methods of winding up a company: a voluntary winding-up and a winding-up by the court: s.73.

(a) Voluntary winding-up

A voluntary winding-up is initiated by a resolution of the company in general meeting by two possible resolutions: (i) a special resolution; and (ii) an extraordinary resolution to the effect that the company cannot by reason of its liabilities continue in business and that it is advisable to wind up: s.84.

(b) Members' and creditors' voluntary winding-up

In a members' voluntary winding-up the directors make a statutory declaration of solvency under s.89 and declare that the company will be able to pay its debts in full within a maximum period of 12 months from the commencement of the winding-up: s.90.

The declaration must be made either within the five weeks immediately preceding the resolution, or on the same day as (but before) the passing of the resolution. If the resolution is passed, the declaration must be registered within 15 days of the resolution. Directors are liable to fines where such declarations are made without reasonable grounds.

The resolution must be advertised in the *London Gazette* within 14 days: s.85. The commencement of the winding-up dates from the time of the resolution: s.86, and, from then on, the company ceases to carry on business except in so far as is required for a beneficial winding-up: s.87.

(i) *Progress of a members' voluntary winding-up*

The company in general meeting appoints one or more liquidators: s.91. If the liquidation extends beyond a year, the liquidator must call company meetings at the end of each year from the commencement of the winding-up and present interim reports to the meeting: s.93. When the company's affairs are wound up, the liquidator calls a final meeting and presents a final report as to the winding-up: s.94(1). Within one week of the meeting, a copy of the accounts and a return as to the holding of the meeting are sent to the Registrar of Companies: s.94(3). The company is automatically dissolved three months after the registration of the return of the final meeting: s.201.

Dissolution is the termination of the legal existence of a registered company or LLP. It usually follows a winding-up.

If the liquidator decides that the company is in fact insolvent, he/she must call a meeting of the creditors within 28 days, giving them seven days' notice: s.95. The meeting must be advertised in the *London Gazette* and in two newspapers circulating in the relevant locality. The liquidator presides over the creditors' meeting and submits a statement of affairs, and the liquidation proceeds as a creditors' winding-up.

(ii) *Progress of creditors' voluntary winding-up*

A creditors' voluntary winding-up is usually commenced by an extraordinary resolution of the members, and there is no statutory declaration of solvency.

The company must call a creditors' meeting as well as a general meeting. The creditors' meeting must be summoned for not later than the fourteenth day after the date the winding-up resolution is passed. Creditors must be given seven days' notice and the meeting must be advertised in the *London Gazette* and in two newspapers circulating in the relevant locality. The notice must state either the name and address of an insolvency practitioner who, before the meeting, will furnish free of charge such information as the creditors may reasonably require, or a place in the relevant locality where, on the two business days before the meeting, a list of names and addresses of creditors is available for inspection free of charge: s.98.

At the meeting, the directors must lay before the meeting a statement of the company's affairs and appoint a director to preside: s.99. At their meetings, members and creditors may nominate a liquidator. The liquidator will be the creditors' nominee, but where the meetings have nominated different people, any director, member or creditor may apply to the court within seven days for the members' nominee to be a liquidator instead of or jointly with the creditors' nominee, or for the appointment of some other person: s.100.

The creditors may appoint a liquidation committee of not more than five persons, in which case the members may appoint not more than five representatives to the committee. The liquidation committee works with the liquidator and sanctions the liquidator's powers where required: s.101. The directors' powers cease on the liquidator's appointment except so far as the liquidation committee or the creditors authorise them to continue: s.103.

The winding-up procedure continues as for the voluntary members' winding-up except that annual meetings and final meetings of creditors as well as members must be called: ss.105 and 106. The dissolution is achieved in the same way: s.201.

(b) Compulsory winding-up by the court

Compulsory winding-up is where a registered company, partnership or limited liability partnership is put into liquidation by order of the court following a winding-up petition.

The county courts have jurisdiction for the winding-up of companies unless the paid-up share capital exceeds £120,000, in which case jurisdiction lies with the Chancery Division of the High Court: s.117. The process begins with the presentation of a petition by one of a group of recognised persons on one of the statutory grounds.

(c) Grounds for the winding-up

The grounds for winding up a company are:

(a) the company has by special resolution resolved that it shall be wound up by the court;
(b) the company was a public company incorporated as such, has not been issued with a certificate under s.117 CA 1985 and more than a year has elapsed;
(c) it is an old public company;
(d) the company does not commence business within a year from incorporation or suspends business for a whole year;
(e) the number of members is reduced below two (this does not apply to a private company limited by shares or by guarantee which may have only one member);
(f) the company is unable to pay its debts;
(g) it is just and equitable that the company should be wound up: s.122(1).

In addition, the Secretary of State may present a petition on the grounds of public interest: s.124A, arising from (a) a company investigation under Part XIV, CA 1985; (b) a report or information obtained under the FSMA 2000; (c) information obtained under s.2 Criminal Justice Act 1987; or (d) any information obtained under s.83 CA 1989 (powers exercisable for purpose of assisting overseas regulatory authorities), for the company to be wound up if the court thinks it just and equitable. A petition can also be made by the FSA under s.367 FSMA 2000.

Inability to pay debts is statutorily defined in s.123:

(i)   if a creditor for a sum of £750 serves at the registered office of the company a written demand for payment and the company for three weeks neglects to pay the sum or to secure or compound for it to the reasonable satisfaction of the creditor: s.123(1)(a);

(ii) if execution or other process issued on a judgment, decree or order of any court in favour of a creditor is returned unsatisfied in whole or in part: s.123(1)(b);

(iii) if the company is unable to pay its debts as they fall due: s.123(1)(e);

(iv) if the value of the company's assets is less than the amount of its liabilities, including contingent and prospective liabilities: s.123(2).

The serving of a statutory demand under s.123(1)(a) has long been recognised as a useful procedure whereby an unpaid creditor can place the company in a predicament where it must either settle the debt in question or be deemed unable to pay its debts and be wound up by the court on a creditor's petition. The disadvantage is the three-week delay. Increasingly, creditors favour the more direct approach of s.123(1)(e) and present a petition stating that the company is indebted to them for an amount exceeding the statutory minimum required for a statutory demand; that the debtor has given no notification that the amount is disputed; and that the company is unable to pay its debts and should be wound up, as in *Taylor's Industrial Flooring Ltd v. M & H Plant Hire (Manchester) Ltd* [1990] BCLC 216.

(d)   Persons entitled to petition

A winding-up petition can be presented by the company, the directors, the Secretary of State, the DTI, the receiver, contributory(ories) or creditor(s): s.124.

Contributory means every person liable to contribute to the company's assets in the event of its being wound up: s.79(1).

The apparent limitation to members holding partly paid shares is not true and all members and past members can petition. Apart from the right to petition under s.122(1)(e), members can only petition in respect of shares held and registered in their name which (i) were originally allotted to them; (ii) have been held by them for at least six months out of the previous 18; or (iii) have devolved on them through the death of a former holder: s.124(2).

In spite of the provision that 'the court shall not refuse to make a winding-up order on the ground only that the company's assets have been mortgaged to an amount equal to or in excess of those assets, or that the company has no assets': s.125(1), petitioners must have a financial interest in the winding-up: *Re Chesterfield Catering Co. Ltd* [1977] Ch 373. Petitions will also be rejected on just and equitable grounds if there is an alternative available remedy and the petition is unreasonable.

Creditors can petition only in respect of claims for £750 and more, but joint petitions are possible. The debt must be undisputed, except where the company accepts that it is liable for an amount of at least £750 and the dispute relates to a claim in excess of that sum: *Re Tweeds Garage* [1962] Ch 406. The court may reject the petition if it is opposed by more important creditors.

(e)   Effect of a winding-up order

The commencement of winding up is the date of the presentation of the petition (unless the company is already in voluntary winding-up): s.129(2), and dispositions of the company's property, share transfers or alterations in the members' status after the commencement of the winding-up are void unless the court otherwise orders: s.127.

The court will approve *bona fide* transactions with third parties before the hearing, particularly for companies not trading at a loss. Applications can be by the company, the third party and any interested parties before or after the transaction and before or after the winding-up order. Payments to existing creditors will not be approved since they may turn out to be preferential in the event of a winding-up order being made.

The Court of Appeal held that payments into and out of an overdrawn account were dispositions under s.127: *Re Gray's Inn Construction Co. Ltd* [1980] 1 WLR 711, but that payments into an account in credit were not: *Re Barn Crown Ltd* [1994] 4 All ER 42. Banks generally freeze bank accounts on learning of the presentation of a petition against a company customer. Failing this, the court must decide whether the bank should refund any unapproved payments into and out of the account to the liquidator, subject to the liquidator's obligation first to try to recover sums paid out from the payee. The legal confusion surrounding this area was resolved by the Court of Appeal in 2001.

In *Bank of Ireland v. Hollicourt (Contracts) Ltd* [2001] 1 All ER 289, the company's account was in credit on the presentation of the petition but the bank continued to operate the account because it became aware of the petition only three months later. Following the winding-up order, the liquidator sought recovery of £156,000 in respect of payments out of the account. The Court of Appeal held that there was no liability on the bank to refund payments made to creditors by cheques. The payments were not dispositions under s.127 since the bank honours the cheques as the company's agent.

(f)   Appointment of a liquidator

At any time after the presentation of the petition, the court may appoint a provisional liquidator to carry out the functions conferred by the court: s.135. On the making of the winding-up order, the Official Receiver becomes the liquidator until another person is appointed: s.136(2). The Official Receiver is a civil servant attached to a court with responsibilities for personal and corporate insolvency.

Official Receivers may summon separate meetings of contributories and creditors for the purpose of choosing a person to be liquidator in their place: s.136(4). They have 12 weeks in which to decide whether to call the meeting: s.136(5), but one or more creditors, representing a quarter of the total debts, can request the convening of the meeting. Where the meetings are convened, the creditors' appointee will be the liquidator, subject to rights of appeal as for the creditors' voluntary winding-up: s.139.

At any time, the Official Receiver can apply to the Secretary of State to appoint a person in their place and, if there is no appointment following the convening of the meetings of creditors and contributories, it is their duty to decide whether to refer the matter to the Secretary of State. Where the winding-up order is made immediately upon the appointment of an administrator ceasing to have effect, the court may appoint the administrator as liquidator: s.140. Where there is a supervisor of a CVA in place, the court may appoint the supervisor as a liquidator. In neither case will the Official Receiver become liquidator.

Creditors and contributories may also decide to establish a liquidation committee.

(g) The powers of the liquidator

The liquidator has the right to exercise any of the powers in Parts I and II of Schedule 4 with the sanction of the court or the liquidation committee (payment of debts, compromise of claims and so on; institution and defence of proceedings; carrying on the business of the company); and, with or without that sanction, to exercise any of the powers in Part III of Schedule 4: s.167.

(h) The conclusion of the winding-up

The liquidator calls a final creditors' meeting, which receives the final report and decides whether the liquidator should be released. The return of the meeting and notice of vacation of office are registered with the Registrar of Companies, and after three months the company is dissolved: s.205.

(i) Proof of debts

Creditors must prove the existence of their debt in order to share in the company's assets. All debts can be proved, liquidated and unliquidated, certain and uncertain, contingent, present and future, with the exception of certain non-provable debts. If the total amount of the debt is uncertain, the liquidator must assess the value and creditors have a right of appeal to the court.

(j) Priority of debts

Debts are ranked in order of priority and satisfied in that order from the company's assets. Where there is a supervisor of a CVA already in place, the court may appoint the supervisor as the liquidator. In neither case will the Official Receiver become liquidator.

Priority is given to preferential debts under s.175(1). The category of preferential debts was considerably reduced by the Enterprise Act (EA) 2002, which abolished Crown priority status: s.251(1) EA 2002. Thus claims by the Crown in respect of unpaid tax or VAT and debts due to Customs and Excise are now classified as unsecured debts. The sole remaining category of preferential debts relates to employee benefits as follows:

(a) remuneration for up to four months prior to the liquidation subject to a maximum of £800 per employee;
(b) accrued holiday remuneration; and
(c) sums loaned to the company and used for the specific purpose of the payment of employees' remuneration and accrued holiday remuneration.

The expenses of the liquidation, as well as including the liquidator's remuneration and the costs involved in any legal action for enforcing claims on behalf of the company, also include rent and rates payable on property of factories etc. in which the liquidator continues production etc. in the interests of increasing the assets available for creditors. In *Exeter City Council v. Bairstow and others* [2007] EWHC 400 (Ch) the same right to claim these in priority to other claims was extended to administration. Claims for pre-petition rent and rates arrears count as unsecured debts.

Secured creditors with fixed charges have four options in respect of proof of debts:

(a) to realise the security and prove for any outstanding balance as an unsecured creditor;

(b) to value the asset as security, declare the value to the liquidator and claim in respect of any outstanding balance as an unsecured creditor;

(c) to rely on the security as full satisfaction of the debt and lodge no proof;

(d) to surrender the security to the liquidator and prove for the whole debt as an unsecured creditor.

Where the creditor opts for (b), the liquidator can opt to buy in the asset at the valuation in the event that it would have an enhanced value in association with other company assets.

For the significance of the inclusion of a 'whole debt clause' in a guarantee in respect of guarantors seeking to prove in a liquidation see Chapter 15, p.356.

All claims are subject to set-off in respect of debts owed to the company by the proving creditor. If the creditor's contract expressly provided for payment of interest, they could claim for the total interest from the date of supply of the goods or services up to the date of the winding up order. If the debt arose under a written contract which did not provide for interest, the creditor can claim for interest for the same period at only the rate payable in respect of judgment debts. If payable under an oral contract with no express provision for interest, the creditor could claim for interest at the same rate, but only having served a written demand for payment and for the period between the date of the written demand and the winding up order.

(k) Assets of the company

All the company's assets belonging to it at the commencement of the liquidation are available for the creditors, including payments from contributories in respect of partly paid shares.

(l) Unavailable assets

(i) Property held as agent, trustee or bailee

Property held by the company as agent, trustee or bailee for another and property which the company holds for the benefit of another person is not available for distribution.

In *Re Kayford Ltd* [1975] 1 All ER 604, money sent in by customers of a mail order company and paid into a special account pending delivery of the goods ordered was held on trust to be returned to the customers.

(ii) Retention of title

Property in the company's possession under a contract containing a retention of title clause pending full settlement will not pass to the liquidator if correctly stored and marked to indicate that it belongs to the supplier. Where such goods are sold and the clause extends into the proceeds of sale which must be held in a separate account, these sums of money will not pass (see Chapter 15, p.359).

(iii) Property disclaimed by the liquidator

The liquidator can disclaim onerous property including (i) unprofitable contracts; and (ii) property which is unsaleable or not readily saleable, or property which may give rise to a liability to pay money or perform any other onerous act. The disclaimer terminates the rights, interests and liabilities of the company from that date and persons suffering loss as a result must prove as creditors in respect of the loss. Special rules relate to the disclaimer of leases.

Disclaimers can take place at any time, but interested persons can serve written notice on liquidators requiring them to elect to disclaim or not when the period is reduced to 28 days from the notice or such longer period as the court may allow: ss.178–182.

In *Hindcastle v. Barbara Attenborough Associates Ltd* [1996] 2 WLR 262, the House of Lords held that the disclaimer of a lease releases the company from liability but does not affect the rights and liabilities of any other person. A director who had guaranteed payment of the rent therefore remained liable under his guarantee. This reversed the decision in *Stacey v. Hill* [1901] 1 KB 660.

(m) Avoidance of transactions prior to the winding-up

The liquidator may increase the assets available for distribution by avoiding transactions entered into prior to the winding-up.

(i) Dispositions after the presentation of the winding-up petition

The liquidator may recover property disposed of by the company between the date of the presentation of the petition and the winding-up order unless the disposition was authorised by the court: s.127. This will then be available for the creditors.

(iii) Transactions at an undervalue

Administrators and liquidators can ask the court to set aside transactions at an undervalue within a relevant time before the onset of insolvency: s.238. This refers to transactions within two years prior to the onset of insolvency or those between the making of an administration application and the making of the order, and between the filing with the court of a copy of a notice of intention to appoint an administrator under paragraph 14 or 22 and the making of the appointment: s.240(1). The company must at the time have been unable to pay its debts for the purposes of s.123, but this is presumed for transactions to connected persons: s.240(2). The onset of insolvency is precisely fixed depending on whether it is an administration or liquidation: s.240(3).

A company enters into a transaction at an undervalue if:

(a) it makes a gift to a person, or enters into a transaction on terms whereby it receives no consideration;
(b) it enters into a transaction where the consideration is significantly less than the value of the consideration supplied by the company: s.238(4).

An order will not be made if the court is satisfied that the company entered into the transaction in good faith and where there were reasonable grounds for believing that it would benefit the company: s.238(5). The creation of a charge is not a transaction at an undervalue since it is not a gift, neither does it deplete the company's assets: *Re M C Bacon Ltd* [1990] BCLC 324 (for facts see below). There is no territorial limit on s.238 proceedings. In *Re Paramount Airways Ltd* [1991] 3 WLR 318, the administrator was able to claim in respect of funds paid into a bank account in Jersey.

The nature of the orders made is listed in s.241, which protects purchasers of the property in good faith and for value: s.241(2) and (2A).

(iv) Voidable preferences

The administrator or liquidator can set aside payments and charges which have been made to put a creditor or guarantor or surety of a creditor into a better position in the event of the company going into an insolvent liquidation. Such payments and charges must have taken place within the relevant time prior to the onset of insolvency, which is two years for connected persons and six months for outsiders: s.240(1)(a) and (b), and the company must have been unable to pay its debts within the meaning of s.123.

The section also catches transactions made between the making of an administration application and the making of the order: s.240(1)(c), and the filing with the court of a notice of intention to appoint an administrator under paragraph 14 or 22 and the making of an appointment.

Preferences are voidable only where the company was motivated by a desire to confer a benefit on the person preferred. For a connected person, defined in s.249, an intention to advantage the person is presumed: s.239(6): *Re DKG Contractors Ltd* [1990] BCC 903; and *Re Beacon Leisure Ltd* [1991] BCC 213.

The onset of insolvency is as for transactions at an undervalue.

In *Re M C Bacon Ltd* [1990] BCLC 324, the company had an unsecured overdraft limit of £300,000. In 1986 it lost its major customer and two of the directors retired from active management. In May 1987 a bank report found the company to be technically insolvent. As a condition of continuing to operate the bank account, the bank demanded fixed and floating charges over the company's assets. In September 1987 the company went into liquidation and the liquidator sought to set aside the charge as a transaction at an undervalue or as a voidable preference. The court concluded that the company did not necessarily desire that which it intended to achieve and held that the charge was not voidable. In *Re M C Bacon Ltd (No 2)* [1990] 3 WLR 646, the liquidators were unable to claim the costs of the abortive action as part of the expenses of the liquidation.

The court may order retransfer of property, release or discharge of security, repayments to administrator or liquidator, revival of guarantees and so on: s.241. Third parties who are *bona fide* purchasers in good faith and for value are protected: s.241(2) and (2A). The proceeds of a successful claim are held on trust for the unsecured creditors: *Re Yagerphone Ltd* [1935] 1 Ch 392.

(v) Avoidance of floating charges

Floating charges created in favour of outsiders within one year before the onset of insolvency are invalid under s.245(3)(a) unless the chargee can prove that the company was unable to pay its debts at that time or became unable to pay its debts as a consequence: s.245(4). For connected persons, the period is extended to two years and is not conditional upon the company being unable to pay its debts at the time of the creation of the charge. The onset of insolvency is precisely determined for administrations and liquidations: s.245(5).

There is an exception as regards the aggregate of:

(a) the value of money paid, or goods or services supplied to the company at the same time as, or after, the creation of the charge;
(b) the value of the discharge or reduction at the same time as, or after, the creation of the charge of any debt of the company;
(c) any interest payable in pursuance of (a) or (b): s.245(2)(a).

The exception in respect of cash, goods and services paid or supplied to the company at the same time as, or after, the creation of the charge means that contemporaneous advances or supplies of goods and services can at least partially, if not entirely, validate the floating charge. Where the consideration consists of goods or services, the security will be valid only to the extent that the charge was reasonable: s.245(6).

In *Re Shoe Lace Ltd* [1992] BCLC 636, the court decided that the degree of contemporaneity depended upon the ordinary meaning of the words used. On that basis, although loans had been made between April and early July in consideration of the proposed creation of a debenture, they could not be said to have been made at the same time as the creation of the debenture, which was finally executed on 24 July 1990. The floating charge was therefore invalid. The Court of Appeal endorsed the High Court's decision on appeal under the name *Power v. Sharp Investments Ltd* [1994] 1 BCLC 111.

An advance made before the formal execution of a debenture will not be regarded as being made at the same time as the creation of the charge unless the interval is so short that it can be regarded as minimal.

There are advantages of this for banks and suppliers under the terms of a current account.

In *Re Yeovil Glove Co. Ltd* [1965] Ch 148, the bank's act in meeting company cheques totalling some £110,000 subsequent to the creation of the debenture was held to be new cash, even though the charge was created in respect of an existing debt with no obligation on the bank to make further advances and the overdraft remained virtually unchanged. This shows the advantageous operation of the rule in *Clayton's Case* (1816) 1 Mer 572, which provides that credits to a current account discharge debts in the order in which they were incurred in the absence of specific appropriation.

A loan by an unsecured creditor under a floating charge on the understanding that the loan will be for immediate settlement of the unsecured creditor's existing debt does not fall within the exception: *Re Destone Fabrics Ltd* [1941] Ch 319. If a company redeems a charge prior to liquidation or administration, the liquidator or administrator cannot require the chargeholder to repay the money received, although it may be recoverable as a preference: *Mace Builders (Glasgow) Ltd v. Lunn* [1987] Ch 191.

(vi) Extortionate credit transactions

The administrator or liquidator may apply to the court in respect of extortionate credit transactions within the three years prior to the entry into administration or commencement of the liquidation: s.244. There is a presumption that the transaction is extortionate. The court can (i) set aside the whole or part of the transaction; (ii) vary the terms of the transaction or terms under which a security is held relating to the transaction; (iii) require any person to refund sums paid by the company; (iv) require the surrender of any security; or (v) provide for accounts to be taken between any persons.

(vii) Transactions defrauding creditors

These are transactions at an undervalue made at any time with the aim of putting assets beyond the reach of creditors or prejudicing their interests: s.423(3). They update the mechanism established by s.172 Law of Property Act 1925, which was held in *Re Shilena Hosiery Ltd* [1980] Ch 219 to relate to companies.

In *Arbuthnot Leasing International Ltd v. Havelet Leasing Ltd (No 2)* [1990] BCC 636, the court held that the fact that the directors were acting on legal advice in respect of a complicated transfer of assets out of the reach of creditors did not prevent the transaction from being contrary to the section.

Potential applicants include individual claimants who are victims: s.424. Possible court orders are similar to those in s.241: s.425. The test for intention under s.423(3) is more difficult to satisfy than that under s.238 or 239.

(viii) Unregistered charges

See Chapter 12, p.264.

(n) Remedies for mismanagement

Liquidators may also increase the assets available for distribution by way of the personal liability of directors of the company to restore property or contribute to the assets of the company.

(i) Summary remedy against defaulting directors

The directors of an insolvent or nearly insolvent company may owe a common law duty to creditors to preserve the assets from dissipation: *Winkworth v. Edward Baron Development Co. Ltd* [1987] 1 All ER 114; and *West Mercia Safetywear v. Dodd* [1988] BCLC 250.

In *Re Purpoint Ltd* [1991] BCLC 491, the director was held liable to contribute £12,666.79p towards the company's assets, including an amount for the purchase by the company of a car on HP when (a) it was unnecessary for the company's business; and (b) the company was insolvent; and cash sums were withdrawn by the director and unaccounted for.

In *Re DKG Contractors Ltd* [1990] BCC 903 it was held that creditors are entitled to have the company's assets kept intact, and that a fraud against the creditors cannot be authorised. Payments totalling over £400,000 paid to the director in the 10-month period before liquidation were ordered to be repaid under s.212. Orders in respect of the same sum under s.239 (voidable preference) and s.214 (wrongful trading) were concurrent.

Where misfeasance proceedings are successful, a director can be ordered to return property to the company or compensate it for any loss caused. An action can be commenced by the Official Receiver, liquidators or creditors or, with leave of the court, contributories even though they will not personally benefit from any order: s.212(5).

In *Re Eurocruit Europe Ltd* [2007] EWHC 1433 (Ch) the court held that the limitation period of a claim brought by a liquidator under s.212 was the same as that applicable to the underlying claim, namely the date the damage was suffered by the company rather than when the cause of action accrued to the liquidator on his appointment. The court struck out proceedings against a director of a company which had ceased to trade on 21 September 1999 in respect of proceedings issued by the liquidator on 10 October 2005 following his appointment on 12 October 1999.

(ii)   Fraudulent trading

If during the winding-up it appears that any business of the company has been carried on with intent to defraud creditors of the company or creditors of any other person or for any fraudulent purpose, the court may declare any persons who were knowingly parties to the carrying on of the business liable to contribute to the company's assets: s.213(1) and (2).

The phrases 'intent to defraud' and 'fraudulent purpose' mean that a person can be liable only where their conduct was deliberately and actually dishonest according to the notions of ordinary decent business people: *Re EB Tractors Ltd* [1987] BCC 313.

In *Re William C Leitch Brothers Ltd* [1932] 2 Ch 71, intent was established where directors carried on business with no reasonable prospect of the debts being paid. In *Re Gerald Cooper Chemicals Ltd* [1978] Ch 262, a person could be liable if only one creditor was defrauded and by one transaction.

This section is directed against 'any persons who were knowingly parties to the carrying on of the business in the manner above-mentioned'.

In *Re Maidstone Buildings Provisions Ltd* [1971] 1 WLR 1085, a company secretary who failed to advise the directors that the company was insolvent and should cease trading was not a party to the carrying on of the business.

Passive participants cannot be liable unless fraudulent trading is claimed against those actually carrying on the business.

In *Re Augustus Barnett & Son Ltd* [1986] BCLC 170, a parent company successfully applied for a claim against it to be struck out on the ground that there had been no allegation that the board of the subsidiary in liquidation had carried on business with intent to defraud creditors. The subsidiary had been able to continue trading only because of statements by the parent of continued financial support, including 'letters of comfort' agreeing to financial support.

The offence of wrongful trading was designed to overcome the technical problems of establishing liability for fraudulent trading.

(iii)   Wrongful trading

The offence of wrongful trading establishes an objective duty of care alongside the subjective duty, but only as regards a director of a company (a) which has gone into insolvent liquidation; and (b) where, at some time before the commencement of the winding-up of the company, that person knew or ought to have concluded that there was no reasonable prospect that the company would avoid going into insolvent liquidation: s.214(2). Under this section, directors owe a statutory duty of care to creditors and can be made liable to contribute towards the assets of the company in liquidation. A director has a defence if s/he took 'every step with a view to minimising the potential loss to the company's creditors as he ought to have taken': s.214(3). For the purposes of s.214(2) and (3), the facts which a director of a company ought to know or ascertain, the conclusions which he ought to reach and the steps which he ought to take are those which would be known or ascertained or reached or taken by a reasonably diligent person having both:

(a) the general knowledge, skill and experience that may reasonably be expected of a person carrying out the same functions as are carried out by that director in relation to the company;

(b) the general knowledge, skill and experience that director has: s.214(4).

Section 214 provides a remedy against former directors: s.214(1), and shadow directors: s.214(7). Shadow directors are defined in s.251. The section specifically does not rule out a parent company from qualifying as a shadow director, and it is therefore more difficult for a group of companies to place one or more of its subsidiaries in insolvent liquidation unless every step has been taken to minimise loss to creditors. Persons identified as *de facto* directors can also be liable: see above, Chapter 11, p.236.

The first successful examination of s.214 came in *Re Produce Marketing Consortium Ltd* [1989] BCLC 513. The court held that the directors ought to have concluded that as at July 1986 there was no reasonable prospect of the company avoiding insolvent liquidation (it went into liquidation in October 1987), and the two defendants were jointly and severally liable to contribute £75,000 to the company's assets.

Where the court cannot, because of the company's inadequate records, establish when the directors should have been aware that the company could not survive, the court can fix the start date. The measure of compensation has been identified as the debts incurred subsequent to that date: *Re Purpoint Ltd* [1991] BCLC 491; *Re DKG Contractors Ltd* [1990] BCC 903. In the *Produce Marketing* case the court held that directors could not apply for total or partial exemption from liability under s.214 under s.727 CA 1985. In *DKG Contractors*, however, the application of the section to s.214 liability was not ruled out.

The value of any wrongful trading award is kept for the benefit of the unsecured creditors by analogy with preferences: *Re Yagerphone* (1935). Directors ordered to contribute under ss.213 and 214 can be disqualified by the court: Company Directors Disqualification Act (CDDA) 1986 s.10.

In *Re Oasis Merchandising Services Ltd* [1997] 2 WLR 764, the liquidator commenced s.214 proceedings against five directors. But as the company and its creditors were unable or unwilling to fund the action, the liquidator, with the consent of the liquidation committee and the Companies Court, assigned the fruits of the action to a specialist litigation support company in return for its funding the action. The court stayed the action as being champertous (an illegal bargain whereby an outsider agrees with a litigant to pay for the action and share in the proceeds recovered) and an abuse of the process. An appeal was dismissed on the ground that the liquidator's statutory rights are not assignable.

(o) Criminal liability arising from insolvency

Criminal charges can be brought under the following sections: (i) s.206: fraud in anticipation of winding-up; (ii) s.207: transactions in fraud of creditors; (iii) s.208: misconduct in the course of winding-up; (iv) s.209: falsification of company books; (v) s.210: material omissions from statement of affairs; and (vi) s.211: false representations to creditors.

(p) Disqualification of directors arising from insolvent liquidation

As well as being disqualified under s.10 CDDA for up to 15 years, directors may be disqualified under s.2 CDDA where convicted of an indictable offence in connection with the promotion, formation, management or liquidation of a company. On summary conviction the maximum period is five years, and on indictment the maximum period is 15 years. A director of a company in the course of winding-up may be disqualified under s.4 CDDA where s/he has been found guilty of fraudulent trading (whether convicted or not) under s.458 CA 1985, or has been guilty of any fraud or breach of duty in relation to the company.

The court has a duty to disqualify unfit directors of insolvent companies for a minimum period of two years: s.6 CDDA. The tests for unfitness are established in Part II of Schedule 1, but these have been extended by judicial decision to include negligence and non-payment of company debts. The key case on liability arising from non-payment of company debts with particular regard to the non-payment of Crown debts is *Re Sevenoaks Stationers (Retail) Ltd* [1990] 3 WLR 1165, which lays down criteria for the period of disqualification (see Chapter 11, p.242). Section 6 is weakened by the fact that proceedings can be initiated only by the Secretary of State or, if s/he so directs, where a company is being wound up by the court, by the Official Receiver. The court continues to have jurisdiction to hear cases on disqualification even though the winding-up of the company is concluded: *Re The Working Project Ltd* [1995] 1 BCLC 226.

(q) Dissolution of a defunct company

A company can be dissolved without being wound up when it appears to have ceased to function. The Registrar sends a letter to the registered office asking whether the company is still functioning. If there is no reply within one month, the Registrar, within 14 days, sends a registered letter notifying the company that, if no answer is received within one month, a notice will be published in the *London Gazette* with a view to striking the company's name off the register.

In the event of a confirmative reply or no reply, the notice is published and the company is struck off within three months of that date: ss.652–653 CA 1985. Application can be made within 20 years for the company to be restored to the register, and in that event the company will be deemed to have continued in existence as if its name had not been struck off.

Within two years of the dissolution, the court may declare it void on an application by the liquidator or any other interested person: s.651 CA 1985.

13.6 Insolvent general partnerships

The position regarding insolvent partnerships is complicated since there is the possibility of a bankrupt partner or partners with or without an insolvent partnership and an insolvent partnership with or without a bankrupt partner or partners. There is also the complication of distinguishing between partnership creditors and the separate private creditors of the individual partners, and the assets of the firm and those of the individual partners.

The IA 1986 rules were applied to partnerships by the Insolvent Partnerships Order (IPO) 1994, replacing the 1986 Order which was largely ineffective. One major change from the 1986 Order retained in the current legislation recognised partnerships as a distinct entity and provided that, in general, they should be wound up as unregistered companies under Part V IA 1986. As a result, partners became subject to the CDDA 1986 as directors of the unregistered company.

The partnership is also treated as a distinct entity in the sense that it can be placed in administration and be subject to a partnership voluntary arrangement (PVA).

(a) Winding-up of insolvent partnership without concurrent petition against any partner

A petition can be brought by a creditor, an insolvency practitioner (liquidator, administrator or trustee in bankruptcy), the Secretary of State or any other person other than a partner: Art. 7 IPO 1994. In addition a petition can be brought by a partner (any one if there are fewer than eight and otherwise with permission of the court): Art. 9. Petitions can be on three grounds, only one of which relates to insolvency: (i) that the partnership has ceased to carry on business; (ii) that it is unable to pay its debts; or (iii) that it is just and equitable to wind the partnership up. Inability to pay its debts is in accordance with s.123 IA 1986. Detailed rules for the proceedings are in Schedules 3 and 5 IPO 1994.

In *Investment and Pensions Advisory Service Ltd v. Gray* [1990] BCLC 38, the court decided that the private assets of the partners are not available to creditors unless they have been the subject of insolvency proceedings. As a result, this procedure will not be used by creditors where there is any doubt about the partners' ability to cover the firm's debts.

(b) Winding-up of insolvent partnership with concurrent petition against any partner

A member or a creditor may bring concurrent petitions to wind up the partnership and bankrupt one or more of the partners: Arts 8 and 10 and Schedules 4 and 6 IPO 1994. The partnership can be wound up only if it is unable to pay its debts. The petitions are presented in the same court on the same day. The petition against the firm is heard first.

This procedure involves two sets of creditors – the joint and the separate creditors – and two available funds – the joint and the separate estates. In this case it is necessary to establish the priority between the two groups of creditors and even within the two groups; priority in each case will depend on whether the creditors are secured or preferential. There is also the category of deferred creditors under s.3 Partnership Act 1890 in respect of loans falling within s.2(3)(d) and (e).

The rules provide that the joint estate is primarily available for the joint creditors and the separate estates for the separate creditors, with any unmet claims being transferred to the other estate. Where the joint creditors remain unpaid in full out of the joint estate, however, their claim for the unpaid balance is apportioned amongst the several estates where they rank equally with the ordinary, separate creditors.

(c) Joint bankruptcy petitions

There is an alternative to winding up an insolvent partnership where all the partners are insolvent: Art. 11 and Schedule 7, IPO 1994. The partners can present a joint bankruptcy petition to the effect that the firm is unable to pay its debts, and the personal bankruptcy provisions of the IA 1986 (as amended by the Schedule) apply. A single trustee in bankruptcy is appointed to administer the joint and separate estates. The same priority rules apply to the joint and separate creditors as in a winding-up with concurrent bankruptcy petitions. The procedure is less complex, however, and, where the unsecured joint and separate estates do not exceed £20,000, the court can apply the summary procedure for the administration of the estates.

Hot Topic . . .
THE GLOBAL DIMENSION

With the increasing globalisation of trade, cross-border insolvency has become an important issue. The insolvency of companies which have been engaged in cross-border trading has led to developments to deal with insolvency at an international level. In 1997, the United Nations Commission on International Trade Law (UNCITRAL), established to allow the UN to play a greater part in 'reducing the disparities caused by the domestic rules governing international trade', adopted a Model Law on Cross-Border Insolvency. This was designed to allow countries to adapt the law to their own conditions and needs. UNCITRAL has issued 'A Guide to the Enactment of the Model Law' for states wishing to incorporate the Model Law. In the UK, s.14 Insolvency Act 2000 allows the Secretary of State to give effect to the Model Law by way of statutory instrument. There has been no secondary legislation to this effect so far.

At the European level, EC Regulation No 1346/ 2000 ([2000] OJ L160/1) was adopted in May 2000. Member States were allowed time to adapt their laws to accommodate the Regulation which came into force across the EU from 31 May 2002. As a Regulation it is directly applicable in all Member States, with the exception of Denmark, without the need to be implemented by domestic legislation. The Regulation applies to insolvency proceedings whether the debtor is a natural or a legal person, a trader or an individual. The proceedings in the UK covered by the Regulation include: winding up by or subject to the supervision of the court, creditors' voluntary winding up (with confirmation by the court), administration, voluntary arrangements under insolvency legislation – IVAs, PVAs and CVAs – bankruptcy or sequestration (in Scotland).

Excluded from the scope of the Regulation are insolvency proceedings concerning insurance undertakings, credit institutions, investment undertakings holding funds or securities for third parties and collective investment undertakings. The reason for their exclusion is that they are subject to special arrangements and, to some extent, the national supervisory authorities have extremely wide-ranging powers of intervention.

The Regulation recognises that it is not practical to introduce insolvency proceedings with universal scope throughout the EU. The Regulation distinguishes between main insolvency proceedings and secondary insolvency proceedings. Main proceedings can be initiated only where the debtor has the centre of his main interests. These proceedings have universal scope and aim at encompassing all the debtor's assets. The Regulation also allows secondary proceedings to be opened to run in parallel with the main proceedings. These may be opened in the Member State where the debtor has an establishment. The secondary proceedings are limited to the assets located in that state. There are mandatory rules of coordination with the main proceedings.

The Regulation applies only to proceedings where the centre of the debtor's main interests is located in the EU. The rules of jurisdiction establish international jurisdiction only, that is to say, they designate the Member State whose courts may open insolvency proceedings. Within that Member State, territorial jurisdiction is established by the national law of the Member State.

The court with jurisdiction to open the main insolvency proceedings should be able to order provisional and protective measures governing assets situated in the territory of other Member States.

Prior to the opening of the main proceedings, the right to request the opening of insolvency proceedings in the Member State where the debtor has an establishment should be limited to local creditors and creditors of the local establishment or to cases where main proceedings cannot be opened under the law of the Member State in which the debtor has the centre of his main interest. If the main insolvency proceedings are opened, the territorial proceedings become secondary.

Creditors with habitual residence, domicile or registered office in the EU have the right to lodge claims in each set of insolvency proceedings relating to the debtor's assets; however, the distribution of proceeds must be coordinated. Creditors are able to keep what they have received in the course of their territorial proceedings but the right to participate in the distribution of assets in other proceedings is subject to whether creditors of the same standing have obtained the same proportion of their claims.

End of Chapter Summary

This chapter is very important in respect of law for business since it is the avoidance of personal insolvency which generally leads individuals to trade under the form of a registered company or under the more recent form of the LLP. It is also significant that, since 1986 (but more significantly 1994), the law of corporate insolvency has been applicable to general partnerships under the Partnership Act 1890 (although the individual partners may also be subject to personal insolvency procedures).

Having read and understood this chapter, you should have a detailed knowledge of the following matters of particular importance:

▶ The alternatives to liquidation in the form of receivership, administration and the company voluntary arrangement (CVA) (and their equivalents for general partnerships).
▶ The powers of administrators, particularly in respect of the disposal of the secured property of the company (or partnership).
▶ The distinction between voluntary members' and creditors' winding-up and compulsory winding-up.
▶ The persons who can petition for the compulsory winding-up of a company and restrictions on their right to petition.
▶ The property available for creditors and the priority of creditors in a liquidation.
▶ The way in which directors can be required by the law to contribute to the assets of the company in liquidation; in particular the law relating to wrongful trading.

The importance of this chapter has been signalled in many earlier chapters, notably Chapters 6–8 and Chapter 12.

Questions

1. Top Drawer plc, a catering company, runs a successful hospitality operation for the principal sporting and social functions – Ascot, Henley, Wimbledon and so on. In 2002 the company established a wholly owned subsidiary, T D Ltd to operate an exclusive range of retail outlets. The directors of T D Ltd were nominees of Top Drawer plc. T D Ltd acquired the necessary premises by way of a loan of £1,000,000 from one of the five banks with which the holding company dealt and the loan was secured by a registered floating charge over T D Ltd's assets. The debenture allowed the bank to serve notice on the company converting its floating charge into a fixed charge.

   The shops were fitted out with the necessary equipment by Main Line Ltd, which supplied the goods subject to a reservation of title clause over them pending full settlement of outstanding debts. The main supplier of the retail operation, H C Ltd, is owed £5,000 by T D Ltd.

   The retail venture lost money and its bank continued to extend credit only on the basis of a letter of accommodation issued by Top Drawer plc and referred to in T D Ltd's annual accounts. In January, T D Ltd's accountants recommended that the directors should consider placing the company in administration. Acting on the advice of the board of Top Drawer plc, however, it continued trading for a further six months, when H C Ltd presented a petition on the ground that the company was unable to pay its debts.

   (i)   How can H C Ltd successfully establish that T D Ltd is unable to pay its debts?

   (ii) If the company goes into insolvent liquidation as a result of the petition, what will be the priority of the bank as a creditor if it had served notice on the company before the presentation of the petition converting its floating charge into a fixed charge?

Questions cont'd

(iii) What would be the position of Main Line Ltd with regard to the cost of shop fittings for the retail outlets if T D Ltd had not yet paid for the work?

(iv) Is there any potential liability of the directors of T D Ltd and Top Drawer plc arising from the way in which T D Ltd was managed?

2. The Insolvency Act 1986 provides three methods whereby a liquidator can seek a contribution to the assets of a company in insolvent liquidation. What are the three methods, and in what ways are they different in respect of (i) the nature of the offence which triggers their operation; (ii) the persons against whom they can be used; and (iii) the defences available?

3. Utopia plc is in insolvent liquidation and the following proofs have been lodged:

(i) A claim for £60,000 by Finance Ltd secured by a floating charge over the company's stocks in respect of wages and salary for the employees of Utopia plc. When the loan was made and the charge was created, Finance Ltd was aware of the presentation of the petition which resulted in the eventual winding-up order against Utopia plc.

(ii) A claim for £80,000 by Dogger Bank plc. On Utopia plc's liquidation, the company's total indebtedness to Dogger Bank plc was £300,000. Of this, £180,000 was in respect of the company's general business account, with the remaining £120,000 in respect of the company's wages and salaries account. Dogger Bank plc had sold freehold property belonging to Utopia plc over which it had a fixed charge. The proceeds of the sale, £220,000, had been appropriated first to discharging the amount outstanding on the business account.

(iii) A claim for £50,000 by Grange Ltd which guaranteed Utopia plc's total indebtedness to Natbest Bank plc subject to a limit of £50,000. Grange Ltd has discharged its liability to the bank.

(iv) A claim for a total of £200,000 from Letters Ltd, the lessor of Utopia plc's factory premises. The claim is for (i) £45,000 for pre-petition arrears; (ii) £15,000 for the period after the liquidator's appointment; and (iii) £140,000 for the remaining five years, taking into account annual rent increases.

(v) A claim for £35,000 by Eden Ltd in respect of goods supplied. The goods claim includes an amount in respect of interest of 5 per cent per annum from the date of supply but fails to take account of the usual trade discount of 2 per cent. Eden Ltd owes £10,000 to Utopia plc under a credit note issued for a previous delivery of faulty goods.

Advise the liquidator concerning the validity and priority of these claims.

Business Assets and Securing Loans

Introduction to Part IV

This part of the book introduces you to the different types of business assets which can be owned by business organisations and entrepreneurs (Chapter 12).

Whilst most of these assets also exist in a non-business context, there is a class of particular significance to business in the form of intellectual property rights. Thus, products developed by the business involving a creative step can be protected by patents; assets in the form of publications, musical compositions and recordings can be protected by copyright; and the goodwill in the form of trade marks and brand names.

Patents are extremely valuable to companies and are vigorously protected. Dyson fought a prolonged legal battle with Hoover over its patented vacuum cleaner system. Drugs companies rely on their patent protection to bring in vast sums of money for successful drugs; Prozac and Viagra are two examples. The companies fight against any breach of their patent rights, including restricting the production of generic equivalents to be used to fight the AIDS epidemic. The end of patent protection for a drug will often mean a collapse in profitability for the company.

Copyright is of major importance to publishers of books and music, and recording and film studios. It enables authors, composers and songwriters to live on the proceeds of their past work and, where the copyright in the back catalogue of a recording artist is owned by the recording company, the ending of the copyright protection represents an enormous loss in the asset value of the company. In 2008, J K Rowling obtained a permanent ban on the publication of a Harry Potter Lexicon. The material had been published on the web for many years and had been praised by Rowling. The judge ruled the publication would have 'irreparably harmed' Rowling as an author, and that the Lexicon had gone beyond the fair use of her work and would have harmed her intention to produce her own encyclopaedia, the proceeds of which are promised to charity. Rowling commented; 'I went to court to uphold the rights of authors everywhere to protect their own original work'.

A brand is a name which customers know and react to. The brand manipulates a buyer's perception of the thing's worth and adds value. The value of the brand is the impression of extra worth that it engenders in customers, whose loyalty is more secure. Branding emerged in the last 100 years, and by 1890 most countries had trade mark legislation establishing a name as capable of legal protection. It was late in the 19th century that manufacturers could take advantage of mass-manufacturing techniques, distribution networks and advertising to win customers on a national or international scale. To distinguish their products, manufacturers gave them distinctive names to differentiate them from 'own label' products of local retailers. George Eastman called his camera 'Kodak' because it was 'short, vigorous, incapable of being misspelt … and meant nothing'. The commercial significance of brands has led to a number of brand-driven takeover deals, with bidders prepared to pay in excess of the asset value of the target company to acquire valuable brand names on the basis that it is almost impossible to create a megabrand from scratch. Thus Nestlé paid £2.55 billion – more than five times the book value of the company Rowntree Macintosh – to acquire the rights to Kit-Kat, After Eight, Smarties and Polo.

The 2008 annual audit of brands by Interbrand reported that the brand value of Google had shot up by 43 per cent from $17.8bn (£9.7bn) to $25.59bn and had gone from 20 to 10 on the branding consultancy's chart of leading brands. Other firms which had significantly added value to their global brand in the previous 12 months included Apple, Amazon and Nintendo. Four of the five highest risers in the top 100 were technology firms. The most valuable brand in the world is Coca-Cola at £66.7bn.

An important aspect of the ownership of any property is that it can be used as a security against loans: see Chapter 15. Particularly important in this respect is the possibility of the business activity being financed by mortgages taken over the personal property of the entrepreneur, including mortgages over life policies, shares and the matrimonial home. Another important area concerns securities issued by limited liability companies (and LLPs) and the distinction between fixed and floating charges. This is discussed in Chapter 12.

The significance of creditors holding a security in respect of debts owed lies in the fact that in the event of the personal or corporate insolvency of the debtor, secured creditors have priority of repayment over unsecured creditors. The priority of creditors in the event of corporate insolvency is discussed at Chapter 13, p.292.

In addition to claims against assets, security for loans can also come in the form of undertakings by third parties that, in the event of the debtor being unable to pay, they will guarantee to make the payment in their place. This is covered by the discussion on guarantees and indemnities.

Since credit is the lifeblood of commerce, these two chapters are of great importance.

Chapter 14

Business property

Learning objectives

After reading this chapter you will know about:

▶ the classification of property in England and Wales;
▶ real property: freehold, leasehold and commonhold;
▶ intangible property including negotiable instruments;
▶ intellectual property: trade marks and brand names, patents and copyright

14.1 The nature and classification of business property

Business assets are important as they can be used as security for raising loans and increasing borrowing capacity. Business property can be tangible and intangible. Tangible property includes land and assets which are capable of physical possession. Intangible property is not capable of physical possession except through the enforcement of ownership rights. Intangible property includes debts and rights under insurance policies. It also includes shares the ownership of which confers the right to attend shareholders' meetings and vote, the right to a dividend and return of the investment on the company's liquidation. Intangible property can be assignable or negotiable in the form of negotiable instruments: cheques and bills of exchange.

Intangible property also includes all intellectual property: trade marks, copyrights and patents. Copyrights and patents give their owner exclusive rights to commercial exploitation of products including inventions, books, music, artistic works and designs; while trade marks protect the identifying characteristics by which consumers identify products or services. The classification of property in England and Wales is shown in Figure 14.1.

14.2 Real property

Absolute ownership of land is vested in the Crown. Below that level, the law distinguishes between 'freehold', 'leasehold' and 'commonhold' property.

Freehold owners are the nearest that English law allows to 'ownership' of land. Leaseholders hold land under a lease, a contract which entitles them to exercise rights of possession for the period allowed by the lease. In addition, the Commonhold and Leasehold Property Act (CLPA) 2002 created commonhold tenure in respect of individual holdings of property, commercial or domestic, where there was an overall freehold owner.

(a) Freehold estates

The normal and most perfect freehold title is the fee simple absolute in possession. The word 'fee' means that the title does not terminate on the death of the current holder but can be passed by will. The word 'simple' indicates that there are no restrictions relating

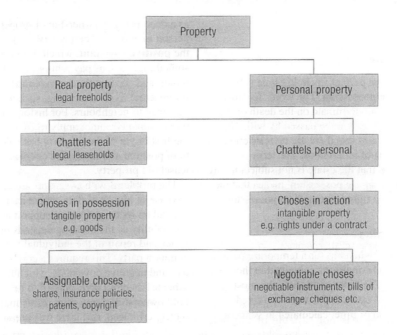

Figure 14.1   Classification of property in England and Wales

to the rights of inheritance. The term 'absolute' indicates that the title is not subject to any condition, and the term 'in possession' means that the title holder has the right to immediate possession.

(b) Leasehold estates

The term of years is one for a fixed determinable period of time, calculated in years or months. It includes the renewable yearly lease. The term of years can also have the qualities of being absolute and in possession. Part 2 of the CLPA 2002 reformed residential leasehold law, giving leaseholders new rights and enhancing their existing ones.

Leaseholders of flats can take over the management of their building and collectively acquire the freehold of it. Leaseholders of flats have the right to buy new, longer leases, and leaseholders of houses can buy the freehold or extend their leases under the Leasehold Reform Act 1967. Leaseholders of houses who have extended their leases under the 1967 Act can buy their freehold or have security of tenure when the extended lease expires.

The CLPA 2002 also provided for greater protection against unreasonable service charges and other payments and for landlords to consult about major works.

(c) Commonhold property

A covenant is a promise contained in a deed passing title from one person to another. There are two types of covenant: the positive covenant is a promise to do something, such as pay rent or keep the property in repair, and the restrictive covenant is a promise not to do something, such as cause a nuisance to neighbours. Positive covenants cannot apply to freehold land once the first buyer of the property has sold it, but both positive and restrictive covenants apply to leasehold property.

Blocks of flats require a combination of positive and negative covenants, which means that they need to be based on leasehold ownership. Long-term residential leasehold was widely criticised, and there was pressure to develop a system to combine the security of freehold with the management potential of positive covenants. The scheme which was developed was commonhold.

Each separate property in the commonhold development is called a unit, which can be a flat, a house, a shop or a light industrial unit. The owner is called a unit-holder. The body owning and managing the common parts is the commonhold association, which must be a private company limited by guarantee, with membership restricted to the unit-holders within the development. The commonhold association must have a standard set of memorandum and articles as prescribed by the Lord Chancellor. The result is that the unit-holders have a direct interest in the unit or units they own and membership of the commonhold association. The commonhold association with its common parts and associated units is registered at HM Land Registry by the developer of the commonhold development or the sponsor of an existing development converting to commonhold.

A unit may consist of two or more separate areas of land, for instance a flat with a garage in a detached block, or a shop with a separate storage unit. Units may be divided vertically, horizontally, or may be free-standing.

The size of the development can be increased or reduced by the purchase or sale of common parts, and rules govern the distribution of capital arising from any sale. The voting rights of unit-holders, the various majorities required for particular purposes, the minimum requirements for the maintenance of accounts and the machinery for fixing and payment of the commonhold assessment (similar to service charges) are set out in the standard articles or the commonhold community statement, which also sets out the procedure for dispute resolution, including internal procedures, alternative dispute resolution (ADR) and, finally, recourse to the courts and tribunals as necessary.

Detailed rules govern the winding-up of commonhold associations including the distribution of any profit. The winding-up of insolvent commonhold associations is under the standard insolvency rules.

(d) Equitable estates

Equitable estates can arise under a trust and where some non-compliance with the legal formalities of law prevents the transfer or creation of a legal title. Legal titles bind subsequent purchasers, even if they have no notice of their existence. Equitable titles are overreached so that the beneficial interest of the equitable title holder transfers to the proceeds of the sale if the legal title is transferred to a *bona fide* purchaser for value without notice of the equitable title.

14.3 Choses (things) in possession

This covers all tangible (or corporeal) property capable of physical possession by the owner: in other words 'goods'.

Goods are transferable by sale under the Sale of Goods Act 1979. Other forms of transfer including hire are covered by the Supply of Goods and Services Act 1982. The supply of goods on hire purchase and conditional sale agreement is covered by the Supply of Goods (Implied Terms) Act 1973. Goods supplied under a credit sale agreement come under the Sale of Goods Act 1979 (see Chapter 18).

14.4   Choses (things) in action

This relates to intangible property which is enjoyed by the enforcement of rights of ownership. Things in action can be assignable or negotiable.

(a)   Assignable things in action

Intangible property rights can be assigned and the assignment may be legal or equitable (formal or informal).

The legal assignment of certain things in action is governed by separate Acts of Parliament, for example shares and insurance polices, but the general law relating to their legal assignment is (s.136 LPA 1925) and requires that the assignment must be:

(i)   absolute (that is, an assignment of the whole debt);
(ii) in writing signed by the assignor;
(iii) expressly notified in writing by the assignee to the debtor.

Thus, if A owes £500 to B, B can assign his/her right to payment to C. A is the debtor, B the assignor and C the assignee. The legal assignee can enforce his/her rights by action against the debtor who can, however, raise against him/her any defence that s/he could have raised against the assignor, such as the right to set-off. The assignment is thus subject to the doctrine of *nemo dat quod non habet* (no one can give what s/he does not have) in that s/he gets no better title than the assignor. If the assignment is informal, the equitable assignee cannot enforce his/her rights in his/her own name but must join the assignor as co-plaintiff in any action. An equitable assignment also requires notice to the debtor and is subject to the doctrine of *nemo dat*.

(b)   Negotiable things in action

Merchants had, over the centuries, developed the practice of transferring among themselves documents representing rights to payment under a 'bill of exchange' free from any requirement of giving notice to the person ultimately obliged to pay. This person was required to pay the current holder of the bill when payment was due. To inspire confidence in this practice, the custom developed that, if a bill was taken in certain conditions, the transferee would take the bill free from defects in title of the transferor.

If the assignee took the bill (i) for value, (ii) in good faith and (iii) without notice of any defect in title of the transferor he was the 'holder in due course' of the bill, the transfer of which was not subject to the doctrine of *nemo dat*. (For bills of exchange, cheques and promissory notes, three further conditions are added by the Bills of Exchange Act 1882 s.29(1).)

Things in action capable of negotiation are called negotiable instruments and include:

(i)   bills of exchange, promissory notes and cheques;
(ii)   treasury bills;
(iii) share warrants and debentures issued or payable to bearer;
(iv)   bankers' drafts;
(v)   circular notes;
(vi)   dividend warrants.

Postal orders and bills of lading are not negotiable instruments. A negotiable instrument is not legal tender (but bank notes are negotiable instruments) and a creditor can refuse to accept a negotiable instrument in discharge of a debt.

Negotiable instruments have the following features:

(i)   they are transferable by mere delivery (or by indorsement plus delivery in the case of a bill of exchange drawn payable to order);
(ii)   there is no need for notice of transfer, and payment is to the holder for the time being;
(iii) legal title passes on negotiation and the holder can sue to enforce payment in his/her own name;
(iv)   the title passes free from equities of which the transferee has no notice;
(v)   a holder in due course has a title free from the defects which affected the transferor.

14.5 Trade marks and brand names

Unregistered trade marks are protected by the common law tort of passing off (see Chapter 4, p. 112), but registered trade marks are protected by statute.

(a) Registered trade marks

A trade mark is 'any sign capable of being represented graphically which is capable of distinguishing goods or services of one undertaking from those of other undertakings'. It may 'consist of words (including personal names), designs, letters, numerals or the shape of goods or their packaging': s.1(1) Trade Marks Act 1994.

A trade mark can include the colour of a product or a motorbike messenger's uniform, the appearance of a firm's delivery van or the pattern on a takeaway hamburger box, or any packaging including distinctive bottle shapes and smells. Symbols include the Bass red triangle, the first UK registered trade mark. Michelin succeeded in registering 'X' for radial tyres, and distinctive combinations of letters can be registered, as with ICI, ICL, GEC, BP and SDP. Problems relating to registration of number combinations led Intel Corporation to give a newly designed chip the name 'Pentium' rather than follow its earlier practice of using numbers.

The law is contained in the Trade Marks Act 1994 and all references in this section will be to that Act unless otherwise stated. It was passed to implement an EC Council Directive (89/104/EEC, [1989] OJ L140/1) which sought to approximate the laws of the Member States relating to trade marks and make provision in connection with Council Regulation (EC) No 40/94, [1994] OJ L11/1, on the EU trade mark. The Act also gives effect to the Madrid Protocol Relating to International Registration of Marks of 27 June 1989. The Act has no effect on the law of passing off: s.2(2).

The Act extends to collective marks distinguishing the goods or services of members of the association which is the proprietor of the mark from those of other undertakings: for example ABTA: s.49 and Schedule 1. It also covers certification marks which indicate that the goods or services are certified by the mark's proprietor in respect of origin, material, mode of manufacture of goods or performance of services, quality, accuracy or other characteristics: s.50 and Schedule 2.

Signs which do not satisfy s.1(1) are excluded, including marks with no distinctive character, or solely designating the kind, quality, intended purpose, value, geographical origin, the time of production of goods or rendering of services, or other characteristics of goods or services, and marks which have become customary: s.3(1). A shape cannot be registered if it results from the nature of the goods themselves, or is necessary to obtain a technical result or give substantial value to them: s.3(2). Registration is also refused for marks contrary to public policy or accepted principles of morality or ones likely to deceive the public as to the nature, quality or geographical origin of the goods or services: s.3(3).

Marks cannot be registered if identical with an earlier trade mark covering identical goods or services, or where similarity of mark and goods or services is likely to cause confusion to the public. This extends to unregistered marks protected by any rule of law (that is, passing off) or protected in any other form (that is, copyright, design right or registered designs): s.5.

The protection offered to well-known or famous marks is of particular interest in respect of refusal of registration. Section 5(3) provides that a trade mark shall not be registered where it is identical or similar to an earlier trade mark, but for goods or services which are not similar to those for which the earlier trade mark is protected where the earlier trade mark has a reputation in the UK (or in the case of a Community trade mark in the EU) and the use of the later mark would take unfair advantage of, or be detrimental to, the distinctive character or repute of the earlier trade mark. This protects famous marks against 'dilution' by either blurring or tarnishing their reputation.

In *Oasis Stores Ltd's Trade Mark Application* [1998] RPC 631, Oasis attempted to register the mark 'Eveready' for contraceptives and condoms. The application was opposed under s.5(3) by Ever Ready plc which owned numerous 'Ever Ready' words in connection with batteries, torches, plugs and so on. The court rejected its claim on the ground that simply being reminded of a similar trade mark with a reputation for dissimilar goods did not necessarily amount to taking an unfair advantage of the repute of that trade mark. In *esure Insurance Ltd v. Direct Line Insurance plc* [2008] EWCA Civ 842 the court dismissed an appeal by esure against a refusal to register as a trade mark a red computer mouse on wheels on the ground that there was indirect confusion between that mark and that already registered by Direct Line, a red telephone on wheels. The court remarked that there was little value in an applicant submitting an expert's report on the possibility of trade-mark confusion where the tribunal was in a position to form its own view.

(b)　The rights of the registered proprietor

The proprietor has exclusive rights in the registered trade mark which are infringed by use of the trade mark in the UK without his/her consent: s.9(1). Infringing acts include the use by a person of a registered trade mark in the course of a trade that is:

(i)　identical with the trade mark in relation to identical goods or services for which it is registered: s.10(1);

(ii) identical with the trade mark and used in relation to similar goods or services to those for which the trade mark is registered; or the sign is similar and is used in relation to identical or similar goods or services for which the mark is registered and there is the likelihood of confusion on the part of the public: s.10(2);

(iii) identical with or similar to the trade mark, and used in relation to non-similar goods or services for which the trade mark is registered where the trade mark has a reputation in the UK and the use takes unfair advantage of or is detrimental to the distinctive character or repute of the mark: s.10(3).

A person uses a sign if s/he (a) affixes it to goods or the packaging thereof; (b) offers or exposes goods for sale, puts them on the market or stocks them for those purposes under the sign, or offers or supplies services under the sign; (c) imports or exports goods under the sign; or (d) uses the sign on business papers or in advertising: s.10(4). A person who applies a mark to material to be used for labelling or packaging goods, as a business paper, or for advertising goods or services is a party to any use of the material which infringes the mark if s/he knew or had reason to believe that the application was not duly authorised by the proprietor or licensee of the mark: s.10(5).

A registered trade mark is not infringed by the use of another registered trade mark in relation to goods or services for which the latter is registered: s.11(1), but subject to the fact that the registration of a trade mark may be declared invalid as being in breach of s.3, in which case it is deemed never to have been registered: s.47(6). There is also no infringement by:

(a) the use by a person of his/her own name or address;

(b) the use of indications concerning the kind, quality, quantity, intended purpose, value, geographical origin, the time of production of goods or rendering of services, or other characteristics of goods or services;

(c) the use of the trade mark where it is necessary to indicate the intended purpose of a product or service (in particular as accessories or spare parts), provided the use accords with honest industrial or commercial practices: s.11(2).

A registered trade mark is not infringed by the use in the course of trade in a particular locality of an earlier right which applies only in that locality: s.11(3), nor by use in relation to goods put on the market in the European Economic Area under that trade mark by the proprietor or with his/her consent: s.12(1), except where there are legitimate reasons for the proprietor to oppose further dealings in the goods, in particular where their condition has been changed or impaired: s.12(2).

Applicants for registration or the proprietor may disclaim right to the exclusive use of any element of the mark, or agree that the rights shall be subject to a specified territorial or other limitation, which will be published and entered in the register: s.13.

(c) Remedies for infringement

Infringement is actionable by the proprietor, and all such relief by way of damages, injunctions, accounts or otherwise is available to him as in respect of the infringement of any other property right: s.14. There are two specific remedies.

Order for erasure of offending sign: the court may order a person who has infringed a trade mark to cause the offending sign to be erased, removed or obliterated from any infringing goods, material or articles in his/her possession, custody or control, or to secure the destruction of the infringing goods, material or articles in question: s.15(1).

Order for delivery up of infringing goods, materials or articles: infringing goods, material and articles are defined in s.17. However, an application for an order under s.16 may not be made after the end of the period of six years from:

(a) in the case of infringing goods, the date on which the trade mark was applied to the goods or their packaging;
(b) in the case of infringing material, the date on which the trade mark was applied to the material;
(c) in the case of infringing articles, the date on which they were made.

The six-year limit is extended where the proprietor of the registered trade mark was under a disability or prevented by fraud or concealment from discovering the facts entitling him/her to apply for an order: s.18(2).

Where infringing goods, material or articles have been delivered up under s.16, an application may be made that they be destroyed or forfeited to such persons as the court thinks fit: s.199(1). If no order is made, the person in whose possession, custody or control they were before being delivered up is entitled to their return: s.19(5). A person threatened with groundless infringement proceedings can claim relief, including a declaration that the threats are unjustifiable, an injunction against continuance of the threats, and damages in respect of any loss sustained. S/he is entitled to relief if s/he can show that registration is invalid or liable to be revoked in a relevant respect: s.21(3).

Unauthorised use of a trade mark in relation to goods is a criminal offence unless the person shows that s/he had reasonable grounds to believe that the use of the sign was not an infringement. The person is liable on summary conviction to imprisonment for a term not exceeding six months or a fine not exceeding the statutory maximum, or both, and on conviction on indictment to a fine or imprisonment for a term not exceeding 10 years, or both: s.92.

(d) Application for registration

Application is to the Registrar and must contain (i) a request for registration; (ii) the name and address of the applicant; (iii) a statement of the goods or services for which registration is sought; and (iv) a representation of the mark. The application must state that the mark is being used by or with the consent of the applicant in relation to those goods or services, or that s/he has a *bona fide* intention that it should be so used; and be accompanied by an application fee and the appropriate class fees: s.32. Goods and services are classified according to a prescribed system, and questions concerning the class of goods or services are determined by the Registrar: s.34. Trade marks are registered in respect of particular goods or classes of goods, and most countries follow the International Classification of Goods Convention: for example sports equipment is Class 28, clothing Class 25.

A person has priority for registering the trade mark for some or all of the same goods or services for six months from filing the first application: s.35(1). If application is made within that period, the relevant date for establishing precedence is the date of filing the first application, and the registrability is not affected by any use of the mark in the UK in the period between that date and the date of the application: s.35(2). See *Inter Lotto (UK) Ltd v. Camelot Group plc* [2003] EWCA Civ 1132; Chapter 4, p.113. Equivalent filing in a Convention country gives rise to the same priority right: s.35(3).

The Registrar carries out a search of earlier trade marks. The applicant must be informed if the requirements for registration are not met, and have the opportunity to make representations or to amend the application. The Registrar can accept or reject the application: s.37. If the registration is accepted, the application is published to give persons the opportunity to oppose the registration within a prescribed time: s.38. The applicant may withdraw his/her application or restrict the goods or services covered by the application. If the application has been published, notification of withdrawal must also be published. Otherwise, an application can be amended only in relation to the name and address of the applicant, errors of wording or copying, or obvious mistakes, and then only where the correction does not substantially affect the identity of the mark or extend the goods or services covered by the application: s.39.

Registered marks are valid for 10 years and renewable for further periods of 10 years under s.42. If registration is not renewed, the Registrar shall remove the trade marks from the register: s.43. A registered trade mark cannot be altered during the period of registration or on renewal, except in respect of alteration of the proprietor's name and address where the mark includes this: s.44. The registered mark is subject to surrender, revocation and invalidity.

(e)   Surrender

The mark may be surrendered in respect of some or all of the goods or services for which it is registered: s.45.

(f)   Revocation

The mark may be revoked on the grounds:

(a) that within the five years following registration it has not been put to genuine use in the UK by the proprietor or with his/her consent and there are no proper reasons for the non-use;

(b) that such use has been suspended for an uninterrupted period of five years without proper reasons;

(c) that, in consequence of acts or inactivity of the proprietor, it has become the common name in the trade for a product or service for which it is registered;

(d) that, in consequence of the use made of it by the proprietor or with his/her consent, it is liable to mislead the public, particularly as to the nature, quality or geographical origin of the goods or services for which it is registered: s.46(1).

Of particular importance here is (c), which occurs once a trade mark ceases to distinguish the goods or service of the proprietor. The easiest way for a trade mark to lose validity is where it becomes a generic name. Thus words such as linoleum, gramophone, aspirin, hovercraft and nylon are all marks which have lost their distinctive link with the products of a particular manufacturer. 'Vaseline' had to be re-established as a distinctive mark. The proprietor will specify stringent regulations for the use of the mark. Trade marks should always be used as an adjective and not a noun and should always be used as registered and not altered. Wherever possible, they should be used in conjunction with the generic description, for example 'Cif – Cream Cleanser', and they should either be capitalised completely or used with an initial capital. Any licensee must be obliged to follow a registered user agreement.

Articles marketed under a registered trade mark should be marked 'Reg Trade Mark' on the object or on the packaging. The practice of using an R in a circle next to the mark has no legal significance, but is likely to be judicially recognised, and it acts as a warning to traders that a monopoly is being claimed. A similar effect is caused by the use of the ™ symbol. An alternative is to mark the protected sign with an asterisk followed by a statement that the symbol is a registered trade mark. It is an offence to say that a mark is registered when it is not: s.95. Common law marks are identified by the words: '"..." is a Trade Mark'. Registration can be invalidated on application to the Registrar or the court and, where a mark is declared invalid, the registration shall be deemed never to have been made.

(g)   Ownership, assignment and licensing

When a trade mark is granted to two or more persons, each is entitled to an equal undivided share in the mark, subject to any agreement to the contrary: s.23. A registered trade mark is transmissible by assignment, testamentary disposition or operation of law in the same way as other personal property, and in connection with the goodwill of a business or independently: s.24(1). An assignment or transmission may be partial, in that it is for only some of the goods or services for which it is registered, or for use in a particular manner or a particular locality: s.24(2). The assignment must be in writing, signed by or on behalf of the assignor or a personal representative or, in the case of a company, by the affixing of a corporate seal: s.24(3). A registered trade mark can be charged as security for a loan: s.24(5).

The Act provides for the registration of transactions affecting registered trade marks. Registrable transactions include: (i) assignment of a mark or any right in it; (ii) the grant of any licence under a registered trade mark; (iii) the grant of any security interest (whether fixed or floating) over a registered trade mark or any right in or under it; (iv) the making by personal representatives of an assent in relation to a registered trade mark or any right in or under it; and (v) an order of the court or other competent authority transferring a registered trade mark or any right in or under it: s.25(2).

Transactions are ineffective against a person acquiring a conflicting interest in or under the mark until application for registration has been made; and a person claiming as a licensee does not enjoy the protection of s.30 or 31: s.25(3). Application must be within six months or, where the court is satisfied that this was not practicable, as soon as practicable thereafter. Assignees or licensees are not entitled to damages or an account of profits occurring between any date of the transfer and the registration of the prescribed particulars: s.25(4). No notice of any trust shall be entered on the register, and the Registrar shall not be affected by any such notice: s.26(1).

A licence to use a registered trade mark may be general or limited, and the limited licence may relate to some but not all of the goods or services for which the mark is registered, or in relation to the use of the mark in a particular manner or a particular locality: s.28(1). The licence must be in writing, signed by or on behalf of the grantor, or by the affixing of a corporate seal in the case of a company: s.28(2). The Act allows for a sub-licence granted by a licensee, and the provisions of the Act apply to both: s.28(4). An exclusive licence means a licence, whether general or limited, authorising the licensee to the exclusion of all other persons, including the grantor, to use a registered mark in the manner authorised: s.29(1).

Where the licensee's rights are infringed, the licensee can bring proceedings in their own name: s.30(1). Unless the licence otherwise provides, licensees can call on the proprietor of the trade mark to take infringement proceedings in respect of any matter which affects their interest: s.30(2), and if the proprietor refuses or fails to do so within two months, licensees may bring proceedings in their own names as if they were proprietor: s.30(3). Where infringement proceedings are brought by a licensee, the licensee cannot proceed with the action without the leave of the court unless the proprietor is joined as a plaintiff or added as a defendant. This does not affect the granting of interlocutory relief on an application by the licensee alone: s.30(4).

An exclusive licence may provide that the licensee shall have the same rights and remedies in respect of matters occurring after the grant as if the licence had been an assignment: s.31(1). Where such provision is made, licensees may bring infringement proceedings against any person other than the proprietor in their own names: s.31(1). Any rights and remedies of an exclusive licensee are concurrent with those of the proprietor and, where the infringement proceedings relate wholly or partly to an infringement in respect of which they have concurrent rights, the proprietor or the exclusive licensee may not without leave proceed with the action unless the other is joined as plaintiff or added as defendant: s.31(4).

Character licensing, granting rights to use imagery in association with products or services, is a major source of income for owners of characters from all major media sources. Thus, from television: Tom & Jerry, Thunderbirds, Mutant Hero Turtles; from publishing, including comics: Dennis the Menace, Harry Potter, Thomas the Tank Engine; from the movies: the Flintstones, Jurassic Park. Licensing allows manufacturers to use the character on shirts, pillows, pencil cases and so on. The Mutant Hero Turtles earned some £60m in licensing rights. The Registrar is, however, unwilling to clutter the register with short-term marks, as can be seen in refusals relating to 'Rawhide' in 1962 (*Rawhide* [1962] RPC 133) and 'Pussy Galore' in 1967 ([1967] RPC 265), and registration could still be refused in similar situations.

Hot Topic . . .

REGISTERING REAL PEOPLE AS A TRADE MARK

Following the death of the actor Marlon Brando, the owners of the Brando estate feared that the actor's name and image could be used for commercial gain without their control. The estate, therefore, applied for trade mark protection with the US patent and trade mark office. The application listed items which the estate thought could be marketed under the Brando name (listed below) which means that Brando is unlikely to suffer the indignity visited on Frank Sinatra, who became the face of a leading credit card campaign.

Brando could become one of the advertising world's most lucrative dead celebrities. Late Hollywood stars like Marilyn Monroe, Humphrey Bogart, John Wayne and Steve McQueen have continued to have lucrative post-death careers promoting products. The Monroe estate accrued $7m from advertising. Elvis Presley is the highest earning late star; according to a 2003 survey by *Forbes* magazine, he earned over £22.3m during 2002.

(a) Brando brands: from mouse pads to confetti

Metal statues and figurines not of precious metal; metal key chains; licence plates and frames; bottle openers; non-luminous and non-mechanical metal signs; tins and cans sold empty; a series of audiovideo recordings; prerecorded performances and acting lessons; juke boxes; sunglasses; refrigerator magnets; mouse pads; telephone cards; magnetically encoded credit cards and debit cards; musical instruments; drums; percussion instruments and accessories; music boxes; posters; postcards; address books; holiday cards; greetings cards; art prints; art reproductions; paper gift bags; writing instruments; loose leaf binders; bookends; non-fiction and reference books about Marlon Brando; children's activity books; gift wrapping paper; bumper stickers; calendars; non-magnetically encoded telephone calling cards; bank cheques; debit gift cards; chequebook covers; comic books; commemorative stamps not issued by the US Postal Office; confetti; decals; letter openers; paper merchandise; bags; pictures; photographic prints; picture books; playing cards; recipe books; rubber stamps; stationery stickers; temporary tattoos; trading cards; metal trading cards; chalk boards for home and/or school use; photo albums; note pads; paper doll books; colouring books; stamps and philatelic goods, namely, pre-stamped postal cards; coin books; shirts; sweatshirts; pants; shorts; jackets; caps; neckwear; belts; coats; underwear; socks; bath robes; pyjamas; kimonos; gloves; footwear; historical figure licensing services.

(b) Diana, Princess of Wales
The Diana, Princess of Wales Memorial Trust, a charity set up to raise money to continue the charitable work of the Princess of Wales, registered a trade mark in the name of the princess in order to control the production of Diana memorabilia and raise money from the granting of licences. In spite of this, the Trust was involved in an unsuccessful legal dispute with the Franklin Mint which produced a variety of items celebrating the Princess.

Persons still living also register their names for trade mark protection. The most famous recent example is David Beckham who registered his name in August 2000.

14.6 Patents

A patent gives the patentee the exclusive right to exploit an invention for 20 years from the date of application to the Patent Office provided renewal fees are paid every year from the fifth year onwards.

The rights granted by the patent are set out in the Patents Act (PA) 1977 as amended by the Patents Regulations 2000 (SI 2000/2037) and the Patents Act (PA) 2004. All statutory references in this section are to the 1977 Act unless otherwise stated. The Patents Regulations 2000 implemented Arts 1–11 of Directive 98/44/EC, [1998] OJ L213/13, on the legal protection of biotechnological inventions and the implementation of Article 27(2) of the Agreement on Trade-Related Aspects of Intellectual Property Rights (TRIPS). The 2004 Act was to update the 1977 Act and bring the UK patents system into line with the revised European Patent Convention and measures to assist the enforcement of patent rights.

Application is to the Patent Office, accompanied by a specification consisting of a detailed description of the invention and a set of claims. The claims define the scope of the invention for which the patentee seeks a monopoly. It is the invention as defined in the claims which is tested for patentability and against which alleged infringements are considered. The Patent Office carries out a search in the relevant technical literature ('prior art') to test for 'novelty' and 'inventive step'. The examination is in two stages: a preliminary and a substantive examination, with separate fees. The applicant is sent the result of the search usually within about 12–15 months.

Depending on the results of the search, the applicant may decide to abandon or modify his/her application or request an examination. The request for examination must be made within six months from the date the application is published by the office. The publication must be within 18 months of filing the application. At the examination stage, the application is examined by a technically qualified Patent Office examiner to see whether it complies with the requirements. An applicant is given one opportunity voluntarily to amend his/her specification during the examination, but s/he may amend it a number of times in accordance with the examiner's requirements. Once the procedure of examination is completed and any objections of the examiner have been met, a patent will be granted, a notice of the grant published in the official journal and a certificate of patent issued. A patent can be revoked after grant.

Where two or more applications are made independently for the same or overlapping inventions, priority is given to the first to file. Under the Paris Convention (1833), most countries have agreed that the date of first filing a patent application in the 'home' country establishes the priority date for applications to other Convention countries, provided the application is made within 12 months.

(a)   International application procedures

British Patent Office applications only result in a British patent effective in England, Wales, Scotland, North Ireland and the Isle of Man. They do not extend to the Channel Islands, although a UK patent may be registered there. Applicants wishing to obtain international patent protection can register nationally or use the Patent Co-operation Treaty and the European Patent Convention.

(i)   The Patent Co-operation Treaty (PCT)

The PCT was agreed in 1970 and currently has 123 contracting states. It provides for the filing of a single application, designating the countries in which patent protection is sought. A single search is carried out and the application is sent to the designated countries for separate examination as a national application. The system is operated by the World Intellectual Property Organisation (WIPO). Applicants apply in one of a number of selected patent offices. The PA 2004 makes changes to the PA 1977 to clarify relations between domestic patent law and the PCT, and implement changes in the latest Regulations, which came into force on 1 January 2004.

(ii)   The European Patent Convention (EPC)

The EPC provides for filing at the European Patent Office in Munich specifying the contracting states in which protection is requested. The application is searched and examined and, if it satisfies the Convention requirements, national patents are granted for those countries. Apart from in the first nine months, when the patent can be challenged at the European Patent Office, validity and infringement can only be contested before the separate national courts. The EPC is not an EU treaty but one between contracting states, of which there are currently 29.

The EPC also ensures harmonisation of patent law within the contracting states. It was originally agreed in 1973 but revised in 2000, and the PA 2004 aims at reflecting these changes in UK patent law. A Europatent takes effect once the *European Patent Bulletin* publishes the fact of its grant. The term of the patent is 20 years and renewal fees are payable at the rates prescribed in each state. Most applications are made directly to Munich and not to the British Patent Office.

(iii)   The Patent Law Treaty (PLT)

The PLT, agreed in 2000, harmonises the procedural requirements of filing and prosecuting a patent application. This involves changes to the PA 1977 to remove or reduce the burden and constraints on patent applicants. The PA 1977 is to be amended by the Regulatory Reform (Patents) Order 2004 to give effect to the PLT.

(b) Patentability

A patent is granted for an invention only where: (a) the invention is new; (ii) involves an inventive step; (iii) is capable of industrial exploitation; and (iv) its grant is not excluded by reference to s.1(2) and (3) PA 1977.

Excluded from patentability as not constituting inventions are: (a) a discovery, scientific theory or mathematical method; (b) a literary, dramatic, musical or artistic work or any other aesthetic creation whatsoever; (c) a scheme, rule or method for performing a mental act, playing a game or doing business, or a program for a computer; and (d) the presentation of information: s.1(2) PA 1977. In addition a patent shall not be granted for an invention the commercial exploitation of which would be contrary to public policy or morality: s.1(3) PA 1977. This is subject to the proviso that the exploitation shall not be regarded as contrary to public policy or morality simply because it is prohibited by any law in force in the UK or any part of it: s.1(4) PA 1977.

In *Astron Clinica Ltd and Ors v. Comptroller General of Patents, Designs and Trade Marks* [2008] EWHC 85 (Pat) the applicants applied for patents for a diverse range of technologies of which the common feature was a computer program which conferred the technical advance. The issue on appeal was whether patent claims could be granted for computer programs. The United Kingdom Intellectual Property Office (UKIPO) considered the registration of a patent for a computer program prohibited by Article 52 of the Convention on the Grant of European Patents implemented by the Patents Act 1977; the European Patent Office (EPO) considered such claims allowable if the program had the potential to bring about a further technical effect. The court held that computer programs were not necessarily excluded by the Convention and that, where claims to a method performed by running a suitably programmed computer or to a computer programmed to carry out the method were allowable, then, in principle, a claim to the program itself should also be allowable.

New s.76A and Schedule A2 relate to the patentability of biotechnological inventions. Under Schedule A2, an invention is not considered unpatentable solely on the ground that it concerns a product consisting of or containing biological material; or a process by which biological material is produced, processed or used. Biological material which is isolated from its natural environment or produced by means of a technical process may be the subject of an invention even if it previously occurred in nature. The following are not patentable inventions:

(a) the human body, at the various stages of its formation and development, and the simple discovery of one of its elements, including the sequence or partial sequence of a gene;
(b) processes for cloning human beings;
(c) processes for modifying the germ line genetic identity of human beings;
(d) uses of human embryos for industrial or commercial purposes;
(e) processes for modifying the genetic identity of animals which are likely to cause them suffering without any substantial medical benefit to man or animal, and also animals resulting from such processes;
(f) any variety of animal or plant or any essential biological process for the production of animals or plants, not being a microbiological or other technical process or the product of such a process.

The schedule further provides, however, that inventions which concern plants or animals may be patentable if their technical feasibility is not confined to a particular plant or animal variety; and an element isolated from the human body or otherwise produced by means of a technical process, including the sequence or partial sequence of a gene, may constitute a patentable invention, even if the structure of that element is identical to that of a natural element.

(i) Novelty

This means that the invention must not form part of the state of the art at the priority date. The state of the art comprises all matter which has, at any time before that date, been made available to the public anywhere in the world by written or oral description.

Available to the public means disclosure to one person who is free in law and equity to use the information as s/he pleases. Certain types of prior disclosure will not invalidate a patent: for example disclosure in breach of confidence or at an international exhibition.

One example is Dunlop, who patented the pneumatic tyre in 1888. Shortly afterwards competitors produced an 1845 patent by a person called Thompson. unable to register a patent in respect of the ballpoint pen since he had previously had some made up and distributed to friends and others.

(ii) Inventive step

There is an inventive step if it is not obvious to a person skilled in the technical field of the invention. In *M Systems Flash Disk Pioneer Ltd v. Trek 2000 International Ltd and anor* [2008] EWHC 102 ,the inventor of the USB memory stick lost an appeal against the revocation of its patent registered in 2000. The claimant had objected to the patent in 2003 claiming that it was neither new nor inventive and that the patent did not describe the invention clearly enough. The defendant filed amendments which were rejected by a Hearing Officer of the Intellectual Property Office (UKIPO). The High Court agreed with his decision.

(iii) Capable of industrial application

Methods of treating humans and animals, whether by surgery, therapy or diagnosis, are unpatentable. Section 4A PA 1977 provides that a patent shall not be granted for an invention of (a) a method of treatment of the human or animal body by surgery or therapy, or (b) a method of diagnosis practised on the human or animal body except for inventions consisting of a substance or composition for use in any such method.

(c) Infringement

Patents are infringed in the UK by doing one of the following without the proprietor's consent:

(i) where the invention is a product, a person disposes of, uses or imports or keeps it for disposal or otherwise;

(ii) where the invention is a process, the person uses it or offers it for use when s/he knows, or it is obvious, that its use would be an infringement; or s/he disposes of, offers to dispose of, uses or imports any product obtained directly by means of that process or keeps any such product whether for disposal or otherwise. It is also an infringement to supply, or offer to supply, 'means essential for putting an invention into effect' to a person not entitled to work the patent, when s/he knows, or it is obvious to a reasonable person in the circumstances, that those means are suitable for putting and are intended to put the invention into effect in the UK.

There are certain limited exceptions, including acts done for private non-commercial purposes, acts done for experimental purposes, and acts done on ships or aircraft temporarily or accidentally within territorial waters or airspace. A person who has him/herself used the invention before the priority date of the patent may do so again or continue to do the acts s/he did before that date.

(i) Patent maintenance

The Patent Office keeps a register of patents open to the public. All goods which are the subject of a patent should bear the words 'Patented' followed by the patent number. If this is not practicable, the packaging should be marked. If there is no marking, then, in the event of proceedings for infringement, damages can only date back to the time when the infringer was made aware that s/he had infringed, provided s/he can prove that at the date of the infringement s/he was not aware and had no reasonable grounds for supposing a patent existed. It is an offence punishable with a fine to hold out that goods are patented or that a patent is applied for when this is not true. Once a patent runs out, a reasonable period of time is given for phasing out stocks of the product bearing any patent marks. Following the grant of the patent, renewal fees have to be paid on an annual basis from the fifth year. The renewal fees rise steeply towards the end of the 20-year period. A patent will lapse on non-payment of renewal fees. Failure by an employee to make the payment means that after that year the patent cannot be restored to the register: *Re Textron Inc.* [1988] 1 FTLR 210. Patent owners can surrender their patents.

(ii) Remedies for infringement

The patent holder is entitled to an injunction, delivery up of infringing articles and damages or an account of profits. Damages are assessed on loss of profits or a royalty basis.

(d) Ownership, assignment and licensing

A patent may be owned by the inventor or their employer or by two or more co-inventors. Any invention made in the normal course of duties of an employee belongs to the employer, but otherwise to the employee. There is compensation to employees: (i) if the invention belongs to the employer who obtains a patent, the employee is entitled to compensation if the patent is of outstanding benefit to the employer; and (ii) an employee may own the invention but assign the patent to the employer, and there is a procedure for assessing the compensation if the parties cannot reach agreement. The matter can be decided by the Patent Office or the court.

An assignment must be in writing and signed by or on behalf of both parties to the transaction; otherwise it is void. A licence may be granted orally and may be non-exclusive or exclusive. All transactions must be registered at the Patent Office. Penalties for non-registration include loss of priority over subsequent transactions and restrictions on the right to recover damages.

Under the Act, a patent owner is required to grant a licence under his/her patent, and persons can apply for a compulsory licence where:

(i)   three years have expired since the date of the patent;
(ii)   the invention, though capable of being worked in the UK, is not being either worked or worked to the full extent possible;
(iii)   demand in the UK is not being met on reasonable terms or to the fullest extent possible;
(iv)   importation has the effect of preventing the invention being worked in the UK.

If the comptroller is satisfied on any of the above grounds, s/he may order the patent to be continued under a 'compulsory licence' and the patent owner must grant a licence. If s/he fails to offer reasonable terms, then these will be settled for him/her.

Assignments and licensing may infringe national or EU competition laws.

14.7 Protection of form and appearance: copyright and design

Copyright exists in every original literary, dramatic, musical or artistic work, and every sound recording or cinematograph film, television or sound broadcast, provided that it is not contrary to public policy. The copyright work is protected for a definite time, depending on its nature. The protection is automatic and arises when the work is created; there is no registration procedure or any formalities except with regard to registered design.

Copyright covers a wide range of subject matter and is of great commercial significance, the most obvious commercially valuable examples being copyrights in films, videos, records, tapes and CDs. The UK law of copyright is found in the Copyright, Designs and Patents Act (CDPA) 1988 as amended by the Duration of Copyright and Rights in Performances Regulations 1995 (SI 1995 No. 3297) and The Copyright and Related Rights Regulations 2003 (SI 2003 No 2498) which transposed the Copyright Directive (2001/29/EC, [2001] OJ L272/32) into UK law. Copyright protection is important on an international scale, and many countries will offer similar protection to that offered in the UK. Where they are signatories to the Universal Copyright Convention 1952, they will offer identical protection as they do to their own nationals.

The protection of form and appearance covered by copyright, design right, design registration and semiconductor chip designs requires the work to be original. Originality does not require the work to have been inventive, and two people could claim copyright for similar works.

(a) Copyright

Works within the scope of the UK copyright law include (i) literary works; (ii) dramatic works; (iii) musical works; (iv) artistic works; (v) the typographical arrangement of published editions; (vi) sound recordings; (vii) films; and (viii) broadcasts and cable programmes: s.1 CDPA 1988. (For database right see Chapter 22, p.539.)

(i) Literary works
A literary work is defined in s.3 as 'any work, other than a dramatic or musical work, which is written, spoken or sung'.

This includes: (a) a table or compilation, and (b) a computer program. The literary work is protected even though it is only spoken or sung and includes speeches, interviews, poetry recitals or the live performance of a monologue. However, it qualifies for protection only once recorded in writing or otherwise: s.1(2).

Writing includes any form of notation by hand or otherwise and regardless of the method by which, or medium in or on which, it is recorded: s.179. Any means of recording is sufficient, including databases, tape, disk and so on. Literary merit is not required and listings of TV programmes, football fixture lists and street directories class as literary works as long as they are of sufficient length.

There is no copyright in respect of a name: *Exxon Corporation v. Exxon Insurance Consultants International Ltd* [1982] Ch 119 ('Exxon'); *Tavener Rutledge Ltd v. Trexapalm Ltd* [1977] RPC 275 ('Kojak'); or for book titles or advertising slogans, or song titles: *Francis, Day & Hunter Ltd v. Twentieth Century Fox Corporation Ltd* [1940] AC 112.

(ii) *Dramatic works*
Dramatic works are not defined, except that s.3(1) specifically includes within the category works of dance or mime. They are not restricted to a play or screenplay and would cover instructions for action or presentation of some kind of performance, including choreography and stage directions. They can be recorded in any form, including a televised performance by ice dancers and possibly figure skating.

(iii) *Musical works*
There is no statutory definition of musical works, but the Act provides that 'music is to be distinguished from any accompanying words to be sung, spoken or performed or actions intended to be performed with the music': s.3(1). Music is not protected until recorded in some way.

(iv) *Artistic works*
Artistic works include graphic works, photographs, sculptures or collages, architecture in the form of buildings or models, and works of artistic craftsmanship: s.4. Artistic quality is not required.

This resulted in extending copyright protection to design drawings; but these are no longer included (see below: Copyright in designs).

(v) *Typographical arrangements of published editions of literary, dramatic and musical works*
The layout, arrangement and appearance of printed pages of such works are given separate protection under s.8, independently of the printed work itself.

(vi) *Sound recordings*
A sound recording is either 'a recording of sounds, from which sounds may be reproduced' or 'a recording of the whole or any part of a literary, dramatic or musical work, from which sound reproducing the work or part may be produced'.

In either case the recording qualifies for protection, regardless of the medium on which the recording is made or the method by which the sounds are reproduced or produced. The soundtrack of a film is now a sound recording for the purposes of the Act; previously it was treated as part of the film.

(vii) *Film*

Film is defined as 'a recording on any medium from which a moving image may by any means be produced', and covers photographic film, videotape and video discs.

There is no need for the recording to be of visual images, and it would seem to cover the recording of signals enabling the generation of abstract pictures on a screen.

(viii) *Broadcasts and cable programmes*

A broadcast is a programme composed of images and sounds seen and heard on television screens, or heard on the radio and broadcast by wireless telegraphy. A cable programme service is defined as a service which consists wholly or mainly in sending by means of a telecommunications system otherwise than by wireless telegraphy of visual images, sounds or other information: s.7.

The difference is merely in the transmission. The broadcast is protected irrespective of whether the material broadcast is protected or merely a live news broadcast or transmission of a sporting event. The independent protection of the broadcast prevents others rediffusing the broadcast and profiting from the broadcaster's investment and effort.

A cable programme service must be intended to present programmes to the public, or be receivable in more than one place. It includes any type of computer network such as a database or information service, but excludes private (domestic or business) cable systems not connected to any other telecommunications system and not used in providing a service to others: s.7(2). It includes a database linking a manufacturer and a dealer network, but not an inter-branch network of the same organisation. The position of interactive databases such as Viewdata or Prestel is not clear: the Secretary of State does have powers to add or remove exceptions but not to amend existing exceptions: s.7(3).

(ix) *Protection of live performances*

A 'performance' means a live performance given by one or more individuals, including a dramatic performance, a musical performance, a reading or recitation of a literary work, a performance of a variety act or a similar presentation.

The unauthorised recording or filming of performances is protected in criminal law but specific civil rights are introduced for the performers and anyone who enjoys exclusive rights to record or film the performer. The performance must be live but need not be before an audience, and includes pirating a 'live' studio performance which is being filmed or otherwise recorded. The 1988 Act was amended by the Copyright and Related Rights Regulations 2003 (SI 2003 No 2498) to include protection for transient and incidental copying.

(b) Copyright infringement

The infringement of the rights of the copyright owner is classified as an act of primary infringement which is committed even though the infringer was not aware that their act constituted an infringement. In respect of other rights, the infringement is classified as a secondary or even tertiary infringement, and liability usually requires that the person infringing must have had knowledge or a reasonable belief that what was done was an infringement.

The marking of products may be sufficient to establish knowledge or reasonable belief, as can be a warning letter from the rights owner.

The law also recognises moral rights, which restrict what can be done with the copyright work. The moral rights exist independently of copyright in the work.

(i) Primary infringement

The copyright holder is protected against (i) the copying of the protected work; (ii) the right of initial public circulation; (iii) performing, showing or playing a work in public; (iv) broadcasting or including the work in a cable programme; (v) renting films, sound recordings and computer programs to the public; and (vi) adapting the work and enjoying the above rights in relation to the adaptation.

Copying the work

Infringement occurs even if only a substantial part of the work is copied; it does not have to be an exact copy and an infringement occurs if there is sufficient objective similarity. For a high-quality work requiring great skill and effort, copying even a small part might be an infringement. It includes making a transient copy of the work, or making a copy as an incidental part of some other use of the work: s.17(6); or using a computer program where all or part of the program is copied into the computer's memory. Where the copyright relates to material in electronic form, copying would be constituted by displaying the information on a screen.

There is a special right for works supplied in electronic form such as computer programs, where the work is 'copy-protected' to make copying difficult or impossible without special equipment: s.296. These are called Technological Protection Measures (TPMs). One form of TPM is the use of encryption and another is the production of CDs which are designed not to be copied (or even played) on PCs. The right is given to the person who issues the copy-protected work to the public, who can exercise it only against someone who supplies a device designed or adapted to circumvent the copy protection, persons who make, import, sell, hire or offer or expose for sale or hire any such device, and anyone who publishes information intended to enable or assist people to circumvent the copy-protection method used. A similar right exists for persons charging for the reception of broadcasts or cable programmes, or who make encrypted transmissions: s.298.

A similar form of protection is Electronic Rights Management Information (RMI) where rightholders protect their work by using codes to identify and track anyone attempting to breach copyright. This is used in connection with software.

Initial circulation

Once the copies are in circulation, anyone can buy and sell them and deal with them in any way except for importation and rental. Sound recordings, films and computer programs can be rented only with the copyright owner's consent, even though copies are in circulation.

Performance in public

The copyright owner has the exclusive right to perform or permit others to perform a copyright work in public: s.19(1). There is a corresponding right for sound recordings, film, broadcast or cable programmes to play or show the work in public: s.19(3).

Broadcasting and inclusion in cable programmes

This exclusive right of the owner of certain copyright works extends to giving other persons permission to broadcast or include the material in a cable programme: s.20. This also includes electronic communication of copyright work to the public.

Adaptations of copyright works

The copyright owner has the exclusive right to make and permit others to make adaptations of literary, dramatic and musical works: s.21(1), and to control what is done to an adaptation of a copyright work. The right of control over the adaptation covers all the basic copyrights. Adaptations include (i) the translation of a literary or dramatic work; (ii) making a dramatic work into a non-dramatic work and vice versa: s.21(3)(a); and (iii) an arrangement or transcription of a musical work: s.21(3)(b). For a computer program the term 'translation' includes a version of the program converted into or out of one computer language or code into another: s.21(4).

(ii) Secondary infringement

The person must know or reasonably believe that an infringement is likely. Infringements include: (i) importing into the UK infringing copies other than for private and domestic use: s.22; (ii) possessing and commercially dealing in infringing copies: s.23; (iii) making, importing or possessing in business anything designed or adapted for making copies of a copyright work: s.24 – this extends to selling or hiring or offering such a thing for sale or hire; and (iv) transmitting a copyright work on a telecommunications system: s.24.

(iii) Tertiary infringement

This only arises once there has been a primary infringement by a person using apparatus for playing sound recordings, showing films or receiving broadcasts or cable programmes and so on; others, including suppliers of the apparatus, persons allowing it to be used on their premises or the supplier of the copy of the work used, can then be liable for tertiary infringement. But they must have known or had reason to believe that there was a likelihood of infringement: s.26.

(c)   Permissible acts in relation to copyright works

The Act makes specific provision excluding copying and other acts for activities including educational purposes, libraries and archives and things done in connection with public administration: that is, copying in connection with judicial proceedings. Fair dealing for research, private study and education is however restricted to research and educational use carried out for a non-commercial purpose, and the use must be accompanied by sufficient acknowledgement of the title and author of the work As regards education, activities likely to be regarded as commercial include fee-paying courses designed to generate fees for the educational establishment, lecturers speaking at conferences in return for a fee and university research sponsored by a commercial enterprise. There are also exceptions in connection with 'fair dealing' in relation to literary, dramatic, musical and artistic works in connection with research and private study, criticism and review, and news reporting: s.29. For the purposes of criticism or review the Act requires sufficient acknowledgement of the author: s.30. What is sufficient is laid down in s.178. The Act excludes incidental inclusion in films, broadcasts and so on of an artistic work, a sound recording, film, broadcast or cable programme: s.31. This will not extend to copyright works which are included deliberately, such as music as part of the soundtrack. Also excluded is the recording of television programmes, whether broadcast or cable, for private and domestic use: s.70.

(d)　Moral rights

Moral rights are the rights of the authors of literary, dramatic, musical and artistic works, and the directors of films, to be identified as such and to object to any derogatory treatment of their work. It prevents anyone else claiming authorship of the work.

Derogatory treatment includes any addition to or deletion from the work: s.80(2). It does not include translating a literary or dramatic work or arranging or transcribing a musical work which involves only a change of key or register. The right to be identified as the author of the work must be asserted; this can be done in the document assigning the copyright, or by serving notice in writing: s.78. There is also a right to privacy for photographs or films made for private and domestic purposes, which can prevent their publication, exhibition to the public, and broadcasting or inclusion in a cable programme. The moral rights are personal to the author or director and cannot be transferred. They can only be exercised by that person or by their personal representatives. An author or director can exercise the rights even after the copyright has been transferred or licensed.

(e)　Ownership of copyrights

The author will be the first person who is the copyright owner; it is therefore important to identify the author. This will depend upon the nature of the work.

(i)　Literary, musical, dramatic and artistic works
The author is the creator of the work: s.9, and the author of the work is the owner of the copyright in it: s.11. For photographs, the author is the creator, generally the photographer. An exception to ownership in respect of literary, musical, dramatic and artistic works relates to works created by employees in the course of their employment, when the copyright belongs to the employer subject to agreement to the contrary.

(ii)　Typographical arrangements of published editions
The creator of the typographical arrangement of a published edition is the publisher: s.9.

(iii)　Sound recording and films
The author is the person by whom the arrangements necessary for the making of the recording or film were made: s.9(2), and the author is the owner of copyright: s.11.

(iv)　Broadcasts and cable programmes
The creator of a broadcast is the person making the broadcast: s.9. The creator of a cable programme is the person providing the cable service: s.9. The creator is the author who is copyright owner: s.11.

(v)　Performances
Each performer is treated as the author or creator of the particular part in the overall performance. The rights in a performance are personal to the performer and cannot be bought or sold: s.192, which means that the performer is the first and only owner of rights in the performance. On the death of the performer, the rights and their control can pass by will and, in the absence of a will, are exercisable by the deceased's personal representatives.

The recording rights in the performance belong to the person with an exclusive recording contract with the performer, or a person who has bought the benefit of the exclusive recording contract, subject in both cases to the person satisfying the nationality requirements of the Act. A licensee from the person with the benefit of the exclusive recording contract may own the recording right if the licence allows for the making of recordings covered by the exclusive recording contract with a view to their commercial exploitation, provided that the licensee meets the nationality requirements of the Act.

(f) Joint ownership

The work is joint if the contributions are not distinct: s.10. Thus a book is a work of joint authorship if it is impossible to identify the individual contribution of the authors. Joint owners can only exercise their rights jointly and cannot grant licences in the copyright work individually or sue individually. However, the moral rights of the authors are exercisable individually: s.88.

The prospective owner of the copyright work can contract to transfer the rights in the work to a person before the work comes into existence. For example, where a work is commissioned and where the agreement is in writing and signed by or on behalf of the prospective owner, the purchaser will be the copyright owner when the work is created: s.91.

(g) Period of copyright protection

The periods of copyright protection in the 1988 Act were amended by the Duration of Copyright and Rights in Performance Regulations 1995, which implement Directive No. 93/98/EEC, [1993] OJ L290/9. Since the periods were in some cases extended (from 50 to 70 years after the author's death), the Regulations make provision for revived copyright.

Protection in a literary, dramatic, musical or artistic work expires at the end of the period of 70 years from the end of the calendar year in which the author dies: s.12(2). However, if the work is of unknown authorship, copyright expires (a) at the end of the period of 70 years from the end of the calendar year in which the work was made; or (b) at the end of the period of 70 years from the end of the calendar year in which the work was first made available to the public: s.12(3). If the identity of the author is discovered before the end of the periods in (a) and (b), then s.12(2) applies. For a literary, dramatic or musical work, being made available to the public includes performance in public, or being broadcast or included in a cable programme service; for an artistic work it includes exhibition in public; for a film, it includes the work being shown in public or being included in a broadcast or cable programme service, but no account shall be taken of any unauthorised act: s.12(5).

Where the country of origin of the work is not a European Economic Area (EEA) state and the author is not a national of an EEA state, the duration of the copyright is according to the country of origin, provided that it does not exceed the period under s.12(2)–(5). If the work is computer-generated, however, the copyright expires at the end of the period of 50 years from the end of the calendar year in which the work was made. For works of joint authorship, the date is calculated from the date of death of the last author or, where only one or more of the joint authors is known, the date of death of the last of them to die.

For sound recordings, copyright expires (a) at the end of the period of 50 years from the end of the calendar year in which it is made, or (b) 50 years from the end of the calendar year in which it is released: s.13A(2).

Hot Topic . . .

COPYRIGHT CLOCK RUNNING OUT FOR ELVIS

Unlike in the USA where the Sonny Bono Copyright Term Extension Act 1998 provides that sound recordings are protected for 95 years from the day of recording, while for post-1976 recordings coverage is the artist's life plus 70 years, in most of the EU the protection period is 50 years from the first release of the recording.

The consequence of this is explained by Peter Jamieson, executive chairman of the British Phonograph Industry: '[t]he end of the sound recording copyright on the explosion of British popular music in the late 50s and 60s, not just the Beatles, but many other British artists, is only a short period away. If nothing is done, they will suffer loss of income not just for their sales in the UK, but their sales across the globe'. Elvis Presley's hits

started to come out of copyright from 2005 and copyright on early hits by Cliff Richard and the Shadows started to expire in 2008.

Sir Cliff Richard launched a campaign to extend the period of protection, and the International Federation of the Phonographic Industry asked the European Commission in 2003 to extend the term of protection for producers and artists to end the discrepancy between the USA and the EU. A review of EU copyright legislation was initiated by then Internal Markets Commissioner, Frits Bolkestein.

The effect of the recordings falling into the public domain will mean that artists and record companies will lose the exclusive rights to their recordings, wiping billions of pounds off the value of record

companies and depriving artists of the income from their back catalogues. In addition, the recordings could be digitally manipulated or used in films or advertisements with the artists having no say in the matter. Sir Cliff commented, 'I am told my recordings could even be used in pornographic films and there's not a thing I could do about it. I will have no control over how my music is used.' The position is particularly difficult for singers like Cliff Richard who do not write their own material. The composers and writers will continue to claim royalties for 70 years after their deaths; only the singer misses out.

Andy Harris, an entertainment lawyer from the Edinburgh firm Tods Murray, expressed doubts whether the campaign will succeed: '[s]ound copyright was only ever meant to last for 50 years because that, it was thought, gave record companies a decent spell of profiting from their artists' music'.

For films, copyright expires at the end of the period of 70 years from the end of the calendar year in which the death occurs of the last to die of: (a) the principal director; (b) the author of the screenplay; (c) the author of the dialogue; or (d) the composer of music specially created for and used in the film: s.13B(2). This is subject to the fact that if the identity of one or more of those persons is unknown, the period shall run from the date of the death of the last person whose identity is known: s.13B(3). If the identities of all the persons are unknown, copyright expires at the end of the period of 70 years from the end of the calendar year in which the film was made, or the end of the year in which it was first made available to the public. Where the country of origin is a non-EEA state and the author of the film a national of a non-EEA state, the duration of copyright in the work is according to the law of the non-EEA state, as long as it does not exceed the provisions under s.13B(2)–(6): s.13B(7).

Copyright in respect of broadcasts and cable programmes expires at the end of the period of 50 years from the end of the calendar year in which the programme was made or included in a cable programme service: s.14.

Copyright in performances expires at the end of the period of 50 years from the end of the calendar year in which the performance took place, or from the end of the calendar year in which it was released, s.191.

The moral rights of authors and directors continue as long as the copyright in the work, but the right to object to being falsely represented as the author of a work lasts until 20 years after the death of the person concerned: s.86.

In *Clark v. Associated Newspapers Ltd* [1998] 1 All ER 959, Sir Alan Clark obtained damages under the law of passing off and s.84, concerning a spoof series in the *Evening Standard* under the title 'Alan Clark's Secret Political Diary'.

14.8 Artists' resale right

The Artists Resale Rights Regulations 2006 (SI 346/2006) implement Directive 2001/84/EC, [2001] OJ L272/32, on the resale right for the benefit of the author of an original work of art and the implementation of the option given by Article 14 of the Berne Copyright Convention (Cmnd 5002).

Regulation 3 creates a new intellectual property right, 'resale right', to be enjoyed by the creator of a work of art (and that of the artist's successors in title) for as long as copyright continues to subsist in the work. The right consists of the entitlement to claim a royalty on the resale of the work following its first transfer by the artist .based on the sale price (in €).

For the purposes of the Regulation 'work' means 'any work of graphic or plastic art such as a picture, a collage, a painting, a drawing, an engraving, a print, a lithograph, a sculpture, a tapestry, a ceramic, an item of glassware or a photograph'. A copy of a work is not regarded as a work unless the copy is one of a limited number which have been made by the author or under his authority: reg. 4(1) and (2).

The UK has taken advantage of a derogation in the Directive, and resale right is currently limited to works by living artists/creators. From 1 January 2010, however, the right will be extended to cover the sale of original works of art by deceased artists up to 70 years after their death.

The people who are jointly and severally liable to pay the resale royalty are (a) the seller, and (b) the agent of the seller; or (c) if there is no such agent, the agent of the buyer; or (d) where there are no such agents, the buyer: reg. 13(1) and (2). Liability arises on the completion of the sale: reg. 13(3).

For joint authorship, the authors are owners of equal shares unless otherwise agreed in writing signed by or on behalf of each party: reg. 5. If from the time it was made the work bears the name of a person purporting to be the author of the work, that person is presumed to be the author unless the contrary is proved: reg. 6(1). The same applies in respect of joint authorship: reg. 6(2).

Resale right is not assignable and any charge on a resale right is void (reg. 7) except for transfer to a UK or EEA charity or a foreign charity of a country listed in Schedule 2. Agreements to share or repay resale royalties are void: reg. 8. Resale right must be exercised through a collecting society, and if the management has not been transferred to a specialist collecting society the society managing the collection of the artist's copyright is deemed to manage the right on his behalf: reg. 14.

Resale right is transmissible by will or by intestate succession by the artist and any person to whom it passes (reg. 9), subject to the fact that it may be transmitted only by a natural person who, at the time of his death, is a national of an EEA state or of a country listed in Schedule 2.

Rates for recognised resale sales are calculated as follows:

4 per cent for the portion of the sale price up to €50,000, then add:
3 per cent for the portion of the sale price between €50,000 and €200,000;
1 per cent for the portion of the sale price between €200,000 and €350,000;
0.5 per cent for the portion of the sale price between €350,000 and €500,000;
0.25 per cent for the portion of the sale price between €500,000 and €2,000,000.

There is no levy beyond this figure since the maximum levy cannot exceed €12,500.

The people who are jointly and severally liable to pay the resale royalty are (a) the seller, and (b) the agent of the seller; and (c) if there is no such agent, the agent of the buyer; or (d) where there are no such agents, the buyer: reg. 13(1) and (2). Liability arises on the completion of the sale: reg.13.

Where there is a work of joint authorship, the resale right belongs to the authors as owners in common and is held in equal shares or in such other shares as may be agreed. The agreement must be in writing and signed by or on behalf of each party to the agreement: reg. 5. Where a name or names purporting to be that of the author or authors appeared on the work when it was made, the person(s) whose name(s) appeared shall, unless the contrary is proved, be the author(s) of the work: reg. 6.

Resale right is not assignable and any charge on resale is void (reg. 7) with the exception of transfer to a UK or EEA charity or a foreign charity in a country listed in Schedule 2. A waiver of a resale right has no effect and an agreement to share or repay resale royalties is void: reg.8. Resale right may be exercised only through a collecting society, and where the holder of the resale right has not transferred the management of his right to a collecting society, the collecting society managing copyright on behalf of artists shall be deemed to be mandated to manage the right: reg. 14.

Resale right is transmissible as personal or moveable property by will or in accordance with the rules of intestate succession, and can be further transmitted by any person into whose hands it passes: reg. 9. This is subject to the restriction that resale right may be transmitted only by a person who, at the time of his death, is a qualifying individual, defined as a natural person who is a national of an EEA state or a national of a country listed in Schedule 2.

14.9 Organisations acting as collecting agencies for their author/creator members

Private organisations run licensing schemes for various categories of authors/creators who are members of them. These allow persons to deal with a copyright work in a way which would otherwise be an infringement in return for payments which are then passed on to the author/creator.

For composers and performers a number of bodies exist. These include the Educational Recording Agency Ltd (ERA), the Musicians Union (MU) and the Performing Artists' Media Rights Association (PAMRA). The last regulates the public performance of music including playing recordings of copyright music on the radio, films and TV.

For writers three bodies collect for their members in respect of the reproduction of their works: the Authors' Licensing and Collecting Society Ltd (ALCS), the Copyright Licensing Agency (CLA), the Educational Recording Agency Ltd (ERA). In addition the Public Lending Right (PLR) monitors the borrowing of published works in public libraries and collects and distributes money to authors.

In respect of paintings and designs, collecting agencies include the Design and Artists' Copyright Society Ltd (DACS) and the National Artists' Association (NAA). These can also collect in respect of the resale right, but the Artists Collecting Society (ACS) formed in June 2006 is the only collecting society incorporated solely for the collection of resale right.

A statutory body called the Copyright Tribunal, created under the 1988 Act, reviews the operation of general licensing schemes.

14.10 Criminal liability

Several criminal offences arise from infringement of copyright. The penalties include fines and imprisonment for up to two years, and the court can order the offender to give up any infringing copies to the copyright holder or have them forfeited or destroyed.

14.11 Product design protection

The law relating to design protection is in the Registered Designs Act (RDA) 1949 (as amended in 1988) and the Design Right (Semiconductor Topographies) Regulations 1989 (SI 1100/1989). The product design is treated separately from the means used to record it, which can be a design drawing, blueprint and technical specification, or a model or prototype. The former is a 'design document' and the latter is defined as something 'embodying a design': ss.51 and 263(1). Designs can be protected by (i) copyright; (ii) design right; or (iii) right in registered designs.

(a) Copyright protection

The CDPA 1988 excludes infringement of a product design from a design document from copyright protection: s.51. However, copyright protection applies to (i) the two-dimensional aspects of design; (ii) situations where the design is for something which is itself an artistic work; and (iii) designs for typefaces. Thus designs for wallpaper, fabric and carpet patterns, motifs, engraving and decorative embossing are within copyright protection, as is the design for a three-dimensional artistic work or work of artistic craftsmanship such as wrought ironwork, jewellery or engravings. The design drawings would qualify as an artistic work.

(b) Design right protection for products

For the purposes of design right protection a design is defined as 'the design of any aspect of the shape or configuration (whether internal or external) of the whole or part of an article'. The definition specifically excludes surface decoration: s.213(3). The design must be recorded in an article or a design document: s.213(6); but a design document includes databases: s.263(1). Excluded from protection are features of shape or configuration which enable an article to fit with another article so that either article can perform its function: s.213(3). Similarly, where one article is intended to form an integral part of another article, the design right will not protect features of shape or configuration which are dependent upon the shape of the other article. These limitations allow the manufacture of competing spare parts, subject to the transitional protection for designs protected by copyright. The methods or principles of construction are also excluded from the design right protection: s.213(3); this will render unprotectable features of a design which are merely dictated by the material used and the method of construction.

Design right does not cover computer programs and recipes and materials. There is nothing to prevent anyone copying the ingredients in a processed food product unless the product is protected by patent, as in the case, for example, of Wall's 'Viennetta' ice cream. The new law will cover circuit diagrams.

(c) Registered design protection for products

Registered design protection is for designs which are attractive, and the design must be registered at the Designs Registry under the Registered Designs Act 1949 as amended by the 1988 Act. Registered design relates to features of shape, configuration, pattern or ornament applied to an article by any industrial process, being features which in the finished article appeal to and are judged by the eye: s.1(1) RDA 1949 as amended. The design is registered in relation to a specified article or articles and needs to be extended to cover any kind of article to which it could be applied, as in the case of a product range. Features of designs of spare parts are registrable in their own right, since 'article' includes any part of an article if the part is made and sold separately: s.44. Two- and three-dimensional design aspects are included, but the Registered Designs Rules 1989 specify that copyright protection must be relied on for wall plaques, medals and medallions, and printed matter primarily of a literary or artistic character, including book jackets, calendars, certificates, coupons, dress-making patterns, greetings cards, labels, leaflets, maps, plans, playing cards, postcards, stamps, trade advertisements, trade forms and cards, transfers and similar articles.

Designs are not registrable if the appearance is not material. Purposes, principles or methods of construction do not qualify for registered design protection, and the integral features exception from design right also applies to registered design. There is, however, no functional combination exception; and features dictated solely by function are not protectable: s.1(1)(b)(i) as amended.

(d) Rights in respect of product designs

(i) Copyright in designs

From 1 August 1989 copyright only applies to the design of things which will be artistic works when made to the design, or attractive two-dimensional designs like wallpaper, fabric, logos and so on.

For product designs made before 1 August 1989, the protection continues for up to 10 years from that date. For designs which are still protected under copyright, once copies of the work (including a typeface) are made by an industrial process, protection is limited to 25 years from the end of the calendar year in which the copied articles are first marketed. Under the Copyright (Industrial Process and Excluded Articles) (No. 2) Order 1989 (SI 1989/1070), an article is treated as being made by an industrial process if at least 50 are made and the article is a copy of an artistic work but not part of a set of articles for registered design purposes. The order also specifies types of things of a literary or artistic character, which will still be covered by the ordinary copyright rules.

(ii) Design right

The owner of the design has the exclusive right to reproduce the design for commercial purposes: s.226. This means making articles to the design, or recording the design in a design document for the purpose of making articles to the design. There is no protection for functional features, integral features, methods or principles of construction, surface decoration or commonplace features.

For there to be an infringement, the reproduction must be for 'commercial purposes', which includes anything done with a view to selling or hiring the article in the course of a business: s.263(3). Primary infringement covers making or authorising anyone to make articles to the design, or recording the design in a design document without consent. Secondary infringement covers importing, possessing and dealing in infringing articles for commercial purposes: s.227. This requires knowledge or a reasonable belief that the articles concerned are infringing articles.

(d) Registered rights

The registered proprietor has the exclusive right to make and import articles to which the design has been applied: RDA 1949, s.7. This is limited to the purposes of selling, hiring or using for the purposes of any trade or business. This means that there is no infringement if the goods are made or imported for private and domestic purposes or for any other purpose that is not for the purposes of a trade or business. The proprietor also has the exclusive right to deal in articles to which the design has been applied. Dealing means selling, hiring, offering or exposing for sale or hire. Registered designs can be infringed without copying, so that if anyone produces an article which is substantially similar to the registered design this will be an infringement. A registered design is also infringed by the making of anything for use in the manufacture of infringing articles: s.7(3).

Protection does not extend to functional features, integral features, methods or principles of construction or where the appearance is not material to the decision to buy. Absence of knowledge or a reasonable belief that the design is registered may enable the person infringing the design to avoid the payment of damages: s.9. There are no criminal offences in relation to registered design rights. There are no criminal offences in relation to infringement of design rights.

(e) Ownership in product designs

For copyright, this is governed by the ordinary copyright rules previously stated. In respect of design right protection, the designer is the person who creates a design: s.214(1). Where the design is computer-generated, the designer is the person by whom the arrangements necessary for the creation of the design are made: s.214(2).

The first/prospective owner of a design right is the designer, unless the design is commissioned or produced in the course of the designer's employment: s.215(1). If it is commissioned, the owner is the person commissioning the design: s.215(2). If the design is created in the course of employment and neither the employer nor the employee has been commissioned by a third party, the owner is the designer's employer: s.215(3). If the only way a design can qualify for design right protection is by satisfying the first marketing requirement, then the owner of the design right is the person who first markets articles made to the design: s.215(4). Thus where the manufactured articles are not first marketed by the design right owner, then the exclusive licensee or the exclusive distributor can become entitled to the design right.

Where a prospective owner of the design agrees to transfer the design right before the design is created, the transferee will become the owner of the design right automatically on creation of the design: s.223(1). Such an agreement must be in writing signed by or on behalf of the prospective owner. No one can be the owner of a registered design unless an application for registration has been made and registration granted. The author of a registrable design is the person who creates it: s.2(3) RDA 1949, or, where the design is computer-generated, the author is the person making the arrangements necessary for the design. The author will be the original proprietor of the design, and the person entitled to apply to register the design: s.2(1).

Where the design is commissioned, the person commissioning is the proprietor entitled to register the design: s.2(1A); and where the design is created by an employee in the course of employment, the employer is the proprietor unless the design was commissioned: s.2(1B). It is possible to transfer the rights to a design or grant a licence in respect of it before registration, and the Act allows a person who obtains an interest in a design in such a way to apply for registration: s.2(1) and (2).

(f) Registering a design in the EU

A registered Community Design is a monopoly right for the appearance of the whole or part of a product resulting from the features of, in particular, the lines, contours, colours, shape, texture and materials of the product or its ornamentation. Applications are filed at the Community Designs Office, known as the Office for Harmonisation of the Internal Market (OHIM). A Community Design Registration covers all 25 Member States of the EU. It can last for up to 25 years subject to being renewed every five years.

(g) Semiconductor chip design protection

Semiconductor chip designs have their own system of protection, now contained in the Design Rights (Semiconductor Topographies) Regulations 1989. The regulations protect the design of the topography of the chip but do not prevent anyone from making a chip with similar functions which is protected in patent law. The regulations specify the aspects of design which are protected.

The owner has the same exclusive rights as the owner of design rights. It is not a primary infringement, however, to reproduce the design for private, non-commercial aims, for analysing or evaluating the design, or for analysing or evaluating the concepts, processes, systems or techniques embodied in it, or for the purposes of teaching the same. This leaves the door open to reverse engineering. The secondary infringement aspects of design right apply to semiconductor chip designs with slight variations. There are no criminal offences created in respect of infringement of semiconductor topography design rights. The protection also excludes functional features, integral features, methods and principles of construction, surface decoration and commonplace features.

The authorship rules for semiconductor chip designs are the same as for design right, including provisions relating to first marketing: s.215(4) and to designs created by employees or designs which are commissioned. Designs can be transferred by prospective owners, and the purchaser becomes the owner of the design right automatically: s.223(1).

End of Chapter Summary

At the end of this complex chapter you should understand the classification of the law of property in England and have a detailed knowledge of the different forms of property which are recognised in English law. Having read and understood the chapter, you should be familiar with the following points:

▶ The distinction between freehold, leasehold and commonhold property.
▶ The concept of tangible and intangible personal property, negotiable instruments and the holder in due course.
▶ The classification of intellectual property rights: trade marks and brand names, patents and copyright and the rights they confer on their owners.

This material is of tremendous significance in commercial law and will be called upon in many of the subsequent chapters. Most immediately, in the next chapter we will see how businesses can use the assets described here as security for loans.

Questions

1. Pop plc is a soft drinks company. The company proposes to market a new drink with a highly distinctive bottle to promote brand identification. There is to be an extensive advertising campaign and the company wishes to ensure that the bottle shape will not be copied by competitors. Advise how the company can achieve the long-term protection it seeks.

2. You are engaged in setting up in business with a couple of friends and need to acquire industrial premises. Your local commercial agent has shown you a number of suitable sites, one of which is described as a freehold, another as a leasehold and the third as commonhold. Explain to your colleagues the significance of the terms.

3. Your friend has invented a new form of powered scooter where the driver straps a power pack to their back and is driven forward by a rotating, plastic, blade. Your friend feels that this could make him a fortune, so seeks your advice on the best way to protect his invention. Advise him what steps he should take. Would there be a problem if he had previously made up a number of prototypes and given them to friends to be tested? Or that, subsequently, somebody came forward with a copy of the *Beano* from 1980 which showed such a device?

4. S Ltd developed and launched on the market a revolutionary new form of lawn mower which operated on solar energy. The machine was named the 'Skymo' and the name was registered as a trade mark. The machine was a runaway success and outsold all of its competitors. Recently the managing director of the company has become aware of the fact that the word 'Skymo' is being used generically to describe the whole range of such machines. In what way could this be a dangerous development, and what should the company do to remedy the situation?

5. Copyright exists in respect of a literary work. How is literature defined for this purpose and what is the nature of the protection afforded by the law to the copyright holder?

Chapter 15

Securing loans

Learning objectives

After reading this chapter you will know about:

▶ mortgages of land, shares, life policies and goods;
▶ remedies and protection of the mortgagee and mortgagor protection;
▶ guarantees and indemnities as security;
▶ retention of title clauses as security for the supplier of goods;
▶ liens as a form of security.

15.1 The nature of a security

Persons lending money or supplying goods or services on credit will generally require some form of security. In the case of loans, this may be in the form of a mortgage or charge on the borrower's property, so that the lender can seize the mortgaged property and realise its value by sale if the borrower defaults on the loan. Suppliers of goods may protect themselves against non-payment by giving themselves the right to recover the unpaid goods.

In other cases, the lender/supplier may obtain an undertaking from a third party that they will guarantee payment of the debt in the event of the default by person to whom the loan or credit has been supplied.

Surety: a person who has given a guarantee or indemnity in respect of a debt or provided security.

In addition, some forms of security arise automatically. Forms of security discussed in this chapter include:

▶ mortgages of real and personal property, tangible and intangible;
▶ guarantees/indemnities given by a third party;
▶ retention of title clauses;
▶ liens over personal property.

15.2 Mortgages of land

The essence of a mortgage is to use the mortgagor's (the borrower's) property as security for a loan by the mortgagee (the lender). In the event of default, the mortgagee recovers the loan and interest by selling the mortgaged property. Mortgages can be legal or equitable (formal or informal).

(a) Legal charge

This creates a legal interest over the property in favour of the mortgagee while the title remains with the mortgagor. The mortgagor can therefore create second and subsequent legal charges over the property. Legal charges are created by deed.

(b) Equitable mortgages

There are three ways of creating an equitable mortgage. It is no longer possible to create an equitable mortgage of land by mere deposit of title deeds / land certificate: s. 2 Law of Property (Miscellaneous Provisions) (LOP(MP))Act 1989 prohibits the creation of an equitable charge of real property without a written contract signed by or on behalf of each party.

(i) Memorandum plus deposit of title deeds/land certificate
The memorandum can be in writing or by deed, and will generally contain an undertaking by the mortgagor to create a legal mortgage on request.

(ii) Memorandum unsupported by deposit of title deeds/land certificate
The memorandum must satisfy s.2 LOP(MP)A 1989, but can be in writing or by deed.

(iii) Agreement to create a legal mortgage
There is a legal agreement to create a legal mortgage under s.2 LOP(MP)A 1989. This creates a binding equitable mortgage convertible into a legal mortgage by specific performance.

(c) Mortgages and reality of consent

Bank finance is the most important source of external capital for small businesses and, where the proprietor is married or in civil partnership, the proprietor's matrimonial / partnership home is frequently charged to finance the family business. Where the home is jointly owned, the wife or partner's consent is required to mortgage the property for the husband's / partner's personal or business debts.

In the case of married proprietors, wives frequently claim that their consent was obtained by misrepresentation or undue influence and, where the bank has actual or constructive notice of the husband's deceit, the mortgage may be set aside. The wife's prior right prevails over that of the bank where the bank knew of it (actual notice) or would have discovered it had it taken the proper steps (constructive notice). The need to take proper steps arises where the bank was aware of certain facts which 'put it on enquiry', in other words, things which should make it suspicious.

In *CIBC Mortgages plc v. Pitt* [1993] 4 All ER 433, the bank advanced money secured against the jointly owned matrimonial home, ostensibly for paying off the mortgage and the purchase of a holiday home. The true purpose was for the husband to invest on the stock exchange, and he had put pressure on his wife to obtain her agreement. The House of Lords rejected her claim to set aside the charge for undue influence. She had to show that the bank had actual or constructive notice of the undue influence, whereas, as far as the bank was concerned, this was a normal advance for the parties' joint benefit.

In *Barclays Bank plc v. O'Brien* [1994] 1 AC 180, the husband was guarantor of his company's £120,000 overdraft and his liability was secured by a second charge on the jointly owned matrimonial home. Although the bank manager laid down that the husband and wife should be fully aware of the nature and effect of what they were signing, and should take independent legal advice, the instructions were not followed by the bank's employees and both parties signed the forms without reading them. In her defence against possession proceedings, the wife contended that her husband had pressurised her to sign and had misrepresented the legal charge as being for a three-week period only and limited to £60,000.

Rejecting the bank's appeal, Lord Browne-Wilkinson held that a presumption of undue influence shifting the burden of proof from the person alleging undue influence to the party denying it would arise between husband and wife only where the wife placed trust and confidence in the husband and where the transaction was manifestly disadvantageous to the wife. In addition, when a wife stands surety for her husband's debts, a creditor is put on enquiry by the combination of two factors: (a) the transaction is not on the face of it to the wife's financial advantage; and (b) there is a substantial risk that the husband has committed a legal or equitable wrong entitling the wife to avoid the transaction. A creditor who is put on enquiry has constructive notice of the wife's rights unless he takes reasonable steps to satisfy himself that her agreement has been properly obtained.

In *Royal Bank of Scotland v. Etridge (No 2)* [2001] 4 All ER 449, the House of Lords considered how the compromise established in the *O'Brien* case between the competing interests of the bank and the borrower's wife had worked in practice. Eight appeals were heard together, in seven of which the wife raised a defence of constructive notice of undue influence to the bank's claim for possession of the family home. The eighth involved an action by the wife against the solicitors who acted for her in the execution of the charge.

The House of Lords held that a mere exaggerated forecast of business prospects by the husband should not be misrepresentation. It abandoned Lord Browne-Wilkinson's formal tests for presumed undue influence as too mechanistic. The burden of proof shifts only where the transaction cannot be justified by reference to people's 'ordinary motives'; and a wife's agreement to charge the matrimonial home for her husband's business debts is not inexplicable where the spouses' fortunes are mutually bound up, even if the wife is less than enthusiastic or hopeful about her husband's business prospects. Undue influence arises only where the husband has misused his influence.

The House of Lords agreed with the *O'Brien* test as to when a bank is put on notice of possible undue influence, but stressed that the bank is put on enquiry once it is aware of the relationship. Where the loan is, however, made to the husband and wife jointly, banks are put on enquiry only when aware that it is, in effect, exclusively for the husband. In this respect, loans to a company are not to be regarded as joint lending merely because of any shareholding or office that the wife holds in the company. Ordinarily, banks can rely on confirmation from the solicitor acting for the wife that the advice has been given. This will not apply if the bank knows that the solicitor has not advised the wife or is aware of facts from which it ought to have realised that she has not received appropriate advice.

Hot Topic . . .

UNDUE INFLUENCE AND MORTGAGES

The *Etridge* case clarified the duties owed to the wife by banks and solicitors. The solicitor does not have to act exclusively for the wife but should have a face-to-face meeting with her in the husband's absence. In advising the wife, the solicitor owes duties to her alone and is concerned only with her interests. If acting for another party, the solicitor must be satisfied that it is in the wife's best interests for him to act for her. The solicitor in explaining the transaction at the bank's request is not the bank's agent.

(a) **Duties owed to the wife by the bank**
▶ To check the name of the solicitor the wife wishes to act for her, and communicate to her the purpose for

which he is to act. In the absence of an appropriate response, the bank should not proceed.

▶ To provide the solicitor with relevant financial information (purpose of loan, level of husband's indebtedness, amount and terms of the advance) to satisfy the bank that the wife has an informed understanding of the transaction.

▶ Where it believes the wife is misled or subject to undue influence, to inform the solicitor of the grounds for this suspicion.

▶ In every case to obtain a written confirmation from the solicitor.

(b) Duties owed by the solicitor to the wife

▶ To explain why he has become involved in the transaction and obtain her confirmation to act. Explain the nature of the documents and the practical consequences which may follow if she signs them.

▶ To point out the seriousness of the risks involved and explain the purpose and amount of the lending and the fact that changes may be made to it without reference to her.

▶ To state that the wife has a choice, and explain the choice open to her.

▶ To check whether she wishes to proceed.

▶ To check whether she is content for him to confirm to the bank that he

has explained to her the nature of the documents and their practical implications, or whether she would prefer that he negotiate with the bank.

In *TSB Bank plc v. Camfield* [1995] 1 All ER 951, the wife had been induced by her husband's innocent misrepresentation that their maximum liability for the business loan was £15,000. The wife sought to have the charge set aside, while the bank claimed it was a valid security for £15,000. The Court of Appeal set the charge aside. In *Barclays Bank plc v. Boulter* [1999] 4 All ER 513, the House of Lords held that the burden was on the wife to prove that the bank did have constructive notice of undue influence or misrepresentation.

Not all cases relate to spouses. In *Banco Exterior International SA v. Thomas* [1997] 1 All ER 46, Mrs D charged her house to the bank and signed a guarantee in respect of the liability of M, a close personal friend. Her former solicitor advised her against this, informed the bank of his views by phone and wrote to say that Mrs D had agreed to proceed against his strong advice. The bank sought to enforce the security and Mrs D (and subsequently her executors) claimed undue influence by M to the knowledge of the bank. The Court of Appeal allowed the bank's appeal and held that it was not the bank's business to ask why Mrs D

wished to stand surety, but merely to ensure that she knew what she was doing, which she did, having received independent legal advice from her ex-solicitor.

In *Credit Lyonnais Bank Nederland NV v. Burch* [1997] 1 All ER 144, the Court of Appeal set aside a mortgage over the defendant's flat and an all-monies guarantee executed in favour of her employer. The court held that the transaction in favour of a company where she was only a junior employee was so obviously disadvantageous to her as to raise a presumption of undue influence. It was not sufficient for the bank's solicitor to advise her to seek independent legal advice before signing; the bank was required to ensure that she obtained this advice. The fact that the defendant did not seek independent legal advice should have indicated to the bank that she was acting under her employer's undue influence.

Where the wife is successful in her claim, the bank will be left with only a charge over the husband's share of the joint property, with no automatic right to realise its interest. The bank can apply to the court under s.15 Trusts of Land and Appointment of Trustees Act 1996 for an order that the property be sold. However, where a wife can establish sufficient hardship and where children are involved, it is unlikely that the bank's interest will prevail.

(d) Priority and protection of mortgagees

Where there is more than one mortgage over the same property, it is necessary to prioritise the mortgagees' claims. The system operates to ensure that subsequent mortgagees discover the existence of earlier mortgagees prior to the finalisation of the charge.

(i) Mortgage protection in registered land

Registered conveyancing always requires some entry on the register of charges. The protection will depend on the nature of the register entry, which in turn depends on the nature of the charge.

Legal mortgages are converted to registered charges by a registration process. The registered charge is entered in the charges register and charges are 'taken to rank as between themselves in the order shown in the register': s.48(1). The first registered charge has priority against all subsequent registered charges. Equitable mortgages are protected by the entry of a notice in the charges register.

Where the land is owned by a company, all mortgages must be registered with the Registrar of Companies within 21 days of the creation of the charge, followed by registration with the Land Registry.

(e)   Protection of the mortgagor

(i)   The equity of redemption

The mortgagor's main protection is the right to redeem his/her property at any time on payment of the principal, interest and costs, irrespective of any contractual date for repayment laid down in the mortgage. It is a proprietary right vested in the mortgagor and it can be conveyed, demised and so on, and passes with the mortgagor's estate on his/her death.

The right is protected by the doctrine that no 'clogs or fetters' should be imposed on the right to remove or seriously restrict the mortgagor's exercise of it. Thus a term purporting to exclude the right is not allowed: *Sammuel v. Jarrah Timber and Wood Paving Corp. Ltd* [1904] AC 323. The right may be restricted for a certain period, but not so as to make the mortgage irredeemable for all practical purposes: *Fairclough v. Swan Brewery Co. Ltd* [1912] AC 566. The courts are prepared to recognise a reasonable restriction where there is no evidence of oppression: restrictions of 20 years and even 40 years have been held to be reasonable.

The equity of redemption can be terminated (i) by waiver by the mortgagor; (ii) by the sale of property by the mortgagee under his/her statutory power of sale; or (iii) where the mortgagee obtains a decree of foreclosure (see p. 347 below).

(ii)   Protection against mortgagee obtaining collateral advantage

The mortgagee may attempt to obtain some collateral advantage over the mortgagor. The most important examples relate to 'solus agreements', whereby a mortgagor may be 'tied' by the terms of the mortgage to obtaining supplies of goods and services from the mortgagee. Petrol companies and breweries acting as mortgagees over commercial premises will often seek this kind of tie. The court treats these as contracts in restraint of trade which are void unless reasonable.

In *Esso Petroleum Co. Ltd v. Harper's Garage (Stourport) Ltd* [1968] AC 269, the court held that a restraint over five years was reasonable, but not one over 21 years. Under EU law, solus agreements are automatically void under Article 81 EC Treaty unless exempted.

(iii)   Oppressive and unconscionable terms

The court can set aside such terms in a mortgage transaction, which can include the rate of interest. The protection is more important where the mortgagee is an individual, a credit company or some foreign financial institution.

In *Cityland and Property (Holdings) Ltd v. Dabrah* [1968] Ch 166, the mortgagor was a tenant buying the freehold of his house from his landlord and was 'obviously of limited means'. He undertook to pay a premium or bonus which represented either no less than 57 per cent of the amount of the loan or interest at 19 per cent. The terms of the mortgage were rewritten.

The court is influenced by the relative bargaining position of the parties (see Unfair Terms in Consumer Contracts Regulations 1999, Chapter 21, p.517).

In *Multiservice Bookbinding Ltd v. Marden* [1979] Ch 84, the court stressed that the mortgagor must show that the bargain was unfair and not merely unreasonable, which involves one party imposing objectionable terms in a morally reprehensible manner. The court considered the legality of index-linked interest rates in a mortgage to a small company, the effect of which meant that the capital repayment after 10 years had become £87,588 as against £36,000 borrowed. The average interest was 16.01 per cent. The court found the bargain hard but not unfair.

(iv) Unfair relationships

The court can consider whether the relationship between the debtor and creditor arising out of the agreement is unfair because of the terms, the way it is operated by the creditor and any other thing done or not done by the creditor before and after the agreement was made: s.140A CCA 1974.

The court can order the creditor to repay (in whole or in part) sums paid by the debtor or a surety, or to do or not to do (or cease doing) anything specified in the agreement. It can reduce any sum payable by the debtor or surety, direct a return of the surety's property provided as security, set aside (in whole of in part) any duty on the debtor or surety, alter the terms of the agreement or related agreement, and direct accounts to be taken: s.140B.

Where a company is in insolvent liquidation, the liquidator has the power to set aside extortionate credit bargains under the Insolvency Act (IA) 1986 (see Chapter 13, p.296).

15.3 Remedies of the mortgagee

(a) Legal mortgages

The mortgagee has five possible remedies: (i) possession; (ii) the power of sale; (iii) foreclosure; (iv) the appointment of a receiver; and (v) suing on the mortgagor's personal covenant to repay.

(i) Possession

A mortgagee rarely exercises the right to possession except where there is an income to be derived from the property, and the stringent controls imposed by equity make the appointment of a receiver more effective.

In *White v. City of London Brewery Co.* (1889) 42 Ch D 237, the mortgagee who took possession and leased licensed premises to a tenant subject to an obligation to buy his beer from the company was liable to account for the additional rent they would have received by letting the premises as a 'free' house.

This right is generally used in conjunction with the mortgagee's statutory power of sale.

The mortgagee's right to possession can have drastic consequences, and there is relief for the mortgagor. The court has the power to grant an adjournment of possession proceedings if there is a likelihood that the mortgagor will, during the period of the adjournment, find not only the arrears of mortgage instalments but any instalment which might have become due during the period: s.8 Administration of Justice Act 1973. In *Bank of Scotland v. Grimes* [1985] NLJ 135, this right was extended to the case of a loan by a bank repayable at the end of 25 years where interest was repayable in monthly instalments.

The court can grant relief only where the mortgagor can produce evidence of an ability to pay up within a reasonable time. The suspension of possession proceedings must be for a definite period: *Royal Trust Co. of Canada v. Markham and Another* [1975] 1 WLR 1416, and a period of six months has been indicated as reasonable for the purposes of the Act, but it could be longer or shorter depending on individual circumstances.

The mortgagor's spouse has a statutory right to tender mortgage payments, and is therefore in a position to resist possession proceedings. The mortgagee has an obligation to inform the mortgagor's spouse of the default and to serve notice of the possession proceedings: s.56 Family Law Act 1996.

(ii) The power of sale

The mortgagee has a statutory power of sale where the mortgage is effected by deed: s.101 Law of Property Act (LPA) 1925. The power of sale arises when the legal date of redemption has passed but is only exercisable where the following conditions are satisfied:

1. default in repayment of mortgage money for three months;
2. arrears of interest for two months;
3. breach of some other provision contained in the mortgage: s.103.

If the power of sale is exercised before it has become exercisable, a *bona fide* purchaser of the property without notice is protected: s.104, but the mortgagee will be liable in an action for damages brought by the mortgagor. In mortgages to banks, the mortgage will generally remove the conditions of s.103 and allow the bank to exercise the power of sale earlier.

The sale by the mortgagee passes a good title to the purchaser free from subsequent mortgages; and claims of second and subsequent mortgagees are transferred to the surplus proceeds of the sale, if any. Where the power of sale is exercised by a second or subsequent mortgagee, the sale can either be subject to or free from the prior charge. Where the sale is free from prior encumbrances, prior mortgagees have priority over the proceeds of sale. The proceeds of sale are to be applied (i) in payment of all costs, charges and expenses properly incurred in connection with the sale; (ii) in discharge of the mortgage money and interest due; and (iii) in payment of the residue to the mortgagor (or subsequent mortgagees).

In *Cuckmere Brick Co. Ltd v. Mutual Finance Ltd* [1971] 2 All ER 633, the claimants charged land on which they had planning permission to build houses to the defendants. The defendants took possession and appointed auctioneers to sell the land. The advertisements failed to mention the planning permission. The claimants drew this to the defendants' attention and sought a delay in the sale; however, the auctioneers, acting on the defendants' instructions, went ahead with the sale and the land was sold at an undervalue. The Court of Appeal held that a mortgagee owed a duty to take reasonable care to obtain the best price possible.

In *Standard Chartered Bank Ltd v. Walker* [1982] 1 WLR 1410, the Court of Appeal held that a bank mortgagee owed a duty to both the borrower and a guarantor of the debt to take reasonable care to obtain the best price possible, and in choosing the time of sale. The sale was on a cold day in February and the goods realised less than half the auctioneer's estimate.

In *American Express Banking Corp. v. Hurley* [1985] 3 All ER 564, the court held that the mortgagee was not responsible for the conduct of the receiver appointed to sell the property unless the mortgagee directed or interfered with the receiver's activities. In spite of the fact that the court found no such interference, it nevertheless held that a mortgagee or receiver owed a duty to the guarantor of the mortgagor's debt to take reasonable care to obtain the true market value of the secured assets.

In the event, however, of a conflict between the mortgagor and the mortgagee, the duty of care owed to the mortgagor is subordinated to the mortgagee's right to act in the protection of his/her own interests.

These cases were based on the idea that there was a common law duty of care owed by the mortgagee. This was disputed in *Downsview Nominees Ltd v. First City Corpn Ltd* [1993] AC 295, however, where the Privy Council held that there was no common law duty of care imposed on the mortgagee, merely an equitable duty of good faith. This approach was, however, rejected by the Court of Appeal in *Medford v. Blake* [1999] 3 All ER 97 (see below), where Sir Richard Scott V-C held that the idea that a receiver owed no duty except a duty of good faith did not make commercial sense.

Where the mortgagee is a building society, the society has a statutory duty to ensure that the sale price is the best which may reasonably be obtained: s.36 Building Societies Act 1962.

In *AIB Finance Ltd v. Debtors* [1997] 4 All ER 677, the High Court held that, where a mortgagee exercised his power of sale over property on which a business is carried out, he had a duty to maximise the value of the asset and therefore had a duty to continue the business so that it could be sold as a going concern. In this case, the mortgaged business premises were sold for £43,500, whereas the debtors claimed that as a going concern the business would have realised around £180,000.

(iii) Foreclosure

A foreclosure order is made by the court on the application of the mortgagee where the date of repayment of the loan secured on the mortgage has passed. The effect of the order is to terminate the mortgagor's equity of redemption and pass the title to the property to the mortgagee. In practice, where a foreclosure application is made, the court will generally order a power of sale under s.91 LPA 1925.

(iv) Appointment of a receiver

The receiver's duty is to receive all the income from the mortgaged property and apply (i) the income in discharge of rents, rates, taxes and other outgoings; (ii) the income in payment of his/her own commission and of fire, life or other insurance premiums payable under the mortgage; (iii) in payment of the interest on the mortgage; and (iv) any surplus towards the discharge of the principal.

Mortgagees have a statutory power to appoint a receiver in the same circumstances and subject to the same conditions as the statutory power of sale. The receiver must be appointed in writing: s.109(1), and will be the agent of the mortgagor unless the mortgage deed provides otherwise: s.109(2). The mortgagor is thus liable for any acts or defaults of the receiver, which makes the appointment of a receiver more attractive to the mortgagee than entering into possession personally.

In *Medford v. Blake*, M was a large-scale pig farmer. His bank appointed a receiver who ran the business until M was able to repay the bank. M had repeatedly told the receiver that he could obtain discounts of £1,000 per week on feedstuffs, but the receiver had failed to obtain the discounts. The court held that the receiver owed a duty of care to manage the business with due diligence and was liable to M for this breach of duty.

(For receivers of companies see Chapter 13, p.272.)

(v) Sue on the mortgagor's personal covenant to repay

Suing on the mortgagor's personal covenant to repay is merely an action to enforce repayment of the debt. Since the mortgage is by deed, the limitation period for actions is 12 years.

(b) Equitable mortgages

A similar category of remedies can be discussed as for legal mortgages.

(i) Entry into possession

It is doubtful whether an equitable mortgagee has any right to possession of the mortgaged property.

(ii) Power of sale

If the mortgage is by deed, the statutory power of sale exists as described above. Where the land is registered, the mortgagee will first of all have to convert his/her mortgage into a registered charge, or the equitable mortgagee will be able to effect a conveyance of the legal estate even though having no legal title him/herself: *Re White Rose Cottage* [1965] Ch 940. Where the mortgage is not by deed, the mortgagee can apply to the court for a power of sale under s.91 LPA 1925.

(iii) Foreclosure

The court has power to order foreclosure on behalf of an equitable mortgagee but will in practice order a sale in lieu of foreclosure.

(iv) Appointment of a receiver

The statutory power applies to equitable mortgages by deed, but in other cases the mortgagee may apply to the court for the appointment of a receiver.

15.4 Mortgages of shares

The mortgagee will generally only be prepared to take a charge over the securities of a public company the shares if which are on either the stock exchange official list or the alternative investment market (AIM). Some public companies do not have their securities listed on any market; stockbrokers carry out transactions by way of matched bargains and it may not be possible to find an immediate buyer. Securities in private companies will generally not be acceptable because of the problems in valuing and realising them. The form of the mortgage depends upon whether the security is registered or bearer.

A company may issue bearer securities for stock and fully paid shares if expressly authorised to by its articles. The company issues a share warrant, which is a negotiable instrument and transferable by mere delivery. Possession of the warrant is the basis of title. It will include dividend coupons which are presented to the company when a dividend is declared. They are very rare but there are no formalities for mortgaging them. A mortgage is created by depositing the warrants subject to an agreement to return them on repayment of the loan plus interest. The mortgagee can transfer them to a third party on default.

Most securities are registered, with the registered holder's name and address in the register of members or debenture holders. Under the CREST registration and transfer system for listed securities, private investors can opt to have paper certificates which will facilitate the mortgaging of those securities.

The certificate is *prima facie* evidence of title to the securities: s.768 Companies Act (CA) 2006. Title ultimately depends upon entry in the appropriate register, and transfers involve the replacement of the transferor's name with that of the transferee. The registered holder for the time being is the person to whom dividend or interest payments are made. Mortgages can be legal or equitable.

(a) Legal mortgages of registered securities

A legal mortgage of registered securities involves a legal transfer of the securities into the name of the mortgagee or its nominee, subject to an undertaking to retransfer on repayment of the loan plus interest.

The transfer is by the stock transfer form introduced by the Stock Transfer Act 1963. This form is used for transfer of stocks and shares in companies and also for most government stocks. The form must be signed by the transferor but does not need to be signed by the transferee.

(b) Equitable mortgages of registered securities

Equitable mortgages of registered securities are created when the mortgagor deposits the share certificate or debenture stock certificate with the mortgagee during the period of the loan.

There is no need for any transfer or memorandum to be signed but, where the mortgagee is a bank, it will generally insist upon a memorandum to establish that the securities are being held as a security, rather than just for safety.

An equitable mortgage is disadvantageous for the mortgagee in that, where there are existing equitable claims against the securities (as where the registered holder held them as trustee for beneficiaries), the mortgagee ranks after earlier equitable claims, even those of which he had no notice. The mortgagor can also obtain a replacement certificate, transfer the securities to a new registered holder and override the mortgagee's equitable claim.

Other problems arise where the company makes a bonus issue which will reduce the market value of the shares. The bonus shares will be sent to the registered holder. There are also problems with rights issues, where the offer is sent to the registered holder. A rights issue could well affect the value of the issued shares.

The equitable mortgagee has some legal protection. S/he can send the company a notice of deposit informing it that s/he holds the securities as mortgagee. This will not have any great effect, since the company cannot enter on its register notice of any trust, expressed, implied or constructive: s. 126 CA 2006. There is an advantage, however, since once the company has been notified of the charge, it will not be able to claim a lien on the shares in respect of advances subsequent to receipt of the notice of deposit. In *Bradford Banking Co. Ltd v. Henry Briggs, Sons & Co. Ltd* (1886) 12 App Cas 29, the court held that the notice of deposit was not a notice of trust for the purposes of s.126 CA 2006 (previously s.360 CA 1985). Liens are not exercisable against fully paid quoted shares, but a company issuing a new share or stock certificate after the service of a notice of deposit would certainly be negligent and liable to the mortgagee.

A more formal possibility is to serve a stop notice on the company. Where a stop notice is served, the company must give 14 days' warning to the mortgagee before registering any transfer of the shares. In that period, the mortgagee can obtain a restraining order or an injunction in an action against the mortgagor. The procedure is seldom used but is useful where there is no possibility of a legal mortgage (where the shares are qualification shares for holding office as director) and there are doubts as to the integrity of the mortgagor. The mortgagee cannot transfer the shares without the signature of the mortgagor on a share transfer form, but will normally require the mortgagor's signature on a form when the mortgage is taken.

15.5   Mortgages of life insurance policies

Life insurance policies are one of the most satisfactory forms of security. The value of the policy is easily established and can only increase as long as the premiums are paid. The value of the policy as a security is the realisable value on the policy's surrender to the insurance company: the surrender value.

The policy acquires a surrender value after premiums have been paid over two or three years, and this will increase during the life of the policy. The surrender value is frequently set out on the policy document and, failing that, the insurance company will supply the information. Since the value can only increase, there is no need for the bank to allow a margin of depreciation.

The risk of the policy being avoided through absence of an insurable interest (see Chapter 19, p.452) is very slight, since reputable insurance companies would waive the issue of illegality to the extent of its surrender value. If the insured commits suicide, this could allow the insurer to refuse to accept liability since the act is a deliberate act of the insured. Some life policies contain a suicide clause to make them payable even on the assured's death by suicide, in which case the only problem is that the terms of the clause are respected. There is an important distinction between the finding of a coroner's court that the insured took their own life while the balance of their mind was disturbed and when they were sane. Even in the absence of a suicide clause, insane suicide does not avoid the policy since the act is not deliberate. Most reputable insurers would generally honour the policy up to its surrender value in any event.

A further problem could be the failure of the insured to pay the premiums, causing the policy to lapse. Where the mortgagee is a bank, the bank may pay the premiums and debit the mortgagor's bank account.

(a)   Legal mortgages

These are created by legal assignment subject to the obligation to retransfer on repayment of the loan plus interest. Legal assignment is governed by the Policies of Assurance Act

1867 and must be in writing, either by endorsement on the policy or by separate instrument in the words or to the effect set out in the Schedule to the Act: s.5.

The assignment in the Schedule is in the following form: 'I, A.B. of ... in consideration of ... do hereby assign unto C.D. of ..., his Executors, Administrators and Assigns, the within Policy of Assurance granted ... In witness, ...' Where the mortgagee is a bank, the bank will use its own form.

The form will contain an assignment clause coupled with a statement that the mortgage secures the payment of all sums due to the bank, including interest and bank charges. There will also be a proviso that the bank will reassign the policy to the customer at his/her own expense on payment of all money due. There will also be a statement that it is a continuing mortgage which will cover the borrowing of the customer for the future up to the limit allowed. The customer will also agree to pay the premiums punctually and produce receipts of payment to the bank, and there will be agreement that, should the customer fail to pay the premiums, they can be paid by the bank and the sums debited from the customer's bank account. The agreement will enable the bank, without the customer's consent, to sell and surrender the policy to the insurance company or any other person, and will exclude the restrictions on the mortgagee's powers under s.103 LPA 1925 (see above p.346).

In addition to the written assignment, there must be notice served on the life office, the company issuing the policy: s.3. Where there is a legal assignment of the policy, the assignee can sue to enforce the rights under the policy in his/her own name and is able to give a legal discharge of the policy to obtain payment of the surrender value.

(b) Equitable mortgages of life policies

Equitable mortgages of life policies can be created by an oral agreement between the parties or, more usually, deposit of the life policy accompanied by a written memorandum of the mortgage terms. The mortgage is valid against the mortgagor's trustee in bankruptcy, executor or administrator, but the insurance company will require a discharge from the assured or his/her personal representatives as well as from the mortgagee before paying out on the policy.

The mortgagee will usually give notice of the mortgage to the insurance company, which ensures priority over any previous mortgagees who have not served notice and of which the mortgagee has no actual or constructive notice. In the absence of notice, priority is determined by the date order of the charges.

15.6 Goods as a security

Charges are possible over goods, and this is frequently used in connection with the financing of foreign trade. Charges can be created in three ways.

(a) Mortgage

A mortgage of goods leaves the possession of the goods with the borrower but transfers the title to the lender. Mortgages of goods are not encountered frequently, since they are regulated by the Bills of Sale Acts 1878 and 1882, which require registration of the charge in the central office of the Supreme Court within seven days of its creation. Since the register is public, and since registration of bills of sale will be published in various trade journals, there is a lot of harmful publicity associated with this form of security. The bill of sale must also comply exactly with the form prescribed by the Bills of Sale Act 1882, s.9, or it will be void.

(b) Pledge

A pledge is where the owner of goods (the pledgor) gives up possession of the goods as a security to the lender (pledgee) whilst retaining the ownership of the goods.

A pledge arises when goods (or documents of title to goods) are delivered to the pledgee by the pledgor as security for a debt, subject to an obligation to return them once the debt is discharged. If the agreement stipulates a fixed date for repayment, the pledgee has an implied power of sale in respect of the goods if the pledgor defaults.

Where there is no fixed date, the pledgee must demand repayment and then exercise their power of sale if there is subsequent failure to pay and after serving of notice on the pledgor of their intention to sell the goods. This is the most frequent form of charge over goods.

(c) Hypothecation

Hypothecation creates a charge over goods without title or possession passing to the lender.

Hypothecation generally arises only where the borrower was not in actual or constructive possession of the goods. Otherwise a pledge would be more usual.

15.7 Guarantees and indemnities

Contracts of guarantee must be distinguished from indemnity contracts. The most obvious difference is that guarantees are required to be evidenced by a memorandum in writing under the Statute of Frauds 1677 s.4 (see Chapter 3, p.71).

A guarantee involves two contracts and three parties. The guarantor is saying to the person about to advance money to the principal debtor, 'Lend AB the money, and if they do not repay you, I will'. The guarantor is only secondarily liable for the debt and liability to pay arises only on the principal debtor's default.

In a contract of indemnity, the indemnor is saying, 'Lend the money to AB and I will see that you are paid'. The indemnor is primarily liable. There is only one contract: between the indemnor and the person lending money, or supplying credit.

In *Pitts v. Jones* [2007] EWCA Civ 1301 it was held that where the court had to distinguish between an oral contract of guarantee and one of indemnity it should ask what the object of the contract was. If the promisor's obligation to pay had arisen as an incident to the central object of the contract, that obligation would be an indemnity, but if it was the central object of the contract, that obligation would be a guarantee. If the promisor had no real interest in the subject matter of the contract, but only a motive for offering his promise, the promise would be a contract of guarantee.

For guarantees, if the contract between the creditor and the principal debtor is void, the guarantor is also released. This used to be important where the principal debtor was a minor or a limited liability company. The situations have been resolved by the Minors'

Contracts Act 1987 s.2, which abolished the rule in *Coutts & Co. v. Browne-Lecky* [1947] KB 104 (see Chapter 3, p.72), and the *ultra vires* reforms in s.35(1) CA 1985 (now s.39 CA 2006) (see Chapter 8, p.195). Bank guarantees contain a clause making the contract both a guarantee and an indemnity.

(a) Contractual considerations of guarantees

There are three contractual considerations to examine: (i) consideration, (ii) disclosure, and (iii) mistake, misrepresentation and undue influence.

(i) Consideration

Unless a guarantee is by deed, there must be consideration for it, although the Mercantile Law Amendment Act 1856 provides that it is unnecessary to set out the consideration in the written instrument constituting the guarantee. In practice, however, the consideration will usually be set out.

The consideration cannot be in the form of a past debt and, in the case of a bank guarantee, there would be a potential problem if the consideration was stated in the form of a specific sum, since it is likely that the guarantee would have no effect unless the bank lent precisely this sum: *Burton v. Gray* (1873) 8 Ch App 932. A bank guarantee will most usually be in the form of a continuing security which will cover advances made by the bank to the principal debtor and be terminable on three months' written notice by the guarantor to the bank, or, in the event of the death of the guarantor, three months after notice of death.

The normal consideration for a bank guarantee will be: '[i]n consideration of the bank making or continuing advances or otherwise giving credit or affording banking facilities for as long as the bank may think fit or granting time to … (hereinafter called "the Principal")'.

(ii) Disclosure

Utmost good faith: contracts of guarantee are not contracts of utmost good faith requiring one or both parties to disclose all material facts.

In *Cooper v. National Provincial Bank Ltd* [1945] 2 All ER 641, the claimant sought without success to have set aside two bank guarantees on the ground that the bank had failed to disclose that the husband of the principal debtor was an undischarged bankrupt who had authority to draw on the account, and that the account had been operated in an improper and irregular way.

A bank guarantee will normally be signed at a tripartite meeting between the bank, the principal debtor and the guarantor, with the principal debtor's presence giving implied authority to the bank to disclose information as a result of any direct questions put by the guarantor.

(iii) Mistake, misrepresentation and undue influence

Contracts of guarantee were vulnerable in the past to the defence of *non est factum* (a claim by the guarantor that it is not his deed) and could be void even though the person signing had been negligent: *Carlisle and Cumberland Banking Co. v. Bragg* [1911]

1 KB 489. The decision in *Saunders v. Anglian Building Society* [1971] AC 1004 means that the defence is unavailable to a person who was negligent in signing the document. Cases can still arise, however, as in *Lloyd's Bank v. Waterhouse* [1991] Fam Law 23 (see Chapter 3, p.58).

A guarantee form should never be allowed to be signed in the absence of the creditor.

In *Associated Japanese Bank (International) Ltd v. Crédit du Nord* [1988] 3 All ER 902, the claimant bank entered into a scheme proposed by a fraudster to buy machines from him for over £1m and lease them back to him. The defendant bank stood guarantor of his liability to the claimant. The fraudster disappeared without making payments and it was discovered that the machines had never existed. The claimant sought to enforce its rights against the defendants under the guarantee. The action failed because the court found that there was an express or implied condition in the guarantee that the machines existed. As an alternative, Steyn J was prepared to hold the guarantee void for common mistake, since both parties to the guarantee believed that the machines existed and would not otherwise have entered into the transaction.

The guarantee may be avoided where the guarantor has been induced to sign by a misrepresentation, even if made innocently: *MacKenzie v. Royal Bank of Canada* [1934] AC 468. There is also authority for saying that silence can amount to a misrepresentation where 'a guarantor put a question or made an observation in the presence and hearing of the bank-agent, which necessarily and inevitably would lead anyone to the conclusion that the intending guarantor was labouring under a misapprehension with regard to the state of the customer's indebtedness': *Royal Bank of Scotland v. Greenshields* 1914 SC 259 at p. 268.

As regards undue influence, there is no general fiduciary duty between a banker and a customer: *National Westminster Bank plc v. Morgan* [1985] 1 All ER 821 (see Chapter 3, p.58). Where the proposed guarantor is, however, the wife of the principal debtor, the creditor should always ensure that a spouse is advised to obtain independent legal advice before signing the guarantee.

In *Bank of Montreal v. Stuart* [1911] AC 120, Mrs Stuart stood as a guarantor in respect of a loan to a company in which her husband was interested. This was signed at the office of, and in the presence of, a solicitor who acted for the bank and for her husband, and who was also an officer and shareholder of the company. She later substituted the initial guarantee for a larger one, and finally entered into a series of transactions under which she surrendered all her estate to the bank and was left without independent means. In all this she never once received independent legal advice. In spite of stating in evidence that she had acted of her own free will to help her husband, the court found that Mrs Stuart, who was an invalid, had acted in passive obedience of her husband, and the transactions were set aside.

(b) Special categories of guarantor

The are four special categories of guarantor.

(i) Children
Guarantees by children cannot be enforced during their minority, but they can ratify the contract on majority or make a fresh enforceable agreement in the same terms: Minors' Contracts Act 1987.

(ii) General partnerships

Unless the firm's articles provide that the giving of a guarantee is within the ordinary course of the firm's business, a guarantee must be signed by all the partners. Guarantees will always provide for the joint and several liability of the partners: see below. The guarantee will not survive a change in the constitution of the firm.

(iii) Limited companies

Problems arise where the guarantee is void because it constitutes financial assistance for the acquisition of shares in a public company contrary to s.678 CA 2006: *Heald v. O'Connor* [1971] 1 WLR 497. The guarantee will also be voidable where the directors executing the guarantee are personally interested in it; this can occur where one company guarantees the account of another company, and a director of the company voting on the resolution is also a director or shareholder of the company for the benefit of which the guarantee is being given. This can also relate to any form of direct security issued by the company in place of an earlier guarantee by the directors.

In *Victors Ltd v. Lingard* [1927] 1 Ch 323, the five directors of a company guaranteed the company's account at the Midland Bank. Some months later, the directors resolved that the company should issue a debenture to the bank as additional security. The articles excluded interested directors from voting on and being reckoned for the purposes of establishing a quorum of the board. The court found that there was a personal interest to the directors since the debenture relieved their liability. In this case the company was estopped from alleging the invalidity of the debentures, but in other circumstances this would have been the case.

Where this situation is likely to arise, the creditor should ensure that the resolution relating to the guarantee (or other issue of securities) is passed by the votes of disinterested directors or, where this is impossible; the decision must be taken by the company in general meeting. Even where the articles allow directors to vote on contracts in which they have an interest, s.177 CA 2006 imposes an obligation to declare that interest at a meeting of the directors by notice in writing in accordance with s.184 or by general notice in accordance with s.185. Where the creditor is aware that this requirement has been breached, the company will be able to avoid the guarantee: *Rolled Steel Products Ltd v. British Steel Corporation* [1986] Ch 246.

(iv) Guarantees by two or more persons

Guarantees by two or more persons give rise to particular problems, notably the nature of the liability of the guarantors, which can be joint, or joint and several. Prior to the Law Reform (Miscellaneous Provisions) Act 1934, the liability for existing and future debts of a guarantor with joint liability came to an end on his/her death under the doctrine of survivorship. The position is unclear since the passing of the 1934 Act. In the case of joint and several liability, the guarantor's liability for existing debts is preserved on death and the creditor can claim against the estate.

To make the co-guarantors jointly and severally liable, the words 'we hereby jointly and severally guarantee' should be used. In the case of a bank guarantee, this will usually be accompanied by a clause allowing the bank to release or discharge one or more of the guarantors from liability without prejudice to its rights and remedies against the remaining guarantor/s, removing the rule whereby discharge of one or more of several co-guarantors releases the others from liability: *Barclays Bank Ltd v. Trevanion, The Banker,* Vol. 27 (1933) p. 98.

The co-guarantors do not need to sign the guarantee in each other's presence, but the failure of all parties to sign discharges those who have already signed.

In *National Provincial Bank of England v. Brackenbury* (1906) 22 TLR 797, a joint and several guarantee was intended to be signed by four guarantors, but only three of the four signed and the court held that they were not liable. In *James Graham & Co. (Timber) Ltd v. Southgate-Sands* [1985] 2 All ER 344, the claimant issued a writ against three guarantors. Before the trial one of the guarantors was made bankrupt and it was discovered that the other signatures were forgeries. The Court of Appeal held there was no liability of one guarantor where the signatures of the co-guarantors were forged. Where one of the guarantors varies the terms of the guarantee without the consent of the others, all the co-guarantors will be discharged. In *Ellesmere Brewery Company v. Cooper* [1896] 1 QB 75, four persons executed a joint and several guarantee which limited the liability of two to £50 each and the other two to £25 each. After the three others had executed the bond, the fourth guarantor executed the bond but marked against his signature '£25 only'. This material alteration discharged the others from liability and, since the others were discharged, the person making the material alteration was also not bound.

See below for the special rules relating to termination of joint and several guarantees.

(c) Rights of the guarantor

The guarantor has rights against (i) the creditor; (ii) the principal debtor; and (iii) co-sureties, but a bank guarantee form will remove virtually all the rights of the guarantor where they conflict with the interests of the bank.

(i) Rights against the creditor

The guarantor can at any time ask the creditor how much s/he is currently liable for under the guarantee. For bank guarantees, because of the duty of confidentiality to the customer, the guarantor will only be told that s/he is liable to the full amount of his/her guarantee or the actual amount of the debt.

Once the debt has become due, the guarantor may pay off the creditor and sue the principal debtor provided s/he obtains an assignment of the guaranteed debt. The guarantor can claim the benefit of any right of set-off of the principal debtor against the creditor. If the guarantor pays off the debt or the part of the whole debt which s/he has guaranteed, s/he is subrogated to all the rights of the creditor in respect of the debt, including any securities given by the principal debtor and co-sureties to the creditor. In bank guarantees, the competing rights of the guarantor will be removed by the inclusion of a whole debt clause: '[t]his guarantee shall be applicable to the ultimate balance that may become due to the bank from the Principal and until repayment of such balance, I will not take any steps to enforce any right or claims against the Principal in respect of any moneys paid by me to the Bank hereunder'.

Where a person has given a guarantee or indemnity to a creditor of a company or an individual now in liquidation or bankrupt, the guarantor cannot prove in the liquidation or the bankruptcy unless s/he has discharged the principal debtor's total obligation to the creditor, even where s/he has agreed to be liable only up to a maximum amount because only one proof can be admitted for the same obligation. If the guarantee is for only part of the principal debtor's debt, the surety may prove once s/he has paid that part in full and the creditor may prove for the remainder. This applies to a guarantee expressed to be for the repayment of 25 per cent of a loan plus interest thereon, or the first £100,000 of the principal debtor's indebtedness to the creditor.

(ii) Rights against the principal debtor

Where the creditor has a right to immediate payment against the guarantor, the guarantor can call upon the principal debtor to pay the debt, even though the creditor has not demanded payment from the principal debtor.

In *Thomas v. Nottingham Incorporated Football Club Ltd* [1972] Ch 596, the court held that as soon as the guarantor gave notice to the creditor terminating the guarantee he was entitled to call upon the principal debtor to pay, even though the guarantor was only liable to pay on demand and no demand had been made.

As soon as the guarantor pays any money under his/her guarantee, s/he has an immediate right of action against the principal debtor and, where the principal debtor is bankrupt or, in the case of a company, in liquidation, has a right to prove for the debt. This is generally restricted by the use in a bank guarantee of a whole debt clause (see above).

(iii) Rights against co-sureties

Where there are co-sureties, a person who pays the debt, or more than his/her proportion of the whole debt, is entitled to contribution from his/her co-sureties, whether there is joint or joint and several liability, and whether they are co-sureties under one instrument or more than one.

In *Stimson v. Smith* [1999] 2 All ER 833, the Court of Appeal held that where a co-surety, not acting officiously or voluntarily, paid a guaranteed liability, he was entitled to a contribution from the co-surety even though the creditor had not made a formal demand as required by the guarantee. Such a procedural or evidentiary requirement was for the surety's benefit and could therefore be waived by him.

Where the principal debtor is solvent, the guarantor must join the principal debtor as co-defendant in any action against co-sureties: *Hay v. Carter* [1935] 1 Ch 397. Any action for contribution must take into account the benefit of securities taken from the creditor and any payments from the principal debtor.

(d)   Termination of the guarantee

Termination is only a problem for a continuing guarantee under which the creditor continues to advance credit or supply goods in reliance on the guarantee until it is terminated. In this case, although the guarantor is released in respect of further advances or deliveries, their existing liability is preserved. The creditor's problem is to ensure that their claim against the guarantor is preserved and will not be discharged through the operation of the rule in *Clayton's Case* (1816) 1 Mer 572, which means that credits will reduce or extinguish the liability of the guarantor, while payments out of the account (or fresh advances on credit) will create new advances for which the guarantor will not be liable. A bank will normally rule off the principal debtor's account and open a new account for future transactions.

In *Westminster Bank Ltd v. Cond* (1940) 46 Comm Cas 60, the bank had inserted a clause into a guarantee allowing it to continue the account with the principal and preserving the guarantor's liability as at the date when the guarantee was determined, notwithstanding any subsequent payment into or out of the account. The court held that the guarantor's liability remained, even though the bank had continued to operate the account without a break for almost six years after the notice of termination. The clause was drafted to cover notice of termination and death of the guarantor, but it could be extended to cover insanity and bankruptcy.

Termination can arise through the following eight circumstances:

(i)   *Payment by the guarantor or the principal debtor*
Payment by the guarantor terminates their liability under the guarantee, as will payment by the principal debtor. In the latter case, however, the guarantee will generally be drafted to exclude termination by payments which are later established as voidable preferences, which can then be reclaimed from the creditor by the trustee in bankruptcy or the liquidator or administrator of a company.

(ii)   *Notice by the guarantor*
In the case of a continuing guarantee, the guarantee will normally provide for its termination by three months' notice by the guarantor. In such a case, the creditor could continue to make advances in reliance on the guarantee, and the guarantor will be liable for the balance outstanding at the end of the period. The same would apply in the event of termination by notice of the guarantor's death, where the guarantee provides that it shall continue for three months after notice of death.

(iii) *Notice of guarantor's death, insanity, bankruptcy or liquidation*
If the guarantee has been acted upon before the death of the guarantor, it will continue until the creditor receives notice of the death. The identical situation will arise in the event of the insanity of the guarantor. Whereas bank guarantee forms usually provide for continuance beyond the notice of death, no such provision is made for insanity, and the guarantee cannot be relied upon once notice is received. If the guarantor is made bankrupt or placed in liquidation, the creditor should no longer rely on the guarantee once notice has been received.

(iv)   *Death of the principal debtor*
The guarantee is terminated to the extent that the total liability of the principal debtor is established. There is only a practical problem concerning the operation of bank guarantees which will normally cover cheques presented after the principal debtor's death and before the bank has notice of the death. Once there is notice, the bank will return the cheques unpaid, marked 'drawer deceased'.

(v)   *Variation of the terms of the principal contract*
A material variation of the principal contract will discharge the guarantor from liability. In this context, the most important variation will be where the creditor gives the principal debtor more time to pay. The rule has been criticised but is strictly applied. However, most guarantees will be drafted to exclude this rule.

(vi)   *Change of parties*
Where there is a change in the constitution of the parties to or for whom the guarantee is given, in the absence of agreement to the contrary the guarantee is revoked as regards

future transactions. This rule is embodied in the Partnership Act 1890 s.18, but the same thing applies to registered companies. and the merger of two or more companies revokes a guarantee given to one of the companies as to future transactions.

(vii) Release of the principal debtor by the creditor

A guarantor is discharged if the creditor releases the principal debtor from his/her liability: *Perry v. National Provincial Bank of England* [1910] 1 Ch 464. This does not apply to compositions under IA 1986, but most guarantees will be drafted to exclude this rule.

(viii) Special rules relating to joint and several guarantees

The notice of the death of one joint and several creditor does not, even when notified to the creditor, prevent the remaining guarantor or guarantors from remaining liable for further advances. In the case of a continuing guarantee, although the termination of the guarantee will usually result in ruling off the principal debtor's account and opening a new account, this may not be necessary where the guarantee contains a clause, as in *Westminster Bank Ltd v. Cond* (1940) (above); further, if the guarantee contains a clause to the effect that the notice of the termination or death of one of the co-guarantors does not terminate the guarantee (which can only be terminated by the notice of all the co-guarantors), the guarantee will continue to cover future advances, even against the deceased guarantor: *Egbert v. National Crown Bank* [1918] AC 903.

Notice of the insanity of one of the co-guarantors will presumably have the same effect on the other guarantor or guarantors, but the liability of the insane guarantor will terminate in respect of further advances. If one joint and several guarantor is made bankrupt the position is the same as for death, and an agreement could make an express provision relating to the continuing liability of the co-guarantors. Once again, the bank would have to rule off the principal debtor's account and channel new transactions through a new account if it wished to prove in the estate of the bankrupt guarantor, unless there was a *Westminster Bank Ltd v. Cond* (1940) clause.

15.8 Property covered by a retention of title clause

A retention of title clause is frequently incorporated into a contract for the sale of goods to protect the seller of the goods in the event of the non-payment of the buyer. The basis is the Sale of Goods Act (SOGA) 1979, under which the property in specific goods in a deliverable state passes to the buyer, which may be at the time of the contract but always on or before delivery: s.18, unless the parties have expressed a different intention: s.17, culminating in 'reservation of disposal', where title does not even pass on delivery: s.19.

A properly drafted clause maintains the contract's status as a sale contract, so the purchaser must be able to use and resell the goods, but gives him/her bailment of them and leaves legal title with the seller until certain conditions are met. The contract will prevent goods passing to the trustee in bankruptcy, liquidator or receiver, and allow unsold and unused goods to be repossessed by the seller. Thus, in *Romalpa* (see below), the sellers reclaimed the unused aluminium; in *Re Peachdart* [1983] 3 All ER 204, unused leather; and in *Clough Mill Ltd v. Martin* [1984] 3 All ER 982, unused yarn.

In *Aluminium Industrie Vaassen v. Romalpa Aluminium Ltd* [1976] 2 All ER 552, aluminium foil was supplied to the defendant for processing, on condition that ownership should not pass until payment of the full price, and that products made from the foil should be kept by the buyers as bailees separately from the other stock as surety for the outstanding price; but that the buyers should have the power of sale of the manufactured articles as the sellers' agents. The court held that the supplier had the right to the unused stocks of foil, a charging order over the goods into which the foil had gone, and the proceeds of sale of the finished goods. The relevant part of clause 13 in the contract read: '[t]he ownership of the material to be delivered … will be transferred to the purchaser when he has met all that is owing … Until the date of payment, the purchaser … is required to store material in such a way that it is clearly the property [of the sellers]'.

But there are three variations on the basic clause, as follows.

(a) Protection against onward sales

If the purchaser resells the product in its original state, the purchaser will get a title under s.25(1) SOGA 1979, since the original purchaser is a 'buyer in possession', which will defeat the claims of the title retention holder: *Four Point Garages Ltd v. Carter* [1985] 3 All ER 12. The supplier can require the buyer to notify the purchaser of the title of the original seller through a variation on the basic clause, '[i]f the purchaser shall resell the goods whilst they are still the property of the seller, he shall notify the purchaser that the goods remain the property of the original seller, until such time as the seller under this contract has received payment for the goods', and prevent the operation of s.25(1). This will still not prevent failure of the clause by the second buyer destroying the identity of the goods.

Where goods sold subject to retention of title are sold and delivered to a sub-buyer also subject to retention of title, unless the sub-purchaser pays for the goods the original seller can claim title to goods remaining in his/her hands: *Re Highway Foods Int Ltd* [1995] 1 BCLC 209.

(b) The 'all-monies' clause

The all-monies clause seeks to retain title until all debts are settled and has been considered in Scottish law in *Armour v. Thyssen Edelstahl Werke AG* [1990] 3 All ER 481, where Lord Keith saw no difference in principle between a clause which passed property on payment of the price and one passing property on the payment of all debts. But it could be contrary to the doctrine of privity of contract and the definition of a sale contract in s.2(1) SOGA 1979, and constitute a charge over book debts requiring registration in the case of a company.

(c) Tracing into the proceeds of sale and/or manufactured goods

The major extension of the basic title retention clause attempts to trace the goods into the proceeds of sale and/or into a manufactured product incorporating the goods. In the *Romalpa* case, the clause effectively provided for rights over manufactured products into which the aluminium could be traced, and the proceeds of onward sale into the bank account of the company. The cases on tracing in equity establish that, where a trustee of property translates that property from its original form into another by sale, or sale and repurchase, the beneficiary is entitled to those proceeds of sale or the repurchased item. Tracing depends on the relationship of trust being set up.

In relation to tracing into the proceeds of sale, the clause must create a constructive trust of the goods and there must be a fiduciary relationship. *Compaq Computers Ltd v. Abercorn*

Group Ltd [1991] BCC 484 established that the court will not imply a right to trace; there must be a specific clause. This must retain equitable as well as legal title and describe the purchaser as both 'bailee' and 'fiduciary', and even specifically as 'trustee', although the term 'agent' can also be used. Thus the purchaser resells the goods as agent/fiduciary for the supplier.

The clause should then claim the proceeds of sale, requiring records of sales specifically to be kept and the proceeds 'to be held in a separate fund for the use of the seller'. In *Hendy Lennox (Industrial Engines) Ltd v. Grahame Puttick Ltd* [1984] 1 WLR 185, there was an insufficient creation of a fiduciary position. In *Re Weldtech Equipment Ltd* [1991] BCC 16, defective drafting created a charge on book debts. In *Re Peachdart* and *Re Andrabell Ltd: Airborne Accessories v. Goodman* [1984] 3 All ER 407, the clause failed because there was no requirement for separate funds. In relation to tracing into manufactured goods, the court takes the view that the title to the goods has passed to the purchaser once the manufacturing process has inextricably mixed the product with others.

In *Re Bond Worth* [1979] 3 All ER 919, an attempt to trace fibres into carpets was held to create a floating charge over the finished product which was void for want of registration under s.860(1) CA 2006. The same thing is seen in *Ian Chisholm Textiles Ltd v. Griffiths and Others* [1994] 2 BCLC 291, in respect of an attempt to trace into dresses made up from fabric. In *Stroud Architectural Systems Ltd v. John Laing Construction Ltd* [1994] 2 BCLC 276, an attempt to create retention of title over glazing units was held to create a floating charge, which was void for want of registration.

Any use of words such as 'charge' or 'security' is likely to lead the court to find a registrable charge: *Pfeiffer Weinkellerei-Weineinkauf GmbH v. Arbuthnot Factors Ltd* [1988] 1 WLR 150; *Compaq Computers Ltd v. Abercorn Group Ltd* [1991] BCC 484; and *Re Interview Ltd* [1975] IR 382.

In other cases the courts have similarly restricted the right to trace on the grounds of loss of identity. In *Borden (UK) Ltd v. Scottish Timber Products Ltd* [1979] 3 All ER 961, resin was used in the manufacture of chipboard, and in *Re Peachdart* leather in the manufacture of handbags. In both cases, once manufacture was undertaken, the product subject to the title retention lost its inherent identity and the right to recover the product was lost.

In *Hendy Lennox (Industrial Engines) Ltd v. Grahame Puttick Ltd* [1984] 1 WLR 185, the product was a diesel engine inserted into a generator by four bolts. Although it became part of a larger finished product, it was possible to disassemble it and recover the engine *in specie*; the product did not lose its identity and could be recovered.

Attempts to draft a clause seeking to trace a right in the goods into which the product has been manufactured are a waste of time, and where goods become attached to land as a fixture they may also have lost their identity.

15.9 Liens

There are two types of lien of importance in this context: possessory and equitable liens.

(a) Possessory liens

Possessory liens give persons in possession of goods, papers and so on the right to retain possession of them until they are paid outstanding charges in respect of those goods, papers and so on. The right is lost once possession is lost.

The holder of the lien does not generally have a right to sell the goods held. The lien can arise through common law or by statute and can be particular or general.

Particular liens are more common and give the right to retain an item until all the liabilities are settled in respect of those goods. Thus agents have a right of lien in respect of goods until settlement of their commission, remuneration and any expenses in respect of those goods. Accountants have a particular lien over clients' books, files and papers: *Woodworth v. Conroy* [1976] QB 884, carriers in respect of charges incurred, innkeepers in respect of goods deposited or left in respect of money owed for board and lodging (Innkeepers Act 1878), and repairers in respect of work carried out. The seller of goods who is in possession of them has a lien and right of stoppage in transit of goods until payment of the purchase price (see Chapter 18, p.442).

General liens give the person in possession the right to retain possession until the settlement of all claims outstanding with the owner. General liens may arise by agreement, a course of dealing or by custom. Solicitors have a general lien over clients' papers. Bankers have a lien in respect of cheques collected on behalf of a client for value, and over the credit balances in clients' accounts for debit balances in other accounts at the same bank. Other persons with a general lien include stockbrokers and factors.

The lien is enforced by retaining the goods which are the subject of the lien. There is generally no right of sale, but there is a right for repairers under the Torts (Interference with Goods) Act 1977, and for unpaid sellers of goods: s.48(3) SOGA 1979 (see Chapter 18, p.443). The lien is lost when possession is lost, even though it may be recovered subsequently: *Westminster Bank Ltd v. Zang* [1966] AC 182. It is also lost on payment or tender of the amount owed and where the holder takes a security in substitution for the lien.

(b)   Equitable liens

An equitable lien exists independently of possession and is an equitable charge on property until claims have been discharged.

An unpaid vendor of land has an equitable lien over the property from the exchange of contracts until payment of the purchase price. Ex-partners have equitable liens over the property of a dissolved partnership. The lien is binding on persons acquiring the property except for *bona fide* purchasers for value without notice, and is enforced by sale.

End of Chapter Summary

Having read and understood this chapter you should have a thorough knowledge of the assets which can be used in a commercial context as security, as well as the nature and significance of the contract under which a third party stands guarantor in respect of an advance.

Of particular significance are the following points:

▷ The formalities for creating legal and equitable mortgages over a variety of assets: land, securities, life insurance policies and goods.
▷ The factors which could affect a life insurance policy and render it void.
▷ The rights of the borrower to repay the sum borrowed and redeem the charged property at any time on payment of the loan plus the interest. This is the borrower's equity of redemption.
▷ The rights of the mortgagee to realise the charged asset on default.

End of Chapter Summary cont'd

▶ The distinction between a guarantee and an indemnity and the factors which affect the validity of a guarantee.

▶ The value of the retention of title clause in respect of contracts for the sale of goods on credit.

▶ The significance of the possessory lien.

This is a crucial chapter since the world of commerce largely exists on credit. Whether a creditor is secured or unsecured and the nature of the security held can be crucial if the borrower later becomes insolvent. These issues are examined in detail in Chapter 13 on corporate insolvency.

Questions

1. With regard to mortgages of registered land, how does the mortgagee protect his/her right to priority over later mortgagees?

2. The mortgagor of real property is protected by the equity of redemption. Explain the operation of this right and how it can be restricted or terminated.

3. What are the risks for the equitable mortgagee of registered shares, and what protection is there for the mortgagee?

4. What is the value of an insurance policy when used as security for a loan? What factors may cause the policy to be avoided by the insurer?

5. What is the essential difference between a guarantee and an indemnity? What do you understand by the term 'utmost good faith', and does it apply to a contract of guarantee?

6. What is the significance of the 'whole debt clause' in a guarantee?

7. What problem arises where a supplier of goods attempts to claim a right to trace those goods into objects manufactured by the purchaser?

8. In respect of a possessory lien, distinguish between a particular and a general lien.

Part V

Business Contracts

Introduction to Part V

This part deals with some of the more significant aspects of relationships crucial to the world of commerce and business.

Chapter 16 deals with the relationship of agency: where one party, the agent, acts on behalf of another, the principal, to bind the principal in contracts falling within the authority of the agent. Of significance in this respect is the distinction made between the actual, the usual and the ostensible authority of the agent, and businesspeople must at all costs be aware of their real significance. Thus principals can find that they can be liable in law for agreements negotiated on their behalf by their agents even though the agents have acted outside the confines of their actual authority: the authority given them by the principal. The chapter deals with all the aspects of agency including the special position of commercial agents.

Chapter 17 deals with an even more important and complex area: the relationship between employer and employee. This is a relationship which is regulated in all its aspects, with the predominant influence coming from EU law in the form of Regulations and Directives. As a result, all employees – full time, part time, casual and temporary – are given equal rights under the law. This extends to protection in respect of hours worked, unfair dismissal and discrimination on the grounds of age, gender, race, disability, sexual orientation and religion. Keeping up with developments in this field is a problem for any employer.

Chapter 18 concerns contracts for the supply of goods and services. This is of importance to all business people as both suppliers and receivers of goods and services. Of particular importance here is the legal distinction made where the receiver is a person dealing as a consumer rather than in the course of business. It is vital to realise that the law protects the private consumer more than the person acting as a dealer in these relationships.

A final chapter (Chapter 19) deals with insurance. This is of vital importance in the commercial context for many reasons. Employers are required to have compulsory insurance in respect of their vicarious liability for the torts committed by their employees in connection with their employment, and all businesses seek the protection of indemnity insurance against the loss of or damage to their assets, including stock. In addition to this, life assurance can be a vital asset for an entrepreneur against which to secure business loans. It is also possible for life assurance to be taken out in respect of debtors and employees.

In this area an important topic is that of the need for an insurable interest in any contract of insurance and the need for the insured to make full disclosure to the insurer before the latter accepts the risk of the insurance.

Chapter 16

Agency

Learning objectives

After reading this chapter you will know about:

- ▶ agents' authority
- ▶ rights and duties of agents
- ▶ liability of agents to third parties
- ▶ termination of the agency
- ▶ Commercial Agents Regulations 1993

16.1 Agency and types of agents

Agents are persons with authority to act on behalf of another called the principal whom they can bind in contracts with a third party within the scope of their authority.

Since the agent is not personally bound by the resulting contract, the agent does not need to have contractual capacity, although in a commercial context it would be unlikely to come across an agent without contractual capacity. Agents can be the principal's employees or independent contractors supplying specialist skills. Companies may appoint other companies as their agent with responsibility for a particular market.

There is confusion between the legal and commercial use of the term 'agent'. In a commercial context the term 'agent' or 'agency' is frequently applied to persons who are not strictly 'agents' in the legal sense. Car dealers described as a manufacturer's agent sell cars as principals, and a buyer has no rights against the manufacturer arising simply out of the purchase contract. The creation by a manufacturer of a 'sole agency' for certain products is not an agency agreement as it prevents the manufacturer from selling the goods personally. Estate agents are not 'agents' in the legal sense, since they have no authority to sell the properties for which they are instructed to find a buyer.

There are five types of agent:

Special agents – have authority on specific occasions or for a specific purpose, for example signing cheques, and the principal is only bound by acts within their actual authority.

General agents – have authority to act within certain limits, for example a general partner can bind the firm and the other partners in contracts in the ordinary course of the firm's business. The principal can be bound by agents acting within their usual, rather than their actual, authority (see below).

Universal agents – have unlimited authority to act for the principal.

Del credere agents – have primary liability for payment on contracts negotiated for their principal in return for a higher rate of commission, for example an advertising agency.

Commercial agents – defined as self-employed intermediaries with 'continuing authority to negotiate the sale or purchase of goods on behalf of another person (the principal), or to negotiate and conclude the sale or purchase of goods on behalf of and in the name of that principal': reg. 2(1) Commercial Agents (Council Directive) Regulations 1993 (SI 1993/3053, [1993] OJ L382/17, as amended by SI 1993/3173).

16.2 Agents' authority

Authority may arise in a number of ways:

- the principal's prior consent;
- the principal's subsequent consent – ratification;
- implied by the law – agency of necessity;
- under the doctrine of apparent authority.

Where agents act without the principal's authority, the principal is not contractually bound to the third party, but the third party can sue the agent for damages for breach of warranty of authority in respect of the lost opportunity.

(a) Principal's prior consent

The authority can be communicated verbally, in writing or by deed. Authority by deed is necessary only where the agent is required to contract on the principal's behalf by deed. In this case, the agent is the donee of a power of attorney and subject to the Powers of Attorney Act 1971. Generally, there is no distinction between verbal and written authority except for specific occasions when agents are required by the law to have authority in writing.

If agents act beyond their actual authority or without authority, their principals are contractually bound only if they subsequently ratify the transaction or where the act is within the agents' apparent authority.

(b) Ratification

Ratification is the subsequent adoption by the principal of an agreement entered into on their behalf by an agent acting either beyond their authority or with no authority.

In order to be effective, ratification is subject to certain conditions:

(i)   Principals can ratify contracts only if they were already in existence when the contract was negotiated on their behalf. Registered companies cannot ratify contracts negotiated on their behalf before their incorporation (see Chapter 8, p.191).

(ii) Agents must have contracted as agents and have named or identified the principal.

In *Keighley, Maxtead v. Durant* [1901] AC 240, the agent purchased wheat at a higher price than authorised but without revealing that he was acting as an agent. The principal purported to ratify the contract but later refused to accept delivery. The House of Lords held that he could not be liable for damages for breach of contract since the ratification was ineffective.

(iii) The principal cannot ratify a void contract or a forgery.

(iv) The principal must have had the capacity to contract both at the time the contract was negotiated and at ratification.

(v)   The principal must generally be aware of all material facts relating to the contract but may ratify the acts of their agent without knowing of them.

(vi) Ratification must be of the whole contract.

(vii) Ratification must be subsequent, within a reasonable time and before the time fixed for performance of the contract.

Except for contracts of insurance, apart from marine insurance, ratification is retrospective in effect except where this would cause excessive hardship to third parties. It can be express or by implication and there are no formal requirements except that ratification must be by deed where the agent has contracted by deed. Ratification generally arises from the principal's conduct, and it can be difficult to identify whether ratification has taken place.

In *Forman & Co. Proprietary Ltd v. The Ship Liddesdale* [1900] AC 190, a shipowner's agent ordered repairs to a ship beyond his authority. The shipowner took the ship back and sold it. The court rejected the claim that this constituted ratification on the ground that the shipowner had little option but to take the ship back and that ratification required some positive, unequivocal act.

In other cases, however, the court has accepted that, where the principal objected when agents purchased goods beyond their authority but later sold some of the goods, this amounted to ratification: *Cornwal v. Wilson* (1750) 1 Ves Sen 509.

Where agents accept an offer 'subject to ratification', the acceptance is a legal nullity until ratification by the principal and, if the offeror revokes the offer before ratification, there is no contract: *Watson v. Swann* (1862) 11 CBNS 756.

(c)   Agency of necessity

This is where the court recognises a person as having the authority of an agent to bind another person even though not appointed as such. This is subject to the following conditions:

- Agents must have responsibility for another's property under a pre-existing agreement;
- There must be an emergency in connection with that property;
- It must be impossible to get instructions from the owner;
- The agent acted in good faith in the owner's interests.

In *Prager v. Blatspiel, Stamp and Heacock Ltd* [1924] 1 KB 556, the defendants, London fur dealers, sold skins to the claimant for delivery in Bucharest, but this was impossible because of the German occupation and, after two years, the defendants resold the skins. The defendants were not agents of necessity because they could not prove that it was impossible to communicate with the claimant, a commercial necessity, and that the action was taken in good faith in the owners' best interests.

In *Gt Northern Railway v. Swaffield* (1874) LR 9 Exch 132, a horse was sent by train and, in the absence of anybody to meet it at its final destination, the railway company, being unable to contact the owner, booked the horse into a livery stable shortly before the arrival of the servant sent to meet it. The railway company was found to have acted under its authority as an agent of necessity.

Third parties seeking to enforce contracts by an agent of necessity against the principal can do so only if there has been strict compliance with the common law rules of agents of necessity, but this is not required for persons claiming to be indemnified as agents of necessity, or defending a claim for wrongful interference.

In *The Winson* [1982] AC 939, a ship was chartered to carry wheat from the USA to Bombay, and during the voyage the ship became stranded on a reef. The salvors unloaded some of the wheat, which was shipped to Manila and warehoused, even though there was then no immediate necessity. The House of Lords found the cargo owners liable to reimburse the salvors' expenses as agents of necessity.

Agency of necessity does not arise in connection with voluntary acceptance of responsibility for another's property. In *Binstead v. Buck* (1777) 2 WB1 1117, a person who took in a lost dog could not claim expenses as an agent of necessity.

(d) Apparent authority

A distinction is made between authority deriving from the agent's status – usual authority – and authority through the principal's representation – ostensible authority.

(i) Usual authority

Usual authority arises from an agent's status and may exceed actual authority.

This is the usual authority of particular trades or professions – solicitor, hotel manager, stockbroker, building site foreman. Principals are contractually bound within their agent's usual authority unless the third party was aware of the actual, more limited, authority.

In *Panorama Developments (Guildford) Ltd v. Fidelis Furnishing Fabrics Ltd* [1971] 2 QB 711, the defendant's company secretary contracted to hire cars for the company but, in reality, the cars were for his own personal use and he had no authority to hire them. The company refused to pay, claiming the agent's lack of actual authority. It was held that a company secretary had implied authority to contract on a company's behalf in respect of administrative matters including hiring cars, and the company was liable.

Principals are bound by acts within their agent's usual or ostensible authority even where they are carried out fraudulently. In *Lloyd v. Grace, Smith & Co.* [1912] AC 716, the defendant firm of solicitors was liable for damages arising from the fraudulent conveyancing work of their managing clerk acting within the course of his employment.

(ii) Usual authority and mercantile agents

A mercantile agent is one 'having in the customary course of [their] business … authority either to sell goods, or to consign goods for the purpose of sale, or to buy goods, or to raise money on the security of goods': Factors Acts 1889 s.1.

Any sale, pledge or disposition by a mercantile agent of goods or the documents of title to goods in their possession with the owner's consent in the ordinary course of their business is binding on the owner even if unauthorised, as long as the person taking under the disposition acted in good faith and without notice of the agent's lack of authority: s.2 Factors Act 1889.

Thus, if a person leaves a car together with the registration documents with a garage which sells cars in the usual course of its business, the garage has implied authority to sell the car. Ownership passes to the purchaser and the original owner can only sue the garage for damages.

(iii) Ostensible authority or 'holding out'

Ostensible authority is where (i) there is a representation by the principal to a third party concerning the authority of an agent; and (ii) the third party acts in reliance on that representation; (iii) the principal is estopped or prevented from denying the truth of the representation.

In *Spiro v. Lintern* [1973] 1 WLR 1002, L had allowed his wife to act as if she had authority to negotiate the sale of his house. S acted in reliance on the authority of the wife, regarded himself as the purchaser and started refurbishing it. L later purported to sell the property to a third party at a higher price, alleging his wife's lack of authority. S successfully applied for specific performance.

In *Freeman and Lockyer v. Buckhurst Park Properties (Mangal) Ltd* [1964] 2 QB 480, a director of the defendant contracted with the claimants, a firm of architects, to draw up plans for a proposed development. When planning permission was refused, the claimants sought to recover their fees from the company, which maintained that it was not liable since the director was unauthorised. The court held that the board had allowed the director to act as if he was the managing director, the claimants had acted in reliance on this representation and the contract fell within the usual authority of a managing director.

In *Hely-Hutchinson v. Brayhead Ltd* [1968] 1 QB 549, the fact that the board allowed a director to act as a managing director was treated as an implied appointment of the director to that position giving him actual authority to bind the company (see Chapter 8, p.195).

Ostensible authority survives beyond the termination of actual authority and ex-agents can continue to bind their ex-principals in post-termination contracts with third parties with whom they have dealt in the past. To avoid this, the principal must notify all persons who have previously dealt with the agent that the agency has been terminated.

In the case of partnerships, unless the firm gives individual notice to all persons who dealt with the partner prior to their retirement and publishes a retirement notice in the *London* or *Edinburgh Gazette* (depending on whether the principal place of business is in England and Wales or Scotland), the partner can continue to bind the firm in respect of post-retirement contracts: s.36 Partnership Act 1890.

16.3 Agents' duties to the principal

Agents owe their principal a duty: (i) of obedience; (ii) of care and skill; (iii) of personal performance; (iv) to account; and (v) of good faith.

(a) Obedience

Agents must obey their principal and cannot exceed their instructions unless given a power of discretion, even where they believe they are acting in the principal's best interests. Failure to obey their instructions will result in liability to compensate the principal for any loss suffered.

In *Bertram, Armstrong & Co. v. Godfrey* (1830) 1 Knapp 381, the claimant instructed his stockbroker to sell certain stocks when they reached a certain price, but the broker failed to sell the stocks believing they would continue to increase in value, and they were later sold at a lower price. The court held that by holding on to the stocks the broker had purchased them himself, and owed the claimant the difference in price plus interest.

Where the instructions are ambiguous, the court looks to see whether the agent has acted reasonably, even though incorrectly.

Only contractual agents are liable for failure to perform their duties, but where agents have a discretion to act or not, they are liable for failure to act only if the power of discretion was exercised unreasonably.

(b) Duty of care and skill

All agents, contractual and gratuitous, must exercise the same degree of care and skill that a reasonable person would exercise in respect of their own affairs. A professional person must display the degree of skill appropriate to the profession under s.13 Supply of Goods and Services Act 1982 (see Chapter 18).

In *Chaudhry v. Prabhakar* [1989] 1 WLR 29, a person was liable for giving negligent advice to a friend in choosing a second-hand car.

(c) Duty of personal performance

Agents must generally carry out any task delegated to them by the principal personally and can only sub-delegate their authority (i) if they have express or implied authority; (ii) in cases of necessity; and (iii) in respect of the delegation of purely ministerial tasks.

Where agents delegate their authority, the sub-agents are the agents' agent and accountable to the agent, who is accountable to the principal. There are legal doubts concerning the ability of the principal to sue the sub-agent.

In *Calico Printers' Association Ltd v. Barclays Bank* (1931) 145 LT 51, Wright J stated: 'the English law has … in general applied the rule that even where the sub-agent is properly employed, there is still no privity between him and the principal; the latter is entitled to hold the agent liable for breach of the mandate which he has accepted, and cannot, in general, claim against the sub-agent for negligence or breach of duty … To create privity it must be established not only that the principal contemplated that a sub-agent would perform part of the contract, but also that the principal authorised the agent to create privity of contract between the principal and the sub-agent.' In this case the agent was held liable for the negligence of the sub-agent.

The position is now subject to the Contracts (Rights of Third Parties) Act 1999. Under s.1(1) and (3) of the Act, a contract may be enforced by a person who is not a party to it if 'the contract so provides or the contract purports to confer a benefit on him, and the contract expressly identifies that person by name … or as answering to a particular description'.

There is also confusion regarding tortious liability as a result of two conflicting decisions.

In *Lee Cooper Ltd v. C H Jeakins & Sons Ltd* [1967] 2 QB 1, it was held that, where agents bailed goods to persons, the bailees owed a duty of care not only to the bailor but also to the bailor's principal. However, in *Balsamo v. Medici* [1984] 2 All ER 304, the court refused to allow an action in tort by a principal against a sub-agent in respect of money received by the sub-agent.

In *Allam v. Europa Poster Services* [1968] 1 All ER 286, the court held that it was possible to delegate authority to serve notice terminating existing licences for advertising sites to the defendant's solicitor since this was a purely ministerial act involving no delegation of confidence or discretion.

In *John McCann & Co. v. Pow* [1975] 1 All ER 129, the court refused to recognise that an estate agent had an implied authority to delegate the finding of a buyer for a client's property to another firm of estate agents, and the agents appointed by the principal could not claim commission in respect of the sale of the property by another agency to which they had delegated the sale of the property.

(d) Duty to account

Agents must account for all money and property received by them as agents. They must keep separate bank accounts, and if their money and the principal's becomes mixed, there is a presumption that everything in the account belongs to the principal.

(e) Duty of good faith

Agents are in a fiduciary relationship to their principal, which imposes the following duties on the agent.

(i) Avoidance of conflicts of interest

Agents must not place themselves in a position where there is a conflict between their personal interests and their duties as agent.

In *Reiger v. Campbell-Stuart* [1939] 3 All ER 235, the claimant instructed the defendant to try to find properties suitable for conversion into flats. The defendant found a suitable property offered at £2,000 and arranged for his brother-in-law to purchase it. He then purported to buy the property from the brother-in-law at £4,500, before selling it to the claimant for £5,000. The claimant successfully sued for an account to her of the secret profit the agent had derived.

Conflicts of interest also arise where agents sell their personal property to the principal or buy property from the principal or act as an agent for both parties to a transaction.

(ii) Full and frank disclosure

There is a duty of full and frank disclosure of all material information of which the agents are aware. When selling goods on the principal's behalf, all offers must be disclosed to the principal, and agents have a duty to obtain the best possible price. In *Keppel v. Wheeler* [1927] 1 KB 577, estate agents were employed to sell a house and obtained an offer of £6,150, which was accepted 'subject to contract' by the owner. They subsequently received a further offer of £6,750. After the completion of the sale at the lower price, the owner of the property successfully sued for damages for breach of duty, which was the difference between the two offers. The agents were, however, entitled to their commission.

The duty has been stated to be absolute: an agent 'must put at his client's disposal not only his skill but also his knowledge, so far as it is relevant; and if he is unwilling to reveal his knowledge to his client, he should not act for him. What he cannot do is to act for the client and at the same time withhold from him relevant knowledge that he has': *per* Megarry J in *Spector v. Ageda* [1973] Ch 30 at p. 48.

In confirmation of this, the Law Commission stated, 'A firm must utilise all the information available to it when acting for a customer. Due to attribution of knowledge within a firm, all parts of the firm must act in the light of all information possessed by the firm' ('Fiduciary Duties and Regulatory Rules' Consultation Paper 124 (1992, HMSO) at s.4.12(v)). In its final report, however, the Law Commission adopted a more relaxed view (Law Com No. 236 (1995, HMSO)). This was reflected in a contemporary decision of the House of Lords.

In *Kelly v. Cooper* [1993] AC 205 (PC), the claimant alleged conflict of interest and failure to disclose against estate agents appointed to sell a property. They did not disclose that the purchaser had bought the neighbouring property through them, which was material in fixing the sale price. The court held that persons in a general agency business, where there was bound to be a conflict of interests between principals, are in a different position from other agents. The contract between the principal and the agent could not be held to include an implied term (a) requiring the agents to disclose confidential information from other vendors; (b) precluding them from acting for rival vendors; or (c) precluding them from earning commission on the sale of a rival vendor's property.

In *Hilton v. Barker Booth and Eastwood (a firm)* [2005] UKHL 8 the defendant firm acted for H, a property developer, in respect of a development to be carried out by him and a contract to sell the developed property to B. BBE acted as solicitor for both parties, albeit with different individual solicitors being responsible for the two parties. During the negotiations and the making of a series of contracts, the firm failed to inform H that B had been made bankrupt and had served a prison term for fraud. In addition, an initial deposit paid ostensibly by B had been advanced by the firm. As a result of B's failure to go through with the deal, H's business failed. In an action against BBE, the House of Lords held that BBE were guilty of a conflict of interests and awarded H damages against the firm.

Hot Topic . . .

CONFLICTS OF INTEREST AND CHINESE WALLS

'Chinese walls' are a set of internal rules and procedures to control and prevent the communication and misuse of confidential information between departments of a multifunction financial intermediary.

This is of particular significance in respect of multi-function financial institutions, firms of accountants or solicitors, particularly following mergers or movements of personnel. In respect of multifunction financial institutions, problems can arise where one department is marketing securities and another is advising investors on their share portfolios. The existence of a Chinese wall prevents the spread of confidential information from one department to another. The Court of Appeal is sceptical about the effectiveness of Chinese walls.

In *Supasave Retail Ltd v. Coward Chance (a firm), David Lee & Co (Lincoln) Ltd v Coward Chance (a firm)* [1991] Ch 259, there were separate actions brought by the liquidators of the two claimant companies. During the preliminary stages of these actions, there was a merger between the firm acting for the liquidators and the firm which had previously acted for some of the principal defendants. The liquidators wanted the newly merged firm to continue to act on their behalf but the defendants objected, on the grounds that confidential information about their defence might leak to the solicitors acting for the liquidators. The firm pleaded that it had established an effective Chinese wall between those members who had acted for the defendants and those acting for the liquidators. The Court of Appeal

rejected the claim that the Chinese wall would prevent seepage of information within the firm.

In *Bolkiah v. KPMG (a firm)* [1999] 2 WLR 215, Prince Jefri of Brunei had retained KPMG between 1996 and 1998 in respect of some private litigation, during the course of which KPMG acquired confidential knowledge of his affairs and assets. In 1998, KPMG were employed as auditors of the Brunei Investment Agency (BIA) tracing money transferred from BIA during Prince Jefri's period as chairman. KPMG felt able to accept the work since it had ceased to act for Prince Jefri more than two months before, but it erected a Chinese wall around the department carrying on the investigation. A High Court injunction restraining the firm from acting was thrown out by the Court of Appeal but reinstated by the House of Lords.

In *Koch Shipping Inc v. Richards Butler (a firm)* [2002] 2 All ER 957, a solicitor with a firm acting for the claimant in arbitration proceedings moved to the defendant firm acting for the other party. The claimant sought an injunction against the defendant firm to restrain them from acting for the other party. The Court of Appeal overturned the injunction on appeal and accepted that the solicitor, who worked on a different floor from those engaged in the arbitration, was responsible and conscientious and could be relied on not to pass on information directly or indirectly when acting for the claimant.

(f) Duty not to make secret profits

Agents must not use or disclose confidential information acquired in their capacity as agents for their own benefit, nor derive a secret profit from their position. Where agents do make a secret profit from their position, they must account to the principal for the profits.

In *Reading v. A G* [1951] 1 All ER 617, a British army sergeant in Egypt was held liable to account to the Crown for money he had been paid for accompanying lorries carrying illicit spirits. Where the secret profit is derived honestly, the agent is still entitled to claim for commission or remuneration: *Hippisley v. Knee Bros* [1905] 1 KB 1. Agents are still liable to account even though their actions have been beneficial for the principal.

In *Boardman v. Phipps* [1967] 2 AC 46, B, a solicitor, and P, as agents for the trustees of an estate, attended the AGM of a company in which the trust held a large shareholding. Believing that the company could be more profitable, they used their own money to acquire a controlling interest in the company. This was done openly but without the consent of the trustees. They made large profits for themselves and the estate. The House of Lords held them liable to account for the profit which they had made, since it had been made by reason of their fiduciary position as agents and the opportunity and knowledge that had come to them in that capacity.

Where the secret profit is in the form of a bribe, principals can take steps against the agents and the briber. Agents receiving bribes are not entitled to remuneration or commission and must account for any payments already received: *Andrews v. Ramsay & Co.* [1903] 2 KB 635. If the bribe has been paid, principals can recover it from the agent. Otherwise, they can recover it from the briber unless they impliedly or expressly assent to the payment: *Anangel Atlas Naviera SA v. Ishikawajima-Harima Heavy Industries Co. Ltd* [1990] 1 Lloyd's Rep 167. In addition, the principal can claim from the agent any properties purchased with bribe money: *A G for Hong Kong v. Reid* [1994] 1 All ER 1. The principal may also sue the agent and third party for any loss suffered under the tort of deceit.

In *Mahesan v. Malaysian Government Officers Co-op* [1979] AC 374, the Privy Council stated that the principal could not recover both against the agent and the briber but must elect between these alternative remedies before judgment.

The agent can be summarily dismissed: *Boston Deep Sea Fishing and Ice Co. v. Ansell* (1888) 39 Ch D 339, and the principal can avoid all contracts negotiated by the agent even though they are not tainted: *Shipway v. Broadwood* [1899] 1 QB 369.

Agents accepting bribes are guilty of conspiracy at common law, and both the agent and the briber are guilty of an offence under s.1 Prevention of Corruption Act 1906 if they acted corruptly. A corrupt motive will be presumed in certain cases under the Prevention of Corruption Act 1916, s.2. The agent is subject to the duty of good faith even after the termination of the agency: *Island Export Finance Ltd v. Umunna and Another* [1986] BCLC 460. (For partners see Chapter 7; for directors, Chapter 11.)

Agents have three rights in respect of the principal: (a) the right to indemnity, (b) the right to remuneration, and (c) the right to a lien over the principal's property in their possession for unpaid remuneration and charges.

16.4 Agents' rights against the principal

Agents have three rights against the principal.

(a) Right to indemnity

Principals must indemnify agents for liabilities or expenses incurred except for: (i) in unauthorised acts; (ii) losses due to an agent's fault; and (iii) losses arising from illegal acts. The right to indemnity is lost where agents are in breach of their duties unless they have acted in good faith (see also p.375).

(b) Right to remuneration

The agent's right to remuneration depends upon the terms of their contract and can be express or implied. Agents can claim remuneration only where they have exactly and completely complied with their instructions. Where remuneration is due but not fixed, agents are entitled to a reasonable amount: s.15 Supply of Goods and Services Act 1982.

In *Kofi Sunkersette Obu v. Strauss & Co. Ltd* [1951] AC 243, the agent's contract provided that the commission, if any, was to be fixed by the principal and, when the principal made no decision on the matter, the Privy Council rejected the agent's claim for commission.

Where commission is to be paid on the completion of a task or tasks, an agent may not be entitled to it even where the task is completed, unless the agent was instrumental in its achievement.

In *Coles v. Enoch* [1939] 3 All ER 327, Coles had sought to purchase a property from the defendant but, unable to raise the money, agreed to act as an agent in finding a purchaser. His attempt to interest a prospective purchaser in Manchester was overheard and, after he had left, the bystander approached the other person and discovered the whereabouts of the property. He then travelled to London and, through his own efforts, traced the property and bought it. The court rejected the claim for commission on the ground that the agent had not been instrumental in concluding the sale.

In *Rolfe & Co. v. George* (1968) 113 SJ 244, a person seeking to sell a property had found a buyer but engaged the claimant as agent in the negotiation of a price. The agent was entitled to commission.

On the other hand, if the contract provides for commission to be earned at an earlier stage, the agent may be entitled to commission even where the deal is not completed. Estate agents' contracts may provide for the payment of commission on the 'introduction of a purchaser ready and willing to buy'. In this case, they are entitled to the commission even if the buyer later backs out of the deal: *Christie, Owen & Davies Ltd v. Stockton* [1953] 2 All ER 1149; *Christie, Owen & Davies Ltd v. Rapacioli* [1974] 2 All ER 311; *Drewery and Drewery v. Ware Lane* [1960] 3 All ER 529; *Peter Long and Partners v. Burns* [1956] 3 All ER 207; and *Scheggia v. Gradwell* [1963] 3 All ER 114. Terms like this followed the decision in *Luxor (Eastbourne) Ltd v. Cooper* [1941] AC 108, where it was held that there was no implied term in a contract against the principal deciding not to go ahead with a sale once a buyer had been found, and thus depriving the agent of his commission.

(c) Right to a lien

Under a particular lien, agents have a right to retain possession of the principal's goods until indemnities and remuneration in respect of those goods have been paid. Where they can claim a general lien, they can retain possession of goods in respect of any outstanding payments due to them from the principal, even though the sums due do not arise from transactions relating to the goods retained. The right to a lien is possessory and is lost if the goods pass out of the agent's possession (see Chapter 15, p. 362).

16.5 Agents' liability to the third party

(a) Bills of exchange and cheques

Agents signing bills of exchange or cheques in a representative capacity who have failed to make this clear may be personally liable on the bills or cheques: s.26 Bills of Exchange Act 1882. Criminal liability may arise where company officers sign a bill of exchange or cheque on behalf of their company but the company's name does not appear or appears incorrectly on the instrument: s.84 Companies Act 2006 (see Chapter 6, p.147).

(b) Deeds

Agents are personally liable on any deed executed by them as agent unless they are appointed by deed.

(c) Contracts for non-existent principals

See p. 370 above and Chapter 8, p.191.

(d) Contracts for undisclosed principals

Where agents enter into a contract on the principal's behalf without revealing to the third party that they are acting as agents, the third party deals with them as if they were the principal. The third party can then elect to sue the agent or the principal. Once they have elected who to sue, however, they cannot change their mind. Commencing a legal action against the agent is presumed to be election, but this can be rebutted if it can be shown that the third party was not aware of the principal's existence when the action was commenced. They can then substitute the principal as defendant. Once a judgment has been obtained, however, it is impossible for the third party to sue the principal, even if the judgment remains unsatisfied.

In *Sika Contracts Ltd v. Gill & Closeglen Properties Ltd* (1978) 9 BLR 11, the claimant was able to enforce against G, a chartered engineer, a contract which G had signed as an agent for the second defendants. G had not indicated that he was signing in a representative capacity and the court refused to imply this from the fact that his professional qualifications followed his name.

In *Yukong Line Ltd of Korea v. Rendsburg Investments Corpn of Liberia (No. 2)* [1998] 1 WLR 294, the court refused to lift the corporate veil of a company and declare that the controller and director of the company was an undisclosed principal for the company at the moment of signing a charterparty or retrospectively, because he transferred funds from the company to avoid a freezing injunction.

Agents can sue or be sued but must defer to the principal if they intervene to claim the benefit of the contract. This is possible only where agents have acted within their actual authority except where they have denied the principal's existence. Undisclosed principals cannot intervene where this is expressly or impliedly excluded in the agreement between the agent and the third party, or where the right to benefit from the contract would force the third party into a contract which they would otherwise have not agreed to.

In *Said v. Butt* [1920] 3 KB 497, knowing the theatre owners would not sell him a ticket to a premiere in person, the claimant arranged for a friend to buy the ticket. He was refused entrance and sued for breach of contract. The court held that the fact of using his friend could not make him a party to a contract with the theatre against its will. In *Dyster v. Randall & Sons* [1926] Ch 932, the defendants could not escape a contract of sale of land purchased by the friend of the claimant who knew that the vendors would not sell to the claimant. In *Siu Yin Kwan v. Eastern Insurance Co. Ltd* [1994] 1 All ER 213, an undisclosed principal could enforce a contract of insurance made by his agent within his actual authority, since this was not a personal contract.

(e) Breach of warranty of authority

If agents act without or beyond their actual authority and the principal does not adopt the contract, the third party can sue the agent for damages for breach of warranty of authority. Liability is strict and it is no defence that they were unaware that they were acting without authority or beyond their authority: *Yonge v. Toynbee* [1910] 1 KB 215 (see p.381).

The donees of a power of attorney who act after the power has been revoked are not liable to the donor or any other party if, at the time, they were unaware that the power of attorney had been revoked: Powers of Attorney Act 1971. The Act also provides that third parties can enforce post-termination contracts if they were unaware of the revocation of the donee's power.

16.6 Termination of agency

The agency relationship can be terminated by (i) mutual agreement; (ii) revocation of the agent's authority; (iii) custom; (iv) complete performance of the contract; (v) expiration of time; (vi) frustration; (vii) death or insanity of either party; (viii) bankruptcy of the principal; and (ix) revocation of the agent's authority.

(a) Mutual agreement and revocation of authority

Either party to the contract may terminate the contract at will and without any notice except where the agency contract constitutes a contract of employment, when reasonable notice must be given: *Parker v. Ibbetson* (1858) 4 CBNS 346. Where the agent has been engaged for a fixed period, earlier revocation may be a breach of contract, entitling the agent to claim damages. Nevertheless, the contract is still terminated and specific performance is not available since the contract is one for personal services. Agents instructed to sell property for a fixed commission cannot prevent the principal deciding not to sell: *Luxor (Eastbourne) Ltd v. Cooper* (see p.378 above).

Principals cannot revoke their authority once the agent has carried out, or is in the process of carrying out, their instructions. Principals cannot revoke the agent's authority if it is combined with an interest, for example where it is given as a security for a debt from the principal to the agent. Neither is it terminated by the principal's bankruptcy, death or insanity. Restrictions also apply for an irrevocable power of attorney, which is not terminated by bankruptcy, death or insanity of the donor: s.4 Powers of Attorney Act 1971. A lasting power of attorney was created by the Mental Capacity Act (MCA) 2005 and transposed into English law the Hague Convention on the International Protection of Adults of 13 January 2000 (Cm 5881). A lasting power of attorney (LPA) must be created in accordance with the Act and The Lasting Powers of Attorney, Enduring Powers of Attorney and Public Guardian Regulations (SI 1253/2007) and be registered with the Public Guardianship Office. LPAs replace the previous enduring power of attorney (EPA) (although EPAs created prior to 30 September 2007 are still legal if registered). The LPA and registered EPAs are not revoked by the supervening mental incapacity of the donor.

Problems arise where the principal effectively terminates the relationship by closing down or merging the business before the end of a fixed term agreement entitling the agent to commission, remuneration or some other benefit.

Generally, the agent will only be able to sue for damages for breach of contract under the terms of an express or implied term in the contract.

In *Rhodes v. Forwood* [1874–80] All ER Rep 476, the agent was authorised to arrange for the sale of all coal dispatched by a colliery owner in Liverpool for seven years on a commission basis. The colliery business was sold before the end of the period and the agent failed in an action for damages for breach of contract. The court held that there should have been express provision to that effect if it had been absolutely intended for the contract to run for seven years.

In *Turner v. Goldsmith* [1891] 1 QB 544, the claimant had a five-year contract as a salesman on commission which specified that he would sell 'any shirts or other goods manufactured or sold by' the defendant. The contract was not terminated when the defendant's factory was destroyed by fire, since it extended beyond goods manufactured by the defendant, and the court held that he was entitled to damages for lost commission.

In *Comet Group plc v. British Sky Broadcasting* [1991] TLR 211, Comet contracted with British Satellite Broadcasting to promote BSB's equipment until February 1991. This operated until BSB's merger with Sky Television in 1990, when it instructed Comet to suspend all further sales. Against Comet's claim for damages for repudiation, BSB claimed that the contract was a form of agency and the contract could not be held to imply that the principal would continue in business until its expiry. The court held that the contract differed from agency in a number of respects and awarded the claimants damages for breach of contract.

(b) Death, insanity or bankruptcy of the principal

Post-termination contracts are void and the agent is liable to the third party for damages for breach of warranty of authority.

In *Yonge v. Toynbee* [1910] 1 KB 215, solicitors instructed to defend an action continued in ignorance of their client's insanity, and were liable to indemnify the other party for post-termination costs. Although the agent's actual authority may be terminated by the principal's insanity, their ostensible authority may continue. In *Drew v. Nunn* (1879) 4 QBD

661, the ostensible authority of a wife to pledge her husband's credit for necessaries continued during his temporary insanity, making him liable to the suppliers.

The agent's authority is not terminated by their own bankruptcy, except where it disqualifies them from continuing, as in the case of company directors and licensed insolvency practitioners.

16.7 Commercial Agents

The Commercial Agents (Council Directive) Regulations 1993 (SI 1993/3053, as amended by SI 1993/3173) have strengthened the position of a commercial agent, defined as 'a self-employed intermediary who has continuing authority to negotiate the sale or purchase of goods on behalf of another person (the principal), or to negotiate and conclude the sale or purchase of goods on behalf of and in the name of that principal': reg. 2(1).

'Self-employed' includes companies as well as individuals, while 'continuing authority' excludes agents appointed for a specified number of transactions. The Regulations do not apply to unpaid commercial agents: reg. 2(2)(a); commercial agents when they operate on commodity exchanges or in the commodity market: reg. 2(2)(b); and commercial agents whose activities as such are considered secondary according to criteria set out in the Schedule to the Regulations: reg. 2(3). Certain agents known as 'canvassing' or 'introducing' agents and generally lacking the power to bind their principals could be within the regulations, but the DTI considers that *del credere* agents fall outside them.

Commercial agents must look after their principal's interests and act dutifully and in good faith: reg. 3(1); must make proper efforts to negotiate and, where appropriate, conclude the transactions they are instructed to take care of; communicate to their principal all the necessary information available to them; and comply with their principal's reasonable instructions: reg. 3(2).

Principals must act dutifully and in good faith: reg. 4(1); and (i) provide the agent with the necessary documentation relating to the goods; (ii) obtain the information necessary for the performance of the agency contract; and (iii) notify the agent within a reasonable period if they anticipate that the volume of transactions will be significantly lower than they could have expected: reg. 4.2(a) and (b). Principals must inform the agent within a reasonable period of their acceptance or refusal of, and any non-execution by them of, a commercial transaction which the agent has procured for them.

Commercial agents, failing agreement on remuneration, are entitled to that usually allowed to commercial agents for the goods where they carry on their activities and, if there is no customary practice, to a reasonable remuneration: reg. 6(1). Regulations 7–12 apply only to cases where a commercial agent is remunerated (wholly or in part) by commission. Agents are entitled to commission on transactions concluded during the period covered by the contracts, which arises whenever the principal and the third party have entered into a contract and extends to sales by the principal in an area where the agent has exclusive right, or to persons within a group in respect of which the agent has exclusive rights: reg. 7.

Agents may be entitled to commission on post-termination sales within a reasonable period resulting from their efforts, and on orders placed pre-termination but concluded afterwards: reg. 8. Regulation 9 apportions commission between a departing and an incoming agent. Commission should be paid as soon as one or more of the following occurs: (i) the principal has accepted or delivered the goods; (ii) the principal should have accepted or delivered the goods; (iii) the third party accepts or delivers the goods; or (iv) the third party pays for the goods: reg. 10 (1); and at the latest when the third party has executed their part of the transaction or should have done so if the principal had executed their part, as they should have done (reg. 10(2)), and not later than on the last day of the month following the quarter in which it became due: reg. 10(3).

Agreements derogating from reg. 10(2) and (3) to the agent's detriment are void: reg. 10(4). The right to commission can be forfeited should any contract not be executed through no fault of the principal, and commission paid is recoverable: reg. 11. The principal must provide a commission statement with the main components in its calculation and, on request, allow access to information to check the commission due: reg. 12 (see also p.251).

The agent and the principal are entitled to receive from the other on request a signed written document setting out the terms of the agency contract, including subsequently agreed terms: reg. 13(1). Where the contract is for an indeterminate period, either party may terminate it by notice: reg. 15(1). The minimum periods of notice are (a) one month for the first year; (b) two months for the second year commenced; and (c) three months for the third year commenced and for subsequent years, and the parties may not agree to a shorter period: reg. 13(2). If longer periods are agreed, the period cannot be shorter for the principal than for the agent: reg. 13(3); and, unless otherwise agreed, the end of the period of notice must coincide with the end of the calendar month: reg. 13(4). Where a fixed period agency contract continues to be performed after that period, it is deemed converted to an indeterminate period contract: reg. 14; and the periods of notice under reg. 15(2) apply.

Rules allowing immediate termination because of the failure of one party to carry out all or part of their contractual obligations and where exceptional circumstances arise (frustration) are preserved: reg. 16. Otherwise, the agent is entitled to indemnity/compensation on termination; the parties can opt for indemnity or compensation but the agent is entitled to compensation in default of an election: reg. 17.

Agents are entitled to an indemnity if and to the extent that (a) they have brought the principal new customers or have significantly increased the volume of business from existing customers, from which the principal continues to derive substantial benefits; and (b) the indemnity is equitable having regard to all the circumstances and, in particular, the commission lost by the commercial agent: reg. 17(3). Indemnity will not exceed one year's commission based on average annual remuneration over the preceding five years, or the average over a shorter period: reg. 17(4). The indemnity does not prevent the agent from seeking damages: reg. 17(5).

Commercial agents are entitled to compensation for the damage suffered as a result of termination of relations with the principal: reg. 17(6). The agent is compensated for damage arising which shall be deemed to occur particularly when the termination: (a) deprives the agent of the commission which proper performance of the contract would have procured while providing their principal with substantial benefits linked to the agent's activities; and/or (b) has not enabled them to amortise costs and expenses incurred on the advice of their principal: reg. 17(7). Problems arise concerning the quantification of the compensation.

In *Lonsdale v. Howard & Hallam Ltd* [2007] UKHL 32 the claimant was a commercial agent in the shoe trade. In 1990 the defendant shoe manufacturers appointed him as their agent. As a result of falling sales, the defendant ceased trading in 2003 and terminated the claimant's agency on the appropriate notice. The county court found that the net annual commission of the claimant was £8,000 and awarded him compensation of £5,000, and this was upheld by the Court of Appeal. The claimant appealed on the basis that the EC Commission had endorsed the method used by the French courts of valuing agencies at twice the average annual gross commission over the previous three years as being appropriate. Dismissing the appeal, the House of Lords held that the ECJ had made it clear that the method of calculating compensation was a matter for each Member State to decide, and that in the instant case the judge had been right in his approach that the damage for which the agent was to be compensated consisted of the loss of the value or goodwill which he could be said to have possessed in the agency.

In *Stuart Light and ors v. TY Europe Ltd* [2003] EWCA Civ 1238 the court held that a sub-agent of the principal, who therefore had no contract with him, had no right to compensation against the principal under reg. 17.

Entitlement to indemnity or compensation arises where termination is by the death of the agent: reg. 17(8); but is lost where the principal is not notified within one year of the termination: reg. 17(9).

A restraint of trade clause in agents' contracts is valid for not more than two years after termination of the contract and only if (a) in writing; and (b) relating to the geographical area or the group of customers and the geographical area entrusted to the commercial agent and to the kind of goods covered by his/her agency under the contract: reg. 20.

In *Page v. Combined Shipping and Trading Co. Ltd* [1997] 3 All ER 656, the claimant entered into a contract in January 1995 to buy and sell commodities on the defendant's behalf in return for half the net profit, for a minimum period of four years. In June 1995, the defendant informed the claimant that its South African parent had decided to cease trading. Treating this as a repudiatory breach, the claimant terminated the contract, sued for loss of commission under reg. 17(6) and sought a freezing injunction to restrain the defendant from removing assets to South Africa. The application was dismissed on the ground that, since the defendant could have operated the contract for the remaining period of time in such a way that the claimant would have made no money, the claimant had lost nothing and had no case for compensation under reg. 17. The Court of Appeal allowed the claimant's appeal and granted the restraint injunction. The court stated that, as the 1993 Regulations were enacted to protect and improve the position of commercial agents, it was arguable that the compensation payable to the agent under reg. 17 was based on the commission which he would have earned if the contract had continued to be performed in the proper manner, and not the commission that he would have earned if the defendant had reduced the trading over the period to nil, thereby reducing his liability to the claimant.

End of Chapter Summary

A knowledge of the law of agency is vital to understanding much of the law of business. The principles of the law of agency are crucial to the understanding of the relationship of partners to their firm and each other. The relationship and duties of the director to the company are based on the law of agency.

Having read and understood this chapter you should have a detailed knowledge of the following matters of particular significance:

End of Chapter Summary cont'd

▶ The way in which agents obtain their authority to act for the principal and the significance of actual, usual and estoppel authority.

▶ The duties of the agent to the principal with particular attention to the problem of conflict of interest.

▶ The rights of the agent against the principal and in particular the rights of commercial agents.

▶ The right of the principal to terminate the relationship of principal and agent and the problems of post-termination dealings by the agent.

▶ The special position of commercial agents.

Questions

1. Gallery d'Art operates a chain of galleries selling works by original artists and a framing service. One gallery is staffed by the manager, Tracy, who has no authority to buy in framing supplies, which are bought centrally, but has authority to buy paintings on behalf of the gallery, subject to a limit of £1,000 per painting.

   Tracy placed an order with a commercial traveller dealing in framing supplies for £4,000. Later the same week, she agreed to purchase five canvases from Damien, an up-and-coming artist, for £2,000 each.

   The Gallery d'Art wishes to avoid the contract for the framing supplies but is anxious to acquire the canvases.

   Advise it.

2. Drake is the owner of a cabin cruiser. He appointed Chandler Ltd as agent to find a buyer for the boat. Under the terms of the agreement, Chandler was to be paid 'a commission of 10% out of the proceeds of the purchase price'. Chandler Ltd placed advertisements in a number of specialist publications. As a result of its efforts, it was contacted by Raleigh who agreed to buy the boat at the asking price. When Chandler Ltd contacted Drake to inform him of the potential sale, Drake informed it that he had decided not to sell the boat after all.

   Advise Chandler Ltd of its position regarding its expenses and commission.

3. Gwen was employed by Organo Ltd, an organic bakery, to buy wheat on its behalf. Gwen negotiated with Bulk Ltd to buy a consignment of wheat on credit without informing Bulk Ltd that she was acting as an agent. Organo Ltd later contacted Bulk Ltd to give it delivery instructions for the consignment. Bulk Ltd refused to deliver the wheat to Organo Ltd. Had it known that Gwen was acting for Organo Ltd, it would have done so on much tighter credit terms, owing to Organo Ltd's poor credit rating.

   Advise Organo Ltd and Gwen of their legal position.

4. A Ltd advertised and sold goods by direct mail for P Ltd and a number of its companies. A Ltd was reimbursed by P Ltd for the cost of placing its advertisements. Because of the volume of advertisements placed by A Ltd, the newspapers in which it advertised gave a 5 per cent discount on the cost of the advertisements. A Ltd, in claiming reimbursement for the cost of advertising for P Ltd, failed to inform P Ltd of the discount and P Ltd paid the full list price.

   P Ltd has recently discovered the existence of the discounts received by A Ltd and has claimed the right to recover the aggregate of the discounts received over the last four years, together with a return of the commission for the sales during the same period.

   Advise A Ltd of the situation.

Chapter 17

Employment contracts

Learning objectives

After reading this chapter you will know about:

- employees and independent contractors
- casual, part-time and temporary workers' rights
- discrimination and employment contracts
- unfair dismissal
- employee protection and takeovers.

17.1 Contracts of service and contracts for services

Contracts of service are between employer and employee; contracts for services are between an employer and a self-employed person, an independent contractor.

Employees enjoy more legal protection than independent contractors. In the UK, a multiple test is used to determine employee status based on the employer's control over the worker, the place of work, who supplies the tools and equipment and the parties' own view of their relationship.

Ready Mixed Concrete v. Minister of Pensions and National Insurance [1968] 2 QB 497 in a dispute as to the company's liability for national insurance contributions for a team of owner-drivers, the drivers owned and maintained their own lorries, which they bought on hire purchase from a Ready Mixed subsidiary, the lorries were painted in the company colours and could only be used for company work. The drivers could delegate the driving, but the company could insist on personal performance. The drivers had no fixed hours and set their own routes, but they had to be available when required and obey reasonable orders 'as if … an employee', and were paid a guaranteed wage and performance-related payments. They were held to be independent contractors.

In *Ferguson v. John Dawson & Partners (Contractors)* [1976] 1 WLR 1213, the claimant was injured falling from an unprotected roof. He was paid as if self-employed without deductions for tax and national insurance, he was under the site agent's control, tools were provided by the company and he was paid hourly. The Court of Appeal held that he was an employee, a main factor being that he had no choice in respect of his status.

In other cases, the question of choice has been crucial and a determining factor, even though there is no change in the substance of the contract.

In *Express & Echo v. Taunton* [1999] IRLR 367. Taunton, a redundant delivery driver, was re-engaged as a self-employed driver. The work was as before and he drove the company's van on routes fixed by the company to the company's instructions. The contract provided, however, that if he was unwilling or unable to drive, he would find a substitute driver. The Court of Appeal held that the essential element of personal service in a contract of service was removed by the substitution clause.

In *Massey v. Crown Life Insurance Co.* [1978] 1 WLR 676, a branch manager requested a change of status to independent contractor and was unsuccessful in establishing employee status for the purpose of a claim for unfair dismissal. In *Catamaran Cruisers Ltd v. Williams* [1994] IRLR 501, W's employer asked him to provide his services through a limited company which was paid a fee. The Employment Appeals Tribunal (EAT) held that Williams had remained an employee.

(a)   Casual workers

The situation is more complex for casual or quasi-casual workers, including home, seasonal and catering workers.

In *Airfix Footwear v. Cope* [1978] ICR 121, a homeworker worked for seven years assembling parts of shoes. Equipment was provided by the company, she was paid on a piecework basis and was responsible for her own tax and national insurance. In a claim for unfair dismissal, the company argued that no employer–employee relationship existed because there was no mutuality of the obligation to offer work and the obligation to accept it. The Court of Appeal held that the regularity of the relationship over the seven-year period was sufficient to establish this mutual obligation.

In *O'Kelly and Others v. Trusthouse Forte plc* [1983] IRLR 369, THF relied on casual workers for banquets. Some were 'regular casuals', and there was sufficient work to ensure full-time employment for them. The claimant regulars were dismissed for trying to organise a union. The following factors indicated employee status: (i) the claimants had no personal investment in the business; (ii) they were under the company's direct control; (iii) they were part and parcel of THF; (iv) they were furthering the business of THF; (v) their uniforms and equipment were supplied by THF; (vi) their work roster was fixed, and permission was required to take time off; (vii) they were governed by a disciplinary and grievance procedure; and (viii) they could benefit from a holiday pay or incentive bonus scheme based on past services. Against this, four factors indicated self-employed status: (i) they were not entitled to notice; (ii) they could refuse to work on a particular roster; (iii) THF had no obligation to provide work or pay them; and (iv) both sides believed they were independent contractors. The Court of Appeal held that they were independent contractors.

(b)   Part-time workers

Part-timers have equal treatment with comparable full-time workers under the Part-time Workers (Prevention of Less Favourable Treatment) Regulations 2000 (SI 2000 No.1551), as amended, implementing the Part-time Workers Directive (97/81/EC, [1997] OJ L14/9). Part-time workers are those paid wholly or partly by reference to the time worked and are not full-time workers, excluding employees under apprenticeship contracts and workers who are not employees: reg. 2(3).

The regulation applies to full-time workers who have become part-time workers: reg. 3, and those who were previously full-time workers returning after an absence of less than 12 months to the same job or one at the same level, under a contract requiring them to work for fewer hours than immediately before their absence: reg. 4(1).

A comparable full-time worker is somebody employed by the same employer under the same type of contract and engaged in the same or broadly similar work, having regard to their similar levels of qualification, skills and experience and working or based at the same or at a different establishment.

Part-time workers are to be treated no less favourably than a comparable full-time worker unless justified on objective grounds: reg. 5(1) and (2). The pro rata principle is applied to determine whether they have been treated less favourably, and workers can ask for a written statement of the reasons for the treatment within 21 days: reg. 6(1). Employees dismissed as a result of having brought proceedings, having requested a written statement or having given evidence or information in connection with such proceedings are unfairly dismissed under Part X Employment Act 1996: reg. 7(2) and (3). Complaints may be made to an employment tribunal within three months (or six months where reg. 13 applies): reg. 8(1) and (2).

Acts by employees in the course of their employment are treated as being done by the employer, whether or not done with their knowledge or approval, and acts by employers' agents with their authority are treated as being done by the employer: reg. 11(1) and (2). In respect of acts by workers, employers have a defence if they can prove they took reasonable steps to prevent the worker from doing that act or acts of that description: reg. 11(3).

The Regulations apply to Crown employees, the armed forces and the police service, but not to holders of judicial office remunerated on a daily fee-paid basis. The regulations mean that part-timers:

▷ must not receive a lower basic rate of pay than comparable full-timers unless justifiable on objective grounds;
▷ have a legal right to overtime payments at the same hourly rate as full-timers once they have worked up to the full-time hours of comparable full-timers;
▷ must be treated equally as regards entitlement to contractual sick and maternity pay;
▷ must not be discriminated against in respect of access to occupational pensions;
▷ must have equal access to training, which should be scheduled so that part-timers can attend;
▷ are entitled to a minimum of statutory annual leave, maternity leave, parental leave, and time off to look after dependants, including any enhancement on a pro rata basis where appropriate;
▷ must not be treated less favourably in the selection of jobs for redundancy.

(c) Fixed-term employees

Fixed-term employees have the right to equal treatment with comparable permanent employees under the Fixed Term Employees (Prevention of Less Favourable Treatment) Regulations 2002 (SI 2002 No. 2034) implementing the EC Fixed-term Work Directive (99/70/EC, [1999] OJ L175/43). Fixed-term employees are employed under a contract which will terminate:

(a) on the expiry of a specific term,
(b) on the completion of a particular task,
(c) on the occurrence or non-occurrence of any other specific event other than attainment of a normal and *bona fide* retiring age in the establishment in his position: reg. 1(2).

The rights and remedies are comparable to those established in respect of part-time workers, including a statement of a right to equal treatment: reg. 3, the right to a written statement of reasons for less favourable treatment: reg. 5, the presumption of unfair dismissal where the reason or principal reason for the dismissal is seeking to enforce the rights under the regulation: reg. 6, and a right to take a complaint to an employment tribunal: reg. 7. In addition, however, where an employee, continuously employed on fixed-term contracts for four years or more, is re-engaged on a fixed-term contract, the new contract operates as a permanent contract unless renewal on a fixed-term basis was objectively justified: reg. 8.

(d) Agency workers

Employment agencies and employment businesses are regulated by the Employment Agencies and Businesses Regulations 2004. They were intended to promote flexibility and increase protection, both for workers who find employment through agencies and for businesses which use them for permanent recruitment or temporary cover (users). Key benefits for users under the Regulations are an increased obligation on employment agencies to vet workers and restrictions on 'temp to perm' fees charged by the employment businesses.

The regulations distinguish between employment agencies and employment businesses. The former introduce workers to a user who then contracts directly with the worker for a permanent or temporary role, whilst the latter enter contracts with the workers and supply their services to the user. Many of the obligations apply to both, and the general obligations are:

- To state clearly in their terms and conditions the basis on which they act and to explain this to workers and users;
- Not to enter contracts on behalf of workers or users without authority and to notify people of their terms and conditions as soon as possible;
- To notify users about all charges – charges to workers are generally prohibited but for exceptional cases e.g. theatrical agencies;
- To explain the type of work the agency or business will find or seek to find for the worker.

Employment businesses are obliged to pay workers even if the user does not pay the employment businesses' invoices, regardless of whether the user has verified the hours worked. Employment agencies are prohibited from paying or being in any way connected with paying fees to those they introduce to a user.

Employment agencies/businesses are prohibited from withholding services in exchange for variation of standard terms. If they make any mutually agreed variations, the employment agency/businesses must within five business days provide workers with a single document setting out the terms as agreed to be varied and the date from which the terms as varied are to take effect. Workers have the right not to suffer any detriment if they decide to seek work through another agency/business or a third party. They are entitled not to be introduced or supplied to a user unless the agency/business has ascertained:

- The identity of the user
- The type of work and its likely duration

- Work hours
- Required qualifications, training and experience
- Expenses payable
- Any health and safety issues, and
- Employment agencies only – the minimum rate of remuneration and other benefits, the payment intervals and length of notice of termination of the employment.

Agency workers are unlikely to be regarded as employees and will not enjoy employment protection rights. They are, however, covered by the Working Time Regulations 1998, reg. 36, and the National Minimum Wage Act 1998, s.36. They are to be treated as having a worker's contract, either with the agency or the principal, depending on who is responsible for paying them.

On 20 May 2008, there was a joint declaration by the government, the CBI and the TUC concerning the draft EU Temporary Agency Workers Directive (COM(2002)149) whereby, after 12 weeks, agency workers will become entitled to 'equal treatment'. This means that the basic working and employment conditions (e.g. pay and holidays) will apply to the agency workers as if they had been recruited directly as permanent staff to do the same job. Equal treatment will not cover occupational social security schemes (e.g. pensions and sickness benefit schemes). The government obtained agreement with its European partners on the terms of the Agency Workers Directive (Directive 2008/94, [2008] OJ L283/36, approved and adopted by the European Parliament on 22 October 2008) and hopes to introduce legislation in the next parliamentary session.

Hot Topic . . .

UK OPT-OUT UNDER THE WORKING TIME REGULATIONS 1998

Britain has an opt-out from the Working Time Directive (Directive 93/104/EC, [1993] OJ L307/18), which establishes a maximum working week of 48 hours. This is done by requiring employees to agree to opt out of the protection offered by the Directive, usually as a condition of their employment. The Confederation of British Industries (CBI) and the government see the opt-out as a cornerstone of flexible labour markets. According to Brussels, a third of the UK workforce has opted out, but only half work more than the current maximum of 48 hours. The TUC claims that this still means that 3.75 million workers have opted out, of whom one in four have claimed that they were given no choice.

On 10 June 2008, the UK obtained agreement from Europe for the continuation of the opt-out from the Working Times Directive.

17.2 Formation of the contract of employment

The contract is regulated by the Employment Rights Act (ERA) 1996 and may be written, oral, implied from conduct or in a combination of those forms. However, the employer must – with some exceptions – provide a written statement of particulars of employment within two months of the start: s.1(1) and (2). This must contain particulars of: (a) the names of the employer and employee; (b) the date when the employment began; and (c) the date on which the employee's period of continuous employment began: s.1(3). It must also contain particulars of:

(a)   the scale or rate of remuneration, or the method of calculating remuneration;

(b)   the intervals at which remuneration is paid (weekly, monthly and so on);

(c)   any terms or conditions relating to hours of work, including normal working hours;

(d)   any terms and conditions relating to any of the following: (i) entitlement to holidays, including public holidays, and holiday pay; (ii) incapacity for work because of sickness or injury, including any provision for sick pay; and (iii) pensions and pension schemes;

(e)   the length of notice which the employee is required to give and entitled to receive to terminate his/her contract of employment;

(f)   the title of the job or a brief description of the work for which s/he is employed;

(g)   where the employment is not intended to be permanent, the period for which it is expected to continue or, if it is for a fixed term, the date when it is to end;

(h)   either the place of work or, where the employee is required or permitted to work at various places, an indication of that and the address of the employer;

(i)   any collective agreements which directly affect the terms and conditions of the employment, including, where the employer is not a party, the persons by whom they were made;

(j)   where the employee is required to work outside the UK for a period of more than one month – (i) the period for which s/he is to work; (ii) the currency in which remuneration is to be paid; (iii) any additional remuneration payable and any benefits to be provided; and (iv) any terms and conditions relating to his/her return to the UK: s.1(4).

The statement must also include a note specifying (a) any applicable disciplinary rules, or refer workers to a reasonably accessible document specifying such rules; (b) (i) the persons to whom they can apply if dissatisfied with any disciplinary decision; and (ii) the persons to whom they can apply for redress of any grievance relating to their employment, and the manner in which the application should be made; and (c), where there are further steps consequent on any such application, explaining those steps or referring to the provisions of a reasonably accessible document explaining them: s.3(1).

This section does not apply to rules, disciplinary decisions or procedures relating to health and safety at work: s.3(2). The rules are relaxed if, on commencement of the employment, the relevant number of employees was less than 20. If there is a change to any of the matters in the statement, the employer must give a written statement of particulars of the change: s.4(1). This must be given not later than (a) one month after the change; or (b), where the change results in the employee being required to work outside the UK for more than one month, the time of leaving the UK, if that is earlier: s.4(3).

(a)   Duty to pay wages

Employers have no obligation to provide employees with work as long as their wages are paid unless those employees are on commission or piecework, or where the publicity generated by the work is as important as the wages. In *Herbert Clayton & Jack Waller Ltd v. Oliver* [1930] AC 209, the employer was in breach of contract where the employee, who had had the leading role in a play, was given a smaller part at the same salary. Another exception is where employees need to maintain a level of expertise.

In *William Hill Organisation Ltd v. Tucker* [1999] ICR 291, T was placed on 'garden leave' for his contractual six-month notice period, during which time he could not work for a competitor. The Court of Appeal held that T's job required continual practice and that a clause in the contract stated that the employer would ensure that the employee had every opportunity to develop his skills.

Employees are entitled to a written, itemised statement of the gross wages, the amounts of any variable and fixed (subject to s.9) deductions and their purpose, the net amount of wages, and, where different parts of the net amount are paid in different ways, the amount and method of each part payment: s.8. Wages are defined as any sums payable to worker in connection with his/her employment, including any fee, bonus, commission, holiday pay or other emolument referable to his/her employment, whether payable under his/her contract or otherwise, including entitlement to statutory sick pay, maternity pay and so on.

Employers are prohibited from making unauthorised deductions from wages: s.13. In the retail trade, there are restrictions on deductions for cash shortages or stock deficiencies: s.18, determining wages by reference to shortages or deficiencies: s.19, and limiting payments from employees for shortages and deficiencies: ss.20 and 21.

The level of pay is governed by the National Minimum Wage Act (NMWA) 1998 implemented by the National Minimum Wage Regulations 1999 (see below p.395).

(b)   Terms implied by common law into a contract of employment

(i)   Duty to maintain mutual trust and confidence
Neither employer nor employee should act in such a way as to damage the mutual trust and confidence which ought to exist between them. This duty is particularly important in connection with constructive dismissal, where employees claim to have been dismissed because of a fundamental breach of the contract of employment by the employer (see p.413).

Hot Topic . . .

EMPLOYERS' DUTY TO EMPLOYEES

Employers must not 'without reasonable and proper cause' conduct themselves in a manner 'calculated and likely to destroy or seriously damage the relationship of confidence and trust between employer and employee': *Woods v. WM Car Services (Peterborough) Ltd* [1981] ICR 666 at p. 670. In *Spring v. Guardian Assurance plc* [1994] 3 All ER 129 at p. 161, Lord Slynn of Hadley noted: 'the changes which have taken place in the employer/employee relationship, with far greater duties imposed on the employer than in the past … to care for the physical, financial and even psychological welfare of the employee'.

In *Malik v. BCCI SA* [1997] 3 All ER 1, two bank employees obtained 'stigma compensation' for being disadvantaged for future employment by the bank's dishonest conduct. The House of Lords held that there was an implied fundamental term that an employer will not 'without reasonable and proper cause, conduct itself in a manner likely to destroy or seriously damage the relationship of trust and confidence between employer and employee'. In a later case relating to the bank, the trial judge found that there were reasons the appellants had been unable to find employment and that stigma was not one of them. The Court of Appeal held that the burden was on the claimant to prove that the failure to obtain employment was the breach of trust and confidence: *BCCI SA v. Ali and Others (No. 2)* [2002] 3 All ER 750.

In *O'Brien v. Transco plc (formerly BG plc)* [2002] All ER 80, O'Brien was engaged in 1995 by BG through an employment agency. In the summer of 1996, BG offered enhanced redundancy terms to all 'permanent employees' within O'Brien's division except him, since BG did not believe him to be a permanent employee. The tribunal's decision that O'Brien had been a 'permanent employee' at the material time and that BG had acted in breach of its duty of trust and confidence was upheld by the EAT and the Court of Appeal. The Tribunal rejected the employer's argument that the duty of trust and confidence was purely negative in form; that it simply prohibited conduct likely to destroy or seriously damage trust and confidence, but did not compel an employer to act to avoid such consequences. The Court of Appeal stressed that the correct approach was to look objectively at the substance of the conduct and, if the effect or likely effect was to destroy or seriously damage trust and confidence, then there was a *prima facie* breach of the term. Once this had been identified, the question was whether the employer had acted 'without reasonable and proper cause'. In this case BG's reasonable belief that Mr O'Brien was not a permanent employee was not grounds for depriving the employee of the improved terms of employment.

(ii) Employees' duty to obey reasonable and lawful orders

The situation for tasks outside the employee's normal job description may depend on the status of the work, whether it is a temporary or permanent requirement, the company's financial position, and even the job market.

In *Secretary of State v. ASLEF (No. 2)* [1972] 2 QB 455, the Court of Appeal found working to rule a breach of an implied term of the employment contract, variously described as a duty not wilfully to obstruct the employer's business or not to obey instructions in a wholly unreasonable way, or a duty to promote the commercial interests of the employer.

In a case involving a teacher, the court stressed the professional nature of the employment and that this sort of duty could be limited to such employees, *Sim v. Rotherham BC* [1987] Ch 216.

(iii) Fiduciary duties of employees

The fiduciary duties arising under the contract of employment can be broken down into a number of specific duties.

Duty not to compete
In *Hivac Ltd v. Park Royal Scientific Instruments Ltd* [1946] Ch 169, a skilled employee was restricted from working, even in a spare-time capacity, for an employer's rival (for company directors see Chapter 11, p.251).

Duty of confidentiality
Employees cannot use for their own benefit or communicate to others any confidential information which came to their knowledge during their employment.

In *Faccenda Chicken Ltd v. Fowler* [1987] Ch 117, F was dismissed for theft and, with other ex-employees, set up a rival operation using sales information – client lists and requirements, delivery routes, times and pricing. The court identified three categories of information: information so readily available that it was never confidential even during employment; information confidential during employment but which employees could use on leaving employment; and information which remained confidential even after the termination of employment. Information concerning clients of the ex-employer was within the second category and could be used by ex-employees unless protected by a valid restraint of trade clause.

In *A-G v. Blake* [1998] 1 All ER 833, an ex-member of the secret service published a book without permission. The Court of Appeal held that the fiduciary duty and the duty of confidentiality lasted only for as long as the relationship and for as long as the information remained confidential. Submitting the manuscript without clearance was not in breach as the material was no longer secret or confidential. An injunction, however, restrained B from receiving further royalties.

An important exception relates to 'whistle-blowers', now regulated by the Public Interest Disclosure Act 1998. In *Babula v. Waltham Forest College* [2007] EWCA Civ 174 it was held that where an employee made a claim for unfair dismissal asserting that it was to be regarded as automatically unfair because he had made a protected disclosure, it was sufficient that he reasonably believed the matters relied on to amount to a criminal offence, or founded a legal obligation. He did not have to be able to point to an actual criminal offence or to an actual legal obligation.

Duty not to make secret profits

Employees must not make secret profits by using the employer's name or equipment or any confidential information. Where the secret profit is innocent, the employer can recover the profit from the employees but not dismiss them or refuse to pay remuneration. Where the secret profit is not innocent or they take bribes, employees can be dismissed (see Chapter 16, p.377).

Duty to disclose misconduct

A senior executive has a duty to report misconduct of other employees to the employer.

In *Sybron Corp. v. Rochem* [1985] Ch 299, the employee was the European operations manager of an American company who received a generous payment from his employer on taking early retirement. It was later discovered that he, in conspiracy with other employees, had been defrauding the company for years by diverting business to a rival company set up for the purpose. The court held that his breach of duty to disclose the misconduct of the employees (which would have revealed his own complicity) entitled the employer to set aside the compensation payments (see Chapter 3, p.62).

(iv) Duty of care

Employers have a common law duty to: (i) take reasonable care for the employees' safety; (ii) provide safe tools and equipment; (iii) provide safe places of work and a safe system of work; and (iv) ensure that employees have properly skilled co-employees.

The employer's failure to insure the employee does not give the employee a civil action against the employer for breach of statutory duty: *Richardson v. Pitt-Stanley and Others* [1995] 2 WLR 26.

17.3 Health and safety at work

Employers owe a statutory duty to their employees and those of any subcontractors under the Health and Safety at Work Act 1974: *R v. Swan Hunter Shipbuilders Ltd and Another* [1982] 1 All ER 204. The duty is generally defined in s.2(1), and particular duties are spelt out in s.2(2), including the provision and maintenance of plant and systems of work which are safe and without risks to health; arrangements for ensuring safety and the absence of risks to health in connection with the use, handling, storage and transport of articles and substances; the provision of such information, instruction, training and supervision as is necessary to ensure the health and safety at work of their employees; the maintenance of any place of work in a condition that is safe and without risks to health; and the provision and maintenance of a working environment that is without risks to health and adequate as regards facilities and arrangements for employees' welfare at work.

In *R. v. Gateway Foodmarkets Ltd* [1997] 3 All ER 78, the Court of Appeal held that s.2(1) imposed strict liability on an employer and that, in the case of a corporate employer, the company was liable unless all reasonable precautions had been taken by its servants and agents. In *R. v. HTM Ltd* [2006] EWCA Crim 1156, following the fatal injury of two employees the defendant company was charged with breach of duty under s.2(1). It sought to establish that it had taken all reasonably practicable steps to ensure the safety of the two employees by training and instructions, that the accident had resulted from the employees' actions and that their actions were unforeseeable. The prosecution argued that foreseeability played no part and that the defendant was precluded by reg. 21(b) of the Management of Health and Safety at Work Regulations 1999 from relying on any act or default of the employees. The court held that a defendant could not be prevented from bringing evidence to show that it had taken all reasonable means to eliminate the risk. Regulation 21 did not apply and the defendants would be entitled to bring forward evidence to show that what had happened was the fault of the employees.

In *Ellis v. Bristol City Council* [2007] EWCA Civ 685 it was held that judges should consider the Health and Safety Commission's Code of Practice when deciding whether a workplace was unsafe. In this case, the Code supported the construction that if a smooth floor was frequently and regularly slippery because of a substance which lay on it, albeit only temporarily, the surface might properly said to be unsuitable if such as to give rise to a risk to the safety of employees using it.

The Provision and Use of Work Equipment Regulations 1998 impose strict liability in respect of 'work equipment', defined as 'any machinery, appliance, apparatus, tool or installation for use at work (whether exclusively so or not)', and 'use' in relation to work equipment meant 'any activity involving work equipment and includes starting, stopping, programming, setting, transporting, repairing, modifying, maintaining, servicing and cleaning': reg. 2(1). Employers must ensure that work equipment is constructed or adapted to be suitable for the purpose for which it is used or provided (reg. 4(1)) and that it is maintained in an efficient state, in efficient working order and in good repair: reg. 5(1). Employers must ensure that, where the safety of work equipment depends on the installation conditions, it is inspected: reg. 6.

In *Smith v. Northamptonshire CC* [2008] EWCA Civ 181 the claimant, a carer, brought proceedings in respect of an injury caused when pushing a wheelchair down a ramp leading from the living room to the patio belonging to a handicapped person. The ramp had been chosen and installed by the NHS. The authority successfully appealed against a finding that the 1998 Regulations applied. The authority had no control over the ramp sufficient to enable it to perform the obligations under the Regulations.

17.4 Statutory employment rights

(a) The right to a minimum wage

The National Minimum Wage Act (NMWA) 1998, implemented by the National Minimum Wage Regulations 1999, covers 'workers'. defined in s.54. This is wider than 'employees' and includes some workers on contracts for services. Agency workers are expressly covered, and the employer is the one responsible for paying the workers or who actually pays them: s.34. Homeworkers are also included, and the Secretary of State has power to extend the legislation to 'any individual of a prescribed description who would not otherwise count within the definition of "worker"'.

The Regulations distinguish between different age groups, and only workers of 22 and above are entitled to the full minimum wage. The regulations exclude from the provisions workers aged 16 and 17, and there are lower rates fixed for workers between 18 and 22, with further complicated provisions relating to apprentices and trainees. Calculations are based on gross pay, but provisions prevent employers from claiming to be paying the minimum wage by including sums payable for other reasons, including any premium overtimes rates. Elements which count include: incentive payments; performance-related pay; bonuses and tips.

Employers must keep adequate records, and workers can claim before an employment tribunal for alleged breaches where the burden is on the employer to disprove the truth of the claim. Workers can also bring claims for dismissal or discrimination for claiming their right to a minimum wage or because they are or will become entitled to it.

(b) The right to equal pay

Article 141 (previously Art. 119) EC Treaty requires that 'men and women should receive equal pay for equal work'. This has been supplemented by the Equal Pay Directive 1975 and the Equal Treatment Directive 1976 which was held to have direct 'vertical' effect in Case 152/84, *Marshall v. Southampton & South West Hampshire Area Health Authority (Teaching)* [1986] ECR 723, allowing enforcement against the state or an organ of the state, and not private individuals or companies.

The Equal Pay Act (EPA) 1970 includes 'all aspects and conditions of remuneration' and covers travel concessions for retired employees: Case 12/81, *Garland v. British Rail Engineering* [1982] ECR 359; access to occupational pension schemes: Case C–57/93, *Vroege v. NCIV Instituut voor Volkshuisvesting BV* [1994] ECR I–4541; age of retirement: Case 152/84, *Marshall v. Southampton & South West Hampshire Area Health Authority (Teaching)* [1986] ECR 723; pension age, and pension benefits and statutory or contractual severance payments: Case 262/88, *Barber v. Guardian Royal Exchange Assurance Group* [1991] 2 WLR 72.

The Pensions Act 1995 provided for equal treatment under occupational pension schemes and the phasing in of a common retirement age of 65 between 2010 and 2020. The exclusion of part-time workers from occupational pension schemes was removed by the Part-time Workers (Prevention of Less Favourable Treatment) Regulations 2000 (SI 2000 No.1551) (as amended), which also removed indirect discrimination of part-timers in calculating redundancy severance pay.

The EPA 1970 allows men and women to claim equal terms with an employee of the opposite sex employed by the same or an associated employer in respect of like work; work rated as equivalent; and work of equal value. Where an equal pay claim succeeds, the woman's contract is deemed to include an equality clause which has the effect that any term of the contract which is less favourable is modified to become as favourable as the man's: s.1, EPA 1970.

Hot Topic . . .

DELAY IN ACHIEVING EQUAL PAY

On 18 September 2008, and in spite of the length of time for which the equality legislation had existed, the Chartered Management Institute reported that women managers will have to wait 187 years to achieve equal pay with men at the current rate of progress. Its annual salary survey showed the average woman in British management earned £32,614 in the 12 months to March 2008, compared with £46,269 for her male counterparts. The survey showed that the pay of women managers will not outstrip that of men until 2195 and that, on current trends, female managers at board level in Scotland will not achieve parity until 2366. The Institute's marketing director said that to have to wait several generations was inexcusable, and that it was time that the lip service of the three decades since sex discrimination was first outlawed was transformed into action. The survey found that the biggest gender gap was in the insurance industry, where male managers earned 45.2 per cent more than women. The gap was smallest in the pharmaceutical industry at 14.9 per cent.

In *Redcar and Cleveland BC v. Bainbridge & Surtees v. Middlesborough Council* [2008] EWCA Civ 885 the court ruled that negotiated proposals by the councils to phase in a system of equal pay which provided protection over several years for male staff, who were due to lose out under the new arrangements, perpetuated unlawful discrimination and could not be justified unless the women were given equivalent benefits. The court accepted arguments from the Equality and Human Rights Commission that employers and unions should be allowed some freedom to negotiate a way out of the problem without causing a financial crisis in the public sector. The judgment by Mummery LJ set out ground rules for negotiations to eliminate discrimination as fast as possible in the financial circumstances of each local authority and NHS trust.

(i) *Like work*

A woman does like work if it is 'of the same or a broadly similar nature' to that of a man.

In *Capper Pass v. Lawton* [1977] QB 852, a woman cook in the directors' dining room who prepared lunches for 10–20 people per day successfully claimed the same rate of pay as two male chefs working in the staff canteen preparing 350 meals a day in six sittings.

(ii) *Equivalent work*

Equivalent work enables comparisons between totally different jobs. If the man's and the woman's jobs have been rated as of equivalent value, then the woman is entitled to equal pay: s.1(5) EPA 1970. In *Redcar and Cleveland BC v. Bainbridge and Ors* [2007] EWCA Civ 929 it was held that a woman, who could base an equal pay claim on a man in the same grade under s.2(1)(b) EPA 1970, where their two jobs were rated as equivalent, could also base a claim on a comparison with a man in a lower grade who received more pay than she did.

(iii) *Work of equal value*

This enables female employees to claim that their work is as valuable as a man's, even though completely different. An independent expert investigates the claim, which is limited to a male employed by the same or an associated employer at the same or at a different establishment sharing common terms and conditions for relevant categories of staff. The woman can freely choose the comparator, and may even choose several.

In Case 129/79, *Macarthys Ltd v. Smith* [1980] ECR 1275, a woman employed as a stockroom manager discovered that she was being paid less than her male predecessor. The ECJ held that, although the Act seems to restrict claims to cases where men and women are employed at the same time, the principle of equal pay should not be limited by the requirement of contemporaneity.

(iv)   Defences

Employers may show that the difference is caused by a material factor other than sex – including length of service, merit, qualifications and so on. The court has accepted arguments relating to market forces, where differences are justified by employees' different routes of entry, grading structures and collective bargaining, and where the employees belonged to different unions.

A further defence is 'red-circling' where an employee (usually male) is moved to a lower rated job because of ill health or job re-grading, but is still paid at the higher rate. Other factors are geographical differences, including the 'London weighting': *NAAFI v. Varley* [1977] 1 WLR 149.

In *Leverton v. Clwyd County Council* [1987] 1 WLR 65, the House of Lords held that there was a genuine material difference between a nursery nurse and clerical staff since, although the nursery nurse had a lower salary, she worked four and a half hours fewer per week and had 50 days extra holiday per year.

In *Hayward v. Cammell Laird Shipbuilders (No. 2)* [1988] AC 894, a canteen cook successfully claimed her work was of equal value with that of three male employees: a painter, a thermal insulation engineer and a joiner. The employer claimed she was £11 better off rather than £25 worse off, on the basis of the total package. The House of Lords rejected the claim on the basis of the overall job package and held that each aspect was to be separately considered and brought up to the best possible standard.

This approach was endorsed by the ECJ in Case 262/88, *Barber v. Guardian Royal Exchange Assurance Group* [1990] ECR I–1889.

(c)   Flexible working

Employees have the statutory right to request flexible working under the Flexible Working (Procedural Requirements) Regulations 2002 (SI 2002/3207) where:

(a) the change relates to:
    (i)   the hours they are required to work,
    (ii) the times when they are required to work,
    (iii) where they are required to work, or
    (iv) such other aspect of their terms and conditions of employment as the Secretary of State may specify by regulations, and
(b) their purpose in applying is to enable them to care for someone who, at the time of application, is a child in respect of whom they satisfy such conditions as to relationship as the Secretary of State may specify: s.80F(1).

The application must indicate the required change and the date from which it operates and explain how the employee thinks the employer would be affected, how this might be dealt with, and how the conditions as to relationship between the employee and the child are met: s.80F(2).

Applications must be made at least 14 days before the child reaches the age of six or, if disabled, 18: s.80F(3). No further application can be made to the same employer within 12 months from the date of a previous application: s.80F(4).

Employers must either hold a meeting to discuss the application or agree to the contract variation in writing within 28 days and notify the employee in writing of their decision within 14 days after the meeting. Employers can refuse applications only on one or more of the following grounds:

(i)   the burden of additional costs,
(ii)   detrimental effect on ability to meet customer demand,
(iii) inability to reorganise work among existing staff,
(iv)   inability to recruit additional staff,
(v)   detrimental impact on quality,
(vi)   detrimental impact on performance,
(vii) insufficiency of work during the periods the employee proposes to work,
(viii) planned structural changes,
(ix)   such other grounds as the Secretary of State may specify by regulations: s.80G(1).

Employees can appeal against the employer's decision: regs. 6–11, and be accompanied by a fellow worker at the meeting to discuss the application or the appeal: regs. 14–16. If the employer refuses to allow or threatens to refuse to allow the employee to be accompanied, the employee may complain to the employment tribunal. Employees and their companions are protected against detriment or dismissal.

Employees may also present a complaint to an employment tribunal (a) that the employer has failed to comply with s.80G(1) in respect of the application, or (b) that rejection of the application was on incorrect facts: s.80H. No complaint may be made in respect of an application which has been disposed of by agreement or withdrawn under reg. 17.

The tribunal can order the application to be reconsidered, and award compensation to a maximum of two weeks' pay. Employees are protected against detrimental treatment following the exercise of their rights and, if dismissed, are regarded as unfairly dismissed if the reason (or the principal reason) is seeking to exercise rights under the regulation.

(d)   Maternity rights

The rights for pregnant workers are in the Pregnant Workers Directive (92/85/EC, [1992] OJ L348/1) which are transposed into UK law by the Employment Rights Act (ERA) 1996, as amended by the Employment Relations Act 1999, the Maternity and Parental Leave Regulations (MPLR) 1999 (as amended) and the Work and Families Act 2006. They provide four protections for pregnant employees:

▸ the right to maternity leave and to return to work,
▸ the right to time off with pay for antenatal care: ss.55–57; and
▸ the right to maternity pay: ss.71–85.
▸ the right not to be dismissed on the grounds of pregnancy: s.99.

(i)   The Right to Maternity Leave

All pregnant employees are entitled to maternity leave of 52 weeks classified as Compulsory Maternity Leave (CML), Ordinary Maternity Leave (OML) and Additional Maternity Leave (AML).

CML is part of OML and is two weeks starting with the date of birth. Employers commit a criminal offence if they allow employees to work during this period: s.72 ERA 1996 and reg. 8 MPLR 1999. OML covers the first 26 weeks of maternity leave. It cannot start until the eleventh week before the expected week of childbirth or the first day of the sixth week before the expected week of childbirth: s.72(1). The latest start date is the day of childbirth: s.72(2).

During OML, the employee is entitled to the benefit of the terms and conditions of employment which would have been applicable to her if she had not been absent (and not been pregnant or given birth to a child): s.71(1). This includes pension scheme membership, use of a company car and the accrual of holiday entitlement, but no entitlement to remuneration: s.71(2).

All employees are entitled to AML for 26 weeks following OML: s.73 ERA and reg. 5 MPLR. Unlike OML, AML does not count as continuous service for pension and other benefits based on length of service, apart from qualifying for statutory employment rights.

The Maternity and Parental Leave etc and the Paternity and Adoption Leave (Amendment) Regulations 2006 allow women (and adopters) to work for up to 10 days during their leave without losing their right to SMP (or adoption pay) for those days. These so-called 'keeping in touch' days are to be mutually agreed between the employee and the employer.

(ii) Right to Return

Employees have the right to return to their previous jobs with their seniority and all other benefits in place as if they had not been absent: s.71(7) ERA 1996, or, if that is not reasonably practicable, to another suitable and appropriate job: reg. 18(2) MPLR. The employee has no need to notify the employer about her date of return and the onus is on the employer to inform her of her return date within 28 days of being notified of the start date of OML. If, however, she wishes to return before the end of the 52 weeks, the employee must give eight weeks' notice of her intention.

Where the right of return is not practicable because of redundancy, the employee is entitled to be offered alternative employment, if any, under a new contract, which must be suitable and appropriate for the employee, and where the provisions in respect of the capacity and place in which she is to be employed and other terms and conditions of her employment are not substantially less favourable to her than if she had returned to work under her right to return: s.81.

If an employee asks to return in a part-time capacity, it would dangerous to dismiss her, since refusal could be indirect discrimination.

(iii) Time off for ante-natal care

The right is subject to the production of a certificate confirming the pregnancy and an appointment card to attend an antenatal clinic, except for the first appointment: s.55.

The employee is entitled to remuneration for the period of absence at the appropriate hourly rate (s.56), and may complain to an employment tribunal if the employer has unreasonably refused her time off or failed to pay the whole or any part of any amount to which she is entitled: s.57.

(iv) Statutory Maternity Pay (SMP)

If by the fifteenth week prior to the expected week of confinement (EWC) the employee has worked for the employer for 26 weeks, she is entitled to SMP for 52 weeks or to maternity allowance for the same period. SMP is nine-tenths of her pay for the first six weeks and then a flat rate for the remaining period.

The Employment Equality (Sex Discrimination) Regulations 2005 have amended the Equal Pay Act 1970 and make it discriminatory to pay a woman less than she would otherwise have been paid because of her pregnancy or maternity leave. This means that any wage increase or bonus payments must be reflected in the maternity pay.

Maternity allowance is paid by the state to women who have been employed or self-employed for at least 26 weeks in the 66 weeks before the expected week of confinement, who have paid National Insurance for 26 weeks and earned on average £30 per week.

(v) Other Rights

Where a woman's job application is rejected due to pregnancy, a claim must be made under the Sex Discrimination Act (SDA) 1975. Selection for redundancy on the grounds of pregnancy is also unfair: *Stockton-on-Tees BC v. Brown* [1988] 2 WLR 935.

In Case C–109/00, *Tele Danmark A/S v Handels- og Kontorfunktionærernes Forbund i Danmark (acting on behalf of Brandt-Nielsen)* [2001] ECR I–6993, the ECJ held that a woman on a six-month contract could not be dismissed for failure to disclose that she was four months pregnant when taken on. The employer could not claim breach of duty of good faith as this would give rise to sex discrimination; employers must assume the economic and organisational consequences of the pregnancy of employees.

(e) Adoption and paternity leave

Chapter 1A ERA 1996 provides for paid adoption leave around the placement of a child for adoption: ss.75A–75D. Ordinary adoption leave is up to 26 weeks and additional adoption leave 26 weeks. Only one spouse is entitled to take the leave, but the other may qualify for paternity leave (see below). The provisions apply only where the child is newly placed with an adoptive parent, not step-family adoptions or adoptions by foster parents.

Statutory adoption pay is financed by the state, with employers able to recover a percentage of what they pay out.

(i) Paternity and adoption leave and statutory paternity and adoption pay

There is a statutory right to two weeks' paternity leave, either post birth or post the adoption of a child: ss.80A and 80B. This can be taken in a single block of either one or two weeks at the choice of the father. The details are in the Paternity and Adoption Leave Regulations 2002 (SI 2002/2788), and the Statutory Paternity Pay and Statutory Adoption Pay (General) & (Weekly Rates) Regulations 2002 (SI 2002/2822 and 2002/2818) (as amended). The weekly rate payable is the smaller of (a) £100, or (b) 90 per cent of the claimant's normal weekly earnings.

The qualifying period for paternity leave is continuous service with the same employer for at least 26 weeks by the fifteenth week before the child is expected to be born, or by the week of an approved match in the case of adoption. An employee has the right to return to a job following a period of one week's or two weeks' paternity leave, and protection from detriment and unfair dismissal in connection with paternity leave. Employees must provide their employer with a self-certificate of their entitlement to statutory paternity pay (SPP). SPP is administered in the same way as SMP, and employers recover a percentage of the amount, generally 92 per cent, but 100 per cent for small employers.

(f)   Parental Leave

The rights were established by the Parental Leave Directive and are in ss.76–80 ERA 1996 and the Maternity and Parental Leave Regulations 1999. The statutory provisions in the Regulations operate as default provisions and apply only if no workplace arrangements exist. The rights apply to parents of children who were under 5 on 15 December 1999.

Under the Regulations, employees with one year's continuous employment can take up to 13 weeks' unpaid parental leave in respect of each child for which the employee has responsibility: regs. 13 and 14. The leave may be taken up to the child's eighteenth birthday. For disabled children, the period is extended to 18 weeks. For adoptive children, leave can be taken up to the earlier of the five-year anniversary of the adoption or the child's eighteenth birthday: reg. 15.

The employee is entitled to the same contractual terms as employees in additional maternity leave, and bound by the same contractual terms: reg. 17.

The default provisions are contained in Schedule 2 and provide for leave to be taken in multiples of one week up to a maximum of four weeks in any year. Employees must give 21 days' prior notice and employers can postpone leave for up to six months if the leave would unduly disrupt the business. They must, however, agree alternative dates on which the leave can be taken.

(g)   Guarantee payments

Where employees are laid off through no fault of their own, they are to receive a guaranteed minimum payment for the workless day(s): ss.28–34. There is a qualifying period of one month: s.29(1), except that, for employees under a fixed-term contract of up to three months, or a contract for the performance of a specific task not expected to last for more than three months, the right arises only if they have been continuously employed for more than three months: s.29(2).

It applies where the employee is laid off because of (a) a diminution in the employer's business in work which the employee is employed to do; or (b) any other occurrence affecting the normal working of the employer's business in relation to the work for which the person is employed: s.28(1). There is no right to payment if the failure to provide the person with work is the consequence of a strike, lockout or other industrial action involving any employee of the employer or an associated employer (another company within the group): s.29(3). There is no right to payment if the employee has unreasonably refused the offer of suitable alternative employment: s.19(4). Employees can claim for no more than five days in a three-month period: s.31.

(h)   Right to remuneration where suspension is on medical grounds

Employees are entitled to remuneration if a business is closed down under health and safety regulations, unless the employer has the right to suspend them. There is a qualifying period of one month, but there is no right to payment if they were unfit to work during the suspension period. There is a defence where employees unreasonably refuse alternative employment: ss.64–65. Women can also be suspended on maternity grounds: ss.66–68. Remuneration is calculated under s.69 and employees can complain to an employment tribunal for failure to pay: s.70.

(i) Right to time off

These rights relate to (i) public duties, for example JPs, members of a local authority: ss.50–51; (ii) redundant workers seeking employment or arranging for training: ss.52–54; (iii) antenatal care: ss.55–57; (iv) trustees of occupational pension schemes: ss.58–60; and (v) employee representatives: ss.61–63.

17.5 Discrimination law and employment

Minorities are protected against discrimination in employment and other areas of life in relation to race, sex, sexual orientation, disability, age and on grounds of religion or belief. The initiative mainly stems from the EU.

(a) Discrimination on the grounds of race or sex

The Sex Discrimination Act (SDA) 1975, as amended by the Sex Discrimination (Indirect Discrimination and Burden of Proof) Regulations (SI 2001 No 2660), makes it unlawful to discriminate directly or indirectly on the grounds of sex and marital status: SDA, s.1(3). The Race Relations Act (RRA) 1976 prohibits discrimination on the grounds of 'colour, race, nationality and ethnic or national origin'.

The terms 'race' and 'ethnic origin' are unclear. The definition of ethnic origin approved by Lord Fraser provides: 'a group is identifiable in terms of its ethnic origins if it is a segment of the population distinguished from others by a sufficient combination of shared customs, beliefs, traditions and characteristics derived from a common or presumed common past, even if not drawn from what in biological terms is a common racial stock'. The definition encompasses Jews, Sikhs, English-speaking Welsh and the Irish. Rastafarians have not been defined as forming such a group.

There are three types of unlawful discrimination: direct, indirect and discrimination by victimisation. It can occur at the point of hiring, during employment or at its termination. Complaints may be brought before an employment tribunal, which may award compensation and make recommendations to the employer.

(i) *Direct discrimination*

This involves treating a person less favourably than another on sexual or racial grounds. In *James v. Eastleigh Borough Council* [1980] 2 AC 751, the council was found guilty under the SDA where Mr James was not allowed free admission to the municipal swimming pool at the age of 61, whereas his wife of the same age was given free access on the basis of having reached pensionable age. There was no intention to discriminate on the grounds of sex. A finding of direct discrimination meant that damages could be awarded without proof of intention, and the defence of justification, available for indirect discrimination, was ruled out.

Discriminatory behaviour cannot be justified by compensation by the employer.

In *Ministry of Defence v. Jeremiah* [1980] QB 87, where an employer required only male employees to carry out particularly obnoxious work and paid them extra for doing so, it was still discriminatory, as was an agreement where women were permitted to leave a factory five minutes before men: *Peake v. Automotive Products* [1978] QB 233.

The RRA s.1(2) also prohibits segregation on racial grounds, and employers are liable where departments or shifts are divided on racial grounds, even though at the employees' request.

Sexual or racial harassment is not in the Acts, but *Porcelli v. Strathclyde Regional Council* [1986] ICR 564 found sexual harassment contrary to ss.1(1) and 6(2)(b) SDA 1975. This includes unwelcome sexual attention; suggestions that sexual relations may further an employee's career (or that refusal may hinder it); insults or ridicule of a sexual nature; lewd, suggestive or over familiar behaviour; and the display or circulation of sexually suggestive material. Employers are vicariously liable for their employees' acts 'in the course of employment': s.41 SDA; s.32 RRA, subject to proving that they have taken all reasonable steps to prevent the discriminatory acts.

In *Jones v. Tower Boot Co. Ltd* [1997] 2 All ER 406, J, a person of mixed race, resigned as a machine operator because of extreme racial harassment, including being called a 'baboon' and branded by a hot screwdriver. Giving judgment for J, the Court of Appeal held that the words 'in the course of his employment' were to be given their natural everyday meaning and not construed restrictively.

(ii) Indirect discrimination

This is the uniform application of a condition or requirement where that requirement puts one sex or racial group at a disadvantage, and where the requirements cannot be justified on non-sexual or non-racial grounds. Thus (i) there must be a requirement or condition applied to all applicants or employees; (ii) the requirement or condition must be so that the proportion of women, married women or members of minority racial groups capable of complying with it is smaller than the comparator group; (iii) the condition must not be justifiable; and (iv) it must be detrimental to the complainant who is unable to comply with it.

In *Price v. Civil Service Commission (No. 2)* [1978] IRLR 3, a requirement that applicants for the post of executive officer should be between the ages of 17 and 28 was discriminatory against women, since these were the ages when many women were likely to be bringing up children.

A 'requirement or condition' does not cover recruitment criteria which are not an absolute bar to appointment. In *Meer v. Tower Hamlets LBC* [1988] IRLR 399, the expressed preference for a candidate who had previous experience working for a local authority was not indirect discrimination.

Problems arise in connection with establishing a comparator group, and the fact that the notion of what is a 'considerably smaller' proportion is not defined. In addition, even where a condition tending to rule out women or minorities is established, there is always the defence that it is justifiable, but the employer would have to show 'objectively justified' grounds to make out the defence, according to the ECJ in Case 170/82, *Bilka-Kaufhaus v. Weber van Hartz* [1986] ECR 1607.

In *Allen and Ors v. GMB* [2008] EWCA Civ 810 the GMB was not justified in indirectly discriminating against a number of female members in resolving gender-based pay inequalities among local authority employees. In 1997, trade unions and local authorities negotiated a national collective agreement to bring all employees under a new system with a common pay and grading structure. Actual pay scales were to be by local agreements following job evaluation. Further to a study in Middlesbrough, new terms and conditions were negotiated. In the negotiations, the GMB gave priority to its members needing pay protection and achieving equality and better pay for the future rather than maximising claims for past unequal pay. Under the deal some women received compensation for historical inequalities in the region of 25 per cent of the full value of successful equal pay claims, and some women none at all.

(iii) Discrimination by victimisation

The Act protects against victimisation for having made complaints of discrimination. Protection also extends to witnesses for the complainant.

In *Derbyshire and ors v. St Helens Metropolitan Borough Council* [2007] UKHL 16, 39 female employees of the authority plus about another 470 employees of the school meals service brought equal pay claims. The claims of the other women were settled by payment of a lump sum but the 39 employees proceeded with their claim before the employment tribunal. Two months before the hearing, the authority sent out two letters: the first to all catering staff stating that the continuance of the claim and a ruling against the council would have a serious impact on all staff; the second sent only to the 39 employees to the effect that the authority was greatly concerned about the outcome of the claim as set out in the first letter. The 39 employees claimed victimisation as a result of the letter contrary to s.4 SDA 1975. The House of Lords held that the tribunal had made no error in law in interpreting ss.4 and 6 and allowed an appeal by the 39 employees.

(iv) Statutory exceptions

Insistence on a particular sex or membership of a minority group can be a genuine occupational qualification: where physiological authenticity requires a man; to preserve decency and privacy; where the work is in a private home and requires close physical or social contact with the employer; where the job requires living in and there are facilities for only one sex; where the job is at an all-male institution; where the job involves the provision of personal services to individuals promoting their welfare or education and the services can be best provided by a man; where the law prohibits the employment of a woman; where the job is in another country the laws or customs of which preclude its being done by a woman; or where the job is one of two to be held by a married couple: s.7 SDA. The SDA also makes provision for a number of occupations: police, prison officers, ministers of religion, midwives and mineworkers.

The equivalent provision in respect of ethnicity includes physical authenticity (actors), restaurants, and where personal services promoting welfare or education are being provided to members of a particular racial group and can most effectively be provided by someone of that same racial group: s.5 RRA. The RRA allows discrimination against seamen recruited outside the UK.

(v) Remedies

The tribunal can (a) make an order declaring the rights of the parties; (b) require the employer to pay compensation; and (c) recommend the employer to take action within a specified period to obviate or reduce the adverse effect of the discrimination. More realistic levels of compensation have been awarded following *Marshall v. Southampton & South-West Hampshire Area Health Authority (Teaching) (No. 2)* [1991] ICR 136. Awards against the military when women were required to leave or have abortions on becoming pregnant have been very high.

If a contract is illegal, the courts will not generally enforce it or allow any statutory rights in respect of it. An exception is made for sex discrimination claims.

In *Leighton v. Michael* [1996] IRLR 67, Leighton worked in a fish and chip shop where PAYE and national insurance were deducted from her wages. The shop was taken over by Michael, who stopped deducting tax in spite of Leighton's protests. The EAT, however, said that neither statute nor public policy disqualified a person from the right not to be discriminated against sexually because their contract was illegal. This will also apply to race discrimination.

(b) Discrimination in respect of sexual orientation

The Employment Equality (Sexual Orientation) Regulations 2003 make it unlawful to discriminate on grounds of sexual orientation in employment and vocational training (regs. 6–21) including direct and indirect discrimination, victimisation and harassment.

Direct discrimination is where a person is treated less favourably on grounds of sexual orientation: reg. 3(1)(a). Indirect discrimination is where a generally applied provision, criterion or practice disadvantages persons of a particular sexual orientation and is not a proportionate way of achieving a legitimate aim: reg. 3(1)(b). Victimisation is receiving less favourable treatment by reason of the fact that a person has brought (or given evidence in) proceedings, made an allegation or otherwise done anything under or by reference to the Regulations: reg. 4. Harassment is subjecting a person to unwanted conduct on grounds of sexual orientation, with the purpose or effect of violating his dignity, or creating an intimidating, hostile, degrading, humiliating or offensive environment for him: reg. 5.

Exceptions relate to national security, benefits dependent on marital status and positive action (regs. 24–26) and where the sexual orientation is a genuine and determining occupational requirement, if it is proportionate in the particular case: reg. 7. An exception also applies for an organised religion to comply with the religion's doctrines or avoid conflict with its followers' religious convictions.

There is the possibility of compensation before an employment tribunal and in the county courts. Once a complainant has established facts from which a court or tribunal could conclude that an act of discrimination or harassment has been committed, the burden of proof is transferred to the defendant. A questionnaire procedure assists complainants in obtaining information from respondents.

(c) Discrimination on the grounds of disability

Part 2 of the Disability Discrimination Act (DDA) 1995 addresses the issue of discrimination against a person suffering from a disability. The Act is amended by the Disability Discrimination Act 1995 (Amendment) Regulations 2003, which implement Council Directive 2000/78/EC, [2000] OJ L303/16 and the Disability Discrimination Act 2005.

The DDA 1995 protects 'a person who has a disability': s.1(2), or a person who has had such a disability: s.2. A disability is a physical or a mental impairment which has a substantial and long-term adverse effect on a person's ability to carry out normal day-to-day activities: s.1(1).

(i) *Impairment*

The term 'physical impairment' is not elaborated on, but 'mental impairment' is qualified in Schedule 1, para. 1(1). A person has a mental impairment if the illness is 'clinically well-recognised'. Schedule 1, para. 1(2) allows the Secretary of State power to include or exclude conditions covered by the term 'impairment', and 'psychopathic or anti-social disorders and addictions' such as 'kleptomania, pyromania, paedophilia, and personality disorders' will be excluded. It remains to be seen whether drug and alcohol addictions will be excluded. Asthma is covered, as is chronic fatigue syndrome (ME). In *Paterson v. Commissioner of Police of the Metropolis, The Times*, 22 August 2007, the EAT held that a chief inspector of police who was dyslexic and found to have been disadvantaged in comparison with his work colleagues in examinations for promotion was disabled under the DDA 1995.

(ii) *Normal day-to-day activities*

There is a prescribed list of normal day-to-day activities in Schedule 1, para. 4: mobility, manual dexterity, physical coordination; continence; ability to lift, carry or otherwise move everyday objects; speech, hearing or eyesight; memory or ability to learn or understand; the ability to concentrate; and the perception of risk or physical danger. The list is exhaustive, but its scope is extended because, if an impairment causes stress, fatigue or pain, these will be taken into account in determining whether or not it produces a substantial effect on a person's ability to perform day-to-day activities.

(iii) *Substantial*

The effect should be 'more than minor' and exclude 'trivial matters'.

(iv) *Long-term effect*

The effect must have lasted for at least 12 months, or be expected to last either 12 months or for the rest of the individual's life (for terminally ill people with a reduced life expectancy): Schedule 1, para. 2.

The Schedule extends protection to people with fluctuating conditions such as epilepsy: Schedule 1, para. 2(2). People with severe disfigurements are deemed to satisfy the condition regarding substantial adverse effect on day-to-day activities: Schedule 1, para. 3, provided the disfigurement is long-term or one which is likely to recur, for example eczema. For a person suffering from a progressive condition who, as a result, has (or has had) an impairment which has (or has had) an adverse effect on his/her ability to carry out a normal day-to-day activity, this effect will be deemed to be substantial, provided that the condition is likely to lead to such an impairment: Schedule 1, para. 8(1). This will cover people suffering, for example, from multiple sclerosis, who may enjoy periods of remission.

The Act relates to discrimination and harassment in respect of employment (Part II); in relation to goods, facilities and services (Part III); education (Part IV); and public transport (Part V).

(v) *Discrimination in employment (Part II)*

The legislation applies to all employers. Regulation 7 removes the previous exemption for small businesses.

Employers discriminate against disabled persons if, because of their disability, they treat them less favourably than they treat or would treat others and cannot show that the treatment is justified. Failure to comply with the statutory duty to make reasonable adjustments for the disabled person is also discrimination. Disabled persons are subjected to harassment where, because of their disability, employers engage in unwanted conduct having the purpose or effect of violating the disabled person's dignity, or creating an intimidating, hostile, degrading, humiliating or offensive environment for him/her.

Following a reference to the ECJ from an Employment Appeal Tribunal decision on 27 November ([2007] ICR 654), people trying to combine work with caring for disabled or elderly relatives have a right to claim against employers who discriminate against them in refusing to offer flexible working. In 2008, the ECJ found that the claimant, who was forced to resign because she wanted more time to care for her disabled son, suffered discrimination by association: Case C–303/06, *Coleman v. Attridge Law & Steve Law* [2007] ICR 1128. This paves the way for carers to claim discrimination not because of their own disability but because of their role in caring for another person.

Protection for employees

It is unlawful for an employer to discriminate against or harass a disabled person: s.4. The discrimination covers: the arrangements made for determining to whom s/he should offer employment; the terms on which s/he offers that person employment, a refusal to offer or deliberately not offering employment: s.4(1). It also covers: the terms of employment; the opportunities for promotion, transfer, training or any other benefit; and refusal to offer or deliberately not offering any such opportunity, or dismissing him/her or subjecting him/her to any other detriment: s.4(2).

The section also prohibits submitting a disabled person to harassment, whether that person is a employee or a person who has applied for employment.

Where a provision, criterion or practice applied by or on behalf of an employer or any physical feature of premises occupied by the employer places the disabled person at a substantial disadvantage, it is the duty of the employer to take such steps as are reasonable to prevent that effect: s.4A.

Employees of the Crown, including the police: s.64, are covered. Police constables are treated as being employed by the chief officer of police: s.64A. New provisions allow, in certain circumstances, for work done wholly outside Great Britain to be treated as employment at an establishment in Great Britain and to make provision about including within Part II employment on board ships, hovercraft and aircraft where the ship is registered in Great Britain, or belongs to or is possessed by Her Majesty's government, and where the hovercraft or aircraft is registered in the UK and operated by a person whose principal place of business is in Great Britain or who is ordinarily resident in Great Britain, or it belongs to, or is possessed by, Her Majesty's government.

Protection for other workers

Sections 4B–4F prohibit discrimination against, and harassment of, contract workers and certain office-holders, and provide for the making of reasonable adjustments for such workers. A contract worker is a person who is employed by person (A) who supplies them under a contract made with the principal (B). Sections 6A–6C and ss.7A–7D prohibit discrimination and harassment, and impose duties to make reasonable adjustments, in relation to partners in firms and barristers (England and Wales) and advocates (Scotland).

Application to trade organisations and so on
Sections 13 and 14 prohibit discrimination and harassment, and impose duties to make reasonable adjustments, in relation to trade organisations. Sections 14A–14D prohibit discrimination and harassment, and impose duties to make reasonable adjustments, in relation to qualifications bodies and persons who provide work placements.

Prohibitions in respect of advertisements
Section 16B prohibits employers and others from publishing or causing to be published advertisements which indicate an intention to discriminate and s.16C prohibits instructions and pressure to discriminate. The Disability Rights Commission (DRC) is given power to enforce ss.16B and 16C.

Positive discrimination in favour of a disabled person is possible, and employers can lawfully advertise posts restricted to disabled people. It is lawful to discriminate between one disabled person and another only in the case of a charity the specific goals of which are to benefit a particular disability: s.18C.

Employers are legally responsible for any acts of discrimination or harassment carried out by their employees, whether or not this was done with their knowledge or approval: s.58, unless the employer has taken 'such steps as were reasonably practicable' to prevent such acts: s.58(5).

(vi) Enforcement

Victims of discrimination or harassment can claim before an employment tribunal: s.17A. Claims must be brought within three months: s.17A, and Schedule 3, para. 3(1). Cases can be heard outside the time limit if it is 'just and equitable': Schedule 3, para. 3(2). Where the complainant proves facts from which the tribunal could conclude in the absence of an adequate explanation that the defendant has acted in a way which is unlawful, the tribunal shall uphold the complaint unless the defendant proves that he did not so act: s.17A(1C).

The tribunal may make such orders as it considers just and equitable: s.17A. The orders will be similar to those available in cases of sex or race discrimination. Legal aid is not available. Unsuccessful claimants will not bear the legal expenses of the successful party unless they knew there was no substance to their claim and no chance of success. Appeals are to the EAT and the Court of Appeal. Legal aid may be available for the appeals.

(vii) Health and safety and disability discrimination

Health and safety grounds are a major justification against employing the disabled. In the event of conflict between the DDA 1995 and statutory health and safety provisions, the latter prevail: s.59. Employers must show that, in spite of reasonable adjustments to the working environment, the disabled applicant represents a risk.

(d) Discrimination on the grounds of religion or belief

The Employment Equality (Religion or Belief) Regulations 2003 implement Council Directive 2000/78/EC, [2000] OJ L303/16 of 27 November 2000 and make it unlawful to discriminate on grounds of religion or belief in employment and vocational training and prohibit direct and indirect discrimination, victimisation and harassment. Religion or belief is defined in reg. 2 as meaning any religion, religious belief or similar philosophical belief.

Direct discrimination is treating a person less favourably on grounds of religion or belief: reg. 3(1)(a). Indirect discrimination is where a provision, criterion or practice which, if applied generally, puts persons of a particular religion or belief at a disadvantage is not a proportionate means of achieving a legitimate aim: reg. 3(1)(b). Victimisation is where a person receives less favourable treatment because he has brought (or given evidence in) proceedings, made an allegation or otherwise done anything under or by reference to the Regulations: reg. 4. Harassment is subjecting a person to unwanted conduct on the grounds of religion or belief with the purpose or effect of violating his dignity or creating an intimidating, hostile, degrading, humiliating or offensive environment for him.

Regulations 6–21 prohibit discrimination, victimisation and harassment in the field of employment and vocational training. They protect employees: reg. 6, contract workers: reg. 8, office-holders (including constables): regs. 10 and 11, and partners in firms. They prohibit discrimination by trade organisations: reg. 15, bodies conferring professional and trade qualifications: reg. 16, training providers: reg. 17, employment agencies: reg. 18, and institutions of further and higher education: reg. 20.

Exceptions relate to national security and positive action: regs. 24–25, and the protection of Sikhs in the wearing of safety helmets: reg. 26. An exception also applies where being of a particular religion or belief is a genuine and determining occupational requirement if proportionate, and for employers with an ethos based on religion or belief where being of a particular religion or belief is a genuine occupational requirement and proportionate: reg. 7.

Remedies include compensation following proceedings in employment tribunals and the county courts. The burden of proof is on the employer once the complainant has established facts from which a court or tribunal could conclude that an act of discrimination has been committed.

From September 2008, faith schools have the right to discriminate on the grounds of religion in selecting their staff, including academic and ancillary staff: s.37 Education and Inspection Act 2008.

(e)   Age discrimination

The Employment Equality (Age) Regulations 2006 came into force in October 2006. The Regulations relate to the concepts of direct and indirect discrimination, victimisation and harassment common to other anti-discrimination regulations (regs. 3, 4 and 6). Unlike in other anti-discrimination legislation, however, an employer may raise the defence of objective justification in respect of direct discrimination claims. There is also an exception where age is a genuine and determining occupational requirement: reg. 8. Employers can also be liable for issuing instruction to discriminate and aiding unlawful acts (regs. 5 and 25) and are liable for the unlawful acts of their employees: reg. 24.

The UK Regulations exclude pensioners, who can be dismissed at 65 without redundancy payments, or at the employer's mandatory retirement age if it is above 65. One of Age Concern's member organisations took the case of the mandatory retirement age to the High Court, which referred it to the ECJ for a ruling. The Advocate-General, Ján Mazák, in a preliminary legal opinion delivered on 23 September 2008 rejected the claim that to compel people to stop work at or after 65 without compensation breached EU equality requirements: Case C–388/07, *The Incorporated Trustees of the National Council on Ageing Concern v. Secretary of State for Business, Enterprise and Regulatory Reform*, not yet reported. The ECJ took the same line on condition that the retirement age was not under 65 and was justified by social policy. The final judgment is due in about six months.

(f) Discriminatory acts by an employer after termination of a contract of employment

In *Relaxion Group plc v. Rhys-Harper etc* [2003] UKHL 33, the House of Lords held as a preliminary point that the SDA 1975, the RRA 1976 and the DDA 1995 protected not only individuals employed at the time of the complaint but also those claiming discrimination or victimisation after the termination of the employer/employee relationship.

(g) The Commission for Equality and Human Rights (CEHR)

From October 2007, the CEHR replaced the Commission for Racial Equality, the Equal Opportunities Commission and the Disability Rights Commission. The CEHR's powers are wider than those of the bodies it replaces and it also deals with discrimination in respect of religion or belief, sexual orientation and age. The CEHR can conduct investigations and assist in litigation. It can also issue unlawful act notices, require persons to develop an action plan and agree not to take legal action if persons agree to discontinue the discriminatory act and take such steps as required by the CEHR.

17.6 Unfair dismissal

Employers must show (a) the reason (or, if more than one, the principal reason) for the dismissal, and (b) that it is either a reason falling within s.98(2) or such other substantial reason of a kind such as to justify the dismissal of an employee holding the position which the employee held: s.98(1). A reason falls within s.98(2) if it (a) relates to the capability or qualifications of the employee for performing work of the kind which he was employed to do; (b) relates to the conduct of the employee; (c) is that the employee was redundant; or (d) that his continued employment would be in breach of a statutory duty of the employee or the employer; and (v) some other substantial reason justifying dismissal: s.98(2) ERA 1996.

Grounds which are automatically unfair are: (i) pregnancy or reasons connected with pregnancy, including failure to offer alternative employment: s.99; (ii) those in connection with duties as a health and safety representative, or bringing to the employer's attention circumstances which the employee reasonably believed were harmful or potentially harmful to health and safety: s.100; (iii) refusal of Sunday work by protected shopworkers and betting workers: s.101; (iii) being trustee of an occupational pension scheme: s.102; (iv) being an employee representative: s.103; (v) following the assertion of relevant statutory rights: s.104; and (vi) redundancy where the circumstances apply equally to other employees who have not been made redundant: s.105.

In addition, the dismissal is unfair (i) if the reason was that the employee (a) was, or proposed to become, a member of an independent trades union, (b) had taken part, or proposed to take part in the activities of an independent trades union at an appropriate time, or (c) was not a member of any trades union, or of a particular trades union, or one of a number of particular trades unions, or has refused, or proposed to refuse, to become or remain a member: s.152; or (ii) if selection for redundancy is related to a person's union membership or activities: Trade Union and Labour Relations (Consolidation) Act

1992 (TULRCA), as amended by the Employment Relations Act 2004. The provisions relating to qualifying period and upper age limit do not apply to the dismissal of an employee on grounds of union membership or activities: s.154.

Dismissal is also unfair if in breach of the SDA, the RRA and the DDA.

Employees may challenge dismissal before an employment tribunal. Dismissal includes (i) termination of a contract of employment by the employer with or without notice; (ii) refusal to renew a fixed-term contract; and (iii) termination of his/her contract by the employee because of the employer's conduct – 'constructive dismissal': s.95(1). An employee is also dismissed where the employer gives notice of dismissal and the employee, during the period of notice, gives notice terminating the contract at an earlier date for the reason for which the employer's notice was given: s.95(2). The date of the termination is determined by s.97. Employees are entitled to a written statement of the reasons for dismissal: s.92.

It is not always clear whether employees have been dismissed or have handed in their notice. They may resign in anger or because threatened with disciplinary proceedings, or fearing that they will otherwise be dismissed, and later try to claim that they were dismissed. They may also accept voluntary redundancy and then claim to have been dismissed. Where dealings between employer and employee are ambiguous, the test seems to be what the employer intended by the words used, and what a reasonable employee would have understood.

The contract may also have been terminated under an automatic termination clause, for example where an employee seeks an extended period of leave abroad and failure to return at the appointed time is deemed to be resignation or termination. In *Igbo v. Johnson Matthey Chemicals* [1986] ICR 505, the Court of Appeal held that, if the contract was terminated, it would constitute a dismissal.

(a)   Termination by frustration

Termination of contracts by frustration is not dismissal. Incapacity through illness is the main source of claims in this respect. The tests for frustration by incapacity were laid down in *Egg Stores (Stamford Hill) v. Leibovici* [1977] ICR 260, and include (i) the length of the employment; (ii) the expected duration of the employment; (iii) the nature of the job; (iv) the nature, length and effect of the disabling event; (v) the need for a replacement; (vi) whether wages have continued to be paid; (vii) the acts and statements of the employer; and (viii) whether, in all circumstances, a reasonable employer could be expected to wait any longer before permanently replacing the employee. This approach was endorsed by the Court of Appeal in *Notcutt v. Universal Equipment Co. (London)* [1986] ICR 414.

The employee's imprisonment may be a frustrating event, although it could be seen as a self-induced breach of contract.

In *Hare v. Murphy Brothers* [1974] 3 All ER 940, a foreman was sentenced to 12 months' imprisonment for assault, and the prison sentence was held to have frustrated his contract. In *Shepherd (FC) & Co. Ltd v. Jerrom* [1985] IRLR 275, a prison sentence of between six months and two years frustrated an apprenticeship contract of four years.

Where an employer dies, goes into voluntary or compulsory liquidation or, in the case of a partnership, is dissolved, employees are treated as having been dismissed and are entitled to redundancy payments if the business is not continued under a new owner or their contract is not continued.

(b) Refusal to renew a fixed-term contract

A fixed-term contract must have a defined beginning and end, with the date known at the outset. Where no termination date is specified, it may be a contract for a particular purpose and not protected. A fixed-term contract may include a term providing for termination by either party giving notice: *Dixon v. BBC* [1979] QB 546 (see p.417).

(c) Constructive dismissal

Claims often arise from the employer exercising a power to vary the contract.

In *White v. Reflecting Roadstuds Ltd* [1991] IRLR 323, W's contract provided that 'the company reserves the rights … to transfer employees to alternative work, and it is a condition of the contract that they are willing to do so when requested'. W's attendance suffered since he found his current employment too physically demanding. After a warning, he was transferred, and claimed this was constructive dismissal. The EAT found the transfer was in accordance with the flexibility clause, which permitted transfer to work at lower rates of pay. Reliance on the clause did not have to be reasonable but had to be on grounds of operational efficiency.

If the variation term is vague or ambiguous, the court or tribunal can assess the reasonableness of the employer's action and, initially, treated a failure to follow good employment practices as constituting constructive dismissal. The Court of Appeal rejected this approach in *Western Excavating (EEC) v. Sharp* [1978] QB 761, and indicated that unreasonable conduct which did not constitute a breach of contract would not justify a claim of constructive dismissal. This made it virtually impossible to base a constructive dismissal claim on the employer's unreasonable use of a contractual power.

In *United Bank Ltd v. Akhtar* [1989] IRLR 505, a mobility clause gave the bank power to transfer Akhtar, temporarily or permanently, elsewhere in the UK. On Monday 2 June he was informed that on the following Monday he would no longer be based in Leeds but in Birmingham, and was notified of this in writing on 5 June. He requested 24 days to sort out his affairs but received no reply, and his pay was stopped from 5 June. The EAT held that the employer was in breach of contract despite the clear mobility provision.

The EAT had taken into consideration the implied term of mutual trust and confidence, and the following cases serve to illustrate breaches.

In *UB (Ross) Youngs Ltd v. Elsworthy* (1993) IDS Brief 498, the contract provided that shift-workers could be transferred to other shifts after consultation and two weeks' notice. A husband and wife, who had been on the same shift, were placed on different shifts. Mrs Elsworthy complained but, as no solution was found, she then resigned. The court held that this was constructive dismissal. The management had not considered her domestic situation and failed to convince the court that their needs could not have been met without putting the Elsworthys on separate shifts. There was breach of mutual trust and confidence.

In *Greenaway Harrison Ltd v. Wiles* [1994] IRLR 380, telephonists who were women with children complained about new shift patterns and were told that they would be dismissed if they failed to agree. The court held that, in the absence of real consultation, although the employer had a legal right to terminate the contracts without notice, the threat amounted to constructive dismissal.

Failure to allow a woman to return to work at the end of maternity leave will constitute dismissal from the date on which she should have been allowed to return, and she will be considered to have been employed up to that date: s.96.

Where there was a gap in time between the employer's repudiatory breach and the employee's acceptance of it by resignation, damages for the loss caused by the repudiatory breach could not be claimed in unfair dismissal proceedings before a tribunal and had to be sought in separate common law proceedings, because they flowed from the employer's antecedent breaches of the duty of trust and confidence. In this case, the damage caused by the manager's conduct prior to the date of the employee's constructive dismissal in March 2005 was damage in respect of which the employee already had an accrued cause of action: *GAB Robins (UK) Ltd v. Triggs* [2008] EWCA Civ 17.

(d)   Remedies for unfair dismissal

A complaint may be presented to an employment tribunal by persons claiming they were unfairly dismissed: s.111. If it is successful, the tribunal must explain the remedies of reinstatement and re-engagement under s.113. And, if the complainant expresses such a wish, the tribunal may make an order under the section.

Reinstatement means that employees return to their old jobs as if they had never been dismissed: s.114. Re-engagement means that they will be taken back in a new job, or in the old job but at a different location, or even by a different company within the group. Employees should enjoy the same advantages as if there has been no interruption in service: s.115. Employers can be ordered to take back an employee, but this happens in about 1 per cent of all cases.

If the terms of a s.113 order are not fully complied with, the tribunal can award compensation to the employee, subject to the s.124 limit. If the employee is not reinstated or re-engaged, the tribunal must award compensation in accordance with ss.118–127, and an additional award of compensation of the appropriate amount, which is to be not less than 26 nor more than 52 weeks' pay, where the dismissal is illegal discrimination under the SDA or the RRA, and in any other case not less than 13 nor more than 26 weeks' pay.

The more usual remedy is compensation under Part X ERA 1996 made up of (i) a basic award calculated following an arithmetical formula according to the number of years' service in much the same way as a redundancy payment; and (ii) a compensatory award of such an amount as the tribunal considers just and equitable having regard to the loss suffered by the employee, and calculated in accordance with s.123, but subject to a limit of £51,700. There is also the possibility of a special award. This is one week's pay multiplied by 104, or £13,775, whichever is the greater, but subject to a limit of £27,500 except where the award is made under s.117 when, unless the employer can satisfy the tribunal that it was not practicable to comply with the reinstatement or re-engagement order, the award shall be increased to one week's pay multiplied by 156, or £20,600, whichever is the greater. Although there is a potential of high awards for unfair dismissal, most awards made are low, which causes dissatisfaction with the remedy.

In *Triggs v. GAB Robins (UK) Ltd* [2007] 3 All ER 590 the claimant employee had an excessive workload and felt she was being bullied by a manager. As a result, she was signed off by her doctor with stress and depression and received sick pay. During her sick leave, she raised the issue of the workload and alleged bullying in a letter to the employer. Having received a response which she considered unsatisfactory, she terminated her contract of employment and brought a claim of constructive unfair dismissal. The tribunal upheld her claim and ruled that she was entitled under s.123 ERA 1996 to recover the loss of her full salary flowing from her dismissal for such period as it saw fit. In respect of an appeal by the employer, the EAT held that the overwork and bullying were a breach of the implied term of trust and confidence, and the employer's failure to carry out an adequate investigation into her grievances contributed materially to the earlier acts so as to constitute constructive dismissal. It also held that the course of conduct formed part of the dismissal and that any ill-health was a consequence of the dismissal leading to loss of earnings at the full rate rather than sick leave.

In *Burlo v. Langley and anor* [2006] EWCA Civ 1778 the claimant was employed as a nanny under a contract which provided for eight weeks' notice by either party and payment of statutory sickness benefit. On 5 March 2004, the employee was injured in a car accident and certified unfit for work until 29 March. By 8 March, the employer wrote saying she was not required to work out her notice. She claimed wrongful and unfair dismissal and the tribunal assessed her compensation at eight weeks' pay at her normal weekly wage. The employers successfully appealed that damages should have been based on statutory sick pay. The court also stated that in calculating compensation for unfair dismissal an employer who has dismissed an employee without notice should make payment in lieu of notice without any deduction for sums earned in other employment during the notice period.

(e) Statutory claim

Employees must establish that they have been continuously employed for two years and an action must be brought within three months of the date of termination. Claims are, however, excluded in respect of (i) employees past normal retiring age: s.109; (ii) persons on strike; and (iii) spouse(s) of the owner(s) of the business.

Employment tribunals have concurrent jurisdiction with the county court. The tribunal can hear claims for a breach of the employment contract or any other contract connected with employment; claims for sums due under such a contract, or claims for recovery of such sums in pursuance of any enactment relating to the terms of performance of such a contract: s.3(2) Industrial Tribunal Act 1996.

Excluded from tribunal jurisdiction are personal injuries claims, and claims for breach of a term: (i) requiring the employer to provide living accommodation for the employee, or imposing an obligation on the employer or employee in connection with the provision of accommodation; (ii) relating to intellectual property; (iii) imposing an obligation of confidence; and (iv) which is a covenant in restraint of trade.

There are three requirements before the claim can be heard by the tribunal: (i) the contract must have terminated; (ii) the claim must be made within three months of termination, or within three months of the last day of employment, subject to extension; and (iii) the claim must either arise out of the termination or still be outstanding at termination, and must not have been settled by the time of application.

Employers cannot initiate claims, but may bring any counterclaim or set-off once a claim has been initiated by the employee. Counterclaims must be brought within six weeks of the employer receiving a copy of the originating application, subject to extension. The limit for damages is fixed at the time of writing at £51,700. There is no qualification period in relation to claims, nor any minimum hours of service, and claims can be brought by any ex-employee.

Claims are likely to be brought in respect of failure to pay wages in lieu of notice, especially by employees with less than two years' service. There are also likely to be claims for failure to follow a contractual procedure relating to redundancy, dismissal and other procedures which are frequently incorporated into the contract of employment. This will allow employees with less than two years' continuity of employment to claim for unfair dismissal for failure to comply with the contractual procedure, whereas they would not qualify for a statutory claim.

Hot Topic . . .

DAMAGES FOR WRONGFUL AND UNFAIR DISMISSAL AT COMMON LAW

The courts have always refused to award damages (i) for injured feelings; or (ii) because the dismissal makes finding new employment more difficult: *Addis v. Gramophone Co. Ltd* [1909] AC 488 and *Bliss v. South East Thames Regional Health Authority* [1987] ICR 700. Awards for injury to feelings within unfair dismissal cases were restricted by *Norton Tools Co. Ltd v. Tewson* [1973] 1 All ER 183, which required the courts to attribute compensation to specific heads of loss. In *Johnson v. Unisys Ltd* [2001] 2 All ER 801, J brought proceedings for unfair dismissal against U in 1994. The tribunal awarded him £11,691.88 compensation, subsequently reduced to the then statutory maximum of £11,000.

J's action for breach of contract and negligence, claiming £400,000 for loss of earnings, breach of the implied term of mutual trust and confidence and of a duty of care, since it was reasonably foreseeable that his dismissal would cause psychological injury, was rejected by the Court of Appeal.

The House of Lords stated that there was no common law remedy for employees to recover damages for unfair dismissal, but that the traditional view that an employment tribunal could compensate only for financial loss was too narrow. Lord Hoffmann said, 'I see no reason why … it should not include compensation for distress, humiliation, damage to reputation in the community or to family life'.

In *Eastwood v. Magnox Electric plc* [2004] UKHL 35 The claimant settled a claim for unfair dismissal and then sought damages for psychiatric injury. The House of Lords held that his claim should proceed where the breach causing the loss occurred prior to the disciplinary procedure of dismissal.

In *Dunnachie v. Kingston upon Hull City Council* [2004] UKHL 36, however, an employment tribunal award included an amount for injury to feelings. This was rejected by the EAT and the Court of Appeal and the House of Lords, the last of which held that Lord Hoffmann's comments were merely obiter and that *Norton Tools* remained good law.

Problems exist for unwary litigants claiming unfair and wrongful dismissal. Since the Employment Tribunals Extension of Jurisdiction (England & Wales) Order (SI 1994/1623, Art.10), employment tribunals have exclusive jurisdiction for unfair dismissal, and concurrent jurisdiction with the civil courts on wrongful dismissal, except that the damages which the tribunal can award in cases of wrongful dismissal are limited to £25,000. In *Roderick Fraser v. HLMAD Ltd* [2006] EWCA Civ 738, RF applied to a tribunal on 25 May 2004 for unfair and wrongful dismissal and reserved his right to pursue his action in the High Court, but did not withdraw his wrongful dismissal claim from the tribunal. He commenced a High Court action on 23 December 2004 for £261,146, but on 31 March 2005 the tribunal found that he had been unfairly and wrongfully dismissed and – in an amended decision on 16 June – assessed damages for breach of contract at £80,090.62 – capped at £25,000 and a compensatory award for unfair dismissal of £16,034.88. On 26 May 2005, HLMAD successfully applied to strike out RF's High Court claim. The Court of Appeal held that his common law claim was barred on the grounds of *res judicata* (estoppel by process).

17.7 Redundancy

The statutory redundancy payments provisions are in Part XI ERA 1996. Employers must make payments to employees who are (a) dismissed by reason of redundancy; or (b) laid off or kept on short time: s.135(1). Eligibility for being laid off or kept on short time is where the period continues for four or more consecutive weeks, or for a series of six or more weeks (of which not more than three were consecutive) within a period of 13 weeks.

Employees must have been in continuous employment for two years prior to the redundancy: s.155. There is no right for employees of the normal retiring age of 65: s.156. The payments must be of at least the statutory minimum. These are:

(i)   for each year of employment at age 41 or over but under 65, one-and-a-half weeks' pay;
(ii) for every year of employment at age 22 or over but under 41, one week's pay;
(iii) for each year of employment at age 18 or over but under 22, half a week's pay.

There is a maximum weekly sum which changes regularly, and a maximum number of years of service which count (20 years at the time of writing: s.162).

The EC Collective Dismissals Directive (EC/75/129, [1975] OJ L48/29), amended by Directive 92/56/EEC. ([1992] OJ L245/3) now the Collective Redundancies Directive 98/59/EC ([1998] OJ L225/16), made it an obligation for employers to consult trades unions over proposed mass redundancies. This is in the Trade Union and Labour Relations (Consolidation) Act 1992 (TULRCA). Where employers propose making 20 or more employees redundant at one establishment within a period of 90 days or less, they must consult all the appropriate representatives of any of the employees to be dismissed: s.188(1) TULRCA 1992. Where they propose dismissing 100 or more employees, the consultation must commence at least 90 days before the first dismissals take effect; in other cases the requirement is at least 30 days: s.188(1A). The appropriate representatives are (a) employee representatives elected by them; or (b), if an independent trades union is recognised by the employer, representatives of the trades union: s.188(1B). Failure to consult entitles a complaint to be taken to an employment tribunal: s.189. Employers must also notify the Secretary of State at the same time as the consultations commence: s.193.

The statutory provisions relating to unfair dismissal and redundancy apply to fixed-term contracts but not performance contracts. Unfair dismissal rights can be excluded where the contract is for a fixed term of one year or more, the dismissal consists of non-renewal and the employee has agreed to the exclusion of these rights in writing before the expiry of the contract. In the case of redundancy rights, the contract period is two years or more. Thus the contract may state, 'The employee agrees to waive any unfair dismissal and redundancy rights which may otherwise arise on the expiry and non-renewal of this contract'. This is not necessary in performance contracts, on the expiry of which unfair dismissal and redundancy rights do not arise.

Note the Fixed Term Employees (Prevention of Less Favourable Treatment) Regulations 2002 (SI 2002/2034) (see p.388 above).

17.8   Transfers of undertakings

The sale of a business has redundancy implications where the purchaser requires fewer employees. However, even where the employees are retained, their existing contracts will be terminated and replaced by new ones, and cessation of employment falls within the definition of redundancy.

The position of such employees is covered by s.218 ERA 1996 (which preserves continuity of employment of a person employed in an undertaking 'at the time of the transfer') or under the Transfer of Undertakings (Protection of Employment) Regulations 1981 (TUPE), which implement the Acquired Rights Directive (EEC/77/187, [1977] OJ

L61/26), now consolidated into Directive 2001/23/EC ([2001] OJ L82/16) which protects employees employed 'immediately before' the transfer. Neither the Act nor the Regulations cover a takeover effected by a transfer of shares, since the identity of the employer remains the same. Since this is the most usual type of transfer in the UK, the value of the Regulations is thereby weakened. TUPE was amended by the Trade Union Reform and Employment Rights Act 1993 after threats by the Commission of infringement proceedings.

The definition of 'undertaking' was widened to cover non-commercial ventures, in accordance with Case C–29/91, *Dr Sophie Redmond Stichting v. Bartol* [1992] ECR I–3189. The transfer of an undertaking, or part of one, may now (a) be effected by a series of two or more transactions; and (b) take place whether or not any property is transferred to the transferee by the transferor: reg. 3.

In the *Sophie Redmond* case, the ECJ held that the Directive applied even though there was no actual transfer of property. The foundation's grant was merely withdrawn and given to another organisation which took over its premises, clients and work and offered employment to some of its employees.

There can be asset reliant transfers and employee reliant transfers, where only the majority of the employees of the transferor are transferred.

Regulation 5 originally provided for the automatic transfer of contracts of employment to the new employer without the employee's consent, contrary to *Nokes v. Doncaster Amalgamated Collieries* [1940] AC 1014. This was rectified by paras 4A, 4B and 5. Under para. 4A, automatic transfer does not occur where the employee 'informs the transferor or the transferee that he objects to becoming employed by the transferee'; however, para. 4B removes the possibility of action against the transferor. Employees are entitled to claim redundancy pay from the transferor under para. 5 only where a substantial change is made in their working conditions to their detriment.

Regulation 5(2) provides for the transfer of the transferor's 'rights, powers, duties and liabilities under or in connection with any such contract'. This will cover breach of contract claims, statutory duties such as breach of the Wages Act 1986, maternity rights, equal pay, unfair dismissal and redundancy discrimination claims, and perhaps even protective awards. It will also cover claims for injuries at work.

In *Secretary of State for Employment v. Spence* [1986] ICR 651, Balcombe LJ said that 'in connection with' covered not only statutory but also tortious liability. This has been acted upon by a county court, which held that the same wording in the National Heath Service and Community Care Act 1990 meant that, if an employee sustained injuries caused by negligence while employed by the transferring employer, liability effectively transferred to the acquiring employer: *Wilson and Others v. West Cumbria Health Care NHS Trust* [1994] IRLR 506.

The fact that TUPE applies only to persons 'employed immediately before the transfer' can operate to the employees' disadvantage where the transfer is identified as having taken place at a time prior to their transfer.

Celtec Ltd v. Astley [2001] All ER 66 concerned A, a civil servant, seconded in 1990 to the Training and Enterprise Councils (TECs), which were given a monopoly over the management of training and enterprise activities previously carried on by the Employment Department. Subsequently the seconded staff were offered employment with the TEC or a return to the civil service. A opted for the TEC (Celtec) in 1993. His claim that he was covered by TUPE was rejected by the EAT since the transfer was in 1990 and A had not moved over until 1993.

To prevent the transferor making employees redundant in collusion with the transferee just prior to the transfer, there is a provision that employees shall be treated as being unfairly dismissed if the transfer or a reason connected with it is the reason, or the principal reason, for their dismissal: reg. 8(1), except with regard to an 'economic, technical or organisational reason entailing changes in the workforce'.

In *Litster v. Forth Dry Dock and Engineering Co. Ltd* [1989] IRLR 161, FDDE was in receivership and its business was to be taken over by a company set up for the purpose. The transferee did not want to take over the workforce of FDDE and, by an agreement between the transferor and the transferee, the employees were made redundant an hour before the transfer. It was held that the dismissal was clearly linked to the transfer and there was collusion between the transferor and transferee.

In *Secretary of State for Employment v. Spence* [1986] ICR 651, the dismissal of employees at 11 a.m. before the successful completion of the sale of the undertaking and their re-employment by the transferee at 2 p.m. on the same day were not unfair under reg. 8(1) and the employees were not able to claim the benefit of TUPE.

The ECJ has held that the directive applied to privatisation of public services where the service transferred had a sufficiently discrete identity: Case C–209/91, *Rask v. ISS Kantineservice A/S* [1992] ECR I–5755. However, in respect of TUPE, the UK courts and the ECJ seem to take a completely different line, with the UK taking a much more liberal approach to the question whether there has been a transfer of an undertaking.

In Case C–13/95, *Süzen v. Zehnacker Gebäudereinigung GmbH Krankenhausservice* [1997] ECR I–1259, the ECJ stated that for the Acquired Rights Directive (Directive 2001/23/EC, [2001] OJ L82/16) to apply on a contract changeover, if the function is asset reliant there must be a transfer of significant tangible or intangible assets or, in a labour-intensive function, the new contractor must take over a major part of the workforce, in terms of numbers and skills.

In *Betts v. Brintel Helicopters Ltd* [1997] 2 All ER 840. BH Ltd had contracts with an oil company for transporting men and goods between the UK and North Sea oil rigs. These expired and were awarded to KLM, which did not take on staff or equipment from BH Ltd and moved operations to another airport. The dismissed pilots claimed to have become employees of KLM under TUPE. The Court of Appeal held that, where one fixed-term contract for services was replaced by another, no such transfer occurred if there was no transfer of significant tangible or intangible assets or the taking over of a major part of the workforce.

However, in *ECM (Vehicle Delivery Service) Ltd v. Cox* [1999] 4 All ER 669, the EAT and the Court of Appeal held that employment tribunals can examine the new employer's motive in not taking on employees. If the employer's motive is to get around TUPE, then TUPE will still apply.

In *ADI (UK) Ltd v. Willer* [2001] All ER 237, ADI had a contract to provide security services at a shopping centre and nine employees were allocated to this. ADI terminated the contract and Firm Security Group Ltd took on the contract. Firm Security took on no employees and no tangible assets were transferred. The EAT held that there was no transfer of an undertaking. In a majority decision, however, the Court of Appeal confirmed the test in *Süzen*, but held that the new employer's motives in not taking on the employees could be taken into account. Thus, where the employees were not taken on but

TUPE would have applied had they been taken on, there will still be a transfer for the purposes of TUPE if it can be established that the reason or principal reason for not taking employees on was to avoid the application of TUPE.

In *RCO Support Services v. Unison* [2002] All ER 50, RCO won the contract to provide the identical cleaning services at a hospital as the previous contractor. It offered to take on the previous contractor's employees, but only on the basis that TUPE did not apply. The offer was not taken up by any of the employees who claimed for unfair dismissal. Their union complained of a breach of the consultation obligations under TUPE. The Court of Appeal upheld the EAT's decision that TUPE applied.

In *Power v. Regent Security Services Ltd* [2007] 4 All ER 354 the appellant employee was employed under a contract which fixed his retirement at 60. The contract was transferred under TUPE but, shortly before the automatic transfer, the employer sent a letter to the employee purporting to offer him the position to which he was entitled but stating that the employment would terminate at the age of 65. When the employee reached the age of 60 the employer purported to terminate his employment. The employee claimed unfair dismissal. The EAT held that the employer was not entitled to refuse to give effect to the contractually agreed retirement age of 65, and the employee could pursue his claim for unfair dismissal.

TUPE also provides for consultation between the employer and the trade union representatives of a recognised trade union of any affected employees.

In *Hollis Metal Industries Ltd v. GMB & Newell Ltd*, UKEAT/0171/07/LEA, Newell Ltd manufactured blinds in England. The factory was bought by Israel-based Hollis Metal Industries which sought to transfer all the work to Israel. The Employment Appeals Tribunal ruled for the first time that TUPE applies to cases where ownership of a company passes to a firm outside the EU although it did not apply in this case.

17.9   Notice

Unless they have agreed to waive it, employees are entitled to notice which is the period specified in the contract or the minimum period of notice in s.86, whichever is the greater. Contracts for an indeterminate period must contain a term relating to notice, failing which one will be implied by the courts. This will be a 'reasonable' period of notice, and in the case of very senior managers could be expected to be six months: *Adams v. Union Cinemas* [1939] 3 All ER 136, with other managers being due three months: *Mullholland v. Bexwell Estates* (1950) SJ 671, and senior clerical workers could expect one month: *Philips v. M J Alkam* (1969). This will be replaced by the statutory period if the latter is longer.

There is no need for notice for fixed-term contracts, and one will not be implied. If there is a notice clause but the contract is terminated immediately, compensation is based on the remaining time: *Laverack v. Woods of Colchester* [1966] 3 All ER 683. Similar rules apply for contracts expressed to terminate automatically on the completion of a task or when money runs out. The period may be where the contract includes a redundancy or disciplinary procedure, when the time to go through the procedural stages, including appeals, is added. In *Dietman v. London Borough of Brent* [1988] IRLR 228, Dietman was entitled to compensation for three months' notice and the three months of the dismissal procedure.

After one month or more of continuous employment, the minimum period of notice is one week; this rises to two weeks after two years of continuous employment and thereafter increases by one week for each additional year up to a maximum of 12 weeks: s.86(1). The common law right to a reasonable period of notice takes priority over the statutory minimum.

17.10 Sick pay

Employers must provide statutory sick pay at rates established by statute: Social Security and Housing Benefit Act 1982.

17.11 Restraint of trade clauses

Terms in employees' contracts restricting their freedom to work after termination of employment are discussed in Chapter 3, p.68.

17.12 The European dimension

Section 5 of the Regulation on Jurisdiction and the Recognition and Enforcement of Judgments in Civil and Commercial Matters (44/2001/EC, [2001] OJ L12/1) deals with jurisdiction over individual contracts of employment. Where an employee enters into an individual contract of employment with an employer who is not domiciled in a Member State, but has a branch, agency or other establishment in one of the Member States, the employer shall, in disputes arising out of the operations of the branch, agency and so on, be deemed to be domiciled in that Member State: Art. 18(2). An employer domiciled in a Member State may be sued in the courts of the Member State where he is domiciled or in another Member State in the courts for the place where the employee habitually carries out his work, or for the last place where he did so, or in the courts for the place where the business which engaged the employee is or was situated: Art. 19. An employer may bring proceedings only in the courts of the Member State in which the employee is domiciled: Art. 20(1).

End of Chapter Summary

This is a complex area of the law which is constantly evolving, largely as a result of European initiatives. For students of law relating to business, it is important simply to be able to grasp the main lines of the law rather than the detail.

Having read and understood this chapter you should have a detailed knowledge of the following essential points:

- The distinction between employees and self-employed persons, and the complex tests employed by the English courts to distinguish the one from the other.
- The mutual duties owed by the employee and the employer under the contract of employment.
- The way in which the rights of non-full-time employees are being brought into line with those of full-time employees.
- The operation of the legal mechanism by which EU law is transposed into English law, including the reference for preliminary interpretation procedure under Article 234 and the significant use of delegated legislation in the form of statutory instruments.

End of Chapter Summary cont'd

▶ The protection afforded to employees who have been unfairly dismissed, and the concept of constructive dismissal.

▶ The protection offered by the law to employees where there has been a transfer of undertakings, particularly as it relates to privatisation of public services.

Questions

1. Name some of the tests which the court applies in distinguishing between employees and independent contractors.

2. The crew of a fishing vessel were defined as 'share fishermen', receiving a share of the profits from the sale of their catch rather than a fixed wage. There were no written contracts of employment and the crew were taxed as self-employed, responsible for their own NI contributions, had no right to sick pay, paid holidays, redundancy payments or compensation for unfair dismissal. The skipper chose the crew but they supplied their own oilskins, gloves, knives and bedding. The owners provided the vessel, fishing gear and safety equipment. If the crew caught no fish on one trip, the cost of fuel and so on was carried forward. Catches were sold at auction by third party sellers who divided the proceeds, with 5 per cent going to the owners and 4 per cent commission to themselves. Further deductions were then made for landing charges, ice, fuel and so on. The crew took 40 per cent of the balance and the owners 60 per cent.

    Applying the principles from other legal decisions you should attempt to reach a decision whether the fishermen are employees or self-employed.

3. Jean is employed by Bakewell plc, a large catering company, and worked for a number of years at their factory in Wedford as a machine operative. She liked the work and it fitted in well with her responsibilities as a wife and mother, since she worked on a shift which allowed her to go home at 4.00 p.m. in time to greet her two young children. Bakewell plc informed the workforce that new shift patterns were being introduced. These would mean that Jean would not be able to be home until 5.00 p.m. The company refused to be flexible and Jean felt obliged to hand in her notice. Advise her on any rights which she may have against the company.

4. NonPC Ltd, a factory on the western edge of town, placed recruitment advertisements in the local paper in Wedford, where there is a large ethnic population which is concentrated in the eastern part of the town. There is also a large Catholic community, most of whom attend St Swithins RC school. The advertisements were for people to work on a production line sorting out defective mouldings of garden gnomes and required applicants to (a) have a GCSE in English Language and (b) be over six feet tall. The advertisement further stated that applicants should list the schools they had attended and that preference would be given to people living within walking distance of the factory. When the company interviewed applicants, the panel refused to consider Rory who used a wheelchair. The workshop was on the fourth floor and was reached by a stairway, there being only a goods lift.

    Consider the issues raised in this scenario.

Chapter 18

Sale and supply of goods

After reading this chapter you will know about:

▶ the definition of contracts for the sale of goods
▶ implied terms in sale of goods contracts and exclusion clauses
▶ passing of property and risk
▶ sale by a non-owner
▶ remedies of the seller and the buyer
▶ implied terms in contracts for the supply of goods and services.

18.1 Contracts for the sale of goods

The law relating to contracts for the sale of goods is found in the Sale of Goods Act (SOGA)1979 as amended, and statutory references in this part of the chapter are to this Act except where otherwise indicated.

Contracts for the sale of goods are contracts 'whereby the seller transfers or agrees to transfer the property in goods to the buyer for a money consideration, called the price': s.2(1).

The word 'property' refers to ownership. The definition takes into account agreements where the ownership in the goods will not transfer immediately, but at some later date. This type of contract is 'an agreement to sell'. The use of the word 'property' excludes from the Act any type of contract relating to goods where ownership does not pass. Thus it excludes contracts relating to hire of goods or contracts of bailment where possession but not ownership passes.

'Goods' includes all personal chattels other than things in action and money, and in particular 'includes emblements, industrial growing crops and things attached to or forming part of the land which are agreed to be severed before sale or under the contract of sale and includes an undivided share in goods': s.61(1).

This includes crops, and other things which are 'attached to or form part of the land', which are 'goods' if they are distinct from the land. Goods must be transferred for a 'money consideration, called the price'. This excludes barter – the exchange of goods – but includes contracts where goods are part-exchanged for goods and money.

If the main purpose of the contract is not the transfer of property, even though there is an element of transfer, the contract is one for labour and materials. In *Robinson v. Graves* [1935] 1 KB 597, a contract to paint a person's portrait was not a contract for the sale of goods, since the main element was the skill of the artist. The same is true where a garage fits parts while servicing or repairing a car, or where a builder supplies bricks and tiles under a contract to build a house: *Young & Marten v. McManus Childs* [1969] 1 AC 454.

Contracts of sale may be in writing, under seal or oral, or partly in writing and partly oral, and may be implied from the conduct of the parties: s.4. Capacity to contract is in accordance with the general law: s.3(1). However, where necessaries are sold and delivered to children or persons suffering from mental incapacity or drunkenness, they must pay a reasonable price: s.3(2).

18.2 Implied terms in sale of goods contracts

Under the Act, as amended, there are implied terms relating to title; compliance with description; satisfactory quality; fitness for purpose; and conformity between sample and bulk. For consumer contracts, the Unfair Terms in Consumer Contracts Regulations 1999 (SI 1999/2083) could also apply (see Chapter 21, p.517).

(a) Seller's right to sell

In the case of a sale, there is an implied term that the seller has a right to sell the goods, and, in the case of an agreement to sell, that s/he will have such a right when the property is to pass: s.12(1). For England, Wales and Northern Ireland, the term is a condition: s.12(5A). In *Rowland v. Divall* [1923] 2 KB 500, the claimant bought a car from the defendant, but after four months discovered that the car belonged to a third party and returned it. He was entitled to treat the contract as discharged for total failure of consideration and recover the purchase price.

If the seller subsequently acquires the title to the goods, the title is transferred to the buyer later than it should have been. Once this has happened, the buyer cannot repudiate the goods under s.12(1) but can repudiate the contract prior to that. In *Butterworth v. Kingsway Motors* [1954] 1 WLR 1286, the buyer purchased a car from a person who had not yet acquired title to it because she had not completed payments to the HP company. The buyer could repudiate the car after 11 months when he discovered the situation, even though the seller completed her payments the following week. (This would now be covered by the Hire Purchase Act 1964, Part III.)

The implied term is also breached where the seller has title but has no right to sell the goods.

In *Niblett Ltd v. Confectioners' Materials Co.* [1921] 3 KB 387, the contract of sale related to tins of condensed milk labelled 'Nissly Brand' which infringed the Nestlé trade mark. Nestlé obliged the buyers to remove the offending labels before they resold the tins. It was held that the sellers were in breach of s.12(1) and (2)(b): an implied term that the buyer will enjoy quiet possession of the goods.

In *Microbeads v. Vinhurst Road Markings* [1975] 1 WLR 218, following the sale of some road-marking machines, the patent for the machines was acquired by a third company, with the result that it could enforce its patent rights against the buyers. The buyers claimed breach of the implied condition as to title and breach of the warranty of quiet possession. The court held that there was no breach of s.12(1), but there was a breach of s.12(2)(b) relating to quiet possession in the future.

Where the contract intended to transfer only a limited title to the buyer: s.12(3), there is an implied term that all charges or encumbrances known to the seller and not known to the buyer have been disclosed before the contract is made: s.12(4), and that the buyer's quiet possession of the goods will not be disturbed by (a) the seller; (b), where the parties intend that the seller should transfer only such title as a third person may have, that person; and (c) anyone claiming through or under the seller or that third person otherwise than under a charge or encumbrance disclosed or known to the buyer before the contract is made: s.12(5). These terms are warranties for England, Wales and Northern Ireland: s.12(5A).

(b)   Compliance with description

Where there is a contract for the sale of goods by description, there is an implied term that the goods will correspond with the description: s.13(1). For England and Wales and Northern Ireland, the term is a condition subject to s.15A in non-consumer cases where the breach is so slight that it would be unreasonable for the buyer to reject the goods, when the breach is to be treated as a breach of warranty unless a contrary intention appears in or is to be implied from the contract.

Where this term is breached, and subject to s.15A, the buyer can repudiate the contract even though the goods are of suitable quality and fit for the purpose. A contract to supply canned fruit in cases of 30 tins could be repudiated because one half of the consignment contained 24 tins to a case: *Re Moore & Co. Ltd and Landauer & Co.* [1921] 2 KB 519. In *Arcos v. Ronaasen (EA) & Son* [1933] AC 470, the contract was for staves for manufacturing barrels described as being 'half an inch thick'. Those supplied varied between half an inch and nine-sixteenths of an inch, and the buyer could repudiate the contract, even though the goods were fit for the purpose. This shows the importance of sellers specifying margins of error in contracts of sale.

The section also extends to sales by sample as well as by description, in which case 'it is not sufficient that the bulk of the goods corresponds with the sample if the goods do not also correspond with the description'. In *Nichol v. Godts* (1854) 10 Exch 191, the sale of oil by way of a sample plus the description 'refined rape oil' fell within the subsection where the bulk corresponded with the sample but not with the description.

Goods are clearly sold by description where the buyer has not seen them and relies on the description applied to them. In *Varley v. Whipp* [1900] 1 QB 513, the claimant bought a piece of farming equipment described as having been used for only one season. On delivery it was seen to be old and had been repaired, and the buyer could repudiate the contract.

The scope of the term was extended by Lord Wright in *Grant v. Australian Knitting Mills* [1936] AC 85, where he stated, 'there is a sale by description even though the buyer is buying something displayed before him on a counter'. In this case, woollen underwear sold over the counter was held to be a sale by description. This position is now covered by s.13(3), which provides that '[a] sale of goods is not prevented from being a sale by description by reason only that, being exposed for sale or hire, they are selected by the buyer'.

(c)   Satisfactory quality

The normal rule for contracts for the sale of goods is *caveat emptor* (let the buyer beware). This is the position where the seller is a private individual, where there is no warranty unless one is specifically incorporated: s.14(1). The position is different where the goods are sold in the course of a business.

For sales in the course of a business, there is an implied term that the goods supplied under the contract are of satisfactory quality: s.14(2). Goods are of satisfactory quality if they meet the standard that a reasonable person would regard as satisfactory, taking account of any description of the goods, the price (if relevant) and all other relevant circumstances: s.14(2A). The quality of goods includes their state and condition, and the following (among others) are, in appropriate cases, aspects of the quality of goods: (a) fitness for all the purposes for which goods of the kind in question are commonly supplied; (b) appearance and finish; (c) freedom from minor defects; (d) safety; and (e) durability: s.14(2B). The term excludes, however, any matter making the quality unsatisfactory (a) which is specifically drawn to the buyer's attention before the contract is made, (b), where the buyer examines the goods before the contract is made, which that examination ought to reveal, or (c), in the case of a contract for sale by sample, which would have been apparent on a reasonable examination of the sample: s.14(2C).

The implied term is a condition for England, Wales and Northern Ireland: s.14(6), subject to s.15A for non-consumer cases.

In *Stevenson v. Rogers* [1999] 1 All ER 613, S carried on business as a fisherman using a boat called *Dolly Mopp* which he had bought many years ago. S bought a boat named *Jelle* in 1983 and sold the *Dolly Mopp* in November 1986. In April 1988 S sold the *Jelle* to R, intending at the time to replace her with a new boat built to his specification. He subsequently changed his mind and, in May 1988, bought another boat as a replacement. R brought an action in respect of the purchase of the *Jelle* regarding the satisfactory quality of the boat. R subsequently appealed a decision of the High Court that the sale was not a sale of goods 'in the course of a business'. The Court of Appeal held that s.14(2) of the 1979 Act embodied a deliberate change in the wording of the equivalent provision in the 1893 Act which had a restrictive effect. The purpose of the change was to widen the protection afforded to a purchaser from a situation where the seller was a dealer in the type of goods sold, to one where he simply made a sale 'in the course of a business'. The court held that s.14(2) was to be construed broadly and at face value, that the boat had been sold in the course of a business and that there was an implied term as to satisfactory quality in the contract of sale.

If the buyer's inspection does not reveal defects simply because the inspection is negligent, the buyer cannot claim in respect of defects which a more thorough examination would have revealed.

In *Thornett & Fehr v. Beers* [1919] 1 KB 486, the buyers of barrels of glue were prevented from claiming in respect of defects in the glue when their examination had only extended to an examination of the barrels themselves.

However, where the examination reveals a defect but the buyer continues with the purchase in the belief that the defect is easily remedied, they can repudiate the goods when the defect turns out to be more difficult to remedy.

In *R & B Customs Brokers Co. Ltd v. United Dominions Trust Ltd* [1988] 1 WLR 321, a person purchased a car knowing that it had a leak, but only later discovered that the leak was major and incurable. Neill LJ stated, 'I am not at present persuaded … that the condition in s.14(2) is excluded if at the time the contract is made the buyer is reasonably of the opinion that the defect can be, and will be, rectified at no cost to himself'. The issue was not resolved by the Court of Appeal, who decided that the buyer could rely on s.14(3) (below) and that the car was not reasonably fit for the particular purpose for which the buyer had informed the seller that he wanted it.

The reference to 'fitness for all the purposes for which goods of the kind in question are commonly supplied': s.14(2B)(a), was considered under the earlier law relating to merchantable quality.

In *Aswan Engineering Establishment v. Lupdine* [1987] 1 WLR 1, the issue was the merchantable quality of heavy duty plastic buckets which, although suitable for most normal purposes, collapsed when left by the buyer stacked in a container in the sun where the heat in the containers reached 70°C. The court held that to be of merchantable quality it was not necessary for the buckets to be suitable for all purposes.

The points in s.14(2B)(b) and (c) appear in line with previous decisions.

In *Rogers and Another v. Parish (Scarborough) Ltd and Another* [1987] QB 933, the Court of Appeal held that a series of small defects in a new Range Rover, which did not make it undrivable or unroadworthy, made it unmerchantable. The court held that the statutory definition extended in the case of motor vehicles to include a pride in the external and internal appearance relative to the market at which the car was aimed. The court's suggestion that the merest cosmetic blemish on a Rolls-Royce might make it unmerchantable is in line with s.14(2A).

The issue of durability in s.14(2B)(e) is of importance, particularly with regard to the sale of second-hand goods.

In *Bartlett v. Sydney Marcus* [1965] 1 WLR 1013, the buyer of a second-hand car, who was warned that the car had a defective clutch which had been taken into account in its pricing, was unable to claim that the car was not of merchantable quality when the clutch failed one month later. In *Crowther v. Shannon* [1975] 1WLR 30, the court held that an 8-year-old Jaguar with 82,000 miles on the clock was not reasonably fit for the purpose when the engine seized after three weeks' driving. In *Bernstein v. Pamsons Motors (Golders Green) Ltd* [1987] 2 All ER 22, the buyer of a new car took the car on two or three short journeys in the first two weeks. After 140 miles and within three weeks of delivery, the car's engine seized. The court held that the car was not of merchantable quality but the buyer had lost the right to repudiate the contract and was entitled only to damages.

The requirement of satisfactory quality applies to all goods supplied under the contract, including things mixed in with the goods: coalite containing a detonator: *Wilson v. Rickett, Cockerell & Co. Ltd* [1954] 1 QB 598. It also covers packaging: in *Geddling v. Marsh* [1920] All ER 631, the sellers of bottled mineral water were liable for injury to a buyer by a defective bottle.

(d)   Fitness for purpose

Where there is a sale in the course of a business and the buyer, expressly or by implication, makes known to the seller a particular purpose for which the goods are being bought, there is an implied term that the goods are reasonably fit for that purpose, whether or not it is a purpose for which such goods are commonly supplied, except where the circumstances show that the buyer does not rely, or that it is unreasonable for him to rely, on the skill or judgement of the seller: s.14(3). The term is a condition for England, Wales and Northern Ireland: s.14(6), but subject to s.15A in non-consumer cases. It is necessary to distinguish between satisfactory quality and fitness for purpose: s.14(2) and (3).

In *Kendall (Henry) & Sons v. William Lillico & Sons Ltd* [1968] 2 All ER 444, groundnuts were supplied to a game farm where pheasants were reared. The groundnuts contained tiny quantities of highly poisonous mould which killed many of the pheasants. The court held that the goods were unfit for the purpose of feeding pheasants under s.14(3), but of satisfactory quality under s.14(2) since they were fit for some purposes for which they were ordinarily and reasonably used and saleable as such.

In order for liability to arise under s.14(3), the buyer must state the particular purpose for which the goods are being bought. The purchaser of a coat who contracted dermatitis because of an abnormally sensitive skin failed in a claim under s.14(3) since the fact had not been drawn to the seller's attention: *Griffiths v. Peter Conway Ltd* [1939] 1 All ER 685. Where the goods have only one normal use, the purpose is communicated by the mere fact of the purchase: the sale of a faulty hot-water bottle in *Priest v. Last* [1903] 2 KB 148.

The buyer must also rely on the seller's skill or judgement, but the reliance does not have to extend to every aspect of the contract.

In *Ashington Piggeries Ltd v. Christopher Hill Ltd (Nordsildmel Third Parties)* [1971] 1 All ER 847, the appellants invented a new compound feed for mink and supplied the formula to the respondents to be made up. The formula contained herring meal and the herring meal supplied by the third parties contained a substance toxic to all animals, but to which mink were particularly sensitive. Although they had supplied the formula, the buyers had relied on the suppliers to select ingredients of a suitable quality. The respondents were in breach of both s.14(2) and (3).

Asking for goods by their trade or brand name generally excludes any implied term relating to fitness for purpose. However, in *Baldry v. Marshall* [1925] 1 KB 260, the claimant asked the defendant car dealers for a car 'suitable for touring purposes'. The defendants recommended a Bugatti, which the claimant then ordered. The car was unsuitable and the claimant was entitled to repudiate the contract.

In ascertaining whether the goods are reasonably fit for the purpose, their price must be taken into account, as well as whether they were second-hand, and other factors. Sellers will not escape liability, however, by producing evidence that they had taken all reasonable precautions to ensure fitness. In *Frost v. Aylesbury Dairy* [1905] 1 KB 1, the defendants were liable for supplying milk containing typhoid germs in spite of taking all reasonable hygiene precautions.

Goods must 'continue to be fit for that purpose for a reasonable time after delivery, so long as they remain in the same apparent state and condition as that in which they were delivered, apart from normal wear and tear'. This statement is from *Lambert v. Lewis* [1982] AC 225, where the buyer's claim in respect of a failed tow-bar coupling was rejected once it became clear that the locking mechanism was broken, thus the seller's obligation was terminated.

(e) Sale by sample

In respect of these contracts, there is an implied term (a) that the bulk will correspond with the sample in quality; (b) that the buyer will have a reasonable opportunity for comparing bulk with the sample; and (c) that the goods will be free from any defect, making their quality unsatisfactory, which would not be apparent on reasonable examination of the sample: s.15(2). This term is a condition for England, Wales and Northern Ireland: s.15(3), subject to s.15A in non-consumer cases.

As regards the requirement that the bulk will correspond to the sample in quality, the court held that the condition is broken even though only a simple process is required to make the bulk correspond with the sample. In *E & S Ruben Ltd v. Faire Bros & Co. Ltd* [1949] 1 All ER 215, the contract related to a quantity of vulcanised rubber. The sample was flat and soft, whereas the bulk was crinkly and folded, although these defects could be cured by warming the material. There was a breach of s.15 and the contract could be repudiated.

Regarding a reasonable opportunity of comparing bulk with sample, in *Polenghi Brothers v. Dried Milk Co. Ltd* (1904) 92 LT 64 the contract was for a quantity of dried milk powder under a contract by sample. The contract specified that payment was to be made in cash 'on the arrival of the powders against shipping or railway documents'. The court supported the buyer's refusal to pay on delivery of shipping documents, contending they had a right to compare the bulk with sample.

As regards the requirement of a reasonable examination of the sample, in *Godley v. Perry* [1960] 1 All ER 36, a retailer was liable to a boy injured by the failure of a catapult, one of a consignment bought from a wholesaler on sale by sample. The wholesaler claimed the retailer's test – pulling back the elastic – was unreasonable. The court held this was all that could have been expected of a potential purchaser.

(f) Waiver of breach of condition

Breaches of condition can always be treated as breaches of warranty, but where a breach of condition has been waived on one occasion it can later be unilaterally reintroduced as a condition on reasonable notice.

In *Charles Rickards Ltd v. Oppenheim* [1950] 1 KB 611, the defendant ordered a car to be built on a Rolls-Royce chassis. The work was not completed within the specified time, but some months later, when the car had still not been delivered, R said that if it was not delivered within four weeks he would refuse to accept it. The court held that he could refuse to accept delivery.

Where a contract is not severable, in that it does not provide for the supply of goods by separate instalments, and the buyer has accepted the goods or part of them, the seller's breach of a condition can only be treated as a breach of warranty unless there is an express or implied term to that effect: s.11(4). This is subject to s.35A, which provides: '(1) [i]f the buyer (a) has the right to reject the goods by reason of a breach on the part of the seller that affects some or all of them, but (b) accepts some of the goods, including, where there are any goods unaffected by the breach, all such goods, he does not by accepting them lose his right to reject the rest'.

Buyers are deemed not to have accepted goods until they have had a reasonable opportunity of examining them and, for sale by sample, comparing the bulk with the sample: s.34. Buyers accept the goods when informing the seller that they have accepted them, when they do an act in relation to them inconsistent with the seller's ownership, or when they retain the goods beyond a reasonable time: s.35. This last point is a serious limitation on statutory protection against defective goods, since after a few weeks at the most the right to repudiate is lost. Thus, in *Bernstein v. Pamsons Motors (Golders Green) Ltd* (above), the right to repudiate a new car was lost within three weeks of delivery.

18.3 Exclusion of implied terms

(a) Consumer contracts

Where one of the parties 'deals as a consumer', the implied terms relating to title, description, satisfactory quality, fitness for purpose and so on can never be excluded. A person deals as a consumer if (i) s/he does not contract in the course of a business or hold him/herself out as doing so; (ii) the other party contracts in the course of a business; and (iii) the goods are of a type ordinarily supplied for private use or consumption. A person does not deal as a consumer in sales by auction or competitive tender.

(b) Non-consumer contracts

Between dealers, the implied terms, except for that relating to title, can be excluded subject to the 'requirement of reasonableness'. The test for reasonableness takes into account: (i) the relative strength of the bargaining positions of the parties; (ii) whether the buyer received an inducement to agree to the term or could have bought elsewhere without the term; (iii) whether the buyer knew or ought to have known of the existence and extent of the term; and (iv) whether goods were manufactured, processed or adapted to the buyer's special order.

In *George Mitchell (Chesterhall) Ltd v. Finney Lock Seeds Ltd* [1983] 1 All ER 108, the court also took account of the fact that the seller could have insured against liability without significantly affecting prices. The case concerned the purchase of cabbage seeds by the claimant. Because of the negligence of the suppliers, the seeds were not those of cabbages, and the farmer lost anticipated profits of £60,000. The defendants claimed protection under an exclusion clause which limited their liability to the cost of the seeds. The court, applying the criteria above, held that they were not protected.

In *St Albans City and District Council v. International Computers Ltd* [1996] 4 All ER 481, the council suffered a loss of £1.3m as a result of an error in computer software supplied under a contract which limited the defendant's liability to £100,000. The court took into consideration (a) the fact that the parties were of unequal bargaining power; (b) that the firm had not justified the figure of £100,000, which was small in relation to the potential loss; (c) that the firm was insured worldwide for a sum of £50m; and (d) that the practical consequences counted in favour of the authority. Accordingly, the firm had failed to discharge its burden to establish that the exclusion clause was a fair and reasonable one. The decision was affirmed by the Court of Appeal.

Where, however, commercial parties are of equal bargaining strength they are generally held to be capable of choosing to be bound by the contracts which they enter and will be regarded as being bound by their terms. In *Granville Oil and Chemicals Ltd v. Davis Turner & Co. Ltd* [2003] 2 Lloyd's Rep 356 the defendant entered into a standard form contract with the claimant to transport paint from Kuwait to Rotterdam and arrange the insurance. The defendant failed to arrange insurance and the paint was damaged in transit. The contract provided that any claim was to be brought within nine months but the claimant failed to bring an action within the time limit. The Court of Appeal held that the nine month limit satisfied the reasonableness test under s.3 UCTA. The court stated that the guidelines in Schedule 2 should be taken into account even though the contract was not one for the sale or hire purchase of goods.

18.4 Passing of property and risk

In respect of non-consumer contracts, the transfer of property means the transfer of risk to the buyer irrespective of whether or not the goods are delivered: s.20(1). This is, however, subject to the fact that where delivery has been delayed through the fault of either buyer or seller, the goods are at the risk of that party in respect of any loss which may not otherwise have occurred: s.20(2). For consumer contracts, the goods remain at the seller's risk until they are delivered to the consumer: s.20(4).

In *Demby Hamilton & Co. Ltd v. Barden (Endeavour Wines Ltd Third Party)* [1949] 1 All ER 435, the sellers agreed to supply 30 tons of apple juice, delivered in weekly truckloads, delivery to be completed by February 1946. In December 1945 the buyer asked them to hold up deliveries. Further deliveries were made in January and April 1946, after which the buyer refused to accept more juice. By November 1946 the remaining juice held by the seller had gone bad. Loss fell on the buyer, since delivery had been delayed through his fault.

For non-consumer contracts, the seller may retain possession but the ownership may have passed to the buyer, and the buyer may obtain possession while the seller retains ownership. To fix the moment at which the title passes, the Sale of Goods Act 1979 contains specific rules in Part II, ss.16–19. These vary according to whether the goods are specific or unascertained.

Specific goods are 'goods identified and agreed upon at the time a contract of sale is made and includes an undivided share, specified as a fraction or percentage, of goods identified and agreed on as aforesaid': s.61.

Sale of a specific painting or a second-hand car is an example of specific goods. Most contracts in supermarkets and other self-service stores relate to specific goods. In 1985, the definition was amended to include an undivided share of goods. Examples of contracts for unascertained goods are those for a specific quantity of a bulk of goods: five cases of wine from a wine merchant's stock, and for generic goods.

Goods may be 'existing goods, owned and possessed by the seller, or goods to be manufactured or acquired by him after the contract of sale': s.5(1). These 'future goods' can be specific or unascertained. If they are to be manufactured or prepared to the buyer's specification they are unascertained, but if they are a specific object to be acquired by the seller they are specific goods. In *Varley v. Whipp* [1900] 1 QB 513, a contract for the sale of a second-hand agricultural machine which the seller did not own at the time of contract was for the sale of specific goods.

(a) Passing specific goods

The basic rule is that property is passed when the parties intend it to be transferred: s.17(1), and that in ascertaining the parties' intentions regard shall be had to the terms of the contract, the conduct of the parties, and the circumstances of the case: s.17(2). The contract rarely provides for the passing of the property, in which case property passes in accordance with Rules 1–4 set out in s.18.

(i) Rule 1

'Where there is an unconditional contract for the sale of specific goods in a deliverable state, the property passes to the buyer when the contract is made, and it is immaterial whether the time of payment or the time of delivery, or both, be postponed.' Goods are in a 'deliverable state' if 'in such a state that the buyer would be bound to take delivery of them'. Problems can arise between the operation of the rule and the intentions of the parties.

In *Dennant v. Skinner and Collom* [1948] 2 KB 164, the buyer successfully bid for a van at an auction, paid by cheque and signed a form to the effect that the property would not pass to him until the cheque was cleared. The cheque was dishonoured and the buyer had in the meantime sold the van to another person. The auctioneer sued to recover the van from the second buyer. The court held that when the buyer signed the statement concerning the transfer of title it had already passed to him 'on the fall of the hammer' under Rule 1.

In spite of the wording of the rule, postponement of payment and delivery will often determine the parties' intentions: in *Ward v. Bignall* [1967] 1 QB 534, Diplock LJ said: 'in modern times very little is needed to give rise to the inference that property in specific goods is to pass only on delivery or payment'.

In *Underwood v. Burgh Castle Brick & Cement Syndicate* [1922] 1 KB 343, there was a contract for the sale of a machine weighing 30 tons and bolted to the floor. The sellers had to unbolt the machine and load it on to a train for delivery and it was damaged while being loaded. On the issue of whether the property had passed to the buyer when the accident occurred, the court held that the machine was not in a deliverable state and that the agreement between the parties relating to delivery of the machine free on rail indicated an intention that property would pass only when the machine was loaded.

(ii) *Rule 2*
'Where there is a contract for the sale of specific goods and the seller is bound to do something to the goods, for the purpose of putting them into a deliverable state, the property does not pass until the thing is done, and the buyer has notice that it has been done.' The reference to 'notice to the buyer' is actual, not constructive, notice.

(iii) *Rule 3*
'Where there is a contract for the sale of specific goods in a deliverable state, but the seller is bound to weigh, measure, test or do some other act or thing ... for the purpose of ascertaining the price, the property does not pass until the act or thing is done and the buyer has notice that it has been done.' A obligation imposed on the buyer to weigh and so on does not trigger the rule.

(iv) *Rule 4*
'When goods are delivered ... on approval or on sale or return or other similar terms the property in the goods passes to the buyer: (a) when he signifies his approval or acceptance to the seller or does any other act adopting the transaction; (b) retains the goods without giving notice of rejection, then if a time has been fixed for the return of the goods, on expiration of that time and, if no time has been fixed, the expiration of a reasonable time.'

The reference to an act adopting the transaction covers cases where the buyer sells or pawns the goods.

In *Kirkham v. Attenborough* [1895–9] All ER Rep 450, K, a manufacturing jeweller, delivered jewellery to W 'on sale or return'. W pledged the goods with A, a pawnbroker, and the price remained unpaid. K sought recovery of the goods from A. The court held that the pledge had adopted the transaction, passing the property to W, who thus passed good title to A.

This can be contrasted with *Re Ferrier* [1944] Ch 295, where the failure to return the goods was not the buyer's fault and was beyond his control. The rule is excluded if the contract provides that the property in goods sold on approval passes only on payment: *Weiner v. Gill* [1906] 2 KB 574.

In *Poole v. Smith's Car Sales (Balham) Ltd* [1962] 2 All ER 482, P, a car dealer, sold a second-hand car to SCS Ltd 'on sale or return' in August 1960. The car had not been returned by October 1960, so P wrote stating that, if it was not returned by 10 November, the car would be deemed to have been sold to them. The car was finally returned at the end of November. The court held that the property had passed to the buyers under Rule 4(b), since a reasonable time had expired without its being returned.

In *Atari Corporation (UK) Ltd v. Electronics Boutique Store (UK) Ltd* [1998] 2 WLR 66, EBS bought computer games under an agreement which provided for 'Payment 30 November 1995. Full sale or return until 31 January 1996'. On 19 January 1996, when the goods had not been paid for, EBS wrote that it had decided to cease stocking certain items which would be placed in its central warehouse for the preparation of a detailed list. EBS appealed to the Court of Appeal against a decision that it had failed to give notice of rejection in time under s.18. The court held that there was a valid notice of rejection; that where goods were delivered on sale or return a notice rejecting unsold goods did not have to be in writing or identify the goods to which it related; and that the goods need not be physically capable of collection when the notice was issued but within a reasonable time.

(b) Passing of an undivided share forming part of a bulk

Where there is a contract for the sale of a specified quantity of unascertained goods where (i) the goods or some of them form part of a bulk; and (ii) the buyer has paid for some or all of the goods forming part of the bulk, then, unless the parties otherwise agree, (i) property in an undivided share in the bulk is transferred to the buyer; and (ii) s/he becomes an owner in common of the bulk: s.20A(1) and (2). The undivided share is calculated according to the quantity of goods paid for in relation to the bulk at that time: s.20A(3), subject to the fact that if the aggregate of the undivided shares should at any time exceed the aggregate of the bulk, the undivided share shall be proportionately reduced so that the aggregate is equal to the bulk: s.20A(4).

Where a buyer has paid for only part of the goods, delivery to him/her out of the bulk shall be ascribed in the first place to the goods for which s/he has paid: s.20A(5). A person who has become an owner in common is deemed to have consented to (a) deliveries to other owners in common; and (b) any dealing with or removal, delivery or disposal of goods by any other owner in common in so far as the goods fall within that co-owner's undivided share: s.20B(1)(a) and (b).

Nothing in this section or s.20A shall (i) impose an obligation on a buyer of goods to compensate any other buyer for any shortfall; (ii) affect any contractual arrangement between buyers for adjustments between themselves; or (iii) affect the rights of any buyer under his/her contract: s.20B(3). The term 'bulk' means 'a mass or collection of goods of the same kind which (a) is contained in a defined space or area; and (b) is such that any goods in the bulk are interchangeable': s.61(1). A new definition of 'delivery' in relation to ss.20A and 20B includes 'such appropriation of goods to the contract as results in property in the goods being transferred to the buyer': s.61(1).

(c)   Passing unascertained goods

The basic rule provides that where there is a contract for the sale of unascertained goods, no property is transferred to the buyer unless and until the goods are ascertained: s.16. Once ascertained, they pass under s.17 or under Rule 5(1) or (2) of s.18.

Rule 5(1) relates to unconditional appropriation plus assent and, for the sale of unascertained or future goods by description, property passes when goods of that description and in a deliverable state are unconditionally appropriated to the contract, either by the seller with the assent of the buyer, or by the buyer with the assent of the seller. The assent may be express or implied, and may be given either before or after the appropriation.

The appropriation must be unconditional: '[a] mere setting apart or selection by the seller of the goods which he expects to use in performance of the contract is not enough. If that is all, he can change his mind and use those goods in performance of some other contract and use some other goods in performance of this contract. To constitute an appropriation of goods to the contract, the parties must have had, or be reasonably supposed to have had, an intention to attach the contract irrevocably to those goods': Pearson J in *Carlos Federspiel & Co. v. Charles Twigg & Co.* [1957] 1 Lloyd's Rep 240.

The case involved contracts to sell cycles and tricycles 'f.o.b. UK port'. The goods were packed and marked with the port of destination but were never sent to Liverpool for shipping. The seller went into liquidation and the buyers sought to recover the goods from the liquidator on the ground that the goods had been unconditionally appropriated. The action failed because the court found an intention that ownership should pass on shipment, and that the appropriating act is usually the last act to be performed by the seller, and the last two acts, the sending of the goods to Liverpool and having them shipped, were not performed.

In *Pignataro v. Gilroy & Son* (1919) 120 LT 480, the court held there was appropriation where the sellers sold 140 bags of rice to the buyer and gave him a delivery order on 28 February 1918 to obtain delivery of 125 bags at Chambers Wharf, and to collect the remaining 15 at the seller's warehouse. The buyer did nothing until 25 March, when he sent someone to collect the 15 bags at the warehouse and discovered that they had been stolen shortly before. The court held that the risk had passed to the buyer, and the seller was not liable for non-delivery.

In *Re Stapylton Fletcher Ltd and Re Ellis Son & Vidler Ltd* [1995] 1 All ER 192, the court held that where cases or bottles of identical wines were held segregated from the trading stock, in store for a group of customers, they would be sufficiently ascertained for the purposes of s.16.

'Delivery to a carrier for delivery to the buyer will usually constitute unconditional appropriation if the seller delivers the goods to … a carrier or other bailee or custodier (whether named by the buyer or not) for the purpose of transmission to the buyer, and does not reserve the right to disposal': Rule 5(2). This does not apply where there are several consignments and the goods are not appropriated on delivery to the carrier.

In *Healy v. Howlett & Sons* [1917] 1KB 337, the seller contracted to sell 20 boxes of fish to a buyer and dispatched by train 190 boxes to various customers, all the boxes being unmarked. The goods went bad during the journey from Ireland to London, and the court held that the property passed only when the railway company allotted the boxes to specific customers during the journey.

Where the seller delivers goods to a carrier but reserves a right of disposal of them, the property will not pass until the condition is complied with. The seller may, for example, deliver the goods to the carrier with instructions that they are not to be handed over until the buyer has paid for them. This reservation of right of disposal is contained in s.19(1). The rule is important with regard to prosecutions for theft. In *Edwards v. Ddin* [1976] 1 WLR 942, a motorist filled his car with petrol and drove off without paying. It was held that the garage owner did not reserve the right to dispose of the petrol once it was in the tank and the property in it had passed to the motorist under s.18, Rule 5.

In relation to appropriation and supermarkets, Parker LCJ stated: 'the intention of the parties quite clearly as it seems to me is that the property shall not pass until the price is paid': *Lacis v. Cashmarts* [1969] 2 QB 400. This applies to goods picked up by the customer and goods weighed and bagged by an employee. Winn J stated: 'the limit of the authority of the meat counter assistant is clearly merely to wrap up and hand over the meat and not to deal in any way with any transfer of property from the owner of the shop to the customer': *Martin v. Puttick* [1968] 2 QB 82.

The fact that the appropriation must be assented to by the other party is not a problem since it can be implied and be given in advance.

(d)   Appropriation by exhaustion of unascertained goods part of a bulk

Where unascertained goods for several customers are transported in bulk for delivery to various destinations, once the last but one delivery has been made, the remaining goods are unconditionally appropriated to the final buyer: *Karlshamns Oliefabriker v. Eastport Navigation Corporation, The Elafi* [1982] 1 All ER 208. The Act was amended in 1995 to incorporate this decision: s.18 Rule 5(3). The position is the same where the bulk is reduced to (or to less than) the aggregate of the quantities due to a single buyer under separate contracts: Rule 5(4).

(e)   Retention of title

Retention of title clauses are a form of security to suppliers and are possible because of s.19(1) which allows the seller of goods to reserve the right of disposal until certain conditions are fulfilled. They provide that property passes to the buyer only when payment has been made, even though the goods have been delivered and the buyer has the right to sell and/or use them. In the event of the buyer's insolvency prior to payment, the supplier can recover the unsold stocks in the buyer's possession (see Chapter 15, p.389).

18.5   Sale by non-owner

The basic legal principle where goods have been sold by a non-owner is the recognition of the owner's rights. This principle is expressed by the phrase *nemo dat quod non habet* (a person with no title cannot pass a good title). The law protects the innocent purchaser only in exceptional circumstances.

The general principle is stated in s.21(1) which establishes only two exceptions: sale by agents and where the owner is estopped by his actions from denying the seller's authority to sell. Further exceptions arise under the Factors Act (FA) 1889 in respect of sales by mercantile agents, and under any common law or statutory power of sale or by court order: s.21(2). These and other exceptions in the FA 1889 and other legislative provisions will now be discussed.

(a) Estoppel authority

This prevents the true owner from claiming that the sale was unauthorised and arises when the owner leads the innocent purchaser to believe that the seller had the right to sell the goods. It must be established that:

(i) the true owner represented – intentionally or negligently – that the seller was entitled to sell the goods;
(ii) the innocent buyer acted in reliance on the representation.

In *Eastern Distributors v. Goldring* [1957] 2 QB 600, the owner of a van wished to raise a loan against it and, together with a motor trader, deceived a finance company by filling in forms as if the van belonged to the trader and the rightful owner wanted to buy it on HP. The finance company acquired the van for cash from the motor trader and transferred it on HP to the true owner. The latter failed to make any instalment payments and later sold the van to an innocent purchaser. In a dispute concerning the rightful ownership of the van, the court upheld the claim of the finance company that, by representing that the van belonged to the motor trader rather than to himself, the defendant was estopped from asserting his ownership.

The representation by the true owner must be either intentional or negligent. *Eastern Distributors* can be contrasted with *Mercantile Credit Co. v. Hamblin* [1965] 2 QB 242, where Hamblin contacted a motor trader about raising a loan on the security of her car and completed hire purchase proposal forms, thinking that this was a loan application. There was no estoppel since she had not intended to deceive the finance company into believing the car was the property of the motor trader, and she was not negligent because, knowing nothing about financial matters, she had trusted the motor trader.

The degree of negligence required has been discussed in a number of cases. In *Heap v. Motorists Advisory Agency Ltd* [1922] All ER Rep 251, H was induced by N to allow him to drive away a car ostensibly to show it to a third party. N used the car for a few weeks and then sold it to MAA. H claimed its return under s.21(1). The court held that H was not precluded from denying N's authority to sell. Negligence must be more than mere carelessness and amount to a disregard of the owner's obligations towards a person setting up the defence.

The defence is not available where the innocent purchaser has merely agreed to buy goods. Thus, in *Shaw v. Commissioner of Police for the Metropolis* [1987] 1 WLR 1332, the purchaser from a non-owner agreed to buy a car with the property passing on payment. Since he had not paid, he was unable to claim a good title against the true owner of the vehicle.

(b) Mercantile agents

A mercantile agent is an agent 'having in the customary course of his business ... authority either to sell goods or to consign goods for the purpose of sale, or to buy goods, or to raise money on the security of goods': FA 1889 s.1(1).

In *Lowther v. Harris* [1926] All ER Rep 352, the claimant left some tapestries with a man called Prior, who owned a shop. Although Prior had no authority to sell them, he sold them to the defendant. The claimant sued the defendant in conversion. The issue was whether Prior, who had no general business as an agent and who had only one principal, could be a mercantile agent. The court held that he was. A person can be a mercantile agent even though they act for one principal and act on only one occasion, provided they act in a business capacity.

The basis of the statutory exemption from the *nemo dat* doctrine is stated as follows: '[w]here a mercantile agent is, with the consent of the owner, in possession of goods or the documents of title to goods, any sale, pledge or other disposition of the goods, made by him when acting in the ordinary course of business of a mercantile agent, shall, subject to the provisions of this Act, be as valid as if he were expressly authorised by the owner of the goods to make the same; provided that the person taking under the disposition takes in good faith, and has not at the time of the disposition notice that the person making the disposition has no authority to make the same': s.2(1) FA 1889.

In order to pass a good title, the following must be established:

(i) The mercantile agent must be in possession of the goods or documents of title to goods as a mercantile agent.

A bill of lading is a document of title but not the registration documents for a motor vehicle: *Beverley Acceptance v. Oakley* [1982] RTR 417. The person must take possession as a mercantile agent.

(ii) The possession must be with the owner's consent which is presumed in the absence of evidence to the contrary, and a withdrawal of consent is ineffective unless and until it is drawn to the attention of the person taking the goods: FA s.2(3)(4).

The fact that consent was obtained by means of trickery is not relevant as long as the consent is given to the person in their capacity as a mercantile agent.

In *Pearson v. Rose and Young* [1951] 1 KB 275, the claimant left his car with a man called Hunt to see what offers he could obtain on it. He did not ask or authorise Hunt to sell it, and had no intention of giving the property in the car to him. Hunt sold the car to the defendants. The court held that the claimant could not recover the car since Hunt was a mercantile agent in possession of the car with the consent of the owner, even if he had obtained consent and possession by a trick.

In *Du Jardin v. Beadman Brothers* [1952] 2 All ER 160, a car dealer obtained possession of a second-hand car from the claimant, pretending that he would be able to sell it. He left his own car as security, together with a cheque which was later dishonoured. He secretly took back his own car and then sold the claimant's car to a third party acting in good faith. The court held that the third party acquired a good title. In *Folkes v. King* [1923] 1 KB 282, the claimant delivered his car to a mercantile agent with instructions not to sell it below a certain price. The agent sold it for a lower figure to the defendant who purchased it in good faith. The agent passed a good title under s.2(1).

In *Stadium Finance Co. v. Robbins* [1962] 2 QB 664, the defendant left his car with a dealer under a tentative arrangement that he would try to find a buyer. The defendant took away the ignition key, but left the registration document locked in the car. The dealer, having supplied a substitute key, obtained access to the registration book and sold the car to the claimants who let it out on HP to a person who fell into arrears. The claimants tried to repossess the car but found that it had been retaken by the defendant. The claimants alleged that the property in the car had passed to them since it had been sold in the ordinary course of business by a mercantile agent, but were unsuccessful.

(iii) The sale must be in the ordinary course of the mercantile agent's business.

(iv) The person taking the goods must prove that they had no notice of the agent's lack of authority.

(c) Sale by a person with a voidable title

Where the seller has a voidable title but his title has not been avoided at the time of the sale, the buyer acquires a good title to the goods, provided he buys them in good faith and without notice of the seller's defect of title: s.23 SOGA 1979. This covers goods acquired by misrepresentation and undue influence. It also arises where the contract under which the goods were acquired was subject to a mistake as to the identity of the purchaser in a face-to-face situation: *Lewis v. Averay* [1972] 1 QB 198 (see Chapter 3, p.58).

(d) Sale by a seller in possession

Where the seller has sold goods to one buyer but keeps possession of the goods or the documents of title to them, any subsequent sale or pledge by him to a second buyer who takes delivery of the goods or documents of title in good faith without notice of the previous sale, the second buyer will obtain a good title to the goods: s.24 SOGA 1979. There is an almost identical provision in FA 1889, s.8. Thus, if S sells goods to B and the property passes to B but possession remains with S, if S then sells and delivers them to C, who buys them in good faith, C has a good title to the goods and B can sue S for breach of contract.

(e) Sale by a buyer in possession

Sale by a buyer in possession is where a person has bought or agreed to buy goods and, with the seller's consent, takes possession of them or the documents of title to them, and then – in person or through a mercantile agent – delivers them by sale, pledge or other disposition to a third party. If the third party takes them in good faith without notice of any rights of the original seller, the effect is as if the person making the delivery or transfer were a mercantile agent in possession of the goods or documents of title with the consent of the owner: s.25. There is an identical provision in the Factors Act 1889 s.9.

Thus, if S sells goods to B and possession passes to B but the property remains with S, if B sells and delivers them or documents of title to them to C, who buys in good faith, C obtains title and S can sue B for payment. The section does not confer title to a buyer who purchases from a seller with no title.

In *National Mutual General Insurance Association Ltd v. Jones* [1988] 2 WLR 952, thieves stole a car which was then sold to A, who sold it to C (a car dealer), who sold it to D (another dealer), who sold it to J. Rejecting J's claim that he had acquired a good title to the car against the rightful owner, the court held that the section could only defeat the title of an owner who had entrusted possession of his goods (or documents of title to goods) to a buyer. It could not remove title from an owner from whom the goods had been stolen.

The key words are 'having bought or agreed to buy'. A person has not 'bought or agreed to buy' goods where s/he has taken goods on a 'sale or return' basis, but such deals will be covered by s.18, Rule 4, above. The section does not apply to persons holding goods under a contract of hire. This is important in relation to bailment under an HP contract: *Helby v. Matthews* [1895] AC 471. This ensured the HP contract's popularity with traders and finance companies who could recover the goods from the innocent purchaser.

A person who bought goods under a conditional sale agreement was formerly held to be someone who has 'bought or agreed to buy' for the purpose of s.25, but this has been amended in respect of regulated agreements under the Consumer Credit Act 1974. The protection is now restricted in respect of innocent purchasers of motor vehicles under Part III of the Hire Purchase Act 1964 to the following conditions:

(i) the seller must have hired or bought the vehicle under an HP or conditional sale agreement;
(ii) the purchaser must be a 'private purchaser'.

The buyer must not be a dealer (or a finance house) carrying on business in the motor trade even where they acquire the car for their private purposes: *Stevenson v. Beverley Bentinck* [1976] 1 WLR 1593; however, the Act will protect the first private purchaser from the dealer.

(f) Sale under common law or statutory powers or court orders

Some people are given common law or statutory powers to sell another's property: pawnbrokers in respect of unredeemed pledges; innkeepers can sell the guest's property if the bill is not paid. Under the Torts (Interference with Goods) Act 1977, repairers, improvers, valuers or storers can sell uncollected goods after the expiration of a period of notice to the bailor. The purchaser will obtain a good title if the bailor had no title.

The High Court can order the sale of goods and purchasers acquire a good title under s.21(2)(b) SOGA 1979.

18.6 Performance of the contract

It is the duty of the seller to deliver the goods and of the buyer to accept and pay for them in accordance with the terms of the contract of sale: s.27. Unless otherwise agreed, delivery and payment are concurrent conditions: s.28.

(a) Delivery

Delivery is at the seller's place of business or residence. However, where the contract is for specific goods which to the parties' knowledge are elsewhere, then that is the place of delivery: s.29(2). Whether the buyer has to collect the goods or the seller to send them depends on the contract.

Where the seller is bound to send the goods to the buyer but no time is fixed, the seller must send them within a reasonable time: s.29(3). Where the goods are in the possession of a third person, delivery occurs only when the person acknowledges that s/he holds the goods on the buyer's behalf: s.29(4).

Where the seller delivers fewer goods than s/he contracted to sell the buyer may reject them, but if s/he accepts the goods s/he must pay for them at the contract rate: s.30(1). Where the seller delivers more goods than s/he contracted for, the buyer may accept the goods contracted for and reject the rest or reject the whole: s.30(2). However, where the buyer is not dealing as a consumer, s/he cannot reject the goods under s.30(1) and (2) if the shortfall or the excess is so slight that it would be unreasonable for him/her to do so: s.30(2A). It is for the seller to show that the shortfall or excess was slight for the purposes of s.30(2A): s.30(2B).

Where the seller is authorised or required to send the goods to the buyer, delivery to a carrier, whether named by the buyer or not, for transmission to the buyer is *prima facie* delivery to the buyer: s.32(1). However, the seller must enter into a reasonable contract with the carrier relative to the nature of the goods, failing which, if the goods are lost or damaged in transit, the buyer may refuse to treat delivery to the carrier as delivery to him/herself, or claim damages against the seller: s.32(2). Where the goods are to be sent by sea and it would be usual for them to be insured, the seller must give sufficient notice to the buyer to insure them, failing which the goods will be at the seller's risk during the transit: s.32(3). Where, however, the buyer deals as a consumer, s.32(1)–(3) do not apply and, if the seller is authorised or required to send the goods to the buyer, delivery of them to a carrier is not delivery to the buyer: s.32(4).

Where the seller agrees to deliver goods at his/her own risk at a place other than where they were when sold, the buyer must, unless otherwise agreed, take any risk of deterioration arising from the course of transit: s.33.

(b)   Instalment deliveries

Unless otherwise agreed, the buyer is not bound to accept delivery by instalments: s.31(1). Where there is a contract for the sale of goods to be delivered by stated instalments, which are to be paid for separately, and the seller makes defective deliveries in respect of one or more of the instalments or the buyer neglects or refuses to take delivery of or pay for one or more instalments, it depends upon the terms of the contract and the circumstances of the case whether the breach of contract is a repudiation of the whole contract or whether it is a severable breach giving rise to a claim for compensation but not to a right to treat the whole contract as repudiated: s.31(2).

In *Robert A. Munro & Co. Ltd v. Meyer* [1930] 2 KB 312, the claimants agreed to sell to the defendants 1,500 tons of meat and bonemeal of a specified quality, with delivery by instalments. The claimants delivered some 611 tons of meal which was not of the specified quality. The defendants repudiated the contract. The claimants sued for money due under the agreement and the defendants counterclaimed for damages. The court held that the size of the breach of the contract and the likelihood of its being repeated entitled the defendants to repudiate the contract and claim damages in respect of the inferior meal delivered.

In *Maple Flock Co. Ltd v. Universal Furniture Products (Wembley) Ltd* [1933] All ER 15, the sellers agreed to supply the buyers with 100 tons of flock by instalments. The first 15 deliveries of $1\frac{1}{2}$ tons each were satisfactory, but when a sample of the sixteenth delivery was analysed it was found to contain more chlorine than the contract allowed. The buyers sought to repudiate the contract, but the court held that defective delivery of one instalment did not amount to breach by the sellers of the whole contract. Hewart LCJ stated the test as follows: 'the main tests to be considered are, first, the ratio quantitatively which the breach bears to the contract as a whole, and secondly, the degree of probability or improbability that such a breach will be repeated'.

In *Regent OHG Aisenstadt und Barig v. Francesco of Jermyn Street Ltd* [1981] 3 All ER 327, the claimant contracted to sell 62 suits to the defendant, with delivery by instalments over an agreed period, the number and size of each delivery being at the discretion of the seller. The buyer informed the seller that he wished to cancel the order, but the seller insisted on making deliveries. Five attempted deliveries were rejected by the buyer and, in defence to a claim for damages for non-acceptance, the buyer claimed that, as the deliveries had been one suit short of the contract quantity, he was entitled to reject the whole consignment under s.30(1). The court held that s.30(1) was inconsistent with, and had to yield to, s.31 in the case of a severable contract. Under this section, the short delivery was not sufficient to justify a repudiation of the whole contract.

(c) Acceptance

Where goods that s/he has not previously examined are delivered to a buyer, s/he is not deemed to have accepted them unless and until s/he has had a reasonable opportunity of examining them to see whether they conform to the contract: s.34(1). And the seller is bound to give the buyer a reasonable opportunity of examining the goods to see whether they conform to the contract: s.34(2).

The buyer is deemed to have accepted the goods when (i) s/he intimates to the seller that s/he has accepted them; or (ii) s/he does any act to the goods which is inconsistent with the ownership of the seller: s.35(1). This is subject, however, to subsection (2), under which, where goods were delivered to the buyer and he had not previously examined them, he was deemed not to have accepted them until he had a reasonable opportunity of examining them for the purpose of ascertaining whether they were in conformity with the contract: s.35(2)(a). In *J & H Ritchie Ltd v. Lloyd Ltd* [2007] UKHL 9, R, which carried on a farming business, ordered and paid for agricultural machinery from L. On the second day the machine was used, a vibration was noticed. The machine was taken back by L. The vibration was caused by two missing bearings. The machine was repaired and R was told it was ready for collection and that it was of 'factory gate standard'. L refused to explain the nature of the fault and, when the appellants discovered informally what the problem had been, refused to supply an engineer's report. R rejected the machine and sued for repayment of the purchase price. It was held that a buyer could not be expected to exercise his right of acceptance until he had the information needed to make an informed choice. The seller could not refuse to give the relevant information. As R was deprived of the information needed to make an informed choice, it was entitled to reject the equipment, even though L had later been able to prove that a repair to factory gate standard had been carried out.

A buyer is not deemed to have accepted goods merely because he asked for, or agreed to, their repair by or under an arrangement with the seller: s.35(6)(a).

A buyer is deemed to have accepted the goods when, after the lapse of a reasonable time, he retains the goods without intimating to the seller that he has rejected them: s.35(4). The way in which this can limit the remedies available to the buyer has already been discussed (see p.429 above).

Where the buyer has a right to reject goods because of a breach on the seller's part which affects some or all of them but accepts some of the goods, including some or all of those unaffected by the breach, s/he does not lose his/her right to reject the rest: s.35A (1).

Where goods are delivered to the buyer which s/he refuses to accept, having a right to do so, s/he is not bound to return them and it is enough for him/her to indicate that s/he refuses to accept them: s.36.

When the seller is ready and willing to deliver the goods and requests the buyer to take delivery, and the latter fails within a reasonable time to take delivery, s/he is liable to the seller for any loss and for a reasonable charge for the care and custody of the goods, provided that nothing in this section shall affect the rights of the seller where the refusal of the buyer to take delivery amounts to a repudiation of the contract: s.37.

18.7 The unpaid seller's rights against the goods

The unpaid seller has rights over the goods even though the property has passed to the buyer in addition to the rights of action for non-payment or failure to take delivery. A seller is unpaid when (a) the whole of the price has not been paid or tendered; or (b) a bill of exchange or other negotiable instrument has been received as conditional payment and the condition has not been fulfilled by reason of the dishonour of the instrument or otherwise: s.38(1).

(a) Unpaid seller's lien

If still in possession of the goods, the unpaid seller can retain possession until payment or tender of the price: (i) where the goods have not been sold on credit; (ii) where they have been sold on credit but the term of credit has expired; and (iii) where the buyer becomes insolvent: s.41(1). The seller may exercise his/her right of lien even though s/he is in possession of the goods as agent or bailee of the buyer: s.41(2). Where a part delivery of the goods has been made, the right of lien can be exercised on the remainder unless the right has been waived: s.42. The right to a lien terminates:

(i) on the delivery of the goods to a carrier or other bailee or custodier for transmission to the buyer without reserving the right of disposal of the goods;
(ii) when the buyer or his agent lawfully obtains possession of the goods;
(iii) by waiver of the lien or right of retention: s.43.

(b) Right of stoppage in transit

When the buyer becomes insolvent, the unpaid seller who has parted with possession of the goods has the right of stopping them in transit, resuming possession and retaining them until payment or tender of the price: s.44.

Goods are in transit from the time of delivery to a carrier until the buyer, or his/her agent, takes delivery of them even if the buyer or his/her agent obtains delivery before their arrival at the appointed destination s.45(1) and (2).

Once the goods arrive at the appointed destination, if the carrier acknowledges to the buyer or his/her agent that s/he holds the goods on the buyer's behalf, the transit is at an end, even if the buyer indicates a further destination for the goods: s.45(3). If the goods are rejected by the buyer, the transit is not at an end, even if the seller refuses to take them back: s.45(4). When goods are delivered to a ship chartered by the buyer, it depends on the particular circumstances whether they are in the master's possession as carrier or as agent of the buyer: s.45(5). Transit terminates when the carrier wrongfully refuses to deliver the goods to the buyer or his/her agent: s.45(6). If a part delivery has been made, the remainder may be stopped in transit unless the part delivery shows an agreement to give up possession of the whole of the goods: s.45(7).

The unpaid seller's right is exercised by taking actual possession of the goods or by giving notice of his/her claim to the carrier either in person or to his/her principal. The notice must be given at such time and in such circumstances that the principal, by acting with reasonable diligence, may communicate it to his/her servant or agent in time to prevent delivery: s.46(1). When notice is given, the carrier must redeliver the goods to the seller or in accordance with his/her orders; costs of redelivery are the seller's responsibility: s.46(2).

The right to lien or stoppage is not affected by any sale or other disposition of the goods by the buyer, except (i) where the seller has assented to it; or (ii) where a document of title has been lawfully transferred to the buyer, and s/he transfers it to a person by way of sale who takes it in good faith and for value. Where the transfer is by way of pledge, the right of lien and stoppage can be exercised only subject to the rights of the transferee: s.47.

(c) Unpaid seller's right of resale

The contract of sale is not rescinded by the exercise of the right of lien or stoppage in transit: s.48(1); but where the unpaid seller then resells the goods, the buyer acquires a good title to them over the original buyer: s.48(2). The right of resale arises automatically where the goods are perishable, but otherwise on the expiry of a reasonable time after giving the buyer notice of his/her intention to resell without the buyer paying or tendering the price. The unpaid seller can sue the original buyer for damages for any loss by his/her breach of contract: s.48(3). Where the seller reserves a right of resale in the event of the buyer's default and resells the goods, the original contract of sale is rescinded, but without prejudice to the seller's claim for damages: s.48(4).

18.8 Seller's actions for breach of contract

(a) Action for the price

Where the property has passed to the buyer and s/he wrongfully refuses to pay for the goods, the seller can sue for the price: s.49(1). The right to sue for the price may arise even when the property has not passed, and the goods are unappropriated, where the contract provides for payment on a certain day, irrespective of delivery: s.49(2).

(b) Damages for non-acceptance

Where the buyer refuses to accept and pay for the goods: s.50(1), the damages are the estimated loss directly and naturally resulting from the buyer's breach of contract: s.50(2). Where there is an available market for the goods, the measure of damages is *prima facie* ascertained by the difference between the market price and the contract price at the time when the goods ought to have been accepted or, where no time is fixed, when delivery was refused: s.50(3) (see Chapter 5).

18.9 Buyer's actions for breach of contract

(a) Damages for non-delivery

If the seller wrongfully refuses to deliver the goods, the buyer may sue for damages for non-delivery. The measure of damages is the estimated loss directly and naturally resulting from the seller's breach of contract. Where there is an available market in the goods, the measure of damages is *prima facie* the difference between the contract price and the market or current price at the time when the goods ought to have been delivered or at the time of refusal of delivery: s.51.

(b) Specific performance

In an action for breach of contract to deliver specific or ascertained goods, the court may, if it thinks fit, on the application of the claimant, make an order for the specific performance of the contract: s.52 (see Chapter 5).

(c) Damages for breach of warranty

Where there is a breach of warranty by the seller, or where the buyer elects or is compelled to treat a breach of condition as a breach of warranty, the buyer cannot reject the goods but may (a) set up the breach of warranty in diminution or extinction of the price; or (b) maintain an action against the seller for breach of warranty. The measure of damages is the estimated loss directly and naturally arising from the breach of warranty. In the case of a breach of warranty of quality, the loss is *prima facie* the difference between the value of the goods at the time of delivery to the buyer and the value they would have had if they had complied with the warranty: s.53(3). The fact of setting up the breach of warranty in diminution or extinction of the price does not prevent the buyer from bringing an action for damages for breach of warranty if s/he has suffered further damage. In *Bence Graphics International Ltd v. Fasson UK Ltd* [1997] 1 All ER 979, the defendant supplied vinyl film to the claimant to manufacture decals to identify bulk containers. It was a term of the contract that the film would remain legible for at least five years. The film degraded prematurely, the claimants received many complaints from customers and were forced to retain £22,000 worth of defective material. The Court of Appeal held that the claimant's liability to the ultimate user was contemplated as the measure of damages and that the *prima facie* measure of damages under s.53(3) was displaced.

(d) Additional rights of the buyer in consumer cases

Where the goods do not conform to the contract of sale at the time of delivery, the buyer has the right (a) to require the seller to repair or replace the goods in accordance with s.48B; or (b) in accordance with s.48C, (i) to require the seller to reduce the purchase price, or (ii) rescind the contract. Goods do not conform to a contract if they are in breach of an express term of the contract or a term implied by s.13, 14 or 15.

If the buyer requires the seller to repair or replace the goods, the seller must do so within a reasonable time but without causing significant inconvenience to the buyer; and bear the costs of doing so. The buyer must not require the seller to repair or replace the goods if that remedy is impossible, or disproportionate in comparison to the other remedies or in comparison to an appropriate reduction in the purchase price under s.48C(1).

Where the buyer rescinds the contract, any reimbursement to the buyer shall take into account the use s/he has had of the goods since they were delivered to him/her: s.48C(3).

18.10 Contracts for the supply of goods

The Supply of Goods and Services Act (SGSA) 1982 deals with three areas of the law: (i) contracts for the transfer of property in goods; (ii) contracts for the hire of goods; and (iii) contracts for services. There are implied terms closely modelled on those in the Sale of Goods Act 1979 as amended by the Sale and Supply of Goods Act (SSGA) 1994 and controls limiting the extent to which parties can contract out of these terms.

(a) Contracts for the transfer of property in goods

Contracts for the transfer of property in goods are contracts where there is a transfer of property in goods which are not contracts for the sale of goods or HP contracts. The transferee is protected in respect of title, description, satisfactory quality, fitness for purpose and compliance of bulk with sample through terms implied into the contracts under ss.2–5 SGSA 1982 identical with those in ss.12–15 SOGA 1979. In non-consumer cases where the breach is so slight that it would be unreasonable for the bailee to reject the goods, the breach of implied terms in s.3, 4 or 5(2)(a) or (c) is to be treated as a breach of warranty unless a contrary intention appears in, or is to be implied from, the contract: s.5A.

All other aspects of these contracts relating to the passing of property are covered by common law. The contracts principally protected are (i) collateral contracts relating to the supply of goods; (ii) contracts of exchange or barter; and (iii) contracts where goods are supplied but the essence of the contract is the provision of services: contracts to repair.

(i) Collateral contracts

Collateral contracts are those where, in return for the purchase of one product, the purchaser will be entitled to another: 'free gifts' to purchasers of motor oil. The contract for the motor oil is covered by the SOGA 1979, but the 'free gift' falls under ss.2–5 of the Supply of Goods Act (SGA) 1982.

In *Esso Petroleum Ltd v. Commissioners of Customs and Excise* [1976] 1 All ER 117, the House of Lords rejected a claim by the Commissioners that Esso was liable for purchase tax on World Cup coins which the company was giving away as a sales promotion to every purchaser of four gallons of petrol, on the ground that they were not being 'produced in quantity for sale'.

(ii) Contracts of barter or exchange

Contracts of barter or exchange exclude part exchange contracts, which are sale of goods contracts even if the cash element is very small. A clear case of barter or exchange is where goods are exchanged for tokens to which no money value is attributed: a CD in return for 10 wrappers from a chocolate bar. Claims concerning the quality of the CD are under the SGSA 1982 ss.2–5.

(iii) Contracts for work and materials

Where claims arise under contracts for work and materials, it is important to identify whether the cause of the complaint relates to the failure of a new component or its negligent installation. Claims relating to the former are under ss.2–5, whereas the latter is covered by s.13 SGSA 1982.

The exclusion of the implied terms is restricted in the same way as for the implied terms of the SOGA 1979 under s.7 Unfair Contract Terms Act (UCTA) 1977. The Unfair Terms in Consumer Contracts Regulations 1999 may also apply (see Chapter 21, p.517).

(b) Contracts for hire of goods

In contracts for hire of goods, the hirer obtains possession but not the property in the goods; the relationship is that of bailee and bailor. HP contracts are excluded: s.6(2)(a), but a contract is a contract for the hire of goods whether or not services are also provided under the contract, and irrespective of the nature of the consideration for the hire: s.6(3).

The implied terms are contained in ss.7–10 SGSA 1982. The terms relating to description, satisfactory quality, fitness for purpose, and sample are identical in effect with the equivalent sections in SOGA 1979. The main difference relates to the implied term relating to title. There is an implied condition on the part of bailors that they have a right to transfer possession for the bailment period, or that, for agreements to bail, they will have such a right at the time of bailment: s.7(1).

There is also an implied warranty that the bailor will enjoy quiet possession for the period of the bailment, except for the case of disturbance by the owner or a person entitled to the benefit of any charge or encumbrance disclosed or known to the bailee before the contract is made: s.7(2). These provisions do not affect the bailor's right to repossess goods under an express or implied term: s.7(3). In non-consumer contracts, the bailee is restricted from treating slight breaches as breaches of condition: s.10A. In consumer cases, the transferee has additional rights to the repair or replacement of the goods, to a reduction in the purchase price or to rescind the contract: ss.11M–11S SGSA 1982.

The UCTA 1977 applies to contracts of hire and makes the same distinction between persons dealing as consumers and non-consumer deals.

The implied terms as to title and quiet possession can be excluded in either case but subject to the test of reasonableness. The Unfair Terms in Consumer Contract Regulations 1999 could also apply (see Chapter 21, p.517).

18.11 Contracts for the supply of services

Contracts for the supply of services are contracts under which a person ('the supplier') agrees to carry out a service, but the SGSA 1982 excludes contracts of service and apprenticeship. Contracts are for the supply of a service even though goods are also transferred, or to be transferred, bailed, or to be bailed by way of hire, and irrespective of the nature of the consideration: s.12(1), (2) and (3).

The Secretary of State can exclude the operation of one or more of the sections of the Act to a specified service, or make different statutory provisions: s.12(4) and (5). The duty of a service supplier to carry out the service with reasonable care and skill under s.13 is excluded in respect of (i) the services of an advocate in court or before any tribunal, inquiry or arbitrator and in carrying on the preliminary work directly affecting the conduct of the hearing; and (ii) the services rendered to a company by the company directors in their capacity as directors.

There are three statutorily implied terms in contracts of service: (i) reasonable care and skill, (ii) time for performance and (iii) consideration for the service.

(b)   Reasonable care and skill

The Act provides: '[i]n a contract for the supply of a service where the supplier is acting in the course of a business, there is an implied term that the supplier will carry out the service with reasonable care and skill': s.13.

(c)   Time for performance

The Act provides: '[w]here, under a contract for the supply of a service by a supplier acting in the course of a business, the time for the service to be carried out is not fixed by the contract, left to be fixed in manner agreed between the parties or determined by the course of dealing between the parties, there is an implied term that the supplier will carry out the service within a reasonable time': s.14(1). What is a reasonable time is a question of fact: s.14(2).

(d)   Consideration for the service

The Act provides: '[w]here, under a contract for the supply of a service, the consideration for the service is not determined by the contract, left to be determined in a manner agreed by the contract or determined by the course of dealing between the parties, there is an implied term that the party contracting with the supplier will pay a reasonable charge': s.15(1). What is a reasonable charge is a question of fact: s.15(2).

(e)   Exclusion of implied terms

Where the person to whom the service is supplied is a consumer, or where the supply was on the basis of the supplier's standard form contract, a clause purporting to exclude or limit the supplier's liability is subject to the requirement of reasonableness: s.3 UCTA 1977.

With regard to the implied term of reasonable care and skill, the breach of such a contractual term falls within the definition of negligence: s.1(a) UCTA 1977. As a result, this implied term is also subject to the restriction of exclusion clauses against negligence liability, and any clause which attempts to remove or limit the supplier's liability under s.13 will not cover death or personal injury: s.2 UCTA 1977. The Unfair Terms in Consumer Contracts Regulations 1999 could also apply (see Chapter 21, p. 517).

18.12   Goods supplied under HP and conditional sale agreements

Contracts for goods supplied under HP and conditional sale agreements contain similar clauses relating to implied terms as for the SOGA 1979 and the SGSA 1982. These terms are contained in ss.8–11 of the Supply of Goods (Implied Terms) Act 1973. There are identical controls relating to the exclusion of the implied terms as for the other Acts. In addition, in non-consumer cases, if the breach is slight it is not to be treated as a breach of condition: s.11A.

In *Feldaroll Foundry plc v. Hermes Leasing (London) Ltd* [2004] EWCA Civ 747, the claimant purchased a car from the managing director on HP for his use. The agreement was signed by the managing director on behalf of the company and included a clause excluding all conditions and warranties, express or implied, in respect of the vehicle. It also stated that the car 'will be used for the purposes of my/our business' and an acknowledgement by the hirer that the goods would be used for his own business purposes. In effect the car suffered from a number of defects which made it unsafe to use and it was rejected. In a complex case, the issue was whether the contract was made 'in the course of a business' for the purposes of s.12(1) UCTA 1977. Following its decision in *R & B Customs Brokers Co. Ltd v United Dominions Trust Ltd* [1988] 1 WLR 321, the Court of Appeal held that where a company enters a transaction which is not integral to its business but is merely incidental to it then, for the purposes of s.12(1)(a) UCTA 1977, the company does not make that transaction in the course of a business. As a result, the exclusion clause was void under s.6(2) UCTA 1977. This means that there is a different interpretation of the phrase 'in the course of a business' in UCTA 1977 and SOGA 1979 (see *Stevenson v. Rogers*, above p. 426).

18.13 Discrimination in respect of services, goods and facilities

Racial discrimination in respect of the provision of goods, facilities or services is prohibited: s.20(1) Race Relations Act 1976. Examples are (a) access to and use of any place of public access; (b) hotel, boarding house accommodation; (c) banking, insurance, grants, loans, credit or finance facilities; (d) educational facilities; (e) entertainment, recreation or refreshment facilities; (f) transport or travel facilities; and (g) professional, trade, local or other public authority services: s.20(2).

There is similar protection for disabled persons: s.19(1) Disability Discrimination Act (DDA) 1995 (as amended by the Disability Discrimination Act 2005). 'Services' includes communication and information services, transport (including rail after 2020), services provided by public authorities, group insurance, membership of private clubs, lettings of premises and general qualifications bodies but excluding local education authorities. Discrimination is justified if the provider reasonably believes that: (a) it is necessary in order not to endanger the health or safety of any person (including the disabled person); (b) the disabled person is incapable of entering into an enforceable agreement or of giving informed consent; (c) it is necessary because the provider would otherwise be unable to provide the service to the public (for example a coach refusing to train a disabled athlete); (d) less favourable treatment in terms of standard, manner or terms is necessary in order to provide the service either to the disabled person or to other members of the public (obliging a disabled person attending a concert/theatre to take a particular seat); and (e) the difference in terms reflects the greater cost incurred by the provider: s.19(4).

Service providers must make adjustments to 'a practice, policy or procedure which makes it impossible or unreasonably difficult for disabled persons to make use of a service': s.21(1). Where this involves a physical feature, the provider must take all reasonable steps to (a) remove the feature; (b) alter it; (c) provide a reasonable means of avoidance; or (d) provide a reasonable alternative method of making the service available: s.21(2). It is also an offence for a person selling or letting premises to discriminate against disabled persons: s.22(1).

An unlawful discrimination claim is by civil proceedings for tort within six months in the county court.

End of Chapter Summary

Having read and understood this chapter, you should have a detailed knowledge of the following points of particular importance:

- The implied terms in a contract for the sale of goods, with particular reference to the distinction between the requirement that goods are of satisfactory quality and the requirement of fitness for purpose.
- The significance of the rules relating to the time at which property in the goods passes from the seller to the buyer, together with the passing of the risk; in particular the rules relating to appropriation of goods to a contract.
- The important exceptions to the rule of *nemo dat quod non habet* when persons can pass a title to goods to a third party even though they have no title themselves.
- The real remedies of the unpaid seller of goods, including the right of stoppage in transit and the right to retain the goods pending payment.
- The distinction between contracts for the sale of goods and contracts for the supply of goods and services.

These areas of the law are crucial to the operation of a commercial venture, as can be seen by some of the scenarios in the following questions in which the principles covered in this chapter should be applied.

Questions

1. Q Ltd was a manufacturer of electrically operated model trains, which had a reputation in the trade for their lack of reliability. Q Ltd entered into a contract to sell a consignment of these train sets to W Ltd, a wholesale dealer to the toy trade. The contract contained a term in the following form: 'the manufacturer accepts no liability for any defects or malfunctioning of the goods supplied under this contract'. In effect, in tests carried out by W Ltd, 50 per cent of the consignment proved to be so unreliable that W Ltd was unable to sell them to retailers. Advise W Ltd of any claims against Q Ltd.

2. S Ltd sold a quantity of canned goods to T Ltd. The goods were held at S Ltd's warehouse pending delivery to T Ltd. S Ltd subsequently received a higher offer for the goods from U Ltd and sold them again. U Ltd collected them the next day. Advise T Ltd of its rights in respect of the goods and S Ltd.

3. P Ltd agreed to sell a consignment of bedding to Q Ltd. Under the terms of the contract, P Ltd was to deliver the consignment to Q Ltd's premises within 10 days of the sale. On the twelfth day after the sale, the goods were destroyed in a fire at P Ltd's warehouse. Q Ltd had already resold the bedding at a profit. Advise it of its rights.

4. James placed an order with a food supplier for snacks and sandwiches suitable for a party for vegetarians. When the food was delivered, James was horrified to discover that most of the food was unsuitable for vegetarians and refused to accept delivery of any of it, refusing to take delivery even of the food which was vegetarian. Advise the food supplier whether James has acted within his rights.

5. With regard to contracts between dealers, implied terms can be excluded subject to the 'requirement of reasonableness'. What criteria does the statute set out for establishing the requirement of reasonableness?

Questions cont'd

6. Cold Cuts Ltd is a company supplying frozen foods to retail outlets. On one occasion, the refrigeration unit in a van delivering supplies to two clients broke down shortly after the van left the warehouse. Both clients were taking delivery of the same type of product from a bulk stored in the company's warehouse, and the van was loaded with sufficient to meet the two orders.

   When the van arrived at the first client's premises, the food had defrosted and was no longer acceptable. Cold Cuts Ltd claimed that both clients were liable to pay for the goods since the property in the goods had passed to them when the van was loaded.

   Advise the clients of the position.

   Would your answer be different if the refrigeration unit had broken down after the first consignment had been delivered but before the second delivery had been made?

7. Pete is a plumber who advertises an emergency plumbing service. In the middle of winter, he received a telephone call from an elderly person who had a major leak in her attic due to a burst water pipe from the cold tank. Pete agreed to carry out an immediate repair of the pipe but no agreement was made as to the cost of the work. In fact, the situation was far less desperate than the householder had thought and Pete completed the repair in an hour without needing to replace any piping. After completing the work, Pete handed the householder a bill for £400. Advise the householder on their liability.

8. You have bought goods on sale or return. When does property in the goods pass to you?

9. The Sale of Goods Act 1979 contains a number of exceptions to the rule of *nemo dat quod non habet*. What is the meaning of this rule, and what exceptions are there to it?

10. In addition to being able to sue the buyer for the price, the unpaid seller of goods has remedies against the goods themselves in certain circumstances. What are those remedies, when do they arise, and when are they lost?

11. Tariq was the owner of a petrol-driven lawnmower. The garden shed where the mower was kept was broken into and the mower was stolen. A few weeks later, he saw an advertisement in the local freesheet for an identical mower, and, having given up recovering his own, he went to see the advertised mower with the intention of buying it.

   When he reached the house where the mower was being sold, he realised that it was his own mower and demanded it back. The person selling the mower had bought it in good faith from a car boot sale a few weeks earlier. He refused to allow Tariq to take the mower away, claiming that it was his property.

   Consider Tariq's situation and advise him.

Chapter 19

Insurance

Learning objectives

After reading this chapter you will know about:

- insurable interest in indemnity and life insurance
- formalities and formation of the contract of insurance
- insurance as a contract of utmost good faith
- standard terms in policies of insurance
- life insurance policies
- third party liability and employers' liability policies.

19.1 Introduction

There is often some confusion about the use of the terms 'assurance' and 'insurance', 'assured' and 'insured'. Generally assurance refers to life policies and insurance to indemnity policies, since the death of the insured person is a certainty, whereas indemnity insurance is in respect of an event which may never happen. In this chapter, the words 'insurance' and 'insured' are used throughout for both categories. The person taking out the insurance is the insured (or policyholder) whereas the insurance company is the insurer.

In a contract of insurance, the insurer undertakes to pay a sum of money, or its equivalent, to the insured on the happening of an uncertain future event, which is not within the insured's control and in which the insured has an interest, in consideration of the payment by the insured of a money consideration. The uncertainty relates to either whether it will occur or when it will occur.

There are two categories of insurance: indemnity insurance and contingency insurance. Indemnity insurance is where the contract provides the insured with an indemnity against a future possible loss or liability. This could cover the risk of damage by fire, liability arising out of an accident involving a third party or liability of a company director to contribute to the company's assets under ss.212, 213 and 214 Insolvency Act 1986. Contingency insurance is where the contract provides for the payment of a specific sum of money on the happening of a named event: a personal injury policy or a life policy. A third form of contingency insurance is a contract of annuity where, in return for the payment of a lump sum premium, the insurer agrees to make regular periodic payments of a fixed sum until the death of the insured.

In the case of personal injury and life policies, the insurer must pay the agreed, predetermined sum on the happening of the event, irrespective of the value of the insured's life or the loss that the injury represents to the insured.

There must first be a binding contract under which the insurer is obliged to compensate the insured.

Thus in *Medical Defence Union v. Department of Trade* [1979] 2 All ER 421, the claimant company's membership was doctors and dentists on whose behalf it conducted legal proceedings and indemnified them against claims for damages and costs. Since, under the company's constitution, members had no right to the benefits but could only request assistance, it was not carrying on an insurance business.

A further essential element is that the event insured against must be uncertain. In respect of indemnity insurance, the uncertainty is as to whether the event will take place at all, whereas in respect of life insurance it is as to the time when the event takes place. Indemnity insurance over goods does not offer protection against the normal fair wear and tear of the property. In addition, the dictates of public policy mean that the policy will not extend to cover damage caused by events which are the deliberate act of the insured.

19.2 Insurable interest

Insurable interest is the legal interest which the insured must have in the person or property insured in order for the contract of insurance to be valid. Otherwise, the contract would be indistinguishable from a wagering contract where neither party has an interest in the event. Such contracts were, however, legally enforceable prior to the Gaming Act (GA) 1845.

It was in certain instances necessary to establish the existence of an insurable interest before this date. In the case of marine insurance, it was made a legal requirement by the Marine Insurance Act 1745, and this was followed by the Life Assurance Act (LAA) 1774, which introduced the need for an insurable interest in life policies. There is no statutory requirement in respect of indemnity insurance, but the GA 1845 s.18 made policies illegal as wagering contracts where there was no interest in the goods or property. This section was repealed by the Gambling Act 2005 which makes wagering contracts enforceable. The common law requires there to be an insurable interest in respect of indemnity contracts. Marine insurance is now covered by s.4 Marine Insurance Act 1906.

There is a distinction between indemnity and contingency insurance as to when the insured must have an insurable interest in the subject matter of the policy. For indemnity insurance, the insured's insurable interest must exist at the time of the event triggering the claim under the policy; for contingency insurance it must exist when the contract is taken out.

(a) Insurable interest in life insurance

In respect of life insurance, the insured must have an interest in the life insured, and any person 'for whose use, benefit, or on whose account' a policy is made must have an interest: s.1 LAA 1774. In addition, the names of the insured and any beneficiaries must be inserted into the policy, on pain of the policy being illegal: s.2 LAA 1774. This clearly requires the insurable interest to exist at the time the policy is taken out. In addition, the Act seems to require there to be an interest at the time of the maturity of the policy: s.3 LAA 1774, which was the case until *Dalby v. India and London Life Assurance Co.* (1854) 15 CB 365. This means that, even though there is no insurable interest when the policy becomes payable, the insurer is obliged to pay out under the policy to the insured or an assignee of the policy.

Where persons take out life insurance on a life in respect of which they have no insurable interest the policy is void on the grounds of public policy.

Thus in *Hughes v. Liverpool Victoria Legal Friendly Society* [1916] 2 KB 482, the defendant's agent persuaded the claimant that she was entitled to take out life assurance on a number of people. This was in effect not true and the policies were illegal and void. The claimant was, however, entitled to recover premiums paid since she was the more innocent party.

The purpose behind ss.1 and 2 is clearly to prevent situations where a person takes out life insurance on their own life for the benefit of a third party who has no interest in their life. In effect, however, s.2 seems to be superfluous. If the person for whose benefit the policy is taken out has no interest in the life insured, the policy is void under s.1 even if the person is identified under s.2. If, however, the persons have an interest in the insured life, it is surely irrelevant that they are not identified under s.2.

Section 2 was clearly impossible to apply in respect of group policies taken out by employers to cover the whole of or a class of their employees where the policy was for the employees' benefit. The section does not invalidate a policy for the benefit of unnamed individuals within a class or description if the class or description is stated in the policy and every member is identifiable at any time: s.50 Insurance Companies Amendment Act 1973.

(b) Insurable interest in family relationships

The insured must have had a financial interest in the life of a third party at the time the policy was taken out, except that everybody has an insurable interest in their own life and that of their spouse or civil partner, irrespective of the amount insured. By analogy, this would presumably be extended to engaged couples and unmarried couples living together. This was the view of the Insurance Ombudsman in his annual report for 1989. For all other family relationships, however, the law is very strict and the insured must show that they would suffer financially from the death of the individual whose life is insured.

Children clearly have an insurable interest in the lives of their parents if the latter are obliged financially to support them. There is no such obligation at common law, but an obligation could arise under statute, that is, under a maintenance order against a parent. For an adult child it would be necessary to establish a pecuniary loss arising from the parent's death.

In *Harse v. Pearl Life Assurance Co. Ltd* [1904] 1 KB 558, a son insured the life of his mother with whom he lived and who kept house for him. The insurance was to cover funeral expenses. The Court of Appeal held the policy was illegal for lack of interest since there was no legal obligation on the son to bury his mother on her death.

In respect of parents insuring the life of their child, the only interest that could possibly exist would be to cover funeral expenses. Even where the child is giving financial support to the parents, this does not constitute an insurable interest since this is not a legal obligation: *Halford v. Kymer* (1830) 10 B & C 724.

(c) Insurable interest in business relationships

Creditors have an insurable interest in the lives of their debtors, employers in the lives of their employees and vice versa, and partners in the lives of their co-partners. In all these case, however, the amount of the insurance should be limited to the pecuniary interest of the insured.

In the case of employers insuring the lives of their employees, the value of the employees will vary greatly depending on the length of their service contract. In most cases, the employer's interest will be limited to the period of notice that the employee is require to give. Generally, however, the insured sums may have no bearing on the employee's strict legal value. In *Marcel Beller Ltd v. Hayden* [1978] QB 694, the employee was insured for £15,000, an amount which was not questioned by the court.

(d) Insurable interest in property insurance

The GA 1845 s.18 clearly applied to property insurance and stated that any insurance over property in which the insurer had no interest was void. Whether the LAA 1774 applies to property insurance is a vexed question. It seems right to assume that it applies in respect of real property insurances, but not in the case of goods. Thus, in respect of real property, an insurable interest must exist at the moment of taking out the contract, whereas in respect of goods the interest must be established at the date of loss.

In order to establish an insurable interest in property, it is necessary to establish a legal or equitable interest in the property or a contractual right over it.

Thus in *Macaura v. Northern Assurance Co.* [1925] AC 619, the defendants were not liable under a policy held by the claimant over the timber on an estate in Ireland. Prior to the loss of the timber in a fire, the claimant had transferred the ownership of it to a company, Irish Canadian Sawmills Ltd, in respect of which he was the sole shareholder. The House of Lords held that he had no insurable interest in the timber. Neither as shareholder nor as creditor of the company was he entitled to insure the company's assets. He had no legal or equitable relationship to the timber at all.

In this case, the possession of the property itself, which was standing on Macaura's land, was not sufficient to found an insurable interest. However, a bailee of property has an insurable interest because of the legal liability arising from the bailment, for example in respect of a person hiring and transporting and storing goods.

The interests of mortgagor and mortgagee, vendor and purchaser, landlord and tenant, trustee and beneficiary will certainly be insurable. It is not established whether spouses or other persons living together have an insurable interest in the other person's property. The answer is probably in the negative.

Once the insured is not the sole unencumbered owner of the property, the question of the extent of their interest is important. They will be able to insure the property only to the extent of their loss at its destruction. Mortgagees can recover the extent of their outstanding debt and a vendor may recover nothing if the contract of sale can still be enforced against the purchaser.

In respect of goods and contracts for the sale of goods, the party bearing the risk for their loss has an insurable interest. In respect of HP agreements, the owner has an insurable interest so long as the property or the right to repossess the goods is vested in him. The hirer also has an interest as a bailee. The buyer under a conditional sale agreement has an insurable interest in the full value of the goods.

In respect of contracts for real property, if the LAA 1774 applies, the requirement of the existence of an insurable interest cannot be dispensed with; in respect of goods insurance, there is no reason why the requirement should not be waived or dispensed with.

In this respect, it is important to consider the situation where the insured has insured goods up to their full value even though having only a limited interest in them.

In *Waters v. Monarch Fire and Life Assurance Co.* (1856) 5 E & B 870, the claimants were flour and corn factors who insured the goods in their warehouse whether they belonged to them or were held 'in trust or on commission'. All the goods in the warehouse were destroyed in a fire and the claimants were entitled to recover the full value of the goods. They retained sums to cover their own loss and were trustees of the balance for the other owners.

It is clear that the insured who recovers for the benefit of a third party must account to the third party. It is not clear whether the third party has a direct claim in the event of the insured's unwillingness or inability to claim. The position would appear to be covered by the Contracts (Rights of Third Parties) Act 1999.

Where the insured has no interest, the insured can recover if the insurable interest requirement is waived.

In *Williams v. Baltic Insurance Association of London* [1924] 2 KB 282, the claimant insured his car against third parties and the policy was expressed to cover any friend or relative of the insured driving with his consent. His sister injured some people while driving the car with his consent and the issue was whether the insured could be indemnified in respect of the injuries caused by his sister. The court held that the contract waived any requirement of insurable interest by expressly extending to his sister's liability.

In respect of a policy on real property, whether or not the 1774 Act applies, it seems less likely that a policy will allow the insured to recover for the benefit of a third party. Whether the third party could sue on the policy under the Contracts (Rights of Third Parties) Act 1999 would depend on whether the policy showed an intention to protect the third party's interests. This would be likely in the case of trustee and beneficiary and mortgagor and mortgagee, but less likely in the case of vendor and purchaser or landlord and tenant.

19.3 Formalities and formation of the contract of insurance

Insurance contracts are no exception to the general rules relating to the formation of contracts, but some aspects peculiar to insurance are worth considering.

(a) Offer and acceptance

The offer by the insured will normally be made by way of completing a proposal form, a standard form produced by the insurer. This will be accepted by the insurer as it stands or subject to qualifications, in which case there will be a counter offer. The most common form of counter offer is the acceptance by the insurer subject to the payment of the first premium. Under the general rules applicable to contracts, either party could at this stage withdraw from the proposed contract. In the case of insurance, however, although the proposer may decline to accept, the insurer cannot revoke unless there is a material change in the risk.

In *Canning v. Farquhar* (1886) 16 QBD 727, the insurer accepted a proposal subject to payment of the first premium on 14 December on the terms that no insurance would take effect before the premium was paid. The premium was paid on 9 January but four days previously the proposer had suffered serious injuries in a fall from which he subsequently died. The Court of Appeal held that the insurer was not bound.

As regards acceptance, the general rule is that acceptance is only effective once communicated. This is, of course, subject to exceptions. Where the offer is unilateral, acceptance is acting in accordance with the terms of the offer. In the field of insurance, this occurs where a person purchases insurance at the airport check-in desk. The form is a unilateral offer by the insurer and the proposer accepts by completing the form as required.

(b) Formalities

There are generally no formalities attached to contracts of insurance, and an oral contract is binding as long as it can be proved and there is agreement as to the terms. In effect, insurance contracts are invariably recorded in a policy, but this is of importance only if a term in the insurer's acceptance is that there shall be no liability unless and until a policy has been issued: *Ackman v. Policyholders Protection Board* [1992] 2 Lloyd's Rep 321. There are formality requirements in respect of life insurance and compulsory motor insurance. The provisions regarding life policies are dealt with below (see p.463).

In respect of many types of insurance, and most commonly in motor insurance, insurers may agree to temporary cover on receipt of a proposal. These 'cover notes' are fully effective contracts of insurance and, whereas an acceptance for a full contract of insurance can be made only by the insurer, cover notes will often be issued by the insurer's agents. The fact that the insurer supplies the agent with blank cover notes gives them implied actual or ostensible authority to issue them. In *Mackie v. European Assurance Society* (1869) 21 LT 102, M insured his mill and warehouse through an agent for the Commercial Union. When this policy expired, M contacted W for a new policy. W, who was now an agent for the defendants who had given up fire cover, issued a cover note in the insurer's name for one month. The court held there was a valid temporary contract of insurance. Agents not given blank cover notes by the insurer will not usually be regarded as having authority to bind the insurer. Temporary insurance cover can also be agreed by telephone.

Hot Topic . . .

SEX DISCRIMINATION AND INSURANCE

The UK government announced on 3 January 2005 that Britain had led a successful action to secure an 'opt out' for the insurance industry from an EC gender Directive (2004/113/EC, [2004] OJ L373/37) which forbids businesses to treat men and women differently. As a result, women will continue to enjoy cheaper car insurance than men. The European Commission had attempted to brand the practice as illegal sex discrimination. Malcolm Tarling of the Association of British Insurers said, 'We support equality but we believe that insurers should be free to continue to use factors such as gender when it is relevant in assessing risk'.

Women in their late twenties enjoy the largest discounts in comparison to men. However, the difference between the genders narrows as drivers reach the age of 30 and premiums typically even out. For motorists over the age of 75, men are regarded as a better risk and generally benefit from cheaper insurance.

The opt-out also means that insurers will be able to continue to pay smaller annuities to women, on the grounds that they have longer life expectancy.

19.4 Duration, cancellation and renewal

Indemnity insurance contracts are of limited duration, frequently one year. If, at the end of the period, the contract is renewed, this will be a fresh contract and will be subject to the general duty of disclosure: *Lambert v. Cooperative Insurance Society* [1975] 1 Lloyd's Rep 485.

Indemnity policies generally contain a clause entitling either party to cancel the policy on giving notice to the other party. The period of notice is generally seven or 14 days, but clauses giving a right to immediate cancellation are valid. In *Sun Fire Office v. Hart* (1889) 14 App Cas 98, a policy was terminated under a clause in the policy which allowed the insurer to cancel the policy 'from any … cause whatsoever'. The insured had suffered several fires and had received an anonymous letter threatening arson.

There is no right to renew a policy, and the insurer is under no obligation to warn the insured that the policy is about to expire, although this is generally done. Insurers may allow 'days of grace' during which the policy can be renewed after the expiry date. Since these are a concession by the insurer, the effect of these days of grace depends on the wording of the policy. It is doubtful whether the policy would cover any loss between the expiry and the payment of the premium and whether, after a loss falling within the terms of the policy, the insured could insist on the insurer renewing the policy.

Life policies are different, in the sense that they exist until the death of the insured or, in the case of an endowment or term policy, until the specified fixed date. As long as the premiums continue to be paid, the insurer cannot refuse to renew a life policy. In the same way, such policies do not contain cancellation clauses but they will normally provide for the insured to surrender the policy at any time and, after a certain number of years, the insured will be able to recover a lump sum in the form of the surrender value. An alternative where the insured cannot or does not want to continue to pay premiums is for the policy to become paid-up. In this case, the benefits payable on the death of the life assured will be reduced.

In respect of life policies, where the policy allows for days of grace payment within the days of grace period is effective even if the death of the life assured has already occurred: *Stuart v. Freeman* [1903] 1 KB 47.

19.5 Insurance as a contract of utmost good faith

A contract of insurance is a classic example of a contract of utmost good faith, since the insurer relies totally on the insured to supply information relevant to the risk for which insurance cover is required. As a result, the insured is required to make full disclosure of all known, material factors likely to affect the insurance company in agreeing to accept the risk and fixing the premium by the person taking out the insurance cover. This was spelt out by MacKenna J in *Lambert v. Cooperative Insurance Society Ltd* [1975] 2 Lloyd's Rep 485: '[e]veryone agrees that the assured is under a duty of disclosure and that the duty is the same when he is applying for renewal as it is when he is applying for the original policy'. As regards the extent of the duty, the judge set out four possible tests: (i) to disclose such facts only as the particular assured believes to be material; (ii) to disclose such facts as a reasonable man would believe to be reasonable; (iii) to disclose such facts as a reasonable insurer would regard as material; and (iv) to disclose such facts as a reasonable or prudent insurer might have treated as material. In conclusion, the judge said that the fourth was the proper test.

This decision was cited by the court in *Woolcott v. Sun Alliance and London Insurance Ltd* [1978] 1 WLR 493, where Sun Alliance refused payment on an insurance policy covering W's house against fire on the ground that he had failed to disclose when taking out the insurance that he had earlier convictions for robbery and other offences – albeit some 12 years previously. He had not been asked any questions about his character on the application form and the judge found that, if he had, he would have answered them truthfully.

When taking out insurance, the insured will generally be required to answer a number of questions contained in a proposal form. The fact that these have been answered correctly does not displace the obligation under the duty of utmost good faith.

In *Glicksman v. Lancashire & General Assurance Co. Ltd* [1927] AC 139, G and his partner had insured their business against burglary and had stated in answer to a question in the proposal form that the partnership had never been refused cover by another insurer. Whilst this was true for the firm, G had himself once been refused insurance cover. The House of Lords upheld the defendant's refusal to accept liability.

There have been calls for the law to be reformed but there has been no legislation. There has been some self-regulation by the industry, however, in the Statements of Insurance Practice which state that an insurer will not repudiate his liability against a policyholder who is a private individual on grounds of non-disclosure of a material fact which he could not reasonably be expected to disclose. Intervention by the Insurance Ombudsman has also restricted the worst effects of the doctrine.

Council Directive 73/239/EEC ([1973] OJ L228/3) set out various respects in which there should be coordinated national legislation on insurance business in EU Member States. In *Poole and Ors v. HM Treasury* [2007] EWCA Civ 1021 the court dismissed an appeal by the claimants, Frederick Poole and some 1,000 other Lloyd's Names, in respect of a claim for damages against the Treasury for its failure to transpose the Insurance Directive into UK law so as to provide adequate regulation of the Lloyd's market. The court held that the Directive was not intended to bestow rights on the claimants but was for the protection of the insured.

In the case of life insurance, the information to be disclosed includes the history of the applicant's health, and dangerous occupations and activities. The most common failing is for people taking life cover to mislead the insurance company about their age. Since this will affect the premiums payable, the policy's surrender value will be lower than if the real age had been disclosed. Many insurance companies require proof of age only before paying out against the policy and, where the policy is the security for a loan, the mortgagee should ensure that the insured's age is established by sending in a birth certificate.

There is a risk of the policy being avoided where it restricts the insured's activities: excluding liability for death arising from certain occupations such as aviation, mining and so on, or restricts sporting and leisure activities.

19.6 Content and interpretation of the policy

In respect of contract terms, insurance has traditionally differed from general contracts in the significance of conditions and warranties. In insurance law the term 'warranty' was regarded as a fundamental term which must be strictly complied with and the breach of which would automatically discharge the insurer from liability even if unrelated to the loss. Thus, in the early marine insurance case, *De Hahn v. Hartley* (1786) 1 TR 343, the insured warranted that the ship sailed from Liverpool with 50 hands on board. It left Liverpool with 46 hands but took on an extra six in Anglesey. The insurer was able to avoid all liability.

Similarly, in *Conn v. Westminster Motor Insurance Association Ltd* [1966] 1 Lloyd's Rep 407, C's taxi was badly damaged when it ran off the road at 2a.m. – probably because C was asleep at the wheel. The insurance company refused to accept liability on the ground that C had not complied with the terms of the policy which required him to maintain the vehicle in efficient condition. The front tyres were completely bald and the brakes were defective. Even though this had not caused the accident, the insurer could disown liability.

In *Dawsons Ltd v. Bonin* [1922] 2 AC 413, D insured a lorry with B under a policy which provided that it should be on the basis of the proposal form completed by D. In the proposal, D had stated that the lorry would be garaged at its ordinary place of business in Glasgow, whereas it was normally garaged at a farm on the outskirts of the city. The lorry was destroyed by fire at the farm and the insurers were able to escape liability, since the statement was the 'basis of the contract' even though the misstatement was not material. The wrong information had been filled in by the insurer's local agent and the mistake was not picked up by D. This still did not prevent the insurer from repudiating liability.

It is not easy to distinguish between a warranty and a term simply defining the risk to be covered, when the insurer will be excused from liability only where the breach is related to the loss. In *Farr v. Motor Traders' Mutual Insurance Society* [1920] 3 KB 669, F owned two taxis insured on the basis of a proposal in which the vehicles were to be driven in only one shift per 24 hours. Six months later, one taxi was driven for two shifts on one or two days while the other was being repaired. In respect of a claim following an accident to this particular cab, the insurer claimed that its use on a double shift during August was a breach of warranty and discharged it from liability. The Court of Appeal held that it was merely descriptive of the risk and that the insurer was liable.

The position seems to have been subtly changed by the House of Lords' decision in *Bank of Nova Scotia v. Hellenic Mutual War Risks Association (Bermuda) Ltd, The Good Luck* [1991] 2 WLR 1279, which held that if the insured warrants the accuracy of a statement in the proposal and it proves not to have been true, the insurer is discharged from liability *ab initio*. However, if circumstances change during the currency of the policy which cause the warranty to be breached, the insurer is discharged from liability under the policy from that time onwards.

The term 'condition' is also used in much the same way as in the general law of contract. Thus if the contract makes it a condition that the insurer shall be given notice of the loss within 14 days of it happening, breach of the term will allow the insurer to escape liability.

Where the policy contains a condition precedent requiring claimants to give notice in writing with full particulars immediately after the occurrence of the injury or damage which is the subject of the claim, the insurer can refuse to accept liability under the policy where the condition is not complied with. In *Kosmar Villa Holidays plc v. Trustees of Syndicate 1243* [2008] EWCA Civ 147 it was held that, where insurers acknowledged a claim knowing that the insured had failed to comply with a condition precedent in the notification clause, they elected to waive the insured's failure and accept liability. In this case a client of Kosmar was seriously injured during a holiday. In spite of a clause requiring immediate notification of the details of the claim, Kosmar informed the insurers only a year after the injury.

A rule of construction of importance in insurance is the *contra proferentem* rule under which any ambiguous term is interpreted to the disadvantage of the insurer.

In *Houghton v. Trafalgar Insurance Co. Ltd* [1954] 1 QB 247, the insurer sought to deny liability in respect of a car involved in an accident at a time when it was carrying six people although it was designed to seat five. The policy excluded liability for any damage 'arising whilst the car is conveying any load in excess of that for which it was constructed'. The Court of Appeal held that the clause was ambiguous and should be interpreted as referring only to the weight load and not the number of passengers.

The Unfair Terms in Consumer Contracts Regulations 1999 could also be important here (see Chapter 21, p.517).

19.7 Standard terms in policies of insurance

Many standard terms used in policies of insurance – 'accident', 'all risks', 'damage by fire', and 'loss' (and 'consequential loss') – have been the subject of judicial interpretation over the years.

(a) Accident

The courts have found it difficult to define 'accident'. It must be remembered that insurance covers only unintentional acts and excludes deliberate acts, and it is interesting to see how these two are reconciled. In *Hamlyn v. Crown Accidental Insurance Co. Ltd* [1893] 1 QB 750, H wrenched his knee when he bent down to pick up a marble. The injury was held to be accidental.

In *Marcel Beller Ltd v. Hayden* [1978] QB 694, the claimants insured their employees against death from 'accidental bodily injury'. An employee driving whilst over the alcohol limit lost control of his car on a bend and was killed. The judge rejected the insurers' claim that death was the result of the employee's deliberate act, holding that 'accident' should be interpreted in its ordinary sense.

The judge distinguished this case from the decision in *Gray v. Barr* [1971] 2 QB 554. B had taken a shotgun to G's house where he had gone to look for his wife who was having an affair with G. During a fight with G, the shotgun went off and G was killed. B was sued for damages by G's dependants and sought to claim an indemnity under a policy with the Prudential under which he was covered for liability for injuries to third parties caused by accidents. The trial judge held that G's death had been caused by an accident, but the majority of the Court of Appeal held that it had not.

In respect of accidental damage to property, it is clear that the damage must result from something unintended and unexpected. In the Australian decision, *Robinson v. Evans* [1969] VR 885, E claimed to be indemnified by his public liability insurer following settlement of a tort action brought by R for damage to his crop of brussels sprouts on two separate occasions from fluoride emissions from the chimney of E's brick works. The first occurrence was not an accident since the defendant's managing director knew of the danger. The second instance took place after the chimney had been heightened in the belief that this would solve the problem. The insurers were liable to indemnify the defendant for this second occurrence.

If the real cause of the loss is natural, it will generally not be covered. In *Mills v. Smith* [1964] 1QB 30, however, the court held that a householder's liability policy which indemnified the insured against 'damage to property caused by accident' covered damage done to a neighbour's house by the roots of a tree in the insured's garden. In this respect, it is interesting to note that a change in the wording with a reference to 'an accident' or 'caused by accidental means' might have prevented the court from interpreting the clause so widely.

Hot Topic . . .

DEEP VEIN THROMBOSIS (DVT) – ECONOMY CLASS SYNDROME

There is a lot of interest worldwide in this particular topic, with actions in the USA and Australia as well as the UK. For the purposes of this chapter, our interest lies in the fact that, in order to establish liability on the part of the airlines, the passengers had to claim under Article 17 of the Warsaw Convention 1929 (as amended) which provides: '[t]he carrier is liable for damage sustained in the event of death or wounding of a passenger or any bodily injury suffered by a passenger, if the accident which caused the damage so sustained took place on board the aircraft'. The test case in the UK commenced in November 2001 and the decision that there had been no accident was upheld in the Court of Appeal. The leading judgment of Lord Phillips MR considered the meaning of 'accident'. He stated that the word referred to the cause of the injury and not the injury itself, and that liability 'arises only if a passenger's injury is caused by an unexpected or unusual event or happening that is external to the passenger. ... But when the injury ... results from the passenger's own internal reaction to the usual, normal and expected operation of the aircraft, it has not been caused by an accident.' Lord Phillips said that the word 'accident' naturally suggested 'an untoward event which impacts on the body in a manner which causes death, wounding or injury. The impact of the event may be physical or it may be an impact on the senses which results in bodily injury, but one would normally expect the untoward event to cause the death or injury directly.' He further suggested that inaction or an omission to act by an air carrier could not constitute an accident since inaction was actually a non-event and the antithesis of an accident.

In *Deep Vein Thrombosis and Air Travel Group Litigation* [2005] UKHL 72 the Court of Appeal's decision was confirmed by the House of Lords.

An identical position was reached in the Australian decision in *Povey v. Quantas Airways Ltd* [2005] HCA 33, where it was held that the formation of the blood clots in the veins of the leg could not be the requisite accident because that onset was the damage complained of and no other event or happening, no occurrence external to the passenger could be pointed to.

The argument that inaction or omission to act could not constitute an accident was rejected by the US Supreme Court in *Olympic Airways v. Husain* 124 S Ct 1221 (2004), in which a passenger had requested and obtained non-smoking seats which were only a few rows in front of the smoking section. Being particularly sensitive to second-hand smoke, he asked to be moved on three occasions but was refused by the flight attendant, who asserted untruthfully that there were no spare seats. The passenger collapsed and died as a result of passive smoking and the court held that this was the result of an accident. The majority of the court accepted that the failure to move the asthmatic passenger to an available seat was a cause of damage external to the passenger and, since it was contrary to normal airline industry standards, was therefore neither expected nor usual. An important issue in this finding was the causal chain of the exchanges between the asthmatic and the flight attendant.

(b) All risks

Policies on valuables and contractors' policies are frequently 'all risks'. Basically, they cover all loss to the insured property through accidental cause, but not 'such damage as is inevitable from ordinary wear and tear and inevitable depreciation'. The insured has to establish only that the loss is accidental but not its exact nature. The policy can exclude loss from specific causes: in *Queensland Government Railways and Electric Power Transmission Pty. Ltd v. Manufacturers' Mutual Life Assurance Ltd* [1969] 1 Lloyd's Rep 214, there was a valid exclusion for loss arising from 'faulty design'.

(c) Fire

Actual ignition is necessary and damage from excessive heat is not sufficient, but the law is not concerned with how the fire occurred.

In *Harris v. Poland* [1941] 1 KB 462, H's personal property was insured against loss or damage by fire. She concealed her jewellery in the grate where a fire was laid and later lit the fire, forgetting to remove her jewels. The court allowed her claim on the basis that 'it matters not whether the fire comes to the insured property or the insured property comes to the fire'.

Damage by explosion or lightning is not damage by fire in itself, but if the explosion was caused by fire or fire follows an explosion or lightning, it is covered.

(d)   Loss

The risk of loss is central to the concept of insurance. When the word is combined to form a more complex phrase: 'loss by fire', the actual word 'loss' is less important than when used on its own or in connection with, but as a separate category from, other terms: 'loss, damage or destruction'.

Goods are clearly lost if, after a reasonable time searching for them, it seems unlikely that they will be found, but not if they are in somebody else's hands even though the owner is deprived of possession. But goods would probably be regarded as lost if their recovery were uncertain after all reasonable steps to recover them had been taken. In *Webster v. General Accident Fire and Life Assurance Corp. Ltd* [1953] 1 QB 520, the claimant's car was stolen and passed through a number of hands before reaching a purchaser who had probably obtained good title under the Factors Act. The claimant had taken all reasonable steps to recover the car: contacting the police and motoring organisations, and it was held that the car was lost for the purposes of the claimant's insurance.

Under some policies, goods are insured against 'loss by theft'.

In *Dobson v. General Accident Fire and Life Assurance Corp. plc* [1990] 1 QB 274, the claimant had advertised a watch and diamond ring for sale and handed them over in return for a worthless cheque. The Court of Appeal held that he could recover the value of the goods under his household insurance policy.

This decision was later approved by the House of Lords in *R. v. Gomez* [1993] 1 All ER 1.

Property may be totally destroyed or only damaged, which will affect the amount which the insured can recover. Total loss is where 'the subject matter is destroyed or so damaged as to cease to be a thing of the kind insured'. Thus, after a fire, a house may still have standing walls and foundations but is totally lost. The same is true of cars which are classified as 'write-offs', although in that case it may simply be that they are uneconomic to repair. Where there has been a total loss of goods, the measure of the loss is the market value of the property at the time and place of loss: in other words, the second-hand or resale value. Some policies will however cover for the replacement value of the goods. 'New for old' policies are an exception to the idea that insurance is based on the principle of indemnity.

Where there has been a total loss of real property, there is the question whether the insured is entitled to the market value of the destroyed property or the costs of rebuilding or reinstating the property.

In *Leppard v. Excess Insurance Company* [1979] 1 WLR 512, the insured purchased a cottage which was worth £4,500, including the site value, at the time when it was destroyed by fire, although the cost of rebuilding it would be £8,000. Since the insured had only bought the place to resell it, his loss was held to be the market value of the property. This was in spite of his having completed a proposal form in which he warranted that 'the sums to be insured represent not less than the full value (the full value is the amount which it would cost to replace the property in its existing form should it be totally destroyed)', and that the cottage had been insured for £14,000.

In respect of partial loss of both real and personal property, the basis of indemnity is the cost of repair.

In marine insurance law there is a doctrine of 'constructive total loss', whereby, even if a ship or other insured property is not actually lost or cannot be proved to be lost, the insured can claim as for the total loss. In this case, the insurer will be entitled to the ship or other property if it turns up.

Generally, it is not possible to recover in respect of consequential loss unless it is separately covered. Thus, in *Re Wright and Pole* (1834) 1 A & E 621, the insured was unable to recover in respect of loss of custom and the hire of other premises under an insurance covering his inn which had been destroyed by fire. This cover can be provided by way of interruption insurance, which is taken out by most businesses.

19.8 Causation

In order to claim in respect of a loss, the insured must show that the proximate cause of the loss was an insured peril. This is the effective or dominant or real cause of the loss. In *Symington v. Union Insurance of Canton* (1928) 97 LJKB 646, a consignment of cork insured against loss by fire and stored on a jetty was thrown into the sea to prevent the spread of an existing fire. The proximate cause was held to be the fire.

It can be difficult to identify the proximate cause of the loss where there are two real causes. In *Leyland Shipping Co. v. Norwich Union Fire Insurance Society Ltd* [1918] AC 350, a ship was insured against the perils of the sea except loss due to hostilities. The ship was torpedoed by an enemy vessel during the war and towed into Le Havre where it was safely moored. The authorities subsequently ordered it to be moored outside the harbour where it sank. The proximate cause of its sinking was held to be the torpedoing.

In respect of personal accident claims, policies will often be worded in such a way as to limit the insurer's liability to injury or death arising exclusively from the accident.

In *Jason v. Batten* [1969] 1 Lloyd's Rep 281, the policy provided for the payment of benefits to the insured if he sustained 'in any accident bodily injury resulting in and being – independently of all other causes – the exclusive, direct and immediate cause of the injury or disablement'. The policy excluded liability in respect of death, injury or disablement 'directly or indirectly arising or resulting from or traceable to ... any physical defect or infirmity which existed prior to an accident'. The insured suffered a coronary thrombosis after being involved in a car accident where the blood clot had been present previously. The insurers were not liable.

19.9 Life insurance

There are many forms of life policy, of which the simplest is the whole life policy which pays out a capital sum on the death of the life assured. There is also the term policy which pays out a capital sum on death of the life assured within a specified term. Another variant is the endowment policy which pays out on the death of the insured or at the end of a specified period, whichever comes first. There are also annuity policies where, in consideration of the payment of a lump sum to the insurer, the insurer undertakes to pay an annual sum of money – usually by monthly instalments – to the insured for the rest of their life.

Many of the modern policies of insurance which have been developed over the recent past are investment vehicles and are regulated by the Financial Services Authority (FSA).

There are three special aspects of life insurance: the policyholders' right to cancel a policy during a cooling-off period; the assignment of life policies; and trusts of life policies.

(a) Formalities – disclosure and cancellation

General disclosure requirements applicable to any investment are imposed on life contracts by the FSA. In addition, EC Directives on freedom of services (96/71/EC, [1996] OJ L381/4 and 2006/123/EC, [2006] OJ L376/36) have imposed specific rules relating to pre-contractual disclosure by the insurer to the prospective insured. There are also requirements for disclosure by the insurer during the life of the contract.

Since life insurance contracts are long-term contracts which people may be persuaded to enter by high-pressure sales techniques, policyholders are allowed a cooling-off period during which they can cancel a policy without penalty. This right is contained in the Conduct of Business Rules made by the FSA. The insured has a right of cancellation for a minimum of 14 days from receipt of a notice sent by the insurer but the insurer can specify a longer period of up to 30 days.

(b) Assignment

Life policies acquire an immediately realisable value – the surrender value – within a few years of their being taken out, which means that they can be assigned absolutely or by way of security to a third person who can then obtain the surrender value of the policy from the life office. This is, of course, a consequence of the fact that the insurable interest in respect of life policies is required only at the time of taking out the policy. The assignee is not required to have an insurable interest in the life of the assured.

Prior to the Policies of Assurance Act (PAA) 1867, life policies could not be legally assigned. The assignment of life policies was, however, recognised in equity, but the assignee was required to join the assignor in any action to enforce the policy. In addition, the insurer could not obtain a good discharge against payment from the assignee alone.

The PAA 1867 permits the legal assignment of life policies subject to compliance with the Act's requirements. Where the policy has been assigned in accordance with the PAA 1867, assignees can enforce the policy in their own name: s.1 PAA 1867. Since the life policy is a form of intangible personal property, it can in the alternative be assigned under s.136 Law of Property Act (LPA) 1925. The difference between these two forms of assignment is that the PAA 1867 allows the assignment by way of mortgage, whereas the LPA 1925 requires an absolute assignment. Incomplete legal assignments will always be effective equitable assignments.

An assignment under the 1867 Act must be in the form prescribed in the Schedule to the Act or in words with a similar effect, and it must be endorsed on the policy or contained in a separate instrument: s.5 PAA 1867. Written notice of the assignment must be given to the insurer at its principal place of business: s.3.PAA 1867. Under s.136 LPA 1925, the assignment must be in writing and notice of it must be given to the insurer. In neither case is there any need for the consent of the insurer. It is possible for the policy to provide that it is not legally assignable, but this will still not render ineffective an equitable assignment.

An equitable assignment can also be made in the form of a legal agreement to assign or the deposit of the policy with the assignee as security for a loan. (For assignment of life policies as a security see Chapter 15, p.350.)

(c)   Trusts of life policies

The insured may have established a trust over a life policy for the benefit of another. This will usually arise only in connection with an own-life policy. Where such a trust can be established, there are two advantages for the beneficiary: the capital sum payable on the maturity of the policy will belong to and pass directly to the beneficiary and not be counted as part of the deceased's estate; and, in the event of the insured becoming bankrupt, the policy will not be subject to the claims of the insured's creditors as long as it was not created for the purpose of defrauding the creditors under s.423 Insolvency Act 1986.

The easiest way for a trust to be established is under s.11 Married Women's Property Act 1882. Under this Act, a policy taken out on their own life by a married man or woman and expressed to be for the benefit of the spouse and/or children creates a trust in their favour. The section covers any policy relating to the payment of benefits on the insured's death, including accident policies covering only death by accident and endowment policies for payment on death prior to expiry of the stated period.

The insured is a trustee and must act in the beneficiaries' best interests: policies can only be surrendered in their interests and, on surrender, the money is held on trust for their benefit.

If the beneficiaries are named in the policy, then they have an immediate vested interest in it. Thus in *Cousins v. Sun Life Assurance Society* [1933] Ch 126, a wife who was the named beneficiary in a policy taken out by her husband pre-deceased her husband. The capital sum payable under the policy passed to her estate even though the husband had remarried. If the policy does not name the beneficiaries, however, but is merely expressed to be for the benefit of the deceased's wife and children, the beneficiaries' interest will vest on the death of the insured only in the people fitting that description.

Trust issues can also arise in respect of group insurance policies taken out by employers on the lives of employees or a group of them for their benefit.

In *Bowskill v. Dawson (No. 2)* [1955] 1 QB 13, the employer entered into a trust deed with the trust company which effected the policy for the employees. The deed referred to the fact that sums received by the trust company were to be held on trust for the employees, and the court held that the employees were beneficiaries under the trust deed. There were no such references in *Green v. Russell* [1959] 2 QB 226, where the employer took out a group accident policy for the benefit of employees named in the schedule to the policy. The policy expressly provided that the insurer was to treat the employer as the absolute owner and was not bound to recognise any equitable or other claim or interest in the policy. It was held that the employees had no legal or equitable claim to the policy.

19.10   Liability insurance

Liability insurance covers the insured's potential liability to third parties arising in contract and tort. Such policies are legally required in respect of motor vehicles and employer's liability, but are commonly encountered in respect of householders' liability and professional indemnity. The following are common to all such policies: statutory protection to third parties in the event of the insured's insolvency; standard conditions in liability policies; the sums insured; and the insurer's duty to the victim of the insured.

(a) Bankruptcy/liquidation of the insured

Prior to the Third Parties (Rights Against Insurers) Act 1930, if the insured became bankrupt, entered into a composition or arrangement with his creditors or, in the case of a company or LLP, into liquidation, administration, receivership or CVA, after a claim against it by a third party, the money paid by the insurer went towards the general assets of the insolvent insured and the third party merely proved as an ordinary creditor for the money. The third party is now statutorily subrogated to the position of the insured by s.1(1). This is also the case where the insured dies insolvent: s.1(2).

Liability is incurred by the insured only when the third party obtains a judgment against the insured or an admission of liability.

Thus in *Post Office v. Norwich Union Fire Insurance Co.* [1967] 2 QB 363, the insured were contractors engaged in roadworks during the course of which they damaged a Post Office (PO) cable. The contractors denied liability, claiming it was the fault of a PO engineer. The contractors went into liquidation and the PO sued its insurers before the insured's liability was established. It was held that its action was premature.

This was approved by the House of Lords in *Bradley v. Eagle Star Insurance Co. Ltd* [1989] AC 957, where the claimant contracted a disease during her employment. The employer company had been dissolved in 1976 and she commenced proceedings against its insurer. The action was struck out because of a failure to establish the insured's liability.

A further limitation is that the third party's rights are no better than those of the insured. This means that any claim the insurer may maintain against the insured can be maintained against the third party. This includes the right to avoid the policy for non-disclosure or breach of warranty. Thus in *Pioneer Concrete (UK) Ltd v. National Employers Mutual General Insurance Association Ltd* [1985] 1 Lloyd's Rep 274, the breach of a condition in the policy by the insured requiring immediate notification of legal proceedings against it frustrated the third party's claim.

A further problem is that the operation of the Act can be excluded.

Thus in *The Fanti and The Padre Island* [1991] 2 AC 1, a proviso in the rules of shipowners' mutual insurance clubs provided that the insurers did not pay an indemnity to the insured until the latter had paid the third party making a claim against them – a 'pay to be paid' clause. In these two cases decided together, the insured had been wound up after their liability to third parties had been established but before the claims had been paid. It was held that the third parties did not have direct rights against the insurers in spite of a statutory provision which makes ineffective any provision in the contract of insurance which directly or indirectly avoids the contract or alters the rights of parties: s.1(3).

(b) Standard conditions in liability policies

In respect of admitting liability, the policy will contain a clause along the following lines: '[n]o admission of liability or offer or promise of payment, whether expressed or implied, shall be made without the written consent of the insurer, which shall be entitled at its own discretion to take over and conduct in the name of the insured the defence or settlement of any claim'. Professional indemnity policies also may contain a clause that proceedings by the third party are not to be contested unless a QC so advises.

There will also be a clause requiring the insured to take reasonable precautions to avoid loss. Since the purpose of the clause is to cover the insured against liability for negligence, this would largely negate the main purpose of the policy if taken literally. The court has adopted a commonsense construction of such clauses. Thus in *Woolfall & Rimmer v. Moyle* [1942] 1 KB 66, an employer, the insured, was vicariously liable for the acts of a foreman who had failed to ensure that some scaffolding was safe. The court held that the insured was not personally negligent and had complied with the condition by appointing a competent foreman and reasonably delegating to him certain tasks. In order for the insured to lose protection of the insurance, his omission or act 'must be at least reckless, that is to say, made with actual recognition by the insured himself that a danger exists, and not caring whether or not it is averted'.

(c) Sums insured

The policy may have a financial limit applying to any one contractual period, regardless of the number of claims made, or a limit to each accident, occurrence or claim. In the first case, it has been decided that each separate claim arises out of a separate incident. In *South Staffordshire Tramways Co. v. Sickness and Accident Assurance Association* [1891] 1 QB 402, the claimant's indemnity insurance had a limit of '£250 in respect of one accident'. When one of its buses overturned, injuring 40 passengers, the court held that there had been a separate accident for each passenger. In respect of the destruction of the World Trade Center in New York in 2001, it was held that there were two incidents each giving rise to payment by the insurance company.

If the financial limit is per occurrence, the number of occurrences is the number of negligent acts committed by the insured. If there is one negligent act but lots of individual claims, the financial limit will apply.

In *Forney v. Dominion Insurance Co. Ltd* [1969] 1 WLR 928, a solicitor's professional indemnity policy had a limit of £3,000 per occurrence. His assistant negligently advised a client about a cause of action in tort arising from a car accident where the driver injured some members of his family and caused his own and his father-in-law's deaths. The survivors were advised to sue the estate but the assistant failed to issue the writs in time. The assistant also negligently advised the driver's widow to act as the driver's administratrix, which ruled out her personal claim against the estate. The court held that the acts were two occurrences and the maximum liability of the insurer was £6,000.

(d) Insurer's duty to the victim

Liability insurers frequently negotiate with the victim directly on behalf of the insured and seek to limit their liability. They may induce the victim to agree to a settlement, in which case a fiduciary relationship will arise and the settlement will be voidable on the ground of undue influence, unless the insurers inform the victim of the advisability of seeking independent advice or make an offer which is realistic.

19.11 Employers' liability insurance

Employers have a legal obligation to take out insurance cover in respect of work accidents to their employees under the Employers' Liability (Compulsory Insurance) Act 1969. The Act provides that every employer carrying on any business in Great Britain shall insure and maintain insurance under one or more approved policies with an authorised insurer against liability for bodily injury arising 'out of and in the course of their employment' in Great Britain in that business, but, except in so far as regulations otherwise provide, not including injury or disease suffered or contracted outside Great Britain. For the purposes of the legislation, an employee is anyone who works under a contract of service or apprenticeship, express or implied, written or oral and excludes the need to insure self-employed persons working under a contract for services (see Chapter 17, p.386).

(f) Out of and in the course of employment

There are two aspects to this phrase: 'in the course of employment' and 'out of employment'. The latter requires a causal connection between the employment and the accident, and there are unlikely to be problems here once the employer has been found liable in court or has admitted liability.

The aspect of 'in the course of employment' basically requires the employee to be in the place of work in order for the insurer's liability to trigger. Employees travelling to and from work are not in the course of their employment, even travelling in vehicles provided by their employers unless the terms of their employment contract oblige them to travel.

Hot Topic . . .

ASBESTOS-RELATED CLAIMS – PLEURAL PLAQUES AND THE 'WORRIED WELL'

Asbestos used to be known as 'white gold' or 'the magic mineral', was widely used between 1950 and 1980 and was not completely banned until 1999.

Asbestos-related claims will cost Britain's private and public sectors up to £20bn over the next 30 years. Insurers received 12,370 claims in 2003 and Julian Lowe, who headed a study for the Actuarial Profession, said he expected between 80,000 and 200,000 new claims in the next 30 years.

Insurers face bills of up to £10bn, while companies will be forced to pay out as much as £6bn and the government up to £4bn. The government's liability could be greater, since many of the companies faced with legal action have since collapsed or are in administration.

In *Rothwell v. Chemical and Insolating Co. Ltd and Anor* [2007] UKHL 39 it was held that a person who developed pleural plaques as a result of having been negligently exposed to asbestos in the course of his employment could not sue his employers for negligence. Pleural plaques, a fibrous thickening of the pleural membrane which surrounded the lungs, did not constitute actionable damage because, save in very exceptional cases, they were symptomless and did not themselves cause other asbestos-related diseases. Lord Hoffmann said that proof of damage was an essential element in a claim for negligence and symptomless plaques were not compensatable. Neither did the risk of future illness or anxiety about the possibility of that risk materialising amount to damage for the purpose of a cause of action.

These claimants are classified as the 'worried well' and account for three-quarters of all asbestos compensation claims in the USA. The insurers argued that pleural plaques were simply a marker for asbestos exposure rather than an injury.

In *Vandyke v. Fender* [1970] 2 QB 292, V and F were employees of the same company. They worked some distance from home and the company agreed to provide a car in which F could drive himself and V to work. The company also paid towards the petrol. On a journey to work, V was injured owing to F's negligence. The issue was whether the claim was against the company's liability insurer or the car insurer. The court held that the employer's liability insurer was not liable since the accident did not arise in the course of employment.

In *Paterson v. Costain & Press (Overseas) Ltd* [1979] 2 Lloyd's Rep 204, the claimant was injured as a result of the negligence of the employer's driver on a journey from his office to a construction site to which he had been summoned. The court held that the accident did arise in the course of employment because he was in the vehicle on the express instruction of his employer.

Even if the employees are at the place of work, the accident will not necessarily be in the course of employment if it is not sufficiently incidental to the employment. In *R. v. National Insurance Commissioner, ex parte Michael* [1977] 1 WLR 109, a policemen playing in a football match in his force's team against another force at the force's sports ground was not injured in the course of his employment even though he was expected to play. An injury during a tea break or toilet break will be in the course of employment, as will one within a reasonable time before and after the time of employment.

End of Chapter Summary

Having read this chapter you should have an insight into the topic of insurance and understand the significance of the following:

- The difference between indemnity and contingency insurance.
- The need for an insurable interest on the part of the assured and the distinction in this respect between indemnity and contingency insurance.
- The importance of the need for full disclosure by the assured.
- The meaning of standard terms: accident, all risks, loss and so on.
- The assignment of life policies and surrender value.
- Employers' liability insurance.

The topic of the assignment of life policies is important in connection with securing loans, and employers' liability insurance with the chapter on employment contracts. Both topics are of importance in the business world, as is the whole topic of indemnity insurance.

Questions

1. Explain the concept of the insurable interest and the different requirements of the need for an insurable interest between indemnity and contingency insurance.

2. Credit Ltd is owed £10,000 by Dana and takes out a life insurance policy with Carefree Policies plc on Dana's life to cover the total sum owed. The debt is repaid in accordance with the loan agreement but Credit Ltd continues to pay the premiums on the policy. Advise Credit Ltd of its rights in connection with the policy in the event of Dana's death.

3. James had a policy with Carefree Policies plc, which paid benefits if he sustained injury resulting from and being – independently of all other causes – the exclusive, direct and immediate cause of any accident. The policy excluded liability in respect of death, injury or disablement resulting from or traceable to any pre-existing physical defect or infirmity. Following a car accident, James suffered a heart attack. Carefree Policies plc refuse to pay under the policy on the ground that medical records prior to the accident show that James was taking medication for high blood pressure. Advise James.

4. Prudent Ltd insured their employees against death from 'accidental bodily injury'. Greg, an employee, lost control of his car and was killed. The post-mortem report on Greg showed that, at the time of the incident, he was over the legal alcohol limit. Carefree Policies plc, the insurer, refuse to pay out on the policy, saying that death was not the result of an 'accident' but due to Greg's deliberate act. Advice Prudent Ltd.

5. Prudent Ltd has employer's liability insurance in respect of its employees. Consider the insurance position in respect of the following incidents:
   (i) Angie falls down and breaks her arm in the staff canteen during an extended lunch break.
   (ii) Bob is knocked from his motor scooter and injured on his way to work.
   (iii) Clare has been asked to post the company's mail at the local post office on her way home after work. Before reaching the post office she is injured in a fall.
   (iv) The IT department decided to have a farewell party for a colleague. The party took place after office hours in the company's building. During the celebrations, Don slipped on a dropped cocktail sausage and injured his knee.

Consumer Protection

Introduction to Part VI

This part of the book deals with consumer protection offered under the Consumer Credit Act 1974 (revised by the Consumer Credit Act (CCA) 2006) (Chapter 20) and consumer protection in respect of unfair business-to-consumer commercial practices and false trade descriptions, wrongful pricing and the misdescription of services and accommodation under the Consumer Protection from Unfair Trading Regulations 2008 (Chapter 21). This chapter also discusses consumer protection in respect of unsolicited goods and services, sales at a distance and product safety.

The Consumer Credit Act 1974 deals with all aspects of consumer credit, whereas the credit extended to dealers is still governed by common law. Chapter 20 concentrates on the regulation of credit to consumers. It is significant for businesses to realise the difference between the various forms of credit agreement available to consumers, and in particular the distinctions between the legal effects of HP contracts and conditional sale and credit sale agreements. The protection afforded by s.75 CCA 1974 is of vital importance, in that it imposes liability on the credit provider for defects in the provision of goods and services where the payment is by credit card. This topic is also of relevance to the topic of e-commerce, discussed in Chapter 22, since the main payment methods for online purchases are credit and debit cards.

The Consumer Protection from Unfair Trading Regulations (CPUT) 2008 implement Directive 2005/29/EC ([2005] OJ L149/22) of the European Parliament and the Council and also Article 6(2) of Directive 1999/44/EC ([1999] OJ L171/12) on certain aspects of the sale of consumer goods and associated guarantees (the Sale of Goods Directive). Part 2 sets out the prohibitions on unfair commercial practices which contravene the requirements of professional diligence, misleading actions, misleading omissions, aggressive commercial practices and other commercial practices specified in Schedule 1. It also prohibits the promotion of unfair commercial practices by persons responsible for traders' codes of conduct. Part 3 provides that breaches of the prohibitions are criminal offences subject to specified defences.

The Business Protection from Misleading Marketing Regulations 2008 came into effect on the same date (26 May 2008) as the CPUT Regulations and regulate misleading advertising by traders to traders.

These Regulations harmonise the law throughout the EU and radically amend the previous legislation in the Trade Descriptions Act 1968 and the Consumer Protection Act 1987 (both of which are largely repealed) and a number of other UK regulations.

This is an area of vital importance not only to consumers seeking to enforce their legal rights, but also businesses, which may inadvertently infringe the law through their ignorance of the Regulations as to what claims they can make in respect of the goods and services they offer.

Chapter 20

Consumer credit

Learning objectives

After reading this chapter you will know about:

▶ regulated agreements under the Consumer Credit Act 1974
▶ HP contracts, conditional sale agreements and credit sale agreements
▶ formality of regulated agreements
▶ debtor protection
▶ termination of agreements.

20.1 Introduction

The Consumer Credit Act (CCA) 1974 and later Regulations regulate consumer credit and consumer hire in the UK. They also license traders engaging in consumer credit and hire business and ancillary credit business. A consumer credit business is any business so far as it comprises or relates to the provision of credit under regulated consumer credit agreements. A consumer hire business is one comprising or relating to the bailment of goods under regulated consumer hire agreements: s.189(1). Ancillary credit businesses include credit brokerage, debt adjusting, debt counselling, debt collecting or the operation of a credit reference agency: s.145(1).

Following a review in 2001, the legislation was amended in 2004 by the Consumer Credit (Advertisements) Regulations, the Consumer Credit (Agreements) (Amendment) Regulations, the Consumer Credit (Disclosure of Information) Regulations, the Consumer Credit (Early Settlement) Regulations, the Consumer Credit (Miscellaneous Amendments) Regulations and the Consumer Credit Act (Electronic Communications) Order. The last one enables and facilitates the use of electronic communications for concluding regulated agreements and the sending of notices and other documents. Further reforms required primary legislation which was achieved by the Consumer Credit Act (CCA) 2006, which reformed the Consumer Credit Act 1974.

A primary objective of the CCA 1974 is 'truth in lending', in respect of which it creates a standard measure of the cost of borrowing in the form of the annual percentage rate of charge (APR). This is calculated by taking the total cost of the credit, including interest and other charges. This is then expressed as an annual percentage rate in accordance with regulations under s.20. The rate can be found by reference to the Consumer Credit Tables published by The Stationery Office.

20.2 Agreements within the Act

Agreements are classifiable as (i) consumer credit agreements; (ii) credit-token agreements and (iii) consumer hire agreements.

(a) Consumer credit agreements

These are agreements between an individual ('the debtor') and any other person ('the creditor') by which the creditor provides the debtor with credit of any amount: s.8(1). Credit is defined as a 'cash loan or any other form of financial accommodation': s.9(1). A consumer credit agreement is a regulated agreement if it is not an exempt agreement under s.16. Consumer credit agreements include:

- loans by finance companies and banks;
- bank overdrafts;
- credit card agreements;
- HP, credit sale and conditional sale agreements;
- check trading agreements (where the creditor supplies the consumer with a check/voucher with a specific face value to be paid off by the consumer by a specified number of regular payments. The retailer hands over goods to the face value of the check/voucher and recovers the face value (less a discount) from the creditor).

(b) Credit token agreements

A credit token is a card, check, voucher, coupon, stamp, form, booklet or other document or thing given to an individual by a person carrying on a consumer credit business who undertakes (a) that on the production of it he will supply cash, goods and services (or any of them on credit), or (b) that where, on the production of it to a third party, the third party supplies cash, goods and services (or any of them), he will pay the third party for them in return for payment to him by the individual: s.14(1). A CTA is a regulated agreement for the provision of credit in connection with the use of the credit token: s.14(2).

Credit token agreements relate to the use of some but not all cards used to pay for goods and services:

- Credit cards like Visa and MasterCard are credit tokens where the card issuer agrees to pay the supplier for goods and services supplied to card holder;
- American Express and Diners' Club cards are credit tokens, but the agreement between the card issuer and the card holder is not a regulated credit token agreement since the account must be settled by a single payment at the end of each month.
- Debit cards are credit tokens in that they can be used to buy goods and services but, since the payment is debited from the card holder's account, debit cards are not credit token agreements since no credit is supplied.

(c) Consumer hire agreements

This is an agreement made by a person with an individual ('the hirer') for the bailment of goods which is not an HP agreement, and is capable of subsisting for more than three months: s.15(1). It is a regulated agreement if it is not exempt under s.16. Regulated agreements include certain rental agreements, such as those for television sets.

The term 'individual' includes a partnership of no more than three members or other unincorporated body of persons not consisting entirely of bodies corporate: s.189(1).

Consumer credit and hire agreements may now be greatly affected by the Unfair Terms in Consumer Contracts Regulations 1999 (see Chapter 21, p.517).

Agreements falling outside the scope of the Act are covered by the common law.

20.3 Regulated consumer credit agreements

Credit is provided by fixed sum agreements or running account or revolving credit. Fixed sum credit agreements are for a specific amount of credit and include credit sale, conditional sale and HP agreements. Running account credit agreements provide debtors with cash, goods and services from time to time up to their credit limit. Examples are bank overdrafts and credit card agreements. These agreements can be further classified as: (i) restricted use credit agreements; and (ii) unrestricted use credit agreements.

Restricted use credit agreements are where the credit is tied to a particular transaction, as in HP, conditional sale and credit sale agreements, shop budget accounts, check trading and the use of credit cards for goods and services. Unrestricted use credit agreements impose no restriction on the use of the credit; as with bank loans.

The Act also distinguishes between: (i) debtor–creditor–supplier agreements (DCSAs): s.12; and (ii) debtor–creditor agreements (DCAs): s.13. DCSAs are those where there is a connection between the creditor and the transaction and include:

(i) restricted use credit agreements where the creditor/supplier are the same person;
(ii) restricted use credit agreements under a pre-existing arrangement between the creditor and the supplier, that is, credit cards;
(iii) unrestricted use credit agreements under pre-existing arrangements with the supplier to finance transactions between the debtor and the supplier.

In the case of DCAs there is no connection between the supplier and the creditor, for example the provision of overdraft facilities to be spent as the debtor wishes.

20.4 Exempt agreements

Certain consumer credit and consumer hire agreements are not regulated by the Act: s.16. These agreements can, however, be reopened by the court where they are extortionate under ss.140A–140C, except for those under s.16(6C):s.16(7A). In addition, the Regulations governing advertisements and quotations apply to all organisations involved in house mortgage lending since September 1985. Exempt agreements include the following.

(a) Mortgage lending

Loans by building societies, local authorities and other bodies secured on land to finance the purchase of land or the construction of a dwelling on already owned land are exempt: s.16(2). The exemption also applies to loans for mortgage protection insurance premiums: s.16(1)–(4).

Consumer credit agreements for improvements to existing properties, where there is a mortgage created over the property, are regulated agreements.

(b) Low-cost credit

These are DCAs where the APR does not exceed the highest of the London and Scottish clearing banks' base rates plus 1 per cent, or 13 per cent, whichever is the higher: s.16(5)(b).

(c) Finance of foreign trade

Credit agreements for the import or export of goods and services are exempt agreements: s.16(5).

(d) Normal trade credit

Normal trade credit covers credit where payment is in one instalment and DCSAs for fixed sum credit where repayment does not exceed four instalments, or running account credit payable in one amount, as with American Express and Diners' Club: s.16(5)(a).

(e) Certain consumer hire agreements

Agreements where the owner is a body corporate authorised to supply electricity, gas or water are exempt agreements, where the subject is a meter or metering equipment, or where the owner is a public telecommunications office: s.16(6).

(f) Exemption relating to high net worth debtors and hirers

Consumer credit or consumer hire agreements are exempt where the debtors/hirers are natural persons and there is a declaration that they forgo the statutory protection and remedies accompanied by a previously provided current statement of high net worth that in the previous financial year the debtor/hirer received income of not less than a specified amount, or had net assets with a total value of not less than a specified value: s.16A.

(g) Exemption relating to business

The Act does not regulate consumer credit or hire agreements exceeding £25,000 if the agreement is entered into by the debtor or hirer wholly or predominantly for the purpose of a business carried on, or intended to be carried on, by him: s.16B. This would be presumed if there was a declaration to that effect unless the creditor/owner knew, or had reasonable cause to suspect, that it was not for such a purpose: s.16B(2) and (3).

(h) Exemption relating to investment properties

The Act does not regulate a consumer credit agreement if, at the time the agreement is entered into, any sums due under it are secured by a land mortgage subject to the condition that less than 40 per cent of the land is used, or is intended to be used, as or in connection with a dwelling (a) by the debtor or a person connected with the debtor, or (b), in the case of credit provided to trustees, by an individual who is the beneficiary of the trust or a person connected with such an individual: s.16C(1) and (2). The area of land which comprises a building or other structure containing two or more storeys is to be taken to be the aggregate of the floor area of each of those storeys: s.16C(3). A person is 'connected with' the debtor or an individual who is a beneficiary of a trust if he is: (a) that person's spouse or civil partner; (b) a person (whether or not of the opposite sex) whose relationship with that person has the characteristics of the relationship between husband and wife; or (c) that person's parent, brother, sister, child, grandparent or grandchild: s.16C(4).

Section 126 (enforcement of land mortgages) applies to an agreement which would, but for that section, be a regulated agreement (s.16C(5)) and nothing in that section affects the application of sections 140A to 140C.

20.5   Partially regulated agreements

There are two types of partially regulated agreement: (i) small agreements and (ii) non-commercial agreements. Small agreements are regulated consumer credit agreements (excluding HP or a conditional sale agreement) where the total credit does not exceed £50, or regulated consumer hire agreements where the hirer is not required to pay more than £50: s.17. Non-commercial agreements are made by creditors not in the course of a business: s.189(1).

20.6   Form and contents of the agreement

Regulated agreements must comply with statutory requirements as regards form and content, failing which they are unenforceable by the creditor unless the court dispenses with these requirements where it is just and fair to do so: s.127(1) and (2). This depends on the degree to which the customer has been prejudiced and the culpability of the creditor/owner. The formalities are:

▷ All the terms must be embodied in the written agreement, or in a document referred to in the written agreement: s.61(1)(b), and must be readily legible: s.61(1)(c). Details of any right of cancellation enjoyed by the debtor must be included: s.64(1)(a), and the document must comply with the regulations made under s.60 regarding form and contents, such as names and addresses of the parties, the amounts and dates of payment, and the true cost of the credit.
▷ The agreement must be signed by the debtor or hirer in person, and by or on behalf of the creditor or owner: s.61(1)(a).
▷ Debtors must receive one copy of the agreement when given or sent the agreement to sign: ss.62(1) and 63(1); and, if the agreement is not made on signing, must be given a second copy within seven days of the making of the agreement: s.63(2). For cancellable agreements, the second copy must be sent by post: s.63(3); for credit token agreements (credit card or check trading agreements), the second copy must be given before or at the time the credit token is given to the customer: s.63(4); and a copy of the agreement must be given each time a new credit token is given: s.85.
▷ For prospective regulated agreements to be secured by a mortgage of land, the prospective borrower must receive a copy of the agreement at least seven clear days before being sent the actual agreement to sign: s.61(2); and during that time and for a further period of seven days, the prospective creditor must stay away from the customer to allow a consideration period free from sales pressure, unless the customer specifically requests the prospective creditor to contact him.

Hot Topic . . .

CONSEQUENCES OF NON-COMPLIANCE WITH FORMALITIES

In *Dimond v. Lovell* [1999] 3 All ER 1, D's car was damaged in an accident with a car driven by L. D hired a car under a contract which provided that no hire charges were payable until the conclusion of an action for damages by the company against L in D's name. L's insurer successfully raised as a defence the fact that the agreement with D was a consumer credit agreement unenforceable against D so that she could not claim damages for the car hire. On appeal, D claimed the agreement was enforceable since the prescribed requirements could be varied or waived by an application under s.60(3). The Court of Appeal held that the contract was not enforceable since an agreement to waive or vary the formality requirements had to be made before the agreement was entered into. The court held that D could not recover the hire charges in the absence of an implied trust for the benefit of the hire company. This would not be imposed where it was the company's failure which had rendered the agreement unenforceable.

In *Wilson v. First County Trust Ltd* [2003] 4 All ER 97, the defendant pawnbroker made a loan to W for six months secured against her car under a regulated agreement. On default by W, the pawnbroker sought repayment, failing which the car would be sold. W claimed that the agreement was unenforceable because it did not show the correct amount of the credit. The claim was upheld on appeal to the Court of Appeal. As a result, the borrower was entitled to keep the loan, pay no interest and recover her car.

20.7 Cancellation

When the agreement is signed at the debtors' homes or their own business premises, debtors can cancel regulated agreements during a cooling-off period which runs from the signing until the end of five clear days from receipt of the second copy: s.67. The effect of cancellation varies according to the agreement.

In the case of an HP, conditional sale and credit sale agreement, the customer can recover payments made: s.70; they must return the goods, although they are not obliged to deliver them and can wait until they are collected following a written request: s.72. They have a lien over them for the return of their payments: s.70(2). They must take reasonable care of the goods for 21 days after serving notice of cancellation. Where the goods are perishable, and where goods are supplied to meet an emergency or have been consumed or incorporated into something else, there is no obligation to return them, but they must be paid for: s.69(2).

In the case of an ordinary loan, the customer must repay any credit already received together with interest, except on credit repaid within one month of cancellation: s.71.

20.8 Dealer as creditor's agent

A person negotiating a regulated agreement between a creditor and debtor is the creditor's agent: s.56. This includes the dealer in an HP transaction involving a finance company, or the retailer dealing with a customer paying by credit card. The result is that the creditor is liable for misrepresentations made by the dealer or retailer; any money paid to the dealer or retailer is held to have been received by the creditor; and notice to the dealer or retailer is notice to the creditor regarding withdrawing an offer to enter a regulated agreement: s.57; cancellation of the agreement: s.69; or rescission of the agreement: s.102.

In *Forthright Finance Ltd v. Ingate (Carlyle Finance Ltd third party)* [1997] 4 All ER 99, I agreed to buy an Austin Metro car under a conditional sale agreement with F Ltd. A year later, I negotiated with a dealer to trade it in against a Fiat Panda. The dealers were licensed credit brokers who agreed to buy her Metro, valued at £2,000, and discharge the £1,992 owed to F Ltd. I paid a £1,000 deposit and entered into a conditional sale agreement with C Ltd, a finance company, which recorded the cash price of £2,995, the deposit of £1,000 and the balance of £1,995 on credit. The dealers went into liquidation without having paid the £1,995 to F Ltd. F Ltd obtained a judgment against I, who claimed indemnity against C Ltd under s.56. The district judge ordered C Ltd to indemnify I, but this was reversed on appeal because the antecedent negotiations concerning the Metro did not relate to the goods sold under the agreement, that is, the Panda. The Court of Appeal held that the negotiations were part of a package relating to the Panda, even though the value of the Metro cancelled out the debt due under the agreement. C Ltd was liable under s.56(2) to discharge I's debt to F Ltd.

20.9   Matters arising during the currency of credit or hire agreements

If the debtor under a DCSA has a claim for misrepresentation or breach of contract against the supplier, s/he has an identical claim against the creditor who is jointly and severally liable with the supplier: s.75(1). Subject to agreement between them, the creditor is entitled to be indemnified by the supplier. This does not apply to non-commercial agreements and is restricted to claims relating to single items with a cash price of between £100 and £30,000. This does not apply in the case of hire purchase where the creditor and the supplier are the same person, and as regards credit tokens it does not apply to debit cards or cards such as Diners' Club or American Express.

The creditor is liable for the misrepresentations and breaches of contract of the supplier only if the supplier would have been liable. If the supplier is protected by a valid exclusion clause, the creditor will not be liable. Since the creditor and the supplier are jointly and severally liable, the debtor can sue the supplier and/or the creditor. The fact of obtaining a judgment against one party does not prevent an action being brought against the other under s.3 Civil Liability (Contribution) Act 1978.

The financial restrictions under s.75(3) means that the section does not apply where the contract relates to the purchase of several items costing less than £100 even though the total price is above £100. It should be noted, however, that the creditor's liability under the section is not limited to the amount of credit. If the total price for the goods is paid partly by credit card and partly in cash, the creditor's liability relates to the total purchase price. In addition, where goods supplied are defective and cause injury to the debtor, the creditor's liability extends to cover compensation for the injury suffered by the debtor.

It is not possible to contract out of liability under s.75: s.173(1).

Hot Topic . . .

CREDITORS' LIABILITY FOR SUPPLIERS' DEFAULTS

The joint and several liability of the creditor is particularly advantageous for goods and services purchased abroad using a credit card, when it is more difficult for the debtor to bring claims against the overseas suppliers. In *OFT v. Lloyd's TSB, Tesco Personal Finance, American Express* [2004] EWHC 2600, however, the court held that s.75 protection applied only to purchases of goods or services in the UK and not when credit cards are used in other countries. This was supported on appeal ([2006]

EWCA Civ 268). The House of Lords, however, overturned the Court of Appeal decision and held that the creditor's joint and several liability under s.75(1) CCA 1974 extends to the purchase of goods and services overseas: *OFT v. Lloyds TSB Bank plc and others* [2007] UKHL 48.

The card issuers had contended that the development whereby credit cards can be used to pay a supplier not recruited to the network by, and not in a contractual relationship with, the relevant card issuer was that there were no

'arrangements', pre-existing or in contemplation, between the card issuer and the supplier within the meaning of s.12(b) CCA 1974. This was rejected in the High Court and on appeal, and was not the basis of the appeal to the House of Lords. A further argument was based on the principle that UK legislation is primarily territorial. In his judgment, Lord Mance stated that there was nothing in s.11, 12 or 75(1) purporting to legislate extra-territorially, and that to impose on UK card issuers a liability to UK card holders in respect of liabilities under a foreign supply transaction was not axiomatically to legislate extra-territorially.

20.10 Duty to give notice before taking certain action

Creditors or owners are not entitled to enforce a term of a regulated agreement by (a) demanding earlier payment; (b) recovering possession of goods or land; or (c) treating any right of the debtor/hirer as terminated except after giving not less than seven days' notice of their intention to do so: s.76(1). This applies only where a period for the duration of the agreement is specified and that period has not ended: s.76(2).

20.11 Duty to give information to debtors under fixed-sum credit agreements

On receipt of a written request from the debtor and payment of a fee, the creditor shall within the prescribed period give the debtor a copy of the executed agreement and any other document referred to in it, together with a signed statement showing the total sum paid by the debtor, the total sum remaining unpaid and the total sum which is to become payable: s.77.

The creditor under a regulated agreement for fixed-sum credit must give the debtor statements under s.77A. The statements must relate to consecutive periods (s.77A(1A)) and the first such period must begin with either: (a) the day on which the agreement is made, or (b) the day the first movement occurs on the debtor's account with the creditor relating to the agreement: s.77A(1B). No such period may exceed a year (s.77A(1C)), and a period of a year expiring on a non-working day may be regarded as expiring on the next working day: s.77A(1D). Each statement must be given to the debtor before the end of the period of 30 days beginning with the day after the end of the period to which the statement relates: s.77A(1E).

Defaulting creditors cannot enforce the agreement during the period of non-compliance, and debtors have no liability to pay interest and any default sum for that period: s.77A. There is no liability for annual statements if no further sums were payable under the agreement. If there are two or more debtors or hirers, a debtor/hirer may issue a notice to the creditor dispensing with the need to provide a statement to that debtor/hirer. A dispensing notice is, however, ineffective if it means that no debtor/hirer will receive a statement.

20.12   Duty to give information to debtors under running-account credit agreements

Creditors must issue statements to debtors setting out specified information at intervals of not more than 12 months. Regulations by the Secretary of State may require creditors to include specified information about the consequences of failing to make repayments or making only minimum payments. Creditors in default cannot enforce agreements while in default, and commit an offence if the default continues beyond one month: s.78(6).

20.13   Duty to give information to debtors under consumer hire agreements

Creditors must within the prescribed period give the debtor a copy of the executed agreement and any document referred to in it, together with a statement showing the total sum which has become payable under the agreement but remains unpaid: s.79(1). Owners in default cannot enforce the agreement while the default continues and commit an offence if default continues beyond one month: s.79(3).

20.14   Misusing credit facilities

The debtor under a regulated agreement is not liable for any use of credit facilities by another person who is not their agent or acting by their authority: s.83(1). This section does not apply to non-commercial agreements or to any loss arising from misuse of a cheque or other negotiable instrument.

Section 83 does not prevent the debtor under a credit token agreement from being made liable up to a maximum of £50 for loss to the creditor on losing possession of the token: s.84(1). Nor does it prevent the debtor under a credit token agreement from being liable to any extent for loss to the creditor from the use of the token by a person acquiring possession of it with the debtor's consent: s.84(2). They are not liable for any misuse under s.84(1) or (2) after the creditor has received oral or written notice of the loss of the card: s.84(3). Notice takes effect when received, but oral notice must be confirmed in writing within seven days: s.84(5).

Subsections 84(1) and (2) do not apply to any use of a card which is a credit token in connection with a 'distance contract' (s. 84(3A) and (3B)) as defined in the Consumer Protection (Distance Selling) Regulations 2000 (see Chapter 21). Neither do they apply to the use of a credit token in connection with a distance selling contract within the meaning of the Financial Services (Distance Marketing) Regulations 2004, namely one concluded making exclusive use of distance communications: s.84(3C).

Under the Consumer Protection (Distance Selling) Regulations 2000, a consumer can cancel a payment where there has been fraudulent use of his payment card in connection with a distance contract by a person not acting, or to be treated as acting, as his agent: reg.

21(1). A payment card includes credit, charge and debit cards and store cards: reg.21(6). Where a consumer cancels a payment, the card issuer must recredit the consumer's account: reg. 21(2). The burden of proof that the use of the card was authorised is on the card issuer: reg. 21(3).

Apart from distance contracts, ss.83 and 84 CCA 1974 limit the liability of the card holder for 'loss to the creditor' only where the debtor's account is taken into deficit or an existing deficit has been increased. They do not oblige the creditor to indemnify the debtor for loss suffered by the misue of the credit token. This is, however, ensured for personal customers in the UK in respect of all card products by s.12.10 The Banking Code.

The Banking Code is a voluntary code which sets standards of good banking practice for financial institutions when dealing with personal customers in the UK. A 'personal customer' is defined as any person who is acting for purposes which are not linked to their trade, business or profession. The definition includes personal customers acting as personal representatives, including executors, unless in a professional capacity; and private individuals acting in personal or other family circumstances e.g. as trustees of a fanily trust.

20.15 Early and late payment by the debtor

If the debtor gives written notice to the creditor, they can complete their payments ahead of time: s.94. They may then qualify for a rebate of interest charges under the Consumer Credit (Early Settlement) Regulations 2004 made under s.95. Where they are late in making payments, they may have to pay extra interest to take into account the delay, but they cannot be obliged to pay interest at a higher rate than is payable under the agreement as a whole: s.93.

20.16 Default and non-default notice and regulated agreements

The OFT publishes information sheets for debtors or hirers about arrears and default. Creditors/owners must give debtors/hirers an arrears information sheet at the same time as an arrears notice and a default information sheet at the same time as a default notice: s.86A

For fixed sum credit or hire agreements, creditors/owners must give arrears notices in the specified form together with an arrears information sheet within 14 days from the time when the following conditions are satisfied: s.86B(2):

- The debtor/hirer has made at least two payments under the applicable agreement;
- The total sum paid is less than should have been paid;
- The shortfall is not less than the sum of the last two payments then due;
- The creditor/owner is not already required to provide him with a notice of arrears; and
- The debtor/hirer is not required to pay money under an earlier judgment in relation to the agreement: s.86B(1).

For regulated running account agreements, creditors must give debtors notice in the specified form including an arrears information sheet after the time when:

- The debtor should have previously made at least two repayments;
- The previous two payment were not made;

▶ The creditor has not already been required to provide the debtor with a notice of arrears; and

▶ There is no liability to pay under an earlier court judgment.

The notice must be given no later than the time at which the creditor is required to give the debtor the next regular statement under s.78(4).

If creditors/hirers fail to give notice in accordance with s.86B or 86C they cannot enforce the agreement during the period of default. In addition, debtors/hirers are not liable to pay interest for that period or any default sum which arises during the period in which the creditor/owner failed to give notice or fails to provide a subsequent notice within six months of the previous notice having been provided: s.86D.

Where debtors/hirers incur a default payment, creditors/owners must give them notice in the specified form when it becomes payable. The Secretary of State can provide that this applies only for default sums exceeding a specified amount. Debtors/hirers are liable for interest on default sums only 28 days after the notice was given. If notice was not given, creditors/owners cannot enforce the agreement until notice is given: s.86E. Creditors/owners can claim only simple interest in respect of default sums, including sums payable under small or non-commercial agreements: s.86F.

Creditors wishing to sue for arrears may commence proceedings in the county court, which has exclusive jurisdiction, but, where the debtor has defaulted, creditors must give debtors 14 days' notice if they wish to:

▶ terminate the agreement; or
▶ demand earlier payment of any sum; or
▶ recover possession of any goods or land; or
▶ treat any right conferred on the debtor by the agreement as terminated, restricted or deferred; or
▶ enforce any security.

The notice must specify how the debtor can rectify the breach (s.88); and if the debtor takes such action the breach is regarded as never having occurred: s.89.

Where creditors of a specified duration agreement (such as a hire-purchase agreement) wish to do one of the above other than because of the debtor's default, they must serve seven days' notice of their intention: s.76.

In the case of debtors who have been served with a default or non-default notice, a notice of arrears under s.86B or 86C, or where the creditor brings an action to enforce a regulated agreement, the debtor can ask the court for a time order: s.129. This allows the debtor extra time to rectify any breach and extra time to make overdue payments.

For HP and conditional sale agreements the court can alter the pattern of future payments or allow extra time for them to be made.

In respect of arrears notices under ss.86B and 86C, debtors/hirers can apply only if they have given a notice containing required information to the creditor/owner, 14 days have elapsed since the notice and, in the case of a debtor/hirer who has previously made a time order application, the notice was given after the making of the last application.

The notice must state that the debtor/hirer intends to make a time order application, indicate that he wants to make a proposal to the creditor/owner in relation to making payments under the agreement and give details of that proposal. The notice must be in writing but may be in any form: s.129A.

Where the debtor/hirer has made an offer to pay sums by instalments which is accepted by the creditor/owner, the court may make a time order under s.129. Creditors/owners must notify and inform the debtors/hirers in the specified manner about interest applying to a judgment debt by virtue of a term of the agreement enabling interest to accrue from judgment until payment, and provide further notices at six-monthly intervals. Debtors/hirers are not liable to pay interest for any period during which the creditor/owner has failed to comply with the section: s.130A.

'Default sum' means a sum payable by a debtor/hirer in connection with his breach of a regulated agreement (e.g. a charge in respect of late payment of an instalment or a fee imposed for exceeding a credit limit on a card). It does not include sums which, as a consequence of a breach of the agreement, become payable earlier than they otherwise would have done, and does not include interest: s.187A.

20.17 Unfair relationships

The court can consider whether the relationship between the debtor and creditor arising out of the agreement is unfair because of the terms of the agreement, the way in which the agreement is operated by the creditor and any other thing done or not done by the creditor before or after the agreement was made. In assessing this, all relevant matters are considered: s.140A.

The court can order the creditor to repay (in whole or in part) any sum paid by the debtor or a surety, or to do or not to do (or cease doing) anything specified in the agreement. It can reduce any sum payable by the debtor or surety, direct a return of the surety's property provided as security; set aside (in whole or in part) any duty on the debtor or surety, alter the terms of the agreement or related agreement and direct accounts to be taken: s.140B.

The provisions cover all consumer credit agreements except those secured on land and regulated by the Financial Services Authority (FSA): s.140C. The OFT must give advice and information about the interaction between the unfair relationship provisions and Part 8 Enterprise Act 2002, which allows the OFT to bring proceedings against persons who harm the collective interests of UK consumers: s.140D.

20.18 Death of the debtor

On the debtor's death, termination of the agreement by the creditor is impossible where the agreement is for a specified duration and fully secured. Even if not fully secured, it can be terminated only where there is a power to do so in the agreement and where on application to the court the creditor can show that the debtor's obligations are unlikely to be carried out.

The deceased debtor's relatives can continue HP and other credit and hire agreements of a specified duration if they wish. This is not the case for credit cards and agreements of unspecified duration.

20.19 HP and other instalment sales

An HP contract is a contract of hire together with an option to purchase. The debtor is not a person who has bought or agreed to buy for the purposes of s.25 Sale of Goods Act

(SOGA) 1979, and thus cannot pass a good title to a *bona fide* purchaser without notice of goods that are still subject to the agreement, except for the sale of motor vehicles to private purchasers (see below). Under a conditional sale agreement there is a legal obligation to buy, but the property passes only when all instalments are paid. At common law, such agreements fall within s.25 SOGA 1979 and the purchaser can pass a good title to goods still covered by a conditional sale agreement to a *bona fide* purchaser without notice. This is not true for regulated agreements, which are treated in the same way as HP agreements.

Under a credit sale contract there is a legal obligation to buy, and the property in the goods is transferred to the buyer at the time of the contract under s.18, Rule 1, SOGA 1979 (see Chapter 18, p.431).

In *Forthright Finance Ltd v. Carlyle Finance Ltd* [1997] 4 All ER 90, the claimant finance company, the owner of a Ford car, delivered the car to a dealer under an agreement described as an HP agreement. The dealer was given an option to purchase the car, which was deemed exercised when all the instalments had been paid, at which point the property passed to him unless he elected not to take title. The dealer delivered the car to a customer under a conditional sale agreement financed by the defendant. The trial judge held that the agreement between the claimant and the dealer was an HP agreement, and the defendant was liable in damages for conversion to the claimant. The Court of Appeal upheld the defendant's appeal and found that the agreement was in substance and in form a conditional sale agreement where the dealer had 'agreed to buy' the car and could pass good title under s.25(1) SOGA 1979.

The following topics relate to hire purchase; the points of variance with the other agreements are indicated at the end.

20.20　Involvement of a finance company

Dealers may require the services of a finance company; in which case they sell the goods to the finance company, and the finance company makes an HP contract with the customer/debtor. There is no contract between the dealer and the customer/debtor.

The dealer will normally agree to be liable to the finance company in the event of the debtor's default under a recourse agreement, which is usually an indemnity, but can be a guarantee. In *Goulston Discount Co. Ltd v. Clark* [1967] 2 QB 493, the finance company sued a dealer for £157 damages under a recourse agreement. If the agreement had been in the form of a guarantee, it would be limited to the amount claimable from the debtor (£74 of arrears prior to termination). Since it was an indemnity, the dealer was liable for the whole of the loss suffered (see Chapter 15, p.352).

An alternative is a repurchase agreement when the dealer repurchases the goods from the creditor on the debtor's default.

20.21　Liabilities of the parties

(a)　The dealer

Normally the dealer has no liability to the debtor/hirer where the goods are not satisfactory or fit for the purpose. The debtor/hirer must claim against the finance company/creditor under the Supply of Goods (Implied Terms) Act 1973. However, where the dealer gives the debtor/hirer an express warranty of the fitness of the goods, there is a collateral contract of warranty between them and the debtor/hirer can sue for breach of this contract.

In *Shanklin Pier Ltd v. Detel Products Ltd* [1951] 2 KB 854, the claimants contracted with a company for the repair of their pier and specified that the defendant's paint should be used because the defendant had warranted that it had a life of seven to 10 years. In fact, it had a very short life and the claimants were entitled to claim damages against them.

There will also be a contract where the dealer agrees to carry out a service, such as installation. The dealer could then be liable under ss.13–15 Supply of Goods and Services Act 1982 (see Chapter 18, p.445).

(b) The finance company

Finance companies are liable to the debtor/hirer under the Supply of Goods (Implied Terms) Act 1973 ss.8–11 relating to the same implied terms as found in the Sale of Goods Act 1979 ss.12–15. Exclusion clauses are subject to the Unfair Contract Terms Act 1977 and are inoperative against a debtor/hirer dealing as a consumer (see Chapter 18). The Unfair Terms in Consumer Contracts Regulations 1999 could also apply (see Chapter 21, p.517).

At common law, dealers are not the creditor's agent, but they are for regulated agreements. Thus, where the dealer fills in figures different from those agreed to by the debtor, the debtor is not bound in respect of agreements at common law but is in respect of regulated agreements. In *UDT Ltd v. Western* [1976] QB 513, W agreed to buy a car for £550 under a regulated HP agreement. He paid a deposit of £34 and signed the claimant's standard form in blank, leaving the dealer to fill in the figures. The form sent to the claimants showed a purchase price of £730 and a deposit of £185. When W received a copy of the agreement, he realised that it was not correct but did nothing and paid no instalments. The court held that W was liable.

20.22 Termination of the agreement

An agreement can be terminated in accordance with its terms, or it may be broken. Termination occurs where the debtor/hirer exercises his/her option to return the goods to the creditor, and the agreement is broken where there is default by the debtor/hirer. This would normally provide the creditor with the right to terminate the agreement by notice to the debtor/hirer. S/he may even have a right of termination in some other event, such as death, bankruptcy or imprisonment of the debtor/hirer. For regulated agreements, there are restrictions on the right of termination (see notice of default and death of debtor above).

Where the debtor is in arrears, he/she can escape termination by the creditor by:

(i)   paying off the arrears before the expiry date of the default notice;
(ii) applying to the court for extra time (see above, s.129); or
(iii) falling within the scope of the protected goods provisions: ss.90–91.

Under the protected goods provisions, where at least one-third of the total HP price has been paid the creditor can recover possession only after having first obtained a court order; otherwise the agreement is terminated, the debtor is released from all liability and can recover all sums already paid: ss.90 and 91.

In *Capital Finance Co. Ltd v. Bray* [1964] 1 WLR 323, C Ltd repossessed a car in respect of which B had repaid more than one-third of the total price but later, realising its mistake, left the vehicle outside B's home. When C Ltd sued for outstanding instalments and recovery of the vehicle, the court held that the agreement had been terminated, B was released from liability and could recover money paid under the agreement.

There are exceptions where the repossession is with the debtor's consent or where the debtor has disposed of or has permanently abandoned the goods. In *Bentinck Ltd v. Cromwell Engineering Co.* [1971] 1 QB 324, the debtor left his damaged car at a garage with no instructions for repair, paid no further instalments and later disappeared. The court held that the finance company was not in breach in repossessing the car, even though more than one-third of the total purchase price had been paid.

20.23 The minimum payment clause

The agreement will usually contain a clause requiring the debtor/hirer to pay a minimum amount on terminating or breaching the agreement. Where this sum is excessive, the issue arises whether the contractual rules relating to penalties apply. The situation varies depending on whether the agreement is terminated (i) following breach by the debtor; or (ii) in accordance with the debtor/hirer's option rights.

Where there is breach by the debtor, the distinction between liquidated damages and penalties applies, and if the minimum payment is regarded as a penalty rather than a genuine pre-estimate of the creditor's likely loss, it will not be enforceable and the creditor will have to claim unliquidated damages.

In *Bridge v. Campbell Discount Co. Ltd* [1962] AC 600, B acquired a van from the finance company for a total HP price of £482; the deposit of £105 was made up of part exchange of a car and £10 in cash, and the monthly instalments were £10. The agreement provided for the termination of the contract by the debtor at any time, when a minimum payment clause should operate under which the debtor was to pay the arrears and two-thirds of the HP price as 'agreed compensation for depreciation'. After eight weeks, the debtor indicated that he would be unable to continue the payments and returned the vehicle. He was sued for £206, being two-thirds of the purchase price less the instalments paid. The court held that the letter concerning his unwillingness to pay further instalments did not constitute the exercise of his option to terminate the contract but a notification of his intention to break the agreement, and that, since the agreement was terminated by breach, the rules relating to penalties applied. The minimum payment clause was a penalty and unenforceable, and the case was referred back to the county court to fix the damages suffered by the finance company.

In the case of termination by the exercise of an option the position is less clear, and older authorities suggest that the debtor would be bound by the clause even where the sum was excessive: *Associated Distributors Ltd v. Hall* [1938] 2 KB 83. This case was discussed in the *Bridge* case, where there was disagreement about the current state of the law. In any event, a debtor is taken not to exercise his/her option to terminate unless aware of the consequences: *UDT (Commercial) Ltd v. Ennis* [1968] 1 QB 54.

In the case of a regulated agreement, the debtor can terminate the agreement at any time before the final payment falls due: s.99. In this case, as well as returning the goods, the debtor must pay:

(i)   all arrears of instalments before termination;
(ii)   damages for loss caused by failure to take reasonable care;
(iii) the smallest of the three following:
     (a) the minimum payment;
     (b) the amount necessary to bring payments up to one half of the total HP price;
     (c) the loss sustained by the creditor as a result of termination: s.100.

The right to terminate can be exercised only 'before the final payment falls due', which means that, if the agreement contains an accelerated payments clause under which failure to pay two or more instalments gives the creditor the right to serve notice, making the outstanding balance payable, the debtor cannot serve notice of termination after the notice is served: *Wadham Stringer Ltd v. Meaney* [1981] 1 WLR 39.

20.24   The creditor's claim for damages

Where the agreement is terminated by breach on the part of the debtor or by notice of the creditor after breach by the debtor, and the creditor cannot rely on the minimum payment clause, it is necessary to calculate the damages to which the creditor is entitled. These depend on whether (i) there is a breach of contract by the debtor which is accepted by the creditor; or (ii) there is termination by the creditor because the debtor is in arrears.

Where repudiation is accepted by the creditor, damages are the loss which the creditor has suffered as a result of the debtor's failure to carry out the contract. This arises where the debtor fails to pay several instalments and it is clear that they do not intend to be bound by the contract, or where they write to say that they cannot or will not make further payments.

When a creditor terminates the contract because the debtor is in arrears, the measure of damages is the total amount of the arrears at the date of termination. In *Financings Ltd v. Baldock* [1963] 2 QB 104, B obtained a truck on hire purchase from the claimants. He failed to pay the first two instalments and the finance company terminated the agreement and repossessed the truck, which it later sold. It claimed £538 in respect of the loss it had suffered. The court held that the contract was terminated by the creditor and it was able to claim only the outstanding arrears of £56.

20.25   The powers of the court with regard to regulated agreements

Actions are in the county court and any guarantor is made a party to them. The creditors usually claim for possession and minimum payment or damages. The court has three options: (i) a time order, giving the debtor extra time to pay: s.129; (ii) an immediate return order, together with minimum payment or damages: s.133; and (iii) a transfer order, applicable where the goods are divisible and the debtor has paid enough of the total price to cover both the cost of part of them and at least a quarter of the rest of the total price.

20.26   Protection of the private purchaser of a motor vehicle

Under the Hire Purchase Act 1964 s.27(2) as amended by CCA 1974, a private purchaser in good faith and without notice of a motor vehicle which is still subject to an HP agreement obtains a good title to the vehicle (see Chapter 18, p.439).

20.27   Conditional sale and credit sale agreements

For conditional sale agreements, there is full application of the Act in the same way as for HP contracts. Credit sale agreements are subject to most of the provisions including formality and cancellation. There is no statutory right of termination and the creditor has no right to recover possession of the goods on default. Claims relating to the goods not being of satisfactory quality would be under the SOGA 1979.

End of Chapter Summary

Having read and understood this chapter you should have a detailed knowledge of the following points of particular commercial importance:

- The legal formalities with regard to contracts to provide credit under a regulated credit agreement and the significance of a failure to comply with them.
- The distinction between HP contracts, conditional sale agreements and credit sale agreements with regard to the passing of property.
- The rights of the consumer against the supplier of credit by way of a credit card under s.75 CCA 1974.
- The protection of the debtor under the protected goods provisions.
- The legal implications of the use of a minimum payment clause.

The use of debit cards as opposed to credit cards is dealt with in the following chapter, and the significance of the use of credit and debit cards and the protection afforded to consumers in respect of online e-commerce transactions is considered in Chapter 22.

Questions

1. In order to be a regulated consumer credit agreement the agreement must comply with two conditions. What are they?

2. Lola acquired a motor car under an HP agreement with F Ltd. During the currency of the agreement, Lola sold the car to M Ltd, a dealer, who sold it on to Neil, who took the car in good faith, unaware that it was still covered by an HP agreement. Advise F Ltd of its rights against Neil.

3. Regulated consumer credit agreements can be classified as (i) restricted use credit agreements; and (ii) unrestricted use credit agreements. Give examples of each type.

4. Angela bought a PC on credit from Nixons plc. Within the first week of delivery of the PC, it broke down completely. Against whom will she have a right of action if the transaction was financed in the following ways:
    (i)   an HP agreement with F Ltd was arranged by Nixons plc;
    (ii) it was purchased by Easicash credit card;
    (iii) there was a bank overdraft with HP Bank plc?

5. Distinguish between an HP agreement, a conditional sale agreement and a credit sale agreement.

6. What do you understand by the Protected Goods Provisions under ss.90–91 Consumer Credit Act 1974?

Questions cont'd

7. Angus bought a car on HP financed by F plc. The total credit was £17,000 repayable in monthly instalments over 24 months, and the agreement contained a clause to the effect that on termination by Angus, he would be liable for a minimum payment of two-thirds of the HP price. Four weeks after having entered into the agreement, Angus was made redundant and could no longer keep up the payments. Consider Angus's liability to F plc if:
    (i) Angus gives notice terminating the agreement in the fifth week;
    (ii) Angus fails to pay instalments after the fourth month and F Ltd terminated the agreement.

8. David gave his credit card to Fred, a friend, for safe keeping. Fred used the card in several shops to buy £900 of goods. David's account liability was increased from £600 to £1,500. David phoned the card issuer to explain what had happened and sent written confirmation of the notice as required. By the time of giving the oral notice, David's credit card account debit had been increased from £600 to £900 but had increased to £1,500 by the time the written confirmation of the oral notice had been received. What is David's liability in respect of the misuse of his credit card?
    Would it make a difference to your answer if the card had been misused entirely in respect of contracts for goods over the internet?

Chapter 21

Consumer protection

Learning objectives

After reading this chapter you will know about:

- ▶ the prohibition of unfair commercial practices and the promotion of unfair commercial practices;
- ▶ misleading actions and omissions and aggressive commercial practices;
- ▶ available defences and penalties;
- ▶ the prohibition of misleading advertising including comparative advertising;
- ▶ available defences and penalties for breach;
- ▶ product liability of manufacturers;
- ▶ protection for unsolicited goods and services;
- ▶ cancellable agreements for goods and services;
- ▶ The Unfair Terms in Consumer Contracts Regulations 1999.

21.1 Prohibition of unfair commercial practices

A commercial practice is any act, omission, course of conduct, representation or commercial communication (including advertising and marketing) by a trader which is directly connected with the promotion, sale or supply of a product to or from consumers, whether occurring before, during or after a commercial transaction (if any) in relation to a product. A consumer is any individual who, in relation to a commercial practice, is acting for purposes which are outside his business. A trader is any person who, in relation to a commercial practice, is acting for purposes relating to his business, and anyone acting in the name of or on behalf of the trader. 'Product' means any goods or services and includes immovable property, rights and obligations: The Consumer Protection from Unfair Trading Regulations (cPUT) 2008.

Under earlier legislation the courts had to consider whether a trader was acting for purposes outside his business. A sale 'in the course of a business' had been held to cover the sale of a car by a car hire firm: *Havering London Borough v. Stevenson* [1970] 3 All ER 609.

In *Davies v. Sumner* [1984] 1 WLR 1301, the defendant, a self-employed courier, used his car almost exclusively in connection with his business. The court held, however, that trading in his car in part-exchange for a new car to be used for his business was not a sale in the course of his business. And in *R & B Customs Brokers Co. Ltd v. United Dominions Trust Ltd* [1988] 1 WLR 321, sales by a business of two or three cars over a five-year period were not made in the course of a business.

A person who buys, rebuilds and then sells cars as a hobby does not sell in the course of a business: *Blackmore v. Bellamy* [1983] RTR 303, unless they also run a business and the sale is in the course of that business: *Southwark London Borough v. Charlesworth* (1983) 147 JP 470; see also *Fletcher v. Sledmore* [1973] RTR 371.

The offence will normally be committed by the seller of goods, but it can be a buyer. In *Fletcher v. Budgen* [1974] 2 All ER 1243, a car dealer negotiating for the purchase of a car told the seller that the car was beyond repair and fit only for scrap. The dealer bought the car for £2 and then, having repaired it, advertised it for sale at £136.

A commercial practice is unfair if (a) it contravenes the requirements of professional diligence; and (b) it materially distorts or is likely materially to distort the economic behaviour of the average consumer with regard to the product: reg. 3(3). The term 'average consumer' is to be construed in accordance with paragraphs (2) to (6) of reg. 2. These include taking account of the material characteristics of an average consumer including his being reasonably well informed, reasonably observant and circumspect. In determining the effect of a commercial practice on the average consumer (a) where a clearly identifiable group of consumers is particularly vulnerable to the practice or the underlying product because of their mental or physical infirmity, age or credulity in a way which the trader could reasonably be expected to foresee, and (b) where the practice is likely materially to distort the economic behaviour only of that group, a reference to the average consumer shall be read as to the average member of that group: para. 5. Paragraph 5 is without prejudice to the common and legitimate advertising practice of making exaggerated statements which are not meant to be taken literally: reg. 6.

A commercial practice is also unfair if (a) it is a misleading action under reg. 5; (b) it is a misleading omission under reg. 6; (c) it is aggressive under reg. 7; or (d) it is listed in Schedule 1: reg. 3(4).

(a) Misleading actions

A commercial practice is a misleading action if it satisfies the conditions in paragraph (2) or (3) of reg. 5. Paragraph (2) relates to false information in relation to any of the matters in paragraph (4), or if its overall presentation in any way deceives or is likely to deceive the average consumer in relation to any of those matters, even if it factually correct. Paragraph 4 relates to:

- The existence or nature of the product;
- The main characteristics of the product;
- The extent of the trader's commitments;
- The motives for the commercial practice;
- The nature of the sales process;
- Any statement or symbol relating to direct or indirect sponsorship or approval of the trader or product;
- The price or the manner in which the price is calculated;
- The existence of a specific price advantage;
- The need for a service, part, replacement or repair;
- The nature, attributes and rights of the trader;
- The consumer's rights or the risks he may face.

As regards the main characteristics of the product, these are specified in paragraph 5 and include:

- Availability;
- Benefits of the product;
- Risks;
- Execution;
- Composition;

- Accessories;
- After-sale customer assistance;
- The handling of complaints;
- The method and date of manufacture;
- The method and date of the provision;
- Delivery;
- Fitness for purpose;
- Usage;
- Quantity;
- Specification;
- Geographical or commercial origin;
- Results to be expected from use; and
- Results and material features of tests or checks carried out.

The reference in paragraph 4 to the 'nature, attributes and rights' of the trader include the trader's:

- Identity;
- Assets;
- Qualifications;
- Status;
- Approval;
- Affiliations or connections;
- Ownership of industrial, commercial or intellectual property rights; and
- Awards and distinctions.

A commercial practice is also a misleading action if it causes or is likely to cause the average consumer to take a transactional decision he would not have taken otherwise: reg. 5(2)(b).

A commercial practice satisfies the conditions of paragraph (3) if (a) it concerns any marketing of a product (including comparative advertising) which creates confusion with any products, trade marks, trade names or other distinguishing marks of a competitor; or (b) it concerns any failure by a trader to comply with a code of conduct which he has undertaken to comply with, if (i) the trader indicates in a commercial practice that he is bound by that code of conduct, and (ii) the commitment is firm and capable of being verified and is not aspirational, and it causes or is likely to cause the average consumer to take a transactional decision he would not have taken otherwise, taking account of its factual context and of all its features and circumstances.

(b)   Misleading omissions

A commercial practice is a misleading omission if, in its factual context, taking account of the matters in paragraph (2), (a) it omits material information, (b) hides material information, (c) provides material information in a manner which is unclear, unintelligible, ambiguous or untimely, or (d) fails to identify its commercial intent, unless this is already apparent from the context, and as a result it causes or is likely to cause the average consumer to take a transactional decision he would not have taken otherwise: reg.

6(1). The matters in paragraph (2) are (a) all the features and circumstances of commercial practice; (b) the limitations of the medium used to communicate the commercial practice (including limitations of space or time); and (c), where the medium imposes limitations of space or time, any measures taken by the trader to make the information available to consumers by other means.

In paragraph (1) 'material information' means (a) the information which the average consumer needs, according to the context, to take an informed transactional decision; and (b) any information requirement which applies as a result of a Community obligation: reg. 6(3).

Where the commercial practice is an invitation to purchase, the following information will be material if not already apparent from the context in addition to the material information under paragraph (3); (a) the main characteristics of the product appropriate to the medium by which the invitation is communicated and the product; (b) the identity of the trader, such as his trading name, and the identity of any other trader on whose behalf he is acting; (c) the geographical address of the trader and of any other trader on whose behalf he is acting; (d) either (i) the price, including any taxes, or (ii), where the price cannot reasonably be calculated in advance, the manner in which it is calculated; (e) where appropriate either (i) all additional freight, delivery or postal charges; or (ii), where such charges cannot reasonably be calculated in advance, the fact that such charges may be payable; (f) the following matters where they depart from the requirements of professional diligence: (i) arrangements for payment, (ii) arrangements for delivery, (iii) arrangements for performance, (iv) the complaint handling policy; (g), for products and transactions involving a right of withdrawal or cancellation, the existence of such a right: reg. 6(4).

In *Richards v. Westminster Motors Ltd* [1976] 2 QB 795, an offence was committed under the Trade Descriptions Act (TDA) 1968 where the price at which goods were advertised did not include VAT. In *Read Bros Cycles (Leighton) Ltd v. Waltham Forest LBC* [1978] RTR 397, the court convicted a retailer who advertised a motorbike at one price and, when a customer wished to part-exchange his old bike, then informed the customer that it would cost a further £40. In *Clive Sweeting v. Northern Upholstery Ltd* (1982) 2 TrL 5, a retailer was convicted where he advertised a suite of furniture at a special offer price without indicating that the offer applied only to suites of one colour and not the whole range.

(c)　Aggressive commercial practices

A commercial practice is aggressive if, in its factual context, taking account of all its features and circumstances (a) it significantly impairs or is likely to impair the average consumer's freedom of choice or conduct in relation to the product through the use of harassment, coercion or undue influence; and (b) it thereby causes or is likely to cause him to take a transactional decision he would not have taken otherwise: reg. 7(1). In determining whether a practice uses harassment etc. account shall be taken of (a) its timing, location, nature or persistence; (b) the use of threatening or abusive language or behaviour; (c) the exploitation by the trader of any specific misfortune or circumstance of such gravity as to impair the consumer's judgment, of which the trader is aware, to influence his decision; (d) any onerous or disproportionate non-contractual barrier imposed by the trader where a consumer wishes to exercise contractual rights, including rights to terminate a contract or to switch to another product or another trader; and (e) any threat to take any action which cannot legally be taken: reg. 7(2).

Coercion includes the use of physical force, and undue influence means exploiting a position of power in relation to the consumer so as to apply pressure, even without using or threatening to use physical force, in a way which significantly limits the consumer's ability to make an informed decision: reg. 7(3).

(d) Unfair commercial practices under Schedule 1

Schedule 1 lists 31 commercial practices which are always considered unfair:

1. Falsely claiming to be a signatory to a code of conduct.
2. Displaying a trust mark, quality mark or equivalent without the necessary authorisation.
3. Falsely claiming that a code of conduct has an endorsement from a public or other body.
4. Falsely claiming that a trader or product has been approved, endorsed or authorised by a public or private body.
5. Making an invitation to purchase products at a specified price without disclosing the existence of any reasonable grounds the trader may have for believing that he will be able to offer those products or equivalent products at that price for a period which is, and in quantities which are, reasonable having regard to the product, the scale of advertising and the price offered (bait advertising).
6. Making an invitation to purchase products at a specified price and then (a) refusing to show the advertised items to consumers, (b) refusing to take orders for them or deliver them within a reasonable time, or (c) demonstrating a defective sample of them with the intention of promoting a different product (bait and switch).
7. Falsely stating that a product will only be available, or that it will only be available on particular terms, for a very limited time in order to elicit an immediate decision and deprive consumers of sufficient opportunity or time to make an informed choice.
8. Undertaking to provide after-sales service to consumers with whom the trader has communicated prior to a transaction in a language which is not an official language of the EEA State where the trader is located, and then making the service available only in another language without prior disclosure.
9. Falsely stating or otherwise creating the impression that a product can legally be sold when it cannot.
10. Presenting legal consumer rights as a distinctive feature of the trader's offer.
11. Using editorial content in the media to promote a product where a trader has paid for the promotion without making that clear (advertorial).
12. Making a materially inaccurate claim concerning the nature and extent of the risk to the personal security of the consumer or his family if the consumer does not purchase the product.
13. Promoting a product similar to one made by a particular manufacturer so as deliberately to mislead the consumer into believing that the product is made by that manufacturer when it is not.
14. Establishing, operating or promoting a pyramid promotional scheme where a consumer gives consideration for the opportunity to receive compensation which is

derived primarily from the introduction of other consumers into the scheme rather than from the sale or consumption of products.

15. Falsely claiming that the trader is about to cease trading or move premises.

16. Claiming that products are able to facilitate winning in games of chance.

17. Falsely claiming that a product is able to cure illnesses, dysfunction or malformations.

18. Passing on materially inaccurate information on market conditions or on the possibility of finding the product with the intention of inducing the consumer to acquire the product at conditions less favourable than normal market conditions.

19. Claiming in a commercial practice to offer a competition or prize promotion without awarding the prizes described or a reasonable equivalent.

20. Describing a product as 'gratis', 'free', 'without charge' or similar if the consumer has to pay anything other than the unavoidable cost of responding to the commercial practice and collecting or paying for delivery of the item.

21. Including in marketing material an invoice or similar document seeking payment which gives the consumer the impression that he has already ordered the marketed product when he has not.

22. Falsely claiming or creating the impression that the trader is not acting for purposes relating to his trade, business, craft or profession, or falsely representing oneself as a consumer.

23. Creating the false impression that after-sales service in relation to a product is available in an EEA State other than the one in which the product is sold.

24. Creating the impression that the consumer cannot leave the premises until a contract is formed.

25. Conducting personal visits to the consumer's home, ignoring his request to leave or not to return, except in circumstances and to the extent justified to enforce a contractual obligation.

26. Making persistent and unwanted solicitations by telephone, fax, e-mail or other remote media except in circumstances and to the extent justified to enforce a contractual obligation.

27. Requiring a consumer who wishes to claim on an insurance policy to produce documents which could not reasonably be considered relevant to whether the claim was valid, or failing systematically to respond to pertinent correspondence, in order to dissuade a consumer from exercising his contractual rights.

28. Including in an advertisement a direct exhortation to children to buy advertised products or persuade their parents or other adults to buy advertised products from them.

29. Demanding immediate or deferred payment for or the return or safekeeping of products supplied by the trader, but not solicited by the consumer, except where the product is a substitute supplied in accordance with reg. 19(7) Consumer Protection (Distance Selling) Regulation 2000 (inertia selling).

30. Explicitly informing a consumer that if he does not buy the product or service the trader's job or livelihood will be in jeopardy.

31. Creating the false impression that the consumer has already won, will win, or will on doing a particular act win a prize or other equivalent benefit, when in fact (a) there is no prize or other equivalent benefit, or (b) taking any action in relation to claiming the prize or equivalent benefit is subject to the consumer paying money or incurring a cost.

(e) Offences relating to unfair commercial practices

A trader is guilty of an offence if (a) he knowingly or recklessly engages in a commercial practice which contravenes the requirements of professional diligence under reg. 3(3)(a); and (b) the practice materially distorts or is likely materially to distort the economic behaviour of the average consumer with regard to the product under reg. 3(3)(b): reg. 8(1). A trader who engages in a commercial practice without regard to whether it contravenes the requirements of professional diligence is deemed recklessly to engage in the practice whether or not he has reason for believing that it may contravene those requirements: reg. 8(2).

'Professional diligence' means the standard of special skill and care which a trader may reasonably be expected to exercise towards consumers which is commensurate with either (a) honest market practice in the trader's field of activity; or (b) the general principle of good faith in the trader's field of activity: reg. 2(1).

The Consumer Protection Act (CPA) 1987 had the defence of 'due diligence', whereby companies needed to ensure they had in place the necessary policies and procedures and communicated them to store managers, and some system of control and supervision of the operations at its branches.

In *Berkshire County Council v. Olympic Holidays Ltd* [1994] Crim LR 277, a customer booked a holiday with a travel agent by computer, and the first screen display contained a warning that the reservation was not confirmed; no price was quoted. The customer was given a printout of a second screen display, which included the quoted price, but was invoiced for substantially more. The travel agent was acquitted, on the ground that he had taken all reasonable steps and exercised due diligence. The misleading information was caused by an unexplained fault in the computer which had never occurred before. The agents had tested the software and the same transaction had produced the correct information on a repeated test.

In *DSG Retail Ltd v. Oxfordshire CC* [2001] 1 WLR 1765, a trading standards officer on a visit to a Dixons store saw a number of notices reading: 'Price Check. Price – We Can't be Beaten. We Guarantee to Match Any Local Price'. There was a CD system priced at £299.99 and the same item was on sale at another local store at £186.99. The assistant, on the advice of senior staff, refused a request to buy the system at the lower price. On another visit, the officer saw 38 similar 'price check' signs on display, together with seven notices setting out the conditions for the price check promise. Dixons were convicted under s.20(1) CPA 1987 for the CD system and the apparently unqualified price promise. On appeal, the court held that the refusal to honour the price promise for the CD player was evidence of failure to exercise due diligence. In respect of the 'price check' signs, the evidence that conditions applied to the promise which were not apparent on the face of the general notices was sufficient evidence that they were misleading price indications.

Recklessness does not imply dishonesty; the prosecution has to show only that the defendant did not have regard to the truth or falsity of their statement, even though it cannot be proved that they deliberately closed their eyes to the truth.

In *MFI Warehouses v. Nattrass* [1973] 1 All ER 762, the court found the defendants negligent in respect of an advertisement which the chairman had considered for five to 10 minutes without appreciating its implications. However, in *Airtours plc v. Shipley* (1994) 158 JP 835, the company appealed successfully against its conviction for stating that a hotel had a swimming pool by establishing that the brochure had been produced within the set guidelines and procedures of the company's errata policy.

The defendant must have had this knowledge or recklessness at the time the false statement was made. In *Cowburn v. Focus Television Rentals Ltd* [1983] Crim LR 563, the defendants advertised: 'Hire 20 feature films absolutely free when you rent a video recorder'. In effect, people were entitled to only six films, and packaging and postage had to be paid. Following a complaint, the defendants made sure that the customer received 20 films and reimbursed the cost of postage and packaging. They were still convicted, since the statements were false when made and had been made recklessly.

The requirement of contemporaneity excludes promises and forecasts about the future. In *Beckett v. Cohen* [1972] 1 WLR 1593, the accused agreed to build a garage 'within 10 days'. The court held that he was liable for breach of contract for failure to do so, but not criminally liable. This is of particular importance in connection with holiday brochures. In *Sunair Holidays Ltd v. Doss* [1970] 2 All ER 410, the divisional court held that a statement in a brochure 'all twin-bedded rooms with ... terrace' was accurate when made because the appellants had contracted with the hotel for the provision of such rooms for their clients, and there was no offence when the hotel provided a room without a terrace.

In *British Airways Board v. Taylor* [1976] 1 All ER 65, concerning an overbooking system for flights, the House of Lords held that 'I have pleasure in confirming the following reservations for you – London/Bermuda Flight BA 679 – Economy Class – 29 August Dep. 1525 hours Arr. 1750 hours' was a false statement within s.14(1) TDA 1968.

In *Wings Ltd v. Ellis* [1984] 3 All ER 577, the travel company recalled brochures after discovering a mistake but, months later, a customer booked a holiday on the basis of an old brochure. The House of Lords held that the statement was made when the brochure was published and again when read. The defendants had not made a false statement knowingly or recklessly when the brochure was published, but they did when it was read because they then knew that the statement was untrue.

A trader is guilty of engaging in a commercial practice which is a misleading action under reg. 5 unless the practice satisfies the condition in reg. 5(3)(b): reg. 9. A trader is guilty of an offence in engaging in a commercial practice which is a misleading omission under reg. 6: reg. 10. A trader is guilty of an offence if he engages in a commercial practice which is aggressive under reg. 7: reg. 11. A trader is guilty of an offence if he engages in a commercial practice under Schedule 1: reg. 12.

Persons guilty of an offence under reg. 8, 9, 10, 11 or 12 shall be liable on summary conviction to a fine not exceeding the statutory minimum or on conviction on indictment to a fine or imprisonment for a term not exceeding two years or both: reg. 13. No proceedings shall be commenced later than three years from the date of the offence or one year from the date of the discovery of the offence, whichever is the earlier: reg. 14(1).

Where an offence committed by a body corporate is with the consent or connivance of an officer or attributable to negligence on his part, the officer as well as the body corporate is guilty of the offence and liable to be proceeded against: reg. 15(1). 'Officer' includes a director, manager, secretary or other similar officer or a person purporting to act as such: reg. 15(2).

In any proceedings for an offence under reg. 9, 10, 11 or 12 it is a defence for the person to prove:

(a) that the commission of the offence was due to:
1. A mistake;
2. Reliance on information supplied to him by another person;
3. The act or default of another person;
4. An accident; or
5. Another cause beyond his control; and
(b) that he took all reasonable precautions and exercised all due diligence to avoid the commission of such an offence by himself or any person under his control: reg. 17(1).

Persons cannot rely on ground (2) or (3) without leave of the court unless they have served notice in writing on the prosecutor identifying or assisting in the identification of the other person within seven days before the date of the hearing: reg. 17(2).

The words 'another person' cause problems where the defendant is a company. In *Beckett v. Kingston Bros (Butchers) Ltd* [1970] 1 QB 606, the defendant successfully avoided prosecution under TDA 1968 by establishing that the fault lay with the employee. Companies can therefore escape liability unless the employee can be identified as the company's *alter ego*: identified as being the company (see Chapter 6, p.151).

In *Tesco Supermarkets Ltd v. Nattrass* [1971] 2 All ER 127, a branch of Tesco advertised a special offer on soap powder, but had run out of the special price packets. The branch manager had failed to supervise the actions of an assistant who put out normally priced packets. The JPs and the Divisional Court had held that the company was liable because the branch manager was its *alter ego*. The company appealed and the House of Lords held that the branch manager was not sufficiently high in the management hierarchy to be regarded as the company's *alter ego*.

Lord Reid stated, 'Normally the board of directors, the managing director and perhaps other superior officers of a company can carry out the functions of management and speak and act as the company. Their subordinates do not. They carry out orders from above and it can make no difference that they are given some measure of discretion. But the board of directors may delegate some part of their functions of management, giving to their delegate full discretion to act independently of instructions from them ... But here the board never delegated any part of their functions. They set up a chain of command through regional and district supervisors, but they remained in control. The shop managers had to obey their general directions and also to take orders from their superiors. The acts or omissions of shop managers were not acts of the company itself.'

The alternative of making the company vicariously liable has been rejected as being unjustified.

In order for the defence to apply, the person must establish that they took all reasonable precautions and exercised all due diligence.

In respect of an identical defence under the TDA 1968, a second-hand car dealer advertised a car as being 'in good condition throughout'. He had obtained an MOT certificate but the car was badly corroded. The dealer claimed that he had been misled by others. Donaldson LJ stated, 'What he has to do is show that it was a latent defect, that is to say, a defect which could not with reasonable diligence have been ascertained': *Barker v. Hargreaves* [1981] RTR 197.

In *Harringey London Borough v. Piro Shoes Ltd* [1976] Crim LR 462, the defence was rejected in connection with shoes wrongly labelled 'all leather' when the company instructed their managers to remove the label before the shoes left the shop. The court held that, since the offence under the TDA 1968 was committed by the mere fact of the goods being 'exposed for sale', the instructions should have been to remove the label before the goods were displayed. The offence was therefore committed by another person but the defendants had not taken 'all reasonable precautions'.

In *Sharratt v. Geralds The American Jewellers Ltd* (1970) 114 SJ 147, the defendants were charged in respect of supplying a wristwatch marked 'diver's watch' and 'waterproof'. They had not tested the watches, but relied on the manufacturer's reputation. Allowing an appeal against the magistrates' finding that they had exercised all due diligence, Lord Parker CJ stated, 'There was clearly an obligation to take any reasonable precautions that could be taken … The elementary precaution of dipping the watch in a bowl of water would have prevented the offence.'

In *Garrett v. Boots Chemists Ltd*, 16 July 1980, Lord Lane CJ stated, 'What might be reasonable for a large retailer might not be reasonable in the village shop'. The failure of Boots to test a random sample of pencils for their lead content constituted a failure to take all reasonable precautions.

There is also the defence of innocent publication of an advertisement if the person proves that:

(a) he is a person whose business it is to publish or to arrange for the publication of advertisements;
(b) he received the advertisement for publication in the ordinary course of business; and
(c) he did not know and had no reason to suspect that its publication would amount to an offence.

'Advertisement' includes a catalogue, circular or price list: reg. 18.

Where a person commits an offence under reg. 9, 10, 11 or 12, or would have committed an offence but for a defence under reg. 17 or 18, and the commission of the offence or what would have been offence is due to the act or default of some other person, that other person is guilty of an offence, subject to reg. 17 or 18, whether or not he is a trader and whether or not his act or default is a commercial practice. and he may be charged with and convicted of the offence whether or not proceedings are taken against the first party: reg. 16.

In *Coupe v. Guyett* [1973] 2 All ER 1058, the defendant, a car repair workshop manager employed by the owner, Miss Shaw, recklessly made a false statement as to repairs. Miss Shaw took no active part in it. She was charged under s.14(1)(b) TDA 1968 and the defendant was charged under s.23 TDA 1968, similar to reg. 16. Miss Shaw was acquitted on the ground that she neither made, nor authorised, nor was aware of the false statement. The defendant was acquitted on the ground that a s.23 conviction was not possible since the owner had committed no offence. On appeal, the court held that if the justices had acquitted Miss Shaw solely on the basis of the statutory defence then it would have been possible for them to convict the defendant.

Private individuals can be 'other persons': for instance, a motorist who 'clocks' a car before selling it to a dealer causing the dealer to commit an offence under TDA 1968: *Olgiersson v. Kitching* [1986] 1 WLR 304.

(f) Enforcement

The duty is on the local weights and measures authority (in Northern Ireland the Department of Enterprise, Trade and Investment): reg. 19. The authorities have the power to make test purchases (reg. 20) and to enter and investigate with or without a warrant: regs. 21 and 22. People obstructing enforcement are guilty of an offence: reg. 23.

21.2 Trade descriptions

The Business Protection from Misleading Marketing Regulations 2008 prohibits misleading advertising (reg. 3), comparative advertising (reg. 4) and the promotion of misleading and comparative advertising (reg. 5) in respect of traders. 'Advertising' means any form of representation in connection with a trade, business, craft or profession in order to promote the supply or transfer of a product, and 'advertiser' is construed accordingly. 'Comparative advertising' means advertising which in any way – explicitly or by implication – identifies a competitor or a product offered by a competitor. 'Product' means any goods or services and includes immovable property, rights and obligations. 'Trader' means any person who is acting for purposes relating to his trade, craft, business or profession and anyone acting in the name of or on behalf of a trader: reg. 2(1).

(a) Prohibition of advertising which misleads traders

Misleading advertising is prohibited (reg. 3(1)). Advertising is misleading which:

(a) in any way, including its presentation, deceives or is likely to deceive the traders to whom it is addressed or whom it reaches; and by reason of its deceptive nature is likely to affect their economic behaviour; or
(b) for those reasons, injures or is likely to injure a competitor: reg. 3(1).

In determining whether advertising is misleading, account shall be taken of all its features, and in particular of any information it contains concerning:

(a) the characteristics of the product;
(b) the price or manner in which the price is calculated;
(c) the conditions on which the product is supplied or provided; and
(d) the nature, attributes and rights of the advertiser.

The characteristics of the product include:

- Availability;
- Nature;
- Execution;
- Composition;
- Method and date of manufacture;
- Method and date of the provision;
- Fitness for purpose;
- Uses;

- Quantity;
- Specification;
- Geographical or commercial origin;
- Results to be expected from use; or
- Results and material features of tests or checks carried out.

The nature, attributes and rights of the advertiser include the advertiser's:

- Identity;
- Assets;
- Qualifications;
- Ownership of industrial, commercial or intellectual property rights; or
- Awards and distinctions.

(b) Comparative advertising

Comparative advertising is permitted on the following conditions:

(a)   it is not misleading under reg. 3;

(b)   it is not a misleading action or misleading omission under reg. 5 or 6 of the Consumer Protection from Unfair Trading Regulations 2008;

(c)   it compares products meeting the same needs or intended for the same purpose;

(d)   it objectively compares one or more material, relevant, verifiable and representative features of those products, which may include price;

(e)   it does not create confusion among traders (i) between the advertiser and a competitor, or (ii) between the trade marks, trade names, other distinguishing marks or products of the advertiser and those of a competitor;

(f)   it does not discredit or denigrate the trade marks, trade names, other distinguishing marks, products, activities, or circumstances of a competitor;

(g)   for products with a designation of origin, it relates in each case to products with the same designation;

(h)   it does not take unfair advantage of the reputation of a trade mark, trade name or other distinguishing marks of a competitor or of the designation of origin of competing products;

(i)   it does not present products as imitations or replicas of products bearing a protected trade mark or trade name: reg. 4.

In *Boehringer Ingelheim Ltd and Ors v. Vetplus Ltd* [2007] EWCA Civ 583 the court held that no interim injunction would issue to inhibit comparative advertising whereby one trader promoted his goods over those of a rival unless the claimant could show the advertising was misleading and he would probably win a permanent injunction at trial. Jacob LJ said that a man who made a damaging statement involving the use of another's trade mark which he reasonably believed to be true at the time but which later turned out to be untrue would not be acting in accordance with honest practice if he was not prepared to compensate the owner of the damaged mark. He could express his honestly held opinion, but only on the basis that he would compensate his trade rival if it was proved to be wrong. The court held that this position was confirmed by the Comparative Advertising

Directive (97/55/EC, [1997] OJ L290/18), and a comparative advertiser would only be acting in accordance with honest practices if in accordance with the conditions of Art. 3a Misleading Advertising Directive (84/450/EC,[1984] OJ L250/17).

(c) Promotion of misleading and comparative advertising which is not permitted

A code owner shall not promote in a code of conduct misleading or non-permitted comparative advertising: reg. 5. A code owner is defined as a trader or body responsible for (a) the formulation and revision of a code of conduct; or (b) monitoring compliance with the code by those who have undertaken to be bound by it: reg.2.

(d) Offences

A trader is guilty of an offence if he engages in advertising which is misleading under reg. 3: reg. 6. A person guilty of an offence under reg. 6 shall be liable on summary conviction to a fine not exceeding the statutory maximum; or on conviction on indictment to a fine or imprisonment for a term not exceeding two years or both: reg. 7.

Where an offence committed by a body corporate is with the consent or connivance of an officer, or attributable to any neglect on his part, the officer as well as the body corporate is guilty of the offence: reg. 8(1). 'Officer' includes a director, manager, secretary or other similar officer; and a person purporting to act as such: reg. 8(2).

No prosecution shall be commenced three years from the date of the commission of the offence or one year from the date of discovery of the offence whichever is the earlier: reg. 10.

In any proceedings it is a defence for the person to prove:

(a) that the commission of the offence was due to:
    1. A mistake;
    2. Reliance on information supplied to him by another person;
    3. The act or default of another person;
    4. An accident; or
    5. Another cause beyond his control; and
(b) that he took all reasonable precautions and exercised all due diligence to avoid the commission of such an offence by himself or any person under his control: reg. 11(1).

Persons cannot rely on ground (2) or (3) without leave of the court unless they have served notice in writing on the prosecutor identifying or assisting in the identification of the other person within seven days before the date of the hearing: reg.11(2).

There is also the defence of innocent publication of an advertisement if the person proves that:

(a) he is a person whose business is to publish or to arrange for the publication of advertisements;
(b) he received the advertisement for publication in the ordinary course of business; and
(c) he did not know and had no reason to suspect that its publication would amount o an offence: reg. 12.

Where a person commits an offence under reg. 6, or would have committed an offence but for a defence under reg. 11 or 12 and the commission of the offence or what would have been the offence is due to the act or default of some other person, that other person is guilty of an offence, subject to reg. 11 or 12, whether or not he is a trader and whether or not his act or default is a commercial practice, and he may be charged with and convicted of the offence whether or not proceedings are taken against the first party: reg. 9.

(e)　Enforcement

The duty is on the local weights and measures authority (in Northern Ireland the Department of Enterprise, Trade and Investment): reg. 13. Where the enforcement body is the local weights and measures authority, it may bring proceedings only if it has notified the OFT at least 14 days before proceedings are brought; or the OFT consents to proceedings being brought in a shorter period. The enforcement authority must also notify the OFT of the outcome: reg. 14. The enforcement authority may bring proceedings for an injunction (including an interim injunction) to secure compliance with the Regulations: reg. 15. It may accept an undertaking from the person concerned that he will comply with the Regulations: reg. 16.

The authorities have investigative powers under Part 4, including the power to require persons to provide specified information or to produce any specified documents: reg. 21. They also have the power to make test purchases (reg. 22) and the power of entry and investigation with or without a warrant: regs. 23 and 24. People obstructing officers are guilty of an offence: reg. 25.

21.3　The Trade Descriptions Act (TDA) 1968

The TDA 1968 still applies in some very specialised situations, including falsely indicating that goods or services are as supplied to the royal family or simulating the Queen's Award to Industry logo: s.12.

21.4　Distance selling

The Consumer Protection (Distance Selling) Regulations 2000 (SI 2000/2334) implement Directive 97/7/EC ([1997] OJ L144/19) of 20 May 1997 with the exception of Article 10.

'Distance contract' means any contract concerning goods or services concluded between a supplier and a consumer under an organised distance sales or service provision scheme run by the supplier who, for the purposes of the contract, makes exclusive use of one or more means of distance communication up to and including the moment at which the contract is concluded.

The phrase 'means of distance communication' includes any means which, without the simultaneous physical presence of the supplier and the consumer, may be used for the conclusion of a contract between those parties. An indicative list in Schedule 1 includes:

- Unaddressed printed matter
- Addressed printed matter
- Letter
- Press advertising with order form

- Catalogue
- Telephone with human intervention
- Telephone without human intervention
- Radio
- Videophone
- Videotext
- Email
- Fax machine
- Television (teleshopping).

The Regulations do not apply to distance contracts excluded by reg. 5(1) including contracts:

- For the sale or other disposition of an interest in land except for a rental agreement;
- For the construction of a building where the contract also provides for a sale or other disposition of an interest in land on which the building is constructed, except for a rental agreement;
- Relating to the supply of financial services;
- Concluded by means of an automated vending machine or automated commercial premises;
- Concluded with a telecommunications operator through the use of a public pay-phone;
- Concluded at an auction.

Schedule 2 gives a non-exhaustive list of financial services including investment services, insurance and reinsurance operations, banking services, and services relating to dealing in futures or options.

The Regulations have limited application to contracts for the supply of groceries by regular delivery and contracts for the provision of accommodation, transport, catering or leisure services where the supplier undertakes, when the contract is concluded, to provide these services on a specific date or within a specific period (reg. 6).

The supplier must provide the consumer with the information referred to in reg. 7 prior to the conclusion of the contract. This includes information on the right to cancel the distance contract, the main characteristics of the goods or services, and delivery costs where appropriate. The supplier must confirm in writing, or another durable medium available and accessible to the consumer, information already given and give additional information, including the conditions and procedures relating to the right to cancel the contract: reg. 8. The supplier must inform the consumer prior to the conclusion of a contract for services that he will not be able to cancel once performance has begun: reg. 8(3).

The Regulations provide a 'cooling-off period' to enable the consumer to give notice of cancellation to the supplier which has the effect of treating the contract as if it had not been made. Where the supplier supplies the information under reg. 7 on time, the cooling-off period is seven working days from the day after the date of the contract in the case of services, or from the day after the date of delivery of the goods. If the supplier fails to comply with the information requirement, the cooling-off period is extended by three months. Where the supplier complies with the information requirement later than he should have done but within three months, the cooling-off period begins from the date he provided the information: regs. 10–12.

Certain contracts are excluded from the right to cancel unless the parties have agreed otherwise:

(a) those for the supply of services if the performance of the contract has begun with the consumer's agreement (i) before the end of the cancellation period under reg. 12(2); and (ii) after the supplier has provided the information in reg. 8(2);
(b) those for the supply of goods or services the price of which is dependent on fluctuations in the financial market which cannot be controlled by the supplier;
(c) those for the supply of goods made to the consumer's specifications or clearly personalised or which, by reason of their nature, cannot be returned or are liable to deteriorate or expire rapidly;
(d) those for the supply of audio and video recordings or computer software if they are unsealed by the consumer;
(e) those for the supply of newspapers, periodicals or magazines; or
(f) those for gaming, betting or lottery services: reg. 13.

If the consumer cancels, the consumer must be reimbursed within a maximum period of 30 days: reg. 14. Where the consumer cancels the contract, any related credit agreement is automatically cancelled: reg. 15. On cancellation, the consumer must restore goods to the supplier if the supplier collects them and in the meantime take reasonable care of them: reg. 17. There is no obligation on the consumer to return goods, but if he is required to under the contract and does not do so, he must pay the cost to the supplier of recovering them.

The contract must be performed within 30 days subject to agreement between the parties. However, where the supplier is not able to provide the goods or service ordered, substitutes may be offered if certain conditions are met: reg. 19. Where the consumer's payment card is used fraudulently in connection with a distance contract, the consumer is entitled to cancel the payment. If the payment has already been made the consumer is entitled to a recredit or to have all sums returned by the card issuer. The debtor's potential liability under a regulated consumer credit agreement for the first £50 of loss to the creditor from misuse of a credit token in connection with a distance contract is removed in an amendment to the CCA 1974.

21.5 Unsolicited goods and services

The Regulations prohibit the supply of unsolicited goods and services to consumers. Reg. 24 replaces with amendments s.1 Unsolicited Goods and Services Act 1971. It also creates an offence in similar terms to that in s.2 of the 1971 Act but extended to the supply of unsolicited services and limited to supply to consumers. These relate to persons making a demand for payment for unsolicited goods or services: reg. 24(4), or threatening legal proceedings, placing or threatening to place any person on a list of defaulters or debtors, or invoking or threatening any other collection procedure in respect of unsolicited goods or services: reg. 24(5). The scope of s.2 of the 1971 Act and Art. 4 of the 1976 Order (which apply only to goods) is amended to restrict their application to the unsolicited supply of goods to businesses (see p.516).

The UK enforcement authorities for the Regulations are the OFT and the Trading Standards Departments. An enforcement authority must consider complaints about a breach of the Regulations: reg. 26, and is authorised to seek an injunction to prevent further breaches: reg. 27.

21.6 Product liability

Manufacturers may be liable for their products in five ways: (i) the Sale of Goods Act (SOGA) 1979; (ii) negligence; (iii) the Consumer Protection Act (CPA) 1987; (iv) The General Product Safety Regulations (GPSR) 1994; and (v) a collateral contract of guarantee.

(a) The Sale of Goods Act 1979

Protection in respect of defective goods based on the implied term of satisfactory quality in s.14(2) SOGA 1979 has been discussed. However, since the basis of liability is contractual, the manufacturer is liable only where the buyer dealt directly with it. The buyer will generally sue the retailer, who will then claim an indemnity against his wholesaler, who will eventually claim against the manufacturer.

Where a person buys goods as a gift for somebody else, handing over the gift does not transfer the statutory protection: *Heil v. Hedges* [1951] 1 TLR 512. The Consumers' Association has suggested that the rights could be assigned by writing on the gift tag: 'To Grandad with all my love and all my rights under the Sale of Goods Act 1979', but admits that this is legally doubtful!

(b) Tortious liability: negligence

Donoghue v. Stevenson [1932] AC 562 established the manufacturer's liability to the ultimate consumer where the consumer could establish negligence. The burden of proof is on the consumer, however, who is unlikely to be aware of the manufacturing process and any potential breaches of manufacturing safeguards. The doctrine of *res ipsa loquitur* is important here.

In *Chapronière v. Mason* (1905) 21 TLR 633, the doctrine was successfully applied when a stone was found in a bath bun, but was unsuccessful in *Daniels v. White* (1968) 160 LT 128, where carbolic acid was found in a bottle of lemonade, since the manufacturers established that they had a safe manufacturing operation with adequate quality control.

(c) The Consumer Protection Act (CPA) 1987, Part I

This implements a European Directive on product liability (Directive 85/374/EEC, [1985] OJ L210/29). Persons injured by a defective product have a right of action against the manufacturer irrespective of whether or not the manufacturer was negligent. The basis of the claim is s.2, which requires the claimant to establish:

(a) that the product contained a defect;
(b) that the claimant suffered damage;
(c) that the damage was caused by the defect;
(d) that the defendant was producer, own-brander or importer into the EU of the product.

(i)   Defective product

A product is defective 'if the safety of the product is not such as persons generally are entitled to expect; 'safety' in relation to a product includes safety with respect to products comprised in that product and safety in the context of risks of damage to property, as well as in the context of risks of death or personal injury': s.3(1) CPA 1987. In determining whether a product is defective all the circumstances must be taken into account, including:

(a) the manner in which, and purposes for which, the product has been marketed, its get-up, the use of any mark in relation to the product and any instructions for, or warnings with respect to, doing or refraining from doing anything with or in relation to the product;

(b) what may reasonably be expected to be done with or in relation to the product; and the time when the product was supplied by its producer to another;

(c) nothing shall require a defect to be inferred from the fact alone that the safety of a product which is supplied after that time is greater than the safety of the product in question: s.3(2) CPA 1987.

Products include goods or electricity and include a product which is comprised in another product, whether by virtue of being a component part or raw material or otherwise: s.1(2) CPA 1987.

Agricultural products are excluded unless they have undergone an 'industrial process' giving them 'essential characteristics'. This includes any processing of the product such as freezing, canning or otherwise transforming the product – meat into sausages, potatoes into frozen chips – when the processor is the producer for liability purposes.

(ii)   Damage to the claimant

Damages can be claimed for death or personal injuries and for loss of, or damage to, property (including land) which is:

(a) of a description of property ordinarily intended for private use, occupation or consumption; and

(b) intended by the person suffering the loss or damage mainly for his/her own private use, occupation or consumption: CPA 1987 s.5(3).

It is not possible to claim damage to business property, and private property loss or damage cannot be claimed unless it exceeds £275.

There can be no claim for any damage to the defective product itself or to any product supplied with it or comprised within it. Where a defective product is incorporated into a larger product there will be two defective products, and the claimant can sue either producer, but cannot claim for damage to the defective component nor to the larger item supplied with the defective component comprised in it.

(iii)   The defendant

A claim can be brought against the producer, the own-brander or the importer. Own-branders are liable only if they have branded their goods in such a way as to hold themselves out as being the producer. Liability can be escaped where the product is labelled in such a way as to remove this impression: 'Manufactured for Safeburys by A plc'. The term 'importer' is restricted to the person responsible for importing the product into the EU. Thus, if a product is imported into France by A and then imported from France into the UK by B, only A will be liable as an importer.

Where it is difficult to identify the importer or producer, and the supplier fails to identify them when requested, the supplier may be liable as if they had been the producer.

(iv) Defences
The following defences are provided by s.4 of the CPA 1987:

(i)   The defect is due to compliance with any statutory requirement or rule of the EU.
(ii) The defendant did not supply the product; for example it was stolen from his premises.
(iii) The defendant supplied the product otherwise than in the course of a business and the defendant did not produce it (or own-brand it or import it into the EU) with a view to profit.
(iv) The defect did not exist in the product at the time it was supplied by the defendant.
(v)   A component manufacturer is not liable where the defect is attributable to the design of the larger product in which the product is included, or where the defect is attributable to instructions given by the manufacturer of the larger product.
(vi) That the defect was not discoverable at the time they supplied the product. The defendant must show 'that the state of scientific and technical knowledge at the relevant time was not such that a producer of products of the same description as the producer in question might be expected to have discovered the defect if it had existed in their products while they were under their control'. This is the 'development risks' defence.

The burden of proof is on the defendant. A further defence of contributory negligence is also established in s.6(1), again with the burden of proof on the defendant. The basis of this defence is that the claimant has failed to take reasonable care and is thereby partly responsible for his/her own injuries.

(v) Exclusion of liability
Persons are prohibited from escaping liability by way of an exclusion clause: 'The liability of a person … shall not be limited or excluded by any contract term, by any notice or by any other provision': s.7.

(vi) Limitation of actions
There are two rules regarding claims under the Act:

(i)   Proceedings must be commenced within three years of the injury or damage occurring or, if not discovered until later, within three years of the claimant becoming aware of the injury or damage;
(ii) No proceedings may be commenced more than 10 years after the supply of the product.

(d) The Consumer Protection Act 1987, Part II

This part of the Act:

(i)   enables the Secretary of State to prevent the marketing of unsafe goods;
(ii) makes it an offence to supply consumer goods which fail to comply with a general safety requirement;
(iii) entitles a consumer to bring an action for damages against a trader for damage or loss resulting from the infringement of safety regulations.

(i)   Preventing marketing of unsafe goods

The Secretary of State can issue two types of instruction under s.13.

(ii) The prohibition notice

This can be issued only when the Secretary of State is made aware that dangerous goods are on the market and, to prevent any delay in protecting the public, the local trading standards office can serve a 'suspension notice' where he/she has reasonable grounds to think that safety requirements have been infringed: s.14. This prohibition operates for up to six months but, where no infringement is discovered, the trader may be entitled to compensation: s.14(7). Failure to comply with a prohibition notice is a criminal offence. Customs officers have power to seize and detain goods at ports for up to two working days to allow trading standards officers to satisfy themselves whether the goods infringe trading standards: s.31.

(iii) The notice to warn

This is served on a manufacturer when it appears that a product has a dangerous design fault and states the steps required by the manufacturer, which may be to publish a warning notice in the newspapers or even to contact individual purchasers. Failure by the manufacturer to comply with the notice to warn is a criminal offence.

(iv) Supplying consumer goods in breach of a general safety requirement

Consumer goods are those 'which are ordinarily intended for private use or consumption'.

Excluded from this definition are water, food, aircraft (except hang-gliders), motor vehicles, controlled drugs, licensed medicinal products and tobacco.

This offence is created by s.10. The general safety requirement is that goods should be reasonably safe. In deciding whether goods are unsafe, the court will have regard to all the circumstances, including the purpose for which the goods were marketed, their 'get-up', any instructions or warnings given, and any published standards of safety. It is a defence for a trader to prove that it complied with the requirements of safety regulations or any approved standard of safety.

The offence is not committed only by a trader supplying the goods, but also by a trader who agrees or offers to supply them or exposes or possesses them for supply. There is a limited defence for a retailer who neither knew, nor had reasonable grounds for believing, that the goods were not reasonably safe. There is no application to goods intended for export from the UK, or goods not supplied as being new.

The general defence of due diligence is also available for anyone charged with an offence under s.10 or an offence under safety regulations. The essence is that the defendant took all reasonable steps and exercised all due diligence to avoid committing the offence: s.39. For an importer or wholesaler this may require proof of tests on more than infrequent random samples of the goods.

(v) *Actions for losses arising from infringement of safety regulations*

Actions can be brought against a manufacturer even where the claimant did not purchase the goods from the manufacturer, and even if they did not buy the goods. There is no need to establish the negligence of the manufacturer, and the claim is independent of Part I of the Act. Civil liability cannot be excluded or restricted by any exemption or exclusion clause.

(vi) *Limitations on criminal and civil liability under the Act*

Liability under Part II only attaches to persons who are acting 'in the course of carrying on a business'.

(e) The General Product Safety Regulations (GPSR) 1994

These Regulations parallel Part II CPA 1987. Regulation 5 GPSR 1994 disapplies the provisions of s.10 CPA 1987 to the extent that they impose general safety requirements which must be complied with if products are to be (a) placed on the market, offered or agreed to be placed on the market, or exposed or possessed to be placed on the market by producers; or (b) supplied, offered or agreed to be supplied, or exposed or possessed to be supplied by distributors.

For distributors the Regulations disapply s.10 CPA 1987 in relation to the supply of goods, and thus merely replace the statutory provisions; for producers the disapplication relates to 'placing on the market', which may be narrower than the s.10 CPA 1987 'supply', which is broadly defined in s.46 CPA 1987.

'Producer' means manufacturers who are established in the EU, and extends to any person presenting themselves as a manufacturer by affixing their name, trade mark or other distinctive mark to the product, or to a person who reconditions the product. Where the manufacturer is not established within the EU, the producer is the importer, the manufacturer's representative, and other professionals in the supply chain whose activities may affect the safety of the product placed on the market. This last category must be contrasted with 'distributors', who are professionals in the supply chain and whose activity does not affect the safety properties of a product: reg. 2(1). Thus the distinction between producers and distributors is blurred, and many persons may be brought within the definition of producer (for example persons transporting and storing food, since the conditions in which the goods are stored or transported may affect their safety). It could also cover people fitting or installing electrical and other products.

The Regulations cover a wider range of products than the CPA 1987, extending to 'any product intended for consumers or likely to be used by consumers, supplied whether for consideration or not in the course of a commercial activity and whether new, used or reconditioned': reg. 2(1). There is an exclusion in respect of any product 'which is used exclusively in the context of a commercial activity even if it is used for or by a consumer': reg. 2(1). This clearly covers infrastructure such as escalators in shops, ski lifts and railway carriages, but whether it extends to shampoos supplied to salons or supermarket trolleys is unclear. Regulation 2(1) adds that 'this exception shall not extend to the supply of such a product to a consumer', which is not very clear.

No producer shall place a product on the market unless it is a safe product: reg. 7. This is described in reg. 2(1) as: 'any product which, under normal or reasonably foreseeable conditions of use, including duration, does not present any risk or only the minimum risks compatible with the product's use, considered as acceptable and consistent with a high level of protection for the safety and health of persons, taking into account in particular:

(a) the product's characteristics: composition, packaging, instructions for assembly and maintenance;
(b) the effect on other products, where it is reasonably foreseeable that it will be used with other products;
(c) the product's presentation: labelling, instructions for use and disposal and any other indication or information provided by the producer;
(d) the categories of consumers at serious risk when using the product, in particular children, and the fact that higher levels of safety may be obtained or other products presenting a lesser degree of risk may be available shall not of itself cause the product to be considered other than a safe product.'

If a product conforms to the specific rules of UK law, which it must satisfy before it can be marketed, there is a presumption that the product is safe: reg. 10(1). Where specific rules exist, safety is to be assessed having regard to: (a) voluntary UK national standards giving effect to a European standard (for example BSI standards); or (b) Community technical specifications (for example standards of the European Committee for Standardisation (CEN)), or, failing either, UK standards or codes of good practice in the product sector or the state of art and technology: reg. 10(2).

Producers are also required to provide consumers with the relevant information to enable them to assess the risks inherent in a product throughout its normal or reasonably foreseeable period of use where such risks are not immediately obvious, and to adopt measures to enable the consumer to be informed of the risks which the product may represent and to take appropriate action, including withdrawing the product, to avoid those risks. These measures include marking products or product batches for the purposes of identification; sample testing; complaint investigation and informing distributors about such monitoring: reg. 8.

Distributors have a duty to help ensure compliance with reg. 7, and in particular shall not supply products which the distributor knows or should have presumed, on the basis of information in their possession and as a professional, are dangerous products; and shall participate in monitoring the safety of products by passing on information on the product risks and cooperating in the action to avoid those risks: reg. 9.

Regulation 12 creates offences for producers and distributors contravening reg. 7 or 9(a). It is also an offence under reg. 13 for a producer or distributor to offer or agree to place on the market any dangerous product, or to expose or possess such product for placing on the market, or to offer or to agree to supply any dangerous product or expose or possess any such product for supply. For the purposes of reg. 12, producers have strict liability, whereas distributors are liable only if they know or ought to have known that the product was dangerous. However, reg. 13 creates strict liability offences for both producer and supplier. For both offences, however, it is a defence for persons to show that they took all reasonable steps and exercised all due diligence to avoid committing the offence: reg. 14(1).

A distributor cannot use the due diligence defence in reg. 14(1) or in s.39(1) CPA 1987, where they have contravened reg. 9(b), which requires participation in product monitoring and cooperating in avoidance of risks: reg. 14(5).

Persons charged under GPSR 1994 who allege that the offence was caused by the act or default of another, or in reliance on information given by another, cannot rely on the defence without leave of the court, unless notice under reg. 14(3) is served seven days before the hearing on the person bringing the proceedings: reg. 14(2).

Where the offence is caused by the act or default of another person in the course of a commercial activity, the other person is guilty of an offence: reg. 15(1). Where a body corporate is guilty of an offence in respect of an act or default committed with the consent or connivance of, or attributable to neglect of, any director, manager, secretary or other officer, s/he shall also be guilty of that offence and liable to be prosecuted and punished: reg. 15(2). Actions must be commenced within 12 months of the date of the offence: reg. 16, and persons guilty of any offence shall be liable on summary conviction to imprisonment for three months or a fine not exceeding level five on the standard scale, or both: reg. 17.

For enforcement of the GPSR 1994, s.13 CPA 1987 applies to products as it applies to relevant goods under that section with regard to prohibition notices and notices to warn: reg. 11(a). The requirements of the Regulations constitute safety provisions for the purposes of suspension notices, forfeiture and power to obtain information under ss.14, 16 and 18 CPA 1987: reg. 11(b). The Regulations are enforceable by the weights and measures authorities in Great Britain: reg.11(c).

(f) Collateral contract of guarantee

The manufacturer of goods, even though they do not market them directly, may make a collateral contract with the consumer, and 'guarantees' and 'warranties' issued by them may form the basis of the contract between consumer and retailer. The manufacturer may be liable in respect of these promises.

The guarantee or warranty previously sought to remove any purchaser's rights under the law, but this is regulated by s.5 Unfair Contract Terms Act 1977, which provides:

(1) In the case of goods of a type ordinarily supplied for private use or consumption, where loss or damage:
   (a) arises from the goods proving defective while in consumer use; and
   (b) results from the negligence of a person concerned in the manufacture or distribution of the goods, liability for the loss or damage cannot be excluded or restricted by reference to a guarantee of the goods.

A guarantee is 'anything in writing if it contains or purports to contain some promise or assurance (however worded or presented) that defects will be made good by complete or partial replacement, or by repair, monetary compensation or otherwise': s.5(2)(b).

The section 'does not apply as between the parties to a contract under or in pursuance of which possession or ownership of the goods passed': s.5(3). This appears to allow a manufacturer to exclude themselves from liability where the consumer purchased the goods direct from them, but merely means that the attempted exclusion from liability will be under some other section.

21.7 Contracts for unsolicited goods and services

The reference to unsolicited goods relates to the practice whereby dealers send goods to people without their having requested them, subject to a proviso that, if the person does not return the goods within a stated period, they will be deemed to have purchased the goods and will be invoiced for them.

The Unsolicited Goods and Services Act 1971 was amended by the Consumer Protection (Distance Selling) Regulations 2000 (see above p.508). These provide that persons receiving the goods are entitled to treat them as an unsolicited gift and use, deal with or dispose of the goods as if they were an unconditional gift: reg. 24(2). The rights of the sender of the goods are extinguished: reg. 24(3).

The Act also regulates entries in trade or business directories: s.3, and makes it a criminal offence to send unsolicited books describing or illustrating human sexual techniques: s.4.

21.8 Cancellable agreements for goods and services

The Cancellation of Contract made in a Consumer's Home or Place of Work etc. Regulations (SI 2008/1816) replace the Consumer Protection (Contracts Concluded away from Business Premises) Regulations 1987 (SI1987/2117) and give cancellation rights in respect of contracts for goods or services made during a visit by a trader to a consumer's home or place of work, or to the home of another individual; or on an excursion organised by the trader; or after an offer made by the consumer during such a visit or excursion: reg. 5. The Regulations re-implement Council Directive 85/577/EEC ([1985] OJ L372/31) to protect the consumer in respect of contracts negotiated away from business premises.

The Regulations do not apply to (a) contracts listed in Schedule 3; (b) any cancellable agreement; a consumer credit agreement which may be cancelled by the consumer in accordance with the terms of the agreement; a contract made during a solicited visit or a contract made after an offer made by a consumer during a solicited visit where the contract is (i) a regulated mortgage, home purchase plan or home reversion plan if the making or performance of such a contract is a regulated activity for the purposes of the Financial Services and Markets Act 2000; (ii) a consumer credit agreement secured on land which is either regulated under the CCA 1974; or, to the extent that it is not regulated under the CCA 1974, exempt under that Act; or (iii) any other consumer credit agreement regulated under the 1974 Act: reg. 6.

Contracts excepted from the Regulations under Schedule 3 are:

1. A contract for the construction, sale or rental of immovable property or a contract concerning other rights relating to immovable property other than for (a) the construction of extensions, patios, conservatories or driveways; (b) for the supply of goods and their incorporation in immovable property; and for the repair, refurbishment or improvement of immovable property.
2. A contract for the supply of foodstuffs or beverages or other goods intended for current consumption in the household and supplied by a regular roundsman.
3. A contract for the supply of goods or services provided that each of the following conditions is met: (a) the contract is concluded on the basis of a trader's catalogue which the consumer has the opportunity of reading in the absence of the trader's

representative; (b) there is intended to be continuity of contact between the trader's representative and the consumer in relation to that or any subsequent transaction; and (c) both the catalogue and the contract contain a prominent notice informing the consumer of his rights to return the goods within a period of not less than seven days of receipt or to cancel the contract within that period without obligation other than to take reasonable care of the goods.

4. A contract of insurance.

5. Any contract under which credit not exceeding £35 is provided other than a hire purchase or conditional sale agreement.

6. Any contract not falling within paragraph 5 under which the total payments made by the consumer do not exceed £35.

7. Any agreement the making or performance of which by either party constitutes a relevant regulated activity, which means an activity of the following kind: (i) dealing in investments as principal or as agent; (ii) arranging deals in investments; (iii) operating a multilateral trading facility; (iv) managing investments; (v) safeguarding and administering investments; (vi) establishing, operating or winding up a collective investment scheme: para. 8(1).

A solicited visit is one made at the express request of the consumer, but excludes (a) visits made after he or a person acting in his name or on his behalf: (i) telephones the consumer (other than at the consumer's request) and indicates that he, or the trader on whose behalf he is acting, is willing to visit the consumer; or (ii) visits the consumer and indicates that he or the trader is willing to make a subsequent visit to the consumer; or (b) a visit during which the contract made relates to goods and services other than those concerning which the consumer requested the visit: reg. 3.

A consumer has the right to cancel a contract within the cancellation period and must be given written notice of that right at the time the contract is made: reg. 7. The cancellation period runs for seven days from the day of receipt of a notice in writing of the right to cancel: Schedule 4 para. 3. If the consumer serves notice of cancellation within the cancellation period the contract is cancelled and treated as if it had never been entered into. A cancellation notice sent by post is deemed to have been served at the time of posting whether or not it is actually received, and where sent by e-mail to have been served on the day it was sent: reg. 8. On the cancellation, any sum paid by or on behalf of the consumer shall be repayable (reg. 10) and any related credit agreement is cancelled: reg. 11. A consumer who has acquired possession of goods shall, on cancellation, be under a duty, subject to a lien, to restore the goods to the trader and meanwhile to take reasonable care of them. But he has no duty to deliver the goods except at his own premises: reg. 13.

There is no right to contract out of the Regulations: reg. 15. Regulations 17–23 relate to the enforcement of the Regulations. It is an offence for a trader to enter into a contract to which the Regulations apply without complying with the notice requirements of reg. 7. A person guilty of such an offence is liable on summary conviction to a fine of up to £5,000.

21.9 Unfair terms in consumer contracts

The Unfair Terms in Consumer Contracts Regulations 1999 (SI 1999/2083) implement Council Directive 93/13/EEC ([1993] OJ L95/29) and replace the 1994 Regulations to reflect more closely the wording of the Directive.

They relate to terms in contracts between a seller or a supplier and a consumer: reg. 4(1), who is defined as any natural person who, in respect of contracts covered by the Regulations, is acting for purposes which are outside his trade, business or profession: reg. 3(1). The Regulations do not apply to contractual terms which (a) reflect mandatory statutory or regulatory provisions (including provisions under the law of any Member State or in EU legislation having effect in the UK without further enactment) or (b) the provisions or principles of international conventions to which the Member States of the EU are party: reg. 4(2). The Regulations apply to all kinds of contracts – not just for the sale of goods – and cover contracts for the sale of land, mortgage and loan documentation, insurance contracts and contracts for transport or professional advice. Contracts 'for the supply of goods' include contracts for lease or hire.

A contractual term which has not been individually negotiated shall be regarded as unfair if, contrary to the requirement of good faith, it causes a significant imbalance in the parties' rights and obligations arising under the contract, to the detriment of the consumer: reg. 5(1). A term shall always be regarded as not having been individually negotiated where it has been drafted in advance and the consumer has therefore not been able to influence the substance of the term: reg. 5(2). In addition, notwithstanding that a specific term or certain aspects of it has been individually negotiated, these Regulations shall apply to the rest of a contract if an overall assessment of it indicates that it is a pre-formulated standard contract: reg. 5(3). It is for the seller or supplier to show that a term was individually negotiated: reg. 5(4).

An assessment of the unfair nature of the term shall take into account the nature of the goods or services and refer to all circumstances attending the conclusion of the contract and to all the other terms of the contract or of another contract on which it is dependent: reg. 6(1). In so far as it is in plain intelligible language, the assessment of fairness of a term shall not relate (a) to the definition of the main subject matter of the contract, or (b) to the adequacy of the price or remuneration, as against the goods or services supplied in exchange: reg. 6(2).

In respect of written contracts, a seller or supplier shall ensure that any written term of a contract is expressed in plain, intelligible language, and, if there is any doubt about the meaning of a written term, the interpretation most favourable to the consumer shall prevail, subject to a proviso that this shall not apply in proceedings brought under reg. 12: reg. 7. The effect of the Regulations is that any unfair term concluded with a consumer by a seller or supplier shall not be binding on the consumer. However, the contract shall continue to be binding on the parties if it is capable of continuing in existence without the unfair term: reg. 8.

The Regulations apply notwithstanding any term which applies under the law of a non-Member State if it has a close connection with the territory of the Member States: reg. 9. Further, it is the duty of the OFT to consider any complaint that any contract term drawn up for general use is unfair, unless the complaint is frivolous or vexatious; or a qualifying body has notified the OFT that it agrees to consider the complaint: reg. 10(1). The qualifying bodies are listed in Schedule 1 and include the regulators in respect of gas, electricity, telecommunications, rail services and water, all weights and measures authorities in Great Britain and the Consumers' Association. The OFT and any qualifying body may apply for an injunction against any person appearing to be using, or recommending the use of, an unfair term drawn up for general use in contracts concluded with consumers: reg. 12(1). A qualifying body can apply for an injunction only where it has given 14 days' notice to the OFT of its intention to apply, or where the OFT consents to the application within a shorter period: reg. 12(2). The OFT must give reasons for the decision to apply or not to apply for an injunction and, in reaching a decision not to apply in respect of a term which it considers to be unfair, may have regard to undertakings given as to the continued use of such a term in contracts concluded with consumers: reg. 10(3).

Schedule 2 contains an illustrative list of terms which may be regarded as unfair, and includes:

(a) excluding or limiting the liability of a seller or supplier in the event of the death of a consumer or personal injury resulting from an act or omission of the seller or supplier;

(b) inappropriately excluding or limiting the legal rights of the consumer in the event of total or partial non-performance or inadequate performance of any of the contractual obligations;

(c) making an agreement binding on the consumer whereas provision of services by the seller or supplier is subject to a condition the realisation of which depends on his own will alone;

(d) permitting the seller/supplier to retain sums paid by the consumer where the latter decides not to conclude or perform the contract, without providing for him to receive equivalent compensation from the seller/supplier where the latter cancels the contract;

(e) requiring a consumer who fails in his obligation to pay a disproportionately high sum in compensation;

(f) authorising the seller/supplier to dissolve the contract on a discretionary basis with that same facility not given to the consumer, or permitting him to retain sums paid for services not yet supplied where he dissolved the contract;

(g) enabling the seller/supplier to terminate a contract of indeterminate duration without reasonable notice except where there are serious grounds for doing so;

(h) automatically extending a contract of fixed duration where the consumer does not indicate otherwise, when the deadline fixed for the consumer to express this desire not to extend the contract is unreasonably early;

(i) irrevocably binding the consumer to terms with which he had no real opportunity of becoming acquainted before the conclusion of the contract;

(j) enabling the seller/supplier to alter the terms of the contract unilaterally without a valid reason which is specified in the contract;

(k) enabling the seller/supplier to alter unilaterally without valid reason any characteristics of the product or service;

(l) providing for the price of goods to be determined at the time of delivery or allowing a seller/supplier to increase their price without giving the consumer the right to cancel the contract if the price is too high in relation to that agreed on the conclusion of the contract;

(m) giving the seller/supplier the right to determine whether the goods or services are in conformity with the contract, or exclusive right to interpret any contract term;

(n) limiting the seller/supplier's obligation to respect commitments undertaken by his agents or making his commitments subject to compliance with a particular formality;

(o) obliging the consumer to fulfil all his obligations where the seller/supplier does not perform his;

(p) giving the seller/supplier the possibility of transferring his rights and obligations under the contract, where this may reduce the guarantees for the consumer, without his agreement;

(q) excluding or hindering the consumer's right to take legal actions or exercise any other legal remedy, particularly by requiring the consumer to take disputes exclusively to arbitration not covered by legal provisions, unduly restricting the evidence available to him or imposing on him a burden of proof which, according to the applicable law, should lie with another party to the contract.

21.10 Consumer protection and e-commerce

For consumer protection in the context of e-commerce see Chapter 22, p.529.

End of Chapter Summary

The material contained in this chapter is of tremendous relevance to the world of commerce, dealing as it does with the protection afforded to consumers in a variety of different contexts. Once again, the influence of EU law is strong here.

Having read and understood this chapter, you should have a detailed knowledge of the following points of particular significance:

▷ Consumer protection from unfair commercial practices.
▷ Prohibition against misleading and comparative advertising.
▷ The law relating to defective products.
▷ The law relating to unfair terms in consumer contracts.

This chapter relates in many respects to the chapter relating to the sale and supply of goods, and there are many cross-references between them.

Questions

1. Marvin is a self-employed courier. He has a Volvo estate car which he uses in his business to deliver goods throughout the London area. Prior to trading in the car, he falsified the odometer (mileometer) reading from 90,000 to 45,000 miles. He then traded in the car to G Ltd. and purchased a new Volvo.

   The car was displayed for sale in G Ltd's showroom, with a sign fixed above the odometer stating 'Mileage not guaranteed'. The car was still there when the showroom was visited by a trading standards officer.

   Consider whether an offence has been committed by (i) Marvin, and (ii) G Ltd, and any defences which may be available.

2. Bona Travel Ltd produced a brochure offering package holidays in the UK and Europe. In respect of a holiday in the Bona Hotel in Nessundorma, Spain, it showed a picture of a large swimming pool with a central bar. This was not a photograph, since the pool and bar were not at that date completed, but Bona Travel Ltd had been assured that they would be completed in time for the Easter holiday visitors. In May, Julian and Sandy stayed at the hotel and the pool was still not completed. Advise them of any claim they have against Bona Travel Ltd and any defence available to Bona Travel Ltd.

Questions cont'd

3. Austin runs a garage and services and repairs cars. Morris, a customer, brought in his car for servicing and repairs to the brakes. When Morris collected his car the next day, he was given an invoice showing the work carried out, including the fitting of new brake pads. On driving his car away, he soon discovered that the brakes were as faulty as before, and an independent test by another garage established that the brake pads had not been changed.

   Advise Morris whether Austin has committed any offence and otherwise advise him of the appropriate action to take.

4. One of the defences under the Consumer Protection from Unfair Trading Regulations 2008 is that the commission of an offence was due to the act or default of another person. This has allowed companies to escape liability on the ground that the fault lay with an employee. Explain the way in which the identification theory is used in these circumstances to obtain a conviction of the company and its limitations.

5. Jamil received through the post a parcel containing a number of books published by Bona Press Ltd. The parcel contained an invoice on which it was stated that, unless the books were returned to Bona Press Ltd within seven working days, Jamil would be liable for £50 plus package and posting. Jamil had never ordered the books and seeks advice concerning his liability to Bona Press Ltd. Advise him.

6. The Unfair Terms in Consumer Contracts Regulations 1999 overlap with what other piece of legislation?

7. To what terms do the Regulations apply in agreements between a seller or supplier and a consumer.

8. Give examples of the types of agreement to which the Regulations do and do not apply.

Part VII

e-commerce

Introduction to Part VII

This one-chapter part deals with the large number of topics raised in connection with e-commerce: payment methods, intellectual property and domain names, and particular issues relating to consumer protection.

Of particular importance in this chapter is the whole notion of electronic contracting and the use of electronic signatures. This makes the topic one which is complex but vital in the modern world where e-commerce is assuming greater importance daily.

e-commerce

After reading this chapter you will know about:

- electronic contracts and the postal rule of acceptance
- electronic contracts and signatures
- terms and electronic contracts
- the proper law of the electronic contract
- payment methods and consumer protection
- registering domain names
- domain names and trade marks
- copyright and the internet.

Hot Topic . . .

E-COMMERCE – THE FASTEST GROWING COMMERCIAL MARKET

Figures published by the DTI (now the Department of Business Enterprise and Regulatory Reform (BERR)) in 1998 valued worldwide electronic trade at US$12bn *per annum*, with an estimated value of US$300–500bn by 2002. The most conservative DTI figures estimated a 2,900 per cent growth in e-commerce in four years.

At the end of 2004, the Office of National Statistics (ONS) reported that e-commerce sales rose to £39.5bn in 2003 from £19bn the previous year. Of this, £11.4bn was in sales to households. Interactive Media in Retail Group (IMRG), the e-retailing umbrella group, estimated that internet sales to shoppers would rise

to around £15bn for 2004, an increase of 40 per cent. It reported that the UK still leads in Europe, with 32.4 per cent of the overall market. In a separate report in 2004 by Forrester Research, European e-commerce sales were set to overtake those in the US for the first time over the Christmas period.

A press release by the ONS on 30 November 2007 stated that the value of internet sales by UK businesses rose to £130.4bn in 2006, an increase of 29.1 per cent on the 2006 figure of £101bn. A key finding was that internet sales represented 6.5 per cent of the total value of all sales by non-financial sector businesses in 2006.

A more recent report published by the UK trade body the Interactive Media in Retail Group (IMRG) showed that £46.6b was spent online in 2007, 54 per cent more than in 2006. A third of all sales happened in the Christmas period, with £15.2b being spent online in December. Four million people shopped online on Christmas Day, spending £84m. It reports that electronics were a major growth area, with the sector enjoying online sales growth of 60 per cent for the month of December. Increases in sales of clothing and alcohol were more modest at 28 and 20 per cent respectively.

In the future, shoppers will probably rely on tools such as Froogle, Google's price comparison tool, or use sites such as Kelkoo, the shopping search and price comparison site, at www.kelkoo.co.uk and www.ukshopping.com.

22.1 Electronic contracts

The key to the development of e-commerce is the ability to contract electronically. The internet is merely a tool of communication like the other tools: the post, the telephone, telex and fax machines. In the same way as the law of contract has incorporated these communication methods and applied the principles of the law of contract to them, it is reasonable to suppose that the law will equally embrace the internet.

(a) Entering an electronic contract

There are two main methods of electronic contracting: electronic mail, or email, and the click-wrap method.

(i) *Email*

Email is the digital equivalent of the letter and can do everything that is done by real mail so that, in the context of the law of contract, it can be used for the purposes of making an offer and communicating an acceptance. In the same way, it can be used for advertisements and circulars. Email is sent and received like real mail. The sender posts the email by putting it in his outbox and the message is then collected by the mail server and forwarded to the receiver where it is lodged to the inbox. The process is quick but not instantaneous, and messages can be delayed and even lost.

(ii) *Click-wrap*

The click-wrap method of contracting is used on the World Wide Web. The operator of a webpage carries an advertisement for goods or services – a webvertisement. The operator offers to supply these goods or services against payment. In order for a contract to be made between the supplier and the customer, there will be a hypertext order form on the webpage, which the customer is invited to complete. Once the form has been completed, the customer will be invited to click on a button marked 'Submit' or 'I Accept' or some similar formula. When this button is clicked, the order is submitted to the operator. The communication can be compared to handing an item to a salesperson in a shop. In this case, the communication will be instantaneous.

The process of the contract negotiation will be the same as in the real world: invitations to treat, offer and counter-offer and final acceptance. Thus advertisements on websites can be compared to their equivalent in the real world: advertisements in magazines and on television and shop displays will constitute invitations to treat. Similarly, with both methods of contracting, it is possible to identify the negotiating stages of the offer and counter-offer. This is most obvious where the email form is being used. The final contract will be concluded between the parties when their acceptance is communicated to the offeror converting the offer into a contract.

At this stage, it is necessary to consider the operation of the postal rule of communication, since both contracting methods are potentially affected by it.

(b) The postal rule and email acceptances

There have been two theories to explain the existence of the postal rule of communication. The first explanation is that the acceptor, in placing his acceptance with a trusted third party, has thereby put it out of his control. The second explanation argues that the rule applies because the means of acceptance are non-instantaneous. Under the first test email communication cannot benefit from the postal rule, but it does under the second. If email is compared to the instantaneous methods of communication to which the postal rule does not apply, it can be seen that email communication has none of the characteristics of these methods and ought, therefore, to benefit from the application of the postal rule.

The main difference between email acceptances and the click-wrap contract is that the latter is instantaneous. It is most comparable to communication by telephone since there are in-built checking mechanisms in the click-wrap sequence which will reveal that there has been a breakdown in communication between the client and the server within a matter of seconds. As the sender of the acceptance can determine whether the message has been successfully received almost instantaneously, the postal rule does not apply. Click-wrap acceptances have to be received in order to be effective.

(c)   The terms of the electronic contract

As in real contracts, the terms of the contract will be those incorporated by agreement of the parties at the time the contract was made. The terms of the contract can be divided into three categories: express terms, terms incorporated by reference and implied terms.

(i)   Express terms

The incorporation of express terms into either form of electronic contract is a simple matter.

Incorporating terms by reference

These are terms which are set out in a separate document and which are incorporated by reference into the final contract. In both forms of contract, it is common to find the incorporation of terms by reference.

In respect of click-wrap contracts, the terms to be incorporated will be on a separate document in a separate webpage. This will be accessible by a hypertext link embedded in the main click-wrap agreement page. The party wishing to incorporate these terms and conditions into the final agreement must make sure that they have been brought to the customer's attention before the contract is concluded in such a way as to make it clear that they are to be incorporated. In order to achieve this, the website has got to be designed so that it is not possible for the customer to press the 'Submit' or 'I Accept' button before the customer indicates knowledge of and acceptance of these terms and conditions. Requiring the customer to click an acknowledgement of the terms and conditions, which will then be incorporated into the final contract even though the customer has not actually read them, usually does this.

Hot Topic . . .

THE PROPER LAW OF THE CONTRACT

The nature of the internet means that there is a far greater potential for cross-border disputes than is the case for reality contracts, where the majority of consumer and even commercial contracts are domestic. Issues relating to private international law and the proper law of the contract are, therefore, more major issues relating to electronic contracts.

The proper law of the contract is determined by the Contracts (Applicable Law) Act 1990 which introduced into UK law the EC Convention on the Law Applicable to Contractual Obligations – the Rome Convention. The choice of law rules are important in: determining whether the contract is formally valid in accordance with the proper law of the contract; whether the contract is materially valid, namely legally valid according to the law of the applicable jurisdiction; and what is the applicable law relating to questions of interpretation, performance and the consequences of breach of the contract. The general principle of the Convention is that the parties can freely choose the applicable law. This can be expressed or can be implied from the circumstances: Art. 3 (1). Generally, the operator of the website can include a choice of law clause in the terms and conditions of the agreement.

If no choice is made, the position is more complicated but is regulated by Art. 4. This provides that the law applicable will be the law of the country which has the closest connection with the contract. This is clarified by Art. 4(2) which states that 'the contract is most closely connected with the country where the party who is to effect the performance which is characteristic of the contract has, at the time of the conclusion of the contract, his habitual residence, or for traders the country in which their principal place of business is located'. The characteristic performance of the contract is usually the act for which payment is made, which may be the supply of goods or services. The effect of this is that the court will usually apply the law of the country where the person who has to provide/supply the required goods or services maintains their principal place of business or is habitually resident.

If Company A in Paris runs a website offering to supply software and that software is bought and downloaded by Company B in Germany, then, in the absence of a choice of law clause, the contract will be governed by French law. This changes if Company B is replaced by Consumer B. The Rome Convention ensures that consumers can rely on their usual consumer protection laws when contracting with overseas traders. Thus, if the contract is for the supply of goods or services to a person who is not buying them in the course of trade, then Art. 5 applies. This means that the law will be regulated by the consumer's place of residence, not the place of residence of the party performing the contract. This is, however, qualified by Art. 5(2). The buyer's habitual place of residence comes into play only if: (1) conclusion of the contract was preceded by a specific invitation from the seller to the buyer or the seller intended to advertise to consumers such as the buyer; (2) the seller received the buyer's order in the country in which the buyer was habitually resident; or (3) the contract is for the sale of goods, and the buyer travelled from the country of his habitual residence to another country to give his order, and the seller arranged for his journey with the intention of inducing him to enter into the contract. If none of these circumstances arises, the proper law of the contract as determined by Arts 3 and 4 will govern the contract.

Transactions concluded over the World Wide Web raise many issues when dealing with Art. 5(2). Is the webvertisement made in the country of the buyer's habitual residence or made in the seller's country of residence? Where is the order received? By placing an advertisement on the Web, does the webvertiser intend to reach consumers in all wired countries? These questions cause a problem, as regards both choice of law and consumer protection.

(ii)   Implied terms

Terms are implied into electronic contracts in the same way as for contracts in the real world. Terms will be implied to give business efficacy to the contract as well as terms implied on the basis of custom and usage. Terms may also be implied by common law as in real contract situations. In that respect, it is necessary only to consider the law applicable to reality contracts of the same nature.

(d)   European regulation of cross-border transactions

The EU examined the issue of contract formation in the Electronic Commerce Directive (Directive 2000/31/EC, [2000] OJ L178/1). The original draft was finalised in November 1998 but in 1999 it became clear that it was in need of review. The amended proposals were published in August 1999 (Draft Directive, COM(1999)427). After substantial amendment it was finally enacted on 8 June 2000. The Directive on electronic commerce (Directive 2000/31/EC) required Member States to amend existing legislation to ensure that current requirements, including requirements of form, which may restrict the use of electronic documentation in the formation of contracts, are removed. The formation of electronic contracts is to be regulated in accordance with Chapter II, Section 3 (Arts 9–11) of the Directive.

The final version differs substantially from the first in determining when a contract is concluded electronically. Instead of specifically providing when a contract is deemed to be concluded, the Directive provides guidelines as to when orders from customers and acknowledgements from service providers are deemed to be received: Art. 11(1). As a result, the Directive says little about contract formation and the legal position of an electronic offer or acceptance.

In the UK, the Directive was implemented by the Electronic Commerce (EC Directive) Regulations 2002 (SI 2002/2013). These provide that, unless non-consumer parties have otherwise agreed, service providers shall, prior to the placing of an order, provide the person using the service with information concerning (a) the technical steps to conclude the contract; (b) whether or not the contract will be filed with the service provider and whether it will be accessible; (c) the technical means for identifying and correcting input errors; and (d) the available languages for concluding the contract. Service providers must also identify the codes of conduct to which they subscribe and how they can be electronically consulted; where terms and conditions apply to the contract, they must be able to be stored and reproduced by the person using the service: reg. 9.

Unless non-consumer parties have otherwise agreed, where the service user places an electronic order, service providers shall (a) electronically acknowledge receipt of the order without undue delay; and (b) provide appropriate, effective and accessible means of allowing the recipient to identify and correct input errors prior to placing the order: reg. 11(1). In the event of a breach of reg. 11(1)(b), the service user can rescind the contract unless the court otherwise orders: reg. 15.

Failure by service providers to comply makes them liable for damages for breach of statutory duty: reg. 13.

Hot Topic . . .

FORMALITY AND THE REQUIREMENTS OF WRITING

The UK government has chosen to leave the authorising or facilitating of the use of electronic communication or electronic storage of information to secondary legislation. The Electronic Communications Act (ECA) 2000 allows the appropriate Minister to introduce statutory instruments 'to modify the provisions of (a) any enactment or subordinate legislation, or any scheme, licence, authorisation or approval issued, granted or given by or under any enactment or subordinate legislation, in such a manner as he may think fit for the purpose of authorising or facilitating the use of electronic communications or electronic storage (instead of other forms of communication or storage) for any purpose mentioned in s.8(2)': s.8(1). These include the doing of anything which is required to be done in writing or otherwise using a document, notice or instrument, and the doing of anything which is required to be or may be authorised by a person's signature or seal, or is required to be witnessed.

In contrast to the provisions of the ECA 2000 in respect of the recognition of electronic signatures, where there is no guidance on such issues as time and place of signature, authenticity of contents and so on (see below), the Minister's power includes that to make provisions for the determination of whether a thing has been 'done' using electronic communication or storage, and the time and place at which it was done, the person by whom it was done, and the contents, authenticity and integrity of electronic data.

22.2 Electronic signatures and encryption

There is concern in the business world that electronic communications are afforded the same qualities of authenticity, integrity and confidentiality as in the real world.

In this respect, a handwritten signature is traditionally regarded as a guarantee of the authenticity and integrity of the document, while the use of a sealed envelope can ensure confidentiality. In respect of e-commerce, the use of electronic signatures and encryption ensures that the electronic message is receivable by only the person for whom it was intended.

There are two principal types of cryptography in use: private or symmetric key cryptography and public or asymmetric key cryptography:

▶ In *private key cryptography* both parties have the same key, which they keep secret. The key is used to encrypt and decrypt messages between the parties. This is a faster system than the public key system as it uses fewer digital symbols.

▶ In *public key cryptography*, there are a public and a private key, which are a pair. The public key is published; the private key is known only to the individual who generated the key pair. Only the private key fits together with the public key to form a compatible pair. Public key systems are slower to operate.

Examples of public key systems are the RSA public key and the Diffie-Hellmann algorithm. RSA has been embedded in the USA in Microsoft Windows, Netscape Navigator and Lotus Notes, among other software packages.

(a)   Electronic signatures

An electronic signature is a string of electronic data used to identify the sender of a data message. The effectiveness of an electronic signature depends on the fact that it must be able to be produced by the sender alone and that any attempt to alter it is incompatible with the integrity of the signature. In order to establish the authenticity of the signature, the electronic signature will generally have attached to it an electronic certificate of authenticity issued by bodies known as Certification Authorities (CAs). The ECA 2000 addresses the issue of the authenticity of electronic signatures and the regulation of the CAs.

(b)   Validity and admissibility of electronic signatures

The British government has addressed the validity of electronic signatures in terms of their evidential admissibility. The relevant provision is s.7(1) ECA 2000:

In any legal proceedings:

(a) an electronic signature incorporated or logically associated with a particular electronic communication or with particular electronic data, and
(b) the certification by a person of such a signature,

shall each be admissible in evidence in relation to any question as to the authenticity of the communication or data or as to the integrity of the communication or data.

The provisions of s.7 apply to all electronic signatures, not simply those issued by approved providers, and regardless of the jurisdiction in which they were issued. However, the provision does not provide that electronic signatures create any presumption as to the provenance, authenticity or date of any data carrying them. The parties must establish this, and the court will decide whether an electronic signature has been correctly used and the weight it should be given.

The Act creates a voluntary approvals regime to cover the providers of all 'cryptography support services', not just for those providing certificates in respect of electronic signatures. These extra services could include the storage of encrypted data and the provision of key escrow and key recovery. Agencies offering these services are referred to as trusted third parties (TTPs). There is a register of agencies, both CAs and TTPs, which have complied with certain conditions to ensure that consumers will be able to rely on them in purchasing cryptography support services. The government uses the umbrella term 'trusted service providers' (TSPs) to describe any agency choosing to offer any cryptographic service, whether as a CA or a TTP.

In respect of the liability of the CAs and other providers of cryptographic services for losses caused by them, the EC Directive on electronic signatures requires that 'Members States shall ensure that by issuing a certificate as a qualified certificate to the public or by guaranteeing such a certificate to the public, a certification-service-provider is liable for damage caused to any entity or legal or natural person who reasonably relies on that certificate': Art. 6 (1).

In spite of this, the British government has decided that the liability of TSPs, both to their customers and to parties relying on their certificates, is best left to existing law and providers' and customers' contractual arrangements. These contracts will include exclusion and limitation clauses which will be subject to the Unfair Contract Terms Act 1977 (see Chapter 3, p.76) and the Unfair Terms in Consumer Contracts Regulations 1999 (see Chapter 21, p.517). Third parties will have to rely on the law of tort and liability based on negligent misstatement.

There is also the issue of the liability of the holder of a private key, should the key's secrecy become compromised and it be used by another with resulting loss. Liability could be based on negligence, but recovery of damages for pure economic loss would be a problem.

(c) Law enforcement agency access

The government has empowered law enforcement agencies to require disclosure of a decryption key, excluding keys which are intended to, and do, create only electronic signatures, rather than encrypted text, necessary to access protected information. This is by the Regulation of Investigatory Powers (RIP) Act 2000.The categories of persons who may require access are specified in s.46(1).

22.3 Payment mechanisms and the internet

Most e-commerce transactions are paid for using existing electronic payment mechanisms: credit cards, debit cards, charge cards and electronic or digital cash.

There are two main concerns in the minds of consumers about e-commerce transactions:

- that someone may use the consumer's payment card information to make fraudulent purchases for which the consumer will be held liable;
- that the merchant, once having been paid, will not perform their side of the contract or will perform it defectively.

There are various technological or practical ways in which consumer confidence can be improved. For credit card transactions, MasterCard and Visa, the two leading card schemes, have developed the secure electronic transaction (SET) protocol for safeguarding payment card details transmitted over the internet. In addition, in the UK, the *Which Online* web trader scheme requires merchants displaying the logo to comply with a code of practice for online traders and provides a legal back-up for any complaints against any one of its members. There is, however, legislative protection to be considered. This will depend on the payment system chosen.

The choice is between the use of credit or debit cards, Paypal or one of the various smart card electronic cash systems.

(a) Payment by credit or debit card

Where the consumer's payment card is used fraudulently in connection with a distance contract by another person not acting, or to be treated as acting, as his agent the consumer is entitled to cancel the payment. If the payment has already been made the consumer is entitled to a recredit or to have all sums returned by the card issuer. In any proceedings where the consumer claims that the use of his payment card was not authorised by him, it is for the card issuer to prove that the use was authorised: reg.21 Consumer Protection (Distance Selling) Regulations 2000. The Regulations also remove the debtor's potential liability under a regulated consumer credit agreement for the first £50 of loss to the creditor from misuse of a credit token in connection with a distance contract For the purposes of the Regulations, 'payment card' includes credit cards, charge cards, debit cards and store cards.

In respect of the fear that online merchants will fail to perform or defectively perform their contractual obligations, consumers are protected by s.75 CCA 1974. In the event of online merchants failing to comply with their contractual obligations, the consumer can obviously sue the merchant directly. This may be difficult because of the global nature of the internet but, where action by the consumer against the merchant is impossible or even difficult, the consumer can fall back on the statutory protection of s.75, which allows him/her to sue the card issuer for any misrepresentation or breach of contract.

The card issuer's liability is entirely dependent on and contemporaneous with the consumer's claim against the merchant. In respect of the liability of the merchant, the consumer must first establish that there is a claim against the merchant before the card issuer's liability arises. This is complicated by the global nature of the internet, in the sense that the law applicable to the contract must first of all be determined. For contracts falling within the scope of the Rome Convention on the Law Applicable to Contractual Obligations 1980 as implemented in the UK by the Contracts (Applicable Law) Act 1990, merchants cannot deprive consumers of 'mandatory rules' defined by Art. 3(3). These are rules of law in the consumer's country which cannot be derogated from by contract.

The consumer's claim is not limited to the purchase price of the goods, but can include consequential loss caused subject to the rules of the applicable law. The section means, therefore, that a credit card holder's bank acts as a guarantor for any misrepresentation or breach of contract claim which the card holder may have against the merchant. This is subject to the fact that:

(i)   the purchase price must be greater than £100 and less than £30,000;
(ii) the credit card agreement is used to finance a particular transaction between a debtor and a supplier (restricted use agreements);
(iii) the purchase is made under pre-existing arrangements, or in contemplation of future arrangements, between the card issuer and the merchant.

The card-issuing banks in the UK have argued that credit card holders cannot use s.75 to make a claim against their bank where the goods or services were purchased from a merchant recruited to the card network by a bank other than the card holder's bank, particularly where the merchant is located overseas. The House of Lords, however, overturned the Court of Appeal decision supporting this claim and held that the creditor's joint and several liability under s.75(1) CCA 1974 extends to the purchase of goods and services overseas: *OFT v. Lloyds TSB Bank plc and others* [2007] UKHL 48 (see Chapter 20, pp.482).

Debit card and charge card holders do not benefit from the protection of s.75 CCA 1974. The card holder would have to proceed directly against merchants in respect of misrepresentations or breach of contract.

(b) PayPal

PayPal is an e-commerce business allowing for payments and money transfers through the internet. It performs payment processing for online vendors, auction sites and other corporate users against payment of a fee.

It was founded in 1998 and is located in San Jose in the USA. On 3 October 2002 it was purchased by eBay for $1.5 billion and became a wholly owned subsidiary of eBay, which now requires everyone on its UK site to offer PayPal. Persons subscribe to PayPal by email, are identified by their email address and a password and identify a payment card from which payments are to be made giving the card numbers to PayPal. When payment is made, PayPal instantly confirms the payment to the vendor of the goods or services and debits the amount from the designated payment card. The vendor has the advantage of guaranteed payment and can instantly despatch the goods or supply the service, while the purchaser is protected against the risk of the card details falling into the wrong hands.

PayPal has become a global leader in online payment with more than 164 million accounts worldwide. It is available in 190 markets and 17 currencies around the world, enabling global ecommerce across different locations, currencies and languages.

(c) Electronic or digital cash

Electronic or digital cash involves a system whereby digitally represented units of value, denominated in a particular currency and stored on an electronic device (smart card or computer hard drive), are transferred from a buyer to a seller.

One such system is Mondex, which was originally developed by National Westminster Bank in the UK and later sold to MasterCard International. Mondex International Ltd concludes shareholder franchise agreements with selected banks in a particular region which oblige the banks to develop and implement the Mondex scheme in that area. Mondex operates in the USA, Canada, New Zealand, Hong Kong and South Africa. In the UK, HSBC, NatWest and Bank of Scotland have franchise agreements with Mondex International Ltd.

The Mondex digital cash is a stored value system based on smart cards. The key benefits of Mondex are:

1. Security – Mondex is a safe way to carry money. A lock function, available on the card with a Mondex device, enables the cardholder to prevent unauthorised access. The cardholder chooses the code and it can be changed at any time.

2. Convenience – Mondex offers cardholders a quick and easy method of payment.
3. Flexibility – Mondex can be used for purchases of any size and, technically, there is no limit to the amount of cash held in the card, but limits are set within each country according to local regulation and market demand.
4. Control – cardholders can spend only what is on their card, so there is no risk of incurring debts. The 'purse' keeps an up-to-the-minute record of the amounts and the place where the payment took place.

Another system is Visa Cash, a smart card electronic cash system owned by Visa. The system works via a chip embedded in a bank card and looks similar to the 'Chip and PIN' cards issued around the world. The card is loaded with cash via specialised ATMs, and the cash can then be spent by inserting the card into the retailer's card-reader and pressing the button to confirm the amount. No PIN entry is required nor any signature, which makes for a speedy transaction.

Many of the electronic cash card systems have failed. One such is Dexit which was launched in Canada in 2001 for on-line and off-line payments, but which went in restructuring in 2006.

The most successful rechargeable contactless stored value smart card for on-line or off-line systems is the Hong Kong Octopus card launched originally in 1997 to collect fares for the city's mass transit system. The Octopus card has developed into a widely used payment system for virtually all public transport in Hong Kong and for payments at convenience stores, fast-food restaurants, on-street parking meters, car parks and other point of sale applications such as service stations and vending machines.

(d) Digital cash and credit/debit cards compared

Using digital cash is disadvantageous to consumers since, if it is used to pay for goods or services to the operator of a sham site, the consumer will suffer an immediate loss in not being able to reclaim the cash, which the merchant will be able to spend immediately. It is advantageous to merchants to be paid by digital cash. This avoids the problem of payment cards and the risk that the buyer is fraudulently using someone else's card. The merchant will not receive payment in this situation because of the charge back clause.

The advantage to consumers is that digital cash offers expanded shopping opportunities because:

▶ It is a relatively cheap payment system for low-cost goods and services.
▶ It can hold multiple currencies simultaneously.
▶ It may increase consumer confidence in not having to send card details over the internet (see also PayPal).
▶ There is no risk for banks and the need for credit checks is avoided, which opens the e-commerce sector to consumers without payment cards.
▶ Absence of charge backs means that banks should be more willing to sign up merchants and expand the e-commerce sector.

22.4   Domain names

A domain name is not the same as an email address or address references on the World Wide Web, which are known as universal resource locators (URLs). The domain name will, however, be included as a part of each of these. The domain name system (DNS) was introduced to associate easily remembered names with the underlying numeric addresses under the internet protocol. Domain names are registered in a hierarchical system with a limited number of country code and generic top-level domains (TLDs).

(a)   Country code TLDs

Examples of the country code TLDs are:

.uk   United Kingdom
.fr   France
.d   Germany.

These TLDs are then divided into second level domains (SLDs) and so on. Thus the primary .uk name server contains a number of SLDs, including the following:

.co.uk   UK commercial entities
.org.uk   UK non-commercial organisations
.net.uk   UK network operators
.ac.uk   UK universities.

To these basic roots are added the individual name, which goes to make up the full domain name of the organisation to which the name belongs, for example www.bbc.co.uk.

In the UK, the body with the monopoly for maintaining the domain name registry is a non-profit-making company limited by guarantee called Nominet.uk (www.nominet.org.uk). There are similar bodies in all developed countries, but the rules relating to registration and maintaining registration of the name vary from country to country. There are also EU domain names (.eu) which are administered by EURid.

(b)   Generic TLDs

Examples of generic TLDs are:

.com   commercial organisations
.net   for network organisations
.org   for miscellaneous non-commercial organisations.

(c)   Registering a domain name

Generic domains are regulated by the US National Standards Institute (NSI) and are, in theory, for global organisations. They are registered with the Internet Corporation for Assigned Names and Numbers (ICANN) but registration is possible through a UK registration agent. Registration can be for up to 10 years and is renewable.

For commercial entities to establish an electronic business presence they need to establish a website under an effective name. This name will generally be based on the name of the company or its key brands. Having an appropriate domain name will mean a potential increase in sales of the company's products or services.

All countries maintain a registry of national domain names. The registration procedure is simple, but companies should use the services of a domain registration agent to handle the formality. The domain registration agents have established registration facilities in national registries worldwide, and this will enhance the chance of the company obtaining the domain name of its choice. Some companies may even use more than one registration agent. Prior to choosing a name, it is necessary to make a search to establish that the intended name is available. This is done through the website of the domain registration agent: in the UK www.nominet.org.uk. Once the name has been checked as available, the actual registration process is also completed over the internet through an agent's website and the process can take a matter of seconds. Registration is valid for two years and is renewable.

Hot Topic . . .

DOMAIN NAMES AND TRADE MARKS

Disputes concerning domain names and trade marks have arisen because of two things: trade mark law is territorial and the internet is global, and because no two domain names can be identical, whereas two or more companies in the same or different countries may be entitled to use the identical name.

This fact can give rise to disputes concerning entitlement to a domain name. An example is the dispute between Prince plc in the UK and Prince Sports Inc. in the USA. Prince plc registered the domain name prince.com first and was challenged by Prince Sports Inc.: *Prince plc v. Prince Sports Group Inc.* [1998] FSR 21. Following litigation, the domain name remains with Prince plc.

Problems have arisen because of the practice of what is called 'cybersquatting'. This involves a situation where people have registered domain names where the name is the same as or very similar to the trading name or registered trade mark of a well-known company. The usual aim is to offer the domain address to the owner of the name or registered trade mark in return for a payment. An example of this was the case of Michael Laurie who registered the domain name

'harrods.com'. The name was handed back to Harrods, the London store, after a judgment in favour of the store.

Other problems arise where a domain name is registered which features as part of the domain name a rendition of a famous trade mark with intent to attract visitors to the website, drawn by the famous name. One of the most famous examples is that of Porsche, where the Porsche name was attached to hundreds of domain names, not all concerning cars, for example porschegirls.com. In cases like these, the owner of the registered trade mark will often pursue aggressive policies to prevent the use of any domain name including or alluding to the famous trade mark. Cases of this nature are often called 'reverse domain name hijacking'.

In both of these situations, the main legal weapons used have been the law of registered trade marks and the law of passing off.

Infringement of a registered trade mark under the Trade Marks Act (TMA) 1994 can arise in the following ways:

(1) If a sign which is identical to a registered trade mark is used in the course of trade in connection with

identical goods and services for which the mark is registered, then there is infringement. There is no need to show any likelihood of public confusion: s.10(1) TMA 1994.

(2) If an identical or similar sign is used in conjunction with identical or similar goods for which a mark is registered, then there is infringement if there is a likelihood of public confusion: s.10(2) TMA 1994.

(3) If a similar or identical mark is used in relation to goods or services which are not similar to those for which it is registered, where the trade mark has a reputation and the use of the sign without due cause takes unfair advantage of or is detrimental to the distinctive character or repute of the trade mark: s.10(3) TMA 1994.

In *Avnet Inc. v. Isoact Limited* [1998] FSR 16, Avnet sold goods by catalogue and carried advertisements for different manufacturers. It registered the trade mark 'Avnet' in the UK in class 35 for advertising and promotional services. Isoact Ltd was an internet service provider (ISP) with particular interests in aviation. In connection with its business, it used the words Aviation Network and Avnet. Isoact Ltd registered the domain name avnet.co.uk and allowed customers to display their own advertisements on the site. Avnet brought an action alleging trade mark infringement, arguing that the sign was used in connection with identical goods and services. The court decided that Isoact was not providing advertising or promotional services within class 35 of the Trade Mark Register, but provided the services of an ISP, activities which would (if registered) probably fall within class 42. Therefore, since the services were different, there was no infringement under s.10(1) and Isoact could keep and use the domain name.

In *British Telecommunications and Others v. One in a Million and Others* [1999] 4 All ER 476, a number of domain names including marksandspencer.com, bt.org and britishtelecommunication.net were registered by, among others, One in a Million. The case was decided primarily on the law of passing off, and by some extension of existing principles the court determined that, by registering the domain names, the defendants had created instruments of deception. Thus the domain names had to be handed back to the trade mark and brand owners. The court also held that the domain names were registered to take advantage of the distinctive character and reputation of the marks, which was both unfair and detrimental, and therefore in breach of s.10(3) TMA 1994.

The significance of this decision is that it seems to accord special protection to domain names containing trade marks which are famous or even well known. The protection seems more complete in respect of domain names than is the case of the protection against dilution of a trade mark itself.

In *Oasis Stores Ltd's Trade Mark Application* [1998] RPC 631, there was an application to register the mark 'Eveready' for contraceptives and condoms. The application was opposed by Ever Ready plc, the owner of numerous 'Ever Ready' words and device marks for batteries, torches, plugs, smoke alarms and so on. Ever Ready plc claimed that registration of the mark would be contrary to s.5(3) TMA 1994 which prevents the registration of a sign which is similar to a registered mark for dissimilar goods and services, where the registered mark has a reputation and the registration of the sign would take advantage of or be detrimental to the mark without due cause. The court held that simply being reminded of a similar trade mark with a reputation for dissimilar goods did not necessarily amount to taking an unfair advantage of the repute of that mark.

Judging by the decision in *One in a Million*, these guidelines do not seem to apply to domain name cases involving famous names.

22.5 Copyright and the internet

While several of the categories of works protected by the Copyright, Designs and Patents Act 1988 are applicable to website contents – text (literary), images still (artistic) and moving (film), and sounds (audio recordings) – the Act made no specific provision for databases as a separate category.

The Copyright and Rights in Databases Regulations 1997 (SI 1997/3032) implement the provisions of Council Directive 96/9/EC ([1996] OJ L33/23) of March 1996. The Directive harmonised the law relating to copyright in databases and introduced a new right to prevent extraction and re-utilisation of the contents of a database. It required copyright protection of databases which, by virtue of the selection or arrangement of the contents, constitute the author's own intellectual creation.

Part II (regs. 5–11) amends and modifies Part I of the Act in order to align its provisions with those of the Directive. In particular, the Regulations:

(a) modify the definition of literary work in s.3 by including database, as defined in the Directive (regs. 5 and 6);

(b) introduce a new s.3A defining the meaning of 'original' in relation to databases, so that a database is accorded copyright protection only where the conditions of that section are satisfied;

(c) make provision for adaptation and translation in relation to a database under s.21;

(d) amend s.29 to remove research for a commercial purpose from the general application of the fair dealing provision in relation to a database;

(e) introduce a new s.50D containing specific exceptions to the exclusive rights of the copyright owner which permit any person having a right to use a database to do any acts which are necessary for access to and the use of the contents of the database without infringing copyright;

(f) introduce a new s.296B which renders void any term in an agreement which seeks to prohibit or restrict the doing of any act permitted under s.50D.

In relation to database right, the Directive provides a right for the maker of a database in which there has been a substantial investment in obtaining, verification or presentation of the contents to prevent extraction and/or re-utilisation of the whole or a substantial part of the contents of the database. This right applies irrespective of the eligibility of the database for protection by copyright and without prejudice to rights existing in the contents of the database.

Part III (regs. 12–25) provides for database right, and in particular:

(a) for the interpretation of certain terms, in particular database, extraction, insubstantial, investment, jointly, lawful user, maker, re-utilisation and substantial; and excludes public lending from database right: reg. 12;

(b) for a new property right, 'database right', for a database in respect of which there has been a substantial investment: reg. 13;

(c) that the maker of a database is the person who takes the initiative and risk of investing in obtaining, verifying or presenting the contents and that the maker is the first owner of the database right: regs. 14 and 15;

(d) for the acts infringing database right: reg. 16;

(e) that the duration of protection of database right is 15 years from the end of the calendar year in which it was completed, and that substantial changes give rise to a further term of protection: reg. 17;

(f) that database right subsists only when the database was made or, if the making extended over a period, for a substantial part of that period, its maker or one of its makers meets the qualifying conditions: reg. 18;

(g) that lawful users are entitled to extract or re-utilise insubstantial parts of a database and render void any term or condition in an agreement which seeks to prohibit or restrict such extraction or re-utilisation: regs. 19 and 20;

(h) specific exceptions to database right for a lawful user and other acts which may be done in relation to a database: reg. 20 and Schedule 1;

(i) permitted acts on assumption as to expiry of database right and certain presumptions relevant to database right: regs. 21 and 22;

(j) apply in relation to database right certain provisions of Part I of the Act as they apply to copyright, in particular dealing with the rights in copyright works, rights and remedies of right owners and exclusive licensees: reg. 23;

(k) licensing of database right and extension of the Copyright Tribunal's jurisdiction in database right licensing proceedings: regs. 24 and 25 and Schedule 2.

In relation to a database created on or before the date of publication of the Directive (27 March 1996) which was a copyright work immediately before the commencement of the Regulations, copyright continues for the remainder of the term of copyright: reg. 29. In relation to a database completed on or after 1 January 1983 in which database right subsists as at 1 January 1998, the database qualifies for a term of protection of 15 years from 1 January 1998: reg. 30.

End of Chapter Summary

Many of the issues raised in this chapter relate to previous chapters, but in the context of virtual transactions. Thus there is a discussion of the formation of a virtual contract and consideration of electronic signatures. In addition, the law relating to the payment of virtual contracts refers back to material contained in Chapter 20 concerning payment cards.

Having read and understood this chapter, you should have a detailed knowledge of:

▶ The formation of a virtual contract and the rules relating to the law of the contract.
▶ The law relating to electronic signatures and the requirement that certain contracts must be in writing.
▶ Knowledge of the law relating to domain names including the issue of domain names and the law of trade marks and copyright.

This is very much an emerging area in the law relating to business, and one which everyone active in the commercial world should be familiar with.

Questions

1. Explain how the post rules of communication apply to electronic contracting.

2. Explain the operation of the Rome Convention on the proper law of contracts in the absence of a choice of law clause in the contract. Micromesh Ltd offers software for private and business users via its website. What is the law of the contract where the software is downloaded in Spain by Hidalgo, a Spanish company, and in England by Greg, a private individual. If the software was defective, what protection would Greg have against Micromesh Ltd?

3. What is the UK position regarding the facilitation of electronic contracting and the requirement of writing as a formality?

4. Security plc sought to register a trade mark for a security protection service under the name 'Rightguard'. This word is already a registered trade mark held by Tractor & Rumble plc in respect of a range of men's toiletries. T & R plc opposes the application on the ground that it would take advantage of or be detrimental to the reputation of its trade-marked products. Advise Security plc whether it will succeed in obtaining the registration. Would it be equally successful if it tried to register a domain name for Rightguard having discovered that T & R plc has not already done so?

5. Explain the nature of the protection offered to consumers using payment cards to pay for their goods and services purchased over the internet.

Ab initio   From the beginning.

Accord and satisfaction   Agreement (accord) between parties to a contract that is not completely performed to discharge each other. The mutual promise of release from the contractual obligations constitutes the consideration (satisfaction) for the agreement.

Administration   Alternative procedure to liquidation in corporate insolvency. Company placed in the control of an administrator with the aim of rescuing the business. The procedure can be initiated by the company, the directors or creditors of the company.

Alternative investment market (AIM)   A regulated secondary market operated by the stock exchange for dealing in shares in public companies which do not qualify for listing on the official list.

Annual general meeting   Obligatory meeting of shareholders of a public limited liability company under Companies Act 2006 s.336(1).

Annual return   Return made by a registered company to the Registrar of Companies: Companies Act 2006 s. 854. Contents prescribed by Companies Act 2006 s.855–857.

Articles of association   Internal regulations of a registered company. Usually a modified form of Table A.

Auditor   Person who audits the accounts of a registered company.

Bailment   Transfer of the possession but not ownership of tangible property. By a bailor to a bailee.

Bearer shares   Shares issued by a registered company. Rare in UK.

Bona fide   In good faith; sincere.

Bond   A certificate evidencing a loan made to a company. Bondholder receives interest on capital and capital on maturity.

Call   Demand made by a company to a shareholder of partly paid shares for payment of part or total of the balance outstanding.

Case stated   An appeal from a magistrates' court or crown court in a criminal case on a point of law. There is no retrial. The case is stated to the divisional court which rules on the law applied.

Caveat emptor   'Let the buyer beware'. The buyer must look out for himself.

Charge   A form of security held by a creditor over all or part of the assets of a company or limited liability partnership (LLP). Can be fixed or floating.

Chattel   Tangible, personal property, for example, a watch. Goods.

Cheque   A bill of exchange drawn on a bank and payable on demand.

Choses in action   Intangible personal property or rights, which can be enjoyed or enforced only by legal action, and not by taking physical possession, for example rights as a shareholder, rights as a creditor.

Choses in possession   *See* chattel.

Class rights   Where a company limited by shares has more than one class of share, the rights attached to those shares are called class rights.

Community interest company (CIC)   Companies limited by guarantee or by shares which trade with a social purpose (social enterprises) or carry on other activities which benefit the community.

Company limited by guarantee   Form of registered company used as a vehicle for a charitable or non-profit-making venture.

Compulsory winding-up   Where a registered company, partnership or LLP is put into liquidation by order of the court following a petition usually by a creditor or creditors under Insolvency Act 1986 s.122.

Contra proferentum   Against the party who puts forward a clause in the document.

Contributory   A person liable to contribute to the assets of a company which is being wound up in respect of unpaid capital on partly paid shares.

Conversion   An unauthorised dealing in respect of personal property of a person which constitutes a denial of the title of the true owner.

Conveyance   The document by which land is transferred.

Covenant   A promise set out in a deed.

Creditors' winding up   A liquidation procedure initiated by the members of the company where the company directors do not make a Declaration of Solvency to the effect that the company can pay off its debts within twelve months of the commencement of the liquidation.

De facto   In fact.

De jure   By right; rightful.

De minimis non curat lex   The law does not concern itself with trifles.

Debenture   A written acknowledgement of indebtedness issued by a company or an LLP. In USA, a 'bond'.

Del credere agent   Agents who, for an extra commission, guarantee the due performance of the contract by the persons they introduce to their principal.

Delegatus non potest delegare   A person who is entrusted with a duty has no right to appoint another to perform it in his place.

Directive   Source of EU law. Member States must implement the terms of the Directive by domestic legislation within a specified time.

Director   Member of board of directors of a company. *See also* executive director.

Dissolution   Event signalling the termination of the existence of a registered company or LLP following winding-up.

Dividend   Distribution of share of company's profits to shareholders in accordance with their rights.

Eiusdem generis   General words following a list of specific things are construed as relating to things 'of the same kind' as those specifically listed.

Equity   Term applied to ordinary shares of a company. Derives from fact that the surplus assets of the company on liquidation are divided between the holders of the ordinary shares.

Equity   Alternative source of case law to common law, based on the equitable doctrine developed by the Court of Chancery pre 1873.

Escrow   A document delivered subject to a condition that must be fulfilled before it becomes a deed.

Estoppel   A rule of evidence which applies in certain circumstances and stops a person denying the truth of a statement previously made by him.

Ex gratia   Out of kindness. Gratuitous, voluntary.

Ex parte   Proceedings brought on behalf of one interested party without notice to, and in the absence of, the other.

Executive director   Director who is actively involved in the day-to-day management of a company, usually on a full-time basis or as required under the terms of his or her contract.

Expressio unius est exclusio alterius   When one thing is expressly specified, then it prevents anything else being implied.

Fieri facias **(fi fa)**   Writ addressed to the sheriff: 'cause to be made' a levy on the debtor's goods for the sum due under a judgment.

Floating charge   Equitable security issued by registered companies or LLPs which only become a fixed equitable charge on crystallisation.

Holder in due course   The holder of a negotiable instrument who has taken it for value, in good faith and without notice of any defect in the title of the transferor. The holder in due course takes free from equities and defects of title.

Holding company   A company controlling a subsidiary company; the parent company of a group of companies.

In re   In the matter of.

Insider dealing   Dealing in securities on a regulated market where dealer uses unpublished, price-sensitive information.

Insurable interest   Legal interest that the insured must have in property in order for a contract of insurance to be valid.

Intra vires   An act within one's authority.

Liquidation   Process by which a body corporate, such as a registered company or LLP, is dissolved. Also applies to partnerships.

Liquidator   Person responsible for winding up a company and so on in liquidation.

Loan capital   The capital of a company raised by long-term loans.

Members' voluntary winding-up   A liquidation initiated by the members of the company where the directors make a statutory declaration of solvency that the company will be able to pay its debts in full within 12 months of the commencement of the winding-up.

Negotiable instruments   Personal property in the form of a document transferable by mere delivery or indorsement plus delivery.

Negotiation   Transfers the entitlement in respect of a negotiable instrument, that is, right to receive payment under a bill of exchange or cheque to the indorsee.

Nemo dat quod non habet   No one has power to transfer the ownership of that which he does not own.

Nisi   Unless (also used of a decree or order which will be made absolute later 'unless' good cause be shown to the contrary); provisional.

Non est factum   That the document in question was not his deed.

Novus actus interveniens   A fresh act of someone other than the defendant, which intervenes between the alleged wrong and the damage in question.

Obiter dictum (dicta)   Things said by the way; opinions expressed by judges in passing, on issues not essential for the decision in the case.

Official Receiver   A civil servant attached to a court with designated responsibilities for personal and corporate insolvency.

Ordinary resolution   A resolution at a general meeting of the shareholders of a company, which is carried by a simple majority of members (50 per cent + 1).

Par value   The nominal value of a share.

Pari delicto   Equal fault.

Pari passu   On equal footing.

Parole contract   A contract made orally or in writing (see simple contract).

Per incuriam   Through carelessness or oversight.

Per se   By itself.

Personal representatives   Persons who assume the legal rights in respect of the property of another on death (executors/administrators) and on bankruptcy (trustee in bankruptcy).

Pledge   The giving up of possession of goods as a security by one person (the pledgor) to another (the pledgee).

Prima facie   At first sight.

Promoter   A person who undertakes to form a registered company.

Prospectus   A document issued on behalf of a company inviting the public to subscribe for shares or debentures. Applicable to non-listed companies only.

Proxy   A person nominated by a shareholder to vote for him or her at a company general meeting.

Quantum meruit   As much as he has earned.

Quantum valebant   As much as they were worth.

Quasi   As if; seemingly.

Quorum   The legal minimum number of persons necessary for a meeting to be validly convened.

Ratio decidendi   The reason for a decision; the principle on which a decision is based.

Real property   Freehold estate in land.

Redeemable shares   Shares issued by a limited company that are to be redeemed or are liable to be redeemed at the option of the company or the shareholder subject to certain conditions.

Regulation   A source of secondary EU legislation which is immediately binding on Member States with priority over any conflicting domestic legislation.

Res extincta   The thing that was intended to be the subject matter of a contract, but had previously been destroyed.

Res ipsa loquitur   The thing speaks for itself, that is, is evidence of negligence in the absence of an explanation by the defendant.

Res sua   Something a person believes to belong to another when it is in fact 'his own property'.

Restitutio in integrum   Restoration of a party to his original pre-contract position; full restitution.

Rights issue   Where a company raises further capital by offering the opportunity to existing shareholders to acquire more shares in the company in proportion to their existing shareholding. Usually at a lower price than that at which the shares are currently traded.

Simple contract   A contract made orally or in writing (also called a parole contract). Actions for breach of simple contracts must be brought within six years of the breach or are statute barred.

Specialty contract   Contract made by deed. Actions for breach must be brought within 12 years of the breach after which they are statute barred.

Stoppage in transit   The right of an unpaid seller of goods to recover them while they are still on route to the buyer.

Surety   A person who has given a guarantee or indemnity in respect of a debt or provided security.

Trade marks   'Any sign capable of being represented graphically which is capable of distinguishing goods or services of one undertaking from those of other undertakings'; it may 'consist of words (including personal names), designs, letters, numerals or the shape of goods or their packaging': s.1(1) Trade Marks Act 1994.

Treasury shares   A holding of its own shares by a public limited company. The shares must listed in the UK or an EEA State or traded on a regulated market e.g. AIM.

Uberrima fides   Utmost good faith.

Ultra vires   An act in excess of powers recognised by the law as belonging to the person or body in question.

Volenti non fit injuria   No wrong is done to a person who consents to undergo it.

Index

Page numbers in bold refer to the Hot Topic boxes; an asterisk after a page number denotes a glossary entry. For individual cases, *see* Table of Cases on pages xvii-xxx; for individual Acts of Parliament, Orders, Regulations and Directives, *see* Tables of Statutes, Statutory Instruments and European legislation on pages xxxi-xxxii.